Dedicated to our partners in life

Cross-Cultural Psychology

Research and Applications

THIRD EDITION

John W. Berry

Queen's University, Kingston, Canada

Ype H. Poortinga

Tilburg University, The Netherlands

Seger M. Breugelmans

Tilburg University, The Netherlands

Athanasios Chasiotis

Tilburg University, The Netherlands

David L. Sam

University of Bergen, Norway

CAMBRIDGE
UNIVERSITY PRESS

CAMBRIDGE UNIVERSITY PRESS
Cambridge, New York, Melbourne, Madrid, Cape Town, Singapore,
São Paulo, Delhi, Tokyo, Mexico City

Cambridge University Press
The Edinburgh Building, Cambridge CB2 8RU, UK

Published in the United States of America by Cambridge University Press, New York

www.cambridge.org
Information on this title: www.cambridge.org/9780521762120

First published 2011
Reprinted 2012

Printed in the United Kingdom at the University Press, Cambridge

A catalogue record for this publication is available from the British Library

Library of Congress Cataloguing in Publication data
Cross-cultural psychology : research and applications / John W. Berry . . . [et al.]. — 3rd ed.
      p.   cm.
Includes bibliographical references and index.
ISBN 978-0-521-76212-0 (hardback)
1. Ethnopsychology.   I. Berry, John W.
GN502.C76   2011
155.8 — dc22   2010041959

ISBN 978-0-521-76212-0 Hardback
ISBN 978-0-521-74520-8 Paperback

Contents

x Contents

Part II Relationships between behavior, culture and biology — 221

10 Contributions of cultural anthropology — 223

11 Contributions of evolutionary biology — 249

12 Methodology and theory — 273

Figures

Tables

Boxes

List of additional topics in cross-cultural psychology

Additional Topics in cross-cultural psychology can be found on the website accompanying this book: www.cambridge.org/berry.

www.cambridge.org/berry

This icon in the margin indicates that additional information on topics is available.

Chapter 1
Goals of cross-cultural psychology
Four levels of ethnocentrism in psychology
Research questions in cross-cultural psychology
Psychometric conditions for equivalence of cross-cultural data

Chapter 4
Gender behavior

Chapter 5
Altered states of consciousness

Chapter 6
Genetic epistemology
Cognitive style

Chapter 8
Language development
Some early research on color vision
Bilingualism

Chapter 9
Psychological aesthetics

Chapter 10
Psychological anthropology

Chapter 11
Behavior genetics

Chapter 12
Some forms of control for (quasi-)experimental research in cross-cultural psychology
A classification of inferences
Sources of cultural bias

Chapter 13
Personality and acculturation strategies
Acculturation profiles
Measuring acculturation strategies

Chapter 15
Negotiation

Chapter 17
The link between culture and psychopathology
Examples of culture-bound syndromes
The case of Dhat syndrome
Indigenous psychotherapy in Japan: *Morita* and *Naikan*

Preface to the third edition

The earlier editions of this text (Berry, Poortinga, Segall and Dasen, 1992, 2002 were accompanied by another textbook written by the same four authors: *Human behavior in global perspective: An introduction to cross-cultural psychology* (Segall, Dasen, Berry and Poortinga, 1990, 1999). That text was intended to meet the needs of students who had little prior exposure to psychology or anthropology. However, for the third edition of the present text, there is no longer a parallel book to present these complementary materials. As a result, some of the issues and findings from this other text have been reflected into this edition.

Since the publication of the first edition of this textbook in 1992 (and of the second edition in 2002), there has been massive growth and diversification in the examination of the relationships between cultural and behavioral phenomena. There has been substantial growth in the comparative examination of culture–behavior relationships, which has been traditionally known as *cross-cultural psychology*. Some other developments have focussed on these relationships within cultures, where the concept of *cultural psychology* has been resurrected and redefined. Another development has been the rise of interest in *indigenous psychology*, where local, culturally important perspectives on the study of behavior have been advanced. A third development has been the concern with issues of *cultural diversity* in many culturally plural societies. The cultural, indigenous and the diversity interests all have increasingly evolved toward comparative research and interpretation, leading to some convergence within the field of cross-cultural psychology. One important goal of this text is to bridge these diverse approaches found in the literature. We have tried to take seriously the broad range of orientations found in the psychological study of culture–behavior relationships. However, we do not attempt to provide a single integrated viewpoint.

A second important goal of this text has been to include research carried out across as wide a range of cultural contexts as possible, drawing materials published in English, from many parts of the world. One consequence of this wide casting of the net is that there is an obvious variation in the development and display of behavior in these distinct cultures. However, such a global breadth also provides the possibility of discovering pan-human regularities in basic psychological processes that are shared across these highly variable cultures.

While presenting these various perspectives and findings from different cultures, we nevertheless are explicit about our own position on issues of methodology and theory. This position we refer to as *moderate universalism*, a perspective that is based on evidence for the presence of pan-human basic psychological processes, which are developed and displayed in highly variable ways across cultures.

In this third edition, we have retained the overall structure of previous editions. An introductory chapter lays out some of the basic concepts and tools of the field, serving as an initial presentation of those theories and methods that are required to understand the material that follows. In Part I, we present a survey of the empirical evidence drawn from comparative studies of human behavior across cultures in a number of domains, ranging from development, through social behavior, personality to cognition, emotion, language and perception.

Part II delves further into the bases of our discipline, linking the research we do to our roots in the disciplines of cultural anthropology and biology. These materials establish our claim to be both a cultural science and natural science. The presentation of the links and the interplay between these two traditions establishes our claim to a comprehensive approach to culture–behavior relationship, rather than taking one or the other stances. A third chapter in this Part returns to some of the theoretical and methodological issues initially outlined in Chapter 1. Armed with knowledge from the survey of the empirical evidence from Part I, and with the concepts and findings from our two cognate disciplines in Part II, we now examine in more depth some of the key issues and debates in the study of culture–behaviour relationships.

Part III contains chapters that are essentially applied in character, drawing on many of the findings and ideas presented in Parts I and II. They introduce some new empirical domains and issues, all concerned with "real life" matters such as acculturation, intercultural relations and communications, work organizations and health. The purpose of this Part is to show that our discipline is more than a compilation of empirical findings, theories and methods. These can be used to examine, and possibly improve, the lives of peoples as they carry out their daily activities in their increasingly interconnected and complex cultural settings. A final chapter is devoted to an examination of how cross-cultural psychology might develop further in order to take culture more seriously into its scope of work. It raises questions concerning how our efforts might contribute to a better understanding of personal and national development, and to further internationalizing the discipline so that it breaks out of the constraints of a science largely dominated by one cultural region of the world.

In this third edition, we have continued with a glossary of key terms, as a guide to the various concepts used in the text. These terms are placed in bold when they appear for the first time in the text. We have also added links to materials placed on the Internet, some of which have been "archived" from the second edition. These can be accessed at www.cambridge.org/berry. For a full list of additional topics, please see pages xviii–xix.

www.cambridge.org/berry

Acknowledgements

The two previous editions of this textbook were written by a team of four authors: John Berry, Ype Poortinga, Marshall Segall and Pierre Dasen. Marshall and Pierre did not wish to participate in a new edition, but we sincerely acknowledge their earlier contributions which continue to influence the present edition.

We would also like to express our appreciation to the following colleagues who agreed to read draft chapters and to provide comments: Juri Allik, Ajit Dalal, Pierre Dasen, Ron Fischer, Johnny Fontaine, Heidi Keller, Dan Landis, Chan Hoong Leong, Walter Lonner, Malcolm MacLachlan, Lee Munroe, Anu Realo, Peter Smith, Junko Tanaka-Matsumi, Fons van de Vijver and Colleen Ward.

We also acknowledge the dedicated copy-editing of Julene Knox; her work was both perceptive and precise.

In the first edition we mentioned how the textbook profited from a stay at NIAS (Netherlands Institute for Advanced Studies) by both Berry and Poortinga. The present edition has similarly benefited from a second period at NIAS granted to Poortinga.

As for the previous editions the preparation of the bibliography has been in the hands of Mr. Rinus Verkooijen of Tilburg University. For this edition we also profited from the assistance of Michael Bender and Ms. Cristina Perdomo Mosquera.

1 Introduction

CONTENTS

The field of cross-cultural psychology can be briefly described as the study of the relationships between cultural context and human behavior. The latter includes both overt behavior (observable actions and responses) and covert behavior (thoughts, beliefs, meanings). As we shall discuss later in more detail, there are rather different interpretations even of this broad description, associated with different schools of scientific research. Most researchers studying behavior across cultures argue that differences in overt and covert behavior should be seen as culturally shaped reflections of common psychological functions and processes. In other words, they are postulating a "psychic unity" of the human species (e.g., Jahoda, 1992). This is the position adopted by the authors of this text. Other researchers, often belonging to a school referred to as cultural psychology, emphasize that psychological functioning is essentially different across cultural regions of the world. For example, Kitayama, Duffy and Uchida (2007, p. 139) argue that different "modes of being" are found in various cultures. Sometimes the two approaches are even presented as two distinct fields of science.

In this book we use the label "cross-cultural psychology" as the overarching name for the field. More specific terms, such as cultural psychology, culture-comparative psychology and indigenous psychology will be used when it is necessary to distinguish orientations within this broader field. The common designation is justified by the shared assumption that culture is an important contributor to the development and display of human behavior. All those involved in the field believe that research in psychology has to be "culture-informed"; they share the idea that human behavior cannot exist in a cultural vacuum and that all psychological research has to take this principle into account.

In order to understand divergent interpretations and to form your own opinion, it is necessary to learn about the background of debates in cross-cultural psychology. This introductory chapter is meant to provide an overview of major theoretical perspectives, and to draw attention to some important methodological issues. It should facilitate the reading of subsequent chapters that deal with cross-cultural research in various domains of psychology and in which similar issues of theory and method tend to occur time and again. The first three sections of this chapter provide an overview of the most important theoretical debates that influence how researchers approach cross-cultural studies. The fourth and the fifth sections briefly discuss methodological issues that are recurrent in debates about cross-cultural similarities and differences.

In the first section we present a few definitions of the field, in order to highlight some of the emphases found in the literature. We conclude with our own definition, which we see as rather comprehensive. It reflects our intention to write a textbook that covers more or less the full range of topics and approaches found in cross-cultural psychology. We also refer to another characteristic, namely the goals of cross-cultural psychology, a topic discussed on the Internet (Additional Topics, Chapter 1).

In the second section we present three recurrent themes of theoretical debate in the contemporary literature on behavior and culture. The first of these themes is on the question of whether culture should be seen as something that is part of the person, or as the set of external conditions in which a person is developing and operating. The second theme concerns the question of how far behavior should be seen as culture-specific (or culture-relative) versus how far it should be seen as culture-general (or universal). The third theme of debate is how in psychological terms cultural differences are organized. Here the issue is whether cultural differences form meaningful patterns that allow for broad categorizations (e.g., individualist and collectivist cultures) or whether instead observed differences are quite unrelated (e.g., driving on the left/right hand side of the road presumably has nothing to do with a stronger or weaker preference for hierarchy in interpersonal relationships). We also explicate our own position on these three themes. In later chapters this should help the reader to evaluate where our orientation may have biased our presentation.

In the third section we briefly describe "interpretive positions" on the three themes as they have coalesced into "perspectives" on cross-cultural psychology. We present three such perspectives, labeled culture-comparative psychology, cultural psychology and indigenous psychology. In additional text placed on the Internet (Additional Topics, Chapter 1) we elaborate on the ethnocentrism of the dominant (western) mainstream in psychology and how it necessitates the development of psychology in local contexts. www.cambridge.org/berry

In the fourth section we turn to issues of method that tend to be more salient in cross-cultural psychology than in other fields of psychology. We first address the question of on what basis separate cultures are being distinguished in cross-cultural research and how cultures are sampled. Thereafter, we describe the main methodological distinction in design and analysis, between qualitative approaches and quantitative approaches.

The fifth section deals with threats to interpretation of data. We mention three such threats: possible lack of equivalence and bias in data, overgeneralization of results, and insufficient distinction between culture-level and individual-level variance.

Definitions: What is cross-cultural psychology?

Like other fields of study, cross-cultural psychology can be defined in various ways. Such definitions are often carefully formulated to represent what their authors wish to convey as essential. We mention five examples:

1. "Cross-cultural research in psychology is the explicit, systematic comparison of psychological variables under different cultural conditions in order to specify the antecedents and processes that mediate the emergence of behaviour differences" (Eckensberger, 1972, p. 100).
2. "Cross-cultural psychology is the empirical study of members of various culture groups who have had different experiences that lead to predictable and significant differences in behavior. In the majority of such studies, the groups under

study speak different languages and are governed by different political units" (Brislin, Lonner and Thorndike, 1973, p. 5).

3. "Cross-cultural research is any type of research on human behavior that compares behavior of interest across two or more cultures" (Matsumoto, 1996, p. 5).

4. "Cultural psychology [is] the study of the culture's role in the mental life of human beings" (Cole, 1996, p. 1).

5. Cultural psychology "has a distinctive subject matter (psychological diversity, rather than psychological uniformity); it aims to reassess the uniformitarian principle of psychic unity and develop a credible theory of psychological pluralism" (Shweder, 2007, p. 827).

In most of these definitions, the term **culture** appears, referring to cultural conditions or cultural groups. For the time being, we can define culture as "the shared way of life of a group of people"; in Chapter 10, we will consider more elaborate meanings of the term.

Each of the five definitions highlights a particular feature of culture. In the first, the key idea is that of identifying cause and effect relationships between culture and behavior ("... specify the antecedents and processes that mediate..."); the second is more concerned with identifying the kinds of cultural experiences ("... speak different languages" etc.) that may be factors in promoting human behavioral diversity across cultures. The third definition emphasizes that cross-cultural research is culture-comparative research. In the last two definitions, the adjective "cross-cultural" is replaced by "cultural"; this single change signifies an important shift from the first three definitions. The core issue is whether or not it makes sense to consider "culture" and "behavior" as distinct entities. In the "cultural" approach to the field, there is an emphasis on the mutual, interactive relationship between cultural and behavioral phenomena.

In the culture-comparative approach, which is represented by the first three definitions, cultural conditions are seen as existing independently of particular individuals. These conditions are related to differences in behavior patterns, without necessarily implying that there are differences in underlying functions and processes. In the last two definitions, behavior differences across cultural groups are taken also to imply differences in psychological functions and processes. This is particularly strong in the last definition, which makes it a goal of the field to challenge the concept of the "psychic unity" of humankind. This last definition appears to postulate the existence of different psychologies in different cultures – a position that is similar to that implied by the "indigenous psychology" approach (see below). In our view, the field of cross-cultural psychology incorporates both perspectives represented in these definitions (Berry, 1997, 2000; Poortinga, 1997; see also Chapter 12).

Limited attention is given in these five definitions to some other interests. For example, cross-cultural psychology is concerned not only with diversity, but also with uniformity: what is there that might be psychologically common to a range of cultures, or even universally to the human species (Brown, 1991; Lonner, 1980)? This brings us to the question of how far proximal biological variables, including, for example, dietary habits, nutritional deficiencies and distal biological variables, including the phylogenetic roots of the human capacity to develop culture, should be included in cross-cultural psychology (see Chapter 11). Related to this evolutionary view of culture as human adaptation to the environment, there are other kinds of contextual variables (not always included in the conception of culture) that have been considered to be part of the cross-cultural enterprise. These include ecological variables (Berry, 1976), which become prominent when human populations are seen as being in a constant process of adaptation to their natural environment, and which emphasize factors such as economic activity (hunting, gathering, farming, etc.) and population density. This "ecocultural" perspective will be considered later in this chapter.

Also not included in the five definitions cited is the study of various ethnocultural groups within a single nation state who interact and change as they adapt to living together. The justification for such an ethnic psychology being included in cross-cultural psychology is that most ethnocultural groups maintain distinctive cultural features, sometimes for several generations after contact or migration. This suggests that a comprehensive definition should also signal cultural change (which often results from contact between cultures), an aspect that will be considered more fully in Chapter 13.

We are now in a position to propose a general **definition of cross-cultural psychology** that will be used in this book:

Cross-cultural psychology is the study: of similarities and differences in individual psychological functioning in various cultural and ethnocultural groups; of ongoing changes in variables reflecting such functioning; and of the relationships of psychological variables with sociocultural, ecological and biological variables.

A field of science is not only characterized by its definition; also of importance are the aims and goals. You can find a brief discussion on the Internet (Additional Topics, Chapter 1), including a statement of our own perspective, to make clear to the reader where we stand.

www.cambridge.org/berry

Themes of debate

Theme 1: Culture as internal or external to the person

To what extent should culture be conceptualized as part of the person (internal culture), and to what extent as a set of conditions outside of the person (external culture)? When we talk about European culture or Indian culture, we can refer to the mode of subsistence (how people make a living), the political organization of society and/or other aspects of the ecological and social context; this is external culture. We can also refer to the ideas, philosophies, beliefs, etc. of the members of a culture; this is culture internal to the person. Much of the language, religion, knowledge and beliefs of a person's social environment become internalized; the pre-existing features of one's culture become part of oneself in the processes of enculturation and socialization. External conditions include factors such as climate, mode of economic existence and poverty as opposed to affluence, social institutions and practices, formal education, and influences resulting from contact with a new society, as in the case of migration. For example, there has been extensive research into happiness as a function of material affluence, with the latter including not only personal wealth, but also the Gross National Product of the society (Diener, Diener and Diener, 1995; Veenhoven, 1999).

For a long time, both cultural anthropologists and cross-cultural psychologists studied behavior mainly as the outcome of the physical and social environment in which people are living; these conditions were seen as antecedent factors to psychological functioning. A major shift occurred among anthropologists when culture came to be defined in terms of subjective meanings (Geertz, 1973). As a result of this shift, attempts to understand the behavior patterns characteristic of people in a particular culture in terms of prevailing external conditions were largely replaced by an approach to culture as the shared meanings that are constructed by its members in the course of their interactions. A similar shift can be found in cross-cultural psychology. In such research studying cross-cultural differences in modes of cognition (Peng and Nisbett, 1999) or the experiencing of emotions (Feldman-Barrett *et al.*, 2007) external conditions receive little emphasis.

When asked for an opinion a large majority of cross-cultural psychologists will acknowledge that culture should be both "out there," and "in here." However, in actual studies researchers tend to ignore either the external or the internal aspect of culture, emphasizing only one side in the type of data that are being collected and analyzed.

Theme 2: Relativism–universalism

To what extent are psychological functions and processes common to humankind (universalism), and to what extent are they unique to specific cultural groups (relativism)? This question is perhaps the most debated issue in cross-cultural psychology and central to many of the theoretical distinctions that can be found throughout this book. It is also one of the most tenacious questions, with proponents of both positions being able to present data to support their views. To give just one example, take the interaction between language and thought.

Most people's thinking involves mainly language. So, it is a plausible idea that thoughts are different when languages are different. This has become known as Whorf's hypothesis (1956). Color vocabulary became a testing ground for Whorf's theory, because the number of major color categories (indicated in English with names like *red*, *yellow*, *green* and *blue*) varies widely across languages, while at the same time these color names can be linked to physical properties of objects (such as wavelength). There is empirical evidence to the effect that color categories are common, cross-culturally invariant, properties of the perceptual apparatus. However, there are also studies that show that color names can have subtle effects on the categorization of specific hues. Proponents of relativism see the latter findings as support for Whorf's hypothesis whereas proponents of universalism point to the broader picture of universal similarities in color perception (see Chapters 6 and 8 for further information).

For a long time universalism and relativism have been presented as a dichotomy, with universalism postulating the importance of the human organism as a biological and psychological entity, largely invariant across cultures. In contrast relativism asserted the importance of culture (Jahoda and Krewer, 1997). In universalism the focus is on how different ecological and sociocultural environments impact on shared human psychological functions and processes and lead to differences in behavior repertoires. In relativism the focus is on how the functions and processes themselves are the outcome of interactions between organism and context; they are inherently cultural.

With the explicit recognition by virtually all researchers that human phylogenetic history imposes constraints on human behavior (see, e.g., Keller, 2007; Markus and Hamedani, 2007), the earlier dichotomy has lost some of its conceptual distinctiveness and importance. It now makes more sense to postulate a dimension with various positions ranging from exclusive relativism to exclusive universalism. In the former, what is common in human behavior across all cultures is left out of the discussion. In the latter, the role of culture is reduced to the psychologically trivial; that is, human behavior can be studied without attributing any essential role to culture.

To illustrate the range of the continuum we distinguish four positions: extreme relativism, moderate relativism, moderate universalism and extreme universalism. In extreme forms of relativism, all psychological reality is dependent on our own understanding or interpretation (e.g., Gergen and Gergen, 2000). From this perspective, so-called "facts" deriving from research are constructions that cannot reveal an objective reality outside of us; our understanding and interpretation always lead to essential distortions. This position on the relativism–universalism dimension is only marginally present in cross-cultural psychology and will only be touched upon occasionally in this book. The majority of researchers in psychology accept the view that there are observable regularities in human behavior and that their interpretation is not entirely subjective. The rationale for this has been argued, among others, by Jahoda (1986) and by Munroe and Munroe (1997).

The second position – moderate relativism – can be described with the following citation: "Humans are born with the capacity to function in any culture, but as they mature they develop psyches that are organized to function in one specific culture" (Fiske, Kitayama, Markus and Nisbett, 1998, p. 916). This form of relativism emphasizes that psychological functions and processes are the outcome of interactions between organism and sociocultural contexts. One of the more important distinctions reported in the literature is between societies where individuals are characterized by an independent construal of the self, and societies where individuals have an interdependent construal of the self. The former kind of construal implies that a person sees himself/herself as an autonomous individual separate from others; the latter characterizes a person who defines herself/himself as embedded in one's social network (Markus and Kitayama, 1991).

The third position is that of a moderate universalism. It emphasizes that there exist both differences and similarities in behavior across cultures and that psychological research and practice should be informed by both. However, in this approach manifestations of cultural differences in behavior do not automatically imply the need for postulating different psychological functions and processes. A much quoted statement by Przeworski and Teune (1970, p. 92) reads: "For a specific observation a belch is a belch and nepotism is nepotism. But within an inferential framework, a belch is an 'insult' or a 'compliment' and nepotism is 'corruption' or 'responsibility.'" This comment illustrates that the meaning of behavior is dependent on the cultural context in which it occurs, while at the same time it asserts that such meaning can be understood in common terms (i.e., insult, compliment, corruption and responsibility).

Finally, there is the position of extreme universalism, which in the previous edition of this book was referred to as **absolutism** (Berry, Poortinga, Segall and Dasen, 2002). It describes a theoretical orientation that sees behavior as not influenced in any important way by cultural factors. In our opinion such behaviors exist, but are rare and limited to elementary sensory and motor processes. Responses on some of the items of the Ishihara test for color blindness (e.g., Birch, 1997) may be an example. With these items an individual is asked to trace a line that is visible to the non-colorblind, but invisible for those suffering from a certain type of color blindness. The Ishihara test would appear to assess color blindness in all cultural contexts. However, for most psychological tests and scales the cross-cultural comparison of scores at face value can lead to serious misinterpretation.

Theme 3: Psychological organization of cultural differences

Differences in behavior patterns between cultural groups (including responses to tests and questionnaires) usually are not of interest in their own right, but because they are seen as indices of broader aspects of behavior or psychological functioning. Interpretations can be broad and inclusive or they can be more narrow and limited. In this book we shall distinguish between various levels of inference, or levels of generalization, which are derived from psychological data. We shall come across notions such as cultural conventions or practices, behavior domains, attitudes, traits and abilities, styles, cultural dimensions or syndromes, and culture-as-a-system. This third theme may seem to belong to the universalism–relativism debate, but this is only partly so. Universalism–relativism is about the extent to which psychological processes are similar or different across cultures. The organization of cultural differences is about the extent to which various differences in behavior between two cultures should be seen as related to each other or as independent from each other.

The most far-reaching generalizations are in terms of a culture-as-a-system. Such a notion can be very useful if there is a comprehensive set of parameters in terms of which the system can be described or depicted (e.g., a flow diagram or organizational chart), so that it becomes clear what belongs and what does not belong to the system. Inferences made in the past, such as the concepts of "modal personality" (i.e., the dominant features of the typical person belonging to a cultural group, Bock, 1999), and "national character" (a set of personality traits frequently found in a society, Peabody, 1985), belong to this category of inferences. They were vague and have been largely dismissed. There are more recent concepts of similar scope (e.g., the notion of mentality, Fiske *et al.*, 1998); and the notion of "habitus" (lasting, acquired schemes of perception, thought and action, Bourdieu, 1998), but in our view cross-cultural psychologists have never produced a system description of culture that is comprehensive and at the same time lends itself to critical examination with empirical data.

Somewhat less abstract and comprehensive are interpretations in terms of broad cultural dimensions, of which individualism–collectivism and interdependent self versus independent self are the most prominent current examples. Some authors argue that this leads to an oversimplified picture (e.g., Medin, Unsworth and Hirschfeld, 2007). Another concern is with the validity of such high-level generalizations that are difficult to validate properly and virtually impossible to falsify as we shall see when we discuss the psychological organization of cross-cultural differences in Chapter 12.

Less far reaching are generalizations in terms of "styles," a concept used to describe patterns of cognitive abilities; that is, how peoples in certain cultures tend to approach cognitive problems (see the section on cognitive styles in Chapter 6). Styles, attitudes, cognitive abilities and personality traits are concepts from various areas of psychology that are used with a similar meaning in cross-cultural psychology. The construct validity of such concepts, and of interpretations of cross-cultural differences in behavior, is less difficult to establish than for the more comprehensive cultural dimensions noted above. This is because the inferential distance from actual behavior to the underlying concept is smaller and more open to critical appraisal.

With the concept of behavior domains (i.e., categories of situations)[1] the principle of generalization is not applied to psychological functions or processes, but to fields of behavior organized in terms of skills and knowledge of procedures (Cole, 1996). Behavior domains are more descriptive and less inferential than, for example, cognitive styles and personality traits. Finally, customs, practices and conventions are descriptive terms that usually stay close to direct observation of daily life in a particular culture; here the validity of inferences is most open to unambiguous empirical examination.

Explanations that are less comprehensive tend to allow critical empirical scrutiny; as mentioned, they stay closer to the data. The attractiveness of more comprehensive and abstract concepts is that they explain a wider array of cross-cultural differences. This makes the search for more inclusive explanations worthwhile. As we shall see in various chapters, there is a trade-off between the precision of inferences (based on their specificity) and their scope (when seeking broad generalizations).

A few caveats

The three themes that we have discussed in this section represent issues that we will come across frequently in later chapters. Are they the most important themes of debate? A reader with prior knowledge of cross-cultural psychology may be surprised to find that the dichotomy between nature and nurture is not mentioned as one of the themes. There is certainly much debate on theories addressing the extent to which psychological functioning is constrained by our genetic constitution, and how variation can emerge in the course of developmental processes. However, the arguments about nature–nurture have shifted to specific models and theories; the old dichotomy of body and soul, or genetic versus environmental as separate sources of variance largely has been left behind. Cross-cultural researchers have moved from a dualism between psyche and body to a monism where psychological functioning is so much part of the organism that it cannot be defined as a separate principle of existence.

Before concluding this section, we think we should make explicit our own position in respect to each of the three themes mentioned. On the first theme (culture as internal or external), we take the position that culture includes both. It refers to a set of external conditions within which humans develop and act, as well as to constructed psychological meanings. There are meanings and overt behaviors where the relationship with external conditions is unclear, if such a relationship exists at all. However, we also hold the viewpoint that psychological variables and external conditions can be linked closely; sometimes such relationships go back in

---

[1] We use the term "trait" to refer to a characteristic of persons (as in personality traits), and the term "domain" to refer to a class of situations that evoke similar behavior (e.g., situations that evoke a fear reaction, or situations belonging to a field of activity).

historical time (like economic subsistence patterns), and sometimes they are ad hoc solutions to new challenges (such as limiting young children's access to violent TV programs). In short, human behavior can be adaptive to conditions in the external environment both over longer periods of historical time as well as here and now.

On the second theme we tend to be on the universalist side rather than on the relativist side, although we strongly reject absolutism. We believe that there are common psychological processes in all humans, and that cultures shape the development and expression of these underlying features. The basis for our position will become clearer as we discuss the many empirical findings pointing to underlying similarities in human behavior. For example, it is clear that once we comprehend a language, or have a translation, we can understand pretty well the values, emotions and reasoning of cultural "others," as well as being able to communicate ours to them, provided there is a willingness to respect and understand other viewpoints.

On the third theme (psychological organization of cultural differences) even we as authors have some disagreements. None of us is convinced that there is so much coherence in patterns of cross-cultural differences that it is helpful to conceptualize a culture as a psychological system. We have considerable hesitation about currently prominent dimensions, such as collectivism–individualism and the associated independence–interdependence of the self. However, some of us see styles and trait dimensions as an important focus for the explanation of cross-cultural differences, while others place more emphasis on cultural conventions and practices.

Interpretive positions

Views of researchers on themes of debate tend to coalesce into more or less coherent positions, which can be seen as "interpretive positions" or "perspectives" on behavior–culture relationships. An active field of research like cross-cultural psychology can be parceled in various ways (e.g., Bouvy, Van de Vijver, Boski, Schmitz and Krewer, 1994). Here we mention three perspectives to the study of culture and behavior, labeled as: culture-comparative psychology, cultural psychology and indigenous psychology.

Culture-comparative psychology

Psychology gained visibility as a scientific discipline around the beginning of the twentieth century. Although there had been a few earlier studies and many ideas about what we now call cultural differences (Jahoda, 1992), cross-cultural psychology as a separate field of research became established about fifty years later, mainly following culture-comparative research projects. It combined cultural anthropologists' interest in culture with psychological research methods. Through inclusion of data from different cultural contexts such research was meant to contribute to the understanding of the behavior of non-western peoples as well as to the further development of psychology. The "extension of the range of variation" was recognized as an essential characteristic of the field (Whiting, 1954, p. 524).

The culture-comparative perspective is rooted in the idea of universality of psychic functioning. Universality has been discussed extensively in sources from cultural anthropology as well as cross-cultural psychology (e.g., Brown, 1991; Lonner, 1980; Lonner and Adamopoulos, 1997; Munroe and Munroe, 1997). In the broadest sense universality is rooted in basic concerns of the human species, such as hunger and thirst, or the need for some kind of social organization (Malinowski, 1944). These are also found in many other species. Much closer similarity in human functioning across cultures is presumed when universality is defined at the level of psychological concepts as they are formulated in psychological theories. Ultimately the assumption is that any theoretically meaningful psychological concept should make sense everywhere, despite large variations in behavior manifestations. For example, an emotion concept or personality trait which is meant to refer to an aspect of human psychological functioning only makes theoretical sense if its validity can be demonstrated in any culture.

In later chapters we shall see how research findings on visual illusions, social and personality dimensions, emotions and psycholinguistics have been argued to be compatible with the idea of universality. We shall also see that such views have been challenged by the two other perspectives. Perhaps the strongest of these challenges concern the concept of numeracy (being able to deal with numbers). Children in literate societies are taught counting and arithmetic, which play a role in a variety of everyday activities. Does numeracy refer to a skill, even a collection of skills, or does it require a separate mode of cognitive functioning, not found among illiterates? In Chapter 6 we present ways in which this question has been answered.

The main research strategy in culture-comparative studies takes the context in which the members of a culture are living, including both ecological and sociocultural factors, as a set of antecedent conditions (e.g., Segall, 1984). Psychological variables, such as values and attitudes, as well as observable behaviors, are seen as outcomes or consequences of these conditions. Less frequent are studies in which the relationship between antecedent and consequent variables is taken to be moderated or mediated by a third (cultural) variable (Lonner and Adamopoulos, 1997). For example, such a mediating role has been postulated for the temperature of the environment by Van der Vliert (2009). He starts from an ecological perspective contrasting harsh climates (which can be either hot or cold) with temperate climates, taking into consideration precipitation as well as temperature. The second important ingredient in the formation of culture is economic affluence, going from poor to rich. These two influence each other, leading to three "cultural conglomerates": survival cultures (harsh and poor), easygoing cultures (temperate and either poor or rich) and self-expression cultures (harsh and rich).

Comparative empirical research is mostly geared toward selection of cultural populations that differ on some antecedent condition in order to explore differences in behavior outcomes, or to test a priori specified hypotheses about such outcomes (Van de Vijver and Leung, 1997). One research tradition focussing on ecocultural variables (Berry, 1976, in press), including modes of subsistence (such as hunting–gathering, agriculture) and climate, is presented in Box 1.1. In our view this Box is useful for understanding the kind of reasoning underlying the culture-comparative approach.

Box 1.1 **The ecocultural framework**

This framework, presented in Figure 1.1, is a conceptual scheme, rather than a theoretical model from which specific testable hypotheses can be derived. It is a general guide to classes of variables, and their relevance for the explanation of similarities and differences in human behavior to be found across cultures.

This ecocultural framework has been influenced by various ways of thinking about how behavioral, cultural and ecological phenomena might be related, including the work of Malinowski and Rivers. For Malinowski features of a culture are to be understood "by the manner in which they are related to each other within the system, and by the manner in which the system is related to the physical surroundings" (1922, p. x). Here linkages between ecology and culture are proposed. For Rivers, "the ultimate aim of all studies of mankind ... is to reach explanation in terms of psychology ... by which the conduct of man, both individual and collective, is determined ... by the social structure of which every person ... finds himself a member" (1924, p. 1). Here linkages between human behavior and the sociocultural context are proposed. The framework as presented has been influenced by several other writers whose names will appear later in this book (e.g., Kardiner and Linton, 1945; Whiting, 1974; see Additional Topics, Chapter 10). The configuration in Figure 1.1 has been adapted from Berry (1976, in press).

www.cambridge.org/berry

The general flow of the framework is from left to right, with population-level variables (left part) conceived of as influencing individual outcomes (right part). This is intended to correspond to the main interests of culture-comparative researchers who seek to account for individual and group similarities and differences in behavior as a function of population-level factors. It is obvious that a full model would have numerous feedback arrows representing influences from individuals back to the other variables in the framework. The direction from individual to group is represented by two feedback arrows going from right to left. According to many theories, human beings are active participants in their relationships with the physical and social context in which they operate. There is an interactive or dialectical relationship (Boesch, 1991; Eckensberger, 1996; see p. 285, this volume) that can both filter and alter the very nature of this context.

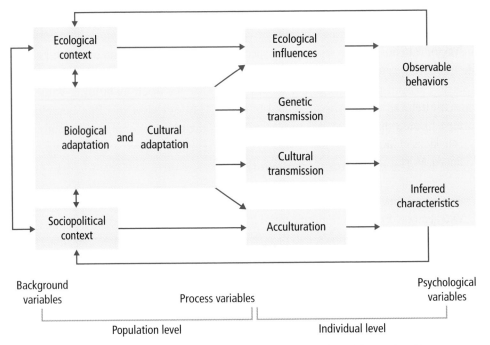

Figure 1.1 An ecocultural framework of relationships among classes of variables employed in cross-cultural psychology.

Box 1.1 continued

At the left of the figure are three major classes of influence. First there is a frame mentioning biological and cultural adaptations linking current behavior patterns to development over historical time as well as to the phylogenetic history of the human species. The framework presumes that individual behavior can be understood only when both cultural and biological features are taken into account (e.g., Boyd and Richerson, 1985, 2005). The other two frames refer to ecological and sociopolitical contexts as they exist in the present time. The three frames are interconnected by arrows reflecting mutual influences. To the right of the figure are the psychological characteristics that are usually the focus of psychological research (including both observable behaviors and inferred characteristics, such as motives, abilities, traits and attitudes). The middle sets of variables (process or mediating variables) represent four kinds of transmission or influences to individuals from population variables.

The ecological context is the setting in which human organisms interact with the physical environment. A central feature is economic activity. For non-industrial cultural groups this refers to reliance on five kinds of economic activity: hunting, gathering, fishing, pastoralism and agriculture. Urban-industrial societies have a way of life in which other dimensions of economic activity have emerged; in particular, socioeconomic status

Box 1.1 continued

has come to be related to cultural or ethnic group characteristics in many societies. The sociopolitical context refers to a host of variables covering norms, beliefs, attitudes and ideas that are the focus of most cross-cultural research reported in the literature.

The framework also illustrates various ways in which features of the population (on the left) become incorporated into an individual's behavioral repertoire (on the right). Four kinds of factors – ecological, biological, cultural and acculturational – are mentioned. Most relationships between the two major background variables and psychological outcomes are mediated by cultural and biological transmission. The latter implies that individuals acquire part of the total gene pool of the population to which they belong through their biological parents. Cultural transmission refers to the processes of socialization and enculturation (see Chapter 2) through which the individual acquires part of the total pool of cultural information available in the society or community. As we will see in Chapters 2 and 3, the distinction between biological and cultural transmission is based more on pragmatic than on conceptual considerations. This is simply because the propagation of one's genes (biological transmission) and the conveyance of parental beliefs, norms and values (cultural transmission) to the next generation go hand in hand and cannot be regarded as two independent transmission processes (in Chapter 11, we will give a more detailed account of the relationship between biology and culture).

Some outcomes can be seen as being mediated by ecological influences, such as modes of food accumulation. Other outcomes result from influences stemming from culture contact in the sociopolitical context of one's group. These come about with contacts between populations due to such historical and contemporary experiences as colonial expansion, international trade, invasion and migration. Such influences are captured by another process variable, that of acculturation, which involves mutual influence between the groups in contact (see Chapter 13).

It is important to note that not all relationships between the two major background variables (biological and cultural variation) and psychological outcomes (observable behaviors and inferred characteristics) are mediated by cultural and biological transmission. Some reactions to external context are best interpreted as rather immediate, such as coping with nutritional deficiency during a famine (leading to reduced performance), or reactions to new experiences with another culture as a migrant or sojourner (leading to new attitudes or values). These direct influences are indicated by the upper and lower arrows that bypass the two forms of population mediation.

Finally, a framework as depicted in Figure 1.1 should not be interpreted rigidly. Individuals can recognize, screen, appraise and alter many of these influences (whether direct or mediated); as a result there are likely to be wide individual differences in psychological outcomes, and return (reciprocal) influences on the background contexts and the various process variables.

During the last few decades the focus has shifted to sociocultural variables, especially values (Smith, Bond and Kağitçibaşi, 2006). In much of this research differences between countries (as proxies for cultures) have been used to create value dimensions, such as individualism–collectivism (Hofstede, 1980, 2001; Triandis, 1995). Usually differences in values are seen as outcomes (consequences) of broad antecedent conditions, such as differences in modes of socialization.

In terms of the three themes of debate outlined in the previous section, culture-comparative research clearly leans toward universalism rather than to relativism. It recognizes culture both as a set of external conditions and as psychological features within the person, often assuming antecedent–consequent relationships between the external context and observed behavior. Inferences or generalizations about value dimensions imply broad generalizations; for example, the contrast between individualistic and collectivistic orientations has been linked to a large variety of behavior differences (Triandis, 1989, 1995). In later chapters we shall see that there are also numerous studies in culture-comparative traditions linking specific cultural features to specific behavior outcomes. As we shall see just now, variation in level of generalization is also found in the other two schools, as is an overall tendency to make rather high-level generalizations.

Cultural psychology

The name cultural psychology was a deliberate choice to identify a field that would be distinct from cross-cultural psychology in the comparative tradition (Shweder, 1990). The motto of cross-cultural psychology had been the "psychic unity of humankind." Shweder (1990, 1991) proposed an alternative motto: "culture and psyche make each other up." This indicates that culture and behavior are to be seen as essentially inseparable and that different psyches will emerge in different cultural contexts. The cultural approach was defined as relativistic, emphasizing unique features not only of behavior manifestations in a cultural group, but also of underlying processes. A clear case is research on emotions. In the ethnographic literature cultural anthropologists reported distinct emotions not found in western societies (e.g., Lutz, 1988; Russell, 1991). Such findings were taken to imply that emotions are not natural categories of common human experience, but sociocultural constructions that are culture-specific. Thus, Kitayama and Markus edited a book with the explicit aim to establish that emotions can be conceptualized as being "social in nature" and "anything but natural" (1994, p.1).

The emergence of cultural psychology followed a shift in cultural anthropology that we have already mentioned, that is, from culture as external context to "culture in the mind of the people" (Geertz, 1973) and from a focus on overt behavior to the construction of meaning (Bruner, 1990). Although this gave a new impetus to the relativist perspective, there are historical roots in earlier traditions, notably psychological anthropology – a field of research in cultural anthropology applying psychoanalytic ideas to the study of personality and culture. In this tradition the members of a culture would be characterized by a typical or modal personality that was qualitatively different from the modal personality of any other cultural group (for a review see Bock, 1999). Another major influence on cultural psychology came from Vygotsky (1978) – a Russian psychologist whose main ideas were published in the 1920s, but only translated into English decades later. In his view "higher mental processes" developed over time in the history of societies. Only to the extent that such processes (a notable example being syllogistic thinking; Luria, 1976) are present in a society can they be transmitted to children in the course of their development. This amounts to culture exerting a mediating influence on the psychological process in the individual between stimulus and response. As we shall see in the section on culture as context for development in Chapter 2 the sociocultural school of Cole (1996; Laboratory for Comparative Human Cognition, 1982) has further developed Vygotsky's ideas, but with interpretations of differences at a far lower level of generalization. Cultures are thought to differ in fields of activity. An example is dealing with computers, which now comes almost "naturally" to urban western youngsters, but is strange and difficult for those less accustomed.

Since cultural psychology as we know it today has been developed only recently, it is not surprising that ideas still tend to shift. The original position that "psyche and culture make each other up" has been followed by another slogan which comes closer to a universalist perspective, namely that there exists "one mind, but many mentalities" (Fiske *et al.*, 1998). Much recent research in cultural psychology has been concerned with a contrast between East Asian societies and US America: namely whether a person defines him/herself primarily as integrated with others or as an individual separate from others. Markus and Kitayama (1991) have referred to this contrast as interdependent construal of the self versus independent construal of the self. Perhaps the strongest claim deriving from cultural psychology has been that self-enhancement was argued to be entirely absent in the Japanese (Heine, Lehman, Markus and Kitayama, 1999; see Box 4.3 for a discussion). Another aspect of this East–West contrast concerns cognition: Chinese thinking is said to be more associative and intuitive, while in Americans reasoning is more formal. Several comparative studies have been reported confirming hypotheses to test this idea (Nisbett, Peng, Choi and Norenzayan, 2001; Peng and Nisbett, 1999). Cultural roots have been inferred that go back to ancient Greek and Chinese philosophies (Nisbett, 2003), reflecting, like the other examples mentioned in this paragraph, a high level of generalization (see Chapter 12).

Current empirical research in cultural psychology tends to follow a comparative design (Kitayama and Cohen, 2007). Unlike in traditional culture-comparative research, differences in psychological variables tend to be interpreted as reflecting differences in psychological functioning that are rooted in the psychological histories of cultural populations rather than in external ecological and sociocultural conditions.

In summary, within cultural psychology, differences in overt behavior tend to be interpreted as implying differences in underlying psychological functions and processes. Initially cultural psychology was defined as a relativist research tradition, but in part it has moved closer to the culture-comparative orientation. While cultural psychologists would not deny the importance of prevailing external conditions these do not feature much in interpretations; culture is something psychological and inside of people rather than referring to external antecedents. Finally, research findings of differences between samples from the East and the West often have been generalized to a single major distinction in the mode of functioning of the self, as either more interdependent with others or more independent from others.

Indigenous psychology

Over the past few decades psychologists outside of Europe and North America have started to conduct research that is more appropriate and relevant to their local contexts than are "western" approaches (for overviews see, e.g., Allwood and Berry, 2006; Kim and Berry, 1993; Kim, Yang and Hwang, 2006). Such developments, collectively called indigenous psychology, can be found in India (e.g., D. Sinha, 1997; Rao, Paranjpe and Dalal, 2008), Central and West Africa (Nsamenang, 1992), Mexico (Diaz-Guerrero, 1993) and the Philippines (Enriquez, 1990). More recently the focus seems to be shifting to psychologies for culturally or even religiously defined regions such as Muslim countries in the Middle East (Dwairy, 2006; Ramadan and Gielen, 1998) or East Asia (Kashima, 2005) rather than for specific countries.

Historically psychology as a science has been imported in the non-western world from the West. Initially psychologists trained in western countries would continue the research they were most familiar with, often replicating western studies (D. Sinha, 1997). They found existing instruments, methods and theories less applicable and especially less relevant to their local context and turned to making psychology more appropriate. Perhaps the boldest attempt was undertaken by Enriquez (1990) and his colleagues in the Philippines. They started out by contacting local people and asking them their ideas about behavior. One salient finding was that the classical situation with the interviewer asking questions and the interviewee giving the responses did not go down well with rural Filipinos. A more successful method was *pagtanong-tanong*, in which interviewer and interviewee are more equal and exchange information interactively. As with participant observation – the main method of ethnography – the respondent more than the researcher is in control of the direction and content of the interaction (Pe-Pua, 2006).

A major emphasis in indigenous psychology is on local psychological concepts for which there are no equivalents in English or other European languages. Examples include *amae* or need for dependency in Japan (Doi, 1973); *nurturant-task leadership* in India (J. Sinha, 1980); and *koro* – the pathological fear of retraction of one's penis into the body in South-East Asia (Simons and Hughes, 1985). As we shall see in later chapters on emotions and personality, studies that have used non-western conceptualizations with western cultural samples tend to replicate original findings, demonstrating the psychological validity of distinctions that are absent from western psychological literature.

The most important reason for developing indigenous approaches, especially among applied psychologists, is that salient issues in low-income societies are relatively rarely addressed by western researchers. In this book we will use the term majority world to refer to the large part of the world population which is living in a context of poverty and illiteracy (Kağitçibaşi, 2007). Psychological correlates of poverty, such as violence and malnutrition, are infrequently mentioned in the subject indices of western textbooks, including textbooks of cross-cultural psychology, and have relatively few entries in research registers like PsychLit (but see, e.g., Carr and Sloan, 2003).[2]

Theory-oriented research and applied research in psychology often are hardly related to each other (Schönpflug, 1993). Such a discrepancy is prominent in the literature on indigenous psychology. Writings on theory often postulate broad generalizations endorsing major differences, notably a collectivist orientation in the East as opposed to the individualism of the West (Kim and Park, 2006; Yang, 2003). In applied studies, many of which are never reported in journals or books with an international readership, the orientation is more pragmatic. There is extensive use of intervention programs, for example in the areas of health behavior and education, based on western principles and methods. However, the specific content of interventions (e.g., names of plants, customs) tends to be adapted to local circumstances (e.g., Leenen *et al.*, 2008; Pick and Sirkin, 2010).

The term "indigenous psychology" can be said to be a misnomer in two ways. First, it assigns a separate status to western psychology as being exempt from this category. Psychology as known today has been largely developed in the West; it is a product of western culture. In our view, it should also be considered as an indigenous psychology. Second, and more important, if there is a need for local forms of psychology there should be more indigenous psychologies, in principle one for each culture or cultural region (however such regions may be defined). This is a contentious issue. Authors who endorse relativism tend to acknowledge the need for multiple psychologies (e.g., Shweder, 1990). Others, like D. Sinha (1997) and Enriquez (1993) have been adamant that indigenous research is needed as an

---

[2] In our view it is a moral imperative for cross-cultural psychology to show a more global concern for human well-being. As mentioned in the Preface, this is the main reason why there is a third part to this book dealing with issues of application.

intermediate stage to make non-western voices and interests explicit, but that ultimately psychology should be a unitary science for all humans. Enriquez (1993) referred to this strategy as the "cross-indigenous approach"; and Yang (2000, p. 257) argued that these multiple psychologies "collectively ... serve the higher purpose of developing a balanced, genuine global psychology." For a further discussion of western dominance in psychology, including cross-cultural psychology, we refer to the Internet (Additional Topics, Chapter 1), where we briefly discuss four levels of ethnocentrism.

www.cambridge.org/berry

The tradition of indigenous psychology in so far as it emphasizes culturally unique psychological concepts clearly leans more toward relativism than to universalism. In this sense indigenous psychology and cultural psychology tend to share a similar perspective. There is also another side to indigenous psychology: namely to overcome western biases in psychological research and application. Making psychology relevant beyond western countries can be compatible with a universalist orientation (e.g., D. Sinha, 1997). A somewhat similar ambiguity can be noted in respect of the distinction between culture inside or outside the person and to issues of generalization. In theoretical accounts authors tend to endorse the cultural psychology perspective of locating culture inside the person, but in applied studies there is more emphasis on external conditions. Also, broad generalizations are found in theoretical discussion, while in applied research and intervention programs local issues tend to be addressed in a pragmatic fashion, often replicating existing programs and methods from the West, with local adaptations of content (e.g., names of plants, local customs) as deemed desirable. The main inspiration for such activities lies in the actual context of poverty and illiteracy rather than in the construction of meaning. Their main goal is to realize changes in actual behavior, rather than mapping out differences in patterns of culture.

Designing cross-cultural research

When conducting empirical research you first have to ask yourself what you want to know and why. In cross-cultural psychology researchers' interest will be in behavior patterns and how they are embedded in cultural context. Some information on types of research questions can be found on the Internet (Additional Topics, Chapter 1). Here we address two issues. The first is the sampling of cultures, that is, the choice of one or more populations in which data are to be collected. The second, much debated issue linked to the conceptualization of culture–behavior relationships, is whether a qualitative or a quantitative approach should be followed in cross-cultural psychology.

Sampling

The notion of "a" culture, as distinct from other cultures, is used in this book in two ways. First, it refers to a population of persons who have certain artifacts and "mentifacts" (i.e., ideas, beliefs, conventions, etc.) more in common among themselves than with outsiders. In the second sense a culture is the repertoire of behavior, including overt and covert aspects, of such a population. In cross-cultural psychology cultures are most frequently national states or societies, but one finds many other groupings of humans also referred to as cultures. For example, in research on acculturation and intercultural relations, ethnocultural groups are cultural populations; they are usually defined in terms of the ancestral culture or country of origin of members. Also, work organizations are sometimes considered to have distinct cultures, as shown by the concept of organizational culture that we discuss in Chapter 16.

Two characteristics are considered relevant in identifying separate cultures. First, the variance between populations in the behavior that is being researched should make up a worthwhile part of the total variance (i.e., the combined within-population variance and between-population variance). We call this *differentiation*. The second characteristic is *permanence*. Malinowski (1944) claimed that a culture has an existence of its own beyond the psychological make-up of its individual members because of its permanence; a culture is still there when all its current members are no longer alive. On the other hand, a notion such as "youth culture" refers to a recently established or even a fleeting group. A group low on differentiation and permanence has little "categorical identifiability" (Schaller, Conway and Crandall, 2004). Any such grouping is not a culture in the sense used in this book.

The distinction between separate cultures, more properly named "culture-bearing units" (or cultunits) (Naroll, 1970a), has to match the kind of grouping for which differences in the psychological variables studied are expected. This means that if societal variables are of interest, the nation state is likely to be the appropriate unit of selection. In a cross-cultural study of psycholinguistics, speakers of different languages make up the relevant cultural populations. A study of the effects of iodine deficiency on cognitive performance by Bleichrodt, Drenth and Querido (1980) included two villages in Spain and two in Indonesia. In this case the high or low presence of iodine in local water supplies determined the units of selection. Ideally the question of which cultural populations to include in a study arises only after it is clear by which variable(s) they are to be distinguished. Once populations have been chosen it has to be considered whether or not for each culture a representative sample will be selected or a certain subgroup (e.g., university students). Finally, it has to be decided how individuals are to be selected within each culture or subgroup (Lonner and Berry, 1986; Van de Vijver and Leung, 1997).

Many culture-comparative studies are carried out with students; they are easily accessible to researchers and possess "test-wiseness," that is, they know how to complete tests and questionnaires. When the findings from student samples are generalized to the cultural populations (usually countries) to which they belong, there is a strong implicit assumption of cultural homogeneity. Such an assumption may be justified (e.g., most citizens of France speak French), but it may also amount to a fallacy. Many psychological variables show systematic variation between educationally or demographically distinguishable groups within countries. Therefore, the size of cross-cultural differences, and even their presence or absence, is likely to depend on the selection of the particular samples chosen to represent the cultures concerned.

It is almost impossible to select a subgroup in one cultural population so that it will precisely match a subgroup in another culture. Strong warnings have been issued against the use of matched samples in culture-comparative studies (Draguns, 1982; Lonner and Berry, 1986). The crux of the objections is that matching on one variable almost without exception leads to mismatching on other variables. Suppose a researcher would like to select samples of West Europeans and of Africans in Nigeria or Kenya matched on education. Educated Africans are more likely than the average citizen of their country to belong to a family with high income and social status, while they may be less likely than other citizens of their countries to value traditional norms and customs.

The following two conclusions emerge, which both clearly go against fairly common research practices in cross-cultural psychology. First, the selection of cultural populations, or culture-bearing units, should be guided by a clear consideration of the basis on which they are to be distinguished. Second, unless there are reasons to assume cultural homogeneity, the representation of a culture by a select sample (e.g., students at one or a few university departments) is likely to lead to a distorted view of cross-cultural differences.

Qualitative and quantitative approaches

In the literature the most important distinction regarding how to carry out cross-cultural research is between qualitative approaches and quantitative approaches. The former are more associated with relativism, and the latter with universalism. Other pairs of terms make similar distinctions, such as idiographic and nomothetic, or phenomenological and experimental. The distinction goes back a long time in cross-cultural psychology (e.g., Jahoda and Krewer, 1997). In many ways, qualitative methods in cross-cultural psychology are rooted in the use of ethnography in cultural anthropology (see Chapter 10). In Box 1.2 we present the well-known dichotomy between emic and etic approaches, formulated in the 1960s.

Box 1.2 **Emic and etic approaches**

One early attempt to deal with qualitative and quantitative approaches is captured in the distinction between **emic** and **etic**. These terms were coined by Pike (1967) in analogy with phonetics and phonemics. In the field of linguistics phonetics refers to the study of general aspects of vocal sounds and sound production; phonemics is the study of the sounds used in a particular language. Berry (1969) has summarized Pike's comments on the emic–etic distinction as it applies in cross-cultural psychology. This summary is presented in Table 1.1.

Many qualitative researchers argue that behavior in its full complexity can only be understood within the context of the culture in which it occurs. In the emic approach an attempt is made to look at phenomena and their interrelationships (structure) through the eyes of the people native to a particular culture. One tries to avoid the imposition of a priori notions and ideas from one's own culture on the people studied. This point of view finds its origin in cultural anthropology where, via the method of participant observation, the researcher tries to look at norms, values, motives and customs of the members of a particular community in their own terms.

The danger of an etic approach is that the concepts and notions of researchers are rooted in and influenced by their cultural background. They are working with "imposed etics" (Berry, 1969, p. 124), or "pseudo etics" (Triandis, Malpass and Davidson, 1971b, p. 6). The goal of empirical analysis is to progressively change the "imposed etics" to match the emic viewpoint of the culture studied. This should lead eventually to the formulation of "derived etics" which are valid cross-culturally.

More extensive listings of distinctive features between emic and etic have appeared in the literature (Pelto and Pelto, 1981; Ekstrand and Ekstrand, 1986), which further subdivide the contrasts listed in Table 1.1. The literature is not very informative when one is looking for empirical procedures to separate the emic from the etic. Berry (1969, 1989; see also Segall *et al.*, 1999) has suggested an iterative approach. In culture-comparative approaches researchers will typically start with an imposed etic. They will scrutinize their conceptions and methods for culture appropriateness in an emic phase. In so far as equivalent concepts and variables are established (see later in this chapter), derived etics will be identified in terms of which valid comparisons can be made, at least across the cultures concerned. Extension of the research can ultimately lead to so much evidence that it can be reasonably concluded that a psychological characteristic is universally present. At the same time, emic explorations within cultural settings should allow the identification of what is culture-specific in psychological functioning. In cultural approaches taking a relativist perspective the emic–etic distinction is sometimes rejected as insufficient. If psychological concepts are seen as essentially cultural, researchers will never be able to move from imposed etics to derived etics; the latter are taken not to exist.

Table 1.1	The emic and etic approaches	
Emic approach	**Etic approach**
Studies behavior from within the system	Studies behavior from a position outside the system
Examines only one culture	Examines many cultures, comparing them
Structure discovered by the analyst	Structure created by the analyst
Criteria are relative to internal characteristics	Criteria are considered absolute or universal

From Berry (1969).

In this book we pay attention to both qualitative and quantitative methods; we see them as complementary although this is not to say that they are exchangeable. The most important principle in the evaluation of the scientific merits of a study is the extent to which it supports one explanation of the data while simultaneously ruling out alternative explanations. This is the guiding principle for the following discussion.

Qualitative research is conducted in natural settings; it is also called field research (Singleton and Straits, 2005). Often multiple methods are applied that are preferably interactive, implying that participants are to be "involved in" the data collection rather than "subjected to" surveys and experimental treatments. The researcher interprets the meaning of the data that are gathered and reflects critically on his or her own role in the research process (Creswell, 2009). Collection of data may be largely unstructured, driven by events as they occur, even with changes in research questions and procedures as the data collection is in progress. Such changes are likely to reflect a better understanding acquired in the course of a study, making qualitative research more adaptable than experiments where procedures are to be followed rigorously. Qualitative research lends itself to single-case analysis, whether at the level of a particular person or at the level of a particular culture, identifying characteristic patterns and configurations (Huberman and Miles, 1994).

Many researchers tend to be critical of qualitative research. First, most qualitative research is heavily dependent on interpretation by the researcher. Methods do not have rule-bound scoring procedures; the insight of the psychologist in the psychological meaning of the respondent's reactions is central (Smith, Harré and Van Langenhove, 1995). Looking at many interpretations in the history of cross-cultural psychology that we now find totally unwarranted, the insights of researchers indeed appear to be on a shaky foundation. A second reason for a critical attitude toward qualitative methods derives from the difficulties in finding formal procedures for establishing the validity of results. There are few parallels in qualitative analysis for procedures that either are open to independent scrutiny by virtue of replicability (like the experiment), or for establishing validity by means of statistical procedures (like the standardized test or questionnaire). In Chapter 12 we will return to the issue of validity when we discuss the epistemological underpinnings of relativism and universalism.

Most culture-comparative research tends to follow a quantitative approach, based in the experimental paradigm of psychology. Some (internal or external) cultural condition forms the independent variable and some behavioral variable is the dependent or outcome variable. The main methods of data collection in quantitative analysis consist of two overlapping categories, one with a focus on assessment instruments (i.e., psychometric tests and questionnaires), and the other with a focus on (quasi-)experimental design.

In a well-designed experiment the researcher has control over the treatments administered to the participants in the various experimental conditions, and the participants should be allocated to these conditions at random. In studies with groups that already exist, participants are nested in their respective groups and their allocation is fixed. Such studies are referred to as "quasi-experiments" (Shadish, Cook and Campbell, 2002). The interpretation of results is problematic when differences in outcomes can be due to some uncontrolled but relevant variable on which the groups happen to differ. In the case of cultural populations the set of variables on which participants differ is immense. Socialization practices, availability of words for certain concepts, education, religious beliefs, access to mass communication media, are only some examples. Also, the control over treatment conditions tends to be very limited in cross-cultural studies. In the laboratory the researcher administers the treatments, although even there control over ambient variables, like the motivation of participants, is imperfect. Many cultural factors extend their influence over a long period of time and their influence on the participants cannot be directly observed. Hence, the effect of a postulated cultural factor that is supposed to underlie a difference in scores is often inferred post hoc. As a consequence, when evaluating cross-cultural comparative studies it is important to consider carefully whether alternatives to the interpretation of the results put forward by the researchers reasonably can be ruled out.

Qualitative and quantitative research methods have been argued by some to be mutually exclusive, but they can also be seen as complementary (e.g., Reichardt and Rallis, 1994; Shadish, 2000; Todd, Nerlich, McKeown and Clarke, 2004). Creswell (2009) recommends mixed methods. Also, the notion of "consilience" in methods has been mentioned as a strategy to strengthen the validity of cross-cultural inferences (Van de Vijver and Chasiotis, 2010; Van de Vijver and Leung, in press). This implies that findings are more convincing when they are based on diverse sources of evidence, multiple sources of data and different research methods. These authors add an important requirement: namely that research should be designed with a view to explicit refutation of alternative interpretations.

Dealing with threats to interpretation

An early series of cross-cultural studies was conducted by Porteus (1937), who administered psychometric tests, especially his own maze test, in various regions of the world. He saw foresight and planning – abilities required to solve the mazes – as the core of intellectual functioning and interpreted score differences in terms of intelligence as an inborn characteristic. His findings led him to conclude that the San people ("Bushmen") in the Kalahari Desert had the lowest intelligence of all peoples, followed by the Australian Aborigines, while white western groups came out as the smartest. This interpretation can be simply dismissed as racially prejudiced, but here the relevant question is whether and how it could be challenged on methodological grounds.

Porteus (1937) assumed that: (1) intelligence was measured by the maze tests in precisely the same way across cultures; (2) scores on the maze tests allowed inferences about the level of innate intelligence of testees; and (3) mean differences between samples of individuals allow statements about the cultures they belong to. The first of these three assumptions entails that scores on the instrument would show comparability or equivalence across groups and be free from cultural bias. The second assumption implies that the scores are not only an indication of how well people can do a certain trick, but also allow a generalization from the scores to the broad concept of inborn intelligence. The third assumption implies that individual scores can be aggregated so that it is meaningful to talk about cultural-level variance in intelligence in addition to individual-level variance. In this section we discuss each of these three assumptions. Although Porteus' inferences about racial differences were particularly gross, we shall see that each assumption entails the risk of overinterpretation of cross-cultural differences.

Equivalence of concepts and data

It has been argued that the cross-cultural comparison of instrument-based data is always scientifically unsound (e.g., Greenfield, 1997). Psychological assessment should take place, if at all, with instruments (tests, etc.) developed within the culture where they are to be used. This viewpoint follows from versions of relativism which hold that psychological processes and functions are not the same across cultures (see Box 1.2). Of course, we agree that comparison of data does not make sense unless what is being measured is the same in the cultures concerned. However, within a universalist framework it is not excluded a priori that instruments address identical concepts cross-culturally. Rather, this is seen as an empirical question. We call scores equivalent or comparable if they can be interpreted in the same way for two persons belonging to different cultures. A lack of comparability, or inequivalence, can be the consequence of many sources of cultural bias (Van de Vijver and Poortinga, 1997; Van de Vijver and Tanzer, 2004). Ultimately, it is the task of a researcher to make it plausible that the interpretation of cross-cultural data is not distorted because of inequivalence. This can be done more easily when different levels of equivalence are distinguished.

Conceptual equivalence addresses the question of whether a domain or trait makes sense in all of the cultural populations to be compared in a study (Fontaine, in press). There are no data analytic procedures that directly address this level of equivalence. If it is rejected a priori, meaningful cross-cultural comparison is ruled out; if accepted, possible empirical evidence should be compatible with the assumption of conceptual equivalence.

Three further levels of equivalence have been distinguished by Van de Vijver and Leung (1997). These distinctions can be illustrated with reference to measurements of temperature. Direct comparison of temperature readings on thermometers does not make sense if some of the thermometers have a Celsius scale and others a Fahrenheit scale. It also does not make sense if a Celsius and a Kelvin scale have been used; these scales have the same metric but differ in origin (the temperature at which the scale value is zero). Keeping this analog in mind, the three hierarchical levels of Van de Vijver and Leung can be described as follows:

- *Structural equivalence* implies that the same trait or domain is measured cross-culturally, but not necessarily on the same quantitative scale (cf. measurements made on a Fahrenheit scale and a Celsius scale).
- *Metric equivalence* (also called equivalence of measurement units) implies that a difference between two scores has the same meaning, independent of the culture in which it was found (cf. measurements on a Celsius scale and a Kelvin scale, where a given difference in temperature spans the same number of degrees on both scales, but absolute temperature readings are not the same because the zero-point for these two scales is not the same).
- *Scale equivalence* (also called full-score equivalence) implies that scores of a given value have in all respects the same meaning cross-culturally and can be interpreted in the same way (cf. temperature readings made with one Celsius thermometer and with another Celsius thermometer).

To distinguish equivalent from non-equivalent data several statistical procedures have been developed. They provide testable conditions for each level that presumably are satisfied by equivalent data, but not by inequivalent or culturally biased data. Such procedures have been widely discussed (e.g., Matsumoto and Van de Vijver, in press ; Van de Vijver and Leung, 1997; Vandenberg and Lance, 2000); we provide a brief overview on the Internet (Additional Topics, Chapter 1).

www.cambridge.org/berry

Distinctions between levels of equivalence have to do with the kind of comparison that can be validly made. If conditions for structural equivalence are met

a researcher can be reasonably sure that an instrument assesses the same psychological domain or construct in individuals of the cultures included in the analysis.
Thus, evidence of structural equivalence also supports conceptual equivalence. If
conditions for structural equivalence are not met, any form of comparison will be
misleading and hard to defend. If conditions for metric equivalence are satisfied,
changes in scores over measurement occasions will have the same meaning (which
is of relevance, for example, in longitudinal studies). If data are fully equivalent,
a single score can be taken to have the same meaning independent of the cultural
background of the person who obtained that score. However, this level is difficult
to establish for hypothetical constructs and in later chapters we shall repeatedly
find that researchers (like Porteus in the example described before) have assumed
full-score equivalence without proper justification.

Generalization

Psychological data are rarely of interest for their own sake; they are meant to
represent a broader domain of behavior or some underlying trait. An often found
distinction in the cross-cultural literature is between performance and competences. Performances are actual behaviors of individuals, including scores on tests
and questionnaires. Competences are qualities of individuals that enable (or constrain) performance. A further distinction can be made between competences and
underlying psychological processes. Sometimes this distinction is made with the
understanding that processes are shared by people in all cultures, while competencies as the cultural realization of these processes may well differ. The distinction
of performance, competence and process illustrates how interpretations of results
can be said to amount to different levels of generalization.

Generalizability theory was developed by Cronbach and colleagues (Cronbach,
Gleser, Nanda and Rajaratnam, 1972). They argued that a measurement forms a
sample from the entire set of possible behaviors that might have been included
in that measurement. In other words, a measurement is of interest in so far as it
represents the set of behaviors to which it is being generalized.[3] The main issue
here is that there is a strong danger of overgeneralization when representation is
poor. In the case of the Porteus mazes there is little doubt that the San testees did
obtain low scores. However, the question is whether performance on these mazes
tests formed a good representation of a San's intellectual capacity. When Reuning
and Wortley (1973) administered a more culture-appropriate version of a maze test
the San could solve mazes of a substantially higher level of difficulty than previously found by Porteus (1937). In Chapter 12 there is a section on the psychological organization of cross-cultural differences where we will discuss some more

---

[3] Cronbach and colleagues (1972) called this set a universe, which corresponds quite closely to the
terms "domain" of behavior and "trait" used here.

formal distinctions between categories of generalizability in the interpretation of cross-cultural data.

Distinguishing culture-level and individual-level variance

Cross-cultural psychologists tend to collect data on individuals in one or more cultural samples and interpret these in terms of similarities and differences between cultures. Thus, there are two levels of analysis: the individual level and the cultural level, with each individual nested in his or her own culture. To such a data set multilevel analysis should be applied. This is important as, with a shift in level, data can shift in meaning. An iconic example derives from educational research, where it is known that girls on average score higher than boys on tests of verbal ability. If a high mean score is obtained by the pupils in a classroom it is likely that there is a high proportion of girls among them. The classroom-level variable "proportion of girls" obviously has a different meaning from the individual-level variable "verbal ability." It may be counterintuitive but structural relationships (correlations) between classroom variables can be statistically independent from relationships between variables at the individual level (Dansereau, Alutto and Yammarino, 1984).

For a comparison of scores across cultures in large data sets (e.g., Hofstede, 1980, 2001; Schwartz, 1992; Schwartz and Boehnke, 2004), each cultural population tends to be represented by a single score for each variable; usually this population score is the mean of the sample score distribution. Thus, the individual scores in a sample are aggregated. The opposite of aggregation is disaggregation. It takes place when population-level information is used to derive information about individuals. In this case statements about individuals are derived from data pertaining to social institutions, including governance and formal education, or to characteristics of societies, such as age distribution and Gross National Product per capita (GNP).

There can be "isomorphism" between the two levels of culture and individual psychological functioning. This is the case when individual-level and cultural-level data have the same structure. Whenever this is not the case, relationships are "non-isomorphic" (Van de Vijver, Van Hemert and Poortinga, 2008a). Isomorphism was assumed in the culture-and-personality school (see Bock, 1999) in which an entire cultural population was characterized in terms of a single personality configuration presumably shared by all its members (e.g., Benedict, 1934). For a description of this school we refer to the Internet (Additional Topics, Chapter 10). Later such strict homogeneity was relaxed, but some of this thinking has persisted in notions of "national character" (Peabody, 1985) and "collective" or "social representations" (Moscovici, 1972, 1982; Jahoda, 1982). The idea that human psychological functioning is essentially cultural has been advanced more recently by cultural psychologists. Its most cogent expression is Shweder's (1990, 1991) formulation, mentioned before, that "culture and psyche make each other up." Universalist approaches do not

www.cambridge.org/berry

assume isomorphism explicitly; they distinguish individual psychological functioning from the cultural context. However, close relationships between the two levels are usually implicitly accepted. If the average score in culture A on an extraversion scale is high, we tend to see the A's as extraverts. One example of a sharp distinction between the two levels is the proposal by Triandis, Leung, Villareal and Clack (1985) to have different terms for individualism–collectivism at country level and at individual level. For the former level they maintained the existing terms; at the individual level they proposed to refer to "idiocentrism" and "allocentrism," although these two terms have not been widely adopted by researchers. The use of different terms is an elegant solution if there is non-isomorphism between levels. This avoids using the same label for concepts that differ in essential aspects.

Applying scores from one level to another level only makes sense when isomorphism can be assumed; otherwise an entangled shift in meaning can lead to invalid interpretations (Adamopoulos, 2008). Recently, statistical techniques have been developed that allow examination of how data at different levels are related to each other (e.g., Muthén, 1994; Hox, 2002). In later chapters we will return to applications in cross-cultural psychology that are beginning to emerge (e.g., Smith and Fischer, 2008, and Lucas and Diener, 2008).

Multilevel analysis requires data sets with numerous samples (Selig, Card and Little, 2008); as such it is likely to have a strong impact on the design of future cross-cultural studies. The statistical techniques are new to many cross-cultural researchers and tend to be complicated, but there is little doubt that they will be mastered as this form of analysis promises a new access to a central issue in cross-cultural psychology: namely to understand the relationships between individual behavior and cultural context.

Conclusions

Cross-cultural psychology as an active field of science is continuously changing. New developments are often reactions against perceived prior imbalances. Culture-comparative psychology was in part a reaction against the psychoanalytic tradition in psychological research conducted by cultural anthropologists (e.g., Kardiner and Linton, 1945). The shift entailed a greater emphasis on psychological uniformity underlying cross-cultural differences in manifest behavior. In turn, the perspectives of cultural psychology and indigenous psychology can be seen as reactions by researchers who believed that univeralism imposes too much of a common mold on human psychological functioning and, in the case of indigenous psychology, insufficiently takes into account issues prevalent in non-western societies.

This chapter presented some definitions of cross-cultural psychology. We showed how a definition can display a particular emphasis or orientation and formulated our own definition, meant to reflect a broad orientation on the field. The second section described three pervasive themes in cross-cultural psychology: viz. (1) culture as external context versus culture as internal to the person; (2) the relativism–universalism dimension; and (3) the question to what extent cross-cultural differences can be meaningfully generalized in terms of broad integrative concepts or dimensions. The third section outlined three interpretive positions on the relationships between behavior and culture: culture-comparative psychology, cultural psychology and indigenous psychology.

In the remaining sections we dealt with various issues of method that are probably more salient in cross-cultural psychology than in other fields of psychology. In a text on the Internet we discussed research questions, arguing that a good study is based on a research question that is precise and can be answered unambiguously. Poor research will make the empty prediction that "this culture will differ in some respects from ours," or "some similarities between groups and some differences" will be found; good research will stipulate which similarities and which differences. We further discussed the selection of "cultunits" and the distinction between qualitative and quantitative approaches to research. We concluded with a section that presents three threats to interpretation of cross-cultural data: viz., lack of equivalence, overgeneralization and insufficient distinction between the cultural and the individual level.

The argumentation in this chapter often had to be incomplete, especially as few references could be made to bodies of empirical evidence that form the basis of various research traditions. We have introduced major themes and perspectives to help the reader evaluate the empirical record as it will be presented in the following chapters.

KEY TERMS

absolutism • aggregation • cross-cultural psychology (definition) • cultunit • cultural bias • cultural psychology • culture • culture, external and internal • culture-as-a-system • culture-comparative research • disaggregation • ecocultural framework • emic • equivalence • etic • external culture: see culture, external and internal • generalization • independent self and interdependent self • indigenous psychology • individualism–collectivism • inference • internal culture: see culture, external and internal • majority world • multilevel analysis • qualitative approaches • quantitative approaches • quasi-experiment • relativism • universalism

FURTHER READING

Berry, J. W., Poortinga, Y. H., Pandey, J., Dasen, P. R., Saraswathi, T. S., Segall, M. H., and Kağitçibaşi, C. (eds.) (1997). *Handbook of cross-cultural psychology* (2nd edn., Vols. I–III). Boston: Allyn & Bacon.

The three-volume handbook consists of thirty-one chapters, which together represent much of cross-cultural psychology. This source is now freely available on Google:

Volume I: http://books.google.com/books?printsec=frontcover&tid=PB3xzjIzyOwC
Volume II: http://books.google.com/books?printsec=frontcover&tid=tLvAmyvsU8UC
Volume III: http://books.google.com/books?printsec=frontcover&tid=EvMnL5An4QEC (all last accessed November 16, 2010)

Online readings in psychology and culture (http://orpc.iaccp.org/)
This wide-ranging collection of contributions is to be found at the website of the International Association for Cross-Cultural Psychology.

Cole, M. (1996). *Cultural psychology: A once and future discipline.* Cambridge, Mass.: Harvard University Press.

This is a sophisticated text written from a culturalist perspective. Cole attempts to integrate biological, sociohistorical and psychological perspectives on behavior.

Creswell, J. W. (2009). *Research design: Qualitative, quantitative, and mixed methods approaches* (3rd edn.). Thousand Oaks, Calif.: Sage.

This is an accessible text starting from a mainly qualitative orientation, but with an open eye for quantitative methods. As the title may already suggest, the author favors mixed methods.

Kitayama, S., and Cohen, D. (eds.) (2007). *Handbook of cultural psychology.* New York: Guildford Press.

As the title indicates, this volume with thirty-six chapters takes the perspective of cultural psychology. The major strength is that it brings together the highlights as well as many lesser-known topics of cultural psychology as it exists in the USA today.

Rao, K. R., Paranjpe, A., and Dalal, A. (eds.) (2008). *Handbook of Indian psychology.* New Delhi: Cambridge University Press.

This overview is informative in showing how there are common themes of discussion that Indian researchers share with colleagues elsewhere, as well as locally salient concepts and issues.

Van de Vijver, F. J. R., and Leung, K. (1997). *Methods and data analysis for cross-cultural research.* Newbury Park, Calif.: Sage.

This is currently the classic text on methodological pitfalls in culture-comparative research.

Part I Similarities and differences in behavior across cultures

With an initial knowledge of the goals, concepts and methods of cross-cultural psychology that were presented in the introductory chapter, this first part of the book seeks to display research findings on the range of psychological domains that have been examined across cultures. The background materials of Chapter 1 should provide the reader with some basis for understanding and critically appraising the research being described in Part I. The order of the chapters has been arranged to begin with a portrayal of human development in infancy and childhood, then continuing into adulthood and older age. The six chapters that follow present some of the core findings from some decades of research into social behavior, personality, cognition, emotion, language and perception. This sequence of topics attempts to illustrate the varying degree of cultural influences on the display of human behavior. In keeping with the perspective of moderate universalism mentioned in Chapter 1, there is a search for cultural variation in development and display of behavior, as well as for possible commonalities in the underlying psychological processes.

2 Individual development: Infancy and early childhood

The notion of development comes into this book at three levels. First, there is phylogenetic development. It deals with variation across species, and the emergence of new species over long periods of time. This form of development will be discussed in Chapter 11. Second, the term "development" can refer to cultural changes in societies. Development in this sense will be touched upon in Chapter 10 (where we discuss the anthropological tradition of cultural evolution), and in Chapter 18 (where we focus on national development). In the present and the following chapter we are mainly concerned with the course of development of the individual through the life span, or **ontogenetic development**. In this chapter, we will focus on cultural similarities and differences in developmental patterns in infancy and early childhood; the next chapter will deal with late childhood, adolescence and adulthood.

Culture as context for development

Individual development can be considered as the outcome of interactions between a biological organism and environmental influences. Although we consider the separation of "nature" and "nurture" to be largely an outdated distinction (see Chapter 11, and the last section of Chapter 12), the relative importance of the biological and the cultural (environmental-experiential) components of behavior has formed the major dimension underlying the differences between various schools of thinking on ontogenetic development in the psychological literature. Thus, there are maturational theories (e.g., Gesell, 1940) that place more emphasis on biological factors. In contrast, traditional learning theory (e.g., Skinner, 1957) emphasizes the role of the environment. In other theories there is much more attention for the interaction between the organism and the environment; an example is the theory of Piaget (1970a), in which stages in cognitive development are distinguished (Additional Topics, Chapter 6). Finally, there are theories in which ontogenetic development is seen as following essentially different pathways as a consequence of differences in the cultural environment in which the individual is growing up (Vygotsky, 1978).

It should be noted that maturational and learning theories do not attribute much significance to cultural factors. In maturational theories development tends to be seen as the realization of a more or less fixed biological program. For learning theorists the environment is very important, but in a mechanistic fashion; the adult organism is more or less the sum of all learning experiences. Mechanistic conceptions of learning view the environment as a large collection of separate and uniform stimuli, a perspective which is in contrast to a culture-informed notion of learning in which the cultural organization of learning experiences is emphasized. In this section we examine in more detail conceptualizations of ontogenetic development that are explicitly informed by culture.

We learn about norms and beliefs and how to read and write via the different routes of cultural transmission (see next section). A fruitful additional aspect of this environmentally based inheritance of information is the culturally modified environment itself (material culture; see Odling-Smee, Laland and Feldman, 2003). According to this view, an important aspect of human culture is the collection of material cultural artifacts which surround us (cars, houses, computers, books, mobile phones, iPods, etc.). Culture is thus not only what we explicitly learn socially, but is also constituted simply by using cultural artifacts which are often built or invented by earlier generations.

There are some theorists in developmental psychology (contextualists) who focus particularly on that materialized cultural knowledge. Contextualists view development as the dynamic interplay of the individuals and their everyday environment.

This approach can be traced back to Vygotsky's (1978) sociocultural theory, which focussed on how cultural transmission takes place. There is probably no developmental theory in which the role of culture is more explicit and encompassing than that of Vygotsky (see the section on contextualized cognition in Chapter 6 and Segall *et al.*, 1999). Vygotsky is also known for his notion that an understanding of phylogenetic development can provide insight into child development (Bjorklund and Pellegrini, 2002). However, it is his sociocultural perspective (referring to historical changes in values, norms and technologies occurring in one's culture) which is noted most by contemporary researchers (see Schaffer and Kipp, 2007). He placed great emphasis on the typically human aspects of behavior and how these have come about, in the course of history at the societal level and ontogenetically at the individual level. He viewed child development as a socially mediated activity in which children gradually acquire knowledge and new ways of behavior through cooperative interactions with more competent members of society. There is an internal reconstruction of external operations, creating *intra*individual processes that are initially *inter*individual.

"Every function in the child's cultural development appears twice: first, on the social level, and later, on the individual level; first, *between* people (*interpsychological*) and then inside the child (*intrapsychological*) … All the higher functions originate as actual relations between human individuals" (Vygotsky, 1978, p. 57; italics in the original). This quotation makes clear that the origins of individual mental functioning are social. A human individual can only acquire higher mental functions that are already there in the sociocultural context.

One of the first developmentalists outside Russia who adopted Vygotsky's ideas was Bronfenbrenner (1979). In his ecological systems theory he defined contexts of development as nested structures, like Russian dolls, each inside the next. The developing child is embedded within four of these spheres, ranging from the immediate setting to the broad culture. For most infants, the innermost context, the so-called microsystem, is the family, that is, mother, father and siblings. The mesosystem consists of the family as a microsystem and other interrelated microsystems like school, neighborhood or day care center. While the exosystem refers to more distant contexts influencing the meso- and microsystem like the parental economic situation, the macrosystem finally as the remotest layer of the ecological system consists of the cultural norms, socialization goals and values. These layers are interacting with each other and influence the development of the child.

Bronfenbrenner's view on development stresses that we have to observe transactions in everyday, natural settings if we want to understand children's development. This very idea lies at the heart of the contextualized cognition school (Cole, 1996). They showed in a number of studies that expertise is related to environmental affordances; this helped to answer the question why

some people seem to fail to attain the highest stage of cognitive development distinguished by Piaget (1970a): the formal operational stage (see Additional Topics, Chapter 6).

Hence, human behavior can be qualified as "culturally mediated." Originally, cultural mediation was thought to have a tremendously broad scope (e.g., Luria, 1971, 1976). Because beliefs, values and intellectual tools may vary substantially across cultures, Vygotsky believed that these new cognitive skills are often culture-specific rather than universal. Later it was demonstrated (e.g., Cole, 1996) that differences, for example between literates and illiterates, are not nearly as extensive as Luria thought (Scribner, 1979; see also Segall *et al.*, 1999). Despite his criticisms of the broad sweep of earlier authors, Cole (1992a, 1996) maintains a position of cultural mediation. In his view the biological organism and the environment do not interact directly, but through a third mediating factor, namely culture. In a schematic representation Cole (1992a) not only makes the classic distinction between organism and environment, he makes a further, equally basic, distinction between the natural environment and culture. For Cole, development is a concept with many levels or time scales: a physical scale; a phylogenetic scale; a culture-historical scale (in which social traditions come about and disappear); an ontogenetic scale; and what he calls a micro-genetic scale. The last entails the here-and-now of human experience. The interactions between these various levels are essential for an understanding of ontogenetic development. In his view stages of ontogenetic development are not just there in individual children, but they emerge in complex social interactions over time. An example is the empirical work in which Cole (1996) has studied how children acquire cognitive skills for computer-based activities in a setting with rich opportunities for written and oral communication (see also Engeström, 2005).

According to this contextualistic approach, each culture provides its children with methods of thinking and problem-solving. These methods, which Vygotsky (1978) called "tools of intellectual adaptation," are internalized by children during interactions with more competent members of their society. In the so-called "zone of proximal development," which defines a range of culturally relevant tasks too complex to be solved by the child alone, a competent expert guides the child to a new level of understanding. To describe this kind of supportive guidance of the activities of the child the term "scaffolding" has been used (Wood, Bruner and Ross, 1976). In many cultures, children do not learn by formal education, that is, by going to school, but by guided participation, an informal "apprenticeship in thinking" (Rogoff, 1990, 2003) in which children's cognition is shaped by actively participating in everyday culturally relevant experiences alongside more skilled partners (Rogoff, Mistry, Göncü and Mosier, 1993). Rogoff's findings make it clear that there is not one single pathway of development, but that different kinds of guided participation are dependent on the different requirements culture places upon its members. Children from cultures with formal teaching through institutionalized educational contexts like schools acquire abstract cultural abilities or techniques like reading and writing mainly through verbal explanations. This context-independent knowledge allows them a more flexible application of their skills. Children from agrarian or pre-industrial cultures learn through participation in everyday activities. They learn specific tasks by observing and imitating adult behavior. These children have better-developed observational skills and in many respects are socially more competent than children from modern middle-class communities (Rogoff *et al.*, 1993).

There are interesting cross-cultural differences in memory tasks that can be directly linked to Vygotsky's notion of culturally mediated cognitive abilities (see also Chapter 6, section on contextualized cognition). African adolescents who rely more on orally transmitted knowledge recall orally transmitted stories better than US-American adolescents (Rogoff, 1990). Western children outperform unschooled peers from non-industrial societies (Cole and Scribner, 1977) in context-free rote memorization and list learning, while unschooled Aboriginal children from Australia are better than their Anglo-Australian peers at remembering locations of objects (Kearins, 1981). Remembering where to find water or game animals and to find the way home through the desert can be a matter of survival in the outback of Australia. In real life the ability to learn large quantities of information quickly can mean the difference between life and death. When your very survival depends on learning relevant features of the environment, you get to learn them fast, while the "laziness' of western children merely reflects the luxury of being able to record everything we need to know in books or computer disks (Dunbar, 1996; Stroup, 1985).

Many cross-cultural psychologists, especially in the school of cultural psychology, are of the opinion that Vygotsky's idea of guided participation is at the core of what happens when children learn. In contrast to other cognitive approaches where the child is seen as a more or less isolated individual performing discovery-based activities on its own, contextualistic views on children's learning are more comprehensive by stressing the importance of socially mediated learning. This social learning also seems to be more effective, because children are more motivated. If they try to solve problems together, they learn more about their own ideas by explaining them to others and often develop solutions they would not have discovered on their own. The notion of an informal apprenticeship by integrating children into the daily activities of adult life is rather common and seems reasonable in agrarian or hunter-gatherer societies where everything that there is to learn can be immediately observed. In industrialized, modern societes, on the other hand, children learn independent of the context to which the solutions and strategies they are taught apply. For many school children this may look like learning for learning's sake and thus can be rather demotivating (Bernhard, 1988).

Knowing that, a straightforward implication to improve modern schooling would be to combine the formal educational contexts with reduced verbal explanations, more peer collaboration and with teachers' active participation (Rogoff, 2003; Schaffer and Kipp, 2007).

The importance of the broader context tends to be emphasized particularly by authors from the majority world,[1] who promote indigenous psychologies (see the section on interpretive positions in Chapter 1). For example, Nsamenang (1992) writes about the factors that have shaped the social history of larger parts of Africa. He refers to the colonial history that led to a derogation of African traditions and religious practices, but also points to the continuation of many beliefs and customs that shape child care and the role and obligations of children. Nsamenang describes, for example, how conceptions of stages of development are not limited to the current life span, but extend into the spiritual realm of the ancestors. This psychological reality is also prominent in other areas of the world, for example in Hinduism (Saraswathi, 1999). Many children in the majority world grow up under conditions of poverty and social disruption, including war (Aptekar and Stöcklin, 1997). Authors like Nsamenang (1992, Nsamenang and Lo-Oh, 2010), Zimba (2002) and Sinha (1997) plead for a psychology that addresses the everyday reality of the developmental context and its consequences for these children. It should be clear that such consequences are not limited to the social domain. They equally lead to stunted growth and cognitive retardation. For example, Griesel, Richter and Belciug (1990) found that there was a gap in cerebral maturity, as assessed by EEG characteristics, between poorly nourished black urban children and children with normal growth in South Africa. The gap was present already with 6- to 8-year-olds, but increased for older children. Corresponding differences were found between these groups of children for measures of cognitive performance (see also Grantham-McGregor et al., 2007).

In particular, the concept of developmental niche (Super and Harkness, 1986) has emphasized that all development takes place in a particular cultural context, paralleling the widely used notion of "ecological niche" that refers to the habitat occupied by a particular species. In this respect, there are clear links to the ecocultural framework in Figure 1.1. As expanded by Super and Harkness (1997, in press), the developmental niche is a system that links the development of a child with three features of its cultural environment: the physical and social settings (e.g., the people and social interactions, the dangers and opportunities of everyday life); the prevailing customs about child care (e.g., the cultural norms, practices and institutions); and caretaker psychology (e.g., the beliefs, values, affective orientations and practices of parents; see the section below on parental ethnotheories). These three

---

[1] For lack of a better distinction we follow Kağitçibaşi (2007) in her way of designating the non-western part of the world, although we are reluctant to use such broad dichotomies.

subsystems surround the developing child, and promote, nurture and constrain its development. They have a number of characteristics: they are embedded in a larger ecosystem; they usually operate together, providing a coherent niche, but can also present inconsistencies to the child if they do not align with each other. Moreover, there is mutual adaptation (interaction) between the child and each subsystem, so that the child influences, as well as is influenced by, each subsystem.

In sum, there is a long history in anthropology and psychology of regarding maintenance systems, like the family, as dependent on environmental conditions and resources (Berry, 1976; Munroe and Gauvain, 2009; Whiting, 1963; see also Chapter 10, the sixth definition of culture as being adaptive to ecosystem, p. 225, and the discussion of cultural evolution as being due to adaptation to changing contexts, p. 229). Accordingly, there is also a long tradition of taking a contextual perspective on human development across cultures (Keller, 2007; Super and Harkness, 1986).

Modes of transmission

Humans as well as cultural groups reproduce themselves. This requires both biological and cultural transmission. The concept of cultural transmission (see Figure 2.1) was used by Cavalli-Sforza and Feldman (1981) to parallel the notion of biological transmission, in which, through genetic mechanisms, certain features of a population are perpetuated over time across generations (Schönpflug, 2009). Biological transmission will be discussed in Chapter 11. Here we merely want to note the central biological feature of transmission, namely the passing on of the species-specific genetic material from two parents to the individual at the moment of conception. By analogy, using various forms of cultural transmission a cultural group can perpetuate its behavioral features among subsequent generations employing teaching and learning mechanisms. Cultural transmission from parents to their offspring is termed vertical transmission by Cavalli-Sforza and Feldman, since it involves the descent of cultural characteristics from one generation to the next. However, while vertical descent is the only possible form of biological transmission, there are two other forms of cultural transmission: horizontal transmission (from peers) and oblique transmission (from others of the parental generation in society). These forms of transmission can be from within a person's own cultural group, and from another cultural group. These distinctions are shown in Figure 2.1. These three forms of cultural transmission involve two processes: enculturation and socialization (see later section). Enculturation takes place through the general "enfolding" of individuals in the context of their culture, leading to the incorporation of culture-appropriate behaviors into their repertoire. Socialization takes place by more specific instruction and training, again leading to the acquisition of culture-appropriate behavior.

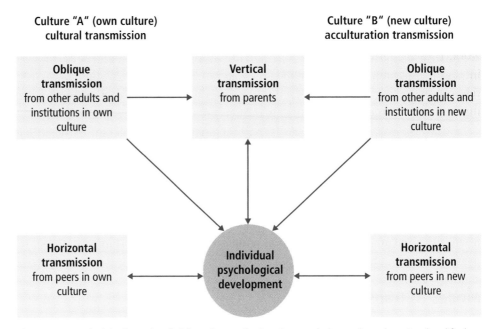

Figure 2.1 Vertical, horizontal and oblique forms of cultural transmission and acculturation (modified from Berry and Cavalli-Sforza, 1986).

In vertical transmission parents transmit cultural values, skills, beliefs, etc. to their offspring. In this case, it is difficult to distinguish between cultural and biological transmission, since one typically learns from the very people who were responsible for one's conception; that is, those who produce a child are usually those who raise the child, so biological parents and cultural parents are very often the same. In horizontal cultural transmission, one learns from one's peers in day to day interactions during the course of development from birth to adulthood; in this case, there is no confounding between biological and cultural transmission. And in oblique cultural transmission, one learns from other adults and institutions (e.g., in formal schooling, social clubs), either in one's own culture or from other cultures. If the process takes place entirely within one's own or primary culture, then cultural transmission is the appropriate term (see left side of Figure 2.1). This form of transmission was shown as a process variable in the ecocultural framework (Figure 1.1). However, if the process derives from contact with another culture, the term acculturation is employed (see right side of Figure 2.1). This latter term refers to the form of transmission experienced by an individual that results from contact with, and influence from, persons and institutions belonging to cultures other than one's own (see the lower line in the ecocultural framework, Figure 1.1). It is a form of later, or secondary, enculturation and socialization (see Chapter 13 for an overview of the concept of acculturation).

These forms of transmission are shown in Figure 2.1 with arrows flowing both toward the developing individual, and other individuals and groups in the framework. These reciprocal influences are particularly important among peers, but also in parent–child relationships (Lamb, 1986). Thus, the double-headed arrows, representing interaction and mutual influence, represent what takes place during cultural transmission and acculturation.

Enculturation and socialization

In the previous section we distinguished two processes of cultural transmission: enculturation and socialization (Berry, 2007a). The concept of enculturation has been developed within the discipline of cultural anthropology, and was first defined and used by Herskovits (1948). As the term suggests, there is an encompassing or surrounding of the individual by his or her culture; the individual acquires, by learning, what the culture deems to be vital. There is not necessarily anything deliberate or didactic about this process; often there is learning without specific teaching. The process of enculturation involves parents, and other adults and peers, in a network of influences (vertical, oblique and horizontal) on the developing individual, all of which can limit, shape and direct him or her. The end result is usually a person who is competent in the culture, including its language, its rituals, values and so on.

The concept of socialization was developed in the disciplines of sociology and social psychology to refer to the process of deliberate shaping, by way of tutelage, of the individual (see Berry, 2007a; Munroe and Gauvain, 2009). It is generally employed in cross-cultural psychology in this same way. When cultural transmission involves deliberate teaching from within one's group, then we are dealing with the process of socialization during early life; re-socialization occurs when the deliberate influences come later in life or from outside one's own culture. The eventual result of both enculturation and socialization is the development of behavioral similarities within cultures, and behavioral differences between cultures. They are thus the crucial cultural mechanisms that produce the distribution of similarities and differences in competence and performance.

The processes of enculturation and socialization take place in a larger ecological and cultural context: the forms (or style) and the content (what) of transmission are generally viewed as adaptive to the ecocultural setting, and are functional in that they ensure that the developing individual acquires the behavioral repertoire that is necessary to live successfully in that setting. It is for this reason that cultural transmission is placed in such a central position in the ecocultural framework (Figure 1.1). Even after the time developing children have become self-sustaining, they typically continue to live in the family and other social groups, and continue to acquire important features of their culture.

On the other hand, the process of cultural transmission does not necessarily lead to exact replication; it falls somewhere between an exact transmission (with hardly any differences between parents and offspring) and a complete failure of transmission (with offspring who are unlike their parents, or culture). It usually falls closer to the full transmission end of this spectrum, than to the non-transmission end. Functionally, either extreme would be problematic for a society: exact transmission would not allow for novelty and change, and hence the ability to respond to new situations, while failure of transmission would not permit coordinated action between generations (Boyd and Richerson, 1985, 2005). The relation between ontogenetic development and societal change will be addressed in more detail in the middle adulthood section in Chapter 3.

Studies of how parents within a certain society characteristically raise their children have been reported in the literature for over a century. As we shall see in Chapter 10, many of these reports have been accumulated in an archive mainly composed of ethnographic reports known as the Human Relations Area Files (HRAF). One approach to the study of cultural transmission is the use of these files to discover the major dimensions of variation in cultural transmission variables around the world. This approach provides us with a broad overview, and allows us to examine cultural transmission in the context of other ecological and cultural variables that have also been included in the archives. We are thus able to examine how enculturation and socialization fit into, or are adaptive to, other features of the group's circumstances.

Studies of cultural transmission employing ethnographic archives have been termed holocultural, since they permit the examination of materials from cultures the whole world over (Munroe and Gauvain, 2009). A well-known early study, carried out by Whiting and Child (1953), attempted to link adult personality to child training by examining the ways in which societies typically explain illness. Ethnographic data from seventy-five societies were derived from the HRAF and five "systems of behavior" (defined as "habits or customs motivated by a common drive and leading to common satisfactions," Whiting and Child (1953), p. 45) were examined: oral, anal, sexual, dependence and aggression. The first three of these five behavior systems were derived from Freud's (1938) theory of psychosexual development, in which sexual gratification is thought to be associated, over the course of development, with different erogenous zones, beginning with the mouth (during the oral stage). Judges made ratings of practices on three dimensions: initial satisfaction or indulgence of the child; the age of socialization; and the severity of socialization.

Two very general conclusions resulted from this study. First, "child training the world over is in certain respects identical ... in that it is found always to be concerned with certain universal problems of behavior" (Whiting and Child, 1953, p. 63). Second, "child training also differs from one society to another"

(Whiting and Child, 1953, p. 64). In this pair of conclusions are reflected the two prototypical and most frequent empirical results found in cross-cultural psychology. They are consistent with numerous findings suggesting common patterns across all cultures (e.g., Lonner, 1980, in press). First there are some common dimensions (cultural universals) that serve to link humankind together, while, second, individuals and groups differ in their typical place on these dimensions. We shall see later (in Chapters 11 and 12) that the first conclusion is essential if we are to have some valid basis on which to make cross-cultural comparisons, and that the second is essential if we are to have sufficient variance in our data to discover evidence that cultural and psychological observations are related in theoretically interpretable ways.

In another classic study, Barry and his colleagues (Barry, Bacon and Child, 1957; Barry, Child and Bacon, 1959) were able (1) to identify common dimensions of child training, (2) to place societies at various positions on these dimensions, (3) to show some characteristic differences between training for boys and girls, and (4) to relate all of these to features of ecological and cultural variation (such as economy and social structure), thus placing socialization in a broader context. Their analyses showed that the different domains of childrearing tended to form two clusters. One cluster (termed "pressure toward compliance") combined training for responsibility and obedience. The other cluster (termed "pressure toward assertion") combined training for achievement, self-reliance and independence. These two clusters appeared to be negatively related. This allowed a single dimension to be created, along which societies were placed, ranging from *compliance* training at one end and *assertion* training at the other end. In this way the initial dimensions were thus reduced to a single one. While this new dimension appears to be consistent with the earlier research, the expectation that there will be concomitant differences in the range of individual variation has not yet been tested empirically. We will also use this comprehensive holocultural approach in the next section when we will deal with cross-cultural patterns in gender-related socialization practices (see also the section on adulthood in Chapter 3).

Gender differences across cultures

In the literature on gender differences a distinction between sex and gender is often made. While sex is used to refer to biological differences of males and females, gender is used to refer to learned beliefs about or social constructions of what it means to be male or female (Best, 2010). These labels are not very useful, since it is impossible to separate biological and cultural influences on sexuality. The quest for the explanation of gender differences in humans is a prime example of how intricate and almost indistinguishable biological and cultural factors are intertwined (see also Chapter 11). Already the intrauterine environment interacts with the chromosomes responsible for the specification of the child's sex (*chromo-somal gender*, xx = girl, xy = boy, see Box 11.1): around the sixth week after con-ception, the "y" chromosome acts like a switch and starts to change the basically female blueprint of the human embryo to a male by initiating the development of testicles. They, in turn, start to produce a huge amount of male hormones called androgens (*hormonal gender*) the uptake of which is dependent on the child's neurophysiological make-up. A calibration of this hormonal tempest has also to take place with the intrauterine hormonal environment, which in turn depends on the mother's general hormonal balance. The general hormonal constitution of the mother is finally influenced by her living conditions (e.g., nutritional status, mari-tal satisfaction or physical and psychological well-being). Which environmental stimuli are able to influence the mother, in turn, depends on her genetic make-up. This is the epigenetic circle: genes determine which environmental aspects can af-fect the behavior, and the environment determines when which genes are activated in which way (see adaptation section in Chapter 11).

These hormonal processes just described lead to the outwardly visible outcomes, in the form of a penis or a vagina (*genital gender*). The genital gender is the start-ing point for the cultural labeling of the child (boy or girl, *social gender*). In each of these steps and long before the social environment can mingle with it, aberrations can occur (Beh and Diamond, 2000; Diamond, 1997; Imperato-McGinley, Peterson, Gautier and Sturla, 1979). Considering the different designations along the develop-mental process of becoming a boy or a girl, two aspects become obvious: first, that the social labeling is only the final, although very important, step in a long chain of epigenetic events, but also, second, that a merely dichotomous, typological view on gender does not always do justice to the epigenetic continuum just described.

The issue of gender differences in socialization and in behavior has received extensive treatment in the cross-cultural literature, leading Munroe and Munroe (1975, p. 116) to conclude that there are modal gender differences in behavior in every society, and that every society has some division of labor by gender. These two phenomena, besides being universal, are also probably interrelated in a functional way. The correspondence between gender differences in socialization emphases and gender differences in behavior is very strong. That the two genders behave in different ways is not surprising, but it still leads to the interesting ques-tion if all societies observed different inborn behavioral tendencies in males and females and then shaped their socialization practices to accentuate or reduce such biologically based tendencies.

As discussed in the previous section, Barry *et al.* (1959) showed that in an HRAF-based study, socialization for males emphasized assertion, and for females it emphasized compliance. With respect to gender differences in behavior Barry *et al.* showed males to be more self-assertive, achievement-oriented and dominant, and females to be more socially responsive, passive and submissive. One key to the explanation is the fact that these behavioral differences, although nearly universal and almost never reversed, range in magnitude from quite large down to virtually nil. A satisfactory explanation, then, needs to account both for the universality of direction of difference and the variation in magnitude of the difference.

Such an explanation takes into account economic facts, including division of labor and socialization practices. The argument begins with an early anthropological finding (Murdock, 1937) that a division of labor by sex is universal (or nearly so) and quite consistent in content. For example, food preparation is done predominantly by females in nearly all societies. Child care is usually the responsibility of females. Sometimes it is shared, but in no society is it the modal practice for males to have the major responsibility. These differences are widely viewed as arising from biologically based differences, especially the female's lesser overall physical strength and, most of all, her child-bearing and child-caring functions (see the adulthood section in Chapter 3). Different economic roles for males and females, with the latter consigned mostly to close-to-home activities, would have been a functional response. A second argument was to suggest that differential socialization evolved as a means for preparing children to assume their sex-linked adult roles. Then, the behavioral differences could best be viewed as a product of different socialization emphases, with those in turn reflective of, and appropriate training for, different adult activities (Barry *et al.*, 1959).

Van Leeuwen's (1978) extension of Berry's (1976) ecological model expands the argument so that it can accommodate other aspects of subsistence mode and variations in degree of sex differences in behavior. Thus, in sedentary, high-food-accumulating societies not only will females be subjected to more training to be nurturant and compliant, but the degree of the difference between the sexes' training will also be high. In low-food-accumulating societies, such as gathering or hunting societies, there will be less division of labor by sex and little need for either sex to be trained to be compliant. Often in such societies (at least in gathering societies, if not hunting ones, as we will see shortly), women's contributions to the basic subsistence activity are integral to it. Hence, women's work is valued by the men, who are then not inclined to derogate women or to insist on subservience from them.

One of the ways in which division of labor varies across cultures is in the degree to which women contribute to subsistence (Schlegel and Barry, 1986). Their participation in such activities may be relatively low or high, depending on the activity. For example, if food is acquired by gathering, women's participation is usually high; in eleven of fourteen (79%) gathering societies for which ethnographic reports were coded, women were high contributors. By contrast, in only two of sixteen (13%) hunting societies did women make a high contribution. Women are more apt to contribute relatively highly to subsistence where the main activity is either gathering or agriculture (other than intensive agriculture), and less highly where the activity is animal husbandry, intensive agriculture, fishing or hunting (Schlegel and Barry, 1986, p. 144).

Does the variation in the subsistence role played by women have any consequences? Schlegel and Barry (1986) found that two sets of cultural features – adaptive and attitudinal – are associated with female contribution to subsistence. Where women play a relatively large subsistence role, the features of polygyny, exogamy, brideprice, birth control and work orientation training for girls prevail. And under these same conditions (the high contribution by females to subsistence), females are relatively highly valued, allowed freedoms and generally less likely to be perceived as objects for male sexual and reproductive needs. In a meta-analysis of data from ninety-three cultures with varying mating systems, Low (1989) also showed that gender-dependent differences in socialization practices varied with the mating system: in more polygynous societies, gender differences were higher, with boys being expected to become more aggressive, courageous and independent, and girls more responsible, obedient and coy. These gender differences decreased with the increase of political or economic power of women. In these, mostly monogamous, cultures, daughters were expected to be less obedient, and more aggressive and ambitious. Low interprets this interesting pattern of gender-culture interaction from an evolutionary perspective: biologically, men and women differ in the amount they have to invest for procreation (Trivers, 1972). In mammals, the parental investment of females is greater than that of the males, leading to the prediction that since females become the limiting resource for males, they as the sex investing less will compete among themselves, leading to higher intrasexual competition within the male sex (see Chapter 11, p. 255). In polygynous societies, attractive (meaning socially successful, see below) males can marry multiple wives, but because every woman who is married to a polygynous husband is no longer available for other men, the majority of males in polygynous societies face the risk of remaining unmarried. This higher reproductive variance for males in polygynous societies increases intrasexual competition in males because the risk of staying unmarried in a polygynous society is higher than in monogamous societies. This, in turn, makes it more likely that these males take risks to get married by being more aggressive and assertive. In monogamous societies, on the other hand, males and females have similar reproductive prospects and that is why, according to Low (1989), they are treated more similarly by their parents.

The basic implication of these findings is that gender is an effect and a cause of socialization at the same time: gender is not only determined by social factors alone; it may also influence them (see, e.g., Snow, Jacklin and Maccoby, 1983: fathers of 1-year-old boys showed more prohibitive behavior than fathers of girls of the same age because the boys made significantly more attempts to touch tempting objects than girls). Self-socialization as a modern developmental concept describing the interindividually varying selective perception of and participation in social contexts is completely compatible with this epigenetic view on gender (Maccoby, 1998). It is important to note that sociocultural factors are essential determinants of gender development (Best and Williams, 1993), but only an interactional view can explain why, for example, the same parental treatment often affects boys and girls differently and why men and women are viewed and behave rather similarly across cultures (Best, 2010). Concerning sex stereotypes, for example, Williams and Best (1990) showed that as early as age 5, children from twenty-five countries consistently associated adjectives like "strong," "aggressive," "cruel" and "adventurous" with men, and "weak," "appreciative," "softhearted" and "gentle" with women (see Chapter 4). The most profound behavioral consistencies can be found in caregiving behavior and aggressive behavior. As, for example, data for caregiving behavior from 189 cultures show (Weisner and Gallimore, 1977; see also Best, 2010), most of the time, mothers, female relatives or daughters are the primary caregivers of infants, and paternal care is relatively rare (see also Chapter 3 on parenting and the family). Regarding physical aggression, Daly and Wilson (1988) reviewed criminological records and found that across cultures and diverse historical periods the ratio of male versus female homicides is about 9:1. As a final example on cross-cultural differences in aggressive behavior, instances of collective aggression like warfare are perpetrated predominantly by coalitions of young men and according to Mesquida and Wiener (1996, 1999) may be conceptualized as a form of male intrasexual competition to acquire resources for the attraction or retention of mates. They were able to show with data sets from twelve tribal societies, but also with UN data sets from a total of 183 nations for the period of 1983 to 1998, that the most reliable factor in explaining episodes of coalitional aggression is the relative abundance of young males. The ratio of the number of men ages 15 to 29 years of age versus men 30 and older in a population appears to be associated with the occurrence and severity of conflicts as measured by the number of war casualties (Mesquida and Wiener 1996, 1999).

What we have seen in this discussion is that females do indeed behave differently from males (see also the adulthood section in Chapter 3). A plausible way to interpret these findings is to distinguish between competence and performance. While differences in competence are rather small, the much bigger differences in performance lead to the conclusion that the underlying processes leading to these differences in performance might be motivational. Men and women all over the world can act similarly, but often they just do not want to do so. It seems clear that these gender differences are strongly influenced by cultural factors, which are operating through socialization practices and are reflective of ecological factors. Both the consistencies in the cross-cultural data and the variations from society to society help us to understand how cultural practices have been defined differently for the two sexes, and how individuals come to behave in accord with them.

Parental ethnotheories

There are several ethnosciences such as ethnobotany, ethnogeology, even ethnopsychology and ethnopsychiatry. The notion of ethnoscience is discussed in Chapter 6 in the section on indigenous cognition, and in Chapter 10's section on cognitive anthropology. These refer to the knowledge and beliefs about a particular area of life held by a particular cultural group. Similarly, groups reveal such knowledge and beliefs about the domain of parenting, which have become known as parental belief systems or parental ethnotheories (Harkness and Super, 1995; Sigel, McGillicuddy-De Lisi and Goodnow, 1992). These are the beliefs, values and practices of parents and other child caretakers regarding the proper way to raise a child, and include such common practices as the provision of affection and warmth, timetables for feeding and elimination, and even for development itself (e.g., when a child should walk, talk, ride a bicycle, choose friends). These beliefs and practices constitute the processes of enculturation and socialization which, as we have seen, have been studied for some time. The advantage of the newer concept of parental ethnotheories is that it links this earlier literature on "childrearing" more closely to ecological and cultural context.

Harkness and Super and colleagues (Super *et al.*, 1996; Super and Harkness, in press) have studied cross-cultural differences in the regulation of sleeping patterns of young children. Parental ethnotheories play a strong role in the extent to which even young babies are left to themselves between feeding times (as in the Netherlands, Rebelsky, 1967) or taken from their cribs when showing signs of distress (as in the USA). Harkness and Super with their colleagues have studied samples of young children (between 6 months and 4½ years of age) and their parents in semi-urban settings in the Netherlands and the USA, using interviews and direct observations. For the Dutch parents imposing regularity in sleeping patterns was an important issue. If children are not getting enough sleep they are believed to become fussy; moreover, young children need sleep for their growth and development. In fact, such ideas are also emphasized in the Dutch health care system. In the USA regular sleeping patterns are seen as something the child will acquire with increasing age, but this is, by and large, not seen as something that can be induced. From diaries kept by parents it emerged that the Dutch children got more sleep during their early years. Direct observations show that, while awake, Dutch children are more often in a state of "quiet arousal," while the US-American children are more often in a state of "active alertness." Super *et al.* (1996; Super and Harkness, in press) suggest that this may reflect the fact that US-American mothers talk to their children more frequently and touch them more (for similar findings see Keller, Chasiotis and Runde, 1992). Dutch parental ethnotheory has it that even young children should be left to themselves; they need to organize their own behavior and keep themselves busy; this is part of a cultural expectation pattern, namely that the children should become "independent." On the basis of a review of the literature Willemsen and Van de Vijver (1997) noted that western parents tended to indicate a lower age of mastery of various skills than non-Western parents. They analyzed possible explanations for this finding on the basis of interviews with Dutch mothers, Turkish migrant mothers living in the Netherlands and Zambian mothers. An interesting finding was that specific context variables could explain about one-third of the cross-cultural variance. Level of education and the number of children were the best predictors: higher-educated mothers mentioned lower ages of mastery, and mothers with many children indicated higher ages.

Keller and her collaborators (2007) also conducted studies on the impact of parental ethnotheories in varying ecocultural contexts. They found that mothers in societies with more emphasis on independent construal of the self (see the subsection on the self in social context in Chapter 5) focussed on the autonomy and independence of the child, whereas mothers in societies with emphasis on dependent self-construal were more focussed on relational aspects in dealing with children. Cross-cultural developmental studies like these help to make understandable how such preferences of the mother become instilled in the infant's behavior. In the studies conducted by Keller and her colleagues (2007), these socialization goals of the mothers were also related to different parental behavioral patterns: mothers from ecosocial contexts emphasizing independence (i.e., urban middle-class mothers from modern (post-)industrialized societies like USA or Germany) had a more exclusive relation to their infant, showed more verbal interactions with a lot of object stimulation (use of toys) during face-to-face interactions and less body contact and body stimulation. On the other hand, mothers from an interdependent ecosocial context (i.e., rural farmers with low formal schooling from Cameroon or India) regarded the child as an apprentice embedded in a tight social network and showed less face-to-face interaction, fewer verbalizations and less object stimulation, but more body contact and body stimulation. Keller (2007) coined the term "parenting strategies" to describe these intriguing relationships between parenting goals and parenting behavior during infancy. In our view, these parenting strategies which are implied to lead to culture-specific developmental pathways are promising concepts in trying to explain adult intercultural psychological and behavioral variation. In Chapter 3 we further discuss childhood as a formative period for adulthood.

These few examples of studies illustrate how different aspects of development come together in the notion of parental ethnotheories. First, the parents are observers of their own children and those in their social environment. Second, parents likely reflect the standards and expectations of the cultural environment they live in, not only in their treatment of children, but also in their perceptions.

Third, parents and other caretakers will influence the development of children through socialization practices that reflect their beliefs. A further finding is that parents often do not realize the ways through which and the extent to which they steer children in a certain direction (Papoušek and Papoušek, 1987). More extensive reviews of these issues can be found in Segall *et al.* (1999) and in Keller (2007).

Infancy and early childhood

Cultural variations in infant development

Biologists consider human beings to be adapted, anatomically and physiologically, to gathering and probably hunting, a way of life that the human species pursued for millions of years. The invention of agriculture that led to a more sedentary mode of living, and later the change to industrialization, are only recent events to which humankind has not been able to make major biological adaptations; the relatively short time has only allowed cultural adaptations (e.g., Konner, 1981, 2007). The level of development at birth depends on the specific adaptation to a particular ecological niche. More than in any other species, human neurological development continues after birth; this permits a large environmental influence on development. Higher primates and human beings are precocious in their sensory systems, but less developed in their motor systems. The relatively slow infant motor development among humans would be a recent adaptation (perhaps a million years ago) due to the invention of means to carry babies, while keeping one's hands free (e.g., Konner, 1981).

Weaning takes place among primates at different times (one year for most monkeys, two years for baboons, and four years for chimpanzees), but this nursing period represents a more or less constant proportion (one-quarter to one-third) of the age until female sexual maturity. Among human nomadic hunters, weaning takes place around three or four years of age (later if there is no new baby), and this corresponds to the same proportion. Most sedentary agricultural societies have a birth spacing (related to the age of weaning) of two to three years. In recent decades, early weaning and bottle feeding have spread to much of the world's population, above all to the large cities of the majority world, with the well-known risks of unclean water and poor food preparation (Grantham-McGregor *et al.*, 2007; see also Chapter 3 on parenting and the family).

The first cross-cultural study of infant performance, one that has had important repercussions, was carried out by Geber and Dean (1957). They examined full-term neonates who weighed more than 2,500 grams in the maternity hospital in Kampala, Uganda. They found a marked precocity in development in relation to western pediatric norms. This has come to be known as African Infant Precocity.[2] In retrospect, Geber and Dean's observations, and the way in which they presented the results, were flawed. The authors did not use statistical tests to establish African differences from the Euro-American norms; and it would have been better to have both African and Euro-American samples tested by the same experimenter. Other factors can also have affected the validity of their results (e.g., differences in mean weight at birth; see Warren and Parkin, 1974). Later studies using stricter methods (e.g., Brazelton, 1973) soon showed that the neonatal precocity found at first was partly exaggerated: there is some precocity, but not as general as previously described.

Differences at birth may be due to genetic factors, but certainly do not preclude pre-birth environmental influences, known as intrauterine experiences of the baby. Differences in birth weight can be due to differences in nutrition of expectant mothers, or to differences in their activity level. While in many western societies expectant mothers are granted maternity leave starting several weeks before the date of birth, this is not the case in most other societies. Moreover, from the moment of birth explicit cultural practices provide for differences in context. For example, in many parts of Africa and the West Indies babies tend to be massaged extensively (e.g., Hopkins, 1977), while in quite a few western countries babies born in hospitals are taken away from the mother for most of the day and placed in cribs. These practices are likely to have consequences for later motor development (Hopkins and Westra, 1990), as we shall see now. Part of the research on infant development across cultures has sought to observe, describe and measure individual behavior (particularly in the psychomotor domain) in a variety of field settings. Following the work of the pediatricians Gesell and Amatruda (1947), who first systematized observations in this domain, various psychologists have constructed developmental scales called baby tests that allow for quantitative measurement (e.g., Bayley, 1969; Brunet and Lézine, 1951/1971; Griffiths, 1970). These scales are composed of a number of items (observable behaviors that are characteristic of a given age) that one can use to determine the infant's developmental age. When developmental age is divided by the chronological age (and multiplied by 100), one obtains a "developmental quotient" (DQ). These scales, in addition to giving a general DQ, also allow the distinguishing of partial DQs in particular areas, such as motor, eye–hand coordination, language and sociability. They can be applied to infants aged between birth and 3 years.

The use of baby tests has been criticized because the overall DQ masks interesting differences between specific items. Super (1976), analyzing each item in the Bayley scale separately for the Kipsigi in Kenya, found that sitting upright

---

[2] The term "African precocity" can be seen as an example of ethnocentrism. The equally appropriate term of Euro-American *retardation* is used nowhere in the literature.

unassisted, and walking, are acquired very early (about one month before the Bayley American norms). These are motor developments recognized as important by Kipsigi mothers; they are named and are specifically trained. In contrast, other motor behaviors, for which infants receive little training, show a delay rather than an advance on the western norm (e.g., crawling; see also Kilbride, 1980). Informed researchers no longer speak of general precocity, but look for a direct link between parental ethnotheories and psychomotor development. There is thus evidence of a strong connection between parental ethnotheories (see below) and (limited) variations in motor development (Bril and Sabatier, 1986; see also Dasen *et al.*, 1978). The general lesson we can learn from this discussion on African Infant Precocity is that there is hardly any evidence for a purely genetic (maturational) effect on individual development but – as we shall see later – there is no evidence for a purely environmental effect either (cf. Chapters 3, 11).

The emphasis on sensorimotor development in earlier studies can be explained in part by the central position of Piaget (1970a, b) in developmental psychology during much of the second half of the twentieth century. Although he stressed development as an interactive process between the individual organism and the environment, Piaget focussed on the child rather than on the social context. A shift in emphasis is reflected in the growing attention for the social context in which children grow up, perhaps best exemplified in research on *parenting* (cf. Bornstein, 1991, 1994; Bornstein and Lansford, 2010). Thus, we now turn to another aspect of development, namely the interaction patterns of parents with their infants. Not only are neonates equipped to start interacting with both the physical and the social environment, parents are also equipped to deal with babies, an idea reflected in the notion of intuitive parenting (e.g., Papoušek and Papoušek, 1987).

Although we are dealing here with behavior of adults, parenting of infants is an area where remarkable cross-cultural invariance has been found. One example is the special intonation patterns of speech that mothers (and also fathers) use when they address the young baby. Among the characteristics of this way of speaking, called "motherese," are a generally higher pitch and larger variations in pitch (Fernald, 1992). Detailed analysis shows that tonal patterns can be distinguished according to communicative intent, for example asking for attention, or comforting the baby (Fernald, 1989). Although there are some cross-cultural variations, these appear to be negligible compared to the similarities (e.g., Papoušek and Papoušek, 1992).

Such communication patterns tend to be interactive as demonstrated, for example, in cross-cultural studies by Keller and colleagues (Keller, Schölmerich and Eibl-Eibesfeldt, 1988; Keller, Chasiotis and Runde, 1992; see also Keller, Otto, Lamm, Yovsi and Kärtner, 2008). They analyzed communication patterns between infants (2–6 months) and parents in US-American, West German, Greek, Trobriand

and Yanomami societies. Quite similar interaction structures were found. For example, infants produce few vocalizations when adults are talking and vice versa; adults respond differently to vocalizations with a positive and negative emotional tone. According to the authors these findings are compatible with the notion of intuitive parenting practices which rest on inborn characteristics regulating behavior exchange between parents and children.

The (for many surprising) similarities do not mean that there are no cross-cultural differences in early parenting behavior. For example, findings by Bornstein *et al.* (1992) suggest that Japanese mothers more than mothers in Argentina, France and the USA use "affect-salient" speech to 5- and 13-month-old babies. This means that they used more incomplete utterances, song and nonsense expressions. The mothers of the other cultures used relatively more "information-salient" speech. This is in line with previous findings to the effect that Japanese mothers empathize with the needs of their infants and try to communicate at the babies' level, while western mothers encourage individual expression in their children. An important, but in our opinion so far rather unanswered, question is to what extent these early differences are small and incidental, and to what extent they form the start of consistent ways in which societies socialize their youngsters. Findings of a recent study by Kärtner, Keller and Yovzi (2010), however, suggest that culture-specific contingency patterns in mother–infant interaction in Cameroon and Germany might already emerge during the second and third month of life.

Recently, approaches to describe and explain cross-cultural differences in rearing patterns have been termed developmental pathways. Such pathways are influenced by the epigenetic interplay of organismic and environmental (cultural) processes (see Chapters 3 and 11). According to some cross-cultural developmental (Keller, 2007) and social psychologists (Kağitçibaşi, 2007; Markus and Kitayama, 1991), cross-cultural differences in developmental outcomes are expressed on the basic personality dimensions of autonomy and relatedness. An emphasis on relatedness over autonomy views the individual as defined through membership in a social system, mainly the family. Harmonious relationships, acceptance of hierarchy (mainly age- and gender-based), cooperation and conformity are landmarks of development viewing the child as an interrelated co-agent with others (Greenfield, Keller, Fuligni and Maynard, 2003). According to Keller (2007), the interdependent self is adapted to rural subsistence-based modes of living. On the other hand, an emphasis on autonomy over relatedness is assumed to be adapted to the urban educated socioeconomic environment and denotes an independent individual who is self-contained, competitive, separate, unique, self-reliant, assertive and having an inner sense of owning opinions (Kağitçibaşi, 2007; Keller, 2007; see also the section on parenting and the family in Chapter 3).

Box 2.1 The component model of parenting (Keller, 2007)

The component model of parenting by Keller (2007) postulates a phylogenetically evolved universal repertoire of parenting systems that are individually modulated by interactional mechanisms. The parenting systems are defined by six particular parenting behaviors, namely: "primary care," "body contact," "body stimulation," "object stimulation," "face-to-face exchange" and "narratives." The four interactional mechanisms which shape mode and style of the expressed parenting behaviors comprise the mode of attention (exclusive or shared), contingency in terms of prompt reactivity, warmth and primary orientation toward positive or negative emotionality. Parenting systems as well as interactional mechanisms are considered as basically independent from each other, allowing alternative strategies through different combinations. These combinations are considered to be adaptive for particular environmental demands and to facilitate the child's acquisition of a contextually based psychology.

Keller and colleagues (Keller, 2007) have repeatedly argued that an interdependent self (see Chapter 5, pp. 121–125) is supported by a proximal style of parenting during the first year of life. Such a style combines high body contact and body stimulation with low verbal mentalizing. Body contact is constituted by close bodily proximity, carrying and co-sleeping. In many different traditional environments, the "back and hip cultures," infants (LeVine, 1990) are carried on the bodies of their mothers or other caregivers for a substantial part of the day. For example, Aka Pygmy and !Kung (San in the Kalahari) mothers carry their infants for about eight hours a day (Barr, Konner, Bakeman and Adamson, 1991; Hewlett, 1991), South American Ache infants spend about 93 percent of their daylight time in tactile contact with mainly the mother (Hill and Hurtado, 1996).

The psychological function of body contact mainly consists of the experience of emotional warmth, which is associated with social cohesion and feelings of relatedness and belongingness (MacDonald, 1992). Warmth contributes to the child's willingness to embrace parental messages and values (Kochanska and Thompson, 1997; Maccoby, 1984), preparing the individual for a life which is based on harmony and respects hierarchy among family members or the primary social group (Keller, Lohaus, Völker, Cappenberg and Chasiotis, 1999). At the same time, parental care in terms of body contact allows continued participation in subsistence labor, for example through farming, fetching water and cooking, although carrying a child might compete for a mother's time with other resource-producing activities (Hill and Hurtado, 1996).

Body stimulation is also based on body communication, but as an exclusive dyadic activity. Mothers stimulate their infants by providing them with motorically challenging experiences through touch and movement. The array ranges from lifting the whole baby up and down in an upright position among West African caregivers to gently exercising arms or legs of the infant among German caregivers (Keller, Yovsi

Box 2.1 continued

and Voelker, 2002). Body stimulation can be related functionally to motor development. The motor precocity of the African infant (Geber and Dean, 1957; Super, 1976), described in the main text, has been interpreted as a consequence of these early stimulation patterns (Bril, 1989). Also Indian baby bathing and massaging have been demonstrated as accelerating developmental progress (Landers, 1989; Walsh Escarce, 1989). Body stimulation might further enhance somatic development in order to prepare an organism for early reproduction. Finally, the verbal environment is skeletal, repetitive and with little elaboration (Fivush and Fromhoff, 1988). It is characterized by commands and instructions with the mother taking a leading role in conversations. A high value is placed on the social context, moral rectitude and the consequences of a certain behavior (Wang, Leichtman and Davies, 2000). Emotions tend to be viewed as disruptive and are expected to be controlled (Bond, 1991; Chao, 1995). The repetitive style has been identified as characteristic for an interdependent sociocultural orientation (Keller, Kärtner, Borke, Yovzi and Kleis, 2005).

An independent self, on the other hand, is supposed to be the long-term outcome of a distal style of parenting. Distal parenting during infancy consists primarily of face-to-face contact, object stimulation and an elaborative verbal environment. Face-to-face exchange is characterized through mutual eye contact and the frequent use of language (Keller, 2007). The parental investment in the face-to-face system consists mainly of the devotion of time and attention in dyadic behavioral exchange. Face-to-face exchange follows the rules of pseudo dialogues providing the infant with the experience of contingency perception. Through the prompt (contingent) answers toward communicative signals, the infant can perceive itself as the cause of the parental action. In this way the infant is informed about his or her uniqueness and self-efficacy. Also, positive emotions are communicated in face-to-face situations (Keller *et al.*, 1999).

The object stimulation system is pervasive in the urban educated middle class and is aimed at linking the infant to the non-social world of objects and the physical environment in general. The elaborative and conversation-eliciting interaction style is characterized by frequent questions, elaborations and the tendency to integrate the child's input so that an equal conversational pattern emerges (Reese, Haden and Fivush, 1993). The narrations are rich, embellished and detailed. The focus is on personal attributes, preferences and judgments. Emotions are often regarded as a direct expression of the self and an affirmation of the importance of the individual (Markus and Kitayama, 1994). The elaborated communication style has been identified as characteristic for an independent sociocultural orientation (Fiske, Kitayama, Markus and Nisbett, 1998; see also Chasiotis, Bender, Kiessling and Hofer, 2010). According to Keller (2007), the prevalence of the distal face-to-face parenting system is especially salient in contexts where a separated agency has to meet the demands of self-contained and competitive social relationships.

Attachment patterns

An important theme in developmental psychology is the attachment between the baby and its mother (Ainsworth, 1967; Bowlby, 1969). From ethology (see Chapter 11), Bowlby derived the idea that behaviors of human infants such as crying and smiling will elicit caregiving reactions from adults. As a result of such interactions, especially with the mother, attachment develops. This provides the child with a secure base from which it can explore the world. The importance of security was demonstrated dramatically in experiments in which rhesus monkeys were reared in isolation (Harlow and Harlow, 1962). In their cages there were two devices: one was constructed of wire and had a nipple from which the young monkey could drink; the other was padded with soft cloth. It was found that the monkey would cling to the "cloth mother" rather than to the "wire mother" when some strange and probably threatening object was put in the cage. Apparently, it was not food but warmth and safety that determined the attachment behavior. Theorists in this area tend to assume that a secure attachment forms the basis for healthy emotional and social development.

Although attachment theory was originally rooted mainly in field observations, the most frequent way of assessment is by means of a standard procedure called the Strange Situation (Ainsworth, Blehar, Waters and Wall, 1978). This consists of a sequence of situations in a laboratory. First the child is with the mother. After a while a stranger comes in. Subsequently the mother leaves, the stranger leaves, and the mother returns. The reactions of the child are observed during each of these episodes. One-year-old children who go to the mother when she returns, and who will accept comfort if they felt distressed, are considered securely attached. Children who avoid the mother or show signs of anger are considered insecurely attached (with a further division in two or even three subcategories; cf. Main and Solomon, 1990).

The cross-cultural equivalence of the Strange Situation as an assessment procedure is questionable. Based on clinical experiences with western childrearing, Bowlby assumed that the mother was the exclusive caretaker for human infants. In the years after Bowlby's (1969) formulation of his theory, this exclusivity of the mother–infant dyad was challenged by identifying the father as an additional, potentially significant caretaking figure across cultures (Lamb, 1986). For example, among the Aka Pygmies the father spends considerable time with the baby at a few months old (Hewlett, 1991).

In the last decades new evidence from primate and human behavioral ecology has shown that assistance from group members other than the genetic parents seems to be crucial for the survival and growth of primate infants (Hrdy, 1999). According to this cooperative breeding hypothesis, this assistance was also essential for child survival during human evolution. In line with that reasoning, in many societies young children are continuously in the company of others, namely older siblings of the child, friends or female relatives of the mother (Hrdy, 1999, 2005; see Chapters 3 and 11). Long periods of bodily contact, with the baby held in a vertical position during the day, are characteristic of many nomadic hunting societies, but are also frequent among agriculturalists. As the infant grows older, there is an increase in cross-cultural differences in the social interactions to which a child is exposed. In some settings children become part of an extended family or village community in which many adults and other children assume caretaking roles. In other settings the role of the mother as primary caretaker remains more central and exclusive. In urban western settings, a new pattern has been developing recently: bringing children from a few months of age onward to a day care center. Is it to be expected that reactions to the Strange Situation can be interpreted in the same way for these one-year-olds as for children who have been in the almost exclusive care of their mother?

What are the consequences of the differences in these cultural practices? Attachment theory as developed by Bowlby and Ainsworth emphasizes the importance of one primary caretaker, which in all societies is usually the mother. For the development of secure attachment patterns she has to be available when the infant needs her. If the child is confronted with various other adults as caretakers, especially relative strangers, this may be detrimental to the formation of secure attachment. Needless to say, this can have serious implications for desirable modes of child care, notably in day care centers. However, the question of what these consequences might be is not easy to answer, because not only the social settings per se, but also socialization goals may differ across cultures. Thus, as we already mentioned earlier, it has been argued that two orientations can be distinguished: in western societies socialization may be more oriented toward self-regulation and autonomy, while in many non-western countries the orientation is more toward social interdependencies (e.g., Bornstein, 1994; Bornstein and Lansford, 2010).

Keller and collaborators (Keller, 2007; Keller *et al.*, 2004) are among those who postulate continuity between these early childrearing themes and later differences in the nature of the self-concept (to be discussed in Chapter 5). Convincing demonstration of the validity of this view requires longitudinal research from infancy to adulthood in societies with quite varying practices. More tenuous evidence is obtained by studying the continuity of attachment styles over shorter periods, or by asking adults to recall their early attachment experiences. In a nine-year follow-up study (children were then 14 years old) a relationship was found between early childrearing and later expressions of aggression in a projective test. A procedure that asks adults about their own past is the Adult Attachment Interview (Main, Kaplan and Cassidy, 1985). A relationship between interview results and adults' caretaking style has been reported in a meta-analysis based on a number of studies (Van Ijzendoorn, 1995), but the interpretation of this finding is debatable (Fox, 1995). Further extension of attachment patterns into adult life is thought to be reflected in the care for elderly parents in need of help (e.g., Ho, 1996; Marcoen, 1995; Marcoen, Grommen and Van Ranst, 2006).

In clinical and developmental psychology, long-lasting effects of early experiences have been debated extensively at least since Freud's (e.g., 1938) claims about the importance of the first six years of life. Culture-comparative research can contribute to this debate, although prevalent ecocultural and sociopolitical contexts often continue to have an influence throughout the lifetime of an individual. This makes it difficult to distinguish between effects that carry over from early in life and direct effects of present conditions. One danger of the sometimes speculative inferences about the long-term effects of quite subtle sociocultural variables is that we may overlook differences in actual ecological conditions. An example to illustrate this comes from a multicountry study by Whiting (1981) on infant-carrying practices in relation to mean annual temperature. Whiting grouped infant-carrying practices into three categories: the use of cradle, arms and sling. Drawing a 10°C isotherm (coldest month) on a world map, and placing the three styles of carrying on the same map, revealed a striking correlation with temperature. In a sample of 250 societies, cradle carrying was predominant in those whose mean temperatures were lower than 10°C, while arm and sling carrying were predominant in warmer societies. The main exceptions were the Inuit, who carry their babies in the parka hood (but away from their bodies). One can speculate on the functional origins of such a relationship between climate and a childrearing practice. In this case, a very down-to-earth consideration may be at work: urine on the clothes is disagreeable in cold climates, while it can evaporate quickly in the heat. One can equally speculate on the long-term effects of such practices on young babies. We return to this issue in Chapter 3 when we discuss childhood as a formative period, and in Chapter 11 when dealing with models of cultural transmission.

Early social cognition

While infancy in other mammals is immediately followed by the juvenile period in which the young are no longer dependent on their parents for survival, Homo sapiens is the only species that has a distinct phase of a "prepubertal" childhood, so that the human primate proportionally has the longest childhood period (Bogin, 1999). This prolonged immaturity (and the distinct human post-reproductive phase in old age; see Chapter 3) form unique aspects of development in humans. Because length of immaturity in primates is related to brain size, which in turn is related to social complexity (Dunbar, 1995), this prolonged period of dependency is considered a preparatory period to adapt to the complex human social environment (see also the childhood as a formative period section in Chapter 3 and the adaptation section in Chapter 11). As human infants are dependent on the caregiving environment, and born with a propensity for social interaction, they show intriguing examples of their bias toward mentalizing the world (Gergely, Nadasdy, Csibra and Biro, 1995): As early as at 3 months of age, infants begin to interpret actions as goal directed; infants try, for example, to imitate intentional rather than accidental acts of other agents and can distinguish between actors who are unwilling from actors who are unable to act in a particular way (Gergely, Bekkering and Kiraly, 2002). At about 8 months of age, according to some authors (Tomasello, 1999), a "revolution" in social understanding takes place. Joint attention, pointing and other communicative gestures by which one indicates an environmental stimulus by non-verbal means are shown for the first time; these are important indicators of the development of the understanding that others have unobservable mental states. Joint attention is a powerful cultural tool since a "triad" of infant, caretaker and object is being built that leads to shared social activities on an object. These behaviors are regarded as precursors for a full-blown mentalistic understanding ("theory of mind," Premack and Woodruff, 1978).

A classic task to measure such mentalistic abilities is the "false location task" (Wimmer and Perner, 1983). This task involves hiding an object at a location and then relocating the object while the actor of the play (usually performed with puppets) is absent. If the child demonstrates that it expects the protagonist to seek the object at the first location, it understands that the protagonist has a false belief differing from its own knowledge. Research has shown that children's understanding of such a task is subject to substantial changes especially during the age-span of 3 to 4.5 years (Wellman, Cross and Watson, 2001). Remarkably, though, recent studies with non-verbal versions show that infants as young as 15 months already expect the protagonist to seek the object in the location in which the protagonist believed the object would be (Onishi and Baillargeon, 2005; see also Surian, Caldi and Sperber, 2007). This is intriguing evidence that there is a profound development of mentalistic understanding even before the acquisition of language.

So how much do infants really know? It seems obvious that infants are biologically prepared for a world consisting of objects and animate beings (Bjorklund and Pellegrini, 2002). In its intuitive understanding of inanimate objects, all the infant needs is a primary representation of the object. In its intuitive understanding of animate beings, however, the infant needs a representation of the mental representations of others (i.e., a meta-representation). Full-blown meta-representational development depends in important ways on social activities such as imitation, intention-reading and identification of goal-directed actions, pretend play and language. What develops most probably is the ability to reflect on one's own representations. Some authors consider this to be impossible before the age of about 18 months, when children can recognize themselves in the mirror, thus obtaining a mental representation of their self (Bischof-Köhler, 1991). Hence, a gap of about 18 months between 1.5 and 3 years seems to exist between the "skeptics" and the "enthusiasts" (as Bischof-Köhler, 1998, referred to them). According to the enthusiasts, full-blown mentalistic understanding is already there in the second year of life; according to the skeptics, this does not occur before the third year.

Thus, it seems likely that infants' understanding of the world is multiply determined. They might possess some innate, or domain-specific knowledge (e.g., theory of mind), while in other cases some more domain-general mechanisms (e.g., memory) might be involved. As an example, let us consider developmental concepts and contextual factors which are ontogenetically related to mentalistic understanding: regarding contextual facilitating factors, pretend play with siblings or peers also facilitates mentalistic understanding, and children from larger families show earlier development of theory of mind (Ruffman, Perner, Naito, Parkin and Clements, 1998). Besides the obvious connection with language acquisition (Goswami, 2008), mentalistic understanding is closely linked to inhibitory control. Inhibitory control is an important element of the control aspects of the increasing awareness of one's own mental states and can be subdivided in delay (delaying gratification of a desire) and conflict inhibition (responding in a way that conflicts with a more salient response). Especially conflict inhibition is ontogenetically linked with theory of mind, but the causal relationship in the developmental trajectory of inhibitory and mentalistic abilities was unclear until recently. In the meantime, there are some indications that a basic inhibitory ability is a prerequisite for the development of mentalistic understanding (Chasiotis, Kiessling, Winter and Hofer, 2006; Pellicano, 2007).

From a cross-cultural perspective, these studies demonstrate a basic assumption of mainstream developmental psychology, namely that everyday knowledge of human psychology is the same everywhere. This universality claim for mentalistic understanding and its development has important implications. If the conviction that other humans are mental beings whose ways of behavior are based on certain states of mind (needs, beliefs or emotions) holds true, it makes sense to view mind as rational and able to control emotions, intentions and thereby actions. However, there are also reasons to assume culture-specific conceptualizations of mind. There might be cultures that explain actions by referring less to inner mental states and more to contextual factors or even to spirits outside the body. In a review discussing cultural variations in theory of mind, Lillard (1998) claimed that the European American model of folk psychology is not universal.

A way to answer the question of universality of the concept of folk psychology is to consider its development. Chasiotis, Kiessling, Hofer and Campos (2006) investigated the relation of theory of mind (measured here as false-belief understanding) and inhibitory control (the ability to suppress a reaction and activate another) since the latter is seen as an important prerequisite of the former. Three samples of preschoolers from Europe (Germany), Africa (Cameroon) and Latin America (Costa Rica) were involved. After controlling for age, gender, siblings, language understanding and mother's education, culture did not have a moderating effect; each culture showed the same relation between conflict inhibition and false-belief understanding. Furthermore, delay inhibition was not a significant predictor of false-belief understanding in any culture. These results are in line with studies involving American or Asian samples (Carlson and Moses, 2001; Sabbagh, Xu, Carlson, Moses and Lee, 2006), thus indicating the possible universality of the relation between conflict inhibition and false-belief understanding. In the study by Chasiotis, Kiessling, Hofer and Campos (2006), Cameroonian children scored significantly lower on theory of mind than the other two cultures; they also showed lower scores in conflict inhibition and higher scores in delay inhibition. The differences in mean scores make the culture-invariant relation between conflict inhibition and false-belief understanding even more interesting because the mean differences are observed against a backdrop of culture-invariant relations between the concepts. These findings suggest that the interdependent parenting goals of obedience and compliance are related to better delay inhibitory performance and lower false-belief understanding in children (see also Chasiotis, Bender, Kiessling and Hofer, 2010).

Conclusions

We began this chapter with the concept of culture as a context for development and described conceptualizations of this context, such as the notion of the developmental niche (Super and Harkness, in press). Then we explained the modes of cultural transmission in more detail, because it is central to much of this chapter, indeed to much of this book. Next, we took a closer look at other developmental issues in the preschool years, and described enculturation and socialization as the processes through which the child acquires knowledge. Thereafter, we considered the primary socialization agents of the child, namely the parents, to see how their beliefs about childrearing lead to cross-cultural differences in parenting behaviors and how these behaviors in turn influence child development. Parenting behaviors are interesting because they may explain how cross-cultural differences in adulthood already emerge during childhood. In the last section we dealt with probably the most important psychological domain characteristic for human children, namely the ability to understand what is psychologically going on in their social environment.

KEY TERMS

attachment • biological transmission • child training • cultural transmission
developmental niche • enculturation • ontogenetic development • parental
ethnotheories • parental investment • socialization • theory of mind

FURTHER READING

Bornstein, M. H. (ed.) (2010). *Handbook of cultural developmental science.* New York: Taylor & Francis.

The handbook documents cultural variation in physical, cognitive, emotional and social development in children, and parents.

Cole, M., and Cole, S. R. (2004). *The development of children* (5th edn.). New York: Freeman.

An introductory text on developmental psychology paying ample attention to the relationship of child and cultural context.

Keller, H. (2007). *Cultures of infancy.* Mahwah, N.J.: Erlbaum.

A comprehensive overview of Heidi Kellers' impressive analysis of cultural variation in developmental pathways in infancy and childhood.

Nsamenang, A. B. (1992). *Human development in cultural context: A third world perspective.* Newbury Park, Calif.: Sage.

A presentation and critique of developmental psychology from an African ecological and cultural perspective.

3 | Individual development: Childhood, adolescence and adulthood

CONTENTS

- Childhood and adolescence
    - Childhood and adolescence as a cultural notion
    - Childhood as a formative period for adulthood
- Adulthood
    - Early adulthood: Mating and partnership
    - Middle adulthood: Parenting and the family
    - Late adulthood
- Conclusions
- Key terms
- Further reading

At virtually the same time as the rise in cross-cultural studies of development, there has been a dramatic increase in interest in **life span development**, which covers not only the period from birth to maturity, but also continues through maturity to eventual demise (Baltes, Lindenberger and Staudinger, 2006). In this chapter, we examine cross-cultural variations in the developmental stages beyond the ones that were discussed in Chapter 2; these are childhood, adolescence and adulthood. After discussing cultural notions of childhood and adolescence, we will present evidence on how childhood experiences can explain cross-cultural variations in adulthood. In the section on adulthood, we will deal with mating, partnership and parenting across cultures. In the final section, we will discuss life span developmental and evolutionary approaches to late adulthood. The chapter concludes with reflections on the cross-cultural applicability of the developmental issues raised in the last two chapters.

Childhood and adolescence

As we have seen in the previous chapter, human development can be described in stages. There, we dealt with the first decade of life, comprising the two earliest stages, infancy and early childhood. While infancy is the period from birth to two years, childhood is mainly defined as the period after infancy and before sexual maturation. Adolescence as a developmental stage is the time in which this maturation takes place, and it can be regarded as a transformation phase to adulthood.

Childhood and adolescence as a cultural notion

Ideas about children and development are found everywhere and, as we have seen in the section on parental ethnotheories in Chapter 2, such ideas can differ across cultures. Also within western societies views about what children are like and how they should behave have changed over time. Kessen (1979) has referred to the US-American child as "a cultural invention," quoting sources in which, for example, obedience of US-American children is emphasized and US-American parents are admonished not to play with their children. Kessen goes so far as to question whether there is a "fundamental nature" to the child. Ariès (1960) has questioned the existence in medieval Western Europe of the emotional ties in the nuclear family that are so characteristic of the family as it is now known in these societies. Descent and arranged marriages were central rather than the romantic love relationship that forms the basis of partnerships today. Ariès based his ideas on historical accounts in which he noted the absence of expressions of emotions with regard to children. However, other authors have quoted numerous sources which do mention such expressions and which give a quite different picture, suggesting that emotional bonds between parents and children did exist (e.g., Peeters, 1988). This suggests that it is meaningful to assume that there exist fundamental ways in which children are the same universally, and in which they interact with adults (see Chapter 2).

Cross-cultural research, particularly by anthropologists, has regularly contributed to the debate, starting with the now controversial descriptions of carefree adolescence on Samoa (Mead, 1928; see Freeman, 1983). While the western view on adolescence typically stresses conflicts with parents, mood disruptions and risky behaviors like drug abuse as being characteristic for that age period (Arnett, 1995, 1999; Dasen, 2000), the anthropological evidence from all over the world (called hologeistic studies, cf. Schlegel and Barry, 1991) clearly shows that, while adolescence is everywhere a time for learning new social roles, with its incumbent psychological tensions, it is often not the period of storm and stress claimed by western developmental and clinical psychologists throughout most of the twentieth century. Adolescence can be relatively brief, about two years for girls and two to four years for boys, longer when more training for adult roles is needed. In some cases, such as in rural India where children have to fulfill adult tasks from a very early age, not much time and attention can be spent on adolescence as the western world, and the more affluent urban Indians, define it (Saraswathi, 1999). One way to reconcile the somehow contradictory views on adolescence might be the notion of distinguishing between narrow and broad socialization (Arnett, 1995, 1999), a concept resembling the independent–interdependent distinction on sociocultural orientations of the self (see the parental ethnotheories section in Chapter 2). Many societies in the majority world use narrow socialization patterns. They have firm expectations of adolescents, and want to restrict their behaviors. This might reduce reckless behavior, but may also reduce independence and creativity. Modern societies show a broad socialization pattern. They have fewer restrictions and their expectations relate more to self-expression and autonomy, thus allowing more reckless behavior as well as other forms of self-expression (like the "psychosocial moratorium" postulated by Erikson, 1968).

Because of its transitional nature, there is a lot of cultural variation in the way the adolescent phase is construed and managed. Every society has some sort of initiation ritual to mark this major turning point in individual development, but while modern cultures in particular consider this phase as a distinct developmental period and even prolong the phase between childhood and adulthood by extended schooling, many non-industrial cultures expect adolescents to take over adult roles immediately by beginning to work or marrying in their early teens. Historically, Freudian psychoanalysis viewed adolescence just as the end of the sexual latency period without any particular function (Freud, 1938). Eric Erikson (1968), as one of the major revisionists of Freud's position and a pioneer of a life span perspective on human development, interpreted the psychoanalytic stages as being psychosocial rather than sexual in nature. Instead of viewing human development as being determined only by sexual maturational processes, Erikson described a shift toward a more sociocultural view on development in which the period of decisive identity formation shifts from early childhood to adolescence (Marcia, 1980).

Early biological views on puberty viewed adolescence as an inevitable period of storm and stress. Recent neurobiological studies show that during adolescence, much remodeling of the brain is going on in areas that affect executive functioning such as emotional regulation, inhibitory control and planning. Brain areas mediating emotional experience change more rapidly than those mediating cognitive regulation (Monk et al., 2003). Neural changes such as the remodeling of the dopaminergic system (or "pleasure" system) may contribute to greater self-focus, and to greater reward-seeking and risk-taking (Blakemore and Choudhury, 2006; Steinberg, 2008). These results, demonstrating a discrepancy between cognitive and emotional maturity, might explain why adolescents sometimes might not act very reasonably although they are at the peak of their cognitive abilities. But this is only half of the story. Other studies showed that the social environment also is important in explaining the variability in adolescent adjustment (Costello and Angold, 2006).

Taking a cross-cultural perspective, Dasen (1999, 2000) has reviewed the cross-cultural literature on adolescence, drawing attention to three methodological approaches: hologeistic studies; ethnographic fieldwork in several societies co-ordinated by Whiting and Whiting (1988); and clinical and developmental psychologists' reports from various non-western countries. In attempting to define which social conditions were providing the smoothest transition from childhood to adulthood, Dasen attributed adolescent stress mainly to rapid social change, with family continuity and integrity being one of the buffer variables. Other reviews of adolescence in a cross-cultural perspective have been provided by Gibbons (2000) and by Sabatier (1999), who deal mainly with large-scale cross-national studies and research on adolescents in migrant groups in multicultural societies. Like Petersen (1988), who dealt with adolescence in mainstream developmental psychology, Sabatier provides a "debunking of myths" concerning migrant adolescents: contrary to popular belief, these adolescents are, as a rule, not particularly prone to mental illness, have a positive self-esteem and are motivated to be successful in school and in learning a trade. According to Sabatier, the idea that acculturation reinforces the generation gap is another myth that has been overturned or at least qualified by recent research findings.

Initiated by hormonal changes in the prepubertal period, the first outward sign of puberty is the growth spurt. This is followed by changes in body proportions: girls' hips and boys' shoulders broaden, girls add more fat and boys more muscles finally leading to sexual maturation. The onset of sexual maturation can be much more easily determined in girls by means of the first menstrual period (menarche). Because of difficulties in measuring the pubertal onset in boys, there is much more evidence for a high variability of the female age of onset of puberty. Age at menarche varies not only within a population, but can also vary between differing historical and cultural contexts. Among some foraging people in New Guinea, age at menarche is around 20 years, in Europe in the eighteenth century it was as late as 16 years, while in modern Europe the mean age is at 12 years. This huge variability cannot be explained merely by genetic differences, but also not by nutritional factors alone (Thomas, Renaud, Benefice, de Meeus and Guegan, 2001). Because it points at an interesting environmental malleability of human somatic development (Belsky, Steinberg and Draper, 1991; Ellis, 2004), we will deal with this variability in the following section.

Childhood as a formative period for adulthood

The nature–nurture controversy has been mainly concerned with how much of observable behavior can be explained by biological factors and how much in terms of environmental influences (see Chapters 1 and 11). Already in 1958 Anastasi pointed out that a more pertinent question may be how nature and nurture relate to each other (Anastasi, 1982). As we shall see in Chapter 11, biological theories about social behavior as advanced in the biological study of behavior are beginning to lead to a theoretical understanding of how such relationships might be conceptualized. In the domain of social behavior there are theoretical approaches in which reproductive development is seen as the epigenetic outcome of *interactional* processes between an organism with genetically given capacities for development and actual environmental experiences.

In cross-cultural developmental psychology such interactions can be studied by linking differences in conditions in early life with differences in characteristic behavior patterns later in life. From that evolutionary perspective, many features of childhood can be considered preparations for adulthood (Bjorklund, 1997; Chasiotis, 2010, in press): if environmental change is slow compared to an individual life span, the optimal mode of adaptation is to establish sensitive learning situations early in life as preparations for adulthood that guide later development (Draper and Harpending, 1988). Accordingly, evidence shows that the first six years of childhood can be considered as psychologically the most important for individual development (Lamb and Sutton-Smith, 1982). Every child is reared in a unique environment characterized by contextual variables like a specific birth order (Sulloway, 1996; Toman, 1971) and socioeconomic conditions. Extensive value surveys in sociology (Inglehart, 1997) and cross-cultural psychology (Allen, Ng, Ikeda, Jawan, Sufi, Wilson and Yang, 2007) provide evidence for the importance of socioeconomic factors for developmental conditions. For example, the financial situation during childhood has been found to be a better predictor of the endorsement of values in adulthood than the current economic situation of the adult respondent (summarized under the notion of "economic determinism" to refer to the impact of the economic situation on psychological outcomes). In the following, empirical evidence will be presented regarding two building blocks of childhood context, birth order and socioeconomic status during childhood, and their explanatory power for cultural differences in pubertal timing, parenting motivation and social values.

Pubertal timing

Evolutionary developmental psychology offers a theoretical framework to conceptualize the influence of the socioeconomic context in childhood on consequent somatic, psychological and reproductive development (Belsky, Steinberg and Draper, 1991; Chisholm, 1993): Belsky, Steinberg and Draper relate factors in the early environment of the child to later sexual and reproductive behavior and draw a contrast between families with limited resources, insecure attachment patterns and stress, and families where there is warmth and security. In the former kind of families there are tendencies for girls to reach sexual maturity at an earlier age, and for both girls and boys to engage earlier in sexual activity. Later in life this pattern is continued and leads to less stable pair bonding (higher rate of divorce) and less parental investment, creating an insecure social environment for the children of the next generation. Cross-cultural support for these results has been found in other studies (Chasiotis, 1999; Chasiotis, Scheffer, Restemeier and Keller, 1998). These are sweeping claims for at least two reasons. First, such intergenerational patterns have been noted before, but were ascribed to social environmental factors that continue across generations; Lewis (1966) spoke about "a culture of poverty" in explaining such patterns. Second, these findings imply that social factors influence biological processes such as sexual maturation and the onset of menstruation. However, whereas in earlier times such influences were thought to be incompatible with biological principles, it is now recognized that processes of physical development may indeed be affected by social conditions (Gottlieb, 1998; Gottlieb, Wahlsten and Lickliter, 1998).

In a research project aimed at investigating the effect of social changes on family development which occurred after the reunification of Germany in 1989, Chasiotis and his colleagues (Chasiotis, 1999; Chasiotis, Keller and Scheffer, 2003; Chasiotis, Scheffer, Restemeier and Keller, 1998) provided support for this perspective. They confirmed the importance of birth order and its interaction with socioeconomic status in childhood by predicting somatic as well as psychological developmental outcomes in a comparison of samples from Osnabrueck (West Germany) and Halle (East Germany). In one study (Chasiotis, Scheffer, Restemeier and Keller, 1998), they used the subsample of all mother–daughter dyads from West and East Germany to test the assumption that the onset of puberty is affected by childhood experiences. The comparison of the two samples of mother–daughter dyads showed that what seems to be inherited is not the timing of puberty per se, but the sensitivity for the prepubertal childhood context. The consideration of social status and birth order in other subsamples of the same research project led to the assumption that childhood context variables could also determine the East–West differences in intergenerational context continuity. Results of a reanalysis (Chasiotis, Keller and Scheffer, 2003) showed that birth order had significant and mainly expected effects of childhood variables on the age at menarche for women who do not have younger siblings (i.e., only children or laterborns). In contrast, participants with younger siblings (i.e., firstborns and middleborns) showed no such effects. In the previous study (Chasiotis et al., 1998) differences in intergenerational context continuity between the parental and filial generations in East and West Germany were interpreted as being caused by different sociocultural milieus prevalent in the former Federal Republic of Germany and the German Democratic Republic. The reanalysis of the data revealed that the intergenerational context discontinuity affecting the onset of puberty was primarily due to different childhood experiences of lastborn daughters and their mothers. It seems that the absence or existence of younger siblings influences the age at menarche, and not the "cultural" origin of the subjects.

Parenting motivation

Although much contextual and cultural variation in parenting behavior has been reported (Keller, 2007), the motivational roots of this culturally divergent parenting behavior are barely known. Chasiotis, Hofer and Campos (2006) proposed that inter-active experiences with younger siblings should be considered an important factor for the emergence of parenting motivation. Taking a cross-cultural, developmental perspective, they suggested that the presence of younger siblings triggers proso-cial, nurturant motivations and caretaking behaviors. In turn, this implicit proso-cial motivation results in positive, loving feelings toward children on a conscious level, which finally lead to parenthood (see also section on adulthood below). Using structural equation modeling, they demonstrated that this developmental pathway is verifiable in both male and female participants, and in all cultural samples from Germany, Costa Rica and Cameroon. A further investigation of the relationship was warranted because the implicit parenting motivation showed cultural variation and was associated with the existence of younger siblings – which was different across cultures. To investigate the impact of this childhood context variable on cul-tural differences, implicit parenting motivation was first regressed on the variable "younger siblings." In the next step, the unstandardized residual of implicit parent-ing motivation of that regression analysis was reentered in an ANOVA (Analysis of Variance) with culture as predictor. The ANOVA with the residual of implicit parent-ing motivation as dependent variable and culture as predictor showed a remark-able decrease in effect size of culture which meant that 62 percent of the original effect size of culture on implicit parenting motivation could be traced back to sib-ling effects. This impressive effect was replicated in three additional samples from Cameroon, Costa Rica and Germany in which the effect size of "culture" decreased to 50 percent, and with three samples from Cameroon, Germany and PR China in which the reduction even approached 100 percent (Chasiotis and Hofer, 2003; see also Bender and Chasiotis, 2010).

Social values

Building on these results of previous studies on implicit prosocial (parenting) mo-tivation, it was further investigated if explicit prosocial values are also influenced by childhood context variables. In two studies, data on social value orientations were collected (Bender and Chasiotis, 2010; Chasiotis and Hofer, 2003). The first study with the Schwartz Value Survey (SVS; Schwartz, 1994a), and samples from Cameroon, Costa Rica and Germany, reveals that 36 percent of the cultural dif-ferences of social values constituting the higher order value type of conservation (consisting of the subscales tradition, conformity and security) can be traced back to sibling effects. After combining the effect of siblings with that of socioeconomic status in childhood (i.e., paternal profession), the amount of explained variance in conservation even increases to 55 percent. Analogous to the findings on economic determinism by Inglehart (1997) and Allen *et al.* (2007), present occupation was not related to conservation value orientation. In the second study (Bender and Chasiotis, in press), the importance of sibling effects for social value orientations was further corroborated in samples from Germany and Cameroon: measuring conservation with the Portrait Values Questionnaire (PVQ; Schwartz, Melech, Lehmann, Burgess, Harris and Owens, 2001), the number of siblings explains 67 percent of the cultural variance in conservation. These strong sibling effects only occur in scales in which intimate relationships with close relatives are almost explicitly mentioned (see, e.g., the definition of the Benevolence scale, Schwartz, in press: "the welfare of people with whom one is in frequent personal contact"), but not in scales dealing with more individualistic, autonomous social values like self-direction and achievement (for similar results on autobiographical memory, see Bender and Chasiotis, 2010).

These results on childhood context effects on diverse psychological variables across cultures imply that the family context during childhood is a powerful tool to explain cross-cultural differences in developmental outcomes. Context variables like socioeconomic status during childhood, birth order or number of siblings can be expected to exert similar influences on somatic, psychological and reproductive developmental pathways across cultures. On the basis of the explanatory power of these childhood context variables for cultural differences in such highly diverse areas as pubertal timing, implicit motivation and social value orientations it can be suggested that many psychological characteristics that are typically attributed to cultural differences may reflect systematic variations in family constellations across cultural contexts. For example, differences in self-construals which are interpreted as due to culture-specific socialization (Markus and Kitayama, 1991) could at least be partially dependent on relevant characteristics shared by participants from cultural samples such as systematic biases due to having (or not having) siblings.

Adulthood

Adulthood is typically divided into early, middle and late adulthood periods. It represents maturity and responsibility across cultures (Levinson, 1978, 1996). According to Erikson's theory of psychosocial stages during life span development (1968), early adulthood is concerned with balancing independence with intimacy, that is, the growing feeling of autonomy with the need to form close relationships.

Research confirms that intimacy is a central concern of young adults (for the US, see Whitbourne, Zuschlag, Elliot and Waterman, 1992; see mating and partnership section below). In middle adulthood, the central theme, in Erikson's terms, is generativity, which is, simply put, the need to be needed (Berk, 2003). In a narrow sense, it describes caregiving behaviors such as teaching and guiding of the next generation, and can express itself already in early adulthood by becoming a parent. More generally, it describes commitments that go beyond oneself and that benefit larger groups, including family, friends or society. Thus, the outcomes of these generative activities can be children (see parenting section), but also ideas or works of art (see late adulthood section). Cross-cultural research on generativity has been lacking until recently. Hofer, Busch, Chasiotis, Kärtner and Campos (2008) showed via structural equation modeling that the relations between implicit prosocial motivation, generativity, explicit generative goals and life satisfaction were the same across three different cultural samples of adults from Cameroon, Costa Rica and Germany. Thus, people all over the world seem to develop this need to be needed in middle and late adulthood (McAdams, 2001b). Finally, late adulthood involves coming to terms with one's life. Wisdom, which is the ability to reflect on and apply practical knowledge combined with emotional maturity, is a strong predictor of life satisfaction in late adulthood and old age (see late adulthood section).

Early adulthood: Mating and partnership

Generally, the term mating system describes how sexual behavior of a group is structured. In anthropology, mating systems usually describe systems of marriage. Besides the socially unstable and more ephemeral mating system of promiscuity or polygynandry, in which two or more males mate with two or more females, there are three types of institutionalized mating systems in human societies: monogamy (one male, one female), polygyny (one male, two or more females) and polyandry (one female, two or more males). In Murdock's *Ethnographic altas* (1967), containing one of the most comprehensive cross-cultural data sets from 849 cultures, the most frequently found mating system across cultures is polygyny: in 83 percent of all known human cultures, a man is allowed to marry two or more wives. Only 16 percent of societies are monogamous, and even fewer (only four societies, or about 0.5 percent of all known human societies) practice polyandry. However, the distribution of these institutionalized mating systems should not be confused with manifest human sexual behavior. First of all, legalized polygyny leads to a higher reproductive variance of males in a society: if more men can have more women (and thus children) than the average, then also more men will remain unwed because there are no potential mating partners left. This means that even within a society where polygyny is legal, most of the men will be monogamous or remain unmarried (see gender differences section in Chapter 2). Secondly, the largest contemporary societies have monogamy as the institutionalized marriage arrangement, so that the most common manifest marriage arrangement all over the world is monogamy. An interesting reason why institutionalized monogamy may lead to more stable and thriving societies might be the fact that, as we discussed in the gender differences section in Chapter 2, leaving lots of men without wives may not only be unfair; it might even be dangerous (Mesquida and Wiener, 1996, 1999).

In contemporary mating and partnership studies from industrial countries a number of changes are underway. It appears that the predominance of monogamous, lifelong relationships is in decline, that divorce rates are rising and that a pattern of sequential or serial monogamy can be observed in which persons have different exclusive partnerships for some period of time or marry repeatedly during their life (for a discussion of the concept of monogamy, see Reichard, 2003). This is often interpreted as a culture-specific sign of the modern western, individualistic way of life in which stable, lifelong relationships are no longer valued. From a cross-cultural perspective, this is unsustainable for many reasons. Looking beyond contemporary societies and taking a historical and cross-cultural perspective, the pattern is in some ways much more complicated, in some other ways quite simple. Starting with the simple patterns, emotional closeness within families in modern societies is not significantly lower compared to the majority world; in fact, the emotional closeness within families across the world is quite similar irrespective of educational, economic or cultural background. In a thirty-nation study, Georgas *et al.* (2006) found that family ties are similarly close all over the world. Another universal feature is that the probability of divorce is much higher in childless couples and does not have much to do with the cultural background either: 40 percent of all divorced couples in pre- as well as in industrial societies are childless (Buckle, Gallup and Rodd, 1996). To explain the seeming rise of serial monogamy in the western world, it is also not useful to compare divorce rates with more recent historical epochs like the Victorian era of the nineteenth century, where monogamy was much more socially and clerically imposed than today. However, taking eco-cultural factors such as subsistence patterns into consideration, it becomes clear that lifelong, exclusive partnerships are mainly characteristic for agrarian societies (MacDonald, 1988). Looking further back to our foraging ancestors by taking contemporary hunter-gatherers into account, it becomes obvious that the seemingly western pattern of instable partnerships and serial monogamy might be phylogenetically quite old and even typical for humans (Shostak, 1981/2000). Thus, the main conclusion here might be that humans all over the world are striving to have at least exclusive, and possibly lifelong, partnerships, but that only about 50 percent are successful in attaining that goal (see also Keller and Chasiotis, 2007).

From an evolutionary perspective, the difference in parental investment (discussed in the gender differences across cultures section in Chapter 2 as part of our mammalian heritage) leads to the prediction of different mating preferences of men and women. In a landmark study (Buss, 1989; Buss *et al.*, 1990) on preferred characteristics of mates in thirty-seven countries, gender differences between the preferences of young men and women were found along the lines of the differential reproductive investment strategies as just described. The results showed that both men and women highly value mutual attraction and love, a dependable character and an understanding and intelligent partner. However, young women expressed relatively more interest in good financial prospects and good earning capacity (i.e., partners capable of looking after them and their offspring well), while young men gave relatively higher ratings to good looks and physical attractiveness (presumably a good appearance reflects health and the capacity to bear children). In an even more comprehensive study, Schmitt (2003, 2005) demonstrated in samples from fifty-two countries with more than 16,000 participants that men showed a preference for more sexual partners than did women. Another line of research is on differences between men and women in the preferred age of a partner and the changes in this preference over the life span (Kenrick and Keefe, 1992). A large number of sources (such as advertisements for partners, and archives) in a range of societies show a similar pattern. During adolescence men tend to be slightly younger than women in a partnership, but this age difference soon reverses; with increasing age women tend to marry men who are older than themselves. An obvious evolutionary explanation is that men, who continue to be fertile much longer than women, have a phylogenetically evolved strategy to prefer partners who can have children.

Middle adulthood: Parenting and the family

In this section, we first describe biological aspects of parenting, starting from an individual perspective, before taking a broader, sociological perspective on the family including societal change.

Parenting

An obvious biological difference related to the already mentioned gender difference in parental investment is that mothers are prepared to nurture their infants with breast milk, which is optimally adapted to infants' needs and protects the infant from infections (Liepke, Adermann, Raida *et al.*, 2002). Breastfeeding also acts as natural contraception, delaying the onset of ovulation (Stern, Konner, Herman and Reichlin, 1986). The composition of human breast milk, low in fat and very low in protein (Lawrence, 1994), implies that infants are supposed to be frequently nursed and therefore be in close proximity to their mothers. In preindustrial societies, weaning age averages between 2 and 4 years (Dettwyler, 1995; Nelson, Schiefenhövel and Haimerl, 2000), so that during that first developmental phase, mothers are necessarily the primary caregivers. This imperative is reflected in the fact that women in all cultures and over historical times care for and interact with their small children substantially more than do fathers or other male relatives (see the gender differences across cultures section in Chapter 2). In the Whiting and Whiting (1975) six-cultures study, children were three to twelve times more frequently in the presence of their mothers than of their fathers. Even in societies with an unusual amount of paternal child care, like the Aka Pygmies, mothers spent substantially more time with their infants than did fathers and other caretakers (e.g., Hewlett 1991).

It is also a universal phenomenon that parents treat their children differently and allocate resources according to the children's value in a particular ecocultural environment. This notion still evokes protest from individuals who believe in human behavior and action as completely intentional and consciously controlled. However, because the interests of parents and infants can differ there is substantial evidence about differential parental investment across cultures and historical epochs (Voland, 1998). Trivers (1974) proposed from an evolutionary perspective that any offspring interest would be to exploit the parental resource as much as possible to maximize the child's own reproductive potential. Mothers and fathers, however, also have to take their own growth and development and that of other offspring or genetic relatives into account. One major issue of this parent–offspring conflict is the time parents invest in a particular child. Weaning is an excellent example of this conflict, since children rarely comply with their mother's intent to wean them. Cameroonian Nso mothers, for instance, put hot pepper or caterpillars on their breasts in order to frighten their children so that they do not want to breastfeed any longer (Yovsi and Keller, 2003).

Especially in circumstances of scarcity of resources and extreme poverty, mothers may "decide" to abort or even kill an infant (Daly and Wilson, 1988; Hrdy, 1999). Schiefenhövel (1988) has reported that Eipo mothers in West New Guinea give birth alone outside the woman's house. The woman decides whether or not to bring the infant to the village or leave it in the bush, wrapped with branches and leaves. These decisions are obviously working as a birth control measure, since the small valley can nourish only a limited number of people. These decisions are also driven by the infant's signs of liveliness. One infant who was destined to die was unwrapped by his mother and taken to the other women when a little foot started kicking through the package. A similar line of argument and evidence is presented by Scheper-Hughes (1995), who observed mother–infant relations among recent rural migrants in a shantytown in Brazil. The unusually high infant-mortality rate during the first year of life was seemingly accepted by the mothers because these infants were seen as too weak to survive the adverse circumstances of extreme poverty with the consequence of malnutrition and ever present diseases. This judgment resulted in detachment of the mother from the infant, to "let it go." Scheper-Hughes saved the life of an extremely malnourished 1-year-old boy whose mother was ready to let him go because she assumed that he "wanted" to die. When he survived, his mother took good care of him, and they developed a good relationship. Also, here, as in the Eipo case that Schiefenhövel observed, the signs of life and health highly influenced maternal acceptance and care. There are numerous other examples, like the fact that name-giving ceremonies are only held with children who are at least a year old, when it is probable that the infant will survive, or the fact that, in conditions of adversity, mother care and mother love start only when the infant has evidenced its ability to survive (see Bjorklund and Pellegrini, 2002). In a similar vein of reasoning, the "healthy-baby-hypothesis" (Mann, 1992) indicates that mothers allocate their resources to the children according to their health status. There is remarkable evidence from preindustrial societies, as we have outlined earlier, that sickly infants do not receive proper care. Today, women in industrial and post-industrial societies have much more support, including governmental assistance, to raise weak children, than did their ancestors and contemporary women in non-industrial societies. Nevertheless, Daly and Wilson (1988) have summarized convincing evidence that even within modern societies children with mental retardation or other congenital defects have a two- to ten-times-higher rate of abuse than do healthy children. Mann (1992) demonstrated that mothers of premature and low-birth-weight twins in the United States demonstrated more positive behavior in terms of playing, kissing, holding and soothing the healthier of the twins, even though the weaker twin was more responsive to the mother (see also Keller and Chasiotis, 2007).

Family and societal change

Middle adulthood is regarded as the phase of establishing a family, a term which nicely illustrates the central theme of this developmental period. As we already saw in Chapter 2, the family can be regarded as a central contextual component for individual development. Moreover, the family can maintain societal processes or can be the starting point of societal change (Kağitçibaşi, 2007). In her theory of family change, Kağitçibaşi challenges the view of modernization theory in which a unidirectional change toward the western individualistic pattern is proposed. Based on her research on cross-cultural differences in the value of children (Kağitçibaşi, 1982; Trommsdorff and Nauck, 2005), three family models can be distinguished: the model of independence, the model of interdependence and the model of psychological interdependence. First, the prototypical family model of interdependence can be found in rural agrarian societies with low levels of affluence, in which children often contribute to the family's economy and provide a security net for their aging parents (Kağitçibaşi, 2005). Having many children is valued, intergenerational interdependence (i.e., feeling close and connected; see Markus and Kitayama, 1991) is necessary for the family's livelihood, and a strong sense of tradition and obedience is dominant in parenting (see also Keller, 2007). Independence in this context is not functional (and thus not valued), because an independent child may leave the family and look after her/his own self-interest when she/he is grown. Second, a prototypical family model of independence can be found in affluent, educated, middle-class, nuclear families (typical for western countries). With alternatives for old-age support, economic dependence on off-spring is often not considered necessary or even desirable. Children – often just one – are therefore raised to be independent and self-sufficient, fostering a sense of separateness and uniqueness (Kağitçibaşi, 2007). Third, the model of psychological interdependence is a synthesis of the other two prototypical models. It is characterized by emotional interdependence between the generations, socialization values emphasizing family loyalties as well as individual loyalties, and childrearing entailing autonomy together with parental control leading to an autonomous-related self (see the parental ethnotheories section in Chapter 2). As a result of economic growth and urbanization, the findings of the value of children studies in eight societies (Trommsdorff and Nauck, 2005) provide evidence for a general shift toward the model of psychological interdependence. According to Kağitçibaşi (2007), a global convergence can be observed, in which a shift from the model of interdependence in the majority (non-western) world as well as from the model of independence in the minority (western) world to the model of psychological interdependence is taking place. We will come back to the practical implications of these views at the end of the next section.

Late adulthood

Baltes has proposed a framework in which biological and cultural factors play distinct roles in life span changes, which is especially applicable in late adulthood. He advances three principles that define the dynamics between biology and culture across the life span. First, he considers that "evolutionary selection benefits decrease with age." In concrete terms: "the human genome in older ages is predicted to contain an increasingly larger number of deleterious genes and dysfunctional gene expressions than in younger years" (Baltes, 1997, p. 367). Second, this biological decline takes place simultaneously with an increase in the "need or demand for culture," including the "entirety of psychological, social, material and symbolic (knowledge-based) resources that humans have generated over the millennia, and which, as they are transmitted across generations, make human development possible" (1997, p. 368). Thus, according to Baltes, there is an increase in culturally rooted functioning over the life span. However, there is a third principle, a countervailing decrease in the "efficiency of culture," in which "the relative power (effectiveness) of psychological, social, material and cultural interventions wanes" (1997, p. 368). In other words, people are less able to make good use of these cultural supports. For example, older adults take more time and practice, and need more cognitive support, to attain the same learning gains.

The application of these three principles has led Baltes to propose a dual-process model of life span development. For example, in the area of cognition, there is a decline in the "cognitive mechanics" (reflecting a person's biological "hardware") with age, as evidenced by speed and accuracy of information processing; but there is a stable level of "cognitive pragmatics" (reflecting the culture-based "software") over the later years, due to the countervailing principles of need for culture and effectiveness of culture. This is evidenced, for example, by the presence of stable reading, writing, language and professional skills, and knowledge about oneself, others and the conduct of one's life. In the remaining parts of this chapter, we will take a closer look at the last age period of human development from a life span perspective.

If we accept this life span perspective on human development (e.g., Baltes, Lindenberger and Staudinger, 2006), we also have to integrate later stages in life. In particular, old age (senescence) is to be explained: why do we age? Historically, aging is a very recent phenomenon: the majority of our ancestors died young. However, this observation confounds mean life span with maximum life span (Hawkes and Blurton Jones, 2005). The modern increase of life span stems from reducing risks earlier in life; it is an increase of the mean age, not of the maximum age, which has not changed throughout our species' history (Austad, 1997). So, why *can* we age? Why do human females live one-third of their lives in a post-reproductive period (Peccei, 2005)? The most prominent answer is the "grand-mother-hypothesis" (Williams, 1957): parents, especially mothers, need support in order to raise their children. Cross-culturally, support comes mostly from female relatives and from peer women or, more rarely, from fathers (Hrdy, 1999). There is evidence that children who did not receive any paternal investment have a higher risk of neglect or even death in diverse cultural contexts (Daly and Wilson, 1988). Even if there is no direct contact, paternal support is crucial for the survival of the offspring (Hill and Hurtado, 1996). From an evolutionary perspective, grandparents should be interested in contributing to the survival of their grandchildren because it contributes to their reproductive success (Voland, Chasiotis and Schiefenhövel, 2005). Voland and Beise (2002) addressed the differential effect of paternal and maternal grandmothers on the survival of their grandchildren. Based on the analysis of historical church documents from East Frisia, Germany, these authors found that the survival chance of grandchildren was higher if the maternal grandmother was alive. With only the maternal grandmother alive, fewer grandchildren died than when both grandmothers were alive.

On the value of cumulative knowledge in old age: The Nestor effect

However, things are even more complicated, since the beneficial effect of grand-mothers depends on several circumstances, such as lineage (the grandmother being mother's mother vs. father's mother), sex of grandchild or patrilocal versus matrilocal societies (e.g., Nosaka and Chasiotis, 2005). As Voland and Beise (2002), for example, found, more than twice as many newborns died if the paternal grandmother lived in the same community with her son's family compared to her not being present in the community. These results impressively document that maternal and paternal grandmothers may engage in different relationships with their grandchildren, with dramatically different consequences. The authors refer to paternal insecurity in explaining grandmaternal inequalities. They also focus on the work load that is expected of the young mother in support of the paternal family, which can result in detrimental effects on pregnancy and children's health that are accepted due to the young age of the women. Not only grandmothers but also siblings and other caretakers are crucial for child survival (Hrdy, 2005).

Moreover, even if it makes evolutionary sense that women grow old, what about men? If they are useless, as an East Frisian proverb suggests ("From an old woman and an old cow you can still expect something; but an old man and an old horse aren't worth anything"; cf. Voland, Chasiotis and Schiefenhövel, 2005, p. 1), why do they also grow old? Speculating about the value of cumulative knowledge in old age, Greve and Bjorklund (2009) state that older members of a group or society know many things worth knowing. Thus, many social institutions preserved – and made useful – this cumulated experience. They propose to name this phenomenon the "Nestor effect," after the elder advisor of Odysseus in Greek mythology. For all human societies, in particular preliterate ones, preservation of knowledge depends on the memories of experienced and, hence, older people. This knowledge includes: caring (birth attendance), healing (recipes, useful plants), threats (famines, droughts), techniques (how to build an axe, how to make fire), geography (where to find a spring). According to Greve and Bjorklund, the memory of the old can be regarded as a "back-up copy" for societies.

The Nestor argument presupposes that humans are capable of retaining old memories (Mergler and Goldstein, 1983), because with age pragmatic knowledge increases (Baltes *et al.*, 2006), and contents of memory that refer to one's youth are less prone to being forgotten (Rubin, Wetzler and Nebes, 1986). Wisdom (which has been defined by Staudinger and Dörner, 2007, p. 674, as "representing a well-balanced coordination of emotions, motivation, and thought, with good judgement and the ability to offer advice in difficult and uncertain matters of life") should, if associated with age, prove an important resource of the elderly. This fits with classical theories of life span development, in particular Erikson's theory (Erikson, 1968), since this approach postulates "integrity" as a final stage beyond generativity.

Moreover, the flow of wealth from the older to the younger generation has been repeatedly demonstrated both in preindustrial and in modern societies (Lee, 2003).

Inheritance may also include non-material goods, such as rights, debts or credits. Aging needs culture (Baltes, 1997), but culture might also need the aged in the first place, since culture depends, to a large degree, on memory as a reservoir of knowledge and experiences (Boyd and Richerson, 2005).

In conclusion, according to the Nestor effect, older members of a family, group or society might be valuable exactly due to their psychological (age-specific) attributes, competencies and abilities. In short: aging and longevity of humans might be an evolutionary adaptation and they became, once evolved, a factor of (cultural) evolution themselves (Greve and Bjorklund, 2009; Voland, Chasiotis and Schiefenhövel, 2005).

Cross-cultural reflections on an applied perspective on development

At the end of our journey through the life span across cultures, it might be interesting to note that a developmental perspective on cross-cultural psychology can also shed light on the discussion how to overcome ethnocentrism in cross-cultural psychology (Additional Topics, Chapter 1; see also Dasen and Akkari, 2008). If the early childhood context is important for individual development, identifying  indicators for a desirable child development outcome is possible, at least from the children's perspective, and might even resemble a middle-class environment (cf. Kağitçibaşi, 2007). Kağitçibaşi (2007) distinguishes between developmental and environmental indicators for a desirable child development. For a 5-year-old, the physical well-being can be assessed by an appropriate nutritional state and growth, the vocabulary use should be sufficient and the child should be able to narrate in a comprehensive manner, and emotionally it should feel loved and secure, show a low aggression level and should be able to do things on its own and to be able to contact others. But also environmental indicators could be identified: the place where the child lives should be clean and safe, and it should possess its own things. There should also be an appropriate environmental stimulation (books, toys, child being read stories), and its parents should have a positive orientation to the child (e.g., parental responsiveness, parental educational aspirations). The caretakers' educational capacity is also important since it is known that a high level of education for the mother ameliorates the developmental circumstances of a child. Lastly, the environment should be characterized as low-conflict and there should be no drug abuse or alcoholism in the family, low spousal conflict and no wife battering or child abuse, and the mother should have a social support network, which in itself decreases the probabilty of spousal abuse (Figueredo, Corral-Vedugo, Frias-Armenta *et al.*, 2001). These are implications if one takes the child's perspective which, according to Kağitçibaşi (2007), are universally valid across cultures.

Furthermore, from an applied perspective, the results on the formative nature of childhood experiences for adulthood also stress the importance of sustainability of sociopolitical actions to improving living conditions: if the childhood context

www.cambridge.org/berry

is formative for adult behavior, then meliorating actions have to be maintained long enough to be effectively transmitted to the next generation. Corresponding to that line of reasoning, there are historical (Voland, Dunbar, Engel and Stephan, 1997) and contemporary demographic findings (Birg, 1995), but also studies in cross-cultural developmental psychology (Chasiotis, 1999; Greenfield, Maynard and Childs, 2003) pointing at an inertia of about thirty years before a behavioral adaptation to a contextual change can be observed.

Conclusions

In the last two chapters we have examined the questions of how the background ecological and cultural contexts of a population become incorporated into the behavior of an individual; we have also examined when and how this happens over the course of individual development. We have argued that all four process variables distinguished in Figure 1.1, and the transmission routes shown in Figure 2.1, are responsible for transmission from context to person. We have also emphasized various forms of cultural transmission and learning during early life, and acculturation that continues (for some) over the life span. With respect to the various routes that cultural transmission can take (vertical, horizontal, oblique) in all cultures, we noted that the relative emphasis on each route can vary from culture to culture. Similarly, the style (ranging from compliance to assertion) varies from culture to culture, and can be seen as a cultural adaptation to ecological factors.

In our treatment of these topics, a number of theoretical issues have been identified. A first major theme is the nature of the interactions between genetic predispositions and cultural or ecological variables; to a large extent this is unknown territory where it would be premature to make strong statements. One possible conclusion is that infants everywhere are set on their life course with much the same apparatus and much the same set of possibilities. Through cultural variations in socialization and infant care practices, some psychological variations begin to appear that can be understood within a framework such as Figure 1.1. This sequence corresponds to the process–competence–performance distinctions outlined earlier, and provides a basis for the position of moderate universalism espoused in this text.

KEY TERMS

generativity • grandmother hypothesis • implicit motivation • life span development • menarche • parent–offspring conflict • senescence

FURTHER READING

Bjorklund, D. F., and Pellegrini, A. D. (2002). *The origins of human nature: Evolutionary developmental psychology.* Washington, DC: American Psychological Association.

This introductory textbook on evolutionary developmental psychology gives a thorough and readable synopsis of this new emerging field with explicit implications for the study of culture.

Dasen, P. R., and Akkari, A. (eds.) (2008). *Educational theories and practices from the majority world.* New Delhi: Sage.

A valuable critique on western ethnocentrism in educational research.

Kağitçibaşi, C. (2007). *Family, self, and human development across cultures: Theory and application* (2nd edn.). Mahwah, N.J.: Erlbaum.

An integration of ideas, findings and applications in child development and societal development, from the perspective of the "majority world."

Voland, E., Chasiotis, A., and Schiefenhövel, W. (eds.) (2005). *Grandmotherhood: The evolutionary significance of the second half of female life.* New Brunswick, N.J.: Rutgers University Press.

An interdisciplinary overview of anthropological, evolutionary and psychological approaches on old-age in women.

4 Social behavior

CONTENTS

- Social context and social behavior
- Values
- Social cognition
- Culture as a social psychological construct
- Conclusions
- Key terms
- Further reading

www.cambridge.org/berry

This chapter deals with what has become the most popular research domain in cross-cultural psychology, namely that of social behavior. We start the chapter by discussing various ideas about the relationships between social context and social behavior that have been put forward in cross-cultural psychology and adjacent fields. This is to give you a taste of the breadth of the field and to put the next section in perspective. We then move to the topic of values, which is arguably the dominant topic in contemporary cross-cultural studies of social behavior. After this, we discuss studies on cultural differences in social cognition and behavior as well as their implications for universality or relativism of social psychological phenomena. The last section deals with different notions of culture as a social psychological construct. We end the chapter with a general discussion. In addition, on the Internet you can find a section on the important, but somewhat understudied area of cultural variation in gender differences in social behavior (Additional Topics, Chapter 4).

If you take at random a recent publication of a cross-cultural study, it is most likely to be about social perception, cognition or behavior. This has not always been the case. In the early days of cross-cultural psychology, studies in perception and cognition were much more frequent. An analysis of empirical studies published in the *Journal of Cross-Cultural Psychology* between 1970 and 2004 by Brouwers *et al*. (2004) showed a steady increase of studies on social psychological topics over time.

This change has also brought about an increase of studies using self-reports (in comparison to experiments or observations) and of studies giving differential socialization as the main reason for choosing cultural samples. Therefore, it is safe to say that the social psychological shift in cross-cultural psychology has not only affected what is studied but also how it is studied and which theoretical explanations are invoked. This is important to note when trying to understand how contemporary researchers address the basic questions that were discussed in Chapter 1.

There may be various explanations for why cross-cultural research into social behavior has become popular. We give you four factors that we think have contributed to the rise of social psychological topics. First, studies in the domain of social behavior tend to show larger cross-cultural differences than studies in other domains. A meta-analysis of studies in various domains of psychology (e.g., psychophysiology, perception, cognition) showed that the largest differences can be found in social behavior (Van Hemert, 2003). Furthermore, this was the only domain in which country-level psychological variables, such as values, explained additional variance over and above economic and political variables. Second, social behavior is relevant for various areas of applied cross-cultural psychology, such as intergroup relations (Chapter 14), intercultural communication (Chapter 15), and work and organization psychology (Chapter 16). Third, the recently emerged field of cultural psychology has been strongly concerned with testing findings from traditional western social psychology in other countries, mostly East Asian (e.g., China, Japan, Korea). Its prominence has led to a marked increase in cross-cultural studies of social psychological phenomena as well as to an increased exposure of mainstream social psychologists to culture-comparative studies. The fourth reason is perhaps the most important, namely the rise of values as a core construct for describing and explaining cross-cultural differences. Values have always been a part of cross-cultural theories, but the work by Hofstede (1980) marks a clear increase in their popularity. The relatively high likelihood of finding cultural differences that can be related to popular value dimensions such as individualism–collectivism may explain why so many researchers are drawn toward studies in the social domain.

This chapter focusses on a selection of topics and findings. The abundance of studies in the social domain simply does not allow us to address everything within the space of a single chapter. Aspects of social behavior that are mostly studied within the context of acculturation, intergroup relations, intercultural communication and work and organization psychology can be found in their respective chapters in Part III of this book. For additional reading, you can consult the Further reading section at the end of this chapter.

Social context and social behavior

In a sense, all human behavior is cultural because the human species is fundamentally a *social* one (Hoorens and Poortinga, 2000). In comparison to other species, even to our close primate relatives, humans seem to be particularly geared toward understanding the intentions and meanings held by other beings in their social environment (e.g., Tomasello, 1999). Our intimate and prolonged interpersonal relations promote the development of shared meanings, and the creation of institutions and artifacts. Thus, it can be expected that the organization of the social context (the social world that people live in) has a profound effect on the types of behaviors that can be observed. However, as can be expected on the basis of the discussion of the various interpretive positions in Chapter 1, there is little agreement about the extent to which also the psychological processes underlying social behavior are cross-culturally similar or different.

The dimension of universalism–relativism that we described in Chapter 1 is prominently present in the domain of social behavior, often as a dichotomy. Evidence supporting both positions can be found in the analysis of social behavior, mostly depending upon the level of abstraction at which the behavior is described. On the one hand, social behaviors are obviously linked to the particular sociocultural context in which they develop. For example, greeting procedures (bowing, handshaking or kissing) vary widely from culture to culture; these are clear-cut examples of the influence of cultural transmission on our social behavior. On the other hand, greeting takes place in all cultures, suggesting the presence of some fundamental communality in this type of social behavior. As we outlined in Chapter 1, we argue in favor of a universalist approach: social psychological processes are likely to be present in all cultures but their manifestation in social behaviors can be strongly influenced by the cultural context. However, various relativist positions, arguing for differences in psychological processes, are well represented in this domain as well. Observations of differences in social behavior have given rise to arguments for indigenous social psychologies (see Chapter 1; Kim and Berry, 1993; Sinha, 1997). Indigenous psychologies attempt to develop social psychologies that are appropriate to a particular society or region. Such activity follows the proposal of Moscovici: "the social psychology that we ought to create must have an origin in our own reality" (1972, p. 23).

Many scholars in the currently popular school of cultural psychology have also taken a relativist stance, but without leaving traditional western social psychological theories and methods. They use these methods to show how social psychological processes (e.g., a need for positive self-regard, attribution processes, social perception) function differently in western and non-western contexts. Though in principle applicable to all kinds of cultures, cultural psychology has focussed almost exclusively on East Asian and western cultural contexts. These are said to be characterized by two distinct definitions of the "self" (Markus and Kitayama, 1991). Some scholars have argued for deeply rooted and enduring psychological differences between these two contexts. For example, Richard Nisbett, one of the main architects of the cultural psychology movement, argued that "there are very dramatic social-psychological differences between East-Asians as a group and people of European culture as a group" (2003, p. 76). Thus, Nisbett can be seen to argue that not only behavior and competencies, but also the underlying psychological processes, are cross-culturally different.

A major question for cross-cultural studies in the social domain is how to conceptualize and study the influence of social context on behavior. As we shall see later in this chapter, the currently most popular conceptualization is that culture is about differences in psychological content, most prominently values and self-construal (see Breugelmans, in press). However, many other conceptualizations have been used. Before we go into studies of culture as values or notions of the self, we first discuss a number of alternative conceptualizations in order to give you a broader perspective on cross-cultural studies of social behavior.

One approach has been to come up with an exhaustive set of the characteristics that can be used to describe any social context and that can be used to distinguish one culture from another. A classic example of such a set can be found in Box 4.1.

Another influential example is the universal model of social relations that has been proposed by Fiske (1991). This model claims that just four elementary relational structures are sufficient to describe an enormous spectrum of forms of human social relations, as well as social motives and emotions, intuitive social thought and moral judgment. These are (1) *communal sharing*, where people attend to group membership and have a sense of common identity, solidarity, unity and belonging, thinking of themselves as being all the same in some significant respect; (2) *authority ranking*, where inequality and hierarchy prevail, highly ranked persons control people, things and resources (including knowledge); (3) *equality matching*, where people are separate but equal, engaging in turn-taking, reciprocity and balanced relationship; and (4) *market pricing*, where individual relationships are mediated by values determined by a "market" system, in which actions are evaluated according to the rates at which they can be exchanged for other commodities. Fiske claims that these models are both fundamental and universal, in the sense that they are the basic constituents for social relations among all people in all cultures.

Box 4.1 **Universals in social behavior**

Aberle and his colleagues (1950) have proposed a set of functional prerequisites of society, defined as "the things that must get done in any society if it is to continue as a going concern." These are of interest because they probably qualify as universals, those activities (in one form or another) that will be found in every culture. There are nine of these:

1. *Provision of adequate relationships with the environment* (both physical and social). This is needed to maintain a sufficient population to "carry" the society and culture.
2. *The differentiation and assignment of roles.* In any group different things need to get done, and people have to somehow be assigned these roles (e.g., by heredity, or by achievement).
3. *Communication.* All groups need to have a shared, learned and symbolic mode of communication in order to maintain information flow and coordination within the group.
4. *Shared cognitive orientation.* Beliefs, knowledge and rules of logical thinking need to be held in common for people in a society to work together in mutual comprehension.
5. *Shared articulated set of goals.* Similarly, the directions for common striving need to be shared, in order to avoid individuals pulling in conflicting directions.
6. *Normative regulation of means to these goals.* Rules governing *how* these goals might be achieved need to be stated and accepted by the population. If material acquisition is a general goal for most people, murder and theft are not likely to be accepted as a means to this goal, whereas production, hard work and trading may be.
7. *Regulation of affective expression.* Similarly emotions and feelings need to be brought under normative control. The expression of love and hate, for example, cannot be given free rein without serious disruptive consequences within the group.
8. *Socialization.* All new members must learn about the central and important features of group life. The way of life of the group needs to be communicated, learned and, to some extent, accepted by all individuals.
9. *Control of disruptive behavior.* If socialization and normative regulation fail, there needs to be some "backup" so that the group can require appropriate and acceptable behavior of its members. In the end, behavioral correction or even permanent removal (by incarceration or execution) may be required.

Another approach has been to look for dimensions along which cultural or social systems can vary. In every social system individuals occupy *positions* for which certain behaviors are expected; these behaviors are called *roles*. Each role occupant is the object of *sanctions* that exert social influence, even pressure, to behave according to social *norms* or standards. If you are unfamiliar with these terms you may wish to consult any introductory sociology text or Chapter 2 of Segall *et al.* (1999). The four highlighted terms constitute some essential elements of a social system. These elements are organized by each cultural group; two key features of this organization are that social systems are differentiated and stratified.

Differentiation means that societies make distinctions among roles; some societies make few, while others make many. For example, in a relatively undifferentiated social structure positions and roles may be limited to a few basic familial (e.g., parent/child), social and economic ones (e.g., hunter/food preparer). In contrast, in a more differentiated society there are many more positions and roles to be found in particular domains (e.g., king, aristocracy, citizen, slave). When differentiated positions and roles are placed in a vertical status structure, the social system is said to be stratified. A number of cross-cultural analyses of stratification are available. For example, Murdock (1967) was concerned with the presence of class distinctions (e.g., hereditary aristocracy, wealth distinctions). At the unstratified end of the dimension are social systems that show few such status distinctions, while at the stratified end of the dimension are social systems that show numerous class or status distinctions (e.g., royalty, aristocracy, gentry, citizens, slaves). An analysis by Pelto (1968) of these and similar distinctions led him to place societies on a dimension called "tight–loose." In stratified and tight societies the pressures to carry out one's roles lead to a high level of role obligation, while in less tight societies there is much less pressure to oblige.

The two dimensions of differentiation and stratification appear in a number of classical studies. For example, Lomax and Berkowitz (1972) factor analyzed numerous cultural variables and found two dimensions, which they termed *differentiation* and *integration*. McNett (1970) found that nomadic hunting and gathering societies tend to have less role diversity and role obligation, while sedentary agricultural societies typically have more diversity and obligation. In urban, industrialized societies, many studies have suggested an even higher level of diversity, but lower levels of role obligation (Boldt, 1978). A study by Henrich *et al.* (2004) on the influence of societal characteristics on prosocial behavior is described in Box 4.2.

There have been many attempts to identify the processes through which social context (i.e., the group) influences the psychology and behavior of individuals. One example that has been very influential in French social psychology is the notion

Box 4.2 **An economic perspective on social behavior**

Cross-cultural work on social behavior is not limited to psychology. One example is a joint project by ethnographers, economists and social scientists to explore economic bargaining behavior in fifteen small-scale societies by Henrich *et al.* (2004). The fifteen societies represented a range of ecocultural and economic contexts such as tropical forest horticulturalists, savanna foragers, desert pastoralists and sedentary farming. Social behavior was measured by participants' choices in a series of economic games, such as the ultimatum game, the dictator game, the trust game and the public goods game (see Camerer, 2003).

Such games typically present participants with a limited set of possible decisions in an interdependent situation; the financial outcome for the participants in the game depends upon the combination of their decisions. One example is the ultimatum game in which one participant is assigned the role of proposer and another participant is assigned the role of responder. The proposer can make only one proposal regarding the division of a fixed amount of money. For example, an amount of $10 could be divided into $5 for the proposer and $5 for the responder, or as $3 for the proposer and $7 for the responder, or as $9 for the proposer and $1 for the responder. The responder can accept the offer, in which case the money is divided according to the proposal, or she can reject the offer, in which case neither participant gets any money. Personal preferences and social norms are typically inferred from participants' behavior in such games. For example, if a large proportion of responders reject unequal proposals (i.e., different from $5/$5) that give the proposer more than the responder then this can be interpreted as a tendency to punish people for unfair behavior. By varying the type of interdependence in different types of games, behavioral economists infer people's preferences and social norms with regard to constructs like fairness, punishment, altruism and trust. This stands in contrast with psychological approaches to such constructs which tend to rely on self-reported, subjective measures. The behavioral economic approach is more akin to behaviorism in psychology.

Henrich *et al.* found several interesting results. One result was that cross-cultural differences in behavior were substantially larger among small-scale societies than previous studies had found with student samples in industrial societies. This attests to the importance of sampling for cross-cultural psychology. Another result was that group-level differences in economic organization and the degree of aggregate market integration (the frequency with which people engage in market exchange, settlement size and sociopolitical complexity) explained a substantial proportion of cross-cultural differences in behavior. This relates to another finding, namely that behavior in the experiments is generally consistent with economic patterns of everyday life. The more people were dependent upon interactions with strangers in their day-to-day life, the more prosocial behavior they exhibited and the more strongly they punished antisocial behavior by others. Thus, social and economic structures of societies can have an important bearing on people's social behavior.

of social representations by Moscovici (1982). Social representations are systems of values, ideas and practices that are on the one hand the outcome of social construction by a group of people, and on the other hand the processes through which people make sense of the material and social world. In this sense, they represent an intermediary level between the individual and the culture. Another example is the notion of memes, which are units or elements of cultural ideas, symbols or practices. The terms "memes" was coined by evolutionary biologist Dawkins (1976) to explain the spread of cultural ideas and practices in a population, by using similar types of analysis to those applied to the spread of genes (i.e., the field of memetics). Other researchers with an evolutionary background have tried to think of the psychological processes that can explain why culture exists at all (see Richerson and Boyd, 2005; Tooby and Cosmides, 1992). These arguments are taken up in Chapter 11.

Researchers with a social psychological background have tried to explain the emergence and propagation of culture in terms of basic psychological processes. For example, Baumeister (2005) described many basic, social psychological processes that are specifically geared toward shaping behavior in a cultural context. In a book edited by Schaller and Crandall (2004) named *The psychological foundations of culture* various authors describe how the emergence and maintenance of cultural variation can be explained by means of fairly simple, low-level psychological processes. For example, Arrow and Burns (2004) presented empirical data describing how random groups of interacting people can spontaneously converge to very different sets of allocation-norms, reminiscent of the four relational structures in Fiske's (1991) model.

To conclude, there is ample evidence for cross-cultural differences in social behavior, but there is little agreement on the explanation of these differences. A central question in this literature is whether differences in social behavior are the consequence of differences in the underlying psychological processes (relativist) or rather the consequence of the same processes operating in different social contexts (universalist). In this section, we have reviewed various conceptualizations of culture that have been used to answer this question. Most of these have enjoyed popularity in specific times or disciplines (e.g., anthropology, biology, social psychology). However, none has been able to match the popularity of the conceptualization of culture as a set of values which is described in the next section.

Values

The study of societal values (the things that societies value) has a long history in sociology and cultural anthropology (e.g., Kluckhohn and Strodtbeck, 1961). The study of individual values has a similarly long history in psychology (e.g., Allport, Vernon and Lindzey, 1960). It has been the combination of both approaches that has been very successful in cross-cultural psychology (e.g., Feather, 1975; Hofstede, 1980; Smith and Schwartz, 1997). Cross-cultural studies of values have had an immense impact; many applied fields such as work and organization psychology, intercultural communication and intercultural training that you will find in Part III of this book have been heavily influenced by this approach. Although cross-cultural research has shown that values can differ across societies, differences in values held by people within a society are typically much larger than differences that are found between societies. This within-culture variation is good to keep in mind when interpreting value differences between cultures.

Values are inferred constructs, whether seen as societal or individual. This means that values are not directly observed, but rather delineated from their manifestations in social organization, practices, symbols and self-reports. Thus, values are eminently psychological. In an early definition by Kluckhohn, the term "values" referred to a conception held by an individual, or collectively by members of a group, of that which is desirable, and which influences the selection of both means and ends of action from among available alternatives (1951, p. 395). This definition was later simplified by Hofstede, who said values are "a broad tendency to prefer certain states of affairs over others" (1980, p. 19). Values are usually considered to be more general in character than attitudes, but less general than ideologies (reflected in political systems).

A classical approach to studying values in psychology is that of Rokeach (1973), who developed two sets of values: terminal values, which were idealized end-states of existence (e.g., "equality," "freedom," "happiness"), and instrumental values, which were idealized modes of behavior used to attain the end-states (e.g., being "courageous," "honest," "polite"). Rokeach developed the Rokeach Value Survey, in which respondents were asked to rank-order the values on the extent to which they are important to them.

The importance of values in cross-cultural psychology was strongly influenced by the landmark study by Hofstede (1980, 1983, 1991). For many years Hofstede worked for a major international corporation, and was able to administer over 116,000 questionnaires (in 1968 and in 1972) to employees in fifty different countries and of sixty-six different nationalities. Three main factors were distinguished and four "country scores" were calculated by aggregating individual scores within each country. Although the statistical analyses pointed to three factors, four dimensions made more sense psychologically to Hofstede. These were (1) *power distance*, the extent to which there is inequality (a pecking order) between supervisors and subordinates in an organization; (2) *uncertainty avoidance*, the lack of tolerance for ambiguity, and the need for formal rules; (3) *individualism–collectivism*, a concern for oneself as opposed to concern for the collectivity to which one belongs; and (4) *masculinity–femininity*: the extent of emphasis on work goals (earnings, advancement) and assertiveness, as opposed to interpersonal goals (friendly atmosphere, getting along with the boss) and nurturance. In later work a fifth dimension was added: long-term and short-term orientation (Hofstede, 2001). This dimension was derived from the Chinese Value Survey, which is an instrument constructed to measure values intentionally from a Chinese rather than a western perspective (Chinese Culture Connection, 1987). Values associated with long-term orientation are thrift and perseverance; short-term values are respect for tradition, fulfilling social obligations and saving face.

Value dimensions can be combined to create value profiles for different countries. An example can be seen in Figure 4.1, which plots the country scores on Power Distance and Individualism. Several "country clusters" can be discerned. In the lower right quadrant is the "Latin cluster" (large Power Distance/high Individualism), termed "dependent individualism" by Hofstede (1980, p. 221); most of the Third World countries are located in the upper right quadrant (a kind of "dependent collectivism"); and most western industrialized nations are in the lower left quadrant ("independent individualism"). The figure also reveals a clear negative correlation between the two value dimensions ($r = -.67$), and both are correlated with economic development indicators, such as Gross National Product ($r = -.65$ with Power Distance; $r = +.82$ with Individualism). In fact, the first dimension (i.e., the dimension that explains the largest proportion of the cross-cultural variation) in all the studies mentioned in this section is closely associated with GNP, a point to which we shall return later.

Of all dimensions, individualism–collectivism has been by far the most influential. This is in part due to the work by Triandis (1995), who has worked on the psychological underpinnings and consequences of this dimension. In short, the difference between individualism and collectivism (I-C) lies in a primary concern for oneself in contrast to a concern for the group(s) to which one belongs. This difference is expressed in a number of ways, for example (1) in the definition of the self as personal or collective, independent or interdependent; (2) in personal goals having priority over group goals (or vice versa); (3) in an emphasis on exchange

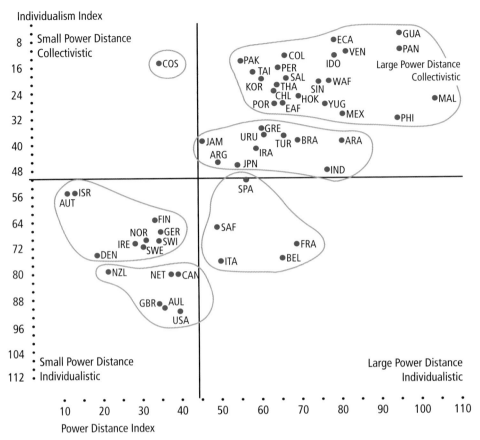

Figure 4.1 Positions of the forty countries on the Power Distance and Individualism scales (from Hofstede, 1980).

rather than on communal relationships; and (4) in the relative importance of personal attitudes versus social norms in one's behavior.

The I-C dimension has been very influential, but it has also been "overextended" to the point that it has become a catchall to explain a very large number of psychological differences across cultures (Kağitçibaşi, 1997a). Of course, this has more to do with the way that the dimension is used than with the nature of the dimension in itself. Often, researchers take I-C differences between cultural samples as a given without actually checking whether the differences in values are actually valid for these samples (i.e., measuring the values) or whether there are alternative explanations to be considered (e.g., Matsumoto, 2006). In addition, I-C may not be a uniform dimension but rather a summary of different types of individualist and collectivist values. According to Allik and Realo, "I-C cannot be defined as a single internally homogeneous concept, but is instead composed of several interrelated, yet ultimately distinguishable, subtypes of I-C" (1996, p. 110).

Triandis (1994b) has made a distinction between horizontal and vertical I-C, introducing the dimension of hierarchy. Triandis and Gelfand (1998) found four distinct factors in an I-C scale, one each for Horizontal Individualism (e.g., "I'd rather depend on myself than on others"), Vertical Individualism (e.g., "It is important that I do my job better than others"), Horizontal Collectivism (e.g., "If a co-worker gets a prize, I would feel proud") and Vertical Collectivism (e.g., "It is important that I respect the decisions made by my groups"). There were negative or weak positive correlations between the horizontal and vertical aspects of both individualism and collectivism. These four types of I-C have been linked to different values, political systems and social orientations by Singelis, Triandis, Bhawuk and Gelfand (1995). Along a different line, Kağitçibaşi (1994) has also argued that there are two types of I-C, namely normative and relational. Normative I-C represents the view that "individual interests are to be subordinated to group interests" (Kağitçibaşi, 1997a, p. 34), while relational I-C is more concerned with "interpersonal distance versus embeddedness" (1997a, p. 36). The distinction is necessary, since "Closely-knit relatedness or separateness can exist within both hierarchical and egalitarian groups" (1997a, p. 36). Thus, hierarchy seems to be an important addition in the understanding of I-C as a cultural construct.

While there is substantial empirical evidence to support any number of conceptualizations of I-C, varying from simple demonstrations of differences in value scales across cultures to complex factor analytic studies (see Kim *et al.*, 1994; Triandis, 1995), there are relatively few critical tests of the construct (e.g., Van den Heuvel and Poortinga, 1999). Fijneman *et al.* (1996) studied willingness to contribute resources to others from various social categories (e.g., father, sister, cousin, close friend, neighbor, an unknown person) in societies previously characterized as collectivist or individualist (Hong Kong, Turkey, Greece, USA, Netherlands). Findings revealed remarkable similarities in patterns of inputs and outputs over social categories in all six countries. In addition, in all these countries both input and output ratings varied across the social categories with degree of emotional closeness in similar ways, suggesting that emotional closeness was a better explanation than I-C. This implies that not only hierarchy, but also relational closeness has an important influence on I-C, as was suggested by Kağitçibaşi (1997a).

A meta-analysis of I-C studies by Oyserman, Coon and Kemmelmeier (2002) supported the view of I and C as independent dimensions. However, they also found some results that seem to challenge the use of I-C for making broad cross-cultural distinctions. For example, they found that, when looking at both dimensions, European Americans were overall more individualistic and less collectivistic than other groups. However, when compared on individual dimensions they were not more individualistic than African Americans, or Latinos, and not less collectivistic than Japanese or Koreans. In comparison to Western Europeans, they were less collectivistic, suggesting that the often-used label "western" fails to capture important value distinctions. Similarly, of all Asian groups only Chinese were both less individualistic and more collectivistic, suggesting that the often-used label "Asian" also fails to capture important regional value distinctions.

Thus, we can conclude that I-C represents an important value dimension but that it tends to be overapplied, becoming a catchall for all possible types of cross-cultural differences. There are different ways to conceive of and measure this construct and there can be substantial regional differences. Hierarchy and relational closeness are two factors that influence the dimension. Although Hofstede's conceptualization is clearly the most influential approach to values, there have been various alternative approaches that may shed some light on value dimensions and cross-cultural differences. Below, we discuss three.

Schwartz (1994a; Schwartz and Bilsky, 1990; Schwartz and Sagiv, 1995) has extended the Rokeach tradition in value research. In an extensive project samples of students and samples of teachers in each of fifty-four societies were administered a scale with fifty-six items that had to be rated on a nine-point scale ranging from –1 (opposed to my values) to 7 (of extreme importance). Considerable effort went into the translation of these items. Moreover, local terms in other languages were sometimes included in the scale, but this did not lead to the discovery of value domains that were not present in the original (western) scale. From this data set ten individual value types emerged. These are shown in Figure 4.2. According to Schwartz and Sagiv (1995) there are two dimensions that organize the ten value types into clusters situated at either end of the two dimensions: these dimensions are Self-enhancement (power, achievement, hedonism) versus Self-transcendence (universalism, benevolence); and Conservation (conformity, security, tradition) versus Openness to change (self-direction, stimulation). It should be noted that these dimensions emerge when data are analyzed on an individual level.

Country-level scores can be obtained by aggregating over individuals within a group (culture or country). When this is done, a different structure emerges according to Schwartz (1994b), namely of seven country-level values: conservatism, affective autonomy, intellectual autonomy, hierarchy, egalitarian commitment, mastery and harmony. These can be organized along three bipolar dimensions: Conservatism versus Autonomy; Hierarchy versus Egalitarianism; and Mastery versus Harmony. The two forms of autonomy in the list of seven values are put together in one cluster, now termed Autonomy. According to Schwartz these dimensions each deal with basic concerns of all societies: (1) how individuals relate to their group (embedded or independent); (2) how to motivate people to consider the welfare of others (vertically structured, or horizontally); and (3) the relationship of people to their natural and social world (dominate and exploit it, or live with it). A recent study by Fischer *et al.* (2010), reanalyzing a large data set collected by

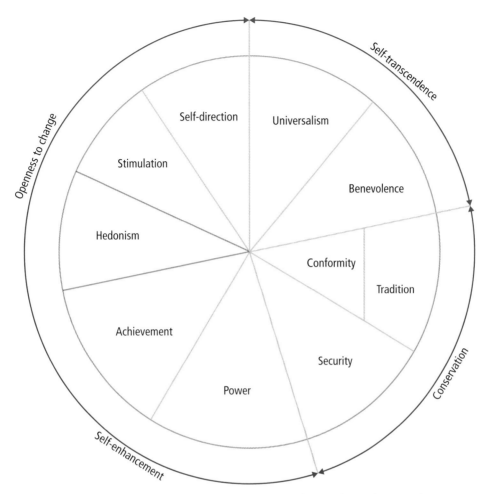

Figure 4.2 Structure of relationships among ten national types of values (from Schwartz and Sagiv, 1995).

Schwartz with multilevel methods that were not used in cross-cultural psychology until recently seems to suggest that the structure of values at the individual level and at the cultural level is actually quite similar.

The World Values Survey (WVS) represents a sociological approach to values and value change (e.g., Inglehart, 2000). It has been carried out four times since 1981 and has sampled values from individuals in ninety-seven countries, covering 88 percent of the world population. Using a wide set of items, it found two basic value dimensions, labeled (1) traditional versus secular-rational, and (2) survival versus self-expression. Traditional countries emphasize parent–child ties and deference to authority, reject divorce, abortion, euthanasia and suicide, have high levels of national pride and a nationalistic outlook. Secular-rational countries emphasize the opposite of these values. Note that this relates to the compliance–assertion dimension discussed in Chapter 2 (see p. 45). The second dimension is characterized by values that emphasize economic and physical security over quality of life. While these two dimensions are the result of national-level factor analyses, the same two dimensions also appear at the individual level of analysis. On the basis of the two dimensions a cultural map of the world has been created (this can be found at www.worldvaluessurvey.org/). Countries that are geographically near or that share a sociocultural history (e.g., ex-Communist or Catholic) tended to cluster together. For example, North-West Europe is high on both secular and self-expressive values, while ex-Communist (East) Europe is high on secular, but low on self-expressive values. South Asia is low on secular and intermediate on self-expressive values, while Latin America is low on secular and high on self-expressive values. An interesting quality of the WVS data is that the repeated assessments allow for observing value change. For example, Inglehart and Baker (2000) have noted that almost all industrialized countries have shown a shift from traditional to secular-rational values. When societies have completed industrialization and move more toward knowledge economies, they tend to move from survival values to self-expression values.

It is clear that the position of countries on these dimensions is strongly related to Gross National Product (GNP). Poor countries are low on both secular and self-expressive values, while high GNP countries are high on both. This replicates a pattern found in the work of Hofstede (1980) where the relationship between a country's individualism score and GNP was substantial (+.82). Whether this means that affluence brings about values (individualism, secularism, self-expression) or that a country's values determine its economic development is a much debated question. The WVS data seem to suggest the former, but Inglehart (2000) noted that culture and economic development probably interact. Rather than one variable influencing the other it is also possible that both come about as a result of other features of a society. Taking an ecocultural perspective, Berry (1994) has suggested that individualism and collectivism are each related to separate aspects of the ecosystem: individualism to the sheer size and complexity of the social system (larger, more complex societies being more individualistic) and collectivism to the social tightness or conformity pressures placed on individuals by their society (tighter more stratified societies being more collectivist). These relationships make clear that we need to take into account GNP and related variables (e.g., level of education, social mobility, societal size and stratification) as potential explanations of cross-cultural differences in values.

Recently, a potential alternative to value approaches has been proposed in the form of social axioms (Leung and Bond, 2004). Social axioms do not tap into abstract values but more directly into beliefs people have about the world. Examples are "People may have opposite behaviors on different occasions," "Hardworking people will achieve more in the end" and "Fate determines one's successes and failures." Initial studies in Hong Kong, Venezuela, Japan, Germany and the US, and later studies involving samples from forty-one cultural groups showed five axiom dimensions at the individual level (social cynicism, social complexity, reward for application, religiosity and fate control). Analyses at country-level yielded two dimensions: social cynicism (containing items from the same construct at individual level) and dynamic externality (containing items from the other four dimensions at individual level; Bond, Leung *et al.*, 2004). At both individual level and at country level meaningful relations have been found between axioms and other psychological and sociodemographic variables, including GNP. Social axioms have not yet been used as widely as dimensions in exploring cross-cultural differences, but they may represent a viable construct linking abstract values and concrete social behaviors.

Thus, we have seen how values have sparked an enormous number of studies on cross-cultural differences. The most influential remain the Hofstede (1980) value dimensions, notably the individualism–collectivism dimension, but we have also seen various alternative conceptions. One of the main assets of large-scale value studies has been that cross-cultural differences in social preferences and perceptions have been globally mapped, showing strong correlations with more "objective" characteristics of cultures such as a nation's GDP. Several questions remain unanswered, such as exactly how many value dimensions should be identified and how these should be conceived of. Some dimensions, such as individualism-collectivism, have been clearly overused in the sense that they have been linked to almost any kind of cross-cultural difference in social behavior. However, it is clear that the study of values has been one of the major advancements in cross-cultural research.

Social cognition

Much of the existing literature on social psychology that is currently available is culture-bound; it has been developed mostly in one society (the USA), which took "for its themes of research, and for the contents of its theories, the issues of its own society" (Moscovici, 1972, p. 19). This culture-bound nature of social psychology became a widely accepted viewpoint in the 1970s and 1980s (e.g., Berry, 1978; Bond, 1988; Jahoda, 1979, 1986). An empirical demonstration of the cultural limits of social psychology was provided by Amir and Sharon (1987). In Israel, they attempted to replicate six studies that had appeared in a single year of an American social psychology journal. By and large half of the hypotheses that were retested did not replicate, while in addition some "new" significant results were found. Various studies were done to test the generalizability of western social psychology, but most of these remained within the realm of cross-cultural psychology. This has changed with the rise of the school of cultural psychology in the 1990s (see Kitayama and Cohen, 2007).

In 1991, Markus and Kitayama published an influential article in which they claimed that the "self" is construed differently in Asian cultures than in European American culture:

Asian cultures have distinct conceptions of individuality that insist on the fundamental relatedness of individuals to each other. The emphasis is on attending to others, fitting in, and harmonious interdependence with them. American culture neither assumes nor values such an overt connectedness among individuals. In contrast, individuals seek to maintain their independence from others by attending to the self and by discovering and expressing their unique inner attributes. (1991, p. 224)

Though clearly reminiscent of psychological descriptions of collectivism and individualism (e.g., Triandis, 1995), Markus and Kitayama differ in that they posit cultural differences to be psychological differences. So, there is not only a differential endorsement of a set of universal values, but the psychological processes themselves are claimed to be fundamentally different. More information about cross-cultural differences in the self can be found in Chapter 5.

A definition of culture in terms of different notions of the self fitted well with other theoretical approaches, such as Shweder's (1990) claim that psychology and culture are mutually constituted. In this view, culture should not be seen as external context but rather as something that is intrinsically interwoven with psychology. Related notions can be found in the work of Nisbett (2003), whose work suggests that East Asians perceive and think about the world in a more holistic way (looking at the bigger picture instead of detail; being able to live with contradiction instead of relying on formal logic) than European Americans (see Chapter 6, section on cognition, East and West).

In this section, we discuss a selection of social psychological behaviors and cognitions that have been found to differ between western and non-western contexts. As we stated at the beginning of this chapter, the point of discussion is often not that the behavioral differences exist but rather what can be inferred from this about differences in psychological processes.

An example of a basic social behavior that has been quite often studied across cultures is conformity. Conforming to group norms will be found in all societies because without it social cohesiveness would be so minimal that groups could not continue to function as a group (one of the functional prerequisites in Box 4.1). However, the extent to which conformity is displayed can vary. Researchers studying conformity have often used the Asch (1956) paradigm, where participants are presented with a line judgment task and had to say which of three lines of differing length were the same length as a standard comparison line. Faced with this task, participants often conformed (about one-third of the time) to unanimous, but obviously incorrect, judgments of line lengths by their fellow participants (who were confederates instructed by the experimenter to deliberately give the incorrect answer). Such studies have been done with people in subsistence economies as well as with people in industrialized societies.

For subsistence economies Berry (1967, 1979) predicted differences between hunting-based groups, with loose forms of social organization and socialization for assertion (lower levels of conformity), and agricultural groups, with tighter social organization and socialization for compliance (high levels of conformity). An Asch-type task of independence versus conformity was administered in seventeen samples from ten cultures. The community norm was communicated to the participants by the local research assistant. Conformity scores were found to be related to a sample's position on an ecocultural index (ranging from hunting/loose/assertion to agriculture/tight/compliance), resulting in a correlation of +.70. This suggests a clear link between societal organization and conformity through child socialization.

The largest group of conformity studies was done in industrialized societies. Bond and Smith (1996) found that the degree of conformity was related to tightness, just as in subsistence societies. However, instead of linking conformity back to ecology and societal organization they related variations in conformity to country-level values. Conformity was higher in societies that held values of conservatism, collectivism and a preference for status ascription, while it was lower in societies valuing autonomy, individualism and status achievement. It is interesting to note that in this study, two *psychological* variables were being related to each other (conformity and values), while in Berry's studies a set of *ecocultural* variables was being related to conformity. In view of the strong relation between GNP and values, we think that conformity and values are related because they are situated in a broader ecocultural context that promotes them as a consistent and functional response to living in tight societies (Berry, 1994).

An example of a basic social cognition that has been studied across cultures is attribution. Social cognitions refer to how individuals perceive and interpret their social world. Given that such interpretations are bound to be embedded in the person's culture, it has been suggested that a more appropriate name might be sociocultural cognition (Semin and Zwier, 1997). Attribution refers to the way in which individuals think about the causes of their own, or other people's, behavior. Based on the differences in ecological and social control that people have over their lives, substantial differences in attribution can be expected. However, perhaps surprisingly, not all cross-cultural studies of attribution show clear patterns of cultural differences.

In western samples, there is a frequently observed preference for attributions to internal dispositions, especially when it comes to the behavior of others, that has become known as the fundamental attribution error. This error, which for a long time was thought to be present in all cultures, seems to be particularly strong in western samples. For example, Morris and Peng (1994) studied articles about crimes from Chinese and American newspapers. They coded the information on whether the crimes were explained by reference to a disposition or to the context or situation. American articles used consistently more dispositional attributions than did Chinese articles. Miller (1984) studied how dispositional biases developed in American and Indian children. She found that American children show an increasing preference for dispositional explanations with age, but that this is not the case for Indian children. In a review of cultural variation in causal attribution across various research traditions, Choi, Nisbett and Norenzayan (1999) concluded that "dispositionism" is a cross-culturally widespread mode of thinking, but that East Asians are more likely to use situational attributions because they believe that dispositions are malleable and that the context is important. This seems to point to a universalistic orientation: the basic psychological process of attribution is present across cultures, but it is developed and used differently, according to some features of the cultural context.

Another attribution bias that is often observed in western samples is the self-serving or egocentric bias. People have the tendency to attribute successes to themselves and failures to the situation. However, many cross-cultural studies did not find evidence for this bias (see Semin and Zwier, 1997). Many groups, such as Japanese and Indians, seem to display the opposite pattern of an unassuming or modesty bias (e.g., Kashima and Triandis, 1986). The same counts for attributions of success and failure by others. Japanese often attribute the successes of others to internal causes and the failures of others to the situation, whereas western samples generally show the reverse pattern.

A crucial question underlying these findings is why these reversals are observed. It could be argued that this is due to the fact that in some cultures people do not strive for a positive evaluation of the self, or to the fact that people act according to social norms that prescribe modest behavior (see conformity). The first explanation would be more in line with a (moderate) relativist position, and the second more with a moderate universalist position. Muramoto (2003) found that Japanese participants show the modesty bias when asked about their own evaluation of past successes and failures, but that they expected close others (friends and family) to give them more credit for success and less blame for failures. This suggests that the modesty would have to do more with norms of self-presentation than with different psychological needs. An illustration of the different explanations that are given for cross-cultural variation in social cognition can be found in Box 4.3.

Box 4.3 **Is self-enhancement a universal phenomenon?**

An illustration of the differences between universalist and relativist interpretations of cross-cultural differences in social behavior can be found in a debate on self-enhancement. Although the debate can be traced back to the seminal paper by Markus and Kitayama (1991), it started with a paper by Heine, Lehman, Markus and Kitayama (1999) on the universality of the need for positive self-regard. From a review of cross-cultural data across various domains they concluded that the Japanese, in contrast to US-Americans, do not have a need to feel positive about themselves. They interpreted this as evidence in favor of fundamental differences in the psychological make-up of Americans and Japanese (see also the section on self in social context in Chapter 5).

In a reaction, Sedikides, Gaertner and Togushi (2003) claimed that the motivation to self-enhance is universally present but that the actual behavior following from this motivation differs among cultures. They posited that people self-enhance on traits and behaviors that are culturally sanctioned; people in individualistic countries self-enhance on individualistic traits and behaviors, whereas people in collectivistic countries self-enhance on collectivistic traits and behaviors. With US-American and Japanese students they found evidence for their claims. Students were asked to imagine working in a sixteen-person business team that consisted of people that were identical to themselves in terms of gender, socioeconomic background and education. Then they were asked to compare themselves with their fellow group members on a set of traits and of behaviors that included both individualistic (e.g., independent, leaving a group when it does not fit your needs) and collectivistic (e.g., compliant, supporting your group no matter what) items. As there was no reason given in the description of the group members to suggest any differences, any ratings of being "better than average" indicated self-enhancement. In line with their hypothesis, they found that US-Americans self-enhanced more on individualistic attributes but that Japanese self-enhanced more on collectivistic attributes.

Heine (2005) replied by attenuating the differences between himself and Sedikides *et al.*, stating that he agreed that the need for positive feelings was universal but that he disagreed that the motive to self-enhance was universal. He argued that the better-than-average effect is actually not a good measure of self-enhancement, explaining why Sedikides *et al.* did find absence of differences but other studies employing other measures did not. Sedikides, Gaertner and Vevea (2005) replied by doing a meta-analysis on studies of self-enhancement, including studies employing different methods. Heine, Kitayama and Hamamura (2007) contested this conclusion, claiming that Sedikides *et al.* had been biased in their selection of studies. From a meta-analysis including a wider array of studies, they claimed evidence for the

Box 4.3 continued

absence of self-enhancement in Japanese. In a final rebuttal, Sedikides, Gaertner and Vevea (2007) included more studies in a new meta-analysis, claiming again evidence for their universality hypothesis. Although the debate ended in a kind of stalemate with both sides claiming that their inclusion criteria for the meta-analysis were the correct ones, it is instructive to see how debates on big theoretical issues often boil down to a disagreement over the interpretation of the meaning of a specific set of data. Recent studies seem to suggest that the motive to make favorable self-evaluations is universally found and that cross-cultural differences in its expression are due to modesty norms in eastern cultures (Kim, Chiu, Peng, Cai and Tov, 2010).

Several other types of social cognition and behavior can be found that show similar differences between American and Asian samples. For example, western individuals often exhibit social loafing, which is the tendency to exert less effort when working as part of a group than working alone. Chinese and Japanese sometimes show the reversed pattern called social striving (Gabrenya *et al.*, 1985). Another example is a study by Kim and Markus (1999), who went to an airport and asked travelers to fill out a simple survey, offering the travelers the choice of a pen as a token of appreciation. There were five pens to choose from, which were identical in all respects but color. East Asians were more inclined to choose the majority pen than westerners. This was interpreted as showing that the samples differed in their *need for uniqueness* because of a culturally different self-construal.

Yamagishi, Hashimoto and Schug (2008) contested this interpretation, claiming instead that the differences were caused by the fact Asians use another default choice strategy than Americans. In this view, Asians choose the majority pen because this is the most rational behavior in their (collectivist) social context, not because they have different preferences. Yamagishi *et al.* showed this by replicating the Kim and Markus (1999) study with slight changes in the conditions. They asked Japanese and Americans which pen they would choose if they were the first of five people to choose, if they were the last of five persons to choose, and if they would buy the pen from a store. In the first conditions, Americans were also more likely to choose the majority pen, whereas in the last two conditions both groups were more likely to choose the unique pen. Thus, the cultural distinction may not be rooted in different psychological processes, but rather in a different situational default strategy.

As we have seen in this section, there are many notable differences in social perception and behavior among cultures, often studied in eastern (East Asian) versus western (US American or European) comparisons. In the topics that we selected the general pattern of findings is that social psychological phenomena that were previously thought to be universal are not always found in other cultural groups. The crucial question is how these findings should be accounted for. Relativist scholars tend to attribute differences in behavior to differences in underlying psychological processes, for example individualist and collectivist values or interdependent and independent self-construals. Thus, behavior (performance) is different because processes are different. Universalist scholars tend to attribute differences in behavior to different ecological (e.g., type of subsistence) or social (e.g., modesty norms) contexts working on the same psychological processes. As we have indicated, we favor the latter interpretation in this book but many researchers in the school of cultural psychology (see Chapter 1) would favor the first interpretation.

Culture as a social psychological construct

There are some issues that have to do with the fact that studies in the social psychological domain often conceive of culture itself as a psychological construct (Breugelmans, in press). We have seen that culture is conceived of as a set of values or as a particular type of self-construal. Values and self-construal are in themselves psychological constructs; individuals have certain values and a particular self-construal. However, we have also seen that these constructs are often used as explanations for cross-cultural differences in other phenomena. In the paper that effectively started the cultural psychology movement, Markus and Kitayama (1991, p. 224) claimed that "[p]eople in different cultures have strikingly different construals of the self, of others, and of the interdependence of the two. These construals can influence, and in many cases determine, the very nature of individual experience, including cognition, emotion, and motivation."

A central issue is how we should establish that differences in psychological constructs such as values and self-construal are actually causes rather than concomitants of other differences in social perception and behavior. This question was addressed by Matsumoto and Yoo (2006), who described four phases in the development of cross-cultural studies. In the first phase, studies were mainly aimed at replicating findings from western (US-American) psychology in other cultures, where differences in behavior were ascribed to "culture" on a post hoc basis. In the second phase, studies tried to find dimensions underlying cross-cultural differences, such as value dimensions. The third phase involved actual manipulation of psychological processes causing cross-cultural differences, such as notions of the self. Matsumoto and Yoo propose that a fourth phase is necessary. These studies should be aimed at verifying that the phenomena supposed to characterize culture (e.g., values or self-construal) are shown to (1) really differ across cultures on the individual level and (2) can explain observed differences in behavior. For example, people in collectivist countries should be shown – rather than assumed – to have a more independent notion of the self, which should explain at an individual level postulated differences in social behavior, such as social loafing.

A second issue has to do with the different dimensions of values at individual and cultural levels. Recent developments in multilevel modeling allow researchers to empirically assess the relationship between concepts at both individual and cultural levels (Van de Vijver, Van Hemert and Poortinga, 2008a). Such models make clear that a straightforward equation of culture-level and individual-level scores can be erroneous. The relationship between scores at different levels is complicated when the properties of constructs are found to be different across levels (i.e., when they are non-isomorphic; see Chapter 1, p. 29). As we have seen in the section on values the number of dimensions that are found differs depending on whether we look at the level of individuals or at the level of countries. This suggests that values have a different meaning at a country level. The question is, of course, what this means. We have mentioned earlier in this chapter that Fischer *et al.* (2010) found that dimensions across levels were similar, contrary to the earlier opinion of established researchers like Hofstede (1980), Schwartz (1994a) and Triandis (1995). It may be noted that these researchers had analyzed their data separately for individual and culture levels. Only with multilevel analyses can dimensions be compared directly across levels.

A third issue is the validity of cross-cultural differences in variables such as values. Value data are almost exclusively gathered by means of self-reports, where participants themselves indicate what they find important. This type of data is sensitive to national differences in response styles, which are correlated with differences in values (Van Herk, Poortinga and Verhallen, 2004). Thus, differences in value scores may be a reflection of differences in acquiescence or scale use rather than of value preferences. We have also seen that cross-cultural differences in values are strongly related to a nation's GNP or affluence. The question is what this correlation means. Some researchers, like Inglehart (2000), suggest that values change according to economic development. This questions the extent to which values can be used as explanatory variables for cross-cultural studies on social perception and behavior.

A fourth issue relates to the stability of values and self-construals as explanatory variables. Relativist scholars tend to emphasize the stability of cross-cultural differences. For example, Nisbett (2003, p. xx) argued that: "My research has led me to the conviction that two utterly different approaches to the world have maintained themselves for thousands of years … Each of these orientations – the Western and the Eastern – is a self-reinforcing, homeostatic system." However, as we shall see in Chapter 13, cultures more often than not are malleable and many people across the globe nowadays have to manage living in ethnically and culturally diverse contexts. In addition, individuals have been shown to be flexible in handling cultural demands in priming studies.

Priming in a cross-cultural context often implies that individuals get a task that temporarily activates an individualistic or collectivistic mind-set; this is expected to influence performance on a subsequent social psychological measure. For example, participants are asked to think of what makes them different from family and friends or to encircle pronouns such as *I, me, mine* in a task. These manipulations should activate an individualistic mind-set. Participants who are asked to think of what makes them similar to family and friends or who encircle pronouns such as *we, us, our* are primed with a collectivistic mind-set. Oyserman and Lee (2008) did a meta-analysis on sixty-seven studies that primed both individualism and collectivism and thirty-two studies that primed one of these constructs and measured the effects of such priming on a number of social psychological variables, such as values, relationality, self-concept, well-being and social cognition.

The priming studies show that by activating psychological constructs differences were found that resemble those found between cultural populations. This can be interpreted to show the validity of these constructs as explanatory variables (Matsumoto and Yoo, 2006), but at the same time it poses some serious questions about the assumed stability of these constructs. If individualism and collectivism can be so easily affected by simple tasks, to what extent can they then be seen as stable explanations for cross-cultural differences in behavior? According to some researchers, the priming studies may mimic the effects of culture but this does not prove that cross-cultural differences are formed in the same way (Fischer, in press). According to Fiske: "Mere accessibility can hardly be an important factor mediating the effects of these constituents of culture on the psyche, unless one postulates that all humans have cognitive representations of all significant aspects of all cultures" (2002, pp. 80–81).

Recent studies seem to suggest that cross-cultural differences may be much less static than we might think on the basis of the values and self-construal studies. According to Oyserman, Sorenson, Reber and Chen: "(r)ather than conceptualise culture as producing fixed and largely immutable patterned ways of thinking and of organising the social world, a situated model allows for the possibility that culturally tuned mind-sets are largely malleable and sensitive to immediate contextual cues." (2009, p. 230)

Other situation-specific explanations for cross-cultural differences in social behavior are increasingly found. Examples that were discussed before in this chapter are the modesty norm by Muramoto (2003) and the situation-dependent default strategies described by Yamagishi *et al.* (2008). Another example is given by Zou *et al.*, who suggested that "key cultural differences in social cognition are carried by differences in individuals' perceptions of their culture's consensual beliefs, beyond any influences of differences in individuals' personal commitments to the beliefs" (2009, p. 580). Zou *et al.* showed in various studies how people's perceptions of cultural consensus or "common sense" are more predictive of behavior than internalized cultural content (e.g., values of collectivism). This notion fits well with recent publications emphasizing the view of culture as a situated norm (e.g., Fischer, Ferreira and Assmar *et al.*, 2009; Gelfand, Nishii and Raver, 2006). The notion of culture as a norm relates to questions of generalizability of cross-cultural differences that we mentioned in Chapter 1 and will raise again in Chapter 12.

Conclusions

In this chapter we have seen that the domain of social behavior has yielded an enormous wealth of cross-cultural studies. We have tried to describe some important lines of research and highlight important issues. A recurring theme throughout the chapter was how to interpret observed cross-cultural differences in social behavior. We found that the distinction between relativism and universalism, which to us is a matter of degree (see Chapter 1), still tends to appear as a dichotomy: relativists tend to look for differences in psychological processes that lead to differences in behavior and universalists tend to look for contextual factors that lead identical processes to produce different behaviors.

The debate is mainly theoretical because all researchers agree that there are substantial cross-cultural differences in social behavior. However, it has important consequences for how we deal with culture. For example, questions of acculturation, intergroup relations, intercultural communication training and management of a culturally diverse workforce will be approached differently when one believes that cultural differences are intrinsically fused with our psychological make-up or when they are seen as psychological processes reacting to different ecological and social contexts.

In this chapter, we have seen that simple societal characteristics such as population density and stratification are systematically related to behavioral differences. Please note the relations with Chapters 2 and 3, because it is often through differential socialization that sociocultural differences in development come about. We have also seen how values can be a tool to describe global cross-cultural differences. Values can be seen to represent a kind of intermediary construct between universalist and relativist positions because the value structure is considered to be universal but value endorsements culture-specific. The biggest threat to the value approach may be that researchers expect too much from it. It is clear that a dimension like individualism–collectivism can describe many differences but that it would be naive to expect that it can capture the full richness of cultural variation.

In addition the assessment of values and the problematic relationships between individual-level and group-level variables need to be addressed.

The third section saw several concrete examples of differences in social cognitions and behaviors. Although this field is currently dominated by cultural psychology, which traditionally has been associated with cultural relativism, we saw ample evidence for a universalist position in the data. The last section noted some tricky issues in the conceptualization of culture as a social psychological construct. However, even if some issues remain unresolved it is clear that the domain of social behavior is a vibrant and productive area for cross-cultural research.

We would like to end by mentioning a point that is shared by all cross-cultural researchers. The evidence in this chapter shows that the current knowledge about social behavior in mainstream psychology is still largely biased toward western culture. Knowledge about the influence of sociocultural context on behavior is needed in order to gain a more rich, indeed a more universal, psychology. Simply assuming that findings with western (student) samples generalize to the majority world is in all likelihood a mistake.

KEY TERMS

gross national product (GNP)   •   priming   •   social axioms   •   social representations   tight–loose   •   values

FURTHER READING

Hofstede, G. (2001). *Culture's consequences* (2nd edn.). Thousand Oaks, Calif.: Sage.

A updated description of the classical study that initiated the many studies on cross-cultural differences in terms of values.

Kitayama, S., and Cohen, D. (eds.) (2007). *Handbook of cultural psychology*. New York: Guilford Press.

Various chapters in this handbook cover cross-cultural differences in social perception, cognition and behavior. The handbook also gives a good overview of the field of cultural psychology.

Smith, P. B., Bond, M. H., and Kağitçibaşi, C. (2006). *Understanding social psychology across cultures: Living and working in a changing world*. London: Sage.

A good introduction to the cross-cultural psychology of social cognition and behavior.

Triandis, H. C. (1995). *Individualism and collectivism*. Boulder, Colo.: Westview.

A classic and comprehensive treatment of the constructs of individualism and collectivism.

5 Personality

CONTENTS

Personality research is concerned with feelings, thoughts and behaviors that are typical of a person and distinguish that person from others. Personality in this sense is the outcome of a lifelong process of interaction between an organism and the ecocultural and sociocultural environment. The effects of these external factors make it likely that there are systematic differences in the person-typical behavior of people who have been brought up in different cultures. Thus, it is not surprising that many traditions in personality research have been extended cross-culturally.

A dominant theme in personality research concerns the question of how person-typical behavior can be explained in terms of more permanent psychological dispositions, and what could be the nature of such dispositions. A global distinction can be made between psychodynamic theories, trait theories and social-cognitive theories. The psychodynamic tradition which has the oldest and widest roots is presented on the Internet with Chapter 10 (Additional Topics, Chapter 10). Most research in this tradition,

www.cambridge.org/berry

which goes by the name of psychological anthropology (formerly called culture-and-personality), has been carried out by cultural anthropologists with a psychoanalytic orientation.

In this chapter we first discuss research on relatively stable characteristics, referred to as personality traits. In trait theories the emphasis is on individual dispositions that are consistent across time and situations. The most important tradition of cross-cultural research is discussed, that is, the five factor model with the associated Big Five dimensions. Some other trait traditions and research on national character are briefly mentioned. The second section deals with approaches that emphasize the learning of socialization history of the individual in the context in which s/he is living. Included are conceptions of the self, which is the way in which a person perceives and experiences himself or herself. Two forms of the construal of the self, independent and interdependent, are distinguished. These self-concepts are said to differ between societies that were characterized as individualist and collectivist in the previous chapter. The third section refers to non-western approaches to personality; some concepts and theories are presented that are rooted in non-western traditions. There are examples from Africa, India and Japan.

Before continuing we would like to call attention to Box 5.1, about a possible relationship among the Ashanti between a man's name and his tendency toward criminal

Box 5.1 **Ashanti personality**

According to Jahoda (1954), among the Ashanti a child is given the name of the day on which it was born. The name refers to the *kra*, the soul of the day. Among boys (no such ideas appeared to exist about girls) the *kra* implies a disposition toward certain behavior. Those born on Monday are supposed to be quiet and peaceful. Boys called "Wednesday" are held to be quick-tempered and aggressive. An analysis by Jahoda of delinquency records in a juvenile court indicated a significantly lower number than expected of convictions among youngsters called "Monday." There was also some evidence that those called Wednesday were more likely to be convicted of crimes against the person of others (e.g., fighting, assault). Although relationships were weak and replication of the study might have been desirable to further establish the validity of the results, Jahoda's conclusion stands that the "correspondence appears too striking to be easily dismissed" (1954, p. 195). A further question is, then, how these findings have to be interpreted: are they a reflection of social stereotypes and prejudices that focus attention on the (expected) misdemeanors of certain youngsters more than of others, or are these social expectations somehow internalized by youngsters, forming their personalities?

behavior. It is an example of one of the myriad and often unexpected interconnections between personality and the sociocultural environment. The Box can serve as a warning that, despite the large number of existing theories, our understanding of the relationship between the behavior of a person and the cultural environment remains limited and tentative.

Trait dimensions

In this section we emphasize **personality traits**. Fiske (1971, p. 299) has defined a trait as "a lasting characteristic attributed to persons in varying amounts of strength." A large number of trait names can be found in the literature; examples are dominance, sociability and persistence. In principle it should be possible to arrive at a comprehensive set of traits which together cover all major aspects of individual-characteristic behavior. Personality traits are usually measured by means of self- or other-report personality questionnaires (for specific traits) or personality inventories (omnibus instruments covering a range of traits). The most important empirical analyses for the distinction of various traits or trait dimensions are multivariate analyses (often factor analysis) of self-report data.

"Big Five" dimensions

The five factor model (FFM) has become the most popular model of trait dimensions. The main postulate is that five dimensions are needed to adequately map the domain of personality. The five dimensions (also called the "**Big Five**") tend to be seen as enduring dispositions, as likely to be biologically anchored (e.g., Costa and McCrae, 1994; McCrae and Costa, 1996, 2008) and as evolved in the human species over time (MacDonald, 1998; McCrae, 2009). The evidence for a biological basis is mainly derived from twin studies; identical twins who share the same genetic material are rather similar in respect of scores on personality variables, even when brought up separately. However, direct evidence linking personality dimensions to specific (patterns of) genes is still largely lacking. In other words, biological research cannot tell us (yet) whether one or the other personality theory is more valid.

The five factors in the FFM were postulated because they were the ones found recurrently on reanalysis of numerous data sets on all kinds of personality inventories in the USA (Norman, 1963). Within each factor different subfactors or facets have been distinguished, but these will not be mentioned here. The inventory used most frequently to assess the Big Five dimensions called the NEO-PI-R (Costa and McCrae, 1992) was developed in the USA and has been translated into more than forty languages. The five factors are labeled as follows:

- neuroticism, with emotional instability, anxiety and hostility; the neurotic person is tense, while the emotionally stable person is secure and relaxed;
- extraversion, with positive emotions as the core, and sociability, seeking stimulating social environments and outgoingness as some of the important characteristics;
- *openness to experience* (earlier called culture), with curiosity, imaginativeness and sophistication;
- *agreeableness*, with compassion, sensitivity, gentleness and warmth; agreeable persons are good to have around;
- *conscientiousness*, with persistence, goal-directed behavior, dependency and self-discipline.

Cross-cultural research has mainly addressed two questions. The first is whether universal validity of the FFM could be established. If the five dimensions represent basic differences in individual functioning they should be replicated everywhere; if they are characteristic of US-Americans, different cultures and languages are likely to show other trait configurations (McCrae, Costa, Del Pilar, Rolland and Parker, 1998). The second question is whether differences in score levels exist across cultures on the various dimensions and what these differences mean.

There are numerous culture-comparative studies based on the NEO-PI-R, including analyses drawing on large numbers of (literate) samples (McCrae, 2002; McCrae and Allik, 2002; McCrae, Terracciano et al., 2005a, b). In general, the five dimensions of the FFM that were identified originally in the USA are also found elsewhere, including non-western societies. Factor analyses on national data sets show similar factors across nations. Such similarity is established by calculating the congruence between factors across countries with Tucker's phi, a measure for structural equivalence (see the section on equivalence and bias in Chapter 1). These coefficients tend to show values of $\varphi = .90$ (phi) or even higher, although exceptions are found more for non-western than for western countries. The findings have been boosted by a large-scale study in which respondents were not asked for self-reports on NEO-PI-R items but for reports on someone they knew. From these other-reports the same five factor structure emerged as found with self-reports, at the individual level as well as at the country level after aggregation of the individual data to country scores (McCrae, Terracciano et al., 2005a, b). All in all, the body of research on the structural equivalence of the Big Five constitutes a major finding that imposes important constraints on the associations between cultural contexts and the make-up of personality, even if the replication of the precise structure is not always perfect.

The evidence on structural equivalence implies that researchers could meaningfully begin to address the second question, namely the search for quantitative differences in scores on the Big Five. Mean differences between cultures are small compared with the interindividual differences within a culture. The variance of the distribution of mean scores of countries on the Big Five factors typically is about one-ninth of the variance of a within-country distribution of individual scores (Allik, 2005; McCrae and Terracciano, 2008). Still, there have been several attempts to relate country variance on personality dimensions to other cultural traits.

It may be noted that in this area of cross-cultural research, more than in many others, the psychometric difficulties of comparison of score levels are appreciated. McCrae and colleagues have described various checks for cultural bias, for example on translations, item bias and the possible effects of response styles. Notably, acquiescence, a response style known to vary with GNP (or education, or individualism–collectivism; Smith, 2004; Van Herk *et al.*, 2004) is unlikely to have an effect on NEO-PI-R scores as half of the items are formulated in such a way that endorsement leads to a low trait score. Translation bias has been checked in studies with bilinguals (see McCrae and Terracciano *et al.*, 2005b). One remaining point of concern is the possible effects of social desirability (e.g., Harzing, 2006), which can be seen as a substantive and valid source of variance, but at the same time may distort the meaning of constructs that are being assessed.

Various other lines of evidence have been explored. McCrae and Terracciano (2008) have argued that various methods (self-reported and other-reports) show similar patterns of differences across the five dimensions and that this would be an unlikely finding unless there is scalar equivalence of scores across countries. Allik and McCrae (2004) have explored patterns of differences across countries and found some similarity between neighboring countries. Hofstede and McCrae (2004) reported correlations of value dimensions and Big Five dimensions which in their interpretation made sense given the meaning of the various dimensions.

Analyses looking into the cultural implications of score differences have made use of all kinds of data sets about countries from international agencies like the UN and the World Bank. These can be correlated with national scores on the Big Five dimensions (or even on the facets within each of the dimensions). McCrae and Terracciano (2008) have mentioned relationships with risk of various kinds of cancer, life expectancy, substance abuse and indices of mental health. Although findings are tentative, especially because of the risk of some uncontrolled third variable, they provide an important rationale for cross-cultural research on personality. Some of the uncertainties are reflected in a study by Rentfrow, Gosling and Potter (2008), who examined predictions about possible relationships between Big Five scores and state-level statistics for numerous indicators across the various states in the USA. Twelve out of thirteen predictions on correlates of the dimension of Agreeableness were in the expected direction, while for Neuroticism only seven out of sixteen predictions were supported. Of course, differences between states within the USA are likely to be smaller than between countries across the globe, but cultural and translational bias also should play a lesser role than in international data sets.

The interpretation of culture-level score differences implies two assumptions, namely that scores meet conditions for fullscale equivalence and that groups of people do indeed differ in levels of extraversion, agreeableness, etc. As mentioned, McCrae and colleagues have gone to some length to rule out effects due to lack of fullscale equivalence. They have argued that this form of equivalence, like construct validity, can only be established through multiple sources of evidence. As mentioned, in their opinion the evidence is largely positive (McCrae, Terracciano *et al.*, 2005a, b; McCrae and Terracciano, 2008). As far as the second assumption is concerned, according to McCrae (2009; see also Hofstede and McCrae, 2004) personality dimensions are not immune to cultural context. The postulate, referred to before, that the Big Five dimensions are biologically rooted apparently is meant to imply cross-cultural invariance of structural relationships, but not of patterns or levels of scores. However, an assumption of universality might also pertain to quantitative aspects of basic personality dimensions (Poortinga, Van de Vijver and Van Hemert, 2002). The fact that trait dimensions like extraversion and neuroticism are not immune to context does not say much about the *likelihood* that cultural contexts will indeed affect the development of such dimensions.

In the data set on other-reports in fifty countries McCrae, Terracciano *et al.* (2005b) analyzed the contributions to the total variance in the Big Five dimensions of sex, age group, culture and their interactions. These effects were robust, but small. On average the main effects of age and culture were the most important, with age explaining 3.1 percent and culture explaining 4.0 percent of the variance. The bulk of the variance (> 90%) has to be attributed to individual differences (including error of measurement). Perhaps culture explains a bit more variance in self-reports; however, the robustness of cultural variance has to do with the stability of results (a country score is aggregated over the respondents in a sample) rather than with the size. Poortinga and Van Hemert (2001) found for the scales in the Eysenck Personality Questionnaire (EPQ; see below) percentages of 14 percent to 17 percent. This kind of finding is not limited to personality scales; for the value types distinguished by Schwartz (1992, 1994a; see the section on values in Chapter 4), Poortinga and Van Hemert calculated percentages ranging from 6 percent to 11 percent, while Fischer and Schwartz (in press) found an average of less than 10 percent for a number of personality and value measures. Such percentages represent a non-negligible part of the variance, but they also indicate that individuals within cultures are substantially more variable than cultures.

Other trait traditions

There are several other models of personality structure. Somewhat older is the research with the Eysenck Personality Questionnaire as the main instrument (e.g., Eysenck and Eysenck, 1975). Traditionally, three personality dimensions were distinguished: psychoticism, extraversion, neuroticism. Later on social desirability was added, that is, the tendency to give responses that are socially acceptable and respectable. In a cross-cultural analysis by Barrett, Petrides, Eysenck and Eysenck (1998) data collected in thirty-four countries were included. Barret *et al.* demonstrated that by and large the factor similarity of the other thirty-three countries in this data set was closely similar to the structure in the UK, especially for extraversion and neuroticism. Thus, cross-cultural research with the EPQ appears to suggest that there are three major dimensions of personality everywhere and not five, as suggested by the findings on the Big Five. However, these two models of personality have also been argued to form different abstractions of the same hierarchical structure (Markon, Kruger and Watson, 2005).

The Big Five and the EPQ dimensions are western instruments and their use elsewhere may amount to creating "imposed etics" (see Box 1.2). The validity of this argument has been investigated through the construction of local personality inventories in non-western countries. For example, a number of studies on personality were conducted in the Philippines by Guanzon-Lapeña, Church, Carlota and Kagitbak using locally constructed instruments. When constructs were compared with the FFM theory, these authors found (1998, p. 265):

our allocation of dimensions to the Big Five domains suggests two things: (a) Each of the Big Five domains is represented by one or more dimensions from each of the indigenous instruments; and (b) None of the indigenous dimensions is so culturally unique that it is unrecognizable to non-Filipinos, or that it cannot be subsumed, at least conceptually, under the Big Five dimensions.

They continue:

This is not to say, however, that there are no cultural differences reflected in the flavor or focus of the dimensions considered most salient to assess in the Philippine context.

Similar findings were reported for the Chinese Personality Assessment Inventory (CPAI), a comprehensive instrument developed from scratch using Chinese sources for developing items. Compared to the FFM an additional factor was identified, labeled Interpersonal Relatedness (IR). Harmony, "face" and relationship orientation are facets of this factor. Thus, a factor beyond the Big Five was found, arguing for cultural specificity of personality structures. However, subsequently, this IR factor was also replicated in a multiethnic sample in Hawaii, and in various ethnic groups in Singapore, suggesting that interpersonal relatedness may be an aspect of personality lacking in the NEO-PI-R, but that ought to have been included in a comprehensive personality inventory (Cheung and Leung, 1998; Cheung *et al.*, 2001; Lin and Church, 2004). As argued by Cheung (2004), the presence of the IR factor in a Chinese scale and its absence in western scales could signify a blind spot in western theories and assessment instruments.

On the other hand, the openness dimension was not represented in the CPAI scales. With a revision of the inventory (CPAI-2) an attempt was made to have this dimension covered. Evidence has been emerging to the effect that the IR dimension predicted significantly more variance of the behavioral correlates of social behavior for Asian Americans than for European Americans, while for scales of the NEO-PI-R better predictions were found for European Americans (Cheung *et al.*, 2008). This suggests that local scales capture better what is salient in a culture.

A complementary body of evidence derives from research with person-descriptive terms. In the "psycholexical" approach such terms (usually adjectives) are selected from the vocabularies of various languages (e.g., Saucier and Goldberg, 2001). Ratings on these terms are then analyzed. Findings indicate that the FFM dimensions are not all cross-culturally replicable. A reanalysis of data sets from six languages in Europe led De Raad and Peabody (2005) to suggest that there were three shared dimensions. In a more extensive analysis with fourteen taxonomies from twelve languages, including Filipino and Korean data, De Raad *et al.* (2010) found that the three factors of extraversion, agreeableness and conscientiousness replicated better (in terms of congruence indices) than the other Big Five factors. They raise the important question of whether a definite universal structure can be achieved that at the same time is comprehensive.

National character

The approaches mentioned so far have in common that traits are identified primarily at the level of individuals. One can also imagine a focus on the cultural group, in other words traits making up a national character. Such ideas are popular; we all have some notions about what the Americans are like, or the Chinese, or the Japanese, etc. Early attempts at a systematic description were pursued by a school in cultural anthropology, called the "culture-and-personality" school, or "psychological anthropology" (Bock, 1999; Hsu, 1972). A summary can be found on Internet (Additional Topics, Chapter 10).

www.cambridge.org/berry

A more recent example is research by Peabody (1967, 1985). He drew a sharp distinction between national stereotypes (often considered to be irrational and incorrect) and national character (considered to be valid descriptions of a population). The latter was defined as "modal psychological characteristics of members of a nationality" (Peabody, 1985, p. 8). To identify national characteristics Peabody asked judges (usually students) to rate trait-descriptive adjectives about people in various nations, including their own. Questions were raised about the validity of national characteristics and judges' opinions about them. Are the usually second-hand impressions of students about other nations valid or do they never amount to more than stereotypes? It has been argued that ratings reflect merely ethnocentric attitudes, that nations change, and that judges rarely have extensive firsthand experience with other countries. Peabody (1985) has discussed such questions and concluded that by and large the objections had to be rejected for lack of supporting evidence.

Terracciano *et al.* (2005; McCrae and Terracciano, 2006) asked samples of respondents (mainly students) from forty-nine nations to describe the personality of a typical member of their nation. They used a scale, the National Character Survey (NCS), consisting of thirty bipolar items with two or three adjectives or phrases to mark each pole. Together the items covered the FFM dimensions as they are operationalized in the NEO-PI-R questionnaire. When aggregated mean scores on the NCS were compared with mean scores for the FFM dimensions in the same nations, in most cases there was no correlation between the two profiles. In other words, if the FFM profiles are a sound standard for personality profiles, Terracciano *et al.*'s findings imply that national character amounts to nothing more than unfounded stereotypes.

The most evident argument against the relevance of this finding is that FFM scores are not a valid standard for assessment of national character (e.g., McGrath and Goldberg, 2006). Notably, ratings of one's own group are subject to reference group effects; that is, in your judgments you use your own cultural environment as an implicit standard (Heine, Lehmann, Peng and Greenholtz, 2002; see Chapter 12, p. 293, this volume). The study by Terracciano *et al.* may have shaken beliefs in the validity of the notion of national character, but it has also been a trigger for further research. For example, Heine, Buchtel and Norenzayan (2008) examined correlations of self-report and other-report scores on the NEO-PI-R and of the national character scores just mentioned with timekeeping scores. Aggregated measures of national timekeeping accuracy were taken from an earlier study by Levine and Norenzayan (1999) and served in the more recent study as estimates of the conscientiousness dimension in the FFM. Heine *et al.* found positive correlations for the national character scores, but not for the FFM consciousness scores.

Oishi and Roth (2009) expanded the list of contradictory findings by demonstrating that nations with high self-reported conscientiousness were not less but rather more corrupt. It does not seem logical that in countries where people describe themselves as purposeful, strong-willed and determined, inhabitants are, by more objectively observed criteria, lackadaisical, less productive and more prone to bribery. However, Oishi and Roth warned that it is too early to give up self-reports since other Big Five dimensions demonstrated expected associations with external criterion variables.

More direct evidence disputing the findings by Terracciano *et al.* (2005) comes from a study in six countries in Eastern Europe (Belarus, Estonia, Finland, Latvia and Poland) by Realo *et al.* (2009; see also Allik, Mõttus and Realo, 2010). These authors administered the same instrument (NCS) as Terracciano *et al.* and asked for self-report ratings as well as ratings of a "typical" co-national and a "typical" Russian. National character stereotypes were shared widely and showed moderate relationships with (aggregated) self-reported personality traits. The six samples had a relatively similar view of the Russian national character. This profile was not related with self-reported personality traits of Russians but correlated somewhat with Russian self-stereotypes. A complication is that in most countries in this study there was firsthand experience with Russians in fairly recent history.

All in all, the impressive findings on trait dimensions have not resulted in a coherent set of dimensions of cross-cultural differences on which researchers agree. At the same time, scales that differentiate reliably between individuals in one culture are more likely than not to do so elsewhere. This suggests that there is a fair or even strong degree of communality in the structure of personality cross-culturally. However, researchers either do not (yet?) know the optimal structure, or that structure may differ (somewhat?) across societies. Future developments will depend on how well differences in score levels can be explained; such explanations hold the key to the further success of trait dimensions.

The person in context

Research on personality is not limited to trait conceptualizations. In traditions based on learning theories the reactions of persons to a situation are explained in terms of their personal reinforcement history. Strict learning theory did not go far in personality research. Soon, principles of transfer and generalization were formulated, going well beyond the mechanism of simple reinforcement. Bandura (1969, 1997) emphasized model learning and imitation, and, later on, self-efficacy. Rotter (1954) developed his social learning theory with internal and external control as very general tendencies of the individual. Mischel (1990) and others started to look for consistencies in behavior patterns (if–then relationships) based on cognitive and affective processes.

There exists an extensive body of cross-cultural research on locus of control, as developed by Rotter (1954, 1966). He believed that an individual's learning history can lead to generalized expectancies. One can see a (positive or negative) reward either as dependent upon one's own behavior or as contingent upon forces beyond one's control. In other words, the locus of control can be perceived as internal or external to oneself. Success in life can be due to "skill" or to "chance" and so can failure. Many events that happen in persons' lives can be taken by them as their own responsibility or as beyond their control. The most important instrument is Rotter's I–E Scale (1966). This consists of twenty-three items that offer a choice between an internal and an external option. Rotter concluded on the basis of factor analysis that the scale represents a single dimension. Hence, it should be possible to express locus of control in a single score that indicates the balance between externality and internality in a person.

Within the USA, where most cross-culturally relevant research has been conducted, it has been repeatedly found that African Americans are more external than European Americans (Dyal, 1984). Low socioeconomic status tends to go together with external control, but the black–white difference remains when socioeconomic differences have been controlled for. In general, locus of control represents a behavior tendency that seems to fit reasonable expectations of individuals belonging to certain groups, given their actual living conditions. Locus of control has been related to an array of other variables. One of the most consistent findings is a positive correlation between internal control and (academic) achievement.

The single dimension postulated by Rotter often could not be replicated in other cultures, also not with other instruments as the I–E scale. A review of ninety studies by Hui (1982) showed no clear evidence of patterns in cross-cultural differences in locus of control. More common has been the finding that there are two factors, pointing to personal control and sociopolitical control as separate aspects, although for non-western rural groups even more fuzzy solutions have been reported (Dyal, 1984; Smith, Trompenaars and Dugan, 1995; Van Haaften and Van de Vijver, 1996, 1999). It seems that locus of control is more determined by local situations than by global, stable environments. The locus of control concept allows a far more explicit role for cultural context in the making of personality than the trait theories discussed earlier in this chapter. It can also be seen as a precursor to other social-cognitive perspectives in which the person is seen as the outcome of the interactions between organism and social environment.

Mischel (1968) challenged trait conceptions, arguing that consistency over situations is largely absent; personality dimensions are poor predictors of future behavior. Instead personality research should take situational variability seriously. Such an alternative is the CAPS (Cognitive-Affective Personality System), a general framework that postulates that behavior is mediated by a set of cognitive affective units (including expectations, goals, competencies) (Mendoza-Denton and Mischel, 2007; Mischel and Shoda, 1995). Stability in behavior patterns derives from "If . . . Then" profiles (*if* situation A *then* this person will do X, but *if* situation B *then* s/he will do Y). There have been few cross-cultural analyses of profiles (but see Mendoza-Denton, Ayduk, Shoda and Mischel, 1997), but it is argued that the CAPS approach is highly compatible with a culturalist approach to personality. Mendoza-Denton and Mischel have proposed the C-CAPS (Cultural Cognitive-Affective Personality System) model and provided examples of how findings from research in cultural psychology, to which we will turn now, fit their approach.

Self in social context

Evidence of cross-cultural invariance of trait dimensions has been rejected in conceptualizations that view personality as studied by trait theorists as an expression of western individualism (Hsu, 1972). Ho, Peng, Lai and Chan have argued that relatedness between persons is a major concern in Confucianism and that interpersonal relationships take precedence over situational demands. They proposed to define personality as: "the sum total of common attributes manifest in, and abstracted from, a person's behavior directly or indirectly observed across interpersonal relationships and situations over time" (2001, p. 940).

A central argument is that the person cannot be separated from the cultural context (Shweder, 1990; Shweder and Bourne, 1984); personality as a set of notions about self and selfhood is a cultural construction, and hence likely to vary cross-culturally. Although the empirical evidence of Shweder and Bourne was limited (Church, 2000), the underlying idea has been widely endorsed. Self is seen by many researchers, particularly in the USA and East Asia, as a cultural product (Heine, 2008). In Chapter 7 we shall see that in research on emotions the most salient findings of cultural specificity come from ethnographic analyses and the same seems to be the case in research on personality. Church (2000) has listed examples, such as Hsu's (1985, p. 33) interpretation of the Chinese word for man (*jen*), which implies "the individual's transactions with his fellow human beings," and Rosenberger's (1994) interpretation of self (*jibun*) in Japanese, meaning "self-part," which also implies that the self is not seen as separate from the social domain.

One theory of self has been formulated by Kağitçibaşi (1990, 1996, 2007). She has differentiated between a relational self and a separated self. The relational self develops in societies with a "family model of emotional and material interdependence." Such societies typically have a traditional agricultural subsistence economy with a collectivistic life style; members of a family have to rely on each other in case of sickness and for security in old age. A separated self is found in individualistic western urban environments with a "family model of independence." Members of a family can live separated from each other without serious consequences for their well-being. A major feature of Kağitçibaşi's theorizing is the distinction of a third category of self, which develops in a "family model of emotional interdependence." This kind of self is called an "autonomous-related self"; it is found particularly in urban areas of collectivist countries. Despite growing material independence, and socialization toward more autonomy, emotional interdependencies between members of the family continue. Kağitçibaşi believes that the main direction of development in the world is toward this third model, allowing for relatedness as well as autonomy in a person's interactions with society at large.

The distinction of Kağitçibaşi between a relational self and an autonomous self comes close to Markus and Kitayama's (1991, 1998) dichotomy between an independent self-construal and an interdependent self-construal (see Chapter 4, p. 100). This major distinction in personality conceptions is seen as summarizing a broad conglomerate of East–West differences in social behavior, cognition, emotion and motivation. In the West personality is rooted in a model of the person as a separate organism, separate, autonomous and atomized (made up of a set of discrete traits, abilities, values and motives), seeking separateness and independence from others. In the East the basic model of the person implies interdependence and relatedness, rooted in a concept of the self not as a discrete entity, but as inherently linked to others. The person is only made "whole" when situated in his or her place in a social unit: "The cultural perspective assumes that psychological processes, in this case the nature and functioning of personality, are not just influenced by culture but are thoroughly culturally constituted" (Markus and Kitayama, 1998, p. 66). In the Euro-American context the person is seen as a unique configuration of internal attributes and behaves accordingly. In East Asian societies personality is experienced and understood as behavior that is characteristic of the person in relationship with others. In one study with a focus on personality Kitayama, Markus, Matsumoto and Norasakkunit (1997, p. 1247) presented a collective constructionist theory of the self in which it is stated that "many psychological tendencies and processes simultaneously result from and support a collective process through which the views of the self are inscribed and embodied in the very ways in which social acts and situations are defined and experienced in each cultural context."

The notion of joint psychological processes is rather old, especially under the label "collective representations" (e.g., Jahoda, 1982), but has not gained much foothold, because no appropriate psychological mechanisms could be specified. Another concept is that of social representations. These have been more widely researched in the school of Moscovici (e.g., 1982; Wagner et al., 1999; see also Chapter 4, p. 91). This school emphasizes shared meanings within and differences in meanings and perceptions between cultural groups. However, Kitayama et al. go much further by specifying differences in psychological processes, rather than differences in social perceptions.

Kitayama et al. (1997) asked Japanese and US students to rate the impact of a large number of events on their self-esteem (*jison-shin* for the Japanese). Situation descriptions had been generated that were seen as relevant for the enhancement or the decrease of self-esteem in a separate study by similar samples of students. American respondents imagined that they would experience more increase in self-esteem to positive situations than decrease in self-esteem to negative situations. This effect was stronger for situation descriptions generated in the USA than for descriptions that came from Japan. On the other hand, Japanese respondents reported that they would experience more reduction in self-esteem in negative situations than enhancement of self-esteem if they experienced positive situations. The differences were quite substantial, suggesting a robust difference in self-criticism and self-enhancement between the two societies.

Kitayama *et al.* recognized that differences might be a matter of expression rather than different modes of self. They proceeded with a second study in which other samples of Japanese and US students were asked to make the same ratings, but this time not with respect to the effect on their own self-esteem, but with respect to the effect on the self-esteem of a typical student: "We assumed that because the respondents were asked to estimate the true feelings (i.e., changes in self-esteem) of the typical student, they would not filter their responses through any cultural rules of public display that might exist" (1997, p. 1256). Very similar results as in the previous study were obtained under these instructions, which was a reason for the authors to argue that the answer pattern was not a matter of display rules, but of true experiences of the self.

There was also at least one puzzling finding. In the first study a third sample was included, consisting of Japanese people who were temporarily studying at a university in the USA. They indicated that they would experience more increase in self-esteem in positive situations, than decrease in self-esteem in negative situations, for situations generated in the USA. Only for situations generated in Japan was the reverse tendency found, consistent with the results of the Japanese sample living in Japan. Such a rapid acculturation effect seems difficult to reconcile with basic differences in self.

The mutual constitution of culture and self remains a central theme in cultural psychological approaches to personality. Kitayama, Duffy and Uchida (2007), in a chapter entitled "Self as cultural mode of being," continue to present two broad types of modes of being. They refer to numerous studies in various domains that are argued to confirm their position. Some of these studies have been presented in Chapter 4; other studies will be mentioned in Chapters 6 (Cognition) and 7 (Emotion).

The article by Markus and Kitayama (1991) has been cited many times; it has had a major impact on cross-cultural psychology and has been at the basis of a body of subsequent research. Is the evidence about sweeping differences between cultures as strong as has been made out? Box 5.2 considers evidence that was derived from the Twenty Statement Test, a projective technique, frequently mentioned as support for East–West differences in construal of the self. In Chapter 4 we mentioned self-enhancement and self-esteem, initially concepts for which large differences were observed between Japan and the USA or Canada (e.g., Heine *et al.*, 1999), but where subsequent studies led to much more modest findings. We can also refer to a study by Matsumoto (1999) that found among eighteen studies testing for differences between Japan and the USA on individualism–collectivism only one which provided support for higher collectivism among the Japanese (see also Takano and Osaka, 1999).

Box 5.2 **The Twenty-Statement Test**

In part Markus and Kitayama (1991) have relied on empirical evidence that with the advantage of hindsight may be less convincing. Substantial differences between country means were reported for a popular method to assess independent and interdependent self-construal, that is, the Twenty-Statement Test, or TST (Kuhn and McPartland, 1954; Triandis, McCusker and Hui, 1990). The TST is a projective test in which respondents complete twenty times the statement "I am … " Cousins (1989) found a much larger proportion of "pure attributes" with Japanese than with US students. Pure attributes are descriptions of self without qualifiers referring to other persons, situations or time, for example "I am honest." The TST was administered a second time in a contextualized format asking for the twenty statements to be completed for the following situations, "at home," "at school" and "with close friends." In these conditions the pattern of scores was reversed; now the US students gave far fewer pure trait answers and the Japanese students far more. Cousins (1989, p. 129) argues: "Lacking contextual cues the TST format – as interpreted from an individualistic perspective – connotes situation-freedom, and lends itself to ego-autonomy … From a sociometric perspective, however, the question 'Who am I?' standing alone, represents an unnatural sundering of person from social matrix and must therefore be supplemented with context."

Thus, Cousins freely interprets the differences in frequencies of trait-descriptive answers in I-C terms, ignoring that the effects are obtained with a subtle shift in instructions in a rather open task that can be interpreted by respondents in multiple ways. In the meantime, the results with the TST or similar techniques have been inconsistent, both for comparisons including European Americans (Oyserman et al., 2002) and for comparisons involving other cultural contrasts (Van den Heuvel and Poortinga, 1999; Watkins et al., 1998).

Projective techniques are notorious for problems with validity. Levine and colleagues (2003; Bresnahan, Levine, Shearman, Lee, Park and Kiyomiya, 2005) have disputed the convergent and discriminant validity of the TST, as well as of two other instruments, the Singelis Self-Construal Scale and the RISC of Cross, Bacon and Morris. It may be noted that these criticisms by Levine and colleagues are not necessarily shared by other authors. Objections were raised by Gudykunst and Lee (2003) and Kim and Raja (2003), who referred mainly to findings and arguments supporting the prevalent "common view," but hardly challenged the psychometric evidence of Levine et al.

There are now several empirical analyses and reviews providing interpretations that are more specific of East–West differences that were initially portrayed as indicative of basic differences in the functioning of the self (e.g., Chiu and Kim, in press). Examples include research on normative prescriptions by Yamagishi et al. (2008; see also Chapter 4, p. 104) and by Chen, Bond, Chan, Tang and Buchtel (2009) on modesty as a self-presentation tactic. Such research suggests that the sweeping interpretations advanced by Markus and Kitayama (1991) and by Kitayama *et al.* (1997) should be open to modification. At the same time, there also seem to be new openings in the traditions of cultural psychology toward accepting that there may be something to culture-comparative and trait traditions (e.g., Heine and Buchtel, 2009). There have been few attempts to combine trait perspectives and social cognitivist views (but see Church, 2000, 2009, who proposed an integrated "cultural trait psychology"). It may well be that such attempts will help to lower the barriers between various conceptualizations and to move research on personality and culture forward.

Some non-western concepts

Notions about personality or personhood[1] exist in many, if not all, cultures. Those proposed from non-western societies are often referred to as indigenous personality concepts. We have argued that this term "indigenous" is somewhat of a misnomer (see Chapter 1, p. 19), as the dominant (western) view in the literature also has a background in a specific cultural context. Concepts found in the mainstream psychological literature have often been defined and validated through research and assessment methods. It can be argued that such concepts are more acceptable than impressionistic notions, wherever the latter may have originated. Many cross-cultural psychologists would be hesitant to accept such an opinion: they tend to give equal credit to concepts about personality based on non-western traditions of reflection on human existence. We shall mention some of these, contributed by authors writing on the culture in which they were brought up. There are unmistakably western influences, but also authentic insights not easily achieved by outsiders (see Sinha, 1997). Moreover, on the Internet (Additional topics, Chapter 5) we consider altered states of consciousness that appear to be important to many non-Western cultures and usually have quite a different meaning than in industrial urban societies. www.cambridge.org/berry

Ubuntu in Africa

A concept that has been gaining rapid acceptance in Africa is *ubuntu*. It refers to a mode of functioning that is considered characteristic for Africa and has been derived from an aphorism which in English means approximately "a person is a person through other persons." *Ubuntu* represents values such as solidarity and compassion (Mbigi, 1997), is supposed to be deeply rooted in African history and

---

[1] The term "personhood" is sometimes preferred when the term "personality" is seen as too closely associated with a trait approach.

tradition, and continues to guide interpersonal relations in poor communities (Broodryk, 2002). Authors like Broodryk and Mgibi contrast *ubuntu* with what they perceive to be western modes of individual and social functioning. From a broader perspective it appears that *ubuntu* reflects similar concerns as the concept of collectivism, and is more or less the opposite of autonomy and independent self-construal. However, local authors tend to portray it as typical for Africa, and as somewhat different from collectivism.[2] A related aspect of African personhood lies in the importance of the broad social context. This is not limited to those presently around, but includes the world of the deceased, the spirits and the gods. Authors like Sow (1977, 1978), and later Nsamenang (1992, 2001) and Mkhize (2004), have emphasized that not directly observable aspects of reality are part of psychological functioning in Africa.

During colonial times, the descriptions of African personality made by western psychiatrists were marked by prejudices and stereotypes. Any indigenous religious beliefs tended to be dismissed as "superstitions" even if they were not more miraculous than supernatural events readily accepted by most Christian believers. An upsurge in the 1960s and 1970s of writings by African authors claiming a separate identity for African people can be seen at least in part as a reaction against the generally negative picture prevalent in colonial times.

The Senegalese psychiatrist Sow (1977, 1978) has provided an extensive theory of the African personality and psychopathology. He distinguished an outer layer, the body, which is the corporal envelope of the person. Next came a principle of vitality that is found in man and animals. This can be more or less equated with physiological functioning. A third layer represented another principle of vitality, but this is found only in humans; it stands for human psychological existence not shared with other species. The inner layer is the spiritual principle, which never perishes. It can leave the body during sleep and during trance states and leaves definitively upon death. The spiritual principle does not give life to the body; it has an existence of its own, belonging to the sphere of the ancestors and representing that sphere in each person.

The concentric layers of the personality are in constant relationship with the person's environment. Sow described three reference axes concerning the relations of a person with the outside world. The first axis links the world of the ancestors to the spiritual principle, passing through the other three layers. The second axis connects the psychological vitality principle to the person's extended family, understood as the lineage to which the person belongs. The third axis connects the wider community to the person, passing through the body envelope to the physiological principle of vitality. These axes represent relations that are usually in a state of equilibrium.

---

[2] Despite several discussions with psychologists from Africa we have not succeeded in finding any consensus on how *ubuntu* differs from collectivism.

According to Sow the traditional African interpretation of illness and mental disorders, and their treatments, can be understood in terms of this indigenous personality theory. A disorder occurs when the equilibrium is disturbed on one or the other of the axes; diagnosis consists of discovering which axis has been disturbed, and therapy will attempt to re-establish the equilibrium. Note that in African tradition illness always has an external cause; it is not due to intrapsychic phenomena in the person's history, but to aggressive interference from outside.

The importance of symbolism is emphasized by others who write on Africa, like Jahoda (1982; cf. Cissé, 1973) in his reference to the very complex personality conceptions of the Bambara in Mali. They distinguish sixty elements in the person that form pairs, each having one male and one female element. Examples are thought and reflection, speech and authority, future and destiny, and first name and family name. Jahoda sees some similarities with psychology as it is known in the West, but also important differences. Bambara psychology forms part of a worldview in which relationships between various elements are established by symbolism rather than by analytic procedures.

Nsamenang (2001) also points out that modern views in psychology about the individual as autonomous differ from the African conception in which the person coexists with the community, with the world of spirits and with the ecological environment. The existence of an indestructible vital force which continues to exist in the world of spirits after death is emphasized (Nsamenang, 1992). Personhood is a manifestation of this vital force through a body. Respect for the person becomes manifest, for example, in the importance attached to greetings; the amount of time spent is not a waste of time and effort, but reflects the social value attached to the greeting; the high value of greetings implies a high regard for persons. Nsamenang (1992, p. 75) further describes how in Africa "a man is not a man on his own," but is rooted in the community in which and for which he exists. The importance of the community is reflected in the saying "Seek the good of the community, and you seek your own good; seek your own good and you seek your own destruction." In Nsamenang's view the primacy of kinship relations will remain paramount, until alternative systems of social security can replace extended family networks.

According to Mkhize (2004) African conceptions of reality differ from western conceptions in time orientation. Western societies emphasize the future; traditional communities concentrate on the past (relationship with those living in the past) and present social relationships. In Africa there is an orientation on external forces (God, fate and ancestors) and on a harmonious coexistence of people and nature. There is a hierarchy of beings with the community of integrated ancestors located between humans and God. Human activity is about harmony with others rather than about personal accomplishments. The relational orientation in traditional cultures is toward family and community and position within the group rather than on the self as a bounded autonomous entity.

The authors mentioned share with many western and Asian researchers who argue for the self in context an emphasis on the embeddedness of personhood in the social environment. The African authors add a dimension: the social environment is not limited to humans who are currently alive, but includes the transcendent: the spirits of the ancestors and God.

Indian conceptions

According to Paranjpe (1984, pp. 235 ff.) the concept of *jiva* is similar to that of personality: "The *jiva* represents everything concerning an individual, including all his experiences and actions throughout his life cycle." Five concentric layers are distinguished. The outermost is the body. The next is called the "breath of life"; it refers to physiological processes such as breathing. The third layer involves sensation and the "mind" that coordinates the sensory functions. Here egoistic feelings are placed that have to do with "me" and "mine." The fourth layer represents the intellect and the cognitive aspects of the person, including self-image and self-representation. The fifth and most inner layer of the *jiva* is the seat of experience of bliss. Paranjpe (1984, 1998) sees many similarities with western conceptions such as those of James and Erikson, but notes an important difference. Apart from the *jiva*, there is a "real self" or *Atman* that is the permanent unchanging basis of life. Paranjpe (1984, p. 268) quotes the ancient Indian philosopher Sankara on this point: "There is something within us which is always the substrate of the conscious feeling of 'I' ... This inner Self (*antar-Atman*) is an eternal principle, which is always One and involves an integral experience of bliss ... The *Atman* can be realized by means of a controlled mind." To achieve the state of bliss one has to acquire a certain state of consciousness.

We have summarized Paranjpe's description of only one school of thinking (Vedanta), but other ancient Indian scholars agree that there are different states of consciousness, including Patanjahli, who described yoga, the system of meditation that nowadays has many adherents outside of India. It is seen as highly desirable to attain the most superior state of consciousness. Restraint and control of the mind to keep it steadily on one object, withdrawing the senses from objects of pleasure and enduring hardship are means toward this desirable condition.

To reach the ultimate principle of consciousness, the ultimate reality, transcending space and time, is a long and difficult process. Should the complete state of detachment and inner quietness be reached, then one's body becomes merely incidental (like one's shirt) and there is a change to fearlessness, concern for fellow beings, and equanimity. Ordinarily people have a low impulse control, which implies that they cannot detach themselves from the always present stimuli and the vicissitudes of life. It will be clear that those trained in detachment will be far less subject to the stresses and strains of life.

On the basis of these considerations Naidu (1983; Pande and Naidu, 1992) has taken *anasakti* or "non-detachment" as the basis for a research program on stress. Contrary to western psychology, where control over the outcome of one's actions is seen as desirable, the ancient Hindu scriptures value detachment from the possible consequences of one's actions. Western studies are on involuntary loss of control, and how this can lead to helplessness and depression. Detachment amounts to voluntarily giving up control and is assumed to have a positive effect on mental health. The methods used to assess and validate the notion of *anasakti* are much the same as those used in western psychometrics. This makes the approach one of the attempts to translate directly an indigenous notion of a philosophical and religious nature into a personality index that could be studied empirically.

Amae in Japan

Amae, pronounced ah-mah-eh, has gained prominence through the writings of the psychiatrist Doi (1973) as a core concept for understanding the Japanese. *Amae* is described as a form of passive love or dependence that finds its origin in the relationship of the infant with its mother. The desire for contact with the mother is universal in young children and plays a role also in the forming of new relationships among adults. *Amae* is more prominent with the Japanese than with people in other cultures. Doi finds it significant that the Japanese language has a word for *amae* and that there are a fair number of terms that are related to *amae*. In Doi's view culture and language are closely interconnected.

He ascribes to the *amae* mentality of the Japanese many and far-reaching implications. The seeking of the other person's indulgence that comes together with passive love and dependency leads to a blurring of the sharp distinction, found in the West, between the person (as expressed in the concept of self) and the social group. As such it bears on the collectivist attitudes allegedly prevalent in Japanese society. Mental health problems manifest in psychosomatic symptoms, and feelings of fear and apprehension can have their origins in concealed *amae*. The patient is in a state of mind where he cannot impose on the indulgence of others. In a person suffering from illusions of persecution and grandeur "*amae* has seldom acted as an intermediary via which he could experience empathy with others. His pursuit of *amae* tends to become self-centered, and he seeks fulfillment by becoming one with some object or other that he has fixed on by himself" (Doi, 1973, p. 132). In an analysis of the social upheavals in Japan, in particular the student unrest, during the late 1960s and early 1970s, Doi points out that more modern times are permeated with *amae* and that everyone has become more childish. There has been a loss of boundaries between generations; *amae* has become a common element of adult-like child and childlike adult behavior.

Amae has been widely endorsed as evidence for the culture-specific nature of personality. The concept has also been challenged, both in respect of its cultural origins and its cultural uniqueness. Burman (2007) has pointed out, partly on the basis of personal communication with Doi, that the notion of *amae* in part was a reaction against a dismissive description of Japanese character after the Second World War. She also comments on the ironic coincidence that this highly Japanese notion has been shaped in terms of a western theoretical frame: Doi was a psychoanalyst who had received his training in the West.

Yamaguchi and Ariizumi define *amae* as "presumed acceptance of one's inappropriate behavior or request" (2006, pp. 164 ff.) and argue that there is an element of inappropriateness (in what is being asked for) and a positive element (it is an expression of love). They draw distinctions between *amae* and both attachment and dependence to further describe the psychological meaning, emphasizing that there is an emotional aspect and a manipulative (motivational) aspect. They conclude from their analysis in which they refer to comparisons of Japanese with Taiwanese and USA students: "The initial evidence indicates that people in other cultures also engage in inappropriate behavior described as *amae* by Japanese" (2006, pp. 172 ff.). In several other empirical studies similarities between Japanese and non-Japanese are also found, as well as a host of, often subtle, differences (Kumagai and Kumagai, 1986; Lewis and Ozaki, 2009; Niiya, Ellsworth and Yamaguchi, 2006; Rothbaum, Kakinuma, Nagaoka and Azuma, 2007). It is difficult to summarize what in the end emerges as culturally specific; the differences that are reported appear to depend on the methods that are being used.

Conclusions

There are many traditions in cross-cultural psychology emphasizing personality differences that should be consistent over a wide range of situations. In the first section of this chapter we have reviewed relevant evidence. The similarities in basic trait dimensions, however defined, provide a common psychological basis that underlies differences in overt culture-characteristic behavior patterns of individuals. However, the structures are not precise and so far it remains rather unclear what to make of cross-cultural differences in score levels on personality dimensions. In the second section we have presented the work of authors who argue that there are essential differences in personality make-up across cultures, or even that what is called personality in western psychology in essence is a cultural characteristic.

Since the early 1990s there has been a large increase in cross-cultural research, also in the domain of personality. Both trait traditions and traditions rooted in learning theory and later in social cognition are prominent, as they are in mainstream psychology. In cross-cultural psychology there is an additional stream of research: the analysis of concepts and approaches that find their origins in non-western traditions of reflection on the person.

The integration of the various bodies of knowledge leaves much to be desired, and in this respect research on personality, unfortunately, is not an exception.

KEY TERMS

amae • "Big Five" dimensions • extraversion • indigenous personality concepts • locus of control • national character • neuroticism • personality traits • *ubuntu*

FURTHER READING

Church, A. T. (2009). Prospects for an integrated trait and cultural psychology. *European Journal of Personality*, 23, 153–182.

> An attempt to bring together trait traditions and traditions with orientations from cultural psychology and with indigenous (non-western) ideas about personality.

Heine, S. J., and Buchtel, E. E. (2009). Personality: The universal and the culturally specific. *Annual Review of Psychology*, 60, 369–394.

> A review chapter rooted in a cultural psychology tradition that reflects also on personality traits.

Kitayama, S., Duffy, S., and Uchida, U. (2007). Self as cultural mode of being. In S. Kitayama and D. Cohen (eds.), *Handbook of cultural psychology* (pp. 136–174). New York: Guilford Press.

> This chapter provides a social psychological perspective on personality rooted in cultural psychology.

McCrae R. R., and Allik, J. (eds.) (2002). *The five-factor model of personality across cultures*. New York: Kluwer.

> This volume provides a broad overview of cross-cultural research on the Big Five dimensions, including a chapter by McCrae based on data from thirty-six cultures.

6 Cognition

CONTENTS

In this chapter, we shift our focus from behavior that is primarily social to behavior that is cognitive. Social cognition was discussed in Chapter 4, where the phenomena of attribution, conformity and self-construal were presented as social psychological manifestations of the cultural context. In Chapter 8, we shall return to a consideration of cultural aspects of cognition, where links between language and culture are explored. In this chapter we focus on the more traditional cognitive phenomena that deal with knowing and interpreting the world, using such notions as intelligence, abilities and styles. We begin with a brief overview of the historical legacy of thinking about how human populations are similar and different in their cognitive lives. In each of the subsequent sections we present four perspectives on relationships between cognition and culture, beginning with a set of conceptualizations that involve a unitary view of cognition (captured in the notion of general intelligence). Thereafter we present cognitive styles, which are general preferences to deal with the world in a particular way. The third perspective is one that focusses on the East–West contrasts in cognition, where there has been much recent research on differences in the cognitive life of western and East Asian populations. Finally, the fourth perspective is contextualized cognition, in which cognitions are seen as task-specific and embedded in sociocultural contexts. Another perspective, that of genetic epistemology, is discussed on the Internet (Additional Topics, Chapter 6).

www.cambridge.org/berry

Cognition is an area of cross-cultural research that has a history of strong controversies. Much of the debate can be seen in terms of the process–competence–performance distinctions made in Chapter 1 (see p. 28). There are obvious differences in cognitive performance across cultures. However, differences between cultural groups in average levels of performance on cognitive tests have been interpreted from two dramatically different perspectives, rooted in either biological or cultural factors. In the first perspective, performance differences are viewed as a more or less direct reflection of variations in inborn competencies. At the group level such interpretations tend to invoke the notion of "race"; differences in performance as assessed by intelligence batteries (i.e., differences in IQ) are usually ascribed to racial differences in underlying cognitive aptitudes.[1] In the second (cultural) perspective, cognitive performances and competencies (and for some authors even processes) are considered to be embedded in culture. Cultural groups are seen to have different performances and competencies that are rooted in ecological demands as well as in sociocultural patterns. That is, cross-cultural differences are expected in competencies and performances, as well as in the organization of cognitive activities.

This second position is consistent with moderate universalism (see Chapter 1, section on Theme 2: relativism–universalism). From this position, we seek to discover cognitive variations in performance that are associated with specific cultural practices, while also seeking underlying similarities in pan-human cognitive processes. Moderate universalism requires us to consider a wide range of studies, from those that view cognitive processes and abilities as essentially untouched by culture (a strong universalist position) to those that are strongly relativist; this latter position views cognitive life as locally defined and constructed, and postulates the existence of cognitive activity that is unique to a particular culture. Moderate universalism considers that basic cognitive processes are shared, species-wide features of all people, everywhere. Culture influences the development, content and use of these processes (as competencies and performances) but does not alter the processes in a fundamental way.

The historical legacy

The relationship between culture and cognition has a long history (reviewed, among others, by Segall *et al.*, 1999, ch. 5). Early on, claims of a "great divide" in intellectual functioning between "civilized" and "primitive" peoples

---

[1] The terms "race" and "racial" are placed in quotation marks when first used, because of the highly problematic nature of categorizations of human groups in such terms.

were commonly made. For example, Levy-Bruhl (1910) considered the thought processes of non-western peoples to be "pre-logical." He claimed that "primitives perceive nothing in the same way as we do" (1910, p. 10). He attributed this difference not to biological but to environmental causes: "The social milieu which surrounds them differs from ours, and precisely because it is different, the external world they perceive differs from that which we apprehend" (1910, p. 10).

Others considered that such differences were due to biological factors, specifically to "race" (e.g., Shuey, 1958). These genetic interpretations have found a resonance in some contemporary writers, such as Rushton (2000), who argues that genetic factors (distributed differently according to "races") are strongly related to cognitive life, especially to intelligence. In his view, higher levels of intelligence were selected for in "Caucasoid" and "Mongoloid" peoples "who evolved in Eurasia, and were subjected to pressures for improved intelligence to deal with problems of survival in the cold northern latitudes" (2000, p. 228).

Less attached to such great divides in the fundamental features of cognition were Boas (1911) and Wundt (1913). While still making the distinction between "primitive" and "civilized" populations, both considered that the underlying cognitive processes were shared by all populations, with differences appearing in the competencies that were developed. In this respect, they were early advocates of a more moderate universalist position as taken in this text. Boas emphasized the identity in thought processes between "civilized" and "primitive" peoples, attributing the differences to a shift from social and emotional content of thought to a more intellectual one: "When the same concept appears in the mind of primitive man, it associates itself with those concepts related to it by emotional states. This process of association is the same among primitive men as among civilized men, and the difference consists largely in the modification of the traditional material with which our new perceptions amalgamate" (1911, p. 239).

Wundt (1913) also argued for the existence of similar cognitive processes among groups of humankind, with differences between populations being due to the "general cultural conditions" in which different groups lived. He suggested that: "the primitive man of the tropics has found plenty of game and plant food in his forests, as well as an abundance of material for clothing and adornment. Hence he lacks the incentive to strive for anything beyond these simple means to satisfy his wants" (1913, p. 110). His main conclusion was that: "the intellectual endowment of primitive man is in itself approximately equal to that of civilized man. Primitive man merely exercises his ability in a more restricted field; his horizon is essentially narrower because of his contentment under these limitations" (1913, p. 113). These views also find resonance in contemporary writings (e.g., Lynn, 2006, to be reviewed below).

While corresponding to a general view of universalism, both Boas and Wundt subscribed to an early form of "environmental determinism." As we discussed in Chapter 1, such simplistic environment–behavior relationships have largely been discounted, and replaced by more interactive and probabilistic conceptions of relationships between human populations and their ecosystems. From this ecocultural perspective, habitats provide both constraints and affordances for human development, but do not determine them.

These historical issues not only set the stage for some current research, but they remain with the contemporary study of the relationships between culture and cognition. They appear frequently in the materials that follow in this chapter.

General intelligence

In this section we look at various approaches to thinking about cognition that take a unitary view of cognitive functioning; that is, they see general intelligence as a coherent characteristic of an individual person. The first is an examination of the idea that there is one basic quality of intelligence, which is referred to as general intelligence, symbolized by "g." We then examine some cross-cultural studies of general intelligence, and finally consider indigenous notions and measures of intelligence.

The notion of "g"

The notion of general intelligence is largely based on psychometric evidence, particularly the consistent finding of positive correlations among results obtained with tests of different cognitive abilities. Spearman (1927) explained this phenomenon by postulating a general intelligence factor, which he referred to as "g" and which represents what all (valid) cognitive tests assess in common. Spearman saw g very much as an inborn capacity. However, other researchers, like Thurstone (1938), found specific, uncorrelated factors, which were seen as incompatible with the notion of one general intelligence factor. A way to organize the enormous amount of available information has been presented by Carroll (1993). On the basis of 460 data sets obtained between 1927 and 1987 he proposed a hierarchical model with three strata. The first includes narrow, specific abilities; the second includes group factors that are common to subsets of tests; and the third consists of a single general intelligence factor.

To examine controversies in the interpretation of group differences in g, we first have to establish what is actually measured across cultures by intelligence tests. Vernon (1969) proposed a hierarchical model that incorporates g and other named factors at varying levels of increased specificity. In his empirical examinations he claimed to find support for this model. Irvine (1979), in a comprehensive overview of early cross-cultural studies, also found evidence for g as well as for more specialized factors, such as reasoning, verbal, figural, mathematical and conceptual reasoning. These analyses fit the hierarchical distinctions of Carroll (1993). All in all, this evidence suggests that intelligence batteries show similar structures in western and non-western countries. Later in this chapter we will present other evidence that is in agreement with this initial interpretation.

The next question is whether differences in levels of scores (performances) indeed reflect differences in some inborn capacity (processes). To identify what basic underlying feature of an individual's cognitive life is responsible for the communality reflected by g, Vernon (1979) called upon a distinction by Hebb (1949) between "Intelligence A" and "Intelligence B." The former is the genetic equipment and potentiality (processes) of the individual, while the latter is the result of its development through interaction with one's cultural environment (i.e., the competence of a person).

However, Vernon went further, introducing the notion of "Intelligence C" to refer to the actual performance of an individual on an intelligence test. This distinction between Intelligence B and C allows another role for culture, since the developed intelligence (B) may or may not be properly sampled or assessed by a test. That is, a test performance (C) may not adequately represent the underlying competence (B). Numerous cultural factors (such as language, item content, motivation and speed) may contribute to this discrepancy. Thus, testers merely obtain data that speak directly to "Intelligence C." Only by drawing inferences from this performance data can researchers say something about "Intelligence B." It should be clear that bias or lack of equivalence in tests will lead to wrong interpretations about competence; this holds even more when inferences are extended to the remote concept of "Intelligence A."

Comparative studies

The explanation of group differences in levels of scores on batteries of general intelligence tests has been very controversial. One aspect of this controversy is the variation in how much the general g factor is part of various tests. This has been found to increase as a function of the complexity of tests, with tests of abstract thinking having highest g-loadings. Spearman (1927) had observed that tests with a higher g component tended to reveal larger performance differences between groups. Elaborating on these observations, Jensen (1985) formulated "Spearman's hypothesis," which predicts larger performance differences between "racial groups" in the USA on tests with a higher g-loading (i.e., tests which presumably form purer measures of intellectual capacity).

Most empirical studies on this hypothesis have been carried out in the USA with persons referred to simply as "black" or "white" (sometimes as African Americans and European Americans). Jensen (1985, 1998) found a substantial relationship between g-loadings of tests and average differences in scores between these two populations. On tests of abstract thinking the mean score difference is in the order of one standard deviation. Jensen interprets this as evidence for clear differences in the intellectual capacity of the two groups. Such views were expanded by Herrnstein and Murray (1994) in a book that argued that social correlates of intelligence score differences were evidence of causal relationships; that is, a group's lower intelligence was seen as the cause of lower social status, education and income. Because these differences have often been interpreted as "racial," the psychometric approach to cognitive competence has become controversial (e.g., Neisser et al., 1996; Sternberg and Grigorenko, 1997a). Numerous arguments have been raised against interpretations of cognitive differences in racial terms. We outline four lines of evidence on such a relationship.

First, there is other test-based empirical evidence, also from the USA, challenging Jensen's (1985, 1998) interpretation. For example, Humphreys (1985) analyzed data from the Project Talent Data Bank with more than 100,000 test takers on a large set of cognitive tests. He found that loadings of g correlated +.17 with race and +.86 with socioeconomic status differences. Scores were analyzed for participants of low and high socioeconomic status and for African Americans and European Americans separately. Performance differences were attributed to adverse environmental factors (low socioeconomic status/SES) which affect all individuals to the same extent, irrespective of race.

Second, tests of higher cognitive complexity are likely to contain more culture-specific elements. Spearman's hypothesis was examined by Helms-Lorenz, Van de Vijver and Poortinga (2003). They administered cognitive tests to second-generation immigrant and Dutch pupils (ages ranging from 6 to 12 years). Three features of tests were examined: the cognitive complexity of a test was derived from previous studies; cultural loadings of a test were rated by psychology students (who assessed the extent to which the test contains cultural elements); and verbal loadings were operationalized as the number of words in a subtest. Factor analysis of the subtest loadings on the first principal component, the theoretical complexity measures, and the ratings of cultural loading revealed two virtually unrelated factors, representing cognitive complexity (g) and cultural complexity (c). They argued: "Our results are at variance with common findings in the literature on SH [the Spearman hypothesis]. The major departure involves the failure to find a positive contribution of cognitive complexity to the prediction of cross-cultural performance differences" (2003, p. 26). In other words, these findings suggest that performance differences between immigrant and Dutch pupils are better predicted by c than by g.

The third line of argument derives from research with cognitively simple tasks. On simple reaction time tasks, response times (RT) are about the same in unschooled as in literate populations (Jensen, 1982, 1985; Van de Vijver, 2008). This supports the notion that there is cross-cultural invariance in information processing at an elementary level. However, on slightly more complex tasks, namely choice reaction time tasks in which respondents have to indicate which one of a set of stimuli is presented, intergroup differences have been reported, for example in South Africa (Verster, 1991). As complexity increases so do these differences (e.g., Sonke et al., 2008; Verster, 1991). Training on a task will shorten the response time, more so as tasks are more difficult (Sonke, Poortinga and De Kuijer, 1999; Sonke et al., 2008; Van de Vijver, 2008). This suggests that cross-cultural differences in RT tasks can be explained in terms of prior exposure or experience (Poortinga, 1985; Posner, 1978).

A fourth line of argument against inferences from tests to "g" is that psychometricians often have taken a rather narrow view of inequivalence and cultural bias (see Chapter 1, "Dealing with threats to interpretation," and Chapter 12 *passim*) in cognitive tests. Analyses of cultural bias have been mainly directed at item bias (Poortinga and Van de Vijver, 2004). As we have seen in Chapter 1, with these procedures each separate test item is examined to see whether across cultures test takers with the same overall test score have equal probabilities to solve the item correctly. Items that are relatively more difficult for one group than for another group can be identified. In this way important aspects of bias can be determined. However, such analyses are not informative about broader issues of inequivalence that affect all items in a test to a similar extent, such as prior experience with the kind of task on which the items of the test are based. A test or battery being free or almost free from item bias certainly does not justify generalization of the results to "Intelligence A."

When cross-cultural comparisons of intelligence are undertaken, many problems of a psychometric and cultural nature are encountered. The basic issues of bias and fairness relate to the validity of the scores obtained: do they really reflect the "intelligence" of the members of a cultural population? The issues of bias and fairness have arisen in recent studies (Georgas, Weiss, Van de Vijver and Saklofske, 2003; Lynn, 2006; Lynn and Vanhanen, 2002).

Lynn (2006) examined over 500 studies that reported IQ mean scores for countries. These scores were not examined for either their cultural validity or equivalence. The main findings were that the average world IQ is around 90, and that there is a gradient across countries, with mean scores declining from north to south. This variation is explained in evolutionary terms: intelligence is related to the need for survival in cold climates. The argument is that as human beings migrated from Africa they encountered a cognitively demanding environment where survival (e.g., keeping warm, hunting rather than gathering) required greater intelligence than in the warmer homelands. As noted previously, this simplistic use of environmental determinism was largely dismissed in the last century, but appears here as an "explanation" for population differences in IQ scores.

Lynn and Vanhanen attempted to show that "the intelligence of the population has been a major factor responsible for the national differences in economic growth and the gap in per capita income between rich and poor nations" (2002, p. xv). The authors draw two implications from their observations. First "the world needs a new international moral code based on the recognition of significant national differences in human mental abilities and consequent economic inequalities," and second "the rich countries' economic aid programs for the poor countries should be continued and some of these should be directed at attempting to increase the intelligence levels of the populations of the poorest countries by improvements in nutrition and the like" (2002, p. 196).

The study by Georgas *et al.* (2003) examines the intelligence of children in eleven cultural populations, using probability sampling. They employed WISC-III, a well-known battery of intelligence tests for children that were originally constructed in the USA (Wechsler, 1997). These populations are largely from western societies (e.g., Canada, Germany, Sweden, USA), but some are from Eastern Europe (Lithuania, Slovenia) and some are from East Asia (Japan, South Korea). The first goal of the project was to examine the structural similarity of the various tests across cultures: do they relate to each other in the same way in all cultures? The second goal of the project was to examine similarities and differences across cultures in the levels of intelligence scores obtained and to attempt to account for any differences. This second goal was pursued using the ecocultural framework.

Findings revealed substantial similarity in the structure of the test scores, which the authors claim to show "the universality of the factor equivalence of the WISC-III across these countries" (Georgas *et al.*, 2003, p. 299). Note that their claim for universality is limited to these countries. Findings also revealed relatively few differences in mean scores across cultures; however, the authors sought evidence for the source of these small differences in two country-level variables which they derived from the ecocultural framework: affluence and education. They found that these two features of the societies explained much of the variance in country-level scores: affluence correlated +.49 with the full scale WISC (+.43 with both the Verbal and Performance subscales), while education correlated +.68 with the full-scale scores (+.55 with Verbal, and +.63 with Performance).

There is a clear and large difference between the Lynn and the Georgas studies with respect to their concern for bias and validity. In the former, published IQ scores are simply assumed to be valid representations of the intelligence of cultural populations, while in the latter psychometric analyses were used to ensure that there was comparability in the data sets across cultures. There is also a clear difference between these two types of studies with respect to the process–competence–performance distinction. In the former, performance differences are readily inferred to imply competence and process differences, while in the latter, interpretations of performance differences are associated with ecological contexts and cultural practices.

Another important issue in understanding general intelligence scores is that they appear to vary over time. This effect, named the "**Flynn effect**" after the author who drew attention to it, shows that there have been massive gains in IQs in many countries over generations in the past century (Flynn, 1999, 2007). Initially, Flynn collected archival data on intelligence test scores from fourteen (mainly western) countries. Some data sets were from military draft registrants and were based on the same test that had been administered for many years. Other data sets came from (representative) standardization samples to norm a test. The military data included virtually all young men in a country, since entire age cohorts were examined for fitness to do compulsory military service. Increases in IQ over time were found in all countries included, with a median value of fifteen IQ points (or 1.0 standard deviation) in a single generation (since 1950). Flynn (1987) suggested that IQ tests do not measure intelligence as a general capacity, but have only a weak link to it. Most likely unidentified factors related to education play a role. Flynn's results are informative for cross-cultural research because they show that average performance on IQ tests in a population is far from stable and can change fairly dramatically in a relatively short time.

The Flynn effect was examined by Brouwers, Van de Vijver and Van Hemert (2009), using a meta-analysis of Raven's Progressive Matrices findings. The analysis employed a cross-cultural and historical design, using data from 798 samples from forty-five countries (N = 244,316), published between 1944 and 2003. Combined educational and economic indicators were used to provide a country-level score on GNP. They discovered "that the Flynn effect can be found in high as well as low GNP countries, although its size is moderated by education-related sample and country characteristics and seems to be smaller in developed than in emerging countries." This pattern suggests that the Flynn effect may be slowing down.

A major paradox in this set of results relates to the well-established finding through numerous studies with twins that IQ scores have a strong hereditary component (e.g., Bouchard, Lykken, McGue, Segal and Tellegen, 1990). If IQ is to some (perhaps large) extent rooted in our genes, how can such massive gains as found by Flynn come about in such a short period of time? In other words, if environmental factors "appear so feeble in twin studies of intelligence, how can they be so potent in IQ gains over time?" (Flynn, 2007, p. 83). Flynn's proposal is that "genetic differences between individuals (within an age cohort) are dominant only because they have hitched powerful environmental factors to their star. Trends over time (between cohorts) liberate environmental factors from the sway of genes and, once unleashed, they can have a powerful cumulative effect" (Flynn, 2007, p. 11;

see Richerson and Boyd, 2005, for a similar argument). That is, environmental and genetic factors are often linked and hence their relative influences are difficult to disentangle when seeking explanations for cultural differences.

Group differences in inborn capacities can only be inferred if the quality of the environment has been similar. As we shall see in Chapter 11 it is widely accepted that individual differences in general intelligence and cognitive abilities can be linked to genetic factors (Ceci and Williams, 1999; Sternberg and Grigorenko, 1997a). But this is very different from claiming that group differences are due (at least in part) to "race." Leading behavior geneticists like Plomin and De Fries (1998, p. 69) have emphasized this: "We cannot emphasize too much that genetic effects do not imply genetic determinism, nor do they constrain environmental interventions." Cognitive developmental processes are likely to reflect interactions between organism and environment, making inferences about the initial state of one of the components rather speculative (see Chapters 2 and 11).

Indigenous approaches

As we have just seen there is wide disagreement among researchers about the interpretation of cross-cultural differences in test scores (performances). Other researchers (who also accept the notion of intelligence as a useful summary label of the level of cognitive performance of individuals) go a step further and argue that intelligence as measured by (western-type) tests provides a highly biased account of what it means to be intelligent in other societies, where the cultural conceptualizations of intelligence may differ. Often such arguments refer to studies with unschooled populations in the majority world. Reviews of **indigenous conceptualizations** of intelligence can be found in Segall *et al.* (1999, ch. 6), Sternberg (2007) and Ruzgis (1994).

An important issue is the relationship between measures of indigenous intelligence and western measures. These have been found to be variable, depending on the tests used. Sternberg and colleagues (Sternberg, 2002; Sternberg, Nokes, Geissler, Prince, Okatcha, Bundy and Grigorenko, 2001) developed a test of practical intelligence (informal tacit knowledge for natural herbal medicines) for use with Dholuo children in Kenya. This test measured their ability to identify local medicines, and to say where they came from, and for what they are used. To assess the intelligence of children, two western tests were employed: the Raven Coloured Progressive Matrices Test, and the Mill Hill Vocabulary Scale. They found no correlation between the indigenous test scores and the scores on Raven's Matrices; however, they did find significant correlations with Mill Hill scores, but they were negative, rather than positive.

One possible interpretation of this surprising finding of a negative correlation was offered by Sternberg *et al.* (2001). This is that Dholuo parents do not value western education, and many of their children drop out of school before graduation in order to engage in farming, where indigenous knowledge is more useful. In this situation, some children have invested more in formal schooling than in acquiring practical knowledge; others do the opposite. This differential distribution of becoming competent in different ways can lead to the observed negative correlation between scores on indigenous tests and on at least one aspect of a western test.

However, standard intelligence tests have been found to predict school and job performance in Zambia (Serpell, 1993) and in other societies in the majority world (Irvine and Berry, 1988). Thus, we need to develop an understanding of a wide range of conceptualizations of intelligence, and to devise and use a wide range of assessment tools in order to gain a comprehensive picture of the range of cognitive abilities developed and expressed across cultures.

Two studies are now presented that illustrate how to approach this task. They are rooted in the field of indigenous cognition (Berry, Irvine and Hunt, 1988). This field assumes the existence of universal processes underlying cognitive functioning, but attempts to understand the cognitive life (competencies and performances) of cultural groups from within their own contexts and from their own points of view. This approach owes much to the broad tradition of ethnoscience (see Chapter 10, section on cognitive anthropology). Many of these studies have concluded that alternative views about human competence incorporate social and moral aspects, in addition to (narrowly) cognitive ones.

One study of how a particular cultural group defines intelligence is presented in Box 6.1. This was done by Berry and Bennett (1992) among the Cree people of Northern Canada. The community educational council had sought an answer to the question: "Toward what goals should we be educating our children?" They knew that the Euro-Canadian educational system was not working well for them and wanted to consider a Cree alternative. The psychometric part of the study is described in Box. 6.1.

Box 6.1 **Indigenous conceptions of intelligence**

This study attempted to discover the Cree conception of what it means to be "intelligent." After eliciting Cree terms, twenty words were written out in the Cree syllabic script on cards. The cards were given to sixty participants, all of whom were able to read the cards. They were asked to put the cards into piles on the basis of similarity of meaning. Multidimensional scaling revealed two dimensions (see Figure 6.1). Reading from left to right (on the horizontal axis) there is a movement from negative to positive evaluation, with the possible inclusion of a moral dimension as well. The vertical dimension may have something to do with openness or sensitivity.

Box 6.1 continued

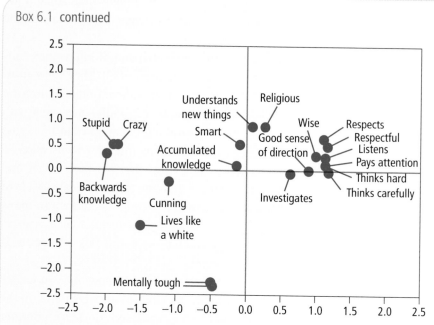

Figure 6.1 Two dimensions of cognitive competence among the Cree.

In Figure 6.1, there is a cluster of words on the right side and slightly above center (i.e., both sensitive and morally good) containing the words rendered in English as "wise," "respects," "respectful," "listens," "pays attention," "thinks hard" and "thinks carefully." This cluster constitutes the core meaning of competence among the Cree. The core idea of respect centers around knowledge of and personal engagement with people, animals, objects (both man-made and natural), the Creator and the land. Such respect for others in one's environment is a central value among many hunting and gathering peoples.

A second core term rendered as "pays attention" was just as often translated as "discipline" or "self-control." The Cree are not saying that individuals have a moral duty to listen to others and carry out what they say; they're telling us that listening to others is smart. The word most directly opposite the core cluster, the word which is therefore most distant from it on both dimensions (i.e., insensitive and morally bad) is rendered as "lives like a white," in the sense of behaving, thinking and comporting oneself like a non-Cree person!

It should be clear from this study that it would be very difficult to assess the Cree concept of intelligence with standard IQ tests. Moreover, if intelligence were measured with a test developed by the Cree, it would be difficult to make comparisons between scores on this Cree test and scores obtained by western groups on their tests. A study like this one leaves us with the question: how would it be possible to decide whether the Cree are more or less intelligent than some other cultural group (particularly urban, western societies), when their vision of the competent person is so different?

Despite such problems, one study did attempt a comparison of indigenous conceptions of intelligence (Fournier, Schurmans and Dasen, 1999). They drew findings from an earlier study by Dasen (1984) among the Baoule of Côte d'Ivoire who had a concept for intelligence (*n'glouele*) and employed similar measures with various samples of residents of a small French-speaking community in the Swiss Alps. Among the Baoule, the concept was explored during interviews with parents. The researchers found that it has numerous meanings that are both social and technological, but that emphasize the social more than the technological aspects of cognitive competence. These social aspects include a willingness to help (responsibility, obedience, honesty, politeness and reflection). The technological aspects include attention, observation, memory and manual dexterity; this last aspect is captured in the phrase "the hands are intelligent."

For a comparison, the Swiss alpine participants were asked how one can recognize whether a child is intelligent. In addition to the kinds of answers found in the Baoule study, some new aspects were found (such as modesty). However, Fournier *et al.* considered that the social/technological classification found in the African study could be used with the Swiss responses, and a comparison could be made. For the Baoule, the proportion of social meanings was 63 percent, and technological 37 percent. In contrast the Swiss responses were predominantly technological, which corresponds to the dominant western view of intelligence. However, there were variations in the ratio of social to technological meanings, depending on the language and age of the Swiss respondents: the more elderly farming participants who responded in patois (a local dialect) had social meanings predominate (65% versus 35%). The authors noted that despite this comparison at the level of meanings of intelligence, it would be impossible to assess the intelligence of these two cultural groups with a common test, just as the testing of any groups with a foreign test would be considered to be invalid.

Cognitive styles

The concept of cognitive styles occupies a middle ground between those that relate all cross-cultural differences in cognitive performance to a single underlying trait (such as "general intelligence") and those that distinguish a myriad of task-specific skills that do not generalize to other tasks (see the later section on contextualized cognition). Cognitive styles are "one's preferred way of processing information and dealing with tasks" (Zhang and Sternberg, 2006, p. 3). They serve as ways of organizing and using cognitive information that allow a cultural group and its members to deal effectively with problems encountered in daily living. Cognitive styles differ from general intelligence approaches in the sense that no absolute criterion (g) is used for the comparison of cognitive competence or performance among cultural groups. They differ from contextualized cognition approaches in the sense that some pattern of relationships among performances on cognitive tasks can be discerned. From an ecocultural perspective (see Box 1.1) cognitive styles are the result of the development of competence and of performances in relation to the adaptive needs of living in specific ecological and sociopolitical habitats.

An early and influential conceptualization of cognitive style has been that of Witkin (Witkin, Dyk, Paterson, Goodenough and Karp, 1962), who developed the dimension of the Field-Dependent/Field-Independent (FDI) cognitive style. In studies of perceptual and orientation abilities in air pilot trainees he noticed that a number of abilities were related to each other in a way that evidenced a "pattern," namely the tendency to rely primarily on internal (as opposed to external) frames of reference when orienting oneself in space. The FDI cognitive style is referred to by Witkin, Goodenough and Oltman (1979, p. 1138) as "extent of autonomous functioning." The construct refers to the extent to which an individual typically relies upon or accepts the physical or social environment as given, in contrast to working on it, for example by analyzing or restructuring it. Those who tend to accept or rely upon the external environment are relatively more field-dependent (FD), while those who tend to work on it are relatively more field-independent (FI). The construct is a dimension. Individuals have a characteristic "place" on this dimension with most falling in the broad middle range.

According to Witkin *et al.* the origins of FDI lie in early socialization experiences: those raised to be independent and autonomous were found to be relatively FI; in families with tighter control during socialization, relatively more FD was found. This socialization dimension, and the associated cognitive style, resemble the socialization dimension discussed in the enculturation and socialization section in Chapter 2 (assertion to compliance), and the distinction between independent and interdependent self-construals discussed in Chapter 5, section on the self in social context.

Two instruments have been central to assessing FDI. In the Embedded Figure Test (EFT), a simple figure has to be found embedded in a complex background. The speed with which a person can disembed the small figure from the background is an indicator of FI. A second test is the Portable Rod and Frame Test (PRFT); here the task is to judge the orientation of a rod that can be rotated inside a tilted square frame. The degree to which a person can rely on his or her own internal cues to judge the verticality of the rod, and ignore the influence of the tilted frame, is an indicator of FI (examples of AEFT can be found on the Internet in the section on cognitive style; Additional Topics, Chapter 6).

www.cambridge.org/berry

Cross-cultural research with the FDI dimension began with studies by Berry (1966), who employed two contrasting cultural groups. First, nomadic hunters and gatherers roam widely in pursuit of plants and animals, track their prey (using disembedding skills), and then return to their camps (organizing spatial information). They are also relatively loose in social structure and emphasize assertion in socialization. They were found to be relatively field-independent. In contrast, sedentary agriculturalists generally do not roam far from their fields, and do not need disembedding or related skills to find the crops that they have planted. They are also tight in social structure and emphasize compliance in socialization. They were found to be relatively field-dependent. However, those who had experienced acculturation, particularly those with more western schooling, were found to be more field-independent than those with less schooling. Thus, both reliance on hunting and more exposure to schooling were predictive of higher field independence (see Witkin and Berry, 1975 for a review).

In order to disentangle the effects of ecological and acculturation antecedents Berry *et al.* (1986) compared African Pygmy hunter-gatherer (Biaka) with agriculturalist villagers (Bagandu) living in the same geographical region as the Biaka. They found that the differences in cognitive style between the two groups were less than anticipated on the basis of their ecological engagement. This was perhaps because the Biaka are employed by the Bagandu for a few months each year as agricultural laborers, while the villagers do some trapping and hunting with the Biaka. Some findings showed that there was a difference between the two cultural groups on the African Embedded Figures Test, when differences in the second predictor (acculturation) were taken into account. The greater experience of western influences (especially schooling) among the Bagandu was predictive of higher field independence.

In some later studies less ambiguous results were obtained. Mishra, Sinha and Berry (1996) looked at three indigenous groups ("Tribals" or Adivasi) in the state of Bihar in India. Two groups were selected to represent a contrast between a nomadic hunting-gathering group and a sedentary agricultural group, while a third group consisted of former hunters who were recently settled as agriculturalists. A variety of tests (both cognitive style, such as embedded figures, and cognitive ability, such as pictorial interpretation) showed that hunting peoples were relatively more field-independent than the agricultural peoples, and those with high levels of intercultural contact (as an indicator of acculturation experience) were also more field-independent. In this study acculturative influences were stronger than those stemming from ecological context differences.

A recent study in India by Mishra and Berry (2008) sampled 400 children from four groups of Adivasi (Bihor and Oaron "tribal" groups) between 9 and 12 years old in the state of Bihar. The samples (100 each) were drawn from hunting-gathering, dry agriculture, irrigation agriculture and urban wage-earning communities. The most important result for cognitive style was that scores on an embedded figures test were highest for the hunting-gathering and wage-earning samples, and lowest in the two agricultural samples.

After some years in which less attention has been paid to FDI in cross-cultural studies, there has been a recent increase of interest in cognitive style because it provides an alternative way to view individual and group differences in cognitive activity (Kozhevnikov, 2007; Sternberg and Grigorenko, 1997b). Most evidence for FDI has been found in studies with subsistence-level populations. However, there have been extensions of sampling to industrial and post-industrial populations, showing that urban participants are more field-independent than agriculturalists, but not usually more that hunters (Berry, 1966, 1976; Berry, Bennett, Denny and Mishra, 2000; Mishra and Berry, 2008). There is a need for more research on urban and acculturating populations in order to examine the relevance of FDI for peoples in an increasingly globalized world.

Cognition East and West

In a recent program of research carried out by Nisbett and colleagues (e.g., Ji, Peng and Nisbett, 2000; Nisbett, 2003, 2006; Peng and Nisbett, 1999) a distinction is made between more holistic and more analytic ways of thinking. The former is seen as characteristic of East Asian populations, the latter of westerners, especially Euro-Americans. The basic proposition is that "there are indeed dramatic differences in the nature of Asian and European thought processes." Nisbett denies that "everyone has the same basic cognitive processes … or that all rely on the same tools for perception, memory, causal analysis, categorization and inference (Nisbett, 2003, p. xviii). These are strong claims, resembling the theoretical position of relativism that was outlined in Chapter 1. In a series of historical observations and empirical studies Nisbett and colleagues have laid the foundations for these claims.

In a historical analysis Nisbett began with observations about ancient Greece and China, arguing that they were "drastically different in ways that led to different economic, political and social arrangements" (Nisbett, 2003, p. 32). He noted that in China, "agricultural peoples need to get along with one another," whereas in Greece "hunting, herding, fishing and trade do not require living in the same stable community" (Nisbett, 2003, p. 34). He further argued that in agricultural communities "causality would be seen as located in the field or in the relation between object and the field" (Nisbett, 2003, p. 36). These observations were then linked to the cognitive style of field dependence (Nisbett, 2003, p. 42), and to the ecocultural basis of cognition (Uskul, Kitayama and Nisbett, 2009).

Examples of the kind of studies carried out by Nisbett and his colleagues have been presented in Nisbett (2003, 2006) and reviewed by Nisbett, Peng, Choi and Norenzayan (2001). Two studies will illustrate their empirical work. In one study, Ji, Peng and Nisbett (2000) examined the perception of co-variation between two objects presented on a split screen. Participants were asked to judge the strength of the relationship between two disparate objects. Chinese participants saw more co-variation than did US-American participants, and they were more confident about their judgments. The authors concluded that this difference represents a more holistic perceptual response to the environment. In the same study, they assessed the cognitive style (FID) of the participants, and found that the Chinese were relatively more FD, confirming the usual findings with agricultural peoples in the cross-cultural study of cognitive style reported in the last section.

In another study, Peng and Nisbett (1999) distinguished between differentiation in thinking (i.e., comparison of opposites and the selection of one as the correct position), and dialectical thinking (i.e., seeking reconciliation between opposites). In a series of experiments they found that Chinese students demonstrated relatively more preference for dialectical solutions when confronted with social conflict situations or logically contradictory information. US-American students were more inclined to polarize conflicting perspectives and to choose one alternative as correct. For example, US-Americans expressed somewhat less preference for dialectical proverbs in Yiddish, and gave higher plausibility ratings to their preferred alternative in the case of contradictory reports of research findings. In the latter case Chinese students were more inclined to give some credit to both reports.

Peng and Nisbett see their results as a reflection of two different cognitive traditions of East and West. They concluded: "We believe that dialectical versus nondialectical reasoning will turn out to be only one of a set of interrelated cognitive differences between Asians and Westerners" (1999, p. 750).

Two empirical studies have challenged the general conclusions drawn by Nisbett and colleagues. The first, by Rayner, Castelhano and Yang (2009), noted that some studies (e.g., Chua, Boland and Nisbett, 2005) reported that Chinese viewers spent less time looking at the focal objects in a scene and more time looking at the background of the scene than did their US-American counterparts. Chua *et al.* postulated that this was because of cultural differences in the prioritization of information (background or foreground). Rayner *et al.* (2009) examined whether there are cultural differences in how quickly eye movements are drawn to highly unusual aspects of a scene, employing US-American and Chinese viewers. Participants were presented with either a normal or an unusual/weird version. There were differences in responses between the normal and weird versions of the scenes. However, there was no evidence of any cultural differences between these two groups. They concluded that "[t]he present study, along with other recent reports, raises doubts about the notion that cultural differences can influence oculomotor control in scene perception" (2009, p. 254).

In a second critical study, Lee and Johnson-Laird (2006) postulated that since East Asians are considered to think holistically and dialectically (Nisbett, 2003), they should tolerate contradictions to a greater degree than westerners do. However, in neither of their experiments did they find any significant differences between the reasoning of East Asians and westerners. Instead, they found East Asians were no more likely than westerners to succumb to illusions of logical consistency, and they were no more likely than westerners to reason solely from their experience. More generally, they venture the view "that deductive competence is a cultural universal" (Lee and Johnson-Laird, 2006, p. 463). They base this view on the worldwide popularity of Sudoku puzzles, which depend solely on deduction. Further, they ask: "What effects, if any, does culture have on reasoning? One effect is likely to concern the contents of inferences: different cultures have different beliefs, and so the premises of their inferences, whether explicit or implicit, are likely to differ too. But, no robust evidence exists for cultural differences in the underlying cognitive processes of reasoning" (Lee and Johnson-Laird, 2006, p. 463). We consider this conclusion to be consistent with our moderate universalist position.

One limitation of two-culture comparisons (such as these East–West studies) is that the differences are uninterpretable (Campbell, 1970; see discussion in Chapter 12, p. 273). Hence, the extension of their work beyond these two cultures by Uskul *et al.* (2009) is an important step. They sampled farmers, fishers and herders in the Eastern Black Sea region of Turkey. This extension replicates the strategy of comparing groups within one ecological zone but who engage it in different cultural ways as reported in the section on cognitive styles. Based on the ecocultural framework, and previous findings, they predicted that farmers and fishers would be more holistic than herders. They used a Framed Line Test (much like the PRFT) which presents a square with a vertical line in the center. Participants were then presented another square of the same or different size; they were asked to draw a line that was identical to the line originally shown. There were two conditions; in one, the request was to draw the line in "absolute" length (absolute task), or in proportion to the height of the new square (relative task). They argued that "the absolute task would be facilitated by the ability to decontextualize or ignore the square frame and, thus, would be interfered with by holistic attention. The relative task would be facilitated by the inability to ignore the square frame" (Uskul *et al.*, 2009, p. 8554). Performance errors were calculated, with overall performance better on the relative task than the absolute task. In keeping with their prediction, farmers and fishers were more accurate in the relative task than herders; and herders were more accurate than the others in the absolute task. They concluded that, in keeping with the ecocultural hypothesis, farmers and fishers are more holistic than herders.

An important question regarding the claims of East–West cognition researchers is about the "depth" of these cognitive performance differences. In summarizing their work, the conclusions reached by Nisbett and colleagues are that "[m]ost of the time, in fact, Easterners and Westerners were found to behave in ways that were *qualitatively* distinct" (Nisbett, 2003, p. 191, emphasis added). This conclusion – that there are *qualitative* differences in basic processes – however, is not supported by their review of their own evidence. For example:

> Americans found it *harder* to detect changes in the background of scenes and Japanese found it *harder* to detect changes in objects in the foreground ... The *majority* of Koreans judged an object to be more similar to a group with which it shared a close family resemblance, whereas an even greater *majority* of Americans judged the object to be more similar to a group to which it could be assigned by a deterministic rule. When confronted with two apparently contradictory propositions, Americans *tended to* polarize their beliefs whereas Chinese *moved toward* equal acceptance of the two propositions. When shown a thing, Japanese are *twice as likely* to regard it as a substance than as an object and Americans are *twice as likely* to regard it as an object than as a substance. (Nisbett, 2003, pp. 191–193, emphases added)

The italicized terms in this passage all refer to *quantitative* rather than to *qualitative* differences in the cognitive *performances* of participants who represent the "East" and the "West." Two issues are important here. First, we see no evidence of qualitative differences in performance: apparently all participants could perform these tasks, but to different degrees; hence there can be no claim of a cognitive process being present in one group but absent in the other. Second, even if there were qualitative differences in *performance*, this would not permit an easy claim of there being differences in underlying basic cognitive *processes*. As argued in Chapter 1, the inferences required to go back from performance to process are complex, which these researchers seem not to examine.

We draw two conclusions from examining the work in this East–West program of research on culture and cognition. First, we consider that the performance differences presented are largely a matter of stylistic rather than qualitative differences in the cognitive life of populations in the East and West. Second, we observe important links between this body of work and the ecocultural approach to understanding the basis for human cognitive diversity, but now using rather novel quasi-experimental cognitive tasks. Taken together, these comments support our view that cultures and individuals develop ways of perceiving and cognizing their environments that allow them to best adapt to the demands that they confront in their daily lives.

Contextualized cognition

In contrast to the approaches discussed so far, that of contextualized cognition is one that criticizes grand theories that attempt to link all cognitive performances together with a presumed underlying general cognitive processor. This holds especially for cultural psychologists like Michael Cole and his colleagues. In a series of monographs (Cole, 1975, 1996; Cole, Gay, Glick and Sharp, 1971; LCHC, 1982; Scribner and Cole, 1981), they outlined a theory and methodology that attempts to account for specific cognitive performances in terms of particular features of the cultural context, and the use of specific cognitive operations; hence the name of contextualized cognition. Overviews of this approach have been presented by Cole (2006), and its application to human development in Cole and Engeström (2007). Much of this work has been stimulated by the sociocultural or sociohistorical tradition (Cole, 1988; Luria, 1976; Vygotsky, 1978; see also Valsiner and Rosa, 2007), and has links with research on "everyday cognition" (Schliemann *et al.*, 1997; see below).

In their 1971 monograph, Cole and his colleagues proposed that "people will be good at doing the things that are important to them, and that they have occasion to do often" (Cole *et al.*, 1971, p. xi), and concluded their volume with the proposition that "cultural differences in cognition reside more in the situations to which particular cognitive processes are applied, than in the existence of a process in one cultural group and its absence in another" (Cole *et al.*, 1971, p. 233). Their context-specific approach is characterized as a

formulation that retains the basic eco-cultural framework, but rejects the central processor assumption as the organizing metaphor for culture's effect on cognition. (LCHC, 1982, p. 674)

Instead of the universal laws of mind that control development "from above," the context-specific approach seeks to understand how cognitive achievements, which are initially context-specific, come to exert more general control over people's behavior as they grow older. The context-specific approach to culture and cognitive development takes "development within domains of activity" as its starting point; it looks for processes operating in the interactions between people within a particular setting as the proximal cause of the increasingly general cognitive competence. (LCHC, 1983, p. 299)

To substantiate their approach, Cole and his colleagues have produced a large volume of empirical studies and literature reviews (see Cole, 1992a, b, 1996). Their early studies (e.g., Cole *et al.*, 1971) were carried out among Kpelle school children and adults in Liberia, and US-American participants in the USA in a set of projects concerned with mathematics learning, quantitative behavior and some more complex cognitive activities (classification, memory and logical thinking). Their general conclusion from these, and many similar studies, is that much Kpelle cognitive behavior is "context-bound," and that it is not possible to generalize cognitive performances produced in one context to other contexts. In later writings (LCHC, 1982, 1983), they claim support for their position by critically reviewing the work of other researchers in such areas as infant development, perceptual skills, communication, classification and memory. Cole (1992a, b, 1996) has emphasized the concept of "modularity," which refers to the domain-specific nature of psychological processes as they have developed in the course of human phylogenetic history. In Cole's theory of cultural-historical psychology "modularity and cultural context contribute jointly to the development of mind" (1996, p. 198). As far as the conceptualization of culture is concerned, Cole's work has been influenced by Vygotsky and his school where ontogenetic development is seen as culturally mediated (see Chapter 2, section on culture as context for development).

Perhaps the major contribution to cross-cultural psychology from Cole's school has been the work challenging the views of Luria and others (e.g., Goody and Watt, 1968) that literacy has served as a "watershed" in the course of human history, meaning that preliterates cannot, while literates can, do certain abstract cognitive operations (Scribner and Cole, 1981). Among the Vai people (also of Liberia) Scribner and Cole were able to find samples of persons who were illiterate as well as samples who were literate in various scripts, namely (1) in a local Vai script, (2) in Arabic taught to those who attend the Quran school or (3) in English taught in western-styled schools. This eliminated the usual confound between schooling and literacy as contributors to cognitive test performance.

Using a battery of cognitive tasks, covering a wide range of cognitive activity (e.g., memory, logical reasoning) Scribner and Cole sought to challenge the idea that literacy transforms the intellect in a general way. They found that there were general performance effects of western-style schooling, but not of other forms of literacy. However, there were some specific test performances that were related to particular features of the Vai script and of the education in Arabic. They concluded with respect to the Vai script that

Instead of generalized changes in cognitive ability, we found localized changes in cognitive skills manifested in relatively esoteric experimental settings. Instead of qualitative changes in a person's orientation to language, we found differences in selected features of speech and communication ... our studies among the Vai provide the first direct evidence that literacy makes some difference to some skills in some contexts. (Scribner and Cole, 1981, p. 234)

In interpreting their results, they noted that Vai literacy is a "restricted" one, in the sense that not many people know and use it, and those who do use it for only limited purposes: "Vai script literacy is not essential either to maintain or to elaborate customary ways of life ... At best, Vai script literacy can be said to engage individuals with familiar topics" (Scribner and Cole, 1981, p. 238) rather than opening up new experiences.

One possible reason for a lack of a general change in intellectual life is the rather limited role that literacy plays in Vai society. A study among the Cree of Northern Ontario (Berry and Bennett, 1989) is relevant to this problem. As for the Vai, Cree literacy is present in a form (a syllabic script) that is not associated with formal schooling. However, most Cree are functionally literate in the script; it is less restricted than among the Vai since it is very widely used by many people, and for many purposes (e.g., telephone books, airline safety sheets and public notices). The results of this study also found no evidence for a general cognitive enhancement (assessed by an elaborated version of Raven's Progressive Matrices), but some evidence for abilities that involved the same mental operations (rotation and spatial tasks) that are important in using this particular script. Thus, also in this study on the effects of literacy there is no evidence that a major shift in ways of thinking has taken place. The "watershed" view of the role of literacy in the course of human history thus has to be rejected, at least with respect to its effects on individual thought; the possible social and cultural consequences of literacy are not addressed by these studies.

Cole and his colleagues have not typically posed the question of inter-test relations of their data, for example in searching for "patterns of abilities" as proposed by Ferguson (1956). Instead they have typically considered the influence of one single cultural experience on one cognitive performance. The problem with considering culture as a set of discrete situation-linked experiences has been identified by Jahoda (1980). However, Cole (e.g., 1992a, b) does appear to subscribe to the view that cultural experiences are intertwined, rather than being a discrete set of situations: "the real stuff of culture is believed to reside in the interaction among elements; the independent variables are not independent" (LCHC, 1982, p. 645).

In the end, then, there may be an evolving rapprochement between Cole and those who seek some degree of generalization from culture-cognition research. Cole remains convinced of his early assertion, namely that non-performance on a particular cognitive task should not be generalized either to an expectation of non-performance on other tasks, or to the absence of the necessary underlying cognitive competence or process.

Cole and his colleagues (e.g., Cole and Engeström, 2007) have promoted the application of their research in the sociocultural tradition to the improvement of human development, not only within the school system, but more broadly in society. Their emphasis is on practice, following the views of Vygotsky (1997, p. 205): "Practice sets the tasks and serves as the supreme judge, as its truth criterion." That is, there is a need to put into practice what is found in research; if it works, it is valid. In a framework that they call "the fifth dimension," Cole and Engeström (2007, p. 495) propose a fundamental interaction between the university, the community and the daily communal activities of individuals. These interventions serve as the validation of the close relationships between cultural contexts and situations, and the development of specific cognitive competencies.

Another branch of the literature on contextualized cognition goes by the name of everyday cognition (e.g., Schliemann, Carraher and Ceci, 1997). This approach is based on descriptive accounts of the cognitive demands and problem-solving strategies found in a particular group. Fascinating skills have been described, often by cultural anthropologists, including, for example, the navigation of boats by the Pulawat across large distances in the Pacific without a compass (Gladwin, 1990), counting among the Oksapmin, who have a number system based on parts of the body (Saxe, 1981) and weaving in various societies (e.g., Childs and Greenfield, 1980; Rogoff and Gauvain, 1984; Tanon, 1994). The social aspects of cognition and learning tend to be emphasized (Lave and Wenger, 1991).

Studies of everyday cognition have generally shown limited transfer and generalization of learning from one class of situations (domain) to another, including from school to non-school situations (Segall *et al.*, 1999). However, one also finds that authors see culture-specific knowledge and skills as the outcome of more general modes of teaching and learning that differ from those prominent in the western school setting. Examples include "scaffolding" (e.g., Greenfield and Lave, 1982) and "apprenticeship" (Rogoff, 2003), which refer to the support that (young) learners receive in everyday situations where they try to master tasks by beginning to carry them out. Such examples of generalized styles of learning in concrete situations, as opposed to (western) learning in school settings away from concrete situations, show that the categories of research traditions are often more overlapping than a textbook, like the present one, will reflect.

In an extension of this tradition, Wang, Ceci, Williams and Kopko (2004) criticize the longstanding approach to understanding cognitive competence in which "the subject is viewed as a solitary actor who possesses a fixed computational processor, and the role, if any, of culturally updated, continuously revised processing is downplayed." Instead, they propose a framework that: "posits the dynamic interplay of four factors that shape the competence: cultural artifacts, cognitive domains, interpersonal contexts, and individual schemata" (Wang, Ceci, Williams and Kopko, 2004, p. 225). In this approach, everyday experiences serve as the starting point for the examination of the developing cognitive competencies of the child. They especially emphasize the "cultural functionality and adaptability of cognitive competence and argue that the development of any cognitive competence is a result of the dynamic interplay between the four aspects of cultural influences in creating competent members of each human society" (Wang, Ceci, Williams and Kopko, 2004, p. 227). In this view, we observe many similarities between a number of the approaches reviewed in this chapter to understanding the links between contexts and competence: competence is developed as an adaptation to the contexts (ecological, cultural, situational) in which individuals carry out their daily lives; competence is expressed in culturally variable ways; and competence changes over time as new contexts are encountered during the course of ontogenetic development.

Conclusions

It is clear from the material in this chapter that ecological and sociocultural factors play a large role in human cognition. It is equally clear that such interactions cannot be fruitfully explored in relation to naive questions about which groups are smarter than others. Rather, some important distinctions between cognitive process, competence and performance reveal the complexity of the relationships. This chapter has been organized according to the extent to which authors generalize from their data, and are willing to make inferences from performances to competencies, and further to underlying processes or capacities. Obviously, interpretations referring to inborn group differences, linked to the notion of race, make the most far-reaching claims. The postulate of a single or unitary cognitive processor (such as g), or of a great divide between populations in the development of this processor, finds little support in the materials reviewed in this chapter. This very general approach carries on the ethnocentric traditions of early comparisons between "primitive" and "civilized" peoples, and has become less and less presented in contemporary research as a valid approach. The three alternatives reviewed all accept that understanding local cultural contexts is an important foundation for the assessment and interpretation of differences in cognitive performance. They differ mainly in the extent to which these contexts are viewed as providing complex patterns of experiences (for example, in the cognitive styles and East–West approaches) or as more discrete situations or activity domains in which individuals have an opportunity to practice and learn specific competencies, and to exhibit them as culturally appropriate performances. How to balance or integrate all these views remains a difficult question.

One important issue arises from these various approaches to examining the relationship between culture and cognition that have been examined in this chapter. There is a strong contrast in assessment procedures between researchers using the general intelligence and cognitive-style approaches, and those employed by "East–West" and contextualized cognition researchers. The first two approaches use multiple items, examine their intercorrelations, and establish their reliabilities and validities. The latter develop and use situations and tasks that are usually single assessments of the presumed underlying cognitive activity. It is difficult to accept their interpretations of what their tasks mean, since they do not establish that the tasks measure what they claim they measure (i.e., there are no validity estimates). Moreover, they do not usually examine possible links among performance on the various tasks intended to assess the same construct (i.e., there are no reliability estimates). We are left with the choice between accepting their interpretation of the many evident performance differences between cultures as indicating differences in competencies or even processes, or of rejecting them because they lack the usual safeguards that attend the meaning of tasks or of making comparisons between cultures.

No simple summary or conclusion is possible in the face of such diversity. Our own reading of this varied set of ideas and data is that the main characteristics of cognitive functions and processes appear to be common to all human beings, as universally shared properties of our intellectual life. Cognitive competencies are developed according to some culturally shared rules; but they can result in highly varied performances that are responsive to ecological contexts, and to cultural norms and social situations encountered both during the course of socialization and at the time of testing.

KEY TERMS

cognitive styles • contextualized cognition • everyday cognition • Flynn effect • "g" • general intelligence • indigenous conceptualizations (of intelligence) • literacy

FURTHER READING

Mishra, R. C. (1997). Cognition and cognitive development. In J. W. Berry, P. R. Dasen and T. S. Saraswathi (eds.), *Handbook of cross-cultural psychology, Vol. II, Basic processes and human development* (pp. 143–176). Boston: Allyn & Bacon.

A review chapter that examines both cognitive development and performance in relation to cultural contexts in which they take place.

Sternberg, R., and Grigorenko, E. (eds.) (2004). *Culture and competence: Contexts of life success*. Washington, DC: APA Press.

A compilation of chapters portraying a number of perspectives on how cultural contexts influence the development of cognitive competence.

Van de Vijver, F. J. R. (1997). Meta-analysis of cross-cultural comparisons of cognitive test performance. *Journal of Cross-Cultural Psychology*, 28, 678–709.

A comprehensive examination of many studies of cognitive abilities across cultures.

7 | Emotion

CONTENTS

In this chapter we focus on various lines of research that have been developed in order to answer the question to what extent emotions are similar or different across cultures. First, we focus on dimensional approaches. Similar to what has been done in cross-cultural research on personality (Chapter 5) and cognition (Chapter 6), some emotion researchers have tried to reveal common dimensions underlying the many emotions that we experience in daily life and to see whether these dimensions are the same (equivalent) across cultures. The second section addresses research on emotion words. In the absence of a clear definition of emotion terms, the words that people use in daily language have become important tools for cross-cultural researchers. The central question here is whether linguistic differences (differences in words) can be used to infer psychological differences (differences in experience; see also Chapter 8). The third section focusses on studies of specific aspects of emotions. Many contemporary researchers no longer try to define emotion in terms of a single criterion. Rather they use a **componential approach**, which assumes that emotions can be defined in many different emotion components (e.g., thoughts, feelings, action tendencies, psychophysiological experiences). An important feature of this approach is that cross-cultural differences are assumed to be independent for each component (Mesquita, Frijda and Scherer, 1997). Special attention is paid to the facial expression of emotions, which has been central to many of the first cross-cultural studies on emotion. We end the chapter with some conclusions and a moderate universalist integration of the available evidence.

One of the first documented cross-cultural studies was on emotions (Darwin, 1872/1998), but systematic studies of this field did not start until the 1970s. By now emotion has become a popular area of cross-cultural research. The increase in the number of studies, however, has not led to more consensus about the extent to which emotions are universal or culture-specific phenomena. One reason for the disagreement is that emotion is an ill-defined construct (Scherer, 2005). Everybody knows what emotions are because we experience them on a daily basis; however, psychologists have been struggling to define emotion in a scientific manner. Many have tried to find what they thought to represent the "essence" of emotions. In the early days of psychology, Wundt (1893) posited that at the core of the experience of feelings are the dimensions pleasantness–unpleasantness, tension–relaxation and activity–passivity (see the section on dimensional approaches below in this chapter). Later psychologists were not satisfied with this definition and looked for other emotion aspects. Perhaps the most well-known examples are James (1884) and Lange (1885), who independently posited that perceptions of changes in the body form the essence of emotional experience. This psychophysiological definition was later also challenged by other researchers who tried to define the essence of emotion in different ways, for example by cognitions (Schachter and Singer, 1962; Valins, 1972), action readiness (Arnold, 1960), facial expression (Ekman, 1992) or social symbols (Averill, 1974). A discussion about the relative merits of each of these definitions goes beyond the scope of this book. What is important for this chapter is that researchers who disagree about cross-cultural similarities and differences in emotions often also define emotions in different ways. Researchers may use the same emotion words, such as "happiness," "anger" or "shame" to refer to very different types of phenomena, such as brain states, behaviors or phenomenological experiences (Kagan, 2007). So, sometimes disagreements that on the surface seem to be about cross-cultural differences are actually rooted in disagreements over the definition of emotion.

Another reason for disagreement among researchers is that there is little consensus on the criteria that should be used to decide whether an emotion is universal or culture-specific. Claims to the effect that cross-culturally an emotion is "similar" or "different" are seldom stated precisely. As we explained in Chapter 1, we hold the position that psychological processes (emotions) are similar across cultures but that their behavioral manifestations (emotion-based behavior) can vary substantially from one culture to another. However, many researchers argue that emotion processes themselves are also different across cultures. So, the question is to what extent cross-cultural differences in performance can be generalized to differences in competences or even processes (see the section on generalization in Chapter 1). The disagreement is difficult to resolve because there is little consensus on the interpretation of the empirical evidence (see Box 7.1). For example, if one culture lacks a word for an emotion that is clearly distinguished in another culture, does this mean that their emotional lives are also different? It is difficult to answer this question especially because – as we noted above – different researchers use different indicators to study emotions across cultures.

Box 7.1 **Same data, different interpretation**

As we have seen in Chapter 1, differences in the interpretation of cross-cultural data do not only depend upon the different interpretive positions that researchers take but also on the way that cross-cultural data are explained. The same data can sometimes be explained differently. An instructive example is the discussion between Russell (1994) and Ekman (1994) on the explanation of cross-cultural data on the recognitions of facial expressions accompanying emotion.

In the 1980s the notion of six or seven basic emotions that could be distinguished on the basis of their facial expressions had become widely accepted as a psychological "fact." However, the idea that some emotions are basic whereas others are blends or mixes as well as the idea that emotions are universal phenomena was not readily accepted by all researchers. One, very elaborate critique of the cross-cultural evidence for basic emotions was written by Russell, who started the summary of his paper with the telling sentence: "Emotions are universally recognized from facial expressions – or so it has been claimed" (1994, p. 102). Russell criticized many aspects of the support for universality, among which was the very notion of universality itself, which he argued to be rather imprecise.

Russell especially questioned the validity of the method through which evidence for universality was gathered. Generally, participants are shown a picture of a person displaying a facial expression which is accompanied by a set of emotion words ("joy," "anger," "fear," "sadness," "disgust" and "surprise"). Participants indicate which emotion is represented in the expression. The idea is that if there were no relation between expression and emotion at all each word would be chosen about as often; participants would essentially choose a word at random. If one word is chosen significantly more frequently than would be expected on the basis of chance (e.g., 1/6 or 16.67% in the case of six alternatives) this is taken as evidence for a systematic relation. Previous research had shown such significant results in many countries, including both western, non-western and even some non-industrialized societies. However, absolute recognition levels were lower in Asian and African than in European and American samples, sometimes even substantially lower. Russell argued that differences in recognition level suggested that the link between emotions and facial expressions may

Box 7.1 continued

not be as universal as assumed. If they were linked, he would expect a very high level of recognition in all countries.

In a sharp rebuttal, Ekman (1994) argued that none of the issues raised by Russell undermined his view on the basic emotions as universal. He argued that Russell put up a straw man of the universalist account in the sense that perfect agreement among people was never expected. He argued in favor of a *neurocultural* view, which emphasized two sets of determinants of facial expressions: a neuro-evolutionary view on the universal aspects and a cultural view (notably in the form of display rules) for the variable aspects. Because both determinants influence recognition of facial expressions the matching of emotion words to facial expressions is inherently imperfect. Therefore, according to Ekman, differences in absolute recognition scores do not say anything about universality. The only thing that matters is whether recognition in each culture is statistically higher than would be expected on the basis of chance. Ekman granted that there were limitations to the studies, but that these cannot explain why recognition was significantly higher than chance in all societies. If anything, they would have introduced error in the measurement lowering recognition scores and making the finding of universal recognition even stronger. In a final reply Russell (1995) conceded some minor points, but, not surprisingly, the major differences of opinion remained substantially unchanged.

It is instructive to see that Russell and Ekman used the same cross-cultural data to come to very different conclusions with regard to the question of whether emotions are universally recognized from facial expressions. This underlines the importance of knowing the theoretical positions of researchers (see Chapter 1, pp. 11–20) in trying to understand debates in the literature. It also illustrates how cross-cultural data are not necessarily the most important; most discussions in cross-cultural psychology of emotions are on the interpretation of data (see Chapter 12).

Van Hemert, Poortinga and Van de Vijver (2007) carried out a meta-analysis of 190 cross-cultural emotion studies in order to see to what extent cross-cultural variance in emotion measures could be explained by different factors. They found 27.9 percent of the variance could be explained by culture-level factors, such as political system, values and religiosity. However, they also found that 13.8 percent of the variance could be explained by method-related factors such as sampling error and sample fluctuations. This means that a substantial proportion of cross-cultural differences need not be the consequence of culture but rather of methodological factors in the study. Finally, they also found that almost 60 percent of the variance remained unexplained. These results are good to keep in mind when reading the empirical evidence in this chapter.

Dimensional approaches

When we ask people to name the emotions they have experienced, we usually obtain a long and diverse list. A common strategy among researchers is to see whether this complexity can be reduced to a limited number of underlying dimensions. Not only does this simplify the analysis of emotions; dimensions also tend to be less susceptible to cultural bias than individual emotions (see Chapter 12, p. 293). An important precursor of research on emotion dimensions has been the landmark research project conducted by Osgood (1977; Osgood, May and Miron, 1975) that originated in an effort to capture the subjective culture of members of various groups. It should be noted that this research did not focus only on the meaning of emotion words per se, but rather on the affective meaning of words in general.

Some words are difficult to translate from one language to another. For example, Triandis and Vassiliou (1972) found that Greeks tend to describe themselves as *philotimous*. There is no direct English equivalent of the concept of *philotimo*. In an attempt to communicate what it means Triandis and Vassiliou wrote: "A person who has this characteristic is polite, virtuous, reliable, proud, has a 'good soul', behaves correctly, meets his obligations, does his duty, is truthful, generous, self-sacrificing, tactful, respectful, and grateful" (1972, pp. 308–309). This description captures the objective or denotative meaning of the word *philotimous* in quite a detailed manner, but on the basis of this description would non-Greeks really understand what the word means, including its emotional and metaphoric tone for Greeks? This question is a matter of the subjective or connotative meaning.

Osgood, Suci and Tannenbaum (1957) developed the Semantic Differential Technique (SDT) in order to capture the connotative meaning of words (see Box 7.2). People are given a word (e.g., *philotimous*) and asked to rate it on a number of seven-point scales, which represent three factors: evaluation (good–bad), potency (strong–weak) and activity (active–passive). Together these factors define a three-dimensional space of affective meaning, in which any word in a language can be positioned.

Osgood *et al.* (1975) applied the SDT in thirty cultures to rate 620 concepts, resulting in the *Atlas of affective meaning*. Some concepts were found to have a similar affective meaning in all cultures. These were called universals. For example, "brightness" scored universally higher on evaluation (i.e., was more positive) than "darkness"; "darkness" scored higher on potency; "red" scored lower than "blue" on evaluation but higher on activity. Some concepts called sub-universals had a similar meaning only in specific clusters of societies, whereas others, called uniquenesses, showed a different meaning in one specific society. An example of a culturally unique meaning is the relatively positive evaluation of "being aggressive" in the USA. Osgood gives as a reason that in this country aggression

Box 7.2 **The Semantic Differential Technique**

The Semantic Differential Technique (SDT) is a method to assess the affective meaning of any word in any language. It involves the rating of a word on a set of bipolar adjectives (see example below). Together, underlying the ratings on these adjectives are three dimensions of affective meaning: evaluation (how positive or negative is a word), potency (how strong or weak is a word) and activation (how active or passive is a word). Rating a word on the bipolar adjectives results in a position in a three-dimensional space of affective meaning; this space has been shown to be universal across many languages. In this way the affective meaning of words in different languages can be compared irrespective of whether the denotative meaning of these words is the same.

The development of the SDT and its cross-cultural application took more than fifteen years (Osgood *et al*., 1975). In a first phase, 100 nouns (e.g., "house," "fruit," "cloud," "hunger," "freedom," "money" and "policeman") were rated on a set of fifty bipolar adjective pairs by 100 teenage boys in each of thirty communities. These adjectives were chosen by means of a computational procedure in which their denotative meaning did not play any role; they were not even translated into English. The assumption was that all local adjective pairs represented the same underlying meaning dimensions. Ratings of all thirty cultures were analyzed together in what is called a "pancultural" factor analysis, showing a very clear three-dimensional structure. When adjectives that loaded very high on these dimensions in each culture were translated into English it was evident that the meaning of the three-dimensional structure was very similar. This meant that the three dimensions of evaluation, and potency, and activity could be used to compare the affective meaning of words across languages and cultures.

For practical purposes, the second phase of the project saw the development of a short form of the SDT for each culture, consisting of the four local scales with the highest loadings on each of the three factors. These short forms were the basis of the data from thirty cultures that formed the basis of the famous *Atlas of Affective Meaning* (Osgood *et al*., 1975).

also implies being competitive in sports and at school and that it does not so much imply intentional injury to others – the more common meaning elsewhere. Another example is the low potency and high activity of the color black among Indian students in Delhi. Local informants rated "black" high on activity; this was ascribed to the association of black with the god Krishna and with hair, and the low potency was ascribed to the lower status of a dark skin.

The work by Osgood showed that the affective meaning of any word can be described in terms of three dimensions. Later studies have examined whether these three dimensions can also be used to capture the meaning of the many emotion words that we have in our languages. For example, Russell (1980) gave participants a list of twenty-eight emotion words and asked them to sort these on the basis of how similar or different they were. Similarity ratings were analyzed by means of multidimensional scaling. He found that only two dimensions were needed to adequately describe the differences of emotion words: evaluation and activity. When all emotions were plotted in this two-dimensional space, a circle-like structure appeared, called the circumplex model of affect. Emotions were positive and active (e.g., delighted), positive and passive (e.g., serene), negative and active (e.g., afraid) or negative and passive (e.g., sad). In a cross-cultural extension Russell (1983; Russell, Lewicka and Niit, 1989) found the same two-dimensional solution in a variety of languages (Chinese, Croatian, Gujarati, Japanese). It has been noted, though, that universality of affective dimensions does not imply that affect is equally important across cultures for describing everyday experiences (see Barrett, Mesquita, Ochsner and Gross, 2007). For example, Japanese respondents (when compared to US respondents) tend to emphasize affective states less frequently in reports of their experiences (Mesquita and Karasawa, 2002).

Fontaine, Scherer, Roesch and Ellsworth (2007) further explored the meaning of emotion words across languages. Instead of asking for similarity sorting, they asked participants in Belgium (Dutch-speaking), Switzerland (French-speaking) and the UK to rate twenty-eight emotion terms on 144 emotion components. They found not a two-dimensional structure like Russell (1980, 1983) did, but rather a four-dimensional structure. The first three dimensions essentially replicated Osgood's SDT dimensions, but a fourth was added, namely an unpredictability factor. These structures were very similar across all cultures, enabling these researchers to compare the extent to which emotion words in different languages refer to a similar or rather different meaning.

To summarize, the meaning of emotion words can be captured in a limited set of dimensions, which are similar across cultures. These universal dimensions can be the starting point for interpreting cultural differences in emotion meaning, such as "being aggressive" in the USA. It is very unlikely that there will be cultures in which none of the dimensions from the Osgood studies will be found. Some studies may find only a selection of these dimensions (Russell, 1983) whereas others may find additional dimensions (Fontaine *et al.*, 2007).

Emotion and language

Dimensional approaches may enable cross-cultural researchers to compare the affective meaning of emotion concepts, but they are less informative about actual emotion experiences in a culture. Emotions are not just experienced as combinations of evaluation, activation and potency, but rather as a relatively coherent set of other features, including appraisals, bodily changes, action tendencies and behaviors. For example, in order to understand what makes experiences of anger and of fear distinct, it seems insufficient to note that they are both negative in evaluation, high in activation, but that anger is strong (high potency) whereas fear is weak. Many researchers study emotions as distinct states or processes rather than as dimensions. However, this leads to the problem of defining what these distinct states or processes are.

As we have seen in the introduction to this chapter, emotions have defied unambiguous definition for a long time; there is no single criterion to distinguish one emotion from another. Many researchers revert to natural language instead when describing different emotions. Most languages possess at least several, and often many words that describe different emotion experiences (see Russell, 1991). When people say that they are happy, sad, disappointed, envious, surprised or proud, there seems to be a tendency among psychologists to assume that each word refers to a distinct emotion experience (Sabini and Silver, 2005). This leads to problems when studying emotions cross-culturally because languages differ substantially in the emotion terms that are used.

Ethnographers have described many emotions that are culture-specific in the sense that no clear equivalent can be found in other languages. These have been termed **culture-specific emotion concepts**. Such descriptions are often very detailed, linking differences in emotion words to culture-specific meanings. In other cases, emotions that were considered as very basic do not seem to be found in particular cultures, such as the absence of a word for sadness in Tahiti (Levy, 1984). A summary table with about twenty cases where a word for a basic emotion appears to be missing in some language can be found in Russell (1991).

Lutz (1988) described emotional life on Ifaluk, a Micronesian atoll. She analyzed two emotions that have no equivalent in the English language: *fago* (an amalgam of what in English is expressed as compassion, love and sadness) and *song* (translated as "justifiable anger"). Like anger, "*song* is considered an unpleasant emotion that is experienced in a situation of perceived injury to self or to another" (1988, p. 156). Unlike anger, *song* is not so much about what is personally disliked as about what is socially condemned. There are other words that refer to forms of anger, but these are clearly distinguishable from "the anger which is a righteous indignation, or justifiable anger (*song*), and it is only this anger which is morally approved" (1988, p. 157). Another example is the elaborate descriptions by Wierzbicka (e.g., 1998) of differences between the German words *Angst* (anxiety), which is fear without an object to be afraid of, and *Furcht* (fear), which has a specific object (being afraid of something). *Angst* is a salient term in German, representing a basic emotion rooted in the writings of the sixteenth-century theologian

Luther, who like many of his contemporaries was struggling with the uncertainties of life and of life after death. A third example is the description by Menon and Shweder (1994) of the meaning of *lajja* in Oriya, a language spoken in India. There seems to be no single emotion word in English to translate this emotion, which can be described as respectful restraint.

Other examples of culture-specific emotion concepts are the Japanese concept of *amae* (see Chapter 5), referring to feelings of depending upon and presuming other people's benevolence to indulge in one's needs (Doi, 1973); the Ilongot (Philippines) concept of *liget*, referring to feelings of energy, anger and passion, but which also covers feelings of grief, being associated with the practice of headhunting (Rosaldo, 1980); the Javanese *wedi, isin, sunkan*, which can all be translated as shame in English (Geertz, 1959); and the Malay concept of *amuk*, referring to an uncontrollable feeling of rage. Sometimes, language-specific concepts are adopted in other languages. For example, amok is now a regular word in the English language. Another example is the German emotion word *Schadenfreude* (pleasure over someone else's misfortunes), which was adopted in English slightly over a century ago.

A central question raised by these observations is what do the linguistic differences mean for the experience of emotions? This question clearly relates to distinctions of the Sapir–Whorf hypothesis in Chapter 8. Relativist scholars tend to attribute more significance to linguistic differences than universalist scholars do. For example, Lutz argued that "emotional meaning is fundamentally structured by particular cultural systems and particular social and material environments. The claim is made that emotional experience is not precultural but *preeminently* cultural" (1988, p. 5, italics in the original). Barrett (2006) proposed a categorization view of emotions, stating that "there is cultural variation in the experience of emotion that is intrinsically driven by cultural differences in emotion categories and concepts" (2006, p. 39). In a similar vein Wierzbicka (1999, p. 26) stated that "whether or not two feelings are interpreted as two different instances of, essentially, 'the same emotion' or as instances of 'two different emotions' depends largely on the language through the prism of which these feelings are interpreted; and that prism depends on culture." An overview of studies suggesting that language does have a bearing on emotion perception and experience has been given by Barrett, Lindquist and Gendron (2007), who summarized their findings as a language-as-context hypothesis. This hypothesis says that "emotion words (implicitly or explicitly) serve as an internal context to constrain the meaning of a face during an instance of emotion perception" (2007, p. 327).

Universalist scholars tend to acknowledge the difference in meaning of emotion words, but do not attach as much psychological significance to these differences. Frijda, Markam, Sato and Wiers (1995, p. 121) summarized the main issue as follows: "One can assume that there exist words ('emotion words') that dictate the way things are seen; or one can assume that there exist things ('emotions') that are given names and thus have words assigned to them." Like many universalist scholars, they tend to be more in favor of the second option, assuming that emotion processes can be cross-culturally similar even if lexicons differ (e.g., Ekman, 1994; Scherer and Wallbott, 1994). It would seem that the burden of proof in this discussion lies more with the universalist than with the relativist position, because we have seen many examples of cultural differences in the meaning of emotion concepts. Tests of the universalist position have been carried out along several lines of research.

One way to look for evidence for universals in emotion experience is to compare the ways that emotions are described in various languages. Kövecses (2000) analyzed emotion metaphors in a variety of languages and came to the conclusion that there was a notable similarity in the type of metaphors, even if the specific content of metaphors differed. For example, anger in Chinese, English, Hungarian and Japanese is described in "container metaphors." The body is a container and anger is a hot substance in the container. Examples are "he was bursting with anger" (English), "anger was boiling inside him" (Hungarian), "anger boils at the bottom of the stomach" (Japanese) and "one's *qi* wells up like a mountain" (Chinese). It is clear that these metaphors can sometimes be quite specific to a language or culture. For example, in Chinese anger is related to an excess of *qi*, which refers to energy flowing through the body. However, at the same time, it is also clear that the metaphors share important characteristics, suggesting that anger is experienced in quite similar ways.

Fontaine, Poortinga, Setiadi and Markam (2002) compared the meaning of emotion words between Indonesia (Bahasa Indonesia) and the Netherlands (Dutch) in an empirical way. In the first phase of their research, they collected a broad array of prototypical emotion words in both countries. The 120 most prototypical terms were then sorted on similarity by students in both countries, yielding the three-dimensional Osgood structure. So far they had worked with local emotion terms. In the second phase they used several independent sources (e.g., dictionaries, bilinguals) to see whether some terms could be considered language equivalent between the two languages. Forty-two pairs were found to be cognitively equivalent (i.e., occupying the same space in a three-dimensional solution). All emotion terms were then entered again into an analysis in which the forty-two equivalent terms had the same position for the two groups and in which no constraints were imposed on the other terms. This common solution accounted for 87 percent of the variance in the Indonesian and Dutch sample. Thus, imposing a common structure hardly affected the cognitive representation of emotional experiences in either of the two samples.

Another way to look for universals is to see whether culture-specific emotion words can be understood by members of another culture. Such a study was carried out by Frank, Harvey and Verdun (2000). Following descriptions of five forms of shame in China by Bedford (1994), they wrote different scenarios that captured these distinct forms and they prepared scales (e.g., feeling helpless, disgraced myself, wishing to hide) on which these scenarios had to be rated. Analyses of the responses by US-American students to these scenarios showed that the distinction between five types of Chinese shame could be largely recovered, suggesting that US-Americans do recognize the varieties of shame distinguished by Chinese.

A final approach is not to look at the meaning of emotion words, but rather at the experience or expression of emotions across cultures. Linguistic differences in the emotion domain are taken as a fact and experiences are compared across cultural and linguistic communities. When similarities in experiential components of emotions are found, this is interpreted to mean that linguistic differences are not very important for emotion experiences. One study that used this approach to directly test the effect of emotion words on emotion experiences was done by Breugelmans and Poortinga (2006; Box 7.3). They showed that Rarámuri Indians from Mexico did have distinct experiences of the emotions shame and guilt, even if their language did not have distinct lexical categories for these emotions. Another study was done by Van de Ven, Zeelenberg and Pieters (2009), who found that English-speaking and Spanish-speaking participants experienced two distinct types of envy (labeled benign envy and malicious envy) even though they do not lexically distinguish between these experiences. In other languages, such as Dutch, Polish or Thai, two different lexical categories do exist for these emotions. Lewis and Ozaki (2009) made a qualitative comparison between experiences of the Japanese emotion *amae* and of the emotion *mardy* that is known in the northern regions of England. They showed that the experiences are to a large extent similar, but that the evaluation of the emotion differs strongly between the two cultures; whereas *amae* is seen as a socially acceptable emotion, *mardiness* is seen as unacceptable and is frowned upon when expressed.

To summarize, it is clear that emotions are categorized in very different ways across cultures and that many cultures distinguish emotion terms that have a unique meaning, perhaps reflecting specific cultural concerns that are considered to be important. However, it is not clear to what extent linguistic differences in emotion categories can be interpreted to denote differences in emotion experience (i.e., whether differences in performance differences can be generalized to differences in competences or processes). The evidence presented in this section gives little support for strong linguistic effects on emotion experience, in the sense that the absence of a lexical category does not imply the absence of an experience. However, on the basis of the studies that we presented, it cannot be ruled out that subtle differences in the meaning of emotion words do affect the way that people experience emotions.

Box 7.3 **Emotion experiences and emotion words**

Can people experience an emotion even if they have no word in their language to express this emotion? Breugelmans and Poortinga (1996) devised a three-phase study to establish whether Rarámuri Indians from northern Mexico experienced shame and guilt as distinct emotions, even though this group had only one term for both emotions (*riwérama*). They also studied a group of rural Javanese from Indonesia who, like the Rarámuri, were a non-western group with low levels of formal education, but who did have two separate words for shame (*isin*) and guilt (*salah*).

In the first phase, the authors gathered descriptions of emotion-eliciting situations in which people experienced *riwérama* from the Rarámuri and in which people experienced *isin* or *salah* from the Javanese. These descriptions were translated and then rated by Dutch and Indonesian students on the extent to which they would elicit various emotions, among which were shame and guilt. There was a strong similarity in ratings by both groups of students, allowing for a selection of the six strongest shame-eliciting situations, the six strongest guilt-eliciting situations and the six strongest shame-and-guilt-eliciting situations. Three situations from each set originated from the Rarámuri and three from the Javanese. These situations were translated back into the local languages and used as stimuli in phase three.

In the second phase, they established the experiential characteristics that distinguished guilt from shame in an international student sample from Belgium, Indonesia, Mexico and the Netherlands. Students were presented with a set of emotion-eliciting situations and asked to what extent they would experience a set of shame characteristics and guilt characteristics. Multidimensional scaling showed that guilt characteristics (e.g., thinking that you did harm to others, that you violated a norm, wanting to apologize, wanting to compensate) clearly clustered together and were distinct from a cluster of shame characteristics (e.g., thinking that you are the center of attention, blushing, wanting to avoid the gaze of others, wanting to hide). This clustering was identical across cultural samples, providing an international standard of guilt experiences and shame experiences that could be used to assess these experiences in the Rarámuri and Javanese without using specific emotion words.

In the third phase, Rarámuri and Javanese reacted to the locally derived situations that were selected in phase one with a set of experiential characteristics that were used in phase two. It was expected that these characteristics would cluster in similar ways with these groups as they did in the international student sample. A comparison of the Javanese with the international student sample resulted in a similar structure for 76 percent of the characteristics. This suggested substantial similarity in the experiences of shame and guilt, but also that testing non-western samples without formal education leads to a substantial number of items (i.e., emotion characteristics) that function in a different way (i.e., non-equivalence). A similar comparison between

Box 7.3 continued
international students and the Rarámuri yielded similar results for 64 percent of the characteristics. Though a slightly larger number of items was non-equivalent with the Rarámuri than with the Javanese, two clear clusters still emerged from the data, representing experiences of guilt and of shame. The authors concluded that "[t]his finding suggests that differences in the emotion lexicon ... cannot be taken as evidence that emotion processes, as identified in terms of associated emotion characteristics, are also different" (Breugelmans and Poortinga, 1996, p. 1117).

Emotion components

As we noted in the introduction, many researchers no longer try to define emotion by means of a single criterion. Rather, they use various **emotion components** to investigate cross-cultural similarities and differences in emotion experience. These components represent what emotion theorists consider to be the most important aspects of the emotion process. Commonly distinguished components are *antecedent events* that elicit the emotion (e.g., seeing a gun), *appraisals* that represent the cognitive evaluation of the situation (e.g., dangerous), *action tendencies* that the emotion motivates (e.g., fleeing), core *affect* (e.g., unpleasant), *bodily sensations* (e.g, heart beating faster), *facial expressions* (e.g., wide eyes, open mouth), *behavior* following from the emotion (e.g., running away) and *regulation* of the emotion (e.g., reappraisal of the situation, coping). Various studies have shown that emotions can quite reliably be distinguished on the basis of their componential profiles (e.g., Frijda, Kuipers and Ter Schure, 1986; Roseman, Wiest and Swartz, 1989; Scherer and Wallbott, 1994).

Brandt and Boucher (1985) did a study on **antecedents of emotions** with respondents from Korea, Samoa and the USA. In each country, informants were asked to write stories about events causing one of six emotions (anger, disgust, fear, happiness, sadness and surprise). A selection of 144 stories was translated and stripped of specific cultural referents and of all emotion terms. Other respondents were then presented with a set of stories and asked to indicate which emotion the person in the story had experienced. There was substantial agreement in the assignment of emotions to stories, both between cultures and within cultures. Contrary to expectation, respondents did *not* do better on stories from their own cultures. This suggests that antecedent events elicit by and large similar emotions for people in different cultures.

For appraisals, the most extensive study was done in thirty-seven countries by Scherer and Wallbott (1994). In a separate analysis of the appraisal data, Scherer (1997) found that the various emotions showed strong differences in appraisal patterns. He also found that certain appraisal dimensions were more prominent in certain countries. Largest differences were found for an item asking whether the event, if caused by a person, would be considered improper or immoral and for an item asking for the unjustness or unfairness of the event. Respondents in Africa tended to rate emotions higher on immorality and unfairness, while in Latin America ratings on immorality tended to be lower. Another study, by Mauro, Sato and Tucker (1992), used a similar design with participants from China, Hong Kong, Japan and the USA. They found that appraisal dimensions did not differ substantially among these samples, especially what they called more primitive dimensions (pleasantness, attentional activity, certainty, coping ability and goal/need conduciveness). Most differences were found on three of the five more complex dimensions (control, responsibility and anticipated effort).

Cultural differences in specific appraisals can cause salient differences in emotion intensity, emotion evaluation and emotion-related behavior. One of the best examples is a series of studies done by Nisbett and Cohen (1996). They provide a detailed description (e.g., historical accounts, crime records and survey results) of what they call a culture of honor in the South of the United States. They then tested the psychological consequences of being a member of an honor culture (Southern USA) or of a non-honor culture (Northern USA) in a series of studies on reactions to insults at the University of Michigan, where both students of Southern origin and students of Northern origin could be found. Under the cover story of another study, male students were asked to walk down a narrow hallway where they bumped into another person (a confederate of the researchers), who then called them an "asshole." After the event dependent variables were measured. Southern students showed higher subjective ratings of anger, larger increases in cortisol (a stress hormone) and testosterone (another hormone, related to aggression), and stronger behavioral reactions (e.g., refusing to make way for a 1.91-meter, 114-kilogram football player in a narrow hallway) than Northerners. Thus, a difference in the importance of a single appraisal, in this case honor, can lead to substantial differences in behavior, even within the same country.

The bodily component of emotion has been one of the oldest, and perhaps one of the most discussed, aspects of emotional experience, going back to the early works by James (1884) and Lange (1885). In the emotion literature, physiological activation and experienced body sensations are often taken as a single component (see Mesquita and Frijda, 1992), but the relationship between the two is far from clear. Averill (1974) argued that the bodily aspects of emotion may have to do more with cultural constructions than with actual physiological changes. Levenson, Ekman, Heider and Friesen (1992) asked Minangkabau people from Sumatra to voluntarily contract facial muscles (e.g., pull your lower lip down; wrinkle your nose). In this way prototypical facial configurations were made up, corresponding to happiness, sadness, disgust, fear and anger. Psychophysiological variables, like heart rate, skin conductance and respiration were recorded. Although configurations were not very precise, patterns of emotion-specific physiological reactions were observed that resembled results found in the USA.

Rimé and Giovanni (1986) analyzed the bodily sensations reported with four emotions (joy, anger, sadness and fear) by participants from nine European countries (see Scherer, Wallbott and Summerfield, 1986). Similar patterns were found for each country, but there were also a few differences. Participants from Northern Europe tended to report more stomach sensations for joy and fear and more muscle symptoms for anger, whereas Southern European participants tended to report more blood pressure changes with anger, joy and sadness. Hupka, Zaleski, Otto, Reidl and Tarabrina (1996) did an extensive study in five countries on body parts where emotions were felt with similar results; some differences were found but by and large patterns were similar across countries. Cross-cultural studies of physiological experiences with embarrassment also reported predominantly similarities (Edelman and Iwawaki, 1987). Most studies on body sensations have been done with university students. In order to test whether more differences would be found with samples that were less influenced by western culture, Breugelmans et al. (2005) studied body sensations experienced with seven emotions among rural Javanese (Indonesia) and Rarámuri Indians (Mexico) in addition to student samples from Belgium, Indonesia and Mexico. They found marked differences in body sensations between emotions within cultures, but strong similarities across cultures, although more differences were found with the rural samples. Differences were mainly found for individual items; for example, unlike other samples, Javanese reported the experience of goose-flesh with the emotion surprise, and the Rarámuri experienced weakness in the knees with almost all emotions.

Cross-cultural differences in the subjective experience or core affect of emotions are difficult to interpret because these are usually measured by means of emotion words which can have markedly different meanings across languages (see previous section). There appears to be evidence to the effect that positive emotions are experienced more frequently or intensely in western cultures than in East Asian cultures. For example, Kitayama, Markus and Kurokawa (2000) found that US-American students reported more frequent positive emotions than negative emotions but that Japanese students reported more frequent interpersonally engaged emotions (e.g., friendly feelings) than disengaged emotions (e.g., pride). East Asians also tend to score higher than US-Americans on measures of emotional distress (Norasakkunkit and Kalick, 2002). Differences in subjective well-being, which is strongly related to the experience of positive and negative emotions, are best explained by norms with regard to the cultural evaluation of emotion, next to differences in Gross Domestic Product (richer countries tend to report higher well-being; see Tov and Diener, 2007). So, the cultural evaluation of affective states does seem to have some effect on the experience of core affect, although confounding variables such as response styles, socially desirable responding or differential meaning of emotion words are difficult to rule out as alternative explanations.

Perhaps surprisingly, hardly any cross-cultural studies have been done on action tendencies or behaviors associated with emotions. A study by Scherer and Wallbott (1994) included some items on verbal, non-verbal and motor expression; and action tendencies have been included in other studies, such as the study by Breugelmans and Poortinga (2006; Box 7.3). Fontaine *et al.* (2006) compared emotion components associated with shame and guilt in Belgium, Hungary and Peru. Among the components were five action tendencies. Participants rated the extent to which they would experience each component in response to a set of (locally derived) shame situations and guilt situations. Multidimensional Scaling across situations revealed a clear shame–guilt structure that was identical across the three countries. Everywhere, shame was more associated with the wish to disappear from sight and guilt was associated with tendencies to ruminate, self-reproach, self-improvement and reparation.

There have been some cross-cultural studies on vocal expressions of emotions. Albas, McCluskey and Albas (1976) collected speech samples meant to express happiness, sadness, love and anger from English- and Cree-speaking Canadian Indian respondents. These expressions were made semantically unintelligible by means of an electronic filtering procedure that leaves the emotional intonation intact. Respondents from both language groups recognized the emotions intended by the speakers far beyond chance level, but performance was better in the own language than in the other language. In another study McCluskey, Albas, Niemi, Cuevas and Ferrer (1975) made a comparison between Mexican and Canadian children (6–11 years of age). With a similar procedure they found that the Mexican children did better than the Canadian respondents, also on the identification of Canadian English expressions, which was tentatively ascribed to a greater importance of intonation in Mexican speech. Van Bezooijen, Otto and Heenan (1983) made a comparison between Dutch, Taiwanese and Japanese respondents, using a single brief phrase in Dutch that had been expressed by different speakers in nine different emotional tones (i.e., disgust, surprise, shame, joy, fear, contempt, sadness, anger, as well as a neutral tone of voice). With one exception all emotions were recognized at better than chance level by all three groups, but the scores of the Dutch respondents were much higher, suggesting a fair amount of loss of information due to cultural and/or linguistic differences between the three samples.

Cross-cultural comparisons of emotion regulation have been predominantly done on the control of emotional expressions, most notably facial expressions. In order to explain cross-cultural differences in the frequency and intensity with which emotions are expressed (see next section), Ekman (1973, p. 176) introduced the notion of display rules. These are "norms regarding the expected management of facial appearance." Each culture has rules about what emotions to express at certain occasions as well as how strongly certain emotions can be shown. A classic study in this area was done by Ekman and Friesen (Ekman, 1973). Japanese and US students were shown stressful films in isolation and in the presence of an experimenter. Without the participants' awareness their emotional expressions were recorded. Highly similar expressions were found in reaction to the same movie episodes when the respondents were alone. However, in the presence of the other person the Japanese respondents showed far fewer negative facial expressions than the Americans, suggesting that they were actively managing the display of their emotions.

In a cross-cultural survey of display rules with over 5,000 respondents in thirty-two countries by Matsumoto, Yoo, Fontaine *et al.* (2008), respondents indicated what they *should do* if they felt each of seven emotions toward twenty-one target interactants in two settings – public and private. Response alternatives were: (1) show more than you feel it, (2) express it as you feel it, (3) show the emotion while smiling at the same time, (4) show less than you feel it, (5) hide your feelings by smiling and (6) show nothing, which correspond to Amplification, Expression, Qualification, De-amplification, Masking and Neutralization. They found that country differences only accounted for about 5 percent of the variation in data, suggesting that norms of emotion display regulation are quite similar across cultures. Differences were found in overall-expressivity endorsement (individualist countries endorsed more expressiveness, especially for positive emotions), and in norms concerning specific emotions in ingroup and outgroup situations.

Some studies have not assessed only a single emotion component, but have rather compared various components at the same time. An important advantage of using several components to measure emotions is that measurements become less susceptible to bias (Chapter 12, see p. 293). If measures of one component are cross-culturally biased but measures of another are not, this still allows for a comparison of the emotion. In contrast, when depending upon a single indicator (e.g., an emotion word) any presence of bias would seriously threaten the validity of comparisons.

In one of the most important studies in this area, respondents from thirty-seven countries on five continents rated personal experiences of seven emotions (joy, fear, anger, sadness, disgust, shame and guilt) on various emotion components, such as appraisals, subjective feelings, physiological symptoms and expressive behavior (Scherer and Wallbott, 1994). Each emotion showed a unique profile across components and these profiles showed a remarkable similarity across cultures. In terms of effect sizes, the main effect of emotion (i.e., the difference between emotions on the components) was clearly much larger than the difference between countries and than the interaction between emotion and country. The interaction is important here because large effect sizes would indicate that componential profiles for emotions would be very different across cultures. Scherer and Wallbott (1994, p. 310) interpreted their results "as supporting theories that postulate both a high degree of universality of differential emotion patterning and important cultural differences in emotion elicitation, regulation, symbolic representation, and social sharing." Matsumoto, Nezlek and Koopmann reanalyzed the data using multilevel techniques. They came to an even smaller estimate of the amount of cultural variation (< 5%). They concluded that "the variance accounted for by country or culture is not very large and ... the bulk of variability found is more aptly ascribed to individual rather than cultural differences" (2007, p. 64).

Reviews of the cross-cultural literature on emotions show that both similarities and differences have been reported for each emotion component (Mesquita and Frijda, 1992; Mesquita, Frijda and Scherer, 1997). So, it would be safe to say that neither an extreme relativist nor an extreme universalist perspective is supported. The most likely pattern in studies of individual components is that there is substantial overall similarity in emotion component profiles and that differences are found for specific components or specific emotions. Mesquita *et al.* rightly pointed out that the similarities in emotion component dimensions are found at a high level of generality, which may obscure differences at more specific levels.

Facial expressions

No emotion component has received more attention than that of facial expressions. In fact, it is safe to say that contemporary cross-cultural research on emotions was largely initiated by Ekman and Friesen's (1969) seminal work on facial expressions. Modern studies of the expression of emotions go back all the way to Darwin (1872/1998). In his book *The expression of the emotions in man and animals* he described a cross-cultural survey among British residents in various countries who sent him descriptions of how emotions were locally expressed. When comparing these descriptions he noted remarkable similarities which he interpreted as evidence that emotions are innate and a product of evolution. Although the book was well appreciated at the time, it has received much less attention than his work on the origin of species.

One reason for the lessened attention for Darwin's work on emotions was the rise of cultural relativism in the social sciences. When in the first half of the twentieth century the biological basis of behavior was challenged by social scientists, the view became popular that there are major cultural differences in emotional expressions. According to authors like Klineberg (1940) and Birdwhistell (1970) human emotional expression is acquired in the process of socialization. Impressive examples were quoted: the widow of a Samurai fighter who died in combat, supposedly will be proud and smile rather than be sad. However, like Darwin, these conclusions were mainly based on casual observation. The best-known studies to systematically test the question of universality of facial expressions of emotion are those conducted by Ekman among the Fore in Papua New Guinea.

Ekman (1980) published a series of photographs that show a similar range of emotional expressions as found in the industrialized countries. These photographs had been selected on the basis of a theory, developed by Tomkins (1962, 1963), that suggested links between central nervous system activity and contractions of the facial muscles. Ekman and Friesen (1969) suspected that most facial expressions reflect a blending of more than a single emotion. However, for some emotions – the so-called basic emotions – there should be a characteristic pattern of the facial muscles. They selected photographs that showed these unblended emotions: happiness, sadness, anger, fear, surprise and disgust. Later on, a distinct muscular pattern was distinguished for a seventh expression: contempt (Ekman and Friesen, 1986).

The first substantive cross-cultural evidence was obtained when respondents in five societies (USA, Brazil, Chile, Argentina, Japan) were shown photographs displaying the six emotions. Participants had to choose one emotion term from a set of six, representing which emotion was expressed in each photograph. The overall rate of correct identification was quite high and no significant differences between cultures were found when the results for the six emotions were combined (Ekman and Friesen, 1969). Although this pleaded strongly against culture specificity, there was still a possibility that the emotional content of photographs from the USA was recognized in other countries because of previous exposure to US movies and other cultural products (i.e., cultural diffusion).

To rule out the alternative explanation, the research was extended to groups isolated from western visual materials and western persons. One famous study was done among the Fore, a group of people in Papua New Guinea. Leaving out a confusion between fear and surprise, the percentage of agreement between the Fore and western respondents on the meaning of (western) facial expressions was as high as 80 percent for a sample of adults and 90 percent for children (Ekman and Friesen, 1971). In the reverse case where facial expressions by the Fore were filmed and later shown to American students these were similar results: high agreement ratings, again with confusion between fear and surprise. This work was later replicated among the Dani, a group living in the mountains of West Irian (West New Guinea). The results again showed that the basic facial expressions of emotion were interpreted in a similar way as in the industrialized urban world. However, the interpretation of universality on the basis of the cross-cultural data has not been undisputed.

Most discussion has been sparked by the fact that overall recognition rates tend to be lower for respondents who have had less previous contact with western culture (see Box 7.1). In the research among the Fore the rates of agreement were mostly similar to the earlier study by Ekman and Friesen (1969) with student samples. However, the task had been simplified from a choice between six emotion words to a choice between three emotion vignettes (short descriptions of situations in which the emotion is elicited). The obvious question is to what extent the lower recognition rates reflected artifacts of the test method (e.g., cultural idiosyncrasies in the stimuli) or "real" cultural differences factors in emotions. Studies designed to probe this problem did not yield clear results (e.g., Boucher and Carlson, 1980; Ducci, Arcuri, Georgis and Sinseshaw, 1982). There appeared to be at least some cultural variation in the ease of recognition of specific emotions. Another methodological factor may be the origin of the faces. In a meta-analysis of emotion recognition within and between cultures Elfenbein and Ambady (2002) found evidence for an ingroup advantage in emotion recognition studies. Emotions were universally recognized at better than chance levels but accuracy was higher when emotions were both expressed and recognized by members of the same national, ethnic or regional group.

Haidt and Keltner (1999) presented posed pictures of fourteen facial expressions to respondents in the USA and India. These included the basic emotions as well as other emotions like shame, embarrassment and compassion. Respondents were asked for free responses (which emotion is displayed?) and were also presented the photographs in a forced-choice format (choose emotions from a list) including a "none of the above" alternative. Although differences in method did matter, the results showed that earlier findings could not be fully ascribed to method artifacts. Six of the seven basic emotions were among the seven best-recognized photographs. Research on facial expressions has not remained limited to the basic emotions. In a ten-country study (with countries as far apart as Estonia, Turkey and Japan) Ekman, Friesen, O'Sullivan *et al.* (1987) demonstrated that blended (or mixed) emotion expressions also are recognized across cultures. In addition, the postural expression of pride seems to be recognized across cultures (Tracy and Robins, 2008).

The extent to which emotion expressions are used as information may vary across cultures. In an elegant study, Masuda *et al.* (2008) showed that the Japanese take into account the emotion expressions by surrounding people when assessing the emotion experienced by a certain individual. In contrast, US-American participants tend to only look at the emotion expressed by the individual. They tested this by presenting participants with a series of cartoons depicting a happy, sad, angry or neutral person surrounded by other people expressing the same emotion as the central person or a different one. The emotions expressed by bystanders did affect ratings of the emotion experienced by the target person made by Japanese students' ratings but not by US-American students. In a second study, they used eye-tracking to see where participants looked when assessing the pictures. They found that Japanese indeed looked more and longer at the faces of the bystanders, next to the face of the target person.

To summarize, cross-cultural studies of emotion components show a remarkably consistent pattern of results. Almost without exception, each component shows evidence for both universal and culture-specific aspects of emotion experiences. However, the extent of cross-cultural variation is limited. In general, about

5 percent of the variance in the data is explained by culture; differences between emotions and between individuals are much more important. This means that patterns of emotion component profiles are similar across cultures and that cultural differences are mainly found in specific items or emotions. It does not mean that cultural differences are insignificant. Differences in the evaluation of specific emotions or the salience of specific appraisals (e.g., honor) can make an important difference in the way that people behave. Similarly, there is strong evidence for a consistent, universal link between facial expressions and certain emotion categories, but culture-specific display rules may influence the ways in which emotions are expressed in specific situations as well as how people deal with facial expressions as information about someone's emotional state.

Conclusions

In this chapter we have reviewed various lines of research that were aimed at answering the question to what extent emotions should be considered similar or different across cultures. We looked at the dimensions underlying emotions, at emotions and language, at different emotion components and at facial expressions. The simple conclusion from this chapter is that all aspects of emotions have both universal and culture-specific aspects. Although this conclusion is clearly true, it is also quite unsatisfactory because it tells us little about the nature or relative degree of cross-cultural similarities and differences.

From a global perspective, the evidence in this chapter seems more in favor of a universalist perspective. The dimensions underlying emotions, the profiles of emotion components and the facial expressions associated with emotions all show very little cross-cultural variation. Cross-cultural differences are mostly found in individual items, components or rules of expression. However, at closer scrutiny cultural variation becomes more important. We have seen how cultures can differ substantially in the emotion categories that they use; how specific differences in the appraisal of honor can have important consequences for subsequent behavior; and how cultures can emphasize the experience and expression of certain types of emotion (e.g., positive emotions). These differences obviously have an impact on people's daily experiences of emotions.

KEY TERMS

affective meaning • antecedents of emotions • basic emotions • componential approach • culture-specific emotion concepts • display rules • emotion components • subjective culture

FURTHER READING

Darwin, C. (1872/1998). *The expression of the emotions in man and animals* (3rd edn.). London: HarperCollins.

Darwin's classic study of the universality of emotion expressions (with comments by Paul Ekman).

Ekman, P. (ed.) (1982). *Emotion in the human face* (2nd edn.). Cambridge: Cambridge University Press.

A comprehensive overview of the early studies and findings on the universality of emotions in the human face.

Mesquita, B., Frijda, N. H., and Scherer, K. R. (1997). Culture and emotion. In J. W. Berry, P. R. Dasen and T. S. Saraswathi (eds.), *Handbook of cross-cultural psychology, Vol. II, Basic processes and human* development (pp. 255–297). Boston: Allyn & Bacon.

A comprehensive review and a classic introduction to the componential emotion theory in cross-cultural research.

Russell, J. A. (1991). Culture and the categorisation of emotions. *Psychological Bulletin*, 110, 426–450.

An overview of the linguistic categorization of emotions in a large variety of cultures.

8 Language

CONTENTS

Compared to communication in other species, human speech is a highly differentiated faculty, enabling us to communicate complex information in an efficient way. There are many aspects to the psychological study of language, including its production and understanding (listening, articulation, memorization), and the use of indirect means of communication through writing and reading. In all of these aspects cross-cultural differences can be observed. In this chapter we will deal with the main theme of cross-cultural psycholinguistic research, namely the extent to which underneath different words and rules of grammar there is commonality between languages.

In the first section research on linguistic relativity is presented, addressing the question of to what extent speaking a particular language influences one's thinking. We look at two topics on which much of the discussion about linguistic relativity has been focussed, namely perception and categorization of colors, and orientation in space. We present the case of relativism and counterarguments based on empirical cross-cultural studies. The second section is on universalist approaches, especially the notion of universal grammar. Again, not only the evidence in favor, but also challenges are presented.

On the Internet we present some additional information. There is an entry on language development (Additional Topics, Chapter 8), pointing out some of the complexities a child has to master in order to acquire a language. There is also a brief account of early

www.cambridge.org/berry

cross-cultural research on color vision (Additional Topics, Chapter 8). Finally, there is a brief discussion on bilingualism and the consequences of the learning and use of more than a single language (Additional Topics, Chapter 8). This topic not only has theoretical implications; it is also highly relevant for ethnocultural and immigrant groups.

Linguistic relativity

Thinking and language are experienced as being intimately connected. It is difficult to imagine how we could think at all, if we had no language in which to think (Hunt and Agnoli, 1991). Therefore, it is not surprising that the question has been raised whether people who speak different languages also think in different ways. Within a relativist perspective, the presumed culture-specific construction of the world is encoded in language. Psychological processes are interpreted, passed on to others and also created through language (Fontaine, in press). Thus, the notion of linguistic relativity implies a close relationship between characteristics of a language and the thoughts that will be found among speakers of that language. This idea has a long history, but today it is usually referred to as **Whorf's hypothesis**, after the linguist Whorf, or as the "Sapir–Whorf hypothesis," after Whorf and the cultural anthropologist Sapir who earlier had launched similar ideas. In Whorf's view (1956, p. 212): "the background linguistic system (in other words, the grammar) of each language is not merely a reproducing instrument for voicing ideas but rather is itself a shaper of ideas, the program and guide for the individual's mental activity, for his analysis of impressions, for his synthesis of his mental stock-of-trade." From this passage it is quite clear that language is seen not only as a means to communicate ideas and thoughts, but as intrinsic to their formation.

Whorf based his theory of linguistic relativity on a comparison of standard average European (SAE) with Native American languages. Between the European languages such as English, French and Italian, Whorf saw much commonality; hence the term SAE. Major differences are seen when one compares European languages with languages from other families. An example is the sense of time among the Hopi Indians. Whorf (1956, p. 57) argued that a Hopi-speaking person has no general notion of time as "a smooth flowing continuum in which everything in the universe proceeds at an equal rate, out of a future, through a present, into a past." The major distinction in Hopi is not between past, present and future, but between the manifested, or the objective, and the unmanifest, or the subjective. The manifest comprises everything that is accessible to the senses, that is, the physical world of the past and the present. The unmanifest includes the future, but also everything that exists in the mind (the Hopi would say the heart) and the realm of religion and magic. In the Hopi verb there is a form that refers to the emergence of manifestation, like going to sleep. However, most of what in English is the present time belongs to the realm of the manifest and is not distinguishable in Hopi from the past.

The SAE notion of time also emerges in the use of plurality and numbers. In English one can as easily speak about ten days as about ten men. Whorf pointed out that ten men can be perceived as a group. Ten days cannot be experienced objectively; we can only experience today. An expression like "ten days" will not be found in Hopi. Rather reference will be made to the day that is reached after the number of ten days has passed. Staying for ten days will be expressed as staying until the eleventh day. Length of time is regarded by the Hopi as "a relation between two events in lateness. Instead of our linguistically promoted objectification of that datum of consciousness we call 'time', the Hopi language has not laid down any pattern that would cloak the subjective 'becoming later' that is the essence of time" (Whorf, 1956, pp. 139–140). The example shows that Whorf extended the principle of linguistic relativity to the level of grammatical characteristics of a language and that he saw these as cultural themes, shared by the speakers of the language.

Some of Whorf's writing has been presented in some detail because of its appeal to many social scientists and linguists. As we shall see, Whorf's hypothesis has led to a large body of research. At the same time, it should be noted that the evidence on which his interpretations were based was rather anecdotal. It has certainly not been demonstrated by Whorf that the Hopi cannot discriminate between past, present and future in much the same way as SAE speakers. Among others, Lenneberg (1953) criticized Whorf's method of translation which led to such strong inferences about cross-cultural differences in thinking. Later on attempts were made to better specify the nature of linguistic relativity. An important distinction is that between the lexical or semantic level, and the level of grammar or syntax (e.g., Fishman, 1960). Another distinction was made between the influence of language on perception and cognition and its influence on verbal communication.

One of the few early experimental studies into linguistic relativity of grammar was carried out by Carroll and Casagrande (1958). They used a feature of the (Native American) Navajo language in which the conjugation of the verb differs according to whether the form or some other feature of an object is referred to. They hypothesized that the concept of form would develop early among Navajo-speaking children. Carroll and Casagrande found that Navajo-speaking children more than English-speaking children of Navajo origin would use form rather than color as a basis for the classification of objects. However, this support for the Whorf hypothesis lost much of its meaning when a control group of Anglo-American children showed an even stronger tendency to classify objects in the way hypothesized for the Navajo-speaking respondents. In Box 8.1 we present another set of studies.

At the grammatical level evidence on the Sapir–Whorf hypothesis was largely negative. Of course, that did not say much about the semantic level. Language in the form of labeling influences the organization and recall of representations in

Box 8.1 **Counterfactuality in the verb and its consequences**

A study (Bloom, 1981) focussed on a particular difference between English and Chinese. English has a conditional construction to indicate that a statement is counterfactual. The sentence: "If I knew French, I could read the work of Voltaire," implies that the speaker does *not* know French. The listener deduces that the premise is false and that the meaning of the sentence is counterfactual. Chinese languages do not have such a conditional mode of expression. If the listener has no advance information the sentence has to be preceded by an explicit negation. For example: "I do not know French; if I knew French, I could read Voltaire." According to Bloom the absence of a counterfactual marker negatively affects the ability of speakers of Chinese to think counterfactually.

He presented Chinese and English-speaking respondents with a story in which counterfactual implications were mentioned following a false premise. The counterfactuals were presented in a conditional form in the English version, but not, of course, in the Chinese version. Bloom found substantial differences when he asked whether the counterfactual events had actually occurred. In Bloom's (1981, p. 29) opinion the differences in linguistic form "may well be highly responsible for important differences in the way English speakers, as opposed to Chinese speakers, categorize and operate cognitively with the world."

Au's (1983, 1984) results from similar experiments were in direct contradiction to those obtained by Bloom. She hardly found any differences between speakers of English and Chinese. More evidence was reported by Liu (1985), working with Chinese speakers who had minimal exposure to English. Using respondents in various school grades and various presentations she concluded that education level, the presentation and the content of the story were crucial variables for the level of performance. But she found no cross-cultural effects of linguistic markers of counterfactuality.

Another study, in which two levels of counterfactuality could be manipulated within a single language, was reported by Vorster and Schuring (1989). They presented a story with counterfactual statements to South African respondents from three languages, namely English, Afrikaans and Sepedi, or northern Sotho. Samples consisted of school children from grades three, five and seven. Vorster and Schuring made use of a feature of the Sepedi language, namely that there are two modes of expressing counterfactuality, of which the one is stronger than the other. It is also noteworthy that these authors asked questions about factual as well as counterfactual statements in the stimulus story. They argued that group differences in responses could not be ascribed to the effects of counterfactuality, if it had not been shown that similar differences were absent for factual statements.

Box 8.1 continued

The results showed that the percentage of correct responses to factual items was very high even for the youngest children. Counterfactual statements led to large percentages of wrong answers, especially with younger children. The crucial finding was that with the less strong counterfactual cueing the Sepedi-speaking children showed a similar pattern of results to the children from Afrikaans- and English-speaking backgrounds, while with the stronger cues the percentages of correct responses were much higher for the Sepedi. The differences in reactions by these Sotho-speaking respondents to the two versions of the same story indicate that the way in which counterfactuality is formulated in a specific instance should be seen as the determining factor, rather than a general mode of thinking. This was clearly not compatible with the Whorfian hypothesis.

memory (e.g., Santa and Baker, 1975). There are numerous examples of differences in word meaning across languages. The Inuit appear to have two words for the semantic category that in SAE languages is represented by the single word "snow."[1] On the other hand, the Aztecs have only one word where SAE languages use cold, snow and ice. This led to two expectations. First, the availability of words for certain categories presumably will make it easier to discriminate certain nuances in the outer world. Second, the availability of more words within a certain category should lead to greater ease of communication. If words are taken as codes, a larger number of words for a given range of phenomena implies a more accurate "codability" (see below) of these phenomena.

The two following subsections further explore cross-cultural research in two areas that have been used as testing grounds for the Whorfian hypothesis: cross-cultural differences in the names of color categories and in spatial frames of reference.

Coding and categorization of color

Color is a physical quality of objects as well as an impression or sensation of the human observer. On the one hand each color can be defined unambiguously in terms of physical qualities, notably the dominant wavelength (hue). On the other hand one can ask respondents to name colors, to remember colors, to provide color categorizations and so on. The physical measurements can then be related to the psychological reports. This makes the domain of color excellently suited for testing Whorf's hypothesis. As we shall see in this section, such relationships are not unproblematic. In early studies color terms were taken as indices of what people in a particular culture were thought to perceive (Additional Topics, Chapter 8). Later on

www.cambridge.org/berry

---

[1] It appears to be an urban legend that the Inuit have "several" words for snow (Pullum, 1989).

sets of chips came into use in which the whole range of visible colors was represented. Most familiar is the Munsell system, in which colors are mapped according to three parameters, namely hue, saturation and brightness (or gray value).

One of the authors advocating the mediation of language in color naming was Ray (1952), who concluded from his studies with Native Americans that each culture has divided the visible spectrum into units on a physically quite arbitrary basis. He rejected even the famous confusion between blue and green (see below), and attributed it to a greater rather than a lower subtlety in classification. Where western cultures use only blue and green, he found a three-way division elsewhere. The middle region is then not identified as blue-green but as a separate color. However, there has been no further empirical validation of Ray's observations.

A new line of research was started by Brown and Lenneberg (1954) with the introduction of the term codability. This was a composite measure of agreement in (1) the naming of a color chip, (2) the length of the name and (3) the response latency in naming. It was expected that more codable colors would be better remembered and more easily identified in a recognition task. Some positive results were found in the USA, but the research was not replicated elsewhere. Lantz and Stefflre (1964) suggested another measure, namely communication accuracy. They asked listeners to identify a certain chip in an array of colors on the basis of color terms that were presented to them. Some terms were found to lead to more accurate identification than other terms. When used in a recognition experiment the more accurately communicable terms also were better recognized. Thus, this work showed an influence of language on communication and memory.

The linguistic relativity hypothesis was radically challenged by Berlin and Kay (1969). These authors asked bilingual respondents resident in the area of San Francisco to generate basic color terms in their mother tongue. A basic term had four main characteristics: (1) it was monoleximic, that is, the meaning could not be derived from the meaning of its parts, as in lemon-colored; (2) the color it signified was not included in another color term (e.g., scarlet is a kind of red); (3) its usage should not be restricted to certain classes of objects; and (4) it had to be psychologically salient. This was evaluated with several indices, such as stability of reference across informants and occasions of usage.

After a listing of basic color terms had been obtained each respondent was given a panel with 329 differently colored chips from the Munsell system and asked to indicate for each term "x" that had been previously generated: (1) all those chips that would be called "x"; and (2) the best, most typical example of "x" in the Munsell display. It is important to note that the respondents worked with terms that they had generated themselves. The experimenter had no idea which shade of color was signified by a particular term.

The results of respondents from twenty languages are summarized in Figure 8.1. The diagram shows that the most typical, or focal, chips for basic colors are neatly

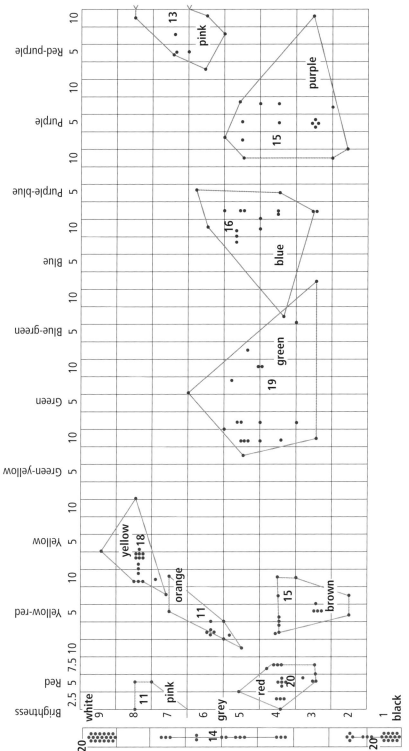

Figure 8.1 Clusters of dots representing foci (averaged over subjects) in each of 20 languages. The number in each cluster indicates the number of languages that had a basic term for the color concerned (numbers in the margins refer to the Munsell color system) (from Berlin and Kay, 1969).

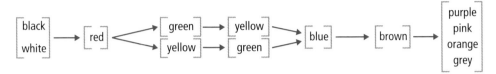

Figure 8.2 The sequence in which terms for focal colors emerge in the history of languages (after Berlin and Kay, 1969).

clustered. Apart from clusters for black and white with terms in all twenty languages, there is also a word in all these languages for the area that is called red in English. Then the number decreases to nineteen for green, eighteen for yellow, sixteen for blue, fifteen for brown and purple, fourteen for gray, and thirteen for pink and eleven for orange. Large parts of the diagram remain outside the areas covered by the basic color terms. Hence, it appeared that there are focal colors. Berlin and Kay (1969, p. 10) concluded that "color categorization is not random and the foci of basic color terms are similar in all languages."

Many cultures do not have names for all the eleven basic colors in English. The second important finding by Berlin and Kay was a strong relationship between the number of basic color terms in a language and the subset of focal colors for which there is a basic term. They claimed that the focal colors become encoded in the history of a language in a (largely) fixed order. The sequence of stages is summarized in Figure 8.2. In the most elementary stage there are two terms, one for white, encoding also for light and warm colors (e.g., yellow) and one for black that includes dark and cool colors (e.g., blue). In the second stage a separate term for red and warm colors emerges. From the third stage onwards the order is not precisely fixed. It is possible that either green or blue (together called "grue") is the next term, but one also finds that a term for yellow is found in a language, but not for grue. It can be seen from the figure that pink, orange, grey and purple are added to a language in the last stage. For Berlin and Kay the various stages are steps in the evolution of languages. To support their evolutionary scheme they drew on a large number of reports in the (mainly ethnographic) literature. There were a few color vocabularies that did not readily fit, but in their view the available information showed a striking agreement with the proposed order.

Berlin and Kay's research was criticized on a number of points. Their definition of basic color terms is somewhat fuzzy, the respondents from San Francisco had all been living for a longer or shorter period in the USA, and many of the categorizations derived for specific terms in specific groups by Berlin and Kay were questioned by cultural anthropologists, who also argued that in this line of work the functional and social meaning of colors, for example in relations to rituals, are ignored (e.g., Sahlins, 1976).

In experimental research Heider (also publishing as Rosch, 1972, 1977) found that focal colors had a higher codability, in the sense that they were named more rapidly and were given shorter names, than non-focal colors by respondents from twenty-three languages. She then turned to unnamed focal colors. She tested the hypothesis that focal colors would also have a higher codability than non-focal colors, even for those focal colors for which there was no basic term in a respondent's language. She studied the Dani, a group in Papua New Guinea with only two basic color terms (i.e., a language at the first stage in the Berlin and Kay sequence). When the Dani were shown color chips they did indeed recognize focal colors better than non-focal colors after a thirty-second interval (as did American students). In a second study with the Dani, eight focal colors and eight non-focal colors were all paired with a separate response word. The number of trials it took a respondent to learn the correct response for each stimulus was the dependent variable. It was found that the focal colors required significantly fewer trials than the non-focal colors. In Rosch's view the results should be explained with reference to physiological factors underlying color vision, rather than linguistic factors.

More direct evidence on the role of possible physiological factors in the linguistic categorization of colors was reported by Bornstein (1973). He related the wavelength of the focal colors found by Berlin and Kay (see Figure 8.2) to the spectral sensitivity of four types of cells found in the brain of Macaque monkeys. These cells were found to be sensitive for wavelengths corresponding to red, yellow, green and blue respectively. In a further study (Bornstein, Kessen and Weiskopf, 1976) the technique of stimulus habituation was used with four-month-old babies, using red, yellow, green and blue stimuli. The authors hypothesized that when the same stimulus was presented repeatedly, looking time would decrease. At the presentation of a different stimulus there would be a dishabituation effect that was stronger as the new stimulus was more dissimilar. All stimulus changes in this experiment were identical in one respect: the size of the change, measured in wavelength, was always equal. However, with some of the changes the new stimulus remained within the same color category as the original stimulus (e.g., both would be designated as red by an adult observer), while with other changes the new stimulus would be classified in another color category (e.g., a shift from red to yellow). It was found that the infants indeed reacted more to the new stimulus when the latter type of change occurred. This indicated that the categories and boundaries between categories for babies long before the onset of speech are much the same as those for adults. In the debate on the primacy of language versus perception in color identification, this quite convincingly suggested the primacy of perception.

Heider's (Rosch [Heider], 1972) findings, indicating that focal colors in English could be identified by the Dani even in the absence of color words, were largely not replicated in a series of studies comparing Berinmo in Papua New Guinea with British respondents. Roberson, Davies and Davidoff (2000) worked with Munsell color chips, as Heider had done. They found five monoleximic color terms for the

Berinmo, including *nol*, a term more or less covering green, blue and purple. In a memory task there was more resemblance between Berinmo patterns of color naming and memory than between Berinmo and British memory patterns. Roberson *et al.* also found that paired associates learning of words and color chips was not faster for (English) focal as opposed to non-focal chips. Again, Heider's results with the Dani were not replicated. The research with the Berinmo was extended with similarity judgments and learning of categories with the English blue–green and the Berinmo *nol–wor* distinction (*wor* corresponds to yellow, orange and brown). It turned out that performance was better for distinctions made in the respondents' own language than for distinctions according to the categories proposed by Berlin and Kay.

It should be noted that the findings of Roberson *et al.* are somewhat more complicated than has been reported here. For example, in one memory task a Berinmo sample showed a better performance for (English) focal than for non-focal chips. Since the Berinmos also gave more incorrect answers on focal chips, Roberson *et al.* explain this as an artifact of response bias. However, the reason for the higher salience of the focal colors is perhaps a better discriminability: focal colors may stand out more than non-focal color chips, which is precisely why researchers like Heider would expect a better memory for focal chips.[2] Nevertheless, one can agree with Roberson *et al.* (2000, p. 394) that they demonstrated quite unambiguously a broad effect of language on color categorization: "the results uphold the view that the structure of linguistic categories distorts perception by stretching perceptual distances at category boundaries."

Evidence extending these results and showing that the acquisition of color terms in children does not follow an invariant order came from a developmental study with children in the UK and the Himba in northern Namibia (Roberson, Davidoff, Davies and Shapiro, 2004). Remarkable similarities were found in the development trajectories of color naming, but these developments were toward culturally distinct sets of color terms. Roberson *et al.* conclude that their results do not support the theory that the eleven basic color terms in English are universal. Instead they argue that a structured organization of categories emerges that varies across languages.

In the meantime most research continues to be based on analysis of color terms. The database on distributions of such terms across the spectrum and their order of emergence in a language has been greatly expanded since Berlin and Kay's initial publication (1969). Adherents to universalistic views focus on unmistakable

---

[2] The color chips in the Munsell system were prepared so that there was equal distance between them on physical characteristics. Some authors have suggested that chips should be selected for equal discriminability, making the focal chips more difficult to recognize. It can be argued that this amounts to the introduction of an unnatural bias against focal chips (cf. Lucy and Schweder, 1979; Poortinga and Van de Vijver, 1997; Roberson *et al.*, 2000).

regularities across languages and have proposed theories of how color naming is rooted in color vision and its physiology (e.g., Hardin and Maffi, 1997; Kay, Maffi and Merrifield, 2003). On the other hand, not only these theoretical views continue to be criticized but also the findings, with (alleged) counterexamples to the presumed regularities as the main empirical evidence (Levinson, 2000; Paramei, 2005; Saunders and Van Brakel, 1997, 2002).

The focus on the role of language as a sociocultural force in color categorization may have diverted attention away from possible factors in the natural environment. As far as the universality of specific basic color categories is concerned, some of the experimental evidence still stands, especially that infants already perceive major color categories (Bornstein, 1997; Bornstein et al., 1976). Moreover, there is a longstanding finding that there is a lower sensitivity for shortwave colors (the blue end of the spectrum) by people living in climates with much sunshine. This was proposed already at the time of Rivers (1901). Bornstein (1973), analyzing color terms in 150 languages, found regional differences in the distribution of such terms and suggested that denser pigmentation of the retina, associated with darker skin color, can act as a filter for blue light and limit perception of color at the shortwave end of the spectrum. Lindsey and Brown (2002, 2004) have reported similar findings. They suggested that high exposure to ultraviolet light leads to a yellowing or browning of the eye lens ("brunescence") at a younger age than in low-ultraviolet environments. This could make "blue" a less communicable color and lead to a single word for the green–blue range of the spectrum. The effect of brunescence of the light on color perception was not supported in a study in which the spectral sensitivity of respondents was actually measured (Hardy, Frederick, Kay and Werner, 2005). These authors note that, taking English as a standard, other basic color terms also tend to be fused in tropical regions. They suggest that linguistic terminology (perhaps related to the need for more distinctions in technology-dependent societies; see Kay and Maffi, 1999) rather than some ecological factor appears to be the crucial variable.

While strong claims of universality as originally made by Berlin and Kay (1969) cannot be maintained, one can think of weaker formulations to account for the regularities that continue to be documented, such as (1) non-random distribution across languages of color terms over the visible spectrum, (2) continuity in all languages of the color area denoted by a term (i.e., the same color term has never been found for two frequency ranges in the color spectrum separated by another color term), (3) salience of the same hues across languages (notably red) and (4) a maximum number of eleven or twelve basic color terms in any language. If Roberson et al. (2000, 2004) had found support for eleven color categories this certainly would have strengthened claims of cross-cultural invariance or universalism, as advanced by Berlin and Kay (1969). However, there are varieties of universalism and the position against which Roberson et al. argue represents a strong version. Their findings as well as their (culture-comparative) research design are incompatible with both strongly relativistic and strongly univeralistic views.

Spatial orientation

Another behavioral domain that has been studied fairly extensively is the relationship between spatial language and spatial cognition. It is evident that humans, like other species, are equipped for moving around in space with an elaborate biological apparatus, including vision, binaural hearing and the vestibular system. The question is to what extent this leads to universally uniform notions about natural space and spatial orientation. According to Levinson (1998, 2003), extensive research in non-western societies has shown that such notions can differ in fundamental ways from those in western societies and that such differences arise from spatial terminology in the language. In Indo-European languages like English the location of objects in the horizontal plane is given from an ego-referenced orientation. For example, English speakers may say "the chair is to the right side of the table"; if they then move to the opposite side of the same display, they would say "the chair is to the left of the table." This spatial frame of reference is viewer dependent, and hence labeled "relative" or "egocentric." In some other languages, the preference is to use absolute orientation with geocentric spatial coordinates that stay the same independently of the position of the observer. They might say "the chair is west of the table." Up-hill/down-hill, the direction of the rising and declining sun, and cardinal directions provide coordinates that are independent of the position of the observer (Levinson, 2003; Taylor and Tversky, 1996).[3] Note that these geocentric references are used not only for wider spatial orientation, but also to describe the location of objects in near, or so-called table, space, inside of dwellings, and even when the reference landmarks are not directly visible.

Majid, Bowerman, Kita, Haun and Levinson (2004, p. 113) in a review of research on spatial frames of reference write about "profound linguistic effects on cognition" and "the emerging view that language can play a central role in the restructuring of human cognition." Such views have been endorsed by several authors (see Gentner and Goldin-Meadow, 2003). The question to be answered is whether such strongly relativist claims are justified.

Levinson and his colleagues devised a number of tasks designed to examine whether a relative or an absolute system of encoding is used not only in language but in non-linguistic cognitive tasks, for example when informants are confronted with a spatial display they are asked to memorize. One such task makes use of

---

[3] A third possibility is to describe the position of an object with reference to another object; for example, "the man is in front of the house," which is also viewer independent. This intrinsic frame of reference, which is found in every language, does not play a role in this discussion.

identical cards, each with a big red circle and a small blue square. Four cards are placed on a table in four different directions (blue square left, right, up or down). A respondent has to remember one of the cards, say blue square to the right/to the east. The respondent is then led to another table, presented with a similar set of cards (with an array of cards at a 180° rotation from an absolute perspective) and asked to point out the card previously chosen. The choice of the card with the blue square to the right (in the above example) indicates a relative choice, and the blue square to left ("east") an absolute one; the two other cards are used to check for task comprehension.

Levinson (2003) and his colleagues (e.g., Majid *et al.*, 2004) reported studies in more than fifteen language groups, using between two and five rotation paradigm tasks in each, although with fairly small samples of mainly adults (eleven to thirty-seven per group). As expected, those groups speaking English, Dutch or Japanese tended to give predominantly relative responses, and those speaking a language in which a geocentric frame was favored (e.g., Arrernte among Australian Aborigines, Tzeltal Mayan in Mexico, Hai//om Khoisan in the Kalahari[4]) gave predominantly absolute responses. Levinson (2003, p. 185) concluded: "These results confirm that language is a good predictor of non-linguistic performance on such non-verbal tasks."

Dasen and colleagues (Dasen and Mishra, 2010; Dasen, Mishra and Niraula, 2003; Wassmann and Dasen, 1998) have carried out an extensive research program that replicates distinctions between an egocentric frame of reference and a geocentric frame of reference, but challenges the exclusive role of language suggested by Levinson (2003) and by Majid *et al.* (2004). They see language as only one aspect of a more general web of ecological, social and cultural factors that may favor the choice of one or the other frame of spatial reference.

In Bali, Wassmann and Dasen (1998) found that the left–right distinction exists in the Balinese language, but is used only to designate objects in contact with the body. Otherwise, objects are located by using a geocentric system based on the main axis up–down (to the mountain–to the sea) and two quadrants more or less orthogonal to this axis (in the south of Bali, this corresponds to sunrise–sunset, but the coordinate system turns as one moves around the island). Many aspects of Balinese life are organized according to this orientation system: the way villages and temples are laid out, the architecture of the compounds, the customary orientation for sleeping, as well as symbolic aspects (each direction is associated with a particular god) and very practical ones (e.g., "Go fetch my shoes that are in the uphill room in the downhill corner"). When spatial language was elicited from adults, the absolute reference system was clearly predominant, and only 3 percent of egocentric descriptors (left/right, in front/behind) were given.

---

[4] The // sign represents a clicking sound found in the language of this group.

Using two tasks devised by Levinson and colleagues (similar to the one described above), it was found that on one of the tasks, easy to encode in language, young children (aged 4 to 9 years) systematically used absolute (geocentric) encoding, as did 80 percent of older children (11 to 15 years) and adults. On another, more visual task, there was an even split between absolute and relative encoding. The impression gained from these results was that the Balinese, whether children or adults, preferentially use an absolute encoding, in accordance with the predominant orientation system in their language and culture. However, depending on task demands, relative encoding was also available.

In India and Nepal, Mishra, Dasen and Niraula (2003) studied children under various ecological conditions (a village and a city in the Ganges plain, and a village in the Nepalese mountains). They found that a relative frame of reference was used more in the city than in the nearby village, where the same language was spoken. Encoding was again found to be task dependent, and when asked for explanations respondents could make use of absolute language to describe a relative encoding and vice versa. Dasen *et al.* concluded that there was no overall linguistic determinant for a frame of reference and that the absolute and relative frames can coexist in the same person. Such plasticity appears to be difficult to reconcile with deeply rooted differences in cognition. It has been suggested that which frame will be followed is not a matter of competence but of "style" (cf. the concept of "cognitive style" as discussed in Chapter 6).

In a detailed account of the studies mentioned (and additional evidence collected on large samples of children in India, Indonesia and Nepal), Dasen and Mishra (2010) lean toward a moderate form of relativism in the sense that behavioral outcomes result from interactions of the individual child with the ecocultural context. The use of a geocentric frame of reference, in both language and cognition, was found to be promoted not only by actual language use (for example, using Balinese rather than Bahasa Indonesian in Bali), but by a greater adherence to traditional culture and Hindu religious practices (which emphasize spatial orientation, Sanskrit using a cardinal orientation system with eight named directions). Mishra, Singh and Dasen (2009) report that some children, particularly those attending a Sanskrit school in Benares, India, were found to be able to maintain geocentric dead reckoning even when outside cues were severely restrained (inside a darkened room, blindfolded, being rotated or led blindfolded to another room). Dasen and Mishra (2010) conclude:

the individuals have in their possession the basic processes needed for either frame, in the same way as basic cognitive processes have been found to be universal in comparative cross-cultural psychology ... Activating one process rather than the other is akin to a cognitive style. And which one is chosen more frequently, or even predominantly, may be due either to individual differences (akin to personality), to task demands ... or to a large variety of ecological and socio-cultural factors.

Another aspect of spatial orientation concerns the description of relations between objects in various languages. Bowerman (1996) has addressed semantic categories referring to positions of objects in relation to each other, like "on," "in," "up" and "under." For example, in English a cookie is *on* the table, but *in* the bowl. The question is to what extent such locative categories are a matter of language, rather than of perceptual mechanisms. There is little doubt that children know about space, even before they master locative prepositions. But Bowerman shows with examples from various languages that prepositions often are not translation equivalent, and sometimes even do not make sense. Thus, in Finnish one says something akin to the English: "The handle is in [rather than on] the pan and the band aid is in [rather than on] the leg." A step further away from English is Tzeltal, a Mayan language, where the equivalent of the prepositions on and in (as in x is "on" the table or "in" the bowl) is not expressed, but locations are indicated with verbs that are differentiated according to the shape of objects. Thus, for a bowl on the table the verb *pachal* is used, and for a small ball the verb *wolol*. In Korean different verbs are used for putting on clothes on different parts of the body (e.g., *ipta* for the trunk, and *sinta* for the feet).[5]

If a broader cross-linguistic perspective is taken categorizations may show considerable similarities. Majid, Boster and Bowerman (2008) studied twenty-eight geographically widely distributed languages, asking speakers to describe videotaped events. There was a core set of cutting and breaking events (involving "non-reversible separations," like tearing a cloth in two pieces and chopping carrots), and a smaller set of "reversible separations," such as opening a teapot. Across speakers, both within and across languages, events described with the same verb were taken as semantically similar. With multivariate analysis (correspondence analysis) seven dimensions were extracted that accounted for 62 percent of the variance. The authors interpreted four of these. For example, the first dimension distinguishing "reversible" versus "non-reversible" events was interpreted as predictability of the locus of separation in the affected object. Loadings on this dimension varied from .60 to .93 across the twenty-eight languages with a mean of .83. Majid *et al.* argued: "Although the precise categories recognized by the languages in our sample differ, they are highly constrained by the four dimensions we have described. These dimensions delineate a semantic space in which the categories recognized by individual languages, as variable as they are, encompass adjacent clips" (2008, p. 243).

A further significant contribution to the debate on the implications for cognitive functioning of linguistic distinctions has come from the study of the Korean verbs *kkita* referring to objects that fit tightly into each other (putting the cap

[5] Bowerman could perhaps have found a similar effect in a language much closer to English, namely Dutch, where one *zet op* (places on) a hat, *doet om* (puts around) a shawl and *trekt aan* (pulls on) trousers and shoes.

on a pen) and *nehta* for loosely fitting relations (putting books in a bag). There is no direct match of this distinction in English (Bowerman and Choi, 2001; Choi and Bowerman, 2007). In habituation experiments McDonough, Choi and Mandler (2003) found that both Korean and English children as young as 9 months showed evidence of making this distinction. Korean adults also did so, but not English-speaking adults. Hespos and Spelke (2004) obtained similar results with 5-month-old infants in both Korean- and English-speaking environments, in other words, long before the onset of speech. Apparently, the categories are available to these infants independent of any representation in language. The fact that English adults do not readily make the distinction according to Hespos and Spelke suggests that the sensitivity to a conceptual distinction available for infants but not marked by their native language becomes reduced. In other words, infants appear to come equipped with a faculty for conceptual distinctions that are not coded in their language and that are strengthened or weakened through interaction with the social environment in the course of development. The environment in many respects seems to act as a set of constraints, a viewpoint to which we will return in the final section of Chapter 12.

It should be realized that once a linguistic categorization is in place, it can have surprising implications. Boroditsky, Schmidt and Phillips (2003) mention a free association task in English given to native speakers of German and Spanish, asking them to provide three adjectives that came to mind with each of a set of object names. These objects had been selected for having an opposite gender in the two languages. The gender of an object name in the original language was found to influence the connotative meaning in English. Thus, for object names that were masculine in German but feminine in Spanish the speakers of German provided adjectives that were rated more masculine. For words masculine in Spanish and feminine in German the opposite trend was found.

At the same time, grammatical differences need not have cognitive consequences as one might expect. A case in point is a study by Bohnemeyer (1998a, 1998b) with speakers of German and Yukatec Maya. In the latter language there are very few ways in which temporality, or the order of events, can be expressed grammatically (for example, the perfect and future of the verb are absent). In order to investigate possible consequences for communication Bohnemeyer prepared video recordings of scenes and combined these in various ways to form sequences of events. One of a pair of participants in the study was shown a video with a particular sequence. The other member of the pair was shown two videos differing in the order of two events and was allowed to ask a single yes/no question to the first participant. From the answer the second person had to infer which of the two videos had been shown to the first person. The German respondents made ample use of event order expressions in their language (in 92% of relevant expressions). The Yukatec speakers hardly did so (in only 1%), but made more frequent use of phasal operators, like "start," "continue" and "end." Despite the obvious grammatical differences German pairs and Yukatec pairs failed the task at nearly the same rate (13% and 15% of the cases respectively). Thus, the absence of expressions of event order in grammar did not markedly affect the distinction of temporality of events in Yukatec Mayan speakers, although they obviously differed from the German speakers in the use of grammatical means of expression.

All in all, during the past decades research on language and culture has been shifting to more precise analyses of more narrowly defined questions. Universalist positions that limit effects of language more or less to the denotative meaning of words do not seem to fit several recent findings. But also claims to the effect that differences in language extend to major psychological differences could not be upheld. Broad generalizations as suggested by Majid *et al.* (2004), in which cross-cultural differences are called cognitively "profound" or "systematic," are not supported. Grand views on both sides of the universalism–relativism dichotomy after initial successes have succumbed under the weight of empirical data; information from controlled empirical studies has led to more nuance and greater complexity. Recently more differentiated approaches are being developed, one example of which is presented in Box 8.2

Universality in language

The Whorfian hypothesis reflects the position that language determines cognition. There are other positions. Piaget (1975) sees language development as a concomitant of the cognitive structures of sensorimotor intelligence. In this sense cognitive development is considered to be a necessary condition for language. However, cognitive development can take place, at least to a certain extent, independent of the availability of (spoken) language. Research with deaf children has shown this quite clearly (e.g., Eibl-Eibesfeldt, 1979; Lenneberg, 1967). Thus, a genetic basis for human language has been assumed, which should show up as universals in language. In a classic work on the biological foundations of language Lenneberg (1967) has argued that the processes by which language (including its structural properties) is realized are innate. Perhaps the most powerful evidence is that deaf children bring language-like structure into their gestures. Goldin-Meadow and Mylander (1998) found that deaf children in both the USA and China used strings of gestures to communicate messages, whereas hearing children and adults tend to use single gestures. These authors concluded that the structural similarities in the children's gestures were striking, despite large variations in environmental conditions, and therefore were likely to be innate.

Box 8.2 A new route for linguistic relativity?

As we have seen in this chapter, most of the proposals about linguistic relativity concern cross-cultural differences in perception and thinking as a consequence of differences in languages, such as grammar and semantic categories. There is another way in which linguistic relativity can be studied, namely by looking at the use of a language under controlled conditions. This was done by Stapel and Semin (2007), who showed with Dutch students effects of different linguistic devices within the same language.

Stapel and Semin hypothesized that the use of concrete terms (action verbs) to describe a situation would influence perception in that attention would be focussed on local properties and details; the use of adjectives would draw attention to global properties of an object. They based their hypotheses on the Linguistic Category Model by Semin and Fiedler (1988), which proposes a sequence from concrete to abstract word categories, ranging from descriptive verbs ("she carries the woman's groceries"), via interpretive action verbs ("she is helping the woman"), and state verbs ("she cares about the woman"), to adjectives ("she is a kind person"). The properties described by adjectives show low contextual dependence; their use is governed by abstract, semantic relations and not by the contingencies of contextual factors. The opposite is true for action verbs, which refer to contextual and situated features of an event.

In the studies, they primed half of the participants with action verbs and half of the participants with adjectives, for example by having students describe a short film of moving chess pieces in terms of verbs or adjectives, by having students read sentences with either action verbs or adjectives or by subliminally flashing action verbs or adjectives on a computer screen. In each of the studies, the dependent variables were perception or categorization tasks. For example, students were presented with a figure that was made up of smaller figures of a different type (e.g., a square made of a number of small triangles). Then they were presented with two other figures that resembled the first figure either at a global level (e.g., a square made up of small squares) or at a detailed, local level (e.g., a triangle made up of small triangles) and asked which figure was most similar to the first. Students in the action verb condition systematically chose more often the figure that matched the first at a local level (i.e., the small figures making up the large figure) whereas students in the adjective condition more often chose the figure that matched the first at a global level (i.e., the large figure made up by the small figures).

Stapel and Semin concluded that their results "provide reliable, empirical evidence for the core of Whorf's (1956) linguistic-relativity hypothesis: Linguistic categories point people to different types of observations" (2007, p. 31). Of course, their research is about differences within one linguistic population. For cross-cultural psychologists the most interesting question is whether differences in perception between

Box 8.2 continued

populations can also be explained though this mechanism. Stapel and Semin see their research as the missing link in cross-cultural studies of linguistic differences. If cultures systematically differ in the extent to which concrete (action verbs) or abstract (adjectives) language is used then this may explain differences in perception. There is some research showing that cultures may indeed differ on this aspect. For example, Maas, Karasawa, Politi and Suga (2006) found that Italians rely more on trait adjectives and Japanese more on behavior-descriptive terms in the description of individuals and groups. The combination of intracultural and cross-cultural research clearly opens new routes for exploration of the relationships between language on the one hand, and how we perceive the world and cognitively deal with it on the other hand.

In line with Lenneberg's ideas Chomsky (e.g., 1965, 1980) suggested that there is a "universal grammar" to which any human language conforms. This grammar corresponds with the nature and scope of human cognitive functioning. According to Chomsky there is an innate organization, a "language acquisition device," that determines the potential for language. At birth the mind is equipped with a mental representation of the universal grammar. Essential in Chomsky's writings is a distinction between the surface structure of a sentence and the deep structure. The surface structure (i.e., the sentence as it appears) can be changed through a series of transformations to the deep structure (i.e., the meaning of the sentence). Chomsky (2000) has confirmed his position that the faculty of language can be regarded as a "language organ," in the same sense as the visual system or the immune system. This faculty is genetically based and the initial state is common to the species. This language acquisition device "takes experience as 'input' and gives the language as an 'output'" (Chomsky, 2000, p. 4). Both input and output are open to examination and form the observational basis for inferences about qualities of the language organ. Thus, Chomsky's approach amounts mainly to an analysis of grammatical features of languages.

The properties of the language acquisition device should be reflected in all human languages. However, so far the grammatical analysis of sentences has not resulted in extensive demonstration of universal characteristics. Few cross-cultural studies have been conducted in psychology aiming to test this theory. Rather, the available evidence is mostly based on detailed rational analyses of abstract structures (such as the deep syntactic structure) in one language. In the tradition of Chomsky universal properties of languages that have been postulated were mainly derived from descriptive surveys of grammatical and other characteristics of languages. Although research has mainly taken the form of linguistic analysis of transformation rules and few cross-cultural psycholinguistic studies have been conducted, Chomsky's ideas have had a wide following. More recently Chomsky (see Hauser, Chomsky and Fitch, 2002) has turned to the evolutionary basis of the faculty of language. However, which functions or properties make language uniquely human largely remains an open question; our understanding of the various constraints that have shaped this evolutionary process remains fragmentary.

The notion of a universal grammar has been challenged by Evans and Levinson (2009). Addressing a list of properties that have been claimed to be shared by all languages (Pinker and Bloom, 1990) they provide evidence of exceptions to all of these. The diversity in human languages at all levels from sounds to meaning is seen as evidence of the importance of cultural and technological adaptation: language is taken as a "bio-cultural hybrid, a product of intensive gene-culture coevolution over perhaps the last 200,000 or 400,000 years" (Evans and Levinson, 2009, p. 431). They refer to a "dual inheritance" theory by Boyd and Richerson (1985, 2005) that will be discussed in Chapter 11 (see p. 266). Evans and Levinson do not deny that there are constraints on how grammars and syntaxes can be constructed, but there appear to be no singular solutions of the type postulated in the concept of universal grammar that have been followed in the development of all languages.

The criticism of universal grammatical structures is of importance in so far as it affects the theoretical status of postulated cognitive processes associated with a universal grammar (see, e.g., Hauser *et al.*, 2002). However, there are regularities in language-related psychological features that do not appear to be much affected by Evans and Levinson's critique of presumed universality of linguistic structures. We can refer here to studies, mentioned in the previous subsection, that have shown similarities in psychological functioning underlying the observable range of variation (for example, the research by Dasen and colleagues, e.g., Dasen and Mishra, 2010, on spatial frames of reference and the study by Majid *et al.*, 2008, on cutting and breaking events). We would also like to refer to the previous chapter on emotions, where instances were presented of cross-cultural differences in linguistic categorization of emotions that were not matched by corresponding differences in various emotion components (e.g., Breugelmans and Poortinga, 2006; Van de Ven *et al.*, 2009).

In the previous chapter we also referred to the work of Osgood (Osgood, May and Miron, 1975) on three dimensions of affective meaning that could be identified across many cultures. Among the features presumably shared by all languages Osgood (1980) postulated the principle of "affective polarity." The three factors of affective meaning that he found, namely evaluation, potency and activation, each have a positive and a negative pole. Affectively negative words will be "marked" more often and positive words will be "unmarked" more often. The marking of a word implies extension with an affix. A clear example in English is the prefix "un" as in *un*happy, or *un*fair. In all thirty language communities studied by Osgood *et al.* (1975) adjectives with a positive meaning, particularly on the evaluation dimension, were also used more frequently and over a wider range of situations than adjectives with a negative meaning.

Another study by Osgood (1979) concerns the use of "and" or "but" in various languages. He argued that the polarity of positive and negative is a basic characteristic of human cognition, already expressed in the ancient Chinese principles of *yang* and *yin*. Osgood anticipated that respondents, when asked to connect two adjectives with either "and" or "but," would use "and" for adjectives with an affectively congruent meaning. When the meaning of two adjectives was affectively incongruent, they should use "but." For example, we tend to speak about noble *and* sincere, beautiful *but* nasty, happy *but* sad and so forth. From his project on affective meaning, mentioned above, Osgood could calculate for various languages a similarity index between pairs of adjectives. Thereafter the correlation was computed between this similarity index and the frequency of using "and" as a connective between two adjectives. The average of this correlation for twelve languages, including among others American English, Finnish, Turkish and Japanese, was $r = .67$, pointing to a shared presence of the cognitive properties involved.

It should be clear that a universalist approach to cross-cultural research in psycholinguistics is not limited to finding similarities; one can also study differences, notably as a function of unequal antecedent conditions to which speakers of a language are being exposed. Apart from the examples given here we can refer to the Internet (Additional Topics, Chapter 8), where some of the tasks are mentioned www.cambridge.org/berry that children have to cope with when acquiring a language. For example, when speakers of Japanese have difficulty distinguishing the English spoken words "lead" and "read" this is understandable as a reflection of differences in antecedent experiences. Another illustration is research on word segmentation, mentioned in the same Internet section. Such differences do not detract from universality of psychological functioning; in fact common functions can be said to make such differences understandable.

Conclusions

There is no aspect of overt behavior in which human groups differ more than in the languages they speak. By itself this does not have any far-reaching implications, since there are few connections between the phonemic features of words and their meanings. In this chapter we explored some of the perceptual and cognitive consequences of lexical and grammatical differences that are also part of linguistic differences, concentrating on two domains where objective reality can be matched with subjective experience and expression, namely color naming and the use of spatial frames of reference. The exploration of the literature for evidence of linguistic relativity was followed by a similar exploration of evidence for similarities that could qualify as universal properties of human language. In both sections we have presented research supporting various positions.

In the beginning of this chapter we presented the Whorfian hypothesis. In its original form the hypothesis has to be rejected. One's thoughts are not nearly as much determined by one's language as Whorf led us to believe. In the meantime the reach of the hypothesis has shifted and research has become more sophisticated. However, this higher level of sophistication has not led to more agreement. Researchers with a relativist orientation tend to remain of the opinion that findings support their viewpoint and the same holds for researchers with a universalist orientation.

KEY TERMS

absolute orientation • basic color terms • color categorization • ego-referenced orientation • linguistic relativity • spatial orientation • universals in language • Whorf's hypothesis

FURTHER READING

Dasen, P. R., and Mishra, R. C. (2010). *Development of geocentric spatial language and cognition.* Cambridge: Cambridge University Press.

This book reports on a thorough research project, providing a balanced account of the relativistic and universalistic features of frames of reference in spatial location.

Evans, N., and Levinson, S. C. (2009). The myth of language universals: Language diversity and its importance for cognitive science. *Behavioral and Brain Sciences*, 32, 429–492.

This article, written from a relativist perspective, provides elaborate linguistic evidence against commonly accepted universals in language.

Hardin, C. L., and Maffi, L. (eds.) (1997). *Colour categories in thought and language.* Cambridge: Cambridge University Press.

The chapters of this book examine the evidence on universals in color naming mostly from a universalist and sometimes from a relativist perspective.

Hauser, M. D., Chomsky, N. A., and Fitch, W. T. (2002). The faculty of language: What is it, who has it, and how did it evolve? *Science* 298(5,598), 1569–1579.

This article provides a distinctly universalist approach to language; it stands in contrast to the above-mentioned article by Evans and Levinson.

9 Perception

CONTENTS

Conventional wisdom would have it that cross-cultural differences in perception are of minor significance. The universal similarities in the anatomy and the physiology of the sensory organs and the nervous system make it likely that sensory impressions and their transmission through the perceptual apparatus are invariant across cultures. In this chapter we shall show that while there are common processes in sensation and perception, there are substantial differences in the outcomes of these processes, and that there can be cross-cultural differences even in the way very simple figures are being perceived. This chapter reviews research mainly from a period before cross-cultural psychology became focussed on sociocultural variables. As argued in Chapter 1, we consider the ecological environment as an important aspect of human functioning in context; we see the topics discussed in this chapter as important for understanding human behavior and its ecocultural and sociocultural variations.

The first section gives a brief review of historical roots of contemporary cross-cultural psychology of perception. This is followed by a section on studies of sensory functions. Then we turn to perception in a more strict sense. When contrasted with sensation, perception implies stimulus selection and other forms of active engagement of the organism. Extensive research, mainly conducted in the 1960s and 1970s, concerns the perception of patterns and pictures. We will examine cross-cultural research on the perception of simple figures, including visual illusions, and on the perception of depth with two-dimensional depictions of three-dimensional objects and scenes. The fourth section on categorization is brief, because much of the research that might be discussed here has been presented in the chapters on emotions and (especially) language. The fifth section deals with the well-established finding that face recognition of members of other groups is more difficult than the recognition of own-group members.

On the Internet there is an entry on psychological aesthetics, a topic developed by Berlyne (e.g., 1980) that showed remarkable similarities in perceptual aspects of appreciation of art, underlying the enormous variations in expressive styles across cultures (Additional Topics, Chapter 9). Most studies have been done on vision, but we also mention some studies in audition, taste and smell.

www.cambridge.org/berry

Historical roots

W. H. R. Rivers (1864–1922) is widely seen as one of the pioneers of cross-cultural psychology. His main work (Rivers, 1901) was based on data gathered during a period of four months by him and some students with Torres Strait Islanders on Murray Island, located between New Guinea and Australia. Measurements were taken on a wide range of topics, such as visual acuity, color vision, visual afterimages, visual illusions, auditory acuity, rhythm, smell and taste, weight discrimination, reaction times, memory and muscular power. The data were organized around three main subjects: visual acuity, perception and visual/spatial perception.

In many respects Rivers' work could be called exemplary for cross-cultural research even today. He showed great concern for issues of method. For example, he worried whether a task was properly understood and tried out different methods to find out which one worked most satisfactorily. He also backed up quantitative data by different kinds of contextual evidence. For example, in his analysis of vision Rivers not only studied color naming and the sensitivity for different colors, but he also asked for preferences and even took note of the colors of the scarves that people would wear on Sundays in church. In addition, Rivers had an open eye for possible alternative explanations. When discussing the then popular notion of the extraordinary visual acuity of non-Europeans, he distinguished between the power of resolution of the eye as a physiological instrument, powers of observation, and familiarity with the surroundings. For example, he examined the eyes of his respondents for defects and diseases and measured visual acuity with and without correcting lenses for deficient eyesight.

Rivers found the visual acuity of the Torres Strait Islanders to be in no way extraordinary. This finding was in contrast with the then prevailing idea that non-European people had more acute sensory faculties (and less well-developed cognitive capacities). On the basis of his own work Rivers concluded "that the visual acuity of savage and half-civilized people, though superior to that of the normal European, is not so in any marked degree" (1901, p. 42). However, he also discussed at length accurate observation of the "savages" and their attention to minute details, concluding that "the predominant attention to objects of sense [is] a distinct hindrance to higher mental development. If too much energy is expended on the sensory foundations, it is natural that the intellectual superstructure should suffer" (1901, pp. 44–45). This complementary relationship between the sensory and the intellectual domain is repeatedly mentioned. It shows that despite his openness of mind, even Rivers was deeply influenced by the ethnocentric ideas prevalent in his time.

In the miscellaneous studies on perception that were published between 1910 and 1950, the notion of "race" remained the dominant explanation of differences, but often without gross implications of inferiority. An example is the work of Thouless (1933) and Beveridge (1935, 1940) on constancies, or "phenomenal regression." From most angles of vision the projection of a circular disc on the retina of an observer forms an ellipse. When asked what they see respondents tend to draw an ellipse that is between the form of the actual retinal projection and a full circle (the phenomenon). This regression toward the phenomenon can be observed not only for form, but also for size, brightness, and so forth. For example, when a gray paper is illuminated at a higher intensity so that it reflects more light than a white paper, it may not appear lighter to the respondent who "knows" that it is gray.

Thouless (1933) found that a small sample of Indian students, compared to Scots, showed a greater tendency to phenomenal regression for two tasks (relative size of two discs, and circular versus ellipsoid form of a disc). He related this finding to Indian art where, in the absence of perspective, objects are drawn as they are rather than as they present themselves to the observer, more so than in European art. Beveridge (1935) found a greater tendency to phenomenal regression among West African college students than among British students for shape and size. In a later study (Beveridge, 1940) he extended the range of tasks and concluded that Africans were probably less affected by visual cues than Europeans, a notion to which we will come back just now.

Somewhat apart stands the work of Oliver (1932, 1933), who argued for the incorporation of indigenous elements in test items and the recognition of difficulties of language and instruction. In a study with the Seashore test for musical abilities he found that West African students, compared with US-American students of a similar level of schooling, acquired higher scores for loudness discrimination, tone duration discrimination and identification of rhythm, but lower scores for discrimination of pitch, discrimination of timbre and tonal memory. The tests for timbre and tonal memory were the only two that correlated with intelligence, presumably because the instructions were difficult to understand.

An important question has been whether observed differences in sensations stand by themselves or whether they generalize to different modalities. For example, in the middle of the last century there was a widespread belief that Africans were more tuned to auditory and kinesthetic stimuli and Europeans more to visual stimuli. Popular knowledge referred to a sense of rhythm and music and a feeling for languages among Africans, including African Americans (e.g., Nursey-Bray, 1970). In the 1960s McLuhan (1971) emphasized the dominance of the visual modality in western people, and Wober (1966) coined the term "sensotypes" to indicate differences between cultural groups in the relative importance of one sensory modality over the others. However, no evidence has been found for the compensation hypothesis in systematic quasi-experimental studies (e.g., Deregowski, 1980a; Poortinga, 1971, 1972). Since the 1970s such notions have largely disappeared from the cross-cultural literature.

Sensory functions

Four classes of explanations of cross-cultural differences in reactions to simple **sensory stimuli** can be distinguished, namely (1) conditions in the physical environment that affect the sensory apparatus directly, (2) environmental conditions that affect the sensory apparatus indirectly, (3) genetic factors and (4) differences in perception.

An example of the direct effect of physical conditions can be found in a report by Reuning and Wortley (1973) on a series of expeditions into the Kalahari Desert.[1] They reported a better auditory acuity in the higher frequency ranges (up to 8,000 Hz) for San in the Kalahari Desert (called "Bushmen," as was common at the time) than the reference values given for Denmark and for the USA. The differences were more striking for older respondents, suggesting that in the Kalahari there is less hearing loss with increasing age. Reuning and Wortley suggested the low levels of ambient noise in the environment as the critical factor in explaining these differences, although they emphasized that other factors, such as diet, could provide alternative explanations.

An example of the indirect effect of environmental conditions, namely poor nutrition, was suspected when black recruits to the South African mining industry

---

[1] The mode of subsistence of the San (hunting and gathering) was severely threatened. The rationale of the project was to map out the competences and abilities with a view to exploring what other ways of economic existence might be feasible. The approach was fairly imposing although it was not perceived in this way at the time.

were found to have a slower dark adaptation than white South Africans (Wyndham, 1975). Deficiencies in the diet were thought to have led to a low level of vitamin A, leading to insufficient functioning of the rods in the retina that are used for vision under conditions of low illumination. A change in diet, however, did not lead to the expected improvement. It was then suggested that many of the mine-workers might be suffering from subclinical forms of liver ailments (cirrhosis), associated with a high incidence of nutritional diseases in early childhood. More recent evidence on the effects of malnutrition has shown a wide range of negative physical and psychological consequences (see the section on poverty, hunger and malnutrition in Chapter 17).

Effects of genetic factors, the third factor mentioned in the literature, have been established for red–green color blindness. Already at the time of Rivers (1901) it was known that the frequency of red–green color blindness was much lower in some non-European groups than in some European groups. Within an evolution-theoretical framework this has been attributed to the disadvantages that color-blind people have when hunting and gathering is the main means of subsistence (cf. Post, 1962, 1971). Another example is the inability to taste substances that contain phenylthiocarbamide or another thiocarbamide group. About 30 percent of Europeans are "taste-blind" for these bitter-tasting substances. Africans and Native Americans are populations that have only a few percent non-tasters (Doty, 1986; Kalmus, 1969). A further illustration of differential sensitivity for the effects of certain chemical compounds is the "alcoholic flush," a reddening of the face that is common among East Asian people after the consumption of only a few alcoholic drinks (Wolff, 1972a, b), but is rarely found in people of European descent.

Most reported differences in sensation have to do with how stimuli are perceived. Here culturally conditioned preferences or dislikes for stimuli play a role rather than the capacity for discrimination or tolerance thresholds. For example, Kuwano, Namba and Schick (1986) have argued that small differences in the evaluation of loudness of neighborhood noise between Japan, Great Britain and West Germany should be interpreted with reference to sociocultural factors (how much you tolerate) rather than in terms of sensory impact or another perceptual variable.

For tastes it has been argued that there is an innate preference for sweet tastes, associated with sugars, and aversion of bitter tastes, associated with toxins (Rozin, 2007). Several differences in preference or hedonistic value have also been found in studies on taste. For example, Chinese respondents rated sucrose at low concentrations as more pleasant than did European American respondents in the USA (Bertino, Beauchamp and Jen, 1983). A stronger preference of African Americans for sweet foods has also been reported. The role of experience is quite obvious here, since sucrose preference can be manipulated by dietary exposure. Also, it has been demonstrated in conditioning experiments that a more or less neutral taste becomes more appreciated when it is coupled with a well-liked flavor (see Doty, 1986, 2001).

Perception of patterns and pictures

In the remainder of this chapter we shall pay attention to perceptual variables. In cross-cultural research the distinction is often fuzzy, but traditionally sensation implies a more passive role for the organism as a recipient for stimuli, whereas perception presumes an active engagement on the part of the organism in the selection and organization of stimuli.

The drawing in Figure 9.1 is taken from a study on pictorial recognition among a remote group in Ethiopia, the Mekan or Me'en, who, at the time, had little previous exposure to pictorial representations (Deregowski, Muldrow and Muldrow, 1972). With few exceptions they identified a leopard, but only after some time and not without effort, for example pointing to the tail a few initially reported a snake. In the process of examination some respondents would go beyond visual inspection; they would touch the cloth on which the pictures were painted and sometimes even smell it.

In all likelihood this is not a matter of (lack of) object recognition in any broader sense. Biederman, Yue and Davidoff (2009) presented unschooled rural Himba in Namibia and students in Los Angeles with pictures of geometric objects, like pyramids or cylinders. They made a distinction between non-accidental properties (e.g., straight contours versus curved contours) and metric properties (e.g., degree of curvature). In a series of trials the respondents had to select the best match of two figures to a standard. Somewhat contrary to their expectation error rates were

Figure 9.1 One of the stimuli used in a recognition task by Deregowski *et al.* (1972). The original figure was much larger (50 by 100 cm) and drawn on coarse cloth.

about the same for the two samples; in each sample error rates were higher for metric differences than for differences in non-accidental properties. Biederman *et al.* concluded that the limited exposure of the Himba to regular artifacts and the absence of words in their language for such forms did not lead to a difference in sensitivity for physical variation.

Pictures such as that of the leopard in Figure 9.1 are fairly complex in shape and texture, and involve culturally rooted artistic styles. Generally more simple figures have been used to analyze principles of perception across cultures. For example, Reuning and Wortley (1973) administered to the San tests for perception of symmetry. Two items are presented in Figure 9.2. Each item consists of a drawing of three narrow rectangles, two black and one gray. The respondent is given a fourth (gray) oblong of the same size as the rectangles. This has to be placed in such a position on the paper that it forms a (bilateral) symmetrical pattern with the three rectangles already there. The item at the top is completed;

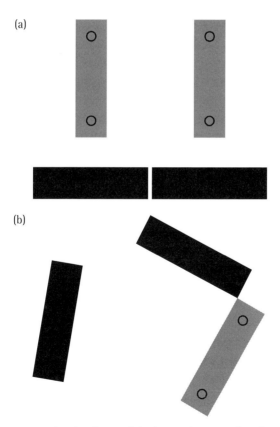

Figure 9.2 Two items, one completed and one as it is given to the respondent, from a test of bilateral symmetry. (The respondent indicates the answer by making a mark with a pencil in two small holes, indicated by small circles on the oblong figure.) After the symmetry completion test, NIPR, Johannesburg.

the other item depicts an incomplete pattern, as it is presented to the respondent. Many San were found to grasp easily the idea of bilateral symmetry.

Visual illusions

One of the richest early research traditions has been on cross-cultural differences in the susceptibility for geometric illusions (see Deregowski, 1989; Segall et al., 1999). An extensive body of research was triggered by the landmark study of Segall, Campbell and Herskovits (1966). This study had its origin in a difference of opinion between the anthropologist Melville Herskovits and the psychologist Donald Campbell, both of whom were Segall's mentors. Herskovits, whose ideas about cultural relativism implied almost unlimited flexibility of the human psyche, believed that even such basic experiences as the perception of the length of line segments would be influenced by cultural factors. Campbell had doubts and thought it required precise empirical scrutiny.

Segall et al. (1966) conducted an extensive study of visual illusions rooted in the work of Brunswik (1956). He believed that repeated experience with certain perceptual cues would affect how these are perceived. This is expressed in the notion of "ecological cue validity." Illusions occur when previously learned interpretations of cues are misapplied because of unusual or misleading characteristics of stimuli (i.e., when usually valid cues happen to be invalid). Segall et al. (1966) generated three hypotheses:

1. The carpentered world hypothesis. This postulates a learned tendency among those raised in an environment shaped by carpenters (rectangular furniture, houses and street patterns) to interpret non-rectangular figures as representations of rectangular figures seen in perspective. If the hypothesis is correct, people in industrial urban environments should be more susceptible to illusions such as the Müller–Lyer and the Sander parallelogram (see Figure 9.3).
2. The foreshortening hypothesis. This pertains to lines extending in space away from the viewer. In pictorial representations these appear as vertical lines. People living in environments with wide vistas have learned that vertical lines on the retina represent long distances. They should be more susceptible to the horizontal–vertical illusion than people living in an enclosed environment, such as a rain forest.
3. The sophistication hypothesis. Learning to interpret patterns and pictures should enhance geometric illusions that are presented two-dimensionally. Exposure to pictorial materials makes people more susceptible to visual illusions.

The design of the study by Segall et al. (1966) was impressive in including several features to guard against possible alternative explanations. For example,

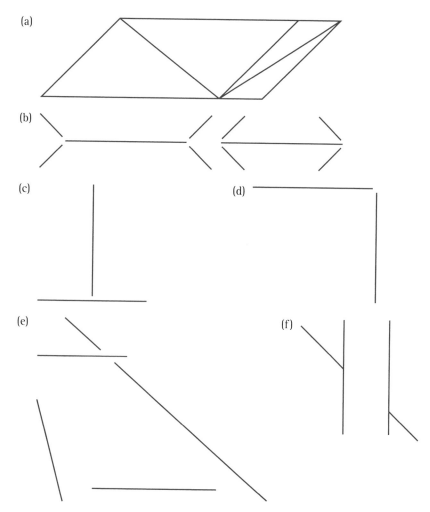

Figure 9.3 Visual illusions used by Segall, Campbell and Herskovits (1966). The respective patterns are (a) Sander parallelogram, (b) Müller–Lyer illusion, (c) and (d) two versions of the horizontal–vertical illusion, (e) modified form of the Ponzo illusion and (f) Poggendorff illusion.

in each location where data were collected a description was made of the prevailing environment in terms of carpenteredness and availability of wide open spaces. Such an elaborate check on the independent variable is still rare in cross-cultural research today. There were also checks on the understanding of the instructions with trial items and on the consistency of the answering patterns of respondents.

Fourteen non-western and three western samples were tested by Segall *et al.* (1966) with a series of stimuli for each of the six illusions presented in Figure 9.3. On both the Müller–Lyer illusion and the Sander parallelogram the western samples were found to be more illusion-prone than any of the non-western samples. Samples drawn from regions with open vistas were more susceptible for the two versions of the horizontal–vertical illusion than samples from regions where such vistas were rare. Also compatible with the second hypothesis was the finding that on the whole non-western respondents were more prone to the horizontal–vertical illusion than western respondents. The patterning of the findings with non-western respondents being more susceptible to some but less to other illusions rules out an explanation in terms of an overall factor, such as test sophistication. All in all, the results were clearly in support of the hypotheses.

Numerous other factors were examined in further research, such as enrichment of the context (Brislin, 1974; Brislin and Keating, 1976; Leibowitz, Brislin, Perlmutrer and Hennessey, 1969), effects of attention (Davis and Carlson, 1970), training in drawing (Jahoda and Stacey, 1970) and skin color. The last variable served as an index of pigmentation of the retina and for some time provided a challenge to the environmental interpretation of the data given by Segall *et al.* (1966).

The reason for implicating retinal pigmentation rested on a series of findings. Pollack (1963) established that at older ages the ability for contour detection decreases. Pollack and Silvar (1967) found a (negative) correlation between contour detection and susceptibility for the Müller–Lyer illusion. They also found correlations between skin color and both retinal pigmentation and contour detection (Silvar and Pollack, 1967). Since most non-western samples in the study of Segall *et al.* came from Africa, an explanation in physiological or genetic terms could not be ruled out. In spite of initial empirical support for the retinal pigmentation hypothesis (Berry, 1971; Jahoda, 1971), most later studies were clearly more in line with the environmental than with the physiological explanation (Armstrong, Rubin, Stewart and Kuntner, 1970; Jahoda, 1975; Stewart, 1973).

Not all the data fitted the carpentered world hypothesis or the foreshortening hypothesis. The most important discrepancy was the finding by Segall *et al.* (1966) that the susceptibility for nearly all illusions decreased with age, while the ever increasing exposure to the environment would lead one to expect the opposite, at least for the Müller–Lyer and related illusions. Nevertheless, as noted above, the three hypotheses have been by and large supported by the available evidence (Deregowski, 1989).

Depth perception

The systematic study of depth cues in pictures was initiated in South Africa by Hudson (1960, 1967) after errors of interpretation were noted among illiterate people in South Africa. Two stimuli of the set he used are shown in Figure 9.4. Hudson wanted to include the depth cues of object size, object superimposition

Figure 9.4 Two of Hudson's (1960) pictures.

and perspective in the pictures. Respondents were asked first to identify the man, the antelope and the other elements in the picture so as to make sure that these were recognized. Thereafter they were asked what the man was doing and whether the antelope or the elephant was closer to him. If there was an answer to the effect that the man was aiming the spear at the antelope or that the antelope was nearer to the man than the elephant, this was classified as a three-dimensional (3D) interpretation. Other answers (that the elephant was aimed at, or was nearer to the man) were taken as evidence of a 2D interpretation.

Hudson's test was administered to various groups in South Africa that differed in education and cultural background. School-going respondents predominantly gave 3D answers; the others responded almost entirely with 2D answers. Hudson's method was criticized on a number of points, but in essence his results were confirmed by later research; the ability to interpret western-style pictorial materials increases as a function of acculturation and school education (Duncan, Gourlay and Hudson, 1973).

Various studies were carried out, mainly in the late 1960s and 1970s, to expand on Hudson's work. The most important development has been the design of alternative methods to measure depth perception in pictorial representations. Deregowski (1980) has made extensive usage of methods in which respondents have to construct a 3D model after a 2D drawing. In one of these tasks respondents were asked to build, with sticks and small balls of plasticine, models of abstract geometrical drawings. In another task drawings of assemblies of cubes had to be copied with real blocks. Maybe the most interesting, because of its simplicity, is a task in which the respondent is given a pair of large wooden calipers. The respondent has to set the calipers at the same angle as that shown in simple drawings of the kind presented in Figure 9.5. The righthand figure can be perceived as a rectangular object photographed at an obtuse angle. If it is seen as such, the perceived angle should not be the same as for the flat figure but more rectangular. If no depth is perceived in the righthand figure, the respondent can be expected to set the calipers at the same angle for both figures. A comparison between Hudson's stimuli and tasks used by Deregowski showed that Zambian domestic servants and school children produced more 3D responses on the latter

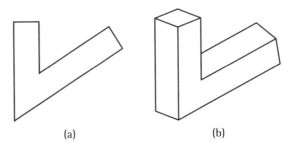

Figure 9.5 The calipers task (Deregowski and Bentley, 1986).

(a)   (b)

(Deregowski, 1980). Thus, the answers of the respondents were shown to vary with the nature of the task.

There are two depth cues that deserve special attention. The first is the gradient of texture. When one is looking along a brick wall details of separate bricks can be seen in the foreground. As the distance to the observer increases fewer and fewer details of texture can be perceived – hence the term "gradient of texture." This is a powerful depth cue in photographs, but one that is absent from virtually all stimulus sets used in cross-cultural studies. This is one reason why these stimuli are lacking in important information and to the first-time observer may display unusual qualities. The second cue is linear perspective. In many pictures, including some of Hudson's, a horizon is drawn on which all lines converge that represent parallel lines from real space. It has been a point of extensive debate whether this depth cue, which has an evident impact on the perception of depth for western respondents, should be seen as a cultural convention. One of the arguments for the conventional character of this cue is the existence of many art traditions in which linear perspective does not occur. In fact, it became only commonly used in Europe during the Renaissance. In addition, linear perspective in drawings does not correspond as closely to reality as is often thought. Parallel lines converge at infinity, but the horizon of our visual field is never at infinity. Standing on a railway the tracks may be seen to come closer together at a large distance, but they do not visibly converge into a single point. On the other hand, it can be argued that drawings based on the prescripts of linear perspective better resemble the optic array of real space than drawings constructed following other principles. In other words, linear perspective is not a convention in the sense of an entirely arbitrary agreement. As a rule it leads to more realistic representation than other conventions (Hagen and Jones, 1978).

Deregowski and Parker (1994) moved a step forward by differentiating between conditions where convergence of parallel lines represents the experiences of observers more adequately, and conditions where divergence is more adequate. A divergent perspective, where parallel lines diverge with increasing pictorial depth, is found frequently in Byzantine art. The task used by Deregowski and Parker required the adjustment of a 3D array in such a way that it appeared as a cube. When the array was placed straight in front of respondents, the adjustments they made were in agreement with a convergent perspective. However, when the array was shifted sideways so that it was no longer in front of the respondent, adjustments were according to a Byzantine divergent perspective. It is unclear why a particular art tradition has developed in a society to emphasize certain modes of representation. However, findings like these show how at first sight quite radically different modes of representation on closer examination provide evidence of close relationships in terms of the underlying perceptual mechanisms (Russell, Deregowski and Kinnear, 1997).

Serpell and Deregowski (1980) have conceptualized picture perception as involving a set of skills. A skilled perceiver can deal with a wide variety of cues and use those cues which are appropriate in a given situation. Basic is the recognition by the perceiver that a situation requires the application of certain skills. This means that one has to learn to treat pictures as a representation of real space. As mentioned before, the Mekan had some initial difficulty with this. Another skill is to know how to interpret impoverished cues. Apparently, western respondents have learned to interpret linear perspective cues as drawn in some of Hudson's pictures. Theorizing about pictorial perception as a set of skills makes clear that cultures can differ in the cues which are used and/or the relative importance attached to each of them. It seems reasonable to assume that culturally specific conditions will facilitate development of specific skills.

All in all, the empirical evidence allows a rather clear practical conclusion. There is little doubt that school children everywhere in the world easily recognize photographs of common objects and clear representational drawings. Relatively simple pictorial material has been shown to be educationally effective in countries ranging from Scotland to India and Ghana (Jahoda et al., 1976). Perceptual difficulties arise more often with pictorially unsophisticated persons, but for complex patterns they are experienced in any cultural group. The interpretation of schematic technical drawings is the most obvious case in point (e.g., Dziurawiec and Deregowski, 1986; Sinaiko, 1975).

The theoretical findings can be evaluated in two somewhat contrasting ways. On the one hand, important insights into the difficulties of pictorial communication have been gained in a few decades of fairly intensive research. On the other hand, an integrated theoretical approach which specifies how perceptual mechanisms and environmental experience interact has not been established. The reasons for this are unclear. There may be principles of organization that remain to be discovered. Alternatively, cultural choices for conventions of depiction may amount to more or less arbitrary selections from an array of workable alternatives. The question to what extent cross-cultural differences can be functionally or causally related to other parameters of culture and to what extent they appear to be non-deterministic is taken up in the final section of Chapter 12.

Categorization

In Chapter 7 we have seen that emotion terms differ across cultures and that there have been extensive discussions on the implications for experiences of emotions. In the previous chapter we have paid attention to categories in color naming. The major question was whether differences between languages in color terms could be demonstrably linked to perceptual categorizations of colors. These topics could also have been approached from the perspective of perception. We will not repeat the same evidence, but note that there have also been studies on odor and taste that have identified cross-cultural differences in categorization. These have been mostly presented as cross-cultural research in perception although sometimes the influence of language on categorization and recognition has been examined explicitly.

A difference in categorization of tastes was reported in a study of Japanese and US-Americans (O'Mahony and Ishii, 1986). The Americans tended to use four categories: sweet, sour, salty and bitter. The Japanese also used a fifth category, *ajinomoto*, which refers to the taste of monosodium glutamate, a well-known taste enhancer. In a subsequent study (Ishii, Yamaguchi and Mahony, 1992), both Japanese and Americans sorted in the same manner, reflecting conceptualization in line with the traditional four taste categories. Also in later studies with Japanese and Australians only quantitative differences in preferences were found.

Ayabe-Kanamura *et al.* (1998) presented Japanese and German women with everyday odorants. There were three types of odors: some were presumed to be familiar to the Japanese only, some to the Germans only and some to both populations. Ratings were asked for intensity, familiarity, pleasantness and edibility. Particularly clear differences between the two populations were found in pleasantness ratings. In general, there was a positive relationship between pleasantness and judgment of stimuli as edible, suggesting that culture-specific experiences, particularly of foods, may significantly influence odor perception. Somewhat unexpectedly, significant differences were also found between the two populations in intensity ratings for some odorants. These differences did not seem simply to be artifacts of the test situation. The authors mentioned the possibility that experience may even influence such basic aspects of odor perception as stimulus intensity. One striking example of a difference in appreciation was that the smell of dried fish was clearly associated with edible food by many Japanese, while the majority of Germans associated it with rotten rather than dried fish. Distel *et al.* (1999) obtained similar results in a study with data from Mexican women in addition to

German and Japanese women, which clearly supported the finding that experience plays a role in appreciation.

Closer to research on the influence of language on odor are studies by Chrea, Valentin, Sulmont-Rossé, Nguyen and Abdi (2005), who asked US-American, French and Vietnamese respondents to sort forty odorants on the basis of similarity in smell. Participants were also asked to sort on the basis of odor names, on the basis of imagined similarity and on the basis of typicality (some smells were rated as more typical than others). Chrea, Valentin *et al.* analyzed the data with multidimensional scaling and found that odor categories were based on perceptual similarities rather than on semantic categories. They argued that there exists a common category structure with boundaries that may differ across cultures. In a further study Chrea, Ferdenzi, Valentin and Abdi (2007) analyzed the codability (explained in Chapter 8, see p. 183) of odorants and its effect on recognition memory, again with French, US-American and Vietnamese samples. They concluded that the codability of odors was partly invariant across the three samples, suggesting that codability in part depends on the perceptual properties of the odors. There were also variations between the cultures as a function of both the olfactory environment and the language. Although the extent of differences still requires further analysis the gist of the findings is similar to that for colour categorization as discussed in Chapter 8.

The claim to the existence of similarities in categorization across all cultures has been reinforced by research on classifications found in folk biology (Atran, 1998). Cross-cultural agreement in the categorization of plants and animals appears to explain about half of the total variance (Medin, Unsworth and Hirschfeld, 2007). In everyday categories reference is most often made to a default level, at an intermediate level of abstraction, called the "basic level" (Rosch, 1978; Rosch and Mervis, 1975). Thus, in general we refer to a "dog" rather than to a "poodle" (subordinate category) or to a "canine" (superordinate category). With greater expertise there may be a shift to subordinate categories, that is, a dog trainer is likely to refer more frequently to a poodle or an Alsatian. It is evident that across cultures such expertise is likely to differ for certain families of plants or animals. Finer categorizations will differ across cultures, often in line with ecological considerations, such as the edibility of certain classes of species, and their place in the diet of a group.

There is debate regarding to what extent similarities in folk biology are the outcome of underlying innate principles of cognition for specific domains (e.g., naive physics and naive biology). The categorizations of very young children already reflect elementary principles of biology and physics, and these appear to guide further cognitive development (e.g., Gelman, 2003; Hirschfeld and Gelman, 1994). At the same time, there are substantial differences and these are of two kinds: in actual categorizations, and in cultural meanings which may be attached to a specific category. The assignment of symbolic or religious significance to some species (e.g., the cat in ancient Egypt or the cow in India) testifies to the importance of such cultural meanings (Medin and Atran, 2004; Medin *et al.*, 2007).

Face recognition across ethnic groups

People from groups with facial features different from one's own group tend to look alike; we also remember faces of individuals from our own ethnic group better (Malpass, 1996). In the USA, where a number of studies have focussed on the recognition of African Americans by European Americans, and vice versa, this cross-ethnicity effect is known as the "cross-race effect" or "own-race bias." Wherever the phenomenon has been investigated, it has been found, although research has been conducted in only a limited number of countries (Meissner and Brigham, 2001).

Differential recognition is usually established in experiments where respondents are shown, one at a time, a series of photographs of own-group members and persons belonging to some other ethnic group. After some time these photographs (or part of them) are presented again together with photographs not shown before (distractors). The respondents have to indicate for each photograph whether or not they saw a picture of that person before. One early experiment by Malpass and Kravitz (1969) used a yes/no recognition task and established a differential recognition effect quite clearly. There have been a number of variations on this basic study. Factors influencing the effect are the delay time between presentation and recognition, and the presentation time of the stimulus faces. Other parameters include the awareness or non-awareness of the respondents that they are taking part in a recognition experiment when first looking at the photographs, and whether the same photographs are presented of the target persons at the recognition task or different photographs. In order to systematically vary features sometimes representations have been developed with facial composite construction kits, a kind of device that is often used by the police to draw up a picture of a suspect on the basis of information of eyewitnesses.

It has become quite common to analyze the results in terms of a signal detection model (Swets, 1964) in which a distinction is made between two parameters, namely sensitivity and criterion bias. Four categories of answers are distinguished: (1) the correct identification of a face seen before (yes–yes); (2) the correct identification of a face not seen before (no–no); (3) the incorrect identification of a face seen before (no–yes); and (4) the incorrect identification of a face not seen before (yes–no). Sensitivity refers to the proportions of correct and incorrect answers. Criterion bias can refer to a tendency of a respondent not to identify a face shown before (resulting in false negatives), or a tendency to "recognize" faces not shown before (false positives). The latter happens more frequently.

In a meta-analysis, in which the majority of the studies came from African American and European American ethnic contrasts, Meissner and Brigham (2001) found that respondents were 1.4 times more likely to identify correctly a previously seen face of the ingroup than a face from an outgroup. Moreover, respondents were 1.6 times more likely to incorrectly identify a not previously presented face of the outgroup than of the ingroup as seen before (false positives). As far as criterion bias is concerned the effects were smaller, but there was a tendency toward a less strict criterion for outgroup faces than for ingroup faces.

It may seem an intuitively plausible explanation that the lower recognition of other ethnic groups reflects stereotypes or negative attitudes toward these groups. However, such social psychological explanations have found little support in experimental findings; rather it appears that perceptual mechanisms are involved. Such mechanisms are postulated in the "contact hypothesis" (see Chapter 14, p. 347). In its simplest form this hypothesis states that correct recognition is a function of frequency of contact. This variable on its own does not seem to have an important role in diminishing differences between own-group and outgroup recognition rates. Only when combined with quality of contact can such an effect be demonstrated (see Sporer, 2001). Thus, Li, Dunning and Malpass (1998) found that European Americans who were ardent basketball fans had better recognition of African American faces than non-fans. This effect was expected by the authors as basketball in the USA has a large number of African American players, and fans have considerable experience identifying individual players. Sporer, Trinkl and Guberova (2007) found that Turkish-Austrian children were faster than Austrian children of Germanic heritage in matching Turkish faces, while for Germanic faces there was no such difference. Apparently, the migrant Turkish children were equally familiar with both kinds of faces, while the Austrian children had relatively less exposure to Turkish faces.

The contact hypothesis can be seen as an instance of perceptual learning models that form the most widely accepted family of theories on the ingroup versus outgroup difference in recognition. According to Gibson (1966), perceptual skills involve learning to differentiate between task-relevant and task-irrelevant cues. In the course of time we learn the perceptual dimensions that are best used for discriminating faces. We gain more experience with the more salient dimensions for distinguishing own-group faces and relatively less with the dimensions of other groups. There is evidence that descriptions of own-group faces and those of other ethnic groups differ somewhat in terms of the categories that are being used (Ellis, Deregowski and Shephard, 1975).

Various forms of perceptual learning theory presume that faces are stored in some hypothetical space in which relevant features (or composites of features) form the dimensions (e.g., Valentine, 1991; Valentine and Endo, 1992). Outgroup faces then become better separated in this space with increasing experience; presumably more similar appearing outgroup faces should be located closer together in the perceptual space than the more differentiated own-group faces. Despite considerable support (e.g., Sporer, 2001) this theorizing has been challenged by MacLin, Malpass and Honaker (2001). With a construction kit these authors prepared faces that were ethnically ambiguous. This can be done by taking the average of each typical feature of two ethnic groups (in this case Hispanic American and African American). Ambiguous faces were provided with an "ethnic marker," namely a Hispanic American hairstyle or an African American hairstyle. In this way, the authors created faces with identical physiognomic features (except hairstyle), which should be equally distinguishable. However, in a recognition task with these faces Hispanic American students better recognized the faces with the Hispanic American hairstyle. MacLin *et al.* suggested that the ethnic marker drives the categorization which takes place according to ethnicity and that recognition is influenced by this perceptual categorization, rather than by higher perceived similarity due to lesser experience with outgroup faces.

Of course, it is difficult to generalize the findings in this section to eyewitness identification in real life. However, the differences in recognition are so large that eyewitness evidence in judicial courts by members of one ethnic group involving other groups may well lead to (unintended) discrimination. In the USA the validity of eyewitness testimony has been shaken since DNA testing in a number of cases has led to revision of convictions (partly) based on such evidence. This has led to reforms in line-up procedures and the interpretation of eyewitness evidence (Wells, Memon and Penrod, 2006).

Conclusions

It is obvious from this overview that not all perceptual variables are equally likely to show cross-cultural differences. On tasks for basic sensory functions, such as perceptual constancies, and stimulus discrimination on psychophysical scales, an approximately equal level of performance is to be expected for all cultural groups, unless there are widespread physical constraints, for example due to malnutrition or overexposure to high levels of noise.

Object recognition in clear representational pictures does not create many problems anywhere in the world, provided the perceiver has had at least some exposure to pictorial materials. Depth is readily perceived in photographs and other pictorial representations rich in depth cues. Culture-specific conventions can play a dominant role in the perception of depth in simple schematic drawings, like Hudson's test. Perceptual habits that are transferred from real space to pattern perception have been cited as antecedents of cross-cultural differences in the susceptibility for certain visual illusions. Some of these illusions are pictorially very simple, consisting only of a few line segments. On the other hand, seemingly difficult perceptual notions such as symmetry appear to be readily grasped by a San group where pictorial representation was largely absent.

As the discrepancy between real space and pictorial representation becomes larger cross-cultural differences increase. With respect to the categorization of stimuli, cultural codes (words) play a role, but categorizations, examined in the domain of odors, show properties that constrain variation. As more emphasis is placed on these common mechanisms, the explanation of cross-cultural differences in perception is shifting to conventions in the sense of cultural agreements which have a certain arbitrariness. Most conventions are limited to fairly specific classes of stimuli. They are not compatible with broad generalizations as have been made in the past, for example in the formulation of compensation hypotheses. However, it would be a mistake to think that an emphasis on conventions means that cross-cultural differences are trivial. If their number is large enough, together they can have a profound influence on the repertoire of behavior. Maybe this is the most important lesson that cross-cultural psychologists can learn from variations in artistic styles (Additional Topics, Chapter 9). Such styles appear to be  www.cambridge.org/berry rather arbitrary from the viewpoint of basic perception, but sometimes they have retained distinctive style characteristics for centuries. All in all, the contents of this chapter make clear how the study of behavior across cultures time and again reveals important cross-cultural differences, but perhaps more than in previous chapters these could be interpreted in terms of common underlying psychological functions and processes.

KEY TERMS

convention • cross-ethnicity effect (in face recognition) • depth cues in pictures • sensory stimuli • visual illusions

FURTHER READING

Deregowski, J. B. (1989). Real space and represented space: Cross-cultural perspectives. *Behavioral and Brain Sciences*, 12, 51–74.

A review article summarizing important classic research on illusions and perception of depth in figures, followed by peer discussion.

Medin, D. L., Unsworth, S. J., and Hirschfeld, L. (2007). Culture, categorization, and reasoning. In S. Kitayama and D. Cohen (eds.), *Handbook of cultural psychology* (pp. 615–644). New York: Guilford Press.

An overview from the perspective of cultural psychology on categorization and related topics.

Meissner, C. A., and Brigham, J. C. (2001). Thirty years of investigating the own-race bias in memory for faces: A meta-analytic review. *Psychology, Public Policy and Law*, 7, 3–35.

An overview of research on face recognition across ethnic groups.

Russell, P. A., Deregowski, J. B., and Kinnear, P. R. (1997). Perception and aesthetics. In J. W. Berry, P. R. Dasen and T. S. Saraswathi (eds.), *Handbook of cross-cultural psychology, Vol. II, Basic processes and human development* (pp. 107–142). Boston: Allyn & Bacon.

The authors review evidence on most topics in cross-cultural perception research, with the exception of face recognition.

Part II   Relationships between behavior, culture and biology

When seeking to understand and explain human behavior across differing populations, there is a need to be informed by concepts and findings from two disciplines beyond psychology that have influenced the development of cross-cultural psychology. First, cultural anthropology has contributed the concept of culture and the ethnographic methods used to study cultural phenomena. It has also examined relationships between culture and behavior, developing its own subdisciplines of psychological anthropology and cognitive anthropology. Second, human biology has also provided important concepts and methods for examining the development and display of behavior in varying contexts. This contribution has been especially important with the rise of the field of evolutionary biology in recent years. Taken together, these two disciplines provide a basis for our claim to be both a cultural science and a natural science. In addition to the conceptual and methodological contributions from these two cognate disciplines, cross-cultural psychology has developed a range of theoretical and practical ways to examine the relationships between context and behavior. The three perspectives presented in the first chapter of the book (culture comparative, cultural and indigenous) are further examined and elaborated. Some basic methodological requirements for making valid comparisons of data from different cultural populations are also explained. These theoretical and methodological principles are necessary in order to take into account both individual and group differences, and to provide the basis for the comparative search for psychological universals.

10 Contributions of cultural anthropology

CONTENTS

The field of anthropology is extremely varied, ranging from cultural and social anthropology, to biological and physical anthropology, and to linguistic and **psychological anthropology**. In this chapter, we emphasize cultural and social anthropology because it has provided a substantial foundation for cross-cultural psychology. However, some of the other fields of the discipline are considered in Chapters 8 and 11.

The core concept of culture has been part of psychology for over a century. The work of Rivers (1901) on perception in New Guinea and of Wundt (1913) on *Völkerpsychologie* were in essence examinations of how culture and behavior are related. More recently the concept of culture was identified as one of the core ideas in the history of international psychology (Pawlik and d'Ydewalle, 2006), and was portrayed there by Berry and Triandis (2006).

The term "culture" has appeared frequently in earlier chapters, with the general meaning provided in Chapter 1: "the shared way of life of a group of people." Also in Chapter 1, we outlined three themes which are intimately rooted in the concept of culture: culture as internal or external to the person (where culture can be found and studied); relativism–universalism (whether people from different cultures can be validly compared); and the psychological organization of cultural differences (whether culture can serve as a way of drawing behavior together into general patterns). These all required an initial understanding of what we mean by culture. In Chapter 1, we also outlined three interpretive positions: culture-comparative psychology, cultural psychology, and indigenous psychologies. These are similarly rooted in the meaning we assign to culture. Hence, a more precise definition of what we mean by culture is essential for our understanding of the field.

In this chapter we first examine various conceptions of culture in more detail. We then consider some aspects of ethnography, including ethnographic fieldwork and the use of ethnographic archives. Finally, we turn to a consideration of two domains of anthropological research that are related to cross-cultural psychology: cognitive anthropology and the study of religion. A portrayal of the field of psychological anthropology (also known as "culture-and-personality") can be found on the Internet (Additional Topics, Chapter 10).

www.cambridge.org/berry

The relationships between anthropology and psychology have been examined by Jahoda (1982) and by Wyer, Chiu and Hong (2009). These books should be read by those wanting an in-depth discussion of these relationships. In this chapter we attend mainly to those features of the anthropological tradition that have had a direct bearing on the development and conduct of cross-cultural psychology, including various conceptions of culture, and the practice of ethnography. However, we do not attempt to portray the field of **anthropology** as a whole. Those seeking an overview of the field should consult recent textbooks (e.g., Ember and Ember, 2007; Robbins, 2006) or the chapter by Munroe and Munroe (1997).

Conceptions of culture

The first use of the term "culture" in an anthropological work was by Tylor (1871), who defined culture as "that complex whole which includes knowledge, belief, art, morals, laws, customs and any other capabilities and habits acquired by man as a member of society." Two rather short but now widely used definitions were later proposed. Linton (1936, p. 78) suggested that culture means "the total social heredity of mankind," and Herskovits (1948, p. 17) that "[c]ulture is the man-made part of the human environment." In contrast to these concise definitions we also have lengthy listings of what is included in culture. One of these is by Wissler (1923), who included speech, material traits, art, knowledge, religion, society, property, government and war. This list is similar to the general categories of culture that are used in the Human Relations Area Files (HRAF); these will be presented later in this chapter (see Box 10.1).

In a classic survey of many definitions, Kroeber and Kluckhohn (1952) suggested that there are six major classes of definitions of culture to be found in the anthropological literature:

1. *Descriptive* definitions are those that attempt to list any and all aspects of human life and activity thought by the writer to be an example of what one means by "culture."
2. *Historical* definitions tend to emphasize the accumulation of tradition over time, rather than enumerating the range of cultural phenomena.
3. *Normative* definitions emphasize the shared rules which govern the activity of a group of people.
4. *Psychological* definitions emphasize a variety of psychological features, including notions such as problem-solving, learning and habits. For example, culture is learned, and the result of this learning is the establishment of habits and collective customs in a particular group.[1]
5. *Structural* definitions emphasize the pattern or organization of culture. This view is related to the descriptive category; however, the overall picture is emphasized here. The central view is that culture is not a mere random list of customs, but forms an integrated pattern of interrelated features.
6. *Genetic* definitions emphasize the origin, or *genesis*, of culture (not genetic in the biological sense). Within this category there are three main features: culture arises as adaptive to the habitat of a group; out of social interaction; and out of a creative process (both individual and interactive) that is a characteristic of the human species.[2]

---

[1] Some cross-cultural psychologists assert that cultures can be studied and described on the basis of psychological data collected from samples of individuals, and then aggregated to the level of their group (e.g., in Chapter 4, where individual value preferences are used to characterize a whole culture, society or nation; see p. 93). The most explicit statement of this belief has been by Triandis, who uses the notion of cultural syndrome to refer to "a pattern of shared attitudes, beliefs, categorizations, self-definitions, norms, role definition and values that is organized around a theme" (1996, p. 408). He argues that cultures can be studied and understood using both anthropological methods at the cultural level, and that "we can also use data from the individual level ... The cultural and individual difference analyses are complementary and allow us to describe cultures" (1996, p. 412). The notion of cultural syndromes has been taken up recently by Oyserman and Sorenson (2009). They present a model that is similar to the ecocultural framework in which cultural syndromes occupy a place intermediate between cultural and biological background phenomena and psychological outcomes.

[2] The ecocultural framework used in this text incorporates many features of these definitions. However, it is most closely related to the genetic definition. It adopts the view that culture is adaptive to both the natural habitat and to sociopolitical contexts (the first two origins), and that the third origin (creative processes) are represented as feedback from human accomplishments to other features of the framework. This dynamic view of how populations relate to their ecosystem treats culture not as a stable end-product, but as part of a constantly changing system, both adapting to, and impacting on, its habitat (Richerson and Boyd, 2005; Triandis, 2009).

Concluding their review with a definition of their own Kroeber and Kluckhohn (1952, p. 181) proposed that

Culture consists of patterns, explicit and implicit, of and for behavior acquired and transmitted by symbols, constituting the distinctive achievements of human groups, including their embodiments in artifacts; the essential core of culture consists of traditional (i.e., historically derived and selected) ideas and especially their attached values; cultural systems may on the one hand be considered as products of action, on the other as conditioning elements of further action.

In this definition, there is an explicit acceptance that culture comprises both concrete observable activities and artifacts, and underlying symbols, values and meanings. This definition reminds us of the theme in Chapter 1 (culture as external or internal to the person), but it proposes that it is both. These two aspects have been termed respectively "culture 1" and "culture 2" by Hunt (2007). For a long time, the first set of characteristics (culture 1) was the main focus of anthropology, and this conception influenced how cross-cultural psychologists drew the concept into their work. In essence, culture was seen as being "out there" and concrete, having an objective reality and a large degree of permanence over time and generations.

The second set of characteristics (culture 2), which are largely "in here" (inside people), or "intersubjective" (created and shared between individuals during social interactions) and more changeable, was initially less influential in the early study of behavior across cultures. This second view, in which culture is to be found within and between individuals in their shared meanings and practices, came to the fore in the 1970s. Culture was not considered to be an objective context for human development and action, but as more subjective, with "culture in the mind of the people" (Geertz, 1973), as a "historically transmitted pattern of meanings embodied in symbols" (Geertz, 1973, p. 89), and as "a conceptual structure or system of ideas" (Geertz, 1984, p. 128). This newer approach has given rise to a more cognitive emphasis in anthropology. For example, Romney and Moore (1998, p. 315) boldly assert that "the locus of culture ... resides in the minds of members of the culture." This conception is now broadly adopted by those who identify with "cultural psychology" (e.g., Cole, 1996; Shweder, 1990).

Most recently in this tradition, Hong (2009, p. 4) has advanced a dynamic constructivist definition of culture as "networks of knowledge, consisting of learned routines of thinking, feeling, and interacting with other people, as well as a corpus of substantive assertions and ideas about aspects of the world" (see also Barth, 2002). This intersubjective conception of culture has been advocated by Corsaro and Johannesen (2007), who refer to the creation of new cultures during social interactions. Wan and Chiu also argue that culture is largely intersubjective, based on social norms which they define as "the assumptions that are widely shared among members of a certain group about the values, beliefs, preferences and behaviors of most members of the group or in the culture of the group" (2009, p. 79). While for them the pendulum has recently swung away from viewing culture only as "out there" to being "in here" and "between individuals," it is important to note that Geertz (1973, p. 12) warned against the "cognitive fallacy" that "culture consists of mental phenomena."

Some convergence between the two views has been articulated: "[c]ulture ... consists of regular occurrences in the humanly created world, in the schemas people share as a result of these, and in the interactions between these schemas and this world" (Strauss and Quinn, 1997, p. 7); and culture is "the entire social heritage of a group, including material culture and external structures, learned actions, and mental representations of many kinds" (D'Andrade, 1995, p. 212). These influential anthropologists take a balanced view of culture, accepting the objective, subjective and intersubjective meanings of the concept.

These debates about how culture is to be conceptualized have created a crisis for many anthropologists, to the point where the very legitimacy of the concept has been questioned (e.g., Abu-Lughod, 1991), while others have defended it (e.g., Bennett, 1999; Munroe and Munroe, 1997). The arguments advanced against the usefulness of the concept are many: it is too static, and cannot deal with the obvious changes under way worldwide; it ignores individual agency in the construction of daily cultural interactions; it places boundaries around phenomena that exhibit continuous variations, etc. These views can all be recognized as part of the postmodernist challenges to positivist and empirical science. Many similar ideas have been advanced within psychology, and are part of the culturalists' challenge to cultural comparativists (see Chapter 12, section on cultural psychology). Fish (2000) and Greenfield (2000) have presented contrasting perspectives on how this postmodernist challenge impacts on our understanding of culture–behavior relationships.

In defence of the concept of culture, those who advocate the validity of the concept point out that there is an actual set of phenomena, and that despite changeability and almost infinite variability of cultures, there continues to be recognizable characteristics (both behavioral and symbolic) of human populations. As phrased by Bennett (1999, pp. 954–955): "Although the concept received bad press, and is a no-word in contemporary cultural anthropology, it remains on the whole the most profitable general way of handling multidimensional behavioral data. Whether we admit it or not, we are all still functionalists ... Classic anthropology's concern for objectivity was not such a bad thing."

Munroe and Munroe also accept the concept of culture as a set of knowable regularities that characterize human groups. Similar to the universalist position adopted in this text, they argued that "universals, generalizations and similarities across cultures could be expected due to our single-species heritage and the necessity of adapting to environmental constraints" (1997, p. 174). Furthermore, in addressing the social constructionists' exclusive focus on variability rather than the commonalities, Munroe and Munroe (1997, p. 176) consider this to be a "one-sided and misleading view, in fact a half-truth."

In this text, we adopt the views that "culture" is still a useful notion, and accept that both views of culture (culture 1 and 2) are valid. We employ the concept of culture as if it has some objective existence that can be used to characterize the relatively stable "way of life of a group of people." As presented in the ecocultural framework, we take the view that such an objective and stable quality of a group (culture 1) can both influence, and be influenced by, individuals and their actions. As previously argued:

> To the cross-cultural psychologist, cultures are seen as products of past human behavior and as shapers of future human behavior. Thus, humans are producers of culture and, at the same time, our behavior is influenced by it. We have produced social environments that continually serve to bring about continuities and changes in lifestyles over time and uniformities and diversities in lifestyles over space. How human beings modify culture and how our cultures modify us is what cross-cultural psychology is all about. (Segall *et al.*, 1999, p. 23)

We also take the view that culture is a set of shared meanings and symbols (culture 2) that are constantly being created and re-created during the course of social relationships. These more subjective (and intersubjective) features of culture are part of the ways in which populations adapt to their longstanding, but ever changing, ecosystems. In our view, both these conceptualizations of culture can be accommodated in the cultural component of the ecocultural framework, as outlined in Chapter 1 (see Box 1.1).

In Chapter 1 ("Distinguishing culture-level and individual-level variance") we considered the idea that different disciplines employ different levels of analysis; they do so legitimately without having to protect themselves from reductionist attacks from more basic disciplines. In anthropology, the concept of culture is clearly a group-level or collective phenomenon. Just as clearly, though, individual-level biological and psychological variables may be related to cultural variables, and from time to time there have been attempts to use them to explain cultural phenomena.

One protection against this reductionism was proposed very early by Kroeber (1917), who argued that culture is *superorganic* – "super" meaning above and beyond, and "organic" referring to its individual biological and psychological bases. Two arguments were presented by Kroeber for the independent existence of culture at its own level. First, particular individuals come and go, but cultures remain more or less stable. This is a remarkable phenomenon; despite a large turnover in membership with each new generation, cultures and their institutions remain relatively unchanged. Thus, a culture does not depend on particular individuals for its existence, but has a life of its own at the collective level of the group. The second argument is that no single individual "possesses" all of the "culture" of the group to which one belongs; the culture as a whole is carried by the collectivity, and indeed is likely to be beyond the biological or psychological capacity (to know or to do) of any single person in the group. For example, no single person knows all the laws, political institutions and economic structures that constitute even this limited sector of one's culture.

For both these reasons, Kroeber considered that cultural phenomena are collective phenomena, above and beyond the individual person, and hence his term "superorganic." This position is an important one for cross-cultural psychology since it permits us to employ the group–individual distinction in attempting to link the two, and possibly to trace the influence of cultural factors on individual psychological development and behavioral expression. Whether "culture" can constitute the "independent variable" in such studies is a matter of debate, and will be addressed in Chapter 12, in the section on analyzing external context and its consequences.

Cultural evolution

As noted in Chapter 11, evolutionary psychology is basically concerned with universals. However, historically, the concept of **cultural evolution** has been concerned with variations over time since Homo sapiens first appeared. It is clear that variable forms of cultural groups have appeared in an identifiable sequence from small hunting and gathering bands, through societies based on plant and animal domestication (agricultural and pastoral peoples), to industrial and now post-industrial societies (e.g., Lomax and Berkowitz, 1972). In the past it has been thought by many that this historical sequence (cultural evolution) somehow displays "progress"; this sequence has become known as "social Darwinism." In this text, we reject this notion of progress over time in forms of culture.

In an attack on the concept of "evolutions as progress," Sahlins and Service (1960) made an important distinction between specific evolution and general evolution. In the former, cultural diversity and change appear, often in adaptation to new ecological (both physical and social) conditions. In the latter, general evolution "generates progress; higher forms arise from and surpass lower forms" (1960, pp. 12–13). We accept the first view of evolution (diversity through adaptive modification) while not accepting the second (progress and higher forms resulting from change). The reason for this position is that there is ample objective evidence for ecologically induced change, but there are only subjective value judgments to provide a basis for claiming one adaptation to be better than another. As Sahlins and Service (1960, p. 15) have phrased it: "adaptive improvement is relative to the adaptive problem; it is to be judged and explained. In the specific context each adapted population is adequate, indeed superior, in its own incomparable way." These criticisms are based upon the position that such judgments do not have any scientific basis, and must inevitably rest on personal preferences about what is "good" and what is "bad" in human existence.

Although we reject the simple parallelism between cultural and biological evolution, this is not to say that there are no links between them. Indeed, there is now ample evidence (see Richerson and Boyd, 2005) that there is a process of co-evolution: that is, cultural practices shape the process of biological evolution; and genetic features of the human species arise, permitting the emergence of culture (see Chapter 11 for a fuller description of this dual inheritance model; see the section on models of cultural transmission).

Cultural relativism

An opposing view to that of "social Darwinism" is cultural relativism, first introduced by Boas (1911) and elaborated by Herskovits (1948). As introduced to cross-cultural psychology by Segall *et al.* (1966, p. 17):

the ethnographer attempts to describe the behavior of the people he studies without the evaluation that his own culture would ethnocentrically dictate. He attempts to see the culture in terms of its own evaluative system. He tries to remain aware of the fact that his judgments are based upon this own experience and reflect his own deep-seated enculturation to a limited and specific culture. He reminds himself that his original culture provides no Olympian vantage from which to view objectively any other culture.

This position of cultural relativism provides a non-ethnocentric stance from which to view cultural and psychological diversity. It promotes a general awareness of the problems inherent in ethnocentric thinking about cultural and psychological differences. There are two issues needing clarification when discussing cultural relativism. The first is the claim that relativism precludes comparison across cultures. As we shall see in Chapter 12, this is not necessarily the case: features of culture or behavior can be compared if there is some underlying dimension that they share (i.e., there is comparability). For example, the proverbial claim that apples and oranges cannot be compared is not a valid prohibition against comparison. Both are fruits, sharing seeds, juice and skin. On these bases they can be compared (Hunt, 2007). A similar argument has been advanced by Raybeck (2005), who advocates the complementary study of cultural specificities and the qualities of humanity that are shared across cultures. He notes that: "it is an axiom of the sciences that contrast is essential to the production of information and, ultimately, meaning. Without contrast, there can be no information" (2005, p. 236). Thus, relativism and comparison are both necessary components of the human sciences, and are the hallmarks of the culture-comparative approach described in this text.

A second issue is that cultural relativism is often taken to imply that "anything goes" with respect to cultural values and practices. However, there are widely accepted limits to cultural and behavioral practices that serve as "universal" principles. For example, the "Universal Code of Human Rights" (United Nations, 1945) and the "Universal Declaration of Ethical Principles for Psychologists" (Gauthier, 2008; see Box 18.1) illustrate these underlying universal principles. However, there are clear variations across cultures in the acceptance of rights, especially with respect to those of women and children.

Cultural universals

One of the more subtle features of cross-cultural psychology is the balance sought between understanding local phenomena, while at the same time attempting to develop panhuman generalizations. These were two of the goals of the field that we proposed in Chapter 1 (Additional Topics, Chapter 1). The position of cultural relativism assists us in the first endeavor (the emic goal), while the postulate of cultural universals (the derived etic goal) provides a basis for the second. Similar to the claim of Aberle *et al.* (1950) that there are certain functional prerequisites for a society (see Box 4.1) is the position that there are certain common features to all cultures: these are basic qualities of culture, and consist of those phenomena that one can expect to find in *any* and *every* culture. Similarly, activities that all individuals engage in (even though obviously carried out in very different ways) are the basis for claims about uniformities in psychological functioning. In other words, there are both cultural universals and psychological universals.

www.cambridge.org/berry

Some concrete cultural universals that have been useful for psychological research are listings based on a wide range of work in many cultures. Such elaborated lists do more than provide a "handy checklist"; they provide a comprehensive set of descriptive categories that may form the basis for comparative work. One candidate for use as a comparative tool is the set of categories developed by Murdock (1949) and used in the Human Relations Area Files (HRAF), which will be discussed later in this Chapter (Box 10.1).

Ethnography

Anthropologists have a long experience of working in virtually all of the world's cultures using a method called ethnography. The legacy of this tradition resides in thousands of published volumes of "fieldwork" in particular cultures. These ethnographic reports are a rich source of information, and serve as an important foundation for cross-cultural psychology. Such culture-specific reports provide valuable culture-level contextual materials for psychologists to use when selecting cultural groups with which to work, and for identifying culturally appropriate content for their research instruments. Two other scientific activities are based on this ethnographic foundation: ethnology and archives.

In the field of ethnology, researchers attempt to understand the patterns, institutions, dynamics and changes of cultures. This search for the larger picture requires the use of ethnographic reports from numerous cultures, comparing them and drawing out similarities and differences. In so doing, ethnologists work with original ethnographic materials (sometimes their own, more often those of others), seeking what may lie behind, or account for, the ethnographic variation. In a sense, while ethnography remains descriptive of explicit culture, ethnology becomes interpretive, using scientific inferences to comprehend implicit culture. In practice, however, most anthropologists do not maintain such a strict distinction between doing ethnography and ethnology. In the case of archives, research is conducted using a vast array of ethnographic reports, sometimes organized into a systematic framework that is amenable to comparative and statistical use (such as the HRAF).

Ethnographic fieldwork

Cross-cultural psychologists will inevitably need to have a good grasp of how to conduct ethnographic work in the field. Longstanding problems, such as how to enter the field, and how to carry out ethnographic research, have been major issues for anthropology, and much has been written to assist the fieldworker (e.g., the classic "Notes and Queries" of the Royal Anthropological Institute, 1951). Other problems, such as interviewing and testing reside in the psychological tradition, while still others, such as sampling and the use of observational techniques, belong to both disciplines. Two discussions of these issues, written expressly for cross-cultural psychologists, can be found in Goodenough (1980) and in Munroe and Munroe (1986b).

The first approach to, and contact with, a cultural group or community can be the single most important act in a program of research; how can it be done with sensitivity and without major gaffes? In a discussion of the problem (Cohen, 1970), experienced fieldworkers concluded that there is no single best approach to the field; each situation requires attention to local standards, and some degree of self-knowledge on the part of the researcher. Indeed, the fieldworker as a sojourner experiences acculturation, and may also experience acculturative stress (see Chapter 13, p. 314) in which self-doubt, loss of motivation, depression and other problems may become great enough to hinder the work.

Perhaps the most effective and ethical way to enter the field is to establish a collaborative relationship with a colleague in another culture. However, much early anthropological research was "extractive" (Gasché, 1992) rather than collaborative: the anthropologist returned home with information and artifacts, much as a geologist would return with mineral specimens, and hence became identified as part of the colonial enterprise. Nowadays many researchers often join forces with colleagues to look at the question together, enhancing the ethical basis of their work (Drenth, 2004). In this way local knowledge and acceptance may be acquired easily and quickly.

While a complete ethnographic study is probably not necessary (and likely to be beyond the capabilities of a psychologist), there is, nevertheless, the need to verify the information contained in a previous ethnography of the people involved in the study. To do this, we need to have some familiarity with ethnographic methods. Full treatments of this topic can be found in Alasuutari (1995), Bernard (1998) and Naroll and Cohen (1970). We focus here on some broad, but central, questions that need to be considered when learning to do cross-cultural psychology in the field (see also Lonner and Berry, 1986).

First, some basic features of the culture need to be examined, in order to understand the general context in which one's research participants developed, and now carry out their lives. The list of features studied by most anthropologists, of what constitutes a culture, has been presented earlier (in the section on definitions of culture and in Box 10.1). Foremost on these lists is the language. This is often the best place to begin learning about another culture; it not only provides cultural knowledge in its own right, but it also provides a vehicle to learn about most other aspects of culture.

While field anthropologists usually acquire a functional fluency in the local language, cross-cultural psychologists rarely do. Herein lies a major difference and a major problem. Anthropologists learn the local language because it is an important part of the culture-to-be-understood; cross-cultural psychologists do not because their research question (unless it is in psycholinguistics) may have little to do with language. However, it can be argued that psychological understanding is so subtle, so dependent on interpersonal communication, that local language learning should be a primary, preliminary objective for cross-cultural psychologists too.

An alternative to this rarely achieved goal is to rely on others as vehicles for understanding; this can be done by way of developing close relationships with colleagues in the other settings. As noted above, much earlier research tended to engage colleagues in other cultures in secondary roles, where they were merely invited to collect data using an already developed set of concepts, hypotheses and instruments. Increasingly a more egalitarian relationship is sought, in which joint conceptualizations and operationalizations are developed between equal partners.

In addition to language, other cultural variables that are implicated in one's research framework need to be examined. For example, economy, material goods, social stratification, political organization, religion and myth may play a role in one's research. The most commonly used approaches to obtaining such information in field anthropology are by intensive interaction with key informants and by the use of observational techniques.

Key informants have a central role in anthropological research because of the presumed normative nature of most aspects of culture. That is, culture is thought to be a widely shared phenomenon, and hence any (or a few) individuals should be able to give a detailed account of their culture. Extensive, followed by intensive questioning, checking and rechecking of previously obtained information, and trying out one's formulations for comment from informants, all contribute to the growing body of knowledge about the cultural group. Over time, with the help of only a few individuals, a comprehensive picture can be built up.

Observations made of daily life also serve to check on the information gained from key informants, and as a way of verifying one's own formulations about the culture (Bochner, 1986; Longabaugh, 1980; Munroe and Munroe, 1994). Discrepancies will be encountered (between formulations and observations), and a return to one's key informants will be required to help sort them out. Hence, there is often an iterative process, moving back and forth between asking informants and direct observations, until one is satisfied that the cultural variables of interest are adequately understood.

Ethnographic archives

By far the most frequently used ethnographic archive in cross-cultural psychology is the vast set of materials known as the Human Relations Area Files (HRAF). If one wanted to locate a set of cultures for a comparative project that met certain criteria, it would be a long and difficult task to wade through hundreds of ethnographic reports searching for specific groups to serve this purpose. Fortunately, a good deal of the ethnographic literature has been organized (assembled, categorized and coded) into these files, even though much of the material is now dated as a result of culture change and acculturation (see Chapter 13, *passim*).

The *Outline of cultural materials* (Murdock *et al.*, 2008) contains seventy-nine topics that are considered to be a universal set of categories to be found in all cultural groups. These have been arranged into eight broad categories by Barry (1980). Box 10.1 provides a selection of these topics.

There are two major dimensions cross-cutting each other: a universe of cultures, and a universe of cultural characteristics. With this massive archive, virtually any feature of a society can be sought and found by the researcher. For example, one can search for a subset of all cultures in a particular part of the world and count the proportion of cultures in these regions that have hunting, as opposed to agriculture, as their basic economic activity. Given the availability of geographical information (on latitude, altitude, temperature and rainfall) for these cultures one could then raise the question, is basic economic activity distributed in a way that is predictable from geographical information? Prior to the availability of the HRAF,

Box 10.1 Cultural topics contained in *Outline of cultural materials*

In Murdock's *Outline of cultural materials* variations in cultural practices around the world are placed in seventy-nine categories; these in turn are organized into eight major sections. It is interesting to compare these aspects of culture to those in Wissler's earlier definition.

Some of the seventy-nine cultural categories of Murdock, as arranged by Barry (1980), are:

1. General Characteristics
   Methodology
   Geography
   Human Biology
   Behavior Processes and Personality
   Demography
   History and Culture
   Change
   Language
   Communication
2. Food and Clothing
   Food Quest
   Food Processing
   Food Consumption
   Drink, Drugs and Indulgence
   Clothing
   Adornment
3. Housing and Technology
   Exploitative Activities
   Processing of Basic Materials
   Building and Construction
   Structures
   Settlements
   Energy and Power
   Machines
4. Economy and Transport
   Property
   Exchange
   Marketing
   Finance
   Labor
   Business and Industrial
   Organization
   Travel and Transportation

5. Individual and Family Activities
   Living Standards and Routines
   Recreation
   Fine Arts
   Entertainment
   Social Stratification
   Interpersonal Relations
   Marriage
   Family
   Kinship
6. Community and Government
   Community
   Territorial Organization
   State
   Government Activities
   Political and Sanctions
   Law
   Offenses and Sanctions
   Justice
   War
7. Welfare, Religion and Science
   Social Problems
   Health and Welfare
   Sickness
   Death
   Religious Beliefs
   Ecclesiastical Organization
   Numbers and Measures
   Ideas About Nature and Man
8. Sex and the Life Cycle
   Sex
   Reproduction
   Infancy and Childhood
   Socialization
   Education
   Adolescence, Adulthood, Old Age

researchers interested in these ecological questions had to go to numerous original sources for their information.

Actual uses of the files have largely been to discover patterns of regular associations (correlations) between two sets of cultural variables across cultures. This "holocultural" or "hologeistic" approach incorporates the "whole-world" range of data and findings (Naroll, 1970a). We have seen one specific example in the search for a relationship between socialization practices and subsistence economy in Chapter 2 (see p. 45). For ease of use many numerical codes have been produced so that each researcher does not have to convert verbal descriptions of a custom (such as childrearing) to a digit each time a category of cultural activity is employed. A massive set of codes is available in both the *Ethnographic atlas* (Murdock, 1967) and in the survey *A cross-cultural summary* (Textor, 1967). More specialized codes are also available (Barry and Schlegel, 1980). Many of these materials are now available in computerized form: http://ehrafWorldCultures.yale. edu. This site was made available in 2008, and has indices for over 700 subjects drawn from the earlier *Outline of world cultures* (Murdock, 1975). One innovation in this site is a search function that allows one to look up subject categories and cultures by typing in key words.

Methods for use with these files have been compiled by Ember and Ember (2009). A number of problems have attended the use of the Human Relations Area Files, leading to many criticisms and equally many attempts to deal with them (Naroll, Michik and Naroll, 1980). We examine briefly some of these problems and the solutions proposed within anthropology. A basic problem is to define what is a cultural group exactly: what are its limits and boundaries, and who is a member? Naroll (1970b) has proposed the notion of "cultunit" (short for "culture-bearing unit"), which is a term for a defined group that exhibits a specific culture. This question of the boundaries of cultunits is related to the issue of their independence. This issue has been termed Galton's Problem (see Naroll, 1970c), and it has been a substantial thorn in the side of those who wish to use correlational analyses in holocultural studies. The essence of the problem is the diffusion of cultural traits from one cultunit to another across boundaries. The presence of a particular practice in adjacent cultunits may be due to borrowing, and not be an independent development. Thus, for example, the correlation across twenty cultunits between the emphasis on compliance in socialization and reliance on agriculture for subsistence (see Chapter 2, p. 45) might be due to one society establishing such a link and then sharing it with other societies. Since correlations of this sort require independence of cases, the apparent linking of these two factors in the twenty cultunits may represent only a single case diffused, rather than twenty independent cases. The solution that has been proposed by Naroll (1970c) is the "double language boundary": two cultunits may be considered to be independent of each other for statistical purposes if there are at least two language borders between any two cultunits in the study. The standard cross-cultural sample (mentioned earlier) was chosen, in part, to meet this independence requirement.

A final problem to be noted here is that of the categories of culture used in the HRAF. In Box 10.1, there were seventy-nine categories or topics presented, into which all cultural data are slotted. The question is whether these categories are a perfect fit, an approximate fit or a poor fit for the whole range of cultural data being reported from around the world. In other terms, are these really *universal* categories of culture, or do some cultural data become selected or distorted, in order to match such a neat conceptual scheme? Are the data within each category truly *comparable* (see Chapter 1, section on equivalence of contents and data)? The solution proposed by Naroll *et al.* (1980) is to make quite explicit all of the coding rules to be employed when taking material from an ethnographic report and entering them into the HRAF. With such rules, coding errors and forced categorization may be avoided. However, numerous data that cannot be categorized may require an expansion or reorganization of the present system of categories.

While cross-cultural psychologists may wish to use the Files to search for systematic co-variation between population-level variables, two other uses are being suggested here. One is that an "initial reading" of a psychological theory or hypothesis (prior to the effort and expense of going to the field) may be possible using variables and data already in the files. In this way one may be able to direct one's activity more effectively toward fruitful questions when one eventually goes to the field. The second one (as we noted at the outset) is that with the help of the files, specific cultures can be identified as providing particular cultural contexts and experiences that are required for a particular comparative psychological study. For example, if our interest were in the effects of variations in socialization practices, we could select a set of societies varying from the extreme assertion to the extreme compliance ends of the dimension, and then go to the field and use psychological assessment procedures with a sample of individuals to assess these practices (that is, to verify the ethnographic account) and to see if the expected behavioral outcomes are indeed present.

Cognitive anthropology

Another branch of anthropology that has close links with psychology is that of **cognitive anthropology**. Most broadly stated, "cognitive anthropology is the study of the relationship between human society and human thought" (D'Andrade, 1995, p. 1). More specifically, its goal is to understand how people in various cultures describe, categorize and organize their knowledge about their natural (and supernatural) world. It shares with psychological anthropology a concern for normative knowledge – what and how people in general know – rather than for psychological processes or individual differences, and differs from the cross-cultural psychological study of cognition (reported in Chapter 6) on these same dimensions.

Another name for this general area is ethnoscience (e.g., Sturtevant, 1964); it is defined as a branch of anthropology that seeks to understand the scientific knowledge that exists in other cultures. In principle, there could be any number of branches, such as ethnobotany, even ethnopsychology (and as we saw earlier in Chapter 2, parental ethnotheories). This initial orientation has led, in psychology, to a concern with indigenous knowledge systems, including practical know-how ("bricolage," Lévi-Strauss, 1962; Berry and Irvine, 1986) and "everyday cognition" (Schliemann, Carraher and Ceci, 1997; Segall *et al.*, 1999, ch. 6) and larger-scale cognitive systems ("indigenous cognition," Berry, Irvine and Hunt, 1988). An example of this general ethnoscience approach is a series of concrete studies of knowledge of natural phenomena by Maya and Menominee indigenous peoples (Atran and Medin, 2008; see below). An excellent overview of the field has been prepared by D'Andrade (1995).

In cognitive anthropology, a key to understanding cognition is to recognize the great importance given to language as a cultural phenomenon (Semin, 2009). As we saw earlier in this chapter, language is one constituent element of culture, and along with tool-making may be one of the few really distinctive qualities of human culture (after all, many non-human species have social organization, territory and even games).

Language is also readily identified with the cognitive life of the human species, since it is clearly implicated in learning, remembering and thinking. Anthropologists interested in human cognition thus sought to gain their particular entry to cognitive phenomena by way of this particular cultural phenomenon – that of language. Historically, two main influences made this language–cognition link the focus of cognitive anthropology. First, as noted in Chapter 8 (p. 180), Whorf (1956) argued that language categories (both the words, and relations among words) serve to codify and organize the world on the one hand, and mold the cognitive life of the individual on the other in basic ways. The empirical evidence for this view is slight (see Chapter 8, p. 180); nevertheless the links are intuitively compelling, and were sufficient to move anthropologists in this direction. Second, formal linguistic analyses (e.g., Greenberg, 1957) provided a model method for examining categories, and the structure of categories, that was easily adopted by cognitive anthropologists. Linguistic analyses of the way people *talked about* a domain (e.g., kinship, animals) thus formed a basis for an analysis of their cognitive organization of the world (i.e., how they *thought about* the domain). This approach is concerned with collective cognition (how people in general understand their world) not with individual cognition (how persons are similar or different from each other, or the nature of the underlying cognitive processes).

The concept of "social representations" has been developed to describe people's shared beliefs about the world. For Moscovici, social representations are "a system of values, ideas and practices ... to enable individuals to orient themselves in their material and social world and to master it ... and to enable communication to take place among members of the community" (1982, p. 3). These ideas have been further developed by Jodelet (2002) and Duveen (2007). However, Jahoda (1982, pp. 214–225) expresses a commonly held view among cross-cultural psychologists that such collective or social representations cannot really provide access to any individual psychological processes, be they cognitive, motivational or attitudinal. In this conclusion we find a key difference between anthropological and psychological data: individual differences and individual processes (the core of psychological enquiry) are simply beyond grasp when one has only population-level data. However, this should not be a basis for dismissing the work of cognitive anthropologists; indeed, like those working in psychological anthropology they have opened up whole new domains for enquiry by cross-cultural psychologists, and have provided a language-based method for studying individual behavior. Later in this chapter, we review two sets of studies using both cultural- and individual-level observation and data, which eliminates this divide.

The view that the language of a group is an important way to understand the cognitive life of a people found an early expression in "componential analysis" (Goodenough, 1956), especially in the study of kinship terms (e.g., Romney and D'Andrade, 1964). Also called "feature analysis," the process begins with selection of a cultural domain, such as family relationships, and the elicitation of terms employed to refer to various members. For example, in English, both gender and the generation distinction are made (e.g., grandmother, grandfather, mother, father, daughter, son) as well the lateral distinctions (e.g., sister, brother); but for some, gender is not distinguished (cousin), nor whether the relationship is by common descent ("blood") or by marriage (e.g., uncle, aunt). In contrast, other languages make more distinction (e.g., whether the cousin is male or female; whether the aunt is by blood or by marriage), and are more inclusive (e.g., uncle can include all adult males that are close to one's parents). Componential analysis has been applied to many other domains, such as "things to eat," or "animals," and even to abstract domains, such as "character traits," and "intelligence" (see Box 6.1). In the view of D'Andrade (1995, p. 3), componential analysis was important because it showed "how to investigate cultural systems of meaning," revealing "native categories that are derived from an emic [see Chapter 1, Box 1.2] analysis of discriminating things in their world, rather than imposing categories from the outside."

Some approaches have shifted away from a focus on language, to a concern with actual behavior (Gatewood, 1985). In the terms of Dougherty and Keller (1982), there is less interest in "taxonomy," and more in "taskonomy." That is, individual differences in how people actually use the cultural knowledge have become the object of study.

Somewhat related to cognitive anthropology is a tradition that goes by the name of everyday cognition (Schliemann, Carraher and Ceci, 1997). This approach is based on descriptive accounts of the cognitive demands and problem-solving strategies found in a particular group. Fascinating skills have been described including the navigation of boats by the Pulawat across large distances in the Pacific without a compass (Gladwin, 1970), counting among the Oksapmin, who have a number system based on parts of the body (Saxe, 1981), and weaving in various societies (e.g., Childs and Greenfield, 1980; Greenfield, 2004; Rogoff and Gauvain, 1984; Tanon, 1994). Studies of everyday cognition have generally shown limited transfer and generalization of learning from one class of situations (domain) to another, including from school to non-school situations (Segall *et al.*, 1999). Still, most authors see culture-specific knowledge and skills as the outcome of more general modes of teaching and learning that differ from those prominent in the western school setting. Examples include scaffolding (e.g., Greenfield and Lave, 1982) and apprenticeship (Rogoff, 1990), as described in Chapter 2 (see p. 38).

Concrete skills and items of knowledge are of direct interest in applied fields. For example, courses on intercultural communication teach participants specific conventions (e.g., not entering a home with your shoes on) next to broader dimensions such as individualism–collectivism (see Chapter 15, section on intercultural training). In cross-cultural health intervention studies skills and knowledge pertinent to specific situations (e.g., smoking, safe sex, nutrition) are needed to make intervention programs locally relevant (Pick, Poortinga and Givaudan, 2003; see Chapter 17, see section on sexually transmitted diseases). Examples of research following the approach of cognitive anthropology concern local beliefs about the aetiology, and probably even more the treatment, of physical diseases, such as malaria prevention (Klein, Weller, Zeissig, Richards and Ruebush, 1995).

Two research studies exemplify how convergence between anthropological and psychological approaches can be achieved. The first is the work of Wassmann and Dasen (1994a, b), who studied number systems and classification rules among the Yupno people of New Guinea. This interdisciplinary collaboration produced evidence for the general (cultural-level) way of counting and classifying objects, and for some individual differences (psychological-level) in how people actually go about these cognitive activities.

Their approach is to gain the advantages of viewing a phenomenon through the use of multiple methods (Wassmann and Dasen, 1994b): first they interview key informants to obtain an understanding at the cultural (or normative) level; second, they make observations of daily behaviors that are in the behavior domain of interest (e.g., counting or sorting); and third, they develop tasks, and ask participants to carry them out, so that individual differences and underlying processes may be discovered. The first is an ethnographic study, the third is a psychological study, and the second represents a technique shared by the two disciplines.

In the first study, Wassmann and Dasen (1994a) noted that the Yupno start counting on the left hand, folding down each finger in turn from the little finger to the thumb; distinct number words exist for 1, 2 and 3; number 4 is "2 and 2," and 5 is called "the finger with which one peels bamboo shoots," namely the thumb; the sum is indicated by showing the closed fist, and saying "one hand." Numbers 6 to 10 are counted in the same way on the right hand, and 11 to 20 on the feet. For numbers 21 to 33, symmetrical body parts are designated two by two, intermixed, to mark each group of five (and number 33), with parts on the central body line. Once the last body part (the penis, called "the mad thing") is reached, the sum is expressed as "one man dead." The process can be repeated on a second person if there is a need to count beyond 33.

Beyond this general (ethnographic) description, the authors were interested in various psychological issues, such as gender and age differences. However, it proved impossible to study women, because Yupno women are not supposed to know the number system and therefore refuse to answer any questions. Neither was it practicable to study children and younger men, because the former only use the decimal system taught in school, and the latter use the traditional system only up to 20, as is done on the coast of New Guinea, where many of them had been working.

One most interesting finding emerged from asking several older men to demonstrate the counting with the number system: although four of them used the system as described above, ending with 33, one of them produced a system ending with 30, two with 32 and one with 37. With one exception (a man starting from bottom up), counting always ended on the penis, but the number of intermediate body parts could vary. This revealed a property of the counting system, namely that it is done in face-to-face situations where variations in the numbering can be taken into consideration.

A second example of combining anthropological and psychological concepts and methods is the research by Atran and Medin (2008) on understandings of biology and botany. They worked with communities of Maya in Guatemala, Menominee in the USA, and the "majority" in the USA. They used ethnographic methods to examine knowledge of, and the ways people categorize, natural objects in their environments. They also worked with samples of individuals from these communities, using tests of knowledge, and categorization tasks. Their research has confirmed the existence of cognitive universals, concluding that:

1. People in all cultures classify plants and animals into species-like groups that biologists generally recognize as populations of interbreeding individuals adapted to an ecological niche ... we call such groups ... generic species ...

2. There is a commonsense assumption that each generic species has an underlying causal nature or essence, which is uniquely responsible for the typical appearance, behavior and ecological preferences of the kind ...

3. The structure of these hierarchically included groups ... is referred to as folk-biological taxonomy ... In all societies that have been studied in depth, folk-biological groups are organized into hierarchically organized ranks.

4. Biological taxonomies not only organize and summarize biological information, they also provide a powerful inductive framework for making systematic inferences about the likely distribution of organic and ecological properties among organisms (Atran and Medin, 2008, pp. 110–111).

They further note:

We have provided evidence for the structural and functional autonomy of folk biology in human cognition ... First ...folk biological taxonomies are universally anchored in the generic-species level ... Second ... people from diverse cultures build topologically similar biological taxonomies that guide inferences about the distribution of biological and ecological properties. Just how these taxonomies are used may vary across groups ... These universal tendencies are most salient outside the center of industrialized societies but nonetheless discernable everywhere. (Atran and Medin, 2008, pp. 113–114)

In this conclusion, we find convergence between research traditions of anthropologists and cognitive psychologists. We also find further evidence for the universalist perspective adopted in this text: underlying cognitive processes are shared across cultures, while the content and products of these processes are highly culturally variable.

Religion

Perhaps the most fascinating thing to emerge from the study of religions is the wide variety of beliefs, and the wide variety of practices and customs that they support. The study of variations in religious beliefs has been primarily the focus of cultural anthropology (Durkheim, 1915; Frazer, 1890/1995; Lévi-Strauss, 1966). In many ethnographies, descriptions of religious beliefs can be found as well as accounts of the function of religion in many societies. In the HRAF, religion is identified as one of the universal categories of culture. Tarakeshwar, Stanton and Pargament (2003) have highlighted religion as an overlooked dimension in cross-cultural psychology and have offered a conceptual framework that incorporates previous distinctions. A similar plea was made by Holden and Vittrup (2009) for a developmental perspective on culture and religion – a topic that they found still to be in a formative stage.

In this section, we distinguish three ways in which religion can be seen to be related to science, including cross-cultural psychology:

1. knowledge about the transcendental (usually referred to as religious or supernatural beliefs) takes precedence over scientific knowledge;
2. science and religion are viewed as separate domains; and
3. science takes precedence over religion, especially in the sense that scientific theories should explain the presence of religious beliefs in humans.

Religious knowledge takes precedence

Religion as such is mainly about the transcendental, a reality or essence that lies beyond observable reality. Believers tend to adhere to a specific religion which implies, definitely for monotheistic religions, a revealed truth that is more or less absolute and should not be doubted. Their religious beliefs take priority over scientific evidence when the two are in conflict. For example, creationist movements generally believe that the world is not more than 6,000 years old; science is mistaken about the age of the world, and counterevidence has been mustered (Numbers, 2006). In some cases religion has been brought into a psychology curriculum; for example, in Indonesia, Setiono and Sudradjat (2008) have proposed that the basis for teaching psychology should be to promote the religious faith and devotion of students.

There is also historical precedence due to religious influences on scientific concepts. Elements from the Christian tradition, within which much of the current behavioral and social sciences initially were formalized, have entered psychology, often through philosophy. Even the notion "psyche" or "soul" that has led to the name of "psychology" is a Greek–Christian concept referring to a non-somatic form of human existence. Such a concept is not shared with all cultures. Religious and philosophical influences are readily observed if concepts originating from other worldviews are considered (see the section on "Self in social context" in Chapter 5). More important, norms and values, and social practices related to these, tend to be justified with reference to religious prescriptions. At present, in some Muslim countries, Sharia law is argued to be prescribed by the Quran. From a perspective of moderate universalism, Sharia law can be seen as representing a strong emphasis on retribution – a principle that similarly is manifest, though perhaps less salient, in all other justice systems meting out punishment to perpetrators.

Religion and science are separate domains

Conflicts between religious and scientific views can be avoided when some kind of separation between the realm of science and the realm of religion can be accepted. One formulation in Christianity has been that the Bible as revealed truth is about the relationship between God and humankind and should not be read as a book of science. Such a separation can come under pressure when the domain of science is expanded and intrudes into the sphere of religious beliefs. The increasing scientific support for evolution theory probably has contributed to a backlash in some countries in the form of demands for the inclusion of the concept of "intelligent design" in school curricula along with that of evolution theory (e.g., Forrest and Gross, 2004).

Most studies of psychology and religion fall into this second category. Analyses like those of Allport (1961) approach religiosity (or spirituality, a search for meaning broader than religion) as a species-wide psychological phenomenon. More often than not such studies reflect a positive attitude toward religion, although most authors would probably agree with that, independent of their personal conviction psychologists do not have the competence to judge the truth claims of religions or anti-religious convictions.

In this tradition numerous empirical studies have made use of psychometric scales, such as the Religious Orientation Scale of Allport and Ross (1967). Such research looks for meaningful dimensions of individual differences and/or for correlates of religiosity and participation in religious organizations. The results are mixed, but they usually show a relationship between religious adherence and spirituality (e.g., Dezutter, Soenens and Hutsebaut, 2006; Miller and Thoresen, 2003; Powell, Shahabi and Thoresen, 2003). By far most of these studies have been conducted in the USA or other western countries; because of this, Gorsuch (1988) has argued that the term "religion" might be replaced by "Christianity."

Relationships found in the West may or may not be consistent across societies. For example, an often reported association between fundamentalist religious convictions and authoritarianism in the USA was not replicated among Christians in Korea (Ji and Suh, 2008). On the other hand, structural validity was found for the (US-American) Spiritual Transcendence Scale in an Indian sample of Hindus, Christians and Muslims (Piedmont and Leach, 2002). So far no consistent picture can be derived, which is not surprising given the small number of cross-cultural studies.

Science takes precedence over religion

Scientific explanation takes precedence over religion when it tries to come up with scientific explanations for religious beliefs and practices (Frazer, 1890/1995; Lévi-Strauss, 1966). For example, Durkheim (1915) argued that religious beliefs and rituals exist because they have a social function. According to him, religious rituals are commentaries on the nature of social life; a ritual expressing a fear of God, for example, is indirectly expressing a fear of the politically powerful within a society. Anthropologists like Frazer and later Lévi-Strauss viewed religion as an attempt to understand and control the world (i.e., as a kind of pre-science; see also

Dunbar, 1996; Horton, 1993). Early in the history of modern psychology, Freud, influenced by Frazer (1890/1995), interpreted religious beliefs as childish: God is a sublimated form of the father as authority figure. In his famous book *Totem and taboo* (1928) Freud referred to religions in non-western countries to argue this viewpoint. In recent times religion has become a focus of evolutionary research. The universal presence suggests that being religious is part of human nature. The question is, what in the human biological make-up predestines humans to developing religion?

Religions tend to require heavy investments of time and materials (e.g., for building houses of worship, ritual sacrifices and maintenance of religious leaders), as well as psychological investments (e.g., emotions and cognitive efforts in praying). In Chapter 11 (section on natural selection) we will see that according to the Darwinian theory of natural selection it should be advantageous for an individual in terms of reproductive fitness to have religion, otherwise it could not be so widely present in humans. However, viewing religion as an adaptation (or set of adaptations) hardly seems to make sense, in view of the high investments. In the literature, three possible hypotheses about the functions of religion are discussed:

1. One possibility is that religion has emerged as a (perhaps somewhat unfortunate) evolutionary by-product of some other important adaptation (e.g., Atran, 2007; Atran and Norenzayan, 2004).
2. Another possibility is that the positive aspects are underestimated and that religion, definitely in the hunter-gatherer groups, brought advantages, such as group cohesiveness, social control or healing rituals (Reynolds and Tanner, 1995; Wilson, 2002). A problem with this view of religion as functional for group cohesiveness is that it only describes the functionality, but cannot explain it: how can religion or religiosity have been evolved at the individual level, if it seems to have advantages mainly at the group level? From a manipulative view of individual genetic self-interest, Alexander (1987), Cronk (1994) and others have argued that religion can be individually advantageous if the other group members are brought by religious norms and values to behave more altruistically than oneself. Models based on these considerations (Maynard Smith, 1982) propose that the more religious group members there are, the more advantageous it becomes to cheat (i.e., to fake commitment and to profit from the benevolence of the majority). The question then becomes: how can religious groups avoid or at least detect cheaters? This leads us directly to the third hypothesis.
3. According to the costly signaling hypothesis (Zahavi, 1975; see Chapter 11, this volume, p. 256), religious commitments are selected for the very reason that they are costly; through circumcision, through donations of large amounts of money, through observing rigid rules of dress or everyday behavior, adherents signal to the religious community that they are true and ardent believers.

Individuals thus profit from belonging to this special and unique group, while the group profits by enhancing intragroup cooperation (Sosis, 2003; Wilson, 2002). Sosis and Bressler (2003) used historical data on the constraints and ritual requirements of eighty-three nineteenth-century communes in the USA. They showed that communes which imposed costlier requirements survived longer than less demanding (often non-religious) communes.

Until now, evolutionary perspectives on religion have mainly taken a distal view by stressing either its manipulative or costly character; they have not yet considered the possible psychological benefits of being religious (Voland, 2009). In conclusion, the analysis of religion from the cross-cultural and evolutionary perspectives has only just started; it is a fascinating topic to which cross-cultural psychology should be able to contribute significantly.

Conclusions

Other than psychology, it is clear that the most important parent discipline of cross-cultural psychology is cultural anthropology. The central concept of culture, and the core themes of where culture is located and of relativism and universalism, have been contributed by anthropology; so too have the methods used in field settings.

While these notions and practices have had to be translated from the language of the collective to that of the individual, the task for cross-cultural psychology has been informed in many ways by this pioneering work in anthropology. We have focussed on the core issues in the anthropological enterprise, including what is currently meant by the concept of culture, how anthropological studies can be carried out (using both field and archival methods), and some major findings from these activities (including the existence of cultural universals as a basis for comparative psychological work).

Occupying the middle ground between the population and individual levels has not been all that easy for cross-cultural psychology. The study of the individual in context (particularly the concern with individual differences) has meant some distancing from, even some conflicts with, our anthropological ancestor. Similarly, our concern for the cultural context of behavior has distanced us from our more experimentally oriented psychological parents.

It should be clear that cross-cultural psychology has been informed in major ways by the anthropological traditions, only a portion of which we have been able to present in this chapter. However, we have sought to present most of the key features of cultural anthropology that should be useful for cross-cultural psychologists when engaging in research across cultures. In particular, knowledge about the debates in anthropology has deepened our understanding of the sources of divergent views that have entered cross-cultural psychology, especially as they relate to the perspectives of the indigenous, cultural and culture-comparative traditions. Perhaps of most relevance has been the portrayal of successful collaborations between anthropologists and psychologists as they seek to understand the intimate links between culture and behavior in all their complexity.

KEY TERMS

anthropology • cognitive anthropology • cultural evolution • cultural relativism • cultural universals • ethnographic archives • ethnography • ethnology • ethnoscience • holocultural approach • Human Relations Area Files (HRAF) • psychological anthropology

FURTHER READING

D'Andrade, R. G. (1995). *The development of cognitive anthropology.* Cambridge: Cambridge University Press.

A comprehensive and critical examination of the origins of and contemporary anthropological research on cognition.

Ember, M., Ember, C., and Peregrine, P. (2007). *Cultural anthropology* (12th edn.). New York: Prentice-Hall.

A widely read, comprehensive textbook of general anthropology that serves as an introduction to the field. It provides excellent coverage of all the main issues that are useful for cross-cultural psychologists.

Moore, C., and Mathews, H. (eds.) (2001). *The psychology of cultural experience.* Cambridge: Cambridge University Press.

A set of essays in the field of psychological anthropology, with a focus on a range of research methods designed to advance the field in new directions.

Munroe, R. L., and Munroe, R. M. (1997). A comparative anthropological perspective. In J. W. Berry, Y. H. Poortinga and J. Pandey (eds.), *Handbook of cross-cultural psychology, Vol. I, Theory and method* (pp. 171–213). Boston: Allyn & Bacon.

A thoughtful overview of what comparative research in anthropology can contribute to cross-cultural psychology.

Robbins, R. (2006). *Cultural anthropology: A problem-based approach.* Belmont, Calif.: Thomson.

A text that presents a series of case studies of contemporary issues in anthropology; many of them concern issues being discussed in cross-cultural psychology.

Ross, N. (2004). *Culture and cognition: Implications for theory and method.* Thousand Oaks, Calif.: Sage.

An innovative presentation of theories and methods for advancing cognitive anthropology.

Valsiner, J., and Rosa, A. (eds.) (2007). *The Cambridge handbook of sociocultural psychology*. Cambridge: Cambridge University Press.

A comprehensive survey of topics in the tradition of Vygotsky's ideas on sociohistorical psychology.

Wyer, R., Chiu, C., and Hong, Y. (eds.) (2009). *Understanding culture: Theory, research and application*. Hove: Psychology Press.

A wide-ranging examination of the relationships between cultural and psychological phenomena, mainly by psychologists. The central (but not the only) theoretical position taken is that of the constructivist and intersubjective conceptions of culture.

11 Contributions of evolutionary biology

CONTENTS

Within cross-cultural psychology it is important to understand the biological, as well as the cultural, bases of behavior. The focus is usually on the sociocultural environment and how it interacts with behavior; this may lead to an unbalanced view. Despite this joint importance, biological aspects are still emphasized rather rarely. Often, biology and culture are seen as opposites; what is labeled as cultural is not biological and what is labeled as biological is not cultural. As we mentioned in Chapter 1, and will describe in more detail here, the two are intricately related in a non-dichotomous way. In the ecocultural framework presented in Figure 1.1 we have included **biological adaptation** and genetic transmission among the concepts that have to be taken into consideration in cross-cultural psychology. For the understanding of behavior, its similarities as well as its cultural variations, the study of the biological basis is as essential as the analysis of sociocultural context.

In the first and second sections of this chapter we give a brief overview of some core concepts of the Darwinian theory of natural and sexual selection. The third section deals with evolutionary-based theories and methods to study animal and human behavior. The fourth and final section of this chapter is devoted to models of cultural transmission which have been developed from a biological perspective in analogy with models of genetic transmission (see the modes of transmission section in Chapter 2; and the section on behavior genetics, Additional topics, Chapter 11).

Natural and sexual selection

Natural selection

The theory of natural selection, formulated originally by Charles Darwin in the nineteenth century (1859) and further developed over the course of more than 150 years, is central to the biological sciences, including their perspective on behavior. Of the core concepts in the theory there are two which are of particular interest in the present context, namely that species change over time and that natural selection is the key to such change.

Essential for the theory of natural selection is the diversity between the individual organisms within a single species. In most species parents produce a large number of offspring. Many of these fail to reach maturity and to procreate in turn. If for some reason a certain heritable trait enhances the probability of survival and reproduction, the frequency of this trait in the population will increase over successive generations. Individual organisms possessing this trait are then said to have a higher reproductive fitness than individuals without the trait. Over many generations such a differential rate of reproduction leads to subtle but systematic changes in the genotype of a population. This is natural selection, which Darwin saw as a causal process under the influence of environmental factors. In short, the evolutionary process of natural selection can be described in three steps: reproduction, variance and selection (Dennett, 1995): The ultimate goal of evolution, which is the dispersion of genes, via 1) reproduction leads to 2) random genetic variations in the progeny. These new variants are subject to 3) selective environmental forces.

At the time of Darwin the reasons for this individual variation were not well understood, although it was known from the breeding of domestic animals and plants that systematic changes in morphological or behavioral traits could be brought about. Through the mating of individuals with desired characteristics a breeder could increase the probability that these characteristics would also be found in subsequent generations. It was only much later, after the discovery of DNA, that these observations could be accounted for in terms of genetic principles. At the present time most biologists share Darwin's opinion that changes in species can be seen as the outcome of interactions between organisms and their environments. We shall briefly describe how these mechanisms of change operate. Since a proper understanding requires some knowledge of genetics, a brief summary of a few basic principles is given in Box 11.1.

Box 11.1 **Genetics**

The account given here is based on the human species, but is, with some variations, valid for all species that multiply through sexual reproduction (cf. Mange and Mange, 1999; Snustad and Simmons, 1997). The genetic material consists of DNA molecules which form long double strands made up of pairs of nucleotides. Each nucleotide contains a base. This base occurs in only four forms, often indicated with the letters A, T, C and G. Various sequences in which the ACTG groups occur correspond (in triplets) with the structure of amino acids. Through a kind of copying process amino acids originate from the DNA. Long strings of amino acids form polypeptides, which, as enzymes, have an effect on specific biochemical reactions.

A gene is a DNA segment that can be recognized by its specific function; the gene is the functional unit of genetic material. Each gene has a certain place (locus) within a chromosome. Of a single gene (identified by locus and function), often more than one variation is found. These variations, which are called **alleles**, form the most important basis for individual variation within a species.

The chromosomes of a pair closely resemble each other, with one exception. Males have an X- and a Y-chromosome, and females two X-chromosomes. This determines biological sex differences. The other chromosomes in a pair show, in the normal case, only small differences. A distinction is often made between genotype – the genetic constitution of an organism – and the phenotype – the characteristics of the organism as they can be observed. The chromosomes contain an enormous amount of information; there are approximately six billion (milliards) of base units. They form genes of varying length, usually extending over thousands of base pairs. For many of the genetic loci there exist more than one allele. This gives an indication of the genetic variability present in the human species. Through sexual reproduction each organism acquires a specific combination of the total pool of genetic material available in the species. Only monozygotic (identical) twins are genetically identical.

The mother exclusively contributes some other genetic materials to the mitochondrion – an organelle in the ovum and other cells that are needed for metabolic processes providing energy for the cell. It is through the analysis of group differences in mitochondrial DNA that the relationships between human groups in various parts of the world have been traced. Most results point to a common "mother" (often called mother Eve) living in Africa between 100,000 and 40,000 years ago (Cann, Stoneking and Wilson, 1987; Ingman, Kaessmann, Pääbo and Gullensten, 2000).

So how do changes in species come about? First of all, new genetic variations emerge from time to time by a small change in a gene. This can happen under the influence of external factors which affect the genetic material; nuclear radiation and certain chemicals are known causal agents. New variations can also be formed without any known external determinant being present. In the complex process of DNA synthesis during sexual reproduction an occasional replication error occurs. Changes in the genetic material lead to so-called mutations. These are relatively rare and most mutants are not viable. In rapidly reproducing micro-organisms mutations provide a realistic prospect for change (cf. the various strains of the influenza virus). In higher organisms with a longer life cycle other factors are likely to have a more appreciable effect on the rate of change. These factors include natural selection, migration, assortative mating and genetic drift. Mating populations can be quite small, for example because they are geographically isolated. Genetic drift refers to random fluctuations in the distributions of variations that will occur in all breeding populations. This genetic drift is negligible in large populations, but not in small groups. A single individual among the founding parents of a group of new settlers can sometimes have an appreciable effect on the frequency of a certain characteristic in the descendants many generations later. This also makes clear why migration, with the consequent introduction of different variations in a breeding population, can have quite remarkable effects.

Non-random mating patterns are very much in evidence among humans, where the choice of a marriage partner is often governed by social rules. In a few societies marriages between blood relatives are encouraged and even customary; this can give rise to inbreeding. It is interesting to note that in most societies close-relative marriages are frowned upon and even prohibited as if these societies know about the deleterious effects of inbreeding. Cultural customs seem indeed to follow a biological rationale here. According to the Westermarck effect (Westermarck, 1921), individuals who live in close domestic proximity during the first few years of life are not sexually attracted to each other as adults. This effect has been observed in many cultures, including the kibbutzim in Israel (Shepher, 1983) and Taiwanese *shim-pua* marriages, in which a poorer family sold their young daughter to a richer family to be married with a son of a similar age and the two youngsters would grow up together (Wolf and Huang, 1979; see also Thornhill, 1991).

Certain changes in the environment can lead to differential reproduction of a given genotype. As mentioned, this is the principle of natural selection. Selection effects have actually been demonstrated in experiments and field studies. Well known are the studies in which it was shown that in certain species of moth the most frequently found color can change from light to dark under the influence of industrial pollution (Kettlewell, 1959). In humans a selective mechanism called heterozygous advantage is known that has caused a high incidence of sickle-cell anemia in some populations. This is described in Box 11.2.

Box 11.2 **Sickle-cell anemia**

Sickle-cell anemia is a genetically transmitted defect in which the hemoglobin (red blood) corpuscles are easily deformed from round to sickle-shaped. It leads to a severe form of anemia and patients usually do not continue to live until they have children. The condition is caused by a single nucleotide in the DNA which occurs in two forms, called "S" and "s." There are three ways in which these two forms (called alleles) can be combined in the genetic material of an individual. The two chromosomes of the relevant pair both can be "S," both be "s," or one can be "s" while the other is "S." The (homozygotic) carriers of s–s suffer from sickle-cell anemia. S–S homozygotes are normal, and the heterozygotic carriers of S–s tend to suffer from a mild form of anemia (e.g., Mange and Mange, 1999). Sickle-cell anemia is a genetically transmitted defect in which the hemoglobin (red blood) corpuscles are easily deformed from round to sickle-shaped. It leads to a severe form of anemia and patients usually do not continue to live until they have children. The condition is caused by a single nucleotide in the DNA which occurs in two forms, called "S" and "s." There are three ways in which these two forms (called alleles) can be combined in the genetic material of an individual. The two chromosomes of the relevant pair both can be "S," both be "s," or one can be "s" while the other is "S." The (homozygotic) carriers of s–s suffer from sickle-cell anemia. S–S homozygotes are normal, and the heterozygotic carriers of S–s tend to suffer from a mild form of anemia (e.g., Mange and Mange, 1999).

What is the reason for this unequal distribution? Vogel and Motulsky (1979) listed three possible explanations:

1. The mutation rate may be different for some external reason (e.g., climate), or due to some other internal genetic factor.
2. Chance fluctuations (genetic drift) have played a role.
3. There is some selective advantage to sickle-cell anemia in areas where it is found frequently.

The size of the populations makes it highly unlikely that the differences in incidence can be due to random error, and for this reason the second possibility has to be rejected. The first alternative has been investigated. For example, in theoretical studies the rate of mutation needed to maintain the high frequencies actually found in certain areas was calculated. Also, the rate of inheritance was studied empirically by comparing children with their mothers. On both counts it could be ruled out that mutations formed a feasible explanation. A selective advantage for the S–s heterozygote was indeed found after it was noted that there was a coincidence between the presence of sickle-cell anemia and malignant forms of malaria. In a number of

Box 11.2 continued

studies, which we will not review here, support for a causal relationship was found. The most important evidence was that the incidence of malaria infections is higher in young children who are S–S homozygotes than in heterozygotes. A ratio of 2:17 between these two categories has been reported (Allison, 1964, quoted by Vogel and Motulsky, 1979). Given the overall high mortality of children due to malaria, this provides a sufficient selective advantage to maintain a high frequency of the "s" allele despite the mortality of the s–s homozygotes. Thus, the high incidence of sickle-cell anemia in equatorial Africa and some other regions of the world very likely reflects a genetic adaptation to long-term conditions in the environment.

Darwin wanted to understand how new species occur; his view was that natural selection acted on the individual level by gradually sorting out unfavorable individual traits (Dennett, 1995; Mayr, 1984). However, his theory was interpreted as if individuals were trying to preserve their species by procreating. The most important landmark of modern evolutionary theorizing is the transformation of this idea of preservation of the species through individual reproduction (or Darwinian fitness) into the conception of inclusive fitness (Hamilton, 1964). Inclusive fitness is the sum of the individual fitness outcomes resulting from own procreation (Darwinian fitness) and the procreation of relatives with whom the individual shares genes. The focus on the concept of inclusive fitness implies that the unit of natural selection is the gene (Dawkins, 1976), although it is not the gene per se that is exposed to selective forces directly but the individual organism that lives or dies, breeds or helps the relatives (Daly and Wilson, 1983; Mayr, 1984). This shift from the species to the individual level has substantial implications for the conception of human nature. It implies that altruism, that is, prosocial orientation and behavior, is not an unconditional human trait, but results from cost–benefit considerations, even if these are implicit and unconscious. There are two main concepts to describe the evolution of cooperative social behavior in self-interested organisms via natural selection: kin selection (Hamilton, 1964) and reciprocal altruism (Trivers, 1971).

Kin selection

According to this conception, individuals' social behaviors will vary according to the degree of genetic relatedness among group members. Individuals will be more cooperative with closely related others as compared to more distantly related or non-related others. The underlying assumption is that genetic closeness fosters cooperation and the reciprocation of investments. Cooperation and altruism based on the perception of reciprocity constitute what is known as Hamilton's rule

(Hamilton, 1964). Considerable empirical evidence has been presented to support this assumption. Dunbar and Spoors (1995) found that in Great Britain adults nominate a high proportion of kin relative to non-kin for help and support (see also Burnstein, Crandall and Kitayama, 1994). In the same vein, Fijneman and colleagues (1996) reported that the family has been identified as the most salient ingroup in the lives of individuals. Based on an extensive cross-cultural research program, Georgas, Berry, Van de Vijver, Kağitçibaşi and Poortinga (2006) concluded that relationships among family members are the most significant relationships in literally all parts of the world (see also Lay, Fairlie, Jackson, Ricci, Eisenberg, Sato et al., 1998; Neyer and Lang, 2003; Rhee, Uleman and Lee, 1996; see also the middle and late adulthood section in Chapter 3).

During the evolutionary past, human social groups presumably consisted of a relatively high proportion of kin (Hinde, 1980). However, the members of the groups not only shared genes to differing degrees, but also past experiences and plans related to the future (Bjorklund and Pellegrini, 2002). They were familiar and thus predictable to each other. Therefore, familiarity can be regarded as the major mechanism that enables individuals to recognize kin (Cheney and Seyfarth, 1999), generalizing to trustworthy individuals in general (see Chapter 2 where it is stressed that establishing familiarity is also the first step in the development of infants' attachment to their caregivers; see p. 58).

Reciprocal altruism

The concept of reciprocal altruism has been proposed by Trivers (1971) in order to capture social relations among genetically unrelated individuals. It predicts that individuals will cooperate with those with whom there is likely to be future social exchange and where there is the expectation, implicit or explicit, that the costs of cooperative and altruistic behaviors that an individual invests are to be reciprocated in the future. It is assumed that these expectations are based on prior experiences of cooperative interactions. It has been demonstrated empirically that even relatively small-scale acts of care can precipitate much greater returns from the individual to whom the original altruistic act was directed (Dickinson, 2000). Cross-cultural field studies (Kaniasty and Norris, 1995) have found that a caring non-relative would be more likely to benefit from someone's altruism than a neglectful non-relative would be.

Sexual selection

About a decade after the publication of his theory of natural selection (1859), Darwin postulated a second selection process, namely sexual selection (Darwin, 1871). While natural selection deals with traits related to the struggle of survival and maintenance (e.g., food acquisition and hygiene), sexual selection acts upon all traits which are related to mating and sexual reproduction. Sexual selection is based on two processes: intrasexual competition and intersexual mate selection (Voland and Grammer, 2003; see the gender differences across cultures section in Chapter 2 and the early and middle adulthood section in Chapter 3). It took more than a century before Trivers (1972) recognized the implications of Darwin's theory to the explanation of animal and human behavior. Trivers (1972, p. 140) argued that in sexually reproducing species like humans "the sex whose typical parental investment is greater than that of the opposite sex will become the limiting resource for that sex. Individuals of the sex investing less will compete among themselves to breed with members of the sex investing more." In mammals, this limiting sex are the females which leads to higher intrasexual competition within the male sex (Daly and Wilson, 1983, 1988). This concept of sex differences in parental investment explains motivational differences and may help to answer the question of why men and women often do not want to act in a similar way, although they in principle are able to do so (see Chapter 2, pp. 45–49).

The handicap principle or the costly signaling theory

From the perspective of costly signaling theory it is argued that many seemingly useless or harmful traits (handicaps), like the peacock's tail, evolved just because they signal their expensiveness and thus the high fitness quality of the bearer of this trait (Zahavi, 1975). For many decades the handicap principle was criticized as being implausible but it has been rediscovered recently (Miller, 2000; Voland and Grammer, 2003) after numerous empirical verifications (Zahavi and Zahavi, 1997); it also has been at the basis of evolutionary hypotheses on complex psychological domains like music, art, language, religion (see the religion section in Chapter 10) and morality. We shall elaborate on the last domain, more specifically on altruism.

Reciprocal altruism as analyzed by Trivers (1972) is restricted to two-person interactions and is thus at most applicable to small and stable groups characteristic for hunter-gatherer societies (Kaplan, Hill, Lancaster and Hurtado, 2000). Modern large-scale societies are characterized by multiple and often anonymous interactions where interactants are unfamiliar and, consequently, unpredictable. If future benefits or reciprocity are uncertain, why should one behave altruistically in the first place? During the last decade, two theoretical concepts were introduced to enhance the understanding of human cooperation: altruistic rewarding and altruistic punishment (Fehr and Fischbacher, 2003).

Altruistic rewarding is the cross-culturally observed trustful exchange that has been widely documented in economic experiments based on game-theoretical assumptions (Buchan, Croson and Dawes, 2002; see Box 4.2). Another cross-culturally robust result is altruistic punishment as the costly rejection of social imbalance, such as unfair sharing (e.g., Henrich, 2001). However, this combination of altruistic rewarding and punishment is often not sufficient to explain social engagement in public or common goods situations involving larger groups with potentially anonymous interactions. Human conditional cooperation is based on the implicit assumptions regarding whether all or most group members will cooperate or not. Such assumptions in turn are mainly determined by the possibility of punishment by third parties (Fischbacher, Gächter and Fehr, 2001). So even more important than altruistic punishment in an interaction between just two parties for encouraging cooperative actions for the common good is the possibility of being punished by a third party who is an outsider and is not directly economically involved (Fehr and Fischbacher, 2004). This is regarded to be a key element of the enforcement of social norms in human societies (Hill, 2002; see section on Modes of cultural transmission below).

Another important reason why humans maintain cooperation with non-kin can be attributed to the mechanism of reputation formation. Reputation through indirect reciprocity (e.g., "image scoring," Nowak and Sigmund, 1998; or social reputation, Milinski, Semmann and Krambeck, 2002; Milinski, Semmann, Bakker and Krambeck, 2001) constitutes another powerful mechanism for the enforcement of cooperation. Reputation-forming behavior can, for example, consist of tough bargaining and insisting on a fair exchange combined with the readiness to pay a costly price to punish deceivers (Fehr and Fischbacher, 2003). From an evolutionary perspective, this kind of cooperation can be easily subsumed under the "costly signal" or "handicap principle" (Zahavi, 1975), because this mechanism explains why we show costly signals, that is, behave altruistically, although we might not gain anything, even indirectly. The underlying assumption is that individuals can afford to show off because they have as a consequence a higher reputation and thus a higher genetic fitness which lowers the costs of showing the particular behavior or trait.

Adaptation

A conclusion of the previous paragraphs on the selective forces leading to the evolution of life is that living organisms including humans did not evolve to survive, but to reproduce. From an evolutionary perspective, our psychological and behavioral make-up is not aimed at merely surviving or well-being but at reproductive success. This perspective can help us in explaining *how* we try to pursue a happy life, as well as *why* some things, like having (grand)children (Voland, Chasiotis and Schiefenhövel, 2005), make us happy while others do not.

To understand how and why individual traits fit to environmental conditions, the Darwinian concept of adaptation is crucial. Adaptation in the broadest sense refers to any process in which an organism reacts to demands of the environment in a way which enhances its well-being, survival or reproduction. In evolutionary biology, the term refers to the adjustment of a population to an environment. But the concept of adaptation can also be found in psychological and anthropological writings (see Chapter 10, p. 229). In the social sciences, social adaptation refers to changes that take place during the lifetime of an organism in response to environmental demands (e.g., Relethford, 1997), while in psychology, adaptation refers to psychological or behavioral changes due to actual changes in the immediate environment.

In order to have a more comprehensive understanding of these different, even confusing, facets of adaptation, the environment that imposes these different demands leading to adaptation has to be defined. This can only be done with reference to the environment of a particular species. Each species occupies an ecological niche in the environment. This niche is defined by the way of life of the individual organisms: how the organisms of that species perceive their environment, how they cope with the prevailing temperature, how they move around in the environment, what food they use and how they collect it and so on. Moreover, organisms are not passively shaped by their environment: they interact with it (see Figure 1.1 and the modes of transmission section in Chapter 2). For example, the carrying capacity of the land can be reduced by overfarming or overcutting of forests; the soil can change because of the excreta that are deposited; and bees contribute to the fertilization of plants from which they draw pollen to make honey and thus help in ensuring a future food supply. It can be said that an organism contributes to establishing its own ecological niche through the way it interacts with the environment. Over a long time period the environment is not constant and the ecological niche will change. From this perspective adaptation is the process of keeping up with the changing environment, which in turn is not organism-independent: if an organism defines the environmental features which can act upon it, without an organism, there is no environment. If we want to know more about an organism, we need an environmental theory explaining these species-specific effects of the environment on the organism (Chasiotis, 2010).

Pleiotropy, spandrels and exaptations

A small change in a single gene can have various effects on the development of an organism. This is called pleiotropy. In a process of natural selection where an evolutionary change takes place in a gene, all effects of that gene will become manifest (directly or indirectly) in the phenotype. Lewontin (1978) refers to the analysis of the adaptive value of a characteristic as an engineering analysis of organism and environment. This is a procedure in which a particular idea is tested in a number of coherent ways. If none of the expectations has to be rejected, more and more confirmatory evidence for that idea is collected. This research strategy is in fact the same as the internal and external validation of theories used by social scientists. The systematic analysis of the various possible explanations for the high incidence of sickle-cell anemia mentioned in Box 11.2 provides an example of this approach.

The example of sickle-cell anemia shows that pleiotropic effects depend on the environment. Another argument against the notion of merely detrimental pleiotropic effects is the idea of antagonistic pleiotropy – a case in which a mutation can have a positive effect on one trait but a negative effect on another. Antagonistic pleiotropy is a central evolutionary concept to understanding many ontogenetic processes. For example, George Williams' (1957) theory on aging (better known as the "Grandmother hypothesis," see Voland, Chasiotis and Schiefenhövel, 2005, and Chapter 3, this volume, pp. 79–81) assumes that there are genes that are beneficial at a younger age (e.g., genes causing higher testosterone levels in males that promote fertility), but which can have disadvantageous effects in older age by increasing the probability of diseases (a higher testosterone level has been related to hypertension and prostate cancer; Gann, Hennekens, Ma, Longcope and Stampfer, 1996).

Despite these more sophisticated views on pleiotropy, some scholars considered the notion of pleiotropy as affecting the principle that each feature, in the behavioral as well as the physical phenotype, must be the adaptive outcome of a selection-driven process. This principle was challenged by Gould and Lewontin (1979) when they introduced the term "spandrels" in this connection. Spandrels are the spaces between the shoulders of adjoining arches as found in buildings, like Gothic church windows or old stone bridges. They have no structural function in the construction and could be left empty, but usually they are filled up, often with sculptures. In a similar sense certain adaptive biological changes may have created spaces for additional functions beyond those that led these changes initially. Moreover, Gould (1991) has suggested that apart from adaptations there can also be exaptations; these are features that now enhance fitness, but originally came about for another function. For Gould the complex brain is a feature of the human organism that has opened up a large scope for what we commonly call culture, including religion, art and technology, for which it hardly can have been developed originally.

It should be noted that Gould's and Lewontin's views have been contested, within evolutionary biology (Alexander, 1990; Mayr, 1983; Voland and Grammer, 2003; Voland, Chasiotis and Schiefenhövel, 2005) as well as in evolutionary psychology (Buss, Haselton, Shackelford, Bleske and Wakefield, 1998), a school of thought to which we shall return later in this chapter. In the meantime given what we know about sexual selection, it is not difficult to notice that Gould's objections on the seeming non-adaptivity of many features of humans like culture, art or religion (see the religion section in Chapter 10) concern selective processes based on natural and not on sexual selection. Furthermore, a more elementary, heuristic argument against the notion of the non-adaptivity of a trait is that it needs an adaptational research framework to be detected: if you want to know whether a trait is an adaptation or not, the only way to find out is to test if it is one (Alexander, 1990; Mayr, 1983).

The argument raised in this subsection is of relevance for cross-cultural psychology for two reasons. First, established evolutionary pathways of development can enhance our understanding of behavior patterns. Second, a too strong presumption of evolutionary adaptation may lead to anthropomorphic language in the interpretation of animal behavior and an underestimation of the importance of culture in shaping the human mind (Bolhuis and Wynne, 2009; Penn, Holyak and Povinelli, 2008). In the next section, dealing with ethology, we will elaborate on this.

Ethology

The study by biologists of animal behavior in natural environments is called **ethology**. Characteristic of this branch of the biological sciences are elaborate and detailed field studies of animals in their natural habitat. The resulting descriptive accounts form the basis for theoretical explanations which are further developed along three lines of enquiry: through additional observations, through experiments to test specific hypotheses and through the comparison of findings across species. To do that, ethologists look at our phylogenetic relatives from two perspectives, **homology** and **analogy**. Homology integrates us in the array of other primate species, all descending from a creature like a modern ape; understanding other primates will help us understand our ancestors with respect to shared phenomena like hunting, tool use and even lethal aggression (Goodall, 1986) or maternal investment (Keller and Chasiotis, 2007). The problem with ape "models," however, is that we do not know which one (chimpanzees, bonobos, gorillas or orangutans) to choose because there is a great variety in behavioral adaptations and social organization. Moreover, all modern apes live in forests, but hominids moved out of the forest and have many features that may not be like those of our common ancestor (Kappeler and Pereira, 2003; Kappeler and Van Schaik, 2004). Analogy, on the other hand, can demonstrate similarities in evolution between primates and humans because we are very similar to other primates in morphology, physiology and behavior. Comparative analyses allow us to deduce rules or patterns of adaptation, for example concerning the effect of contact comfort on the development of attachment (Harlow, 1958; see also Chapter 2, pp. 45–49). Thus, analogy by comparison is more powerful than homology because it may generate general principles about how evolution shapes behavior, social organization and mating and parenting strategies in particular ecologies.

It is particularly in respect of this last strategy that biologists claim to have an advantage over psychologists, who tend to keep their research restricted to a single species and thus are not able to cross-validate their conceptualizations in a broader biological framework. In this section we shall first briefly examine what the ethological approach can contribute, and then move to the application of ethological approaches to humans. Among the topics frequently studied by ethologists are courtship behavior, territoriality, care for offspring, strategies for predator evasion, efficiency in foraging, communication (e.g., acquiring species-specific song in birds) and social organization as found in bees and ants.

Early ethologists (e.g., Lorenz, 1965, and Tinbergen, 1963) were struck by regular patterns in much of the behavior of animals. Often one can observe behavior sequences consisting of a number of distinguishable acts. Once such a sequence is set in motion, it cannot be interrupted and then continued; after interruption it has to be started again from the beginning. Hence the notion was proposed of "fixed action patterns." These patterns are triggered by specific stimuli, which act as releasers of an available behavior process. Another important notion was that of "imprinting." It was observed that young birds tend to react to the first moving object they see after hatching as they normally respond to their parents. For example, animal keepers in zoos have found themselves in the position of substitute parents. They are then followed by young birds in the same way as these chicks normally follow their mother. At adult age such animals have been known to make sexual advances to members of the human substitute parent species, rather than to their own species. For this reason Lorenz (1965) postulated "critical periods" in the process of development. What an animal acquired during such a period was considered fixed and irreversible. A sharp distinction was made between instinct and learning. This divide also marked more or less the boundary between ethology and psychology from the 1930s until the 1970s. The term "instinct" referred to genetically inherited and thus pre-programmed and rather immutable behavior. At that time psychology was dominated by behaviorally inspired learning theories. It was believed by many that through classical conditioning in the tradition of Pavlov and operant conditioning as developed by Skinner, virtually any reaction an individual was capable of making could be linked to any stimulus that could be perceived.

This conclusion proved to be premature. Rats can easily be conditioned to avoid foods which later make them ill if these foods have a certain taste, but conditioning is difficult if the consumption of these foods is accompanied by an electric shock to their feet (Garcia and Koelling, 1966). Conversely, rats have great difficulty in learning to jump for food, but can easily be taught to jump for shock avoidance. Visual cues have also been found to be ineffective in rats for learning food avoidance. For other species, such as monkeys, visual cues are quite effective in learning avoidance of toxic foods. Apparently, cues are most effective when they match the natural life style of a species (e.g., Gould and Marler, 1987). Some ethologists had already argued earlier that the learning abilities of animals were greatly dependent on context. There are predispositions for certain stimulus–response associations, and a reward which will reinforce a certain response may not work well for other responses; this finally led learning theorists like Breland and Breland (1961, p. 683) to conclude in despair: "Under the most controlled circumstances, the animals do as they damn please."

The distinction between learning and instinct has also become more blurred because ethologists withdrew somewhat from the earlier position of Lorenz on imprinting as a special kind of learning dependent on "critical" periods. They now tend to speak about sensitive periods instead (see Chapter 3, pp. 68–72). Genetic factors will facilitate or constrain the learning of certain associations in a relative rather than in an absolute sense. These factors are not necessarily constant; they can cause different effects during various phases of individual development (Archer, 1992; Hinde, 1982). The animal is seen as innately equipped to learn what it needs in the particular ecological niche it occupies. At the same time "instinctive" responses cannot develop without environmental influences, making an ecological approach to behavior necessary. It requires only a small step to argue that learning in the human species, with its own evolutionary history and adapted to its own particular niche, is subject to the same considerations. Moreover, ethologists have asked the question of whether culture is so exclusively human as often thought (see Box 11.3).

From a historical perspective, the advantages of the classic ethological approaches of Lorenz (1965) and Tinbergen (1963) for psychology were more methodological than conceptual. The ethological approach lead to the view that the relationship formation between a parent and his/her child is not based on learning, but on behavioral predispositions on both sides. This focus on actual behaviors lead to methodological innovations like the use of ethograms for infants (for a catalogue of possible behaviors of an organism, see Keller, 1980) and longitudinal observational studies. The main shortcomings are to be found in the theoretical elaboration of their concepts, notably the endorsement of a version of group selection to explain cross-cultural differences (Eibl-Eibesfeldt, 1989) that by current standards is inadequate. The turning point was the classical work by Hamilton (1964) on kin selection, dividing the history of modern evolutionary biology into a pre-Hamiltonian and a post-Hamiltonian ethology (Dawkins, 1979), which came to be known as "sociobiology" (Wilson, 1975).

Evolutionary psychology

Human social behavior was incorporated explicitly in biological thinking by Wilson (1975), who wrote a book about "sociobiology," including a section on

Box 11.3 Emergence of culture in chimpanzees

Ethologists have made extensive observational studies of groups of great apes, especially chimpanzees, sometimes following them for many years. Most widely known is the work of Goodall (1986), but there are a number of similar field sites. Whiten *et al.* (1999) drew up an initial listing (N = 65) of behaviors reported in the literature for chimpanzees. All of these behaviors were assessed by directors of several field sites as to whether or not they had been observed in local groups of chimpanzees. A string of categories were used, namely customary, habitual, present, absent, absent with ecological explanation, absent possibly because of inadequate observation, answer uncertain. Thirty-nine behaviors were found that were absent at some sites, but customary or habitual elsewhere, including some shared between two or more communities. These patterns were especially concerned with sexual advances, grooming and the use of tools. The patterns resembled those of human societies, in which differences between cultures are constituted by a multiplicity of variations in technology and social customs. We can mention as examples field observations reported by one of these researchers. Boesch (1991, 1993, 1995) has suggested that mother chimpanzees influence the development of nut cracking in their infants through stimulation, facilitation and active teaching. Certain contexts may favor teaching with regard to tool use in opening nuts. This can lead to the acceleration of behavior in an inexperienced individual. Eating of leaves of two species of plants was observed for the first time in a group, then spread rapidly within the community. Boesch proposed that there was cultural transmission. Observations by Russon (2002) have shown how young orangutans who grew up in captivity and then were released initially may not know how to obtain certain foods that are difficult to handle (e.g., because of spines), but later have learned this from contacts with other individuals possessing the relevant skills. Is the term "culture" appropriate in view of such behavior patterns? An answer to this question depends ultimately on the defining criteria of the concept. It is quite possible to make a list of criteria that excludes all species except humans (cf. McGrew, 1992; Segall *et al.*, 1999). However, Whiten and colleagues, who have long and firsthand field experience, are clearly inclined to attribute elementary forms of culture to chimpanzees at least (Whiten, Horner and Marshall-Pescini, 2003).

human behavior. At the time, this raised severe objections from social scientists. The anthropologist Sahlins (1977, p. ix), for example, stated: "Within the void left by biology lies the whole of anthropology." Three decades further on much of this kind of evolutionary thinking has become commonplace in psychology and it is beginning to make inroads in cross-cultural psychology as well (Keller, Poortinga and Schölmerich, 2002; Van de Vijver, Chasiotis and Breugelmans, in press).

The evolutionary thinking of ethology and sociobiology (Wilson, 1975) is at the basis of **evolutionary psychology**. A basic assumption in evolutionary psychology is that all human psychological functions ranging from ethnocentrism (e.g., Reynolds, Falger and Vine, 1987) to aesthetics (Dissanayake, 1992) have to be considered in the light of reproductive fitness. According to Tooby and Cosmides (1992) such functions reflect design features of the human mind that have been shaped by evolutionary processes. In the process of selection those features are retained that are functional as opposed to dysfunctional (i.e., less successful in reproduction). Thus, separate successful features are linked together in the reproduction process and in this way a coherent overall design has emerged. There are likely to be a large number of complex evolved psychological mechanisms that are domain specific. Results like those of Garcia and Koelling (1966), mentioned earlier, are seen as evidence of such specificity, and also the fact that one finds phobias for snakes, heights or open spaces, which have always been part of the human environment, but never for electricity sockets, which have been in existence for a few generations only.

Ethologists like Tinbergen (1963) understood the danger of inferences based on insufficent evidence. He proposed four criteria for a behavior pattern to be considered part of the adaptive equipment of a species: (1) its mechanism or cause; (2) its evolutionary history; (3) its ontogenetic development; and (4) the function it supposedly serves. Thus, in an examination of evolutionary studies a major question is whether sufficient evidence exists for the validity of functional explanations. The objection has been raised that findings like those of Buss on gender differences (see gender differences across cultures section in Chapter 2 and adulthood section in Chapter 3) can also be explained in terms of traditional cultural patterns that have created distinctions between men and women (Eagly and Wood, 1999). The question of how these differences are patterned in various societies requires psychological and anthropological explanation. At the same time it is difficult to decide how far objections such as those by Eagly and Wood are to the point, because they address current practices, while evolutionary psychologists seek to address the possible psychobiological roots of such practices.

The notion of the biological givenness of functional entities, also called modules, is also questioned in evolutionary theories emphasizing interactions between organism and environment. According to such interactionist theories reproductive strategies can be modified by factors in the environment of the organism. In Chapter 3 we mentioned the assertion by Belsky *et al.* (1991) that insecure patterns of attachment in infancy lead to an early onset of puberty and sexual partnerships (see pp. 69–71). Similar relationships between early childhood experiences and the onset of puberty have been reported in other studies (Chasiotis, in press). In interactionist approaches genetic mechanisms are capabilities that can be evoked and shaped by specific environmental conditions (see Chapter 3, pp. 68–72).

Models of cultural transmission

In the first section of this chapter we described that genetic information is transmitted from generation to generation. In subsequent sections we have discussed various fields of research in which analysis is focussed on the genetic underpinnings of human psychological functioning. Earlier in the book, in the modes of transmission section in Chapter 2, we discussed the psychological transmission of information between members of a cultural group in the course of ontogenetic development, which does not necessarily require a genetic relationship. Biologists have developed formal models in which the transmission of both genetic and cultural information is dealt with. The distinction between vertical, oblique and horizontal transmission (see Cavalli-Sforza and Feldman, 1981), mentioned in the modes of transmission section in Chapter 2, is an example. Cavalli-Sforza and Feldman have described mathematical models of the non-genetic transmission of aspects of culture. One of the areas which they discuss is the diffusion of innovations, for which mathematical models can be fitted that are similar to those for the spread through a population of an advantageous biological mutation. The scope of most models goes beyond mere description. They are intended to give biological and cultural phenomena a place within a single explanatory framework.

One early attempt to construct models of cultural transmission meeting this requirement was by Lumsden and Wilson (1981). They postulated the notion of a culturegen, which forms the basic unit of culture. A culturegen is a more or less homogeneous set of artifacts, behaviors or "mentifacts" (Lumsden and Wilson's term) that are related. Transmission takes place via epigenetic rules. Epigenesis is the process of interaction between **genes** and the environment. Any regularity in development which gives direction to behavior forms an epigenetic rule. Examples in Lumsden and Wilson's book include principles of perceptual information transmission and incest taboos. However, they go further:

Human beings are thought [by cultural anthropologists] to pursue their own interest and that of their society on the basis of a very few simple structural biological needs by means of numerous, arbitrary, and often elaborate culturally acquired behaviors. In contrast to this conventional view, our interpretation of the evidence from cognitive and developmental psychology indicates the presence of epigenetic rules that have sufficiently great specificity to channel the acquisition of rules of inference and decision to a substantial degree. The process of mental canalization in turn shapes the trajectories of cultural evolution. (Lumsden and Wilson, 1981, p. 56)

These few sentences in no way do justice to the sophisticated arguments presented by Lumsden and Wilson. However, they are sufficient to indicate the kind of concepts, analogous to those found in genetics, in terms of which cultural transmission is described.

Apart from attempts to incorporate cultural and biological transmission within a single framework, one also finds theories that draw distinctions between mechanisms of biological and cultural transmission. None of the authors questions the evolutionary basis of cultural variation and cultural change, but some accept, contrary to orthodox sociobiologists and evolutionary psychologists, that other mechanisms have to be postulated in addition to the natural selection of alternative alleles in the genetic constitution.

One well-known example is the **dual inheritance model** of Boyd and Richerson (1985, 2005). In addition to the genetic inheritance system that has been described in the first section of this chapter they postulate a cultural inheritance system that is based on social learning. What an individual has learned during his or her lifetime is not transmitted genetically; only the capacity for learning, which is part of the genotype, is passed on to his or her offspring and remains in the population. However, during a lifetime a person can pass on cultural information to other members of the group. This information can stay in the possession of the group from generation to generation. The transmission of cultural information has "population-level consequences" according to Boyd and Richerson (1985, p. 4).

The cultural and genetic inheritance systems differ among other things in the nature of parenthood. Cultural traits can be transmitted by "cultural parents" who may well be different from the biological parents, as in oblique transmission (see Chapter 2, p. 41). Also, in the cultural inheritance system, specific experiences gained during an individual's lifetime can be transmitted to that individual's cultural offspring and become part of the inheritance of the group. This is in contrast to genetic transmission, which can only have an effect through a differential rate of reproduction.

The close correspondence between biological and cultural transmission in the theorizing of Boyd and Richerson is especially evident in the mechanisms that they postulate for explaining cultural change. Apart from "mutations" (i.e., error rates due to imperfect memory) and chance variations due to selective retention of information in certain groups, an important place is attributed to social learning and systematic biases in the transmission of information. Social learning is distinguished from individual learning. The latter is based on trial-and-error or conditioning principles. Boyd and Richerson believe that a large cultural repertoire cannot be acquired only by socially controlled conditioning of youngsters. This process would be too uneconomic (Henrich and McElreath, 2007). They attach great importance to Bandura's (1977) social learning theory, in which imitation of behaviors that have only been observed is seen as a sufficient condition for learning. Social learning by observation and imitation leads to cultural stability of behavior patterns. Individual learning, shaped by specific environmental conditions, leads to change.

Boyd and Richerson (1985, 2005; see also McElreath and Henrich, 2007) have constructed models of cultural transmission analogous to models of genetic transmission. The relative incidence of individual and social learning is one of the parameters in these models. The consequences of a change in this parameter, for example in the rate of responsiveness to changes in the environment, can be calculated. The models are further elaborated through the inclusion of the concept of transmission bias. An individual within a culture is exposed to different variants of the available cultural repertoire. Boyd and Richerson assume that the available options can be evaluated and the most adaptive variant selected. This is illustrated with the example of a child learning to play table tennis and observing that there are two ways to hold the bat – the "racquet" grip and the "pencil" grip. No bias occurs when the child randomly chooses one player as a role model, but there are other possibilities. After some practice the child can choose the grip with which the best results are obtained. If it takes too much practice to find this out, another option is to use the most successful player as a model. Yet another option is to simply follow the majority in one's choice.

This last strategy, a conformist one, is linked by Boyd and Richerson to altruism, or cooperation, and to ethnocentrism. The conformist strategy, which makes people follow the most popular variant in a group, leads to a decrease in cultural variation within groups relative to between-group variation. Even though cooperation with group members rather than the pursuit of self-interest can be disadvantageous to the individual (and thus should have disappeared in the process of evolution according to traditional evolution theory), the lower fitness of cooperators within groups can have been offset by a higher survival rate of groups with a high frequency of cooperators. If this is the case, and Boyd and Richerson specify relevant conditions within their models, a high frequency of cooperators is maintained more or less indefinitely. At the same time, the conformist bias can only have this effect if the cooperative behavior is restricted to a limited group. One kind of group which seems to meet the requirement of the models is the cultural group with the associated characteristics of ethnocentrism, including cooperative behavior toward members of the ingroup and uncooperative behavior toward the outgroup.

Complexities are added if a further diversification of levels or modes of transmission is introduced (e.g., Durham, 1982; McElreath and Henrich, 2007; Plotkin and Odling-Smee, 1981). The role of culture as environmental context has been further elaborated by Laland, Odling-Smee and Feldman (2000). In line with traditional evolutionary theory they recognize that through interactions with the environment a species modifies its environment – a process called niche construction (see p. 46). However, Laland *et al.* go further. In human populations niche construction is not only a genotypical characteristic of the species. Two other kinds of processes are involved, namely ontogenetic processes of information acquisition (e.g., learning to read and write) and cultural processes. From this perspective farming with cattle for milk (niche construction) could be at the basis of the genetic change toward tolerance for lactose, as discussed in Box 11.4.

Box 11.4 **Differences in tolerance for lactose**

Lactose is the most important carbohydrate in milk. It cannot be absorbed in the intestine, but needs to be split into two molecules by the enzyme lactase. In newborns the (very rare) absence of the enzyme is lethal unless special food can be provided. Until fairly recently it was considered normal by western medicine that in older children and adults the activity of lactase was maintained. We now know that this is the rule among West Europeans and their descendants in other countries. In many other populations the continuation of lactase excretion in older children and adults is virtually absent, leading to lactose intolerance. Lactose intolerance is manifested by diarrhea, abdominal pain and flatulence after consumption of, let us say, half a liter of cow's milk. This holds for many East Asian groups, Melanesians, Native Americans and for most Africans. Groups of nomadic pastoralists in Africa, such as the Fulani, form a notable exception with high prevalence of lactose tolerance. In Southern Europe and in certain regions of India intermediate values (from 30% to 70%) are found (see Dobzhansky, Ayala, Stebbins and Valentine, 1977, or Vogel and Motulsky, 1979, for further references).

Although there is no perfect correlation the relationship between lactose tolerance in adults and animal husbandry is striking. Two explanations have been suggested – one cultural, and the other referring to physical qualities of the environment (Flatz and Rotthauwe, 1977). In the cultural explanation it is postulated that the consumption of milk, because of its nutritional value in proteins, should give a selection advantage. Once there were a few individuals who can tolerate milk, this trait could slowly spread through the population over a large number of generations. The fact that there are cattle-farming populations with a low frequency of tolerance weakens this hypothesis. In addition, when milk has fermented it is low in lactose content and is digestible in the absence of lactase in the consumer's intestinal tract.

The second hypothesis postulates an advantage of lactose tolerance in areas with relatively little ultraviolet sunlight, such as Northern Europe. Sunlight plays a role in the production of vitamin D, which is needed for calcium metabolism. A too low level of vitamin D leads to rickets, a bone disease. It has been suggested that lactose is an alternative substance to vitamin D in the metabolism of calcium. Another version

Box 11.4 continued

of this hypothesis bears on the direct absorption of vitamin D contained in milk and milk products.

Whatever the precise explanation, lactose intolerance explains why milk is considered repulsive by adults in many countries. Sometimes it is considered good for children and by extension for other weak and sickly persons, but not for strong and healthy people. Obviously such opinions have a much more valid basis than originally thought in western folklore and medicine. Of more interest to us are possible wider ramifications. To what extent has the intolerance for fresh milk been a barrier against the development of animal husbandry in various societies? The form of economic subsistence influences major cultural variables in a number of ways, as we have seen in the modes of transmission section in Chapter 2 and in the discussion of antecedents of susceptibility to visual illusions in Chapter 9. Thus, variations in the digestion of milk may well have been a factor in the shaping of cultures, even if it is not clear at this stage how this biological mechanism has actually operated.

Finally, there are approaches based on the new branch of costly signaling theory, which tries to explain the evolution of culture. The interpretation of cooperative or altruistic acts as costly signaling can explain why we contribute to the public good, but it cannot explain why we should "show off" in social contexts through being altruistic and not, for example, by trying to appear genetically fit by impressing others how particularly brave, powerful or healthy we are (Voland and Grammer, 2003). A supplementary explanatory mechanism to explain why we are especially prone to show prosocial behavior in a context with non-kin others might be cultural group selection (Gintis, Smith and Bowles, 2001; Smith, Bliege Bird and Bird, 2003).

Earlier in this chapter we mentioned evidence of human subjective evaluations of fairness and inequity aversion, that is, the disapproval of unequal transactions. Such behavior goes against the principle of economic rationality which would imply self-interested freeloading without any considerations of fairness (Fehr and Fischbacher, 2003). However, cooperative behavior is likely to be imitated when everybody cooperates. Thus, in special contextual circumstances, like in the human case of cultural transmission through accumulative cultural evolution, norms and institutions may have been maintained through altruistic punishment by third parties (see also Bowles, Choi and Hopfensitz, 2003; Boyd, Gintis, Bowles and Richerson, 2003). This line of reasoning basically conceives of humans as being uniquely prone and able to act altruistically; some authors even start to postulate an "altruistic drive" (Fehr and Fischbacher, 2003; Warneken, Chen and Tomasello, 2006) facilitating within-group cooperation in humans.

This view has been challenged by a fair number of studies showing similar prosocial behaviors in non-primate species (Brosnan, Newton-Fischer and Van Vugt, 2009). Bshary and colleagues could show in pairwise cooperating cleaner fish that they are also able to detect and punish defectors (Raihani, Grutter and Bshary, 2010). This punishment promotes cooperation and thereby yields direct foraging benefits to the punisher. The authors concluded that third-party punishment can evolve via self-serving tendencies in a non-human species, and this finding may also shed light on the evolutionary dynamics of more complex behavior in other animal species, including humans (for an overview, see Bshary, Grutter, Willener and Leimar, 2008).

The main problem with the complex models discussed in this section is that they lack the theoretical strength of traditional evolutionary biology. The definition of higher levels and the specification of relationships between them become increasingly fuzzy as one moves from more biological to more cultural phenomena. From the perspective of cross-cultural psychology it can be argued that ethology and evolutionary psychology, with their emphasis on invariant, genetically based aspects of human psychological functioning, provide minimum estimates of the effects of cultural conditions. Culture-comparative research, if it extends over a sufficient range of cultural populations, tends to lead to maximum estimates of cultural variation. The variety of available models can be seen as evidence that interactions between nature and nurture are difficult to trace. However, this is clearly more so in monocultural than in cross-cultural approaches. We expect that culture-comparative research will increasingly become the testing ground of models and theories as mentioned in this section.

Conclusions

In this chapter we have first outlined principles that provide the foundation for biological thinking about human behavior. These principles are important for cross-cultural psychology because human populations vary in both cultural and biological terms. We then shifted the focus to evolutionary theories of human social behavior. We finished with a brief outline of some models that make distinctions between genetic transmission and other modes of transmission.

Perhaps we should add explicitly what biological thinking as presented in this chapter is *not* about. It is *not* about genes as a deterministic force that pre-empts moral choices. It is also *not* about the explanation of behavior differences between cultural groups. And it is *not* about the dichotomy between nature and nurture, which is a false dichotomy. Biologically speaking we cannot really go against our genes, but the observable behavior repertoire is the outcome of a range of possible responses. The fascinating question is what the space is in which humans can operate and build culture.

The human species is morphologically and physiologically quite similar to other species, but the extensive facility for culture provides for a psychologically unique position. The facilities for conscious reflection and the formulation of long-term goals and plans that can be reached along a variety of routes add a dimension to human behavior not found to the same extent in other species. This can be seen as providing our species with a range of affordances, as we shall argue in the last section of Chapter 12. To define this space, more insight into cross-cultural variations and uniformities of behavior is needed than is presently available. It seems obvious to us that cross-cultural research will have to make a contribution to the further accumulation of such knowledge. At the same time the chapter is meant to provide a warning: we should be careful not to fall into the dogmatic and ideological traps either of some evolutionary psychologists who are inclined to see any coincidence as a causal relationship, or of environmentalistically minded social scientists who cling to the view that the biological basis is largely irrelevant to the study of what is typically human in behavior. Finally, in as much as it makes sense to accept sociocultural evolution as a relevant determinant of cultures that we find today, an important warning is issued by Campbell (1975) which we can ignore only at great future cost. Campbell has argued that in an evolutionary framework cultural inheritance has to be regarded as adaptive. For this reason it has to be treated with respect. He pleads that when we come across puzzling and incomprehensible features of a culture, including our own, we should diligently search for ways in which it may make adaptive sense.

KEY TERMS

adaptation (biological) • adaptation (social) • allele • analogy • dual inheritance model • ethology • evolutionary psychology • fitness (biological) • gene • handicap principle • homology • inclusive fitness • kin selection • natural selection • pleiotropy • reciprocal altruism • sensitive period • sociobiology

FURTHER READING

Boyd, R., and Richerson, P. J. (2005). *The origin and evolution of cultures*. New York: Oxford University Press.

This book describes the further development of the dual inheritance model of cultural transmission.

Dunbar, R. I. M., and Barrett, L. (2007). *Oxford handbook of evolutionary psychology.* Oxford: Oxford University Press.

This book gives an excellent overview of the international "state of the art" in evolutionary psychology with special attention to the interplay of biology and culture.

Odling-Smee, F. J., Laland, K. N., and Feldman, M. W. (2003). *Niche construction: The neglected process in evolution.* Princeton: Princeton University Press.

This book provides an illustration of the models that emerge when the role of the ecological and sociocultural environment is emphasized more than in traditional evolutionary approaches.

12 Methodology and theory

CONTENTS

As noted in Chapter 1, there is much more to a cross-cultural study than collecting data in two countries and comparing the results. Long ago Campbell (1970) warned that two-group comparisons usually are not interpretable: there are too many factors to which an observed difference can be attributed, including a lack of equivalence (cultural bias). In various chapters in Part I we have seen examples of competing interpretations of differences in behaviors across cultures. In the present chapter the scope for interpretation of cross-cultural data will be explored further. Both "culture" and "behavior" are somewhat abstract and diffuse concepts that are not accessible to scientific analysis without further specification. The process of specification is guided by the methods and research questions that are selected by researchers as well as by their theoretical and metatheoretical orientations. Usually method and theory are linked and this is the reason why we have combined them in the present chapter.

The first three sections refer back to the three themes and associated theoretical positions that we outlined in Chapter 1. In the first section we elaborate on the distinction between culture as external context and culture as internal to the person (internal context). The second section on cultural invariance and variations deals with the dimension of universalism versus relativism. We pay attention to the **paradigms** or worldviews that have been associated with qualitative and quantitative approaches, rather than to these methods per se, as we did in Chapter 1. We also return to the three positions of culture-comparative psychology, culture psychology and indigenous psychologies. The third section is on the interpretation of cross-cultural differences. We present distinctions between categories of generalization in the interpretation of cross-cultural data.

In the fourth and final section we discuss whether there are ways of bridging the gaps between the various approaches to understanding relationships between behavior and culture. Two ideas are mentioned. The first is to broaden the theoretical scope of cross-cultural psychology beyond our social science heritage and include some of the biological thinking discussed before, especially in Chapter 11. The second suggestion is to reconsider the way in which we tend to do research and to follow a more comprehensive approach in which direct observation of actual behavior patterns is given a more central place.

Internal and external context

In Chapter 1 we mentioned conditions in the environment, including climate, mode of economic existence, and social institutions and practices, as constituting what was called external culture, or external context. The ecocultural framework (Box 1.1) provided an example of this concept. Affluence was the aspect most frequently referred to in subsequent chapters. National wealth has been associated directly, for example, with differences in value dimensions such as individualism–collectivism (Chapter 4), and with person variables such as happiness (Chapter 5). Indirect links through socialization styles and school education were mentioned in Chapter 2 (parent–child interactions), Chapter 3 (for example in the discussion of adolescence) and Chapter 6 (where in the section on Cognition East and West research was presented on different modes of cognition). Culture conceptualized as an inherent part of the person, or internal culture, was also mentioned in Chapter 1, and illustrated, for example, in Chapter 2 with the contrast between two pathways for individual development (Greenfield, Keller, Fuligni and Maynard, 2003), in the section on the self in social context in Chapter 5 with the independent versus the interdependent construal of the self, and in the section on emotion and language in Chapter 7 with the postulate of culture-specific emotions.

Analyzing external context and its consequences

Variables associated with external context may seem easily accessible, and there are indeed many sources with relevant statistics, especially the websites of international organizations like the UN and the World Bank. Still, researchers have to consider whether the available information matches their questions. For example, climate has often been expressed as the average temperature. Another approach (Van de Vliert, 2009) differentiates between harsh climates (which can be either hot or cold) and temperate climates, taking into consideration precipitation as well as temperature. Van de Vliert's second ingredient in the formation of culture is the dimension of affluence going from poor to rich societies. Climate and affluence influence each other, leading to three "cultural conglomerates": (1) survival cultures (harsh and poor), (2) easygoing cultures (temperate and either poor or rich) and (3) self-expression cultures (harsh and rich). Needless to say, the categorization of countries would have been partly different if Van de Vliert had used hot, temperate and cold climates arranged by average annual temperature.

The operationalization of affluence can also take different forms, although it should be noted that the correlations between various indices tends to be very high. Most frequently used is GNP (Gross National Product per capita). An alternative is PPPI (Purchasing Power Parity Index), which takes into consideration that in low-income countries goods and services tend to be less expensive in US dollar or euro terms. Other indices include estimates of opportunities for citizens and inequalities in society. The Human Development Index (HDI) of the United Nations Development Program (UNDP) combines three factors: life expectancy, education (literacy rate and school enrolment) and standard of living. The Gini coefficient is a measure of the inequality of wealth within a country.

Other variables of external context touched on in previous chapters have included the effect of mode of economic subsistence on social behavior (see the section on gender differences in Chapter 2), the absence of high noise levels leading to less loss of hearing at high frequencies among the San in the Kalahari (Chapter 9, p. 204), and the effects of carpenteredness and open vistas on susceptibility to visual illusions (Chapter 9, p. 208).

In earlier chapters we have also come across research in which the relationship is examined between some psychological trait or disposition and its behavioral consequences. For example, there are numerous studies in which societies are classified as either individualist or collectivist (Klassen, 2004); the consequences that have been investigated include social perception (Chapter 4), cognition (Chapter 6) and, particularly, leadership variables in work organization research, as we shall see in Chapter 16. In such studies it is assumed that external antecedents, such as affluence, have played a role somewhere in the past and have led to current cultural dispositions, while these current dispositions in turn serve as more proximal antecedent variables for behavioral outcomes. Thus, variables reflecting antecedent conditions are seen as causing or facilitating certain consequences in psychological functioning or behavioral outcomes.

An alternative is to consider cultural variables as mediating or moderating variables. A mediating variable accounts for part of the relationship between an independent and a dependent variable. A moderating variable controls the strength of a relationship between an independent and a dependent variable (Baron and Kenny, 1986; Lonner and Adamopoulos, 1997). To analyze such more complicated relationships cross-cultural researchers have begun to turn to multilevel models, which allow distinctions between variance components attributable to the individual level, to the cultural level or to the interaction between these levels.

Antecedent–consequent relationships can be investigated in various research designs with correlations between variables and differences between mean scores of cultural samples as the main statistics. For a further differentiation we can refer to the Internet site (Additional Topics, Chapter 1), where we mention four kinds of designs distinguished by Van de Vijver and Leung (1997, 2000). These are: psychological differences studies, external validation studies, generalization studies and theory-driven studies. The first two of these can be qualified as exploratory research designs, and the latter two as designs for hypothesis testing. The point to note here is that in so far as all four types seek to find lawful relationships between variables (antecedent and consequent), they adhere to the experimental paradigm dominating much of psychology. In this paradigm, research designs tend to have an independent variable (usually some external or internal cultural condition, such as affluence or self-construal) and a dependent variable (usually a measurement of some behavioral outcome, such as sensitivity to visual illusions, self-esteem).

An important tool in the search for antecedent–consequent relationships is meta-analysis (Hedges and Olkin, 1985; Van Hemert, in press). In such cases a researcher will collect as many published studies as possible on a topic, some of which may show large differences between certain cultures, while others perhaps show no differences. An estimate is then made of the size of cross-cultural variations by combining all the findings. There are several publications that make use of this technique, including Oyserman *et al.* (2002), who examined a substantial number of studies on individualism and collectivism (see Chapter 4, p. 93), and Van Hemert, Poortinga and Van de Vijver (2007), who analyzed the size of cross-cultural differences for various kinds of studies on emotions (Chapter 7, p. 160).

In Chapter 1 we have argued that good experiments often are not available in culture-comparative research. An experiment requires that the researcher has control over the various treatment conditions which make up the independent or antecedent variable. In cross-cultural psychology "treatments" often refer to external variables, such as socialization and enculturation, and other long-term influences. In other words, while cultural treatment conditions can be assessed independently, they are frequently inferred rather than measured. In addition, in an experiment the researcher will allocate respondents to treatment conditions via some random procedure. This is the best way to assure that prior existing differences between respondents affecting treatment outcomes are randomly distributed across treatments. Campbell (1969) suggested the term "quasi-experiments" for field studies with existing groups where random allocation of respondents is impossible. In cross-cultural psychology respondents are nested each in their own cultural context. The complexity of contexts, and the innumerable ways in which they can differ from each other, implies that the set of variables on which the samples differ is immense. This makes it difficult to demonstrate the validity of a single explanation. For example, the shift from explanations in terms of construal of the self to explanations in terms of situated norms (Chapter 4, p. 108) demonstrates that the original explanation had not been protected sufficiently against alternative interpretations.

It is a primary task of researchers to demonstrate that their findings, and thus the methods through which they were collected, have **validity**, that is, that they support the interpretations or inferences that are being made (Shadish, Cook and Campbell, 2002). They argue that the concepts of validity and invalidity "refer to the best available approximation to the truth or falsity of propositions, including propositions about cause" (2002, p. 37). The absence of control through manipulation of treatments and random allocation of respondents for many cross-cultural psychologists does not mean that good approximations are out of reach, although they may be more difficult to achieve than in other areas of psychology. For measures that can be taken to enhance valid results in quasi-experimental designs we refer to texts on methodology, especially Shadish *et al.*, and to the Internet (Additional Topics, Chapter 12).

www.cambridge.org/berry

One kind of threat to the validity of interpretations that is prominent in research across cultures has to do with cultural bias in measurements, leading to lack of equivalence of scores, as described in Chapter 1. In subsequent chapters we mentioned bias effects, such as response styles in personality questionnaires (see the discussion on trait dimensions in Chapter 5) and variations in the conceptualizations of intelligence (Chapter 6). It is important to note that many authors tend to ignore issues of bias and that this can lead to serious errors in the estimation of cross-cultural differences. We discuss this issue later in this chapter.

A second point to note is that many cross-cultural studies further examine a trait or dimension on which some cross-cultural difference has been previously established. Such studies can be said to seek **convergent validity**. In so far as they are subject to the same errors as the original study there can be an accumulation of invalid evidence. The remedy is to search for **discriminant validity**. Campbell and Fiske (1959) proposed to use a "multitrait-multimethod matrix." This is a design matrix including various methods of assessment of the target trait to establish convergent validity and measures of different traits, representing alternative explanations, to establish discriminant validity. Multiple methods are used in this design to rule out that findings reflect irrelevant method variance. Unfortunately, this kind of approach is rarely found in cross-cultural research.

Analyzing internal context

When emphasis is placed on culture as internal context, "meanings" and culture-specific modes of psychological functioning are the primary target of analysis. We will distinguish between two categories of research: qualitative methodology and quantitative methodology.

In Chapter 1 we have seen that much qualitative research tends to be geared to the understanding of phenomena in a single culture. In such research, data collection tends to be driven by events as they take place, and changes in research questions and procedures can occur while data collection is in progress. This makes research much more flexible than is possible with the rigid rules of experimental and instrument-bound approaches. Discourse analysis, unstructured interviews, focus groups and ethnography, relying on participant observation and selected informants, are methods of choice (e.g., Creswell, 2009; Willis, 2007). In previous chapters examples of cultural meanings can be found, for instance, in Chapter 7 (section on emotions and language) where we discuss culture-specific emotions. Other examples include non-western personality concepts (Chapter 5) and ethnographies (see Chapter 10).

When the meaning of behavior, including behavior solicited by psychological instruments, is seen as specific to some cultural context there is limited scope for comparison of data. For some authors this implies that the use in other societies of methods and instruments originating from western settings should be rejected (e.g., Greenfield, 1997; Ratner, 2002).

Before, we introduced validity as a touchstone for scientific enquiry. Although sometimes associated with psychometric methods, validity is an issue with many methods. For example, Jahoda (1990) has given examples showing how ethnographers go through a process of postulating hypotheses on the basis of certain field observations and then testing these by checking whether other observations fit. Although these validation procedures are post hoc, they reflect concern for validity. This is also found in concepts like "transparency" and "credibility"; the researcher has to report how an interpretation was arrived at (Guba and Lincoln, 1994).

Greenfield (1997) has emphasized three forms of validity as particularly relevant with qualitative research. The first is interpretive validity (cf. Maxwell, 1992), which is concerned with communication between researcher and the target group. Interpretive validity implies "(1) understanding the communicational and epistemological presuppositions of our subjects, and (2) making sure that all data collection procedures conform to these presuppositions" (Greenfield, 1997, p. 316). In quantitative psychometric traditions this would be seen as a condition for validity rather than as a form of validity, but that is a detail. The relevance can be illustrated with reference to the notion of *pagtanong-tanong* – the need for interactive communication instead of researcher-led interviewing in the Philippines (Pe-Pua, 2006, mentioned as an example with the interpretive position of indigenous psychology in Chapter 1). The second form is ecological validity, which addresses the question of to what extent the data solicited by a research procedure have relevance outside the research context. A parallel can be drawn between ecological validity and the notion of content validity in quantitative psychometric traditions. Greenfield argues that ecological validity is ensured when studying naturally occurring rather than laboratory behavior. Laboratory settings may indeed be artificial and miss out on relevance, but in our view field study by itself cannot guarantee validity; hence it is not clear how on this basis the validity of the interpretations of data can be substantiated (or falsified). The third form of validity that Greenfield has distinguished is theoretical validity, reflecting concerns of what in quantitative research traditions is called construct validity. In the latter traditions interpretive validity is known as structural equivalence (Van de Vijver and Leung, 1997; see the section on equivalence and bias in Chapter 1). All in all, there are evident commonalities between validity concerns raised by Greenfield and traditional distinctions from psychometrics (Van de Vijver and Poortinga, 2002).

In Chapter 1 (see p. 25) we have acknowledged mixed methods (Bond and Van de Vijver, in press) and consilience (Leung and Van de Vijver, 2008) that combine qualitative and quantitative methods as viable pathways through research processes. The argument that qualitative and quantitative methods are complementary rather than contrasting is increasingly gaining acceptance (Karasz and Singelis, 2009). In the perspective from which this book has been written drawing a sharp contrast is seen as counterproductive (e.g., Berry, 2009; Poortinga, 1997).

The essential question that needs to be asked with each and every study is to which extent the interpretation of the findings is made plausible (valid) and is protected against alternative interpretations. Qualitative studies tend to score high on relevance of the research questions, often dealing with applied issues (e.g., Karasz and Singelis, 2009). At the same time, the analysis of validity tends to be stronger in quantitative research. Experimental designs and standard instruments have been invented to move data beyond the impressions of researchers and to reduce their role in the research process. In qualitative research the role that instruments and procedures have in quantitative research tends to fall to the person of the researcher. Even if sometimes unavoidable, we see this as a weakness, contrary to some qualitative researchers (e.g., Creswell, 2009). Unless a permanent record is kept (e.g., on video), non-standardized methods of data collection cannot be replicated and confronted with alternative interpretations.

Although cultural psychology initially was rooted in qualitative traditions quantitative methods have been used increasingly to examine the extent to which there is culture-specific functioning (Kitayama and Cohen, 2007). A characteristic non-comparative experimental method is the priming of aspects of culture (Oyserman and Lee, 2008). As mentioned in Chapter 4, in priming studies the researcher manipulates the salience of a cultural orientation by presenting stimuli associated with that culture. Priming studies meet a major requirement of a true experiment: the researcher explicitly manipulates treatment conditions by exposing participants to various primes. Moreover, many primes can be administered to participants in a broad range of cultures. Some primes depend on specific prior knowledge (notably cultural icons like national flags), but other primes (like asking participants to think of what they have in common with family and friends or how they are different; Trafimow, Triandis and Goto, 1991) should be cognitively accessible almost independent of school education.

Despite the methodological strong points the use of primes has limitations. First, priming effects do not change the objective reality of cultural context with its social relations, icons and practices (Fischer, in press; Fiske, 2002). This means that there is much in culture that cannot be manipulated. A related issue is whether broad cultural dimensions or syndromes like individualism and collectivism can be validated in this way. Priming can be on variables, though probably not on cultural complexes, as noted by Nisbett (2007). Also, priming does not really address what we noted as a weaker point of research on culture and behavior, namely the large-scale absence of searches for discriminant validity of postulated major cultural dimensions. Since primes are mainly selected on the basis of observed differences in cultural repertoires, priming studies have a low a priori probability of disconfirming such differences. Moreover, if a prime should happen to show unexpected results this is likely to be seen as evidence against the relevance of that prime rather than against the presumed underlying dimension (Medin, Unsworth and Hirschfeld, 2007).

Priming studies can also be conducted with samples from more than one culture to examine the relative effect of various primes across cultures (Oyserman and Lee, 2008). This kind of quantitative and comparative design illustrates how much the earlier gaps in methodology between cultural psychology and culture-comparative research in cross-cultural psychology have been closing. Another experimental, and comparative, method in the cultural psychology tradition is the use of brain imaging techniques, especially fMRI (functional magnetic resonance imaging). Cross-cultural differences have been reported mainly between European Americans and East Asians, so far almost the only groups with which studies have been conducted (Chiao and Ambady, 2007). In one such study Hedden *et al.* (2009) analyzed differences in neural reactions to the length of line segments embedded in a frame – a task on which differences in reaction patterns are found in groups with an interdependent and independent construal of the self when instructions are varied (see Kitayama, Duffy, Kawamura and Larsen, 2003). Differences that emerged from the fMRI records collected by Hedden *et al.* were scattered across various areas of the brain. They were interpreted as showing that the same cognitive processes were invoked by the tasks, but that the magnitude of reactions differed according to cultural preferences in the case of tasks making independent versus dependent task demands. The interpretation of scattered fMRI differences is strongly subject to error (Vul, Harris, Winkielman and Pashler, 2009) and findings should probably be seen as preliminary. Moreover, the precise relationship between oxygen levels in the blood (which are measured in fMRI scans) and brain processes remains somewhat unclear. Nevertheless, we expect that fMRI and similar techniques (PET scans, Evoked Responses in the EEG) will be further refined and become more important in cross-cultural psychology.

Cultural invariance and cultural specificity

This section deals with the second theme outlined in Chapter 1, which was described as a dimension that goes from strong forms of relativism to strong forms of universalism. We postulated a dimension rather than a dichotomy recognizing that various positions can be compatible or even complementary. It has been suggested that the choice for a certain position should depend on the research question that is being addressed in a study (Fontaine, in press). Here we shall further elaborate on this dimension that pertains to a classic discussion in cross-cultural psychology (e.g., Box 1.2 on the emic–etic distinction). Controversies were particularly strong in the 1990s and they appear to have subsided somewhat, but some authors continue to argue for a single position because to them the two perspectives of relativism and universalism represent incompatible worldviews or paradigms. Theories and methods based in one paradigm are generally seen as incompatible or "incommensurable" with those from another paradigm. In this section we take relativism and universalism as worldviews. Although relativism is more associated with qualitative and universalism with quantitative methods, we have kept issues of method as discussed in the previous section, separate from the paradigmatic perspectives that are being addressed in the present section.

Relativism

Perspectives associated with cultural relativism have a long history in psychology. In Germany, often seen as the cradle of modern psychology, methods rooted in phenomenology kept an important place until the 1950s. Behaviorism, first in the USA and later in Europe, was a reaction to these "subjective" approaches.

A more "objective" experimental orientation was sought because researchers questioned the speculative nature of subjective interpretations. The elaborate constructions in psychoanalysis about what happens in the unconscious are a case in point. However, many psychologists also started to feel uneasy with behaviorism in which there was emphasis on stimuli and responses (the so-called S–R paradigm), but in which theoretical concepts referring to processes within the person (the S–O–R paradigm) were considered untestable and outside the reach of scientific analysis. Many of these earlier controversies continue to exist; they are indicated with various pairs of terms, like ideographic versus nomothetic, subjective versus objective, and qualitative versus quantitative. Cross-cultural psychology is particularly sensitive to this debate, since there are research traditions where qualitative approaches, as well as traditions where quantitative methods, prevail.

As noted in Chapter 10 a relativist position on culture was identified in anthropology by Herskovits (1948), who built on earlier ideas advanced by Boas (1911). This general orientation seeks to avoid all traces of ethnocentrism and cultural imposition by trying to understand people "in their own terms," without imposing any value judgments, or a priori judgments of any kind. It thus seeks not just to avoid derogating other peoples (an evaluative act), but it also seeks to avoid describing, categorizing and understanding others from an external cultural point of view (a cognitive act). "In their own terms" thus means both "in their own categories" and "with their own values." There is the working assumption that explanations of psychological variations across the world's peoples are to be sought in terms of sociocultural variation, with little recourse to other factors (e.g., external variables, such as climate or affluence).

One way to outline the scope of the debate is by presenting various paradigms (see Box 12.1). A strong form of relativism has been described by Denzin and Lincoln (2000, 2005b). They are among the authors who reject the principle that psychological and social realities are open to the kind of scientific enquiry advocated by Popper (1959, 1963). For them: "[q]ualitative research is a field of inquiry in its own right" (2005a, p. 2): "Qualitative researchers stress the socially constructed nature of reality, the intimate relationship between the researcher and what is studied, and the situational constraints that shape inquiry. Such researchers emphasize the value-laden nature of inquiry. They seek answers to questions that stress *how* social experience is created and given meaning" (2000, p. 8, italics in the original). Qualitative research in this sense is driven by rhetoric with a political and social agenda (Hammersley, 2008). Denzin and Giardina (2006, p. xvi) call for "a methodology of the heart, a prophetic, feminist post-pragmatism that embraces an ethics of truth grounded in love, care, hope and forgiveness." Gergen and Gergen (2000, p. 1026): argue: "The pursuit of general laws, the capacity of science to produce accurate portrayals of its subject matter, the possibility of

Box 12.1 **Four paradigms**

Lincoln and Guba (2000) have described four paradigms, reflecting philosophical positions that are distinguishable in terms of ontology (the nature of existence), epistemology (the nature of knowing) and methodology. These four paradigms are called positivism, post-positivism, critical theory and constructivism. The constructivist paradigm is relativistic: reality is socially constructed, and results of research are created through hermeneutical and dialectical methods in the process of research. In critical theory reality is seen as historically grown views, but for all practical purposes social structures and psychological traits are "out there"; that is, there is a reality independent of our views. In this family of critical theory emphasis is on the epistemological position that methods and knowledge are subjective and value-bound. The first paradigm – positivism – reflects the belief that reality is out there and that through a process of experimental verification research will lead us to finding out the true state of reality.

The second paradigm, post-positivism, remains the leading paradigm in psychology today. It assumes a reality out there of which knowledge will always be imperfect; but we can differentiate more incorrect views from less incorrect views through systematic enquiry. Such enquiry should be based on the epistemological principle of "refutation" or "falsification," developed by Popper (1959, 1963). In his opinion it is beyond scientific research to establish universally valid empirical truths. The statement that "all ravens are black" cannot be the result of observation, since we can never observe all ravens, including future ones. Therefore, the statement can never be completely verified or validated. However, it can be falsified; the statement is demonstrably wrong the moment we observe a non-black raven. According to Popper scientific research proceeds by a process of progressively ruling out incorrect theories through critical experimentation.

A practical difficulty with Popper's position has been identified by Lakatos (e.g., 1974), who pointed out that debates in science often are on the merits of methods and procedures. For example, Galileo's views were challenged by the Roman Catholic clergy of his time because they refused to accept that his observations could be valid. These were made with a lens, a mere piece of glass, which, it was argued by his opponents, could not possibly yield observations superior to the human eye that was created by God. Similar kinds of arguments have been raised in cross-cultural psychology in respect of the use of western concepts and methods in other cultures.

A more principled critique of Popper came from Kuhn (1962), who gave a historical description of changes in scientific worldviews. He showed that evidence which falsifies hypotheses is often ignored; paradigmatic views and major theories tend to be adapted in order to accommodate new evidence, but scientists tend to resist rejection

Box 12.1 continued

of their theories (beliefs) because of negative results. However, such criticisms do not so much address the epistemological principle of falsifiability as the historical reality of fallible scientists hanging on to their theories. Undoubtedly, subjective preferences affect the selection and interpretation of empirical evidence. The question is whether or not these limitations make it necessary to accept relativistic epistemological positions. The perspective taken in this book is that scientific theories can be demonstrated to be wrong on the basis of empirical evidence, and that good research exposes one's preferred theory to falsification. Criticisms make clear why scientific research is difficult, not that the epistemological principle of falsifiability is incorrect. In short, Kuhn being right does not mean that Popper is wrong.

scientific progression toward objective truth, and the right to claims of scientific expertise are all undermined."

We see extreme relativism of this kind as unproductive in empirical science; it has been qualified as a "flight from science and reason" (Gross, Levitt and Lewis, 1996) and has been shown to be incapable of exposing even hoax arguments (cf. Sokal, 1996a, 1996b). Rather, we endorse a dual stance following in the footsteps of Donald Campbell, who advocated using concepts and methods drawn from both traditions. Overman (1988, pp. xviii–xix; see also Berry, 2009) notes that Campbell sought

to reconcile differences between the quantitative tradition and all it stands for and the qualitative tradition and all it stands for. The dominant characteristic of these essays is Campbell's ability to weave a path, not just between quantitative and qualitative knowing, but also between the goal of objectivity and ontological nihilism, between the empirical-behaviorist expectation and the solipsism of phenomenal absolutism. His success depends on our willingness not to be wedded to choosing between the two sets of beliefs, but being able to recognize and operationalize an intermediate position ... Donald Campbell is most notable over his long career as a social science researcher and theorist for having synthesized and reconciled these opposing perspectives.

Cultural psychology

The relativist rejection of the universalist claim of identical processes ("psychic unity") was prominent in the 1990s. It was at the basis of cultural psychology with Shweder's (1990, 1991) adage that "culture and psyche make each other up," although soon replaced by a less far-reaching conceptualization that postulated different "mentalities" but a common mind (Fiske *et al.*, 1998). In Part I of this book (e.g., Chapters 5 and 6) we have referred to research arguing for differences in psychological functioning, notably between East Asians and European Americans. Cultural psychology mostly has followed a post-positivist paradigm, as described in Box 12.1. The reality of the psychological processes and traits that are examined and the methods with which this is happening are not challenged; rather the focus is on the question of identifying psychological functions and traits and how they differ across cultures. At the same time, even moderate relativists do not show much interest in the existence of similarities across cultures, except to assume a moral egalitarian stance (e.g., "all people are equal"), and to explain cultural differences that are being observed as pointing to different functions and processes. Thus, differences are likely to be interpreted in qualitative terms: for example, it has been argued that in East Asians there is an absence (not just a lower salience) of self-esteem (Heine *et al.*, 1999; see Box 4.3); people differ in their form of intelligence, rather than in levels of intellectual competencies (Nisbett, 2003; see Chapter 6, this volume, p. 147); and emotions are culture-specific social constructions rather than invariant psychological states that are differentially emphasized across cultures (Markus and Kitayama, 1994; see Chapter 7, this volume, p. 164).

Researchers in cultural psychology tend to portray their perspective on behavior-culture relationships as a new branch of science (Markus and Hamedani, 2007; Shweder, 2007). We appreciate that it is a matter of definition whether or not earlier culture-comparative traditions are reckoned to belong to the same field. However, we see it as a misrepresentation of history when other approaches within a relativist tradition that go back further in time are being excluded, or at least ignored. First, there is a history that goes back for centuries. Jahoda (1992; Jahoda and Krewer, 1997) has traced similar ideas in the period of the Enlightenment to those that nowadays go by the name of cultural psychology. Second, there are recent traditions that have similar views on the relationships between behavior and culture as reflected in key publications that marked the onset of cultural psychology (Markus and Kitayama, 1991; Shweder, 1990).

Various recent traditions can be found in indigenous psychology as it has been developed in several non-western countries (see below). An example of more western origin is an approach to culture from the perspective of action theory that has been advocated by Eckensberger (1979, 2002; see also Boesch, 1991, 2002). He sees actions as future-oriented, goal directed activities of a potentially self-reflecting agency. Eckensberger (1979) has given an early and far-ranging evaluation of psychological theorizing in cross-cultural psychology. He distinguished five paradigms, which are hierarchically ordered. Most comprehensive is the paradigm of the reflexive human being. As indicated by the name, the reflection of humans on themselves and on their own actions, goals and intentions is characteristic of theories within this paradigm. There is an explicit recognition that actions are elusive: "The content [of an action] cannot be directly derived from the flow of behavior, because each action can be based on several intentions, and each intention can be realized through several modes of behavior (the action is underdetermined, open to multiple interpretations)" (Eckensberger and Plath, 2002, p. 433).

Another example of an approach with relativist leanings is the sociocultural school that goes back to Vygotsky (1978) and Luria (1971). As we have seen in Chapter 2 Vygotsky argued for the historical and contextual nature of human behavior. He formulated his ideas in the period shortly after the Marxist revolution in Russia, but his work became known in the West only some decades later. Vygotsky saw the development of what he called "higher mental functions" as a historical process at the level of societies. These functions, of which abstract thinking received most attention, appear first on the social level as interpsychological categories shared by members of a society.

As mentioned in Chapters 2 and 6, an important change was made to Vygotsky's conceptualization of behavior–culture relationships by Cole (1992a, 1992b, 1996). Cultural mediation in Cole's view does not take place at the level of broad mental functions that manifest themselves in a wide range of behaviors. The evidence rather points to cultural mediation at the level of fields of activity where specific skills and metacognitions are developed. These are acquired in specific activity settings, like the school environment or the work environment, which form activity systems with rich and multiple kinds of interactions.

Unlike most cross-cultural psychologists Cole explicitly attempts not to treat culture as a given that can serve to explain differences in human behavior, but as a state of affairs that needs to be explained. He is concerned about the origins of culture, postulating different time scales in human development, including phylogenetic development, and cultural historical time, as well as the interactions that can take place between levels that are defined at these different time scales. For example, human activities have consequences for societal changes in historical time (and vice versa), and ultimately also for phylogenetic change. Further recent information on sociocultural psychology can be found in Valsiner and Rosa (2007).

Indigenous psychology

A core argument of authors promoting indigenous approaches is that mainstream (western) psychology has tried to fit other people into western categories that are often presumed to hold in all cultures. The worldview underlying such attempts may be criticized on two points. The first criticism is that this amounts to cultural colonization. There is a top–down, one-way transfer of concepts, ideas and methods from the West to other parts of the world. This corresponds to the "transport and test" (imposed etic) feature of cross-cultural psychology that was mentioned in Box 1.2. The second criticism is that mainstream psychology does not take into account the language and worldviews of local people. This refers to the "exploration of other cultures" (emic) feature.

There is a third criticism, falling somewhat outside the scope of this textbook, namely that "western" psychologists, despite their codes of ethics and expressions of concern about human well-being, often have failed to distance themselves from oppressive ideologies and practices. Thus, black psychologists in South Africa have criticized the white psychologists in that country for not having distanced themselves from the Apartheid regime, especially those who expressed egalitarian viewpoints (Nicholas and Cooper, 2001). Another example is the involvement of psychologists with the concentration camp in Guatanamo Bay, where prisoners of the US army were allegedly subjected to inhumane treatments, if not actual torture. The American Psychological Association (APA, 2008) has taken a stance on this, but only years after evidence emerged. As authors living in western democracies we acknowledge the legitimacy of such criticisms.

We also agree to the other two criticisms. Many cross-cultural studies are not more than the extension of existing empirical research traditions to other countries, with a post hoc interpretation of any differences that may emerge. Such research is hardly "culture-informed" in any sense. In Chapter 18 we will argue that to acquire better balance institutions of psychology as a science, such as researchers, departments of psychology and research laboratories, are needed in the majority world (Adair, 2006; Adair, Coelho and Luna, 2002).

The second criticism addresses theoretical issues central to the present chapter. In indigenous psychology behavior is seen as culture-bound by nature and each cultural population needs to develop its own research and applications. For this reason one often finds the plural "indigenous psychologies" being used (e.g., Allwood and Berry, 2006; Kim and Park, 2000). It is easy to see that such an orientation has a relativist rather than a universalist flavor (Hwang and Yang, 2000).

In line with this, the contrast between the cultural and natural sciences approaches has been emphasized by Kim and Park (2006). They argue that there is a need for a "transactional approach" in psychological research, in which human beings are considered as agents in determining their own actions, and in which the transactions (situated in relationships between individuals) are the important unit of activity to be understood rather than the individual. More generally Kim, Yang and Hwang (2006) seek to blur the lines between the indigenous psychology approach and that of cultural psychology, claiming that these two approaches stand in contrast to cross-cultural psychology, which they consider to be exclusively wedded to the natural sciences approach.

However, more than in the literature on cultural psychology, there has been a debate among theorists of indigenous psychology on how to balance culture-specific and culture-common aspects of psychological functioning (e.g., Enriquez, 1993;

Sinha, 1997; Triandis, 2000b; Yang, 2003). Notably, Sinha maintained very explicitly that the two should be seen as complementary rather than as antagonistic. In a similar vein, a "cross-indigenous" approach has been advocated in which ideas from various regions of the world should cross-fertilize each other.

In recent publications there appears to be a trend to place less emphasis on what separates indigenous psychology from "western" psychology and more on what non-western perspectives can contribute to the science of psychology (e.g., Kashima, 2005). There remains an emphasis on understanding, drawing on phenomenological approaches, local philosophies and religion (Kim, 2001), but Kim *et al.* (2006) are adamant that indigenous psychology is part of a scientific tradition that does not seek to develop multiple psychologies. Instead the focus is on multiple perspectives within psychology using whatever methods are appropriate and help to advance a comprehensive understanding of psychological phenomena. Concepts derived from local philosophies can be at the basis of formal theories, but they need to be empirically tested and validated. According to Boski (2006), with the increasingly multinational character of research in cross-cultural psychology indigenous psychology has the ambition of complementing globalization with localization. Hwang (2005, 2006) acknowledges that epistemology and methodology as historically developed in the "West" should be the basis for cultural analysis. Let it be clear that like in other research traditions there is no homogeneity in views among those who identify themselves as indigenous psychologists. An example of a more critical position is that of Mkhize (2004, discussed in Chapter 5, p. 127).

In summary, although there is a wide range of opinions, there also seems to be a growing tendency to endorse a common enterprise, namely to enrich a global science of psychology with local thinking about behavior and psychological functioning.

Universalism

There are few contemporary cross-cultural psychologists who will insist that there is nothing universal to human behavior and the underlying psychological processes and functions. Beyond this general principle disagreements about the extent of cultural invariance and cultural specificity soon start. In the present subsection we are not only concerned with the theoretical status of explanations of human behavior in terms of invariance or universality but also with how we can examine the notion of universality empirically.

Theoretically a psychological concept, or a relationship between concepts, qualifies as a universal if it can be validly used to describe the behavior of people in any culture. Empirically there is not much of interest in cross-cultural psychology that has been examined in all culturally distinguishable groups. A minimum requirement is that samples from societies displaying strong cultural contrasts have been studied. Usually societies with high and low rates of literacy will have to be included, as well as societies varying on dimensions and categories such as affluence, mode of economic subsistence, and religion. Of all the research streams and projects discussed in Part I only a few can be said to have met this requirement, or to have come reasonably close to doing so. Among the positive exceptions we would count the research by Segall *et al.* (1966) on visual illusions that covered a range of natural environments (see Chapter 8), and by Henrich *et al.* (2004, 2005) that extended ultimatum and dictator games to a range of small-scale societies (see Box 4.2). Most research is dependent on questionnaires which require reading skills of respondents and cannot be administered in illiterate societies. In our opinion this implies limitations on the universality of findings in cross-cultural psychology.

Alternatively, those arguing against universality need to provide evidence that a particular psychological process is present in some cultural groups, while being absent in others. As noted already by Cole *et al* (1971, p. 233), "cultural differences in cognition reside more in the situations to which particular cognitive processes are applied than in the existence of a process in one cultural group and its absence in another." If we extend this view beyond cognition to all areas of psychological functioning, we need to be wary of interpreting differences in performance (or competencies) as evidence of differences in psychological processes.

The main issues with universalism are not about evidence needed for deciding that a psychological process or relationship occurs in all cultures, but about the overall orientation of theorists on how culture relates to behavior. There are extreme positions on the universalist side of the dimension as well as on the relativist side. The metatheoretical position of extreme universalism, previously called absolutism (Berry *et al.*, 2002), is one that shows little concern about ethnocentrism in cross-cultural research, or about seeing people "in their own terms." Rather, psychological phenomena are considered to be basically the same across cultures: "intelligence," "honesty" or "depression" are assumed to be the same everywhere and to become manifest in similar behavior.

Methodologically, comparisons of scores on tests and questionnaires are considered to create no essential problems in extreme forms of universalism; they are carried out easily and frequently, based on the use of the same instruments across cultures. These instruments are employed in a standard fashion; linguistic equivalence may be checked, but this is often the only nod in the direction of recognizing the possible role of inequivalence in concepts or instruments. From more moderate perspectives this approach can be argued to lead to serious misrepresentation and "imposed etics" as outlined in Box 1.2. When differences in score levels occur, these are seen as quantitative differences on underlying constructs. The instruments are assumed to meet conditions of fullscale equivalence;

differences in scores are taken to show that different people are just "less intelligent," "less honest" or "more depressed."

The position of moderate universalism adopts the working assumption that basic psychological processes are likely to be common features of human life everywhere, but that their manifestations are likely to be influenced by culture. That is, variations are due to culture "playing different variations on a common theme"; basic processes are essentially the same, but they are expressed in different ways. Methodologically, comparisons are employed, but cautiously, heeding the needs for safeguards about equivalence; comparisons should neither be entirely avoided nor carried out at whim. Assessment procedures are likely to require modification (see Box 12.2). While the starting point may be some extant theory or instrument, one's approach to its use should be informed by local cultural knowledge.

Theoretically, interpretations of invariance and cultural specificities in moderate universalism are made starting from the belief that basic psychological processes are panhuman, and that cultural context influences their development (direction and extent) and deployment (for what purposes, and how, they are used). Thus the major questions are to what extent and in what ways cultural variables interact with behavior. Quantitative interpretations can be validly made along dimensions that fall within a domain in which the phenomena of interest are similar across the cultures examined in a study. For example, in cultures that share the same conception, and encourage the same expression of depression, differences on a test of depression may be interpreted quantitatively. At the same time, in cultures that differ in conception and expression of depression, it may be impossible to obtain equivalent measurements (see Chapter 17, on depression). Differences that are of a qualitative nature require theoretical analysis to define a common dimension on which they can be captured as quantitative differences, before a comparison can be made.

The acknowledgement of inequivalence of cross-cultural data in moderate universalism should not be taken to imply that universals are illusory. Arguments and findings suggesting universals have been presented in reviews from a comparative anthropological perspective by Munroe and Munroe (1997) and by Brown (1991). In the various chapters of Part I we have mentioned several examples, such as basic emotions in Chapter 7, personality dimensions in Chapter 5 and basic cognitive processing in Chapter 6.

So far we have referred mainly to the ontological side of universals (i.e., do they refer to a reality out there?). There is also an epistemological side (i.e., how can we know?). According to Lonner (1980, in press) the search for patterns and regularities as a basis for comparison appears to be unavoidable. In looking for order, students of culture and behavior, including cultural anthropologists and biologists, tend to think in universalistic terms and to pursue universal dimensions. Lonner has distinguished seven levels of universals, ranging from "simple universals" to

Box 12.2 **Cross-cultural transfer and adaptation of methods**

From a universalist perspective, it is a legitimate question to what extent concepts and theories can be transferred meaningfully from one culture to another. This question can also be asked for psychological tools that are meant to form operationalizations of concepts. We have repeatedly challenged the equivalence of methods and concepts across cultures (e.g., Chapters 1, 5, 6), so it should be clear that in our view such transfer can be highly problematic. However, we do not rule out culture-comparative research, which invariably entails some form of transfer of data collection methods, whether qualitative or quantitative.

Transfer as meant here refers to the use of methods and instruments (including tests, questionnaires and intervention programs) developed for one group (the source culture, or culture of origin) to another group (the target culture). Such transfer can, but need not, imply changes (adaptations) to make methods of administration more suited to the target culture. The alternative to transfer is the development of new tools for each target culture. As a rule tools developed for a group will show a better cultural fit than a transferred tool. Still, there are reasons why transfer should be considered. First, the development and standardization of a test or intervention program is costly and time-consuming. Resources are always limited, but particularly in the majority world. Therefore, it makes sense economically to make use of available methods, provided they are sufficiently suitable. Second, transfer of a method comes with research already conducted previously. If a method after transfer is effective in a target group, it stands to reason that theoretical underpinnings and empirical interrelationships also apply in that group; at least this is a good starting proposition for analysis (Poortinga, 1995). Third, transfer of methods adds to an accumulating body of knowledge more than a string of separate methods that are unrelated to each other. Of course, these points are not an argument against the construction of new local methods, but there should be reasonable expectations that a new method will lead to better results than will an existing one.

Transfer of methods may take various forms. A distinction can be made between adoption, adaptation and assembly (e.g., Van de Vijver and Poortinga, 2005). With "adoption" a program is administered in the target group staying close to the original. Program content and materials are left unchanged, and translation is as precise as possible. "Adaptation" refers to the direct transfer of parts (items, subtests, program elements), while other parts that do not transfer well are changed or replaced. "Assembly" amounts to the new development of major parts of an instrument or program for the target culture. There may be common themes and goals in the original and the new versions of a program, but content and/or methods of implementation will be largely different. Which of these three approaches is followed depends in first instance on the need for changes as perceived by researchers or local stakeholders (target population or their representatives).

"cocktail universals." The former category refers to extremely common phenomena, such as human sexuality, aggression and communication; the latter includes events difficult to capture formally but readily understandable in terms of their meaning.

Another categorization was proposed by Van de Vijver and Poortinga (1982). They gave definitions in terms of invariant properties of scales on which cross-cultural differences are expressed. They distinguished four levels of psychometric accuracy in the universality of concepts, with closer cross-cultural similarity in behavior implied as definitions become more precise:

1. *Conceptual universals* are concepts at a high level of abstraction perhaps without any reference to a measurement scale (e.g., modal personality; see Chapter 10, p. 000).
2. *Weak universals* are concepts for which measurement procedures have been specified and for which validity has been demonstrated in each culture investigated, notably through evidence on structural equivalence (e.g., personality dimensions; see the trait dimensions section in Chapter 5). A claim to universality at this level is held, at least implicitly, by psychologists who use the same methods and instruments across cultures, even if they stay away from comparisons of score levels.
3. *Strong universals* are concepts that can be established with a scale that has the same metric across cultures, but a different origin (i.e., meeting conditions for metric equivalence, see Chapter 1, p. 27). Common patterns of findings provide relevant evidence. The detailed evidence on susceptibility to visual illusions, such as the Müller–Lyer and the horizontal–vertical illusion, reported by Segall, Campbell and Herskovits (1966; see Chapter 9), supports standards for metric equivalence. Needless to add, for many other comparisons of score levels the evidence is less convincing.
4. *Strict universals* show the same distribution of scores in all cultures. For such universals instruments are needed that meet requirements for full score equivalence. Given the pervasive interactions of cultural context and human behavior, it is unlikely that any psychological variable will meet this condition.

An important point in these distinctions is that they do away with a dichotomy between universal and culture-specific phenomena. Van de Vijver and Poortinga (1982, p. 393) argued that it seems meaningful "to consider the degree of invariance of data across cultural groups as a function of the similarity in cultural patterns or background variables between them." From the descriptions of the four levels of universals it should be clear that they correspond to levels of equivalence as described in Chapter 1 (Fontaine, in press; Van de Vijver and Leung, 1997, 2000). Evidence of equivalence across a wide range of cultures forms the empirical basis for postulating universality; the level of equivalence that data meet ultimately determines the level of universality. An overview of possible sources of inequivalence or bias is given on the Internet (Additional Topics, Chapter 12).

www.cambridge.org/berry

In Chapter 1 we have seen that conditions of equivalence can be tested across cultures by examining whether a data set meets statistical conditions that generally are satisfied by equivalent data but not by inequivalent data. Two kinds of analyses are widely used. The first is item bias analysis. There are several statistical methods to assess whether an item in an instrument shows or does not show the item distribution in a society that would be expected given its distribution in another society (e.g., Sireci, in press). The second type of analysis seeks to examine structural equivalence. One condition is that factor loadings of items should be similar across cultures. A statistic called "Tucker's φ" (phi) is widely reported. A value of φ > .90, or sometimes φ > .85, is seen as positive evidence for structural equivalence (Van de Vijver and Leung, 1997). In recent times levels of equivalence tend to be examined with other multivariate analysis techniques, such as Structural Equation Models and Analysis of Covariance Structures. Such models allow the testing of a hierarchically ordered string of conditions that are imposing more and more stringent conditions on the equivalence of data across cultures. For information on how to conduct such analyses we refer to the literature (e.g., Cheung and Rensvold, 2002; Van de Vijver and Leung, 1997; Vandenberg and Lance, 2000).

We have to note a paradox here. Although the equivalence of scales for personality dimensions and intelligence tests has been widely challenged, an equally critical attitude is rarely found in respect of scales assessing aspects of social behavior (Van de Vijver, in press). For example, in the ample literature on individualism and collectivism the possibility is hardly mentioned. In an impressive overview by Oyserman *et al.* (2002) on individualism and collectivism the notions of cultural bias or inequivalence are not even mentioned. The paradox is that many researchers who acknowledge important cross-cultural differences tend to take methods as cross-culturally invariant standards in very much the same way as happens in extreme universalism: that is, without concern about inequivalence.

A lack of equivalence of methods is likely to lead to misrepresentation of cross-cultural differences. Often it is assumed that differences are exaggerated because instruments do not fit local knowledge or ideas (Poortinga, 1989; Van de Vijver and Leung, 1997). Heine, Lehmann, Peng and Greenholtz (2002) have argued that cross-cultural differences in ratings of social psychological variables are likely to be underestimated, because respondents in a cultural group will use what they find in their own context as a referent or standard when answering items. In other words, Chinese will rate themselves in respect to other Chinese, and Canadians in respect to other Canadians. To examine this "reference group effect" Heine *et al.* asked respondents with a bicultural background in Japan and Canada whether items in an individualism and collectivism questionnaire were more characteristic of the one or the other culture. In further studies they obtained ratings asking bicultural respondents to compare themselves with the Japanese and with the Canadians. The differences between such ratings were much higher than found with self-ratings of individualism and collectivism. The point to note is that in these studies Heine *et al.* took evaluations of raters as a standard of comparison. However, such evaluations are open to stereotyping, just like ratings of national character (see Chapter 5). Hence, the confirmatory evidence of such findings for differences in individualism is limited. Heine *et al.* have realized this. At the end of their article they recommend more objective measures as standards of comparison, including actual patterns of behavior and psychophysiological recordings.

Although such techniques will enrich the analysis of the relationships between culture and behavior they are also likely to renew the debate about cultural invariance and cultural specificity. We mentioned in the previous section that authors like Chiao and Ambady (2007) emphasize cross-cultural differences reported in fMRI studies and see these as differences in psychological functioning. A concrete example is the interpretation of the study by Hedden *et al.* (2009) by Ambady and Bharucha (2009). Where we mentioned that the same cognitive processes were invoked by the tasks before reporting on the differences, Ambady and Bharucha emphasized that westerners demonstrated greater activation in brain areas associated with attentional control in one task condition and East Asians in the other task condition. For us the scattered differences allowing no clear linkage between the neurological and the behavioral domain are less important than the overall similarity. For Ambady and Bharucha, as for most cross-cultural psychologists, it is the reverse.

Distinguishing between culture level and individual level

As we mentioned in Chapter 1 cross-cultural psychologists tend to deal with data at both the individual and the cultural level. Some kinds of phenomena are "intrinsic" to the cultural level. Examples include social institutions, such as schools and form of government. Other kinds of phenomena are "intrinsic" to the individual level, such as personal characteristics, including one's standing on a personality trait, and cognitive ability. In cross-cultural research we find aggregation of individual data to obtain culture-level scores; country scores on value dimensions such as individualism or independent construal of the self are examples. In such instances culture-level scores are "derived" from individual-level data. There is disaggregation when individuals in a national sample are assigned the score of their country: that is, the individual data are "derived" from the national level. This happens, for example, when every Spaniard is reckoned to belong to the Roman Catholic religion because Spain is a Catholic country.

Intrinsic use of individual or cultural variables (i.e., at the level at which they are collected) usually does not raise concerns about level. Caution is needed with derived scores, which may be open to multiple interpretations. First, a distinction needs to be made between variables with very limited within-culture variation and variables on which individuals within countries have substantially different scores. If there is no or hardly any within-culture variance culture-level scores and individual scores are exchangeable; for example, by far most Spaniards understand Spanish. When individuals differ a derived score can be problematic; a Chinese individual need not be a collectivist when China is a collectivist society (see Triandis and Suh, 2002).

Second, when moving from one level to the other, there can be a shift in meaning. For example, in reaction time tasks with Arabic letters and simple figurative stimuli Iranian students responded faster to the Arabic letters task and slower to the figurative stimuli than Dutch students (Sonke, Poortinga and De Kuijer, 1999). The authors argued that differences in stimulus familiarity can explain this pattern of score differences. Thus, at sample level the pattern of mean reaction times formed a measure of differential stimulus familiarity, while at the individual level both tasks were measures of speed of processing of visual stimuli. When aggregation of scores (as in the present example) or disaggregation implies a shift in meaning, two levels are considered non-isomorphic.

Errors associated with shifts in meaning as a consequence of non-isomorphism have been described systematically by Van de Vijver, Van Hemert and Poortinga (2008a). One well-known example from the literature is Hofstede's (1980, 2001) warning that the four value dimensions which he had identified (see Chapter 4, the values section) held at the level of countries and not at the level of individuals. To infer individual differences from country differences on these dimensions in his opinion amounts to committing an "ecological fallacy." Following this lead, Schwartz (1992, 1994a, b) conducted (separate) analyses for the individual and the culture level on data collected with the Schwartz Value Scale (SVS). He identified two dimensions at the individual level and three at the country level. A more recent multilevel analysis on SVS data in which the two levels were analyzed simultaneously found a two-factor structure at both levels and high correlations between the levels (Fischer, Vauclair, Fontaine and Schwartz, 2010). This suggests a fair deal of isomorphism between the culture level and the individual level for the value domain.

So far we do not know to what extent such findings will be replicated in other domains, since multilevel analysis is a technique that has been used only sparingly in cross-cultural psychology (Van de Vijver, Van Hemert and Poortinga, 2008b). Since various statistical programs are now available it is to be expected that multilevel analysis will be applied more extensively (Smith, 2004). After all, the relationships between individual behavior and the cultural contexts in which they are nested are central to cross-cultural psychology.

Psychological organization of cross-cultural differences

The third theme that we raised in Chapter 1 is how differences between cultures are interrelated. We mentioned categories of interpretations, ranging from highly inclusive to very limited. In the most inclusive category are interpretations portraying cultures as systems. Other successively less inclusive interpretations refer to broad dimensions like individualism, styles, behavior domains and to specific customs or conventions.

Culture-as-a-system is a notion prominent in cultural relativism. Interrelations may not result in neat regular patterns, but strong coherence is suggested. Geertz (cf. Shweder, 1984) argued that culture is not neatly arranged like a spider's web, but he considered the octopus a suitable metaphor. It should be noted that this may be an oddly shaped organism, but it is an organism nevertheless and as such an entirely coherent entity, in which all parts are fully interconnected. If so, it should be possible to prepare reliable organizational charts or organograms of cultures. Replications of ethnographic analyses of one and the same group have led to notoriously discrepant reports (e.g., Kloos, 1988), indicating that a systems approach is not very helpful in advancing the field.

Of course, human behavior repertoire hangs together, if only because an individual physically is a coherent organism. But this does not necessarily imply that differences between cultural populations in psychological functioning are also organized in a coherent fashion. For example, there are many psychologically meaningful cultural variables related to GNP; as a consequence such variables are all interrelated statistically. Does this mean that underlying psychological processes should be seen as interconnected as well? For many variables this may be difficult to decide. We know that a correlation between two variables should not be taken automatically as implying a causal relationship. As we argued before, cross-cultural studies often rely on correlational analyses (including multivariate analyses) and on quasi-experimental designs in which alternative explanations are difficult to rule out.

Another way of looking at cross-cultural differences emerges if the behavior repertoire in a culture is considered as a large number of cultural practices or conventions. In Chapter 1 the term convention was used to refer to explicitly or implicitly accepted agreements among the members of a group as to what is appropriate in social interactions or in some field of activity, like in art (Van de Koppel and Schoots, 1986). Conventions are not trivial. They can make a certain situation very "strong" (Mischel, 1973) so that (almost) all members of a culture will show the same reaction, while in some other culture another reaction is equally prevalent. But conventions have an aspect of arbitrariness from an outsider's perspective. They are not limited to overt actions, but include ways to handle problems (e.g., building stone houses and not wooden houses), and explanations of rules (looking at someone while talking shows honesty and openness, versus not looking someone in the eye is a matter of respect; Girndt and Poortinga, 1997). Conventions can be equated with the words in a dictionary, because of their large numbers. This analogy is relevant in another way: when translating terms on the basis of a dictionary one is likely to go wrong on shades of meaning, and it can be said that in a similar fashion mismatches occur from one cultural repertoire to another, for example in intercultural communication or in the translation of questionnaire items. Even if we basically know certain rules of a society we are likely to err in their proper application. Just as we feel most confident with our mother tongue, we are most at ease with our own cultural repertoire and least likely to commit errors, which amount to transgressions of norms or make our behavior look funny.

As described here conventions exercise a strong effect on the total behavior repertoire, because they occur in large numbers. Some conventions also imply consistent and large cross-cultural differences. A society needs conventions about how to behave in certain situations, and about what is proper; social interactions would become complete chaos without rules. At the same time, there is often no psychological reason why there happens to be a certain convention in a society and not another convention. In so far as conventions have an aspect of arbitrariness this limits the interpretation of cross-cultural differences either in terms of psychologically meaningful variables, or in terms of cultural system properties. The impression we gain when traveling to a faraway country that people there "are" different from us is based on the things we see them "do" differently. From research on the laws of association we know that we easily infer causal relations between events which coincide in space and/or time and that such perceptions of causality can be virtually inescapable even if we cognitively know they are incorrect (Michotte, 1954).

Obviously, conventions do not rule out the possibility that more inclusive psychological clusterings of cross-cultural differences have validity. Explanations at a higher level of generality have a broader reach and are more parsimonious. The principle of parsimony in science entails that more inclusive explanations are to be preferred over less inclusive explanations. There tends to be a trade-off between scope and accuracy and the latter aspect cannot be ignored. Limited generalizability of cross-cultural differences has been acknowledged by several researchers. Hong *et al.* (2000) have recognized that switches between cultural repertoires occur at the level of situations. Bruner (1990) has argued for cultural knowledge as consisting of specific constructs. Cole (1996) sees cultural differences as organized at the level of fields of activity.

We have limited this presentation to the most inclusive **levels of inference** of cross-cultural differences in terms of cultures-as-systems and the least inclusive in terms of conventions. Other, more intermediate generalizations are discussed in an Internet section (Additional Topics, Chapter 12).

Prospects

In this section we raise the question of what cross-cultural psychology may look like in the future, and try to move beyond current thinking and findings, but at the same time giving credit to major traditions and distinctions from within our own field as well as from neighboring disciplines. When we published the second edition of this textbook (Berry *et al.*, 2002) less than ten years ago, the corresponding section was entitled "Beyond current controversies?" It was concerned mainly with ways in which cultural and culture-comparative approaches could coexist. The gaps between culture as internal context and as external context, and between relativism and universalism that we have described as main themes of the field seem to be narrowing. Many researchers have not really given up their positions, but there appears to be a trend away from debates on paradigmatic issues and toward an empirical pragmatism. The largest shift has been that cultural psychologists have moved from a fairly strict relativism (e.g., Shweder, 1990) to also accept culture-comparative research (Kitayama and Cohen, 2007), which presumes common (universal) features of human behavior and some form of equivalence of data. We have noted a corresponding change in indigenous psychology, where contributions to a common psychology have become more and the construction of local psychologies has become less prominent. A broader acceptance of mixed methods, including both quantitative and qualitative research strategies and data, fits this "consilience" (Van de Vijver and Leung, in press).

This is not meant to suggest that the gaps mentioned are closer to a principled solution than they were a decade ago. There remain numerous researchers who continue to argue for a relativist approach (e.g., Eckensberger, 2002; Levinson, 2003; Ratner, 2002) including indigenous psychologists who distance themselves from western research because the culture-specific phenomena and themes that they are identifying with hardly resonate in the dominant western research community. It also does not follow that the field of cross-cultural psychology is without major problems. In a critical review of the achievements Jahoda (in press), one of the forefathers of modern cross-cultural psychology (CCP), argued: "The vagueness of its aims has made it possible for CCP [cross-cultural psychology] to drift over a generation from ambitious (possibly too ambitious) aspirations and practices to severely limited ones. This happened during a period when exciting new fields have emerged which, if embraced by CCP, could greatly enhance its range and scientific status." Jahoda proceeds to outline a more promising future for a cross-cultural psychology with theory-driven experimental research, also including samples from non-literate societies, and applying methods that require more direct contacts with participants than the widely used questionnaire.

Here we outline a future perspective for cross-cultural psychology that emphasizes three points. The first is the need to incorporate biological thinking, which emphasizes culture as a shared human characteristic and not mainly as a source of differences between groups. Historically the field can be defined as the marriage of concepts about culture from cultural anthropology with methods and issues from psychology. Only recently has there been a tendency to recognize biology as an equally valuable parent discipline (see Chapter 11). The second point is the need to distinguish between a cultural context as a set of constraints, and as offering to its members a set of opportunities or affordances that enable or facilitate certain patterns of behavior (see below). The third point is an explicit recognition of both relativist and universalist perspectives and the associated modes of qualitative and quantitative research. It may be noted that these emphases are compatible with the general perspective followed in this textbook, exemplified, for example, in the inclusion of both biological and cultural features in the ecocultural framework (Box 1.1) and a broad definition of the field of cross-cultural psychology.

One possible way to account for the three points mentioned is contained in the following (see Poortinga, 1997; Poortinga and Soudijn, 2002). The starting point is the observation that the range of imaginable actions of a person in a given situation usually is much larger than the observed range. One way to look at this is from a conception of "constraints" that apparently limit the range of alternative actions actually available. On the other hand, in most situations there remain various alternative courses of action open to the person. These can be seen as "affordances" or opportunities. Constraints can be defined at various levels from distal to proximal, and they can be internal within the person as well as external (imposed by the environment). Affordances can be defined as the space of alternatives left by constraints; thus affordances are complementary to constraints. Similar distinctions can be made at several levels; in Table 12.1 they are arranged from distal (far away from the behaving person) to proximal (close to the behaving person).

At the most general level, represented by the top row in Table 12.1, the scope of human behavior is constrained by the phylogenetic history of our species. The environment, or ecological niche, in which humans as a species function imposes constraints on adaptation outcomes. However, when discussing adaptation in Chapter 11 we have seen that, according to some biologists like Gould (1991), current features may not always be the direct outcome of selection-driven genetic transmission processes; they can also result from exaptations and spandrels. Gould portrays the complex brain as a feature of the human organism that has opened up many affordances, like the emergence of different religions, and cultural traditions in art and technology, for which it hardly can have been developed originally. As noted in Chapter 11, these views are contested (e.g., Buss, Haselton, Shackelford, Bleske and Wakefield, 1998), but there is a continuing debate, also among biologists, arguing that the importance of culture in shaping the human mind may have

Table 12.1	Levels of constraints and affordances varying from distal to proximal		
	Constraints		Affordances
	Internal	External	
Distal	*Genetic transmission (species)* adaptations	ecological niche ecological context	pleiotropies and "spandrels"
	Cultural transmission (group) epigenetic rules	sociopolitical context	technology enabling conditions (conventions)
	Genetic transmission (individual) aptitudes	poor fit in cultural niche	capacities
	Cultural transmission (individual) enculturation (skills, beliefs, etc.)	socialization to prevailing conditions	enabling conventions (skills, beliefs, etc.)
Proximal	situation "meaning"	actual situation	perceived choices

Adapted from Poortinga and Soudijn (2002).

been overlooked (Bolhuis and Wynne, 2009; Penn, Holyak and Povinelli, 2008; see also De Waal, 2009). The point to consider is that there may be variation across cultures not only as a consequence of interactions between genes and environment, but also because effects of genes are to some extent non-deterministic, resulting in a range of open choice.

Cultural transmission at the group level (the second row in Table 12.1) can be distinguished from genetic transmission with the help of a notion like epigenetic rules (Lumsden and Wilson, 1981; see the section on models of cultural transmission in Chapter 11) referring to processes of interaction between genes and environment. It is recognized increasingly that the expression of many genes is under the influence of environmental factors (Gottlieb, 1998; Oyama, 2000a, b). Which cultural patterns will develop depends to a large extent on the resources that are available in a given natural environment. There are also patterns that are unlikely to develop, given adverse ecocultural or sociopolitical conditions. In this sense the environment acts as a set of constraints. At the same time, the natural environment provides affordances that have been developed in different ways by various cultural populations, and thus have resulted in different technologies and customs to deal with the environment, including the social environment.

The next row in Table 12.1 addresses transmission as an individual-level phenomenon. One's genetic make-up imposes restrictions on what can be achieved, in terms of physical as well as mental dimensions. One's environment equally does not provide optimum opportunities for development (e.g., less than optimal nutrition), thus providing external constraints. On the other hand, individual capacities need not be seen only in terms of their limiting effects. One's capabilities also form the basis for the development of competencies or skills which can be employed to realize desired achievements; in this sense capabilities can also be viewed as affordances.

The final form of transmission distinguished in the table is cultural transmission at the individual level in the form of enculturation and socialization to prevailing economic conditions and sociocultural context. Enculturation usually refers to all forms of cultural learning, including imitation (see Segall et al., 1999). It is a limiting condition in so far as the individual manages only incompletely to learn from experience. External constraints are added by the limited range of experiences available in a given context, as well as by prevalent socialization practices. The idea of socialization as a constraining process was proposed by Child (1954), who argued that individuals are led to develop a much narrower range of behavior than the potentialities with which they are born.

The last row of the table refers to concrete situations or stimuli which a person is actually facing. In so far as a situation demands certain actions and makes other actions inappropriate (e.g., evasive action in the case of physical danger) there are external constraints. Internal constraints are present in as much as a person attributes certain meanings to a situation. At the same time, in most situations the actor can perceive alternative courses of action that can be conceptualized as affordances.

In psychology, the emphasis is on individual-level explanation. In cross-cultural psychology the focus is on the interaction of individual and cultural context. Constraints can be seen as the defining characteristic of a culture, that is, "[c]ulture becomes manifest in shared constraints that limit the behavior repertoire available to members of a certain group in a way different from individuals belonging to some other group" (Poortinga, 1992, p. 10).

Of course, the table is only schematic; it is a framework and not a theory from which testable hypotheses can be derived directly. Constraints and affordances are often two sides of the same coin and to some extent a matter of perspective. Also there are interactions between the various levels in the table and within rows between constraints and affordances; Super and Harkness's (1997) idea of a multilayered developmental niche (see Chapter 2, p. 40) provides an illustration. What matters here are the implications for the topic of discussion in this chapter. In as much as shared constraints limit the range of behavior alternatives this should lead to interindividual regularities that are open to analysis by observational, experimental and psychometric methods (i.e., quantitative research). To the extent that constraints are known one should be able to predict behavior. For example, ecological constraints can make the development of certain technologies highly unlikely: for example, it is difficult to imagine that any kind of agriculture could have developed in the Arctic area.

In so far as there is freedom from constraints, future events are beyond the reach of prediction; only in retrospect can we try to make sense of the choice that has actually been made in a certain instance. One can either declare unpredictable events out of bounds for scientific analysis, or extend the range of methods to include qualitative modes of analysis, such as description and hermeneutics. Thus, the distinction between constraints and affordances implies complementarity between the two perspectives of universalism and relativism. Culture defined as a set of antecedent conditions is most appropriately analyzed by (quasi-)experimental methods. To the extent that there are no constraining conditions, the rules and conventions that have emerged in a certain group lend themselves to description and interpretive analysis, but escape "lawful" explanation.

A more open attitude toward a biological orientation on culture and cross-cultural differences as argued here does not mean that cross-cultural psychology should turn to the analysis of relationships between genes or genetic expression and behavior. Despite great advances made in genetics and proteomics, the methods of these fields will not be available for the study of complex human behavior in the foreseeable future (if ever), leaving an important niche of much needed expertise for cross-cultural researchers.

Conclusions

As we have seen in previous chapters, there is no common approach in cross-cultural psychology; however, there is a common sphere of interest, namely the relationships between culture and human behavior. In this chapter we have reviewed major perspectives on behavior–culture relationships as they have been formulated in cross-cultural psychology since it became a recognizable subdiscipline in the mid-twentieth century. Major issues of debate can be traced far back in history, as demonstrated by Jahoda (1990) and Jahoda and Krewer (1997).

The first three sections elaborated on the three themes that we introduced in Chapter 1. We discussed views on culture as external versus internal context, on relativism versus universalism and on levels of generalization. In each of these sections we have reflected on issues of theory as well as method. We have presented various viewpoints, but imposed some limits on what makes viable cross-cultural research. We have argued against forms of relativism that see the pursuit of objective knowledge in psychology as a misguided effort. We have also argued against forms of universalism in which it is not explicit that research in cross-cultural psychology has to be culture-informed. Throughout the three sections we have tried to indicate how theoretical and methodological issues are interrelated.

In the final section we have suggested possible ways in which cross-cultural psychology can be reoriented in order to acknowledge more explicitly that culture is (also) a biological feature of human existence and that not only cultural variation but also the extent to which there is cultural invariance forms an important aspect of cross-cultural psychology. We have suggested some ways in which moderate forms of universalism and relativism can be seen as complementary.

KEY TERMS

convergent validity • discriminant validity • levels of inference (or generalization) • mixed methods • paradigm • transfer (of tests) • universality • validity

FURTHER READING

Berry, J. W., Poortinga, Y. H., Pandey, J., Dasen, P. R., Saraswathi, T. S., Segall, M. H., Kağitçibaşi, C. (eds.) (1997). *Handbook of cross-cultural psychology* (2nd edn., Vols. I–III). Boston: Allyn & Bacon.

This three-volume handbook gives a wide-ranging overview of the state of the art in cross-cultural psychology in the 1990s. The full text is freely available on the Internet (see Further reading, Chapter 1).

Cole, M. (1996). *Cultural psychology: A once and future discipline.* Cambridge, Mass.: Belknap.

A book-length discussion of cultural psychology, especially Cole's own sociocultural tradition.

Kitayama, S., and Cohen, D. (eds.) (2007). *Handbook of cultural psychology.* New York: Guildford Press.

We mentioned this text already in Further reading, Chapter 1, as a source for research in the tradition of cultural psychology.

Shadish, W. R., Cook, T. D., and Campbell, D. T. (2002). *Experimental and quasi-experimental designs for generalized causal inference.* Boston: Houghton Mifflin.

This is not a cross-cultural text, but recommended reading for anyone seeking an understanding of the pitfalls in psychological research.

Van de Vijver, F. J. R., and Leung, K. (1997). *Methods and data analysis for cross-cultural research.* Newbury Park, Calif.: Sage.

This book gives a fairly complete account of the essentials of methodology and analysis in culture-comparative research.

Part III | Applying research findings across cultures

A longstanding and fundamental interest of cross-cultural psychology has been the application of the findings of the field to the improvement of both the life circumstances and the quality of life of people everywhere. While the chapters in Part III introduce several new topics of human behavior, they also build upon and apply the findings that were outlined in the first two parts of the book. In a world of increasing interconnections among cultural populations, the three related phenomena of acculturation, intercultural relations and intercultural communication have become substantial parts of the field. The application of research from these domains aims to improve the personal and collective outcomes of such global contact, and to avoid the conflicts that can so often result. Psychology has long been a contributor to the two basic institutions of work and health within cultures. The cross-cultural contribution has been to establish both cultural variations and some basic commonalities that allow international organizations to better understand and serve people in their areas of activity. In a final chapter, we examine ways to promote psychology as a culturally appropriate discipline, where all concepts, methods, findings and applications take the various cultural contexts and meanings into account. Our goal is to encourage psychology to draw upon all the materials that are now available from cross-cultural psychology (and that are sampled in this book), and to promote their inclusion in the scientific and professional training of psychologists and in the daily work that they carry out.

13 | Acculturation

CONTENTS

In the ecocultural framework (Figure 1.1), two major sources of influence on the development and display of behavior were postulated: ecological and sociopolitical. The latter involves contact with other cultures and sets in motion the process of **acculturation**. This chapter examines some core aspects of this process and some of its outcomes.

Related to acculturation psychology is a field that has come to be known as intercultural psychology. These two branches of psychology are sometimes examined together because they both involve intercultural contact. However, they are clearly distinguishable: in acculturation, the focus is on how individuals change in order to live side by side with persons of different cultural backgrounds; and in intercultural work the focus is on how the two parties relate to each other. We are devoting separate chapters to these issues. In Chapter 14, intercultural relations are examined, and a further chapter (Chapter 15) is devoted to an important aspect of both acculturation and intercultural psychologies: intercultural communication.

In this chapter, we will first discuss the concept of acculturation and the different kinds of people undergoing acculturation. We also present a framework for understanding and studying acculturation. This will be followed by the main theoretical perspectives that have been used to study acculturation, as well as the processes, dimensions and outcomes of acculturation. Before concluding the chapter, we will briefly look at some methodological issues in acculturation research.

Definitions and framework

The most widely used definition of acculturation is:

those phenomena which result when groups of individuals having different cultures come into continuous first-hand contact, with subsequent changes in the original culture patterns of either or both groups ... under this definition acculturation is to be distinguished from cultural change, of which it is but one aspect, and assimilation, which is at times a phase of acculturation. (Redfield, Linton and Herskovits, 1936, pp. 149–152)

Although the above definition identifies assimilation to be a phase of acculturation, the two terms are sometimes used synonymously. Indeed, in the US-American sociological literature, acculturation is regarded as a phase of assimilation (see Gordon, 1964). In recent years, following increased global migration, there has also been a proliferation of new terms such as biculturalism, multiculturalism, integration and globalization, and these terms have either been used as alternative concepts or interchangeably with acculturation. While no attempt is made here to clarify the distinctions between all of these terms (see Sam and Berry, 2006, for discussion), we want to emphasize that of the two most widely used terms within this area – assimilation and acculturation – we prefer the term acculturation.

One reason for preferring the term acculturation over assimilation is that it acknowledges the reciprocity of the influence cultural groups have on each other during the contact. A second reason is that acculturation entails a variety of processes and outcomes: groups and individuals within groups adopt different ways to deal with the acculturation experience, and these different ways may result in different outcomes. Because situational factors can alter the experience and course of acculturation, people also have different outcomes in response to their changing experiences. A third reason for our preference for the term acculturation is that, unlike assimilation, acculturation views change as bi-directional and bi-dimensional. The perspective endorsed by assimilation theorists assumes that individuals lose their original culture and identity as they acquire new ones that are similar to the second culture. The assumption is that the more individuals acquire of the new culture, the less they retain of the original culture (LaFromboise, Coleman and Gerton, 1993). A further assumption is that the two cultures in contact are mutually exclusive and that it is psychologically problematic to maintain both cultures (Johnston, 1976; Sung, 1985).

The bi-directional and bi-dimensional perspective proposes that: people do not necessarily move only in the direction of acquiring the dominant culture; and that it is possible for people to independently identify with, or acquire, the new culture without necessarily losing their original culture (Berry, 1980). Change can take place along two independent dimensions, one dimension being the maintenance or loss of original culture and the other being participation in, or adoption of, aspects of the new culture. It is therefore possible for an individual to have more or less of the two cultures in question. The final outcome is one of relative degree of involvement in the two (or more) cultures in contact. This issue is further discussed under cognitive perspectives and under dimensions of acculturation below.

Whereas acculturation as a concept was originally proposed by anthropologists as a group-level phenomenon (Linton, 1949; Redfield *et al.*, 1936), early discussions around the concept also recognized it as an individual-level phenomenon (see Devereux and Loeb, 1943; Thurnwald, 1932). Psychology's strong interest in the individual has contributed toward the formal use of the term **psychological acculturation** (coined by Graves, 1967) and to making the distinction between individual-level changes arising from acculturation and those taking place at the group level. Since our working position is that individual human behavior interacts with the ecological and cultural contexts within which it occurs, there is a need to keep the group and individual levels distinct. This distinction is essential because the kinds of changes that take place at the two levels (i.e., individual and group) are often different (Berry, 1990). Not every group or individual enters into or participates in the group, or changes in the same way as other members of their group during their acculturation. Vast individual differences in psychological acculturation exist, even among individuals who have the same cultural origin and who live in the same acculturative arena (Nauck, 2008).

Acculturating groups

While every person living in a culturally plural society (which is fast becoming the norm in the world) can be said to be undergoing some form of acculturation, research has focussed on some specific groups of people deemed to be undergoing major acculturation, including refugees, asylum-seekers, sojourners, immigrants, expatriates, as well as indigenous peoples and ethnocultural groups. These groups differ in the reasons (both historical and contemporary) for them living together in their plural society. The first reason is voluntariness: groups may find themselves together either because they have sought out such an arrangement voluntarily or alternatively because it has been forced upon them. Second is migration: some groups have remained on home ground, while others have settled far from their ancestral territory (sedentary vs. migrant). And third is permanence: some people are settled into a plural society permanently, while others are only temporary sojourners.

While these three distinctions have provided acculturation researchers with six different kinds of groups to study, the distinctions themselves are not as clearly defined in contemporary societies as they were some decades ago. For instance, some sojourners (e.g., international students) may change their temporary status to one of permanent immigrant status. However, for the purposes of discussion, we will maintain the distinction. Research accruing from the different groups is enormous, and no attempt will be made here to review it all. For a discussion on these groups see Sam and Berry (2006). First, there are indigenous peoples, who have "always been there" in the sense that their roots go way back. The basic characteristic of groups such as Basque and Breton in Europe, and Inuit and Sami in the Arctic, is that they are largely involuntary and sedentary. For discussion on acculturation of indigenous peoples see Kvernmo (2006).

Other peoples who have a long history in a society are the descendants of earlier waves of immigrants who have settled into recognizable groups, often with a sense of their own cultural heritage (common language, identity, etc.); these are termed ethnocultural groups. These ethnic groups can be found the world over, for example in French- and Spanish-origin communities in the new world, in the groups descended from indentured workers (such as Chinese and Indian communities in the Caribbean), from those who were enslaved (such as African Americans), and in Dutch and British groups in Southern Africa, Australia and New Zealand.

In contrast to these two sedentary acculturating groups, there are others who have developed in other places and been socialized into other cultures, who migrate to take up residence (either permanently or temporarily) in another society. Among these groups are immigrants (see Van Oudenhoven, 2006) who usually move in order to achieve a better life elsewhere. For most, the "pull factors" (those that attract them to a new society) are stronger than the "push factors" (those that pressure them to leave). Hence, immigrants are generally thought of as "voluntary" members of plural societies. While immigrants are relatively permanent participants in their new society, the group known as sojourners are there temporarily, for a set purpose (e.g., as international students, diplomats, business executives, aid workers or guest workers). In their case, the process of becoming involved in the plural society is complicated by their knowledge that they will eventually leave, and either return home or be posted to yet another country. Thus, there may be a hesitation to become fully involved, to establishing close relationships, or to beginning to identify with the new society. Despite their uncertain position, in some societies sojourners constitute a substantial element in the resident population (e.g., the Gulf States, Germany and Belgium) and may hold either substantial power, or be relatively powerless. See Bochner (2006) for discussion of the acculturation of sojourners.

Among involuntary migrants, refugees and asylum-seekers (now often called collectively "forced migrants"; Ager, 1999) face the greatest hurdles: they frequently do not want to leave their homelands, and if they do, it is not always possible for them to be granted the right to stay and settle into the new society. People who arrive at the border of a country that has signed the "Geneva Convention on Refugees" have the right to be admitted and given sanctuary (as "asylum-seeker") until his or her claim is adjudicated. If granted permanent admission as refugee, much of the uncertainty that surrounded their life during their flight is reduced. However, most of them live with the knowledge that "push factors" (rather than "pull factors") led them to flee their homeland and settle in their new society; and, of course, most have experienced traumatic events, and most have lost their material possessions. Allen, Vaage and Hauff (2006) have provided a review of refugees and asylum-seekers in societies of settlement, and Donà and Ackermann (2006) of the same groups living in camps.

There are two important reasons why these six kinds of groups (i.e., indigenous peoples, ethnocultural groups, immigrants, sojourners, refugees and asylum-seekers) were introduced according to three factors (voluntary–involuntary, sedentary–migrant and permanent–temporary), rather than simply listed. First, as groups, they carry differential size, power, rights and resources; these factors have an important bearing on how they will engage (as groups or as individuals) in the acculturation process. A second reason is that the attitudes, motives, values and abilities (all psychological characteristics of individuals in these groups) are also highly variable. These factors also impact on how their acculturation and intercultural relations are likely to take place, and how well they adapt. Readers interested in the literature on ethnic minorities may notice that we have refrained from the use of the term, and this is deliberate. The reason is ethnic minorities are not minorities in terms of culture: they have cultures, which are often active and vibrant, like all other cultural groups, and they should not be demeaned by being given a minority status simply because they are small (numerically) and sometimes less powerful.

Quite often so-called ethnic minority groups are either immigrants, refugees or an indigenous group, and we prefer to refer to them by this other status.

To demonstrate that the different acculturating groups and individuals may have different acculturation experiences, Berry, Kim, Minde and Mok (1987) measured stress levels among immigrants, refugees, asylum-seekers, indigenous people and ethnic groups in Canada. The sample consisted of over 1,000 individuals. The study found significant differences in stress levels among the groups (measured with a scale adapted from the Cornell Medical Index by Cawte, 1972, reflecting anxiety and psychosomatic symptoms). These differences in stress level could be related to the voluntary–involuntary, migrant–sedentary and temporary–permanent status of the acculturating group.

Acculturation framework

A framework that outlines and links cultural and psychological acculturation, and identifies the two (or more) groups in contact is presented in Figure 13.1. This framework serves as a map of those phenomena which need to be conceptualized and measured during acculturation research (Berry, 2003). At the cultural level (on the left) we need to understand key features of the two original cultural groups (A and B) prior to their major contact, the nature of their contact relationships, and the resulting cultural changes in both groups that emerge to form ethnocultural groups during the process of acculturation. This requires extensive ethnographic, community-level work; the changes can be minor or substantial, and range from being easily accomplished through to being a source of major cultural disruption.

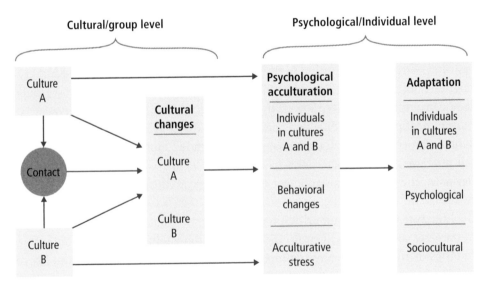

Figure 13.1 A framework for conceptualizing and studying acculturation.

At the individual level (on the right) we need to consider the psychological changes that individuals in all groups undergo, and their eventual **adaptation** to their new situations. This requires sampling and studying individuals who are variably involved in the process of acculturation. These changes can be a set of rather easily accomplished behavioral changes (e.g., in ways of speaking, dressing, eating, and in one's **cultural identity**), or they can be more problematic, producing acculturative "stress" (e.g., uncertainty, anxiety, depression, even psychopathology; Al-Issa and Tousignant, 1997). Adaptation can be primarily internal or psychological (e.g., sense of well-being, of self-esteem) or sociocultural, linking the individual to others in the new society (e.g., competence in the activities of daily intercultural living; Searle and Ward, 1990). General overviews of this process and these specific features can be found in the literature (e.g., Berry, 2006a, 2007; Sam and Berry, 2010; Ward, 2001).

In essence, a key task of acculturation research is to understand the links between the cultural and psychological sets of information, as well as relationships within these sets. Our position is that if cultural and psychological concepts are not distinguished and assessed independently, it is very difficult to obtain a clear picture of the processes and outcomes of the acculturation process.

In principle each culture could influence the other equally, but in practice one tends to dominate the other, leading to a distinction between dominant and non-dominant groups. For a complete picture, mutual influence should be studied; however, for most of this chapter we will focus on the culture receiving the greater influence (i.e., the non-dominant). This is not to say that changes in the dominant culture are uninteresting or unimportant. As we shall see below (and in the section on key concepts in Chapter 14) acculturation often brings about population expansion and greater cultural diversity in societies, attitudinal reaction (prejudice and discrimination) and policy development (for example, in the area of multiculturalism).

The core feature of the acculturation process is that cultural groups become transformed in some ways so that cultural features are not identical to those in the original group at the time of first contact; and frequently, over time, new ethnocultural groups emerge. A parallel phenomenon is that individuals in these groups undergo psychological changes (as a result of influences from both their own changing group and from the dominant group), and with continuing contact further psychological changes may take place. These changes are highly variable, and depend on many circumstances (e.g., discrimination) as well as characteristics of the dominant and non-dominant groups. For both groups, it is important to know the purpose, length and permanence of contact, and the policies being pursued.

Acculturative changes at the group level include political, economic, demographic and cultural changes that can vary from relatively little to substantial alterations in the way of life of both groups. While these population-level changes set the stage for individual change, we have noted previously that there are very likely to be individual differences in the psychological characteristics which a person brings to the acculturation process, and not every person will necessarily participate to the same extent in the process. Taken together, this means that we need to shift our focus away from general characterizations of acculturation phenomena to a concern for variation among individuals in the groups undergoing acculturation.

Theoretical models and perspectives

The definition put forward by Redfield and colleagues (1936) identified acculturation as encompassing all forms of changes; Berry (1980) noted that these group-level changes could be biological, physical, economic and social. With reference to psychological acculturation, which is the main focus of this chapter, Ward (2001; Ward, Bochner and Furnham, 2001) has identified three main areas of individual change during acculturation, and referred to these as the "ABCs of Acculturation." These refer respectively to Affective, Behavioral and Cognitive aspects of acculturation. The ABCs are in turn respectively linked to different theoretical perspectives used in the field: a stress and coping theoretical framework; a culture learning approach and social identification orientation to acculturation. In recent years, concerns have been raised about the limited attention given to (ontogenetic) development in acculturation theories (Sam, 2006a). Except for the recent work by Motti-Stefanidi, Berry, Chryssocoou, Sam and Phinney (in press), many of these concerns have not resulted in a clear theoretical perspective. We will nevertheless present some of the issues pertaining to developmental aspects of acculturation as a separate theoretical position. In addition, this subsection will briefly look at personality and individual factors involved in acculturation, even though they also do not constitute a clear theoretical perspective.

Affective perspectives

The work of Berry on acculturative stress highlights the affective perspective (reviewed by Berry, 2006a). This perspective emphasizes the emotional aspects of acculturation and focusses on such issues as psychological well-being and life satisfaction. This approach corresponds to the acculturative stress component of Figure 13.1. The working hypothesis is that acculturation can be likened to a set of major life events that pose challenges for the individual. These life events may qualify as stressors, and provoke stress reactions in an individual, particularly if the appropriate coping strategies, and social supports are lacking. Drawing upon Lazarus and Folkman's stress model (1984), Berry (2006a; Berry et al., 1987) proposed the acculturative stress model. The core idea is that when serious challenges are experienced during acculturation, and these are appraised to be problematic because one is not able to deal with them easily by simply adjusting to them by changing one's behaviour (see next section), then acculturative stress results. In essence, acculturative stress is a stress reaction in response to life events that are rooted in the experience of acculturation. In line with Lazarus and Folkman's stress model, not all acculturation changes result in acculturative stress because there are a number of moderating and mediating factors (both before and during the acculturation) such as personal characteristics including age and gender, personal resources (such as education) and social support that may influence the perception and interpretation of the acculturation experience. (For a detailed discussion of this see Berry, 1997, 2006a.)

Behavioral perspectives

Stemming from social psychology, and with major influence from Argyle's (1969) work on social skills and interpersonal behavior, the working hypothesis of the cultural learning approach is that during cultural transitions, people may lack the necessary skills needed to engage the new culture (reviewed by Masgoret and Ward, 2006). This may result in difficulties managing the everyday social encounters. To overcome these difficulties, individuals are expected to learn or acquire the culture-specific behavioral skills (such as the language) that are necessary to negotiate this new cultural milieu (Bochner, 1972). Specifically, the cultural learning approach entails gaining an understanding in intercultural communication styles, including verbal and non-verbal components, as well as rules, conventions and norms, and their influences on intercultural effectiveness. This approach corresponds to the "behavioral changes" component of Figure 13.1. In an effort to predict sociocultural adaptation, the cultural learning approach has evolved in two directions: enquiry into sociopsychological aspects of intercultural encounter with a focus on communication styles and communication competence (see Gallois, Franklyn-Stokes, Giles and Coupland, 1988); and an enquiry into cultural differences in communication styles, norms and values (see Searle and Ward, 1990; Ward and Kennedy, 1999). Masgoret and Ward (2006) point out that second-language proficiency and communication competence are the core of all cultural learning approaches, and ultimately of sociocultural adaptation. Language skills are relevant both for the performance of daily tasks in the new cultural society and in establishing interpersonal relationships in the society. Cultural learning approaches assume a direct relationship between language fluency and sociocultural adaptation. Good language proficiency is argued to be associated with increased interaction with members of the new culture, and a decrease in sociocultural maladaptation (Ward and Kennedy, 1999).

The culture learning approach is more applied than theoretical, in its emphasis on social skills and social interaction (Masgoret and Ward, 2006; Ward et al., 2001).

As indicated in Chapter 15, the cultural learning approach forms the basis of intercultural training, providing an underpinning for training and preparation for cross-cultural transitions. As an applied area, the starting point is to identify cross-cultural differences in communication (both verbal and non-verbal), rules, conventions, norms and practices that contribute to intercultural misunderstandings. It then sets out to suggest ways in which confusing and dissatisfying encounters can be minimized (see Chapter 15, p. 316).

A number of factors have been identified in the cultural learning approach that may affect language learning, and subsequently affect sociocultural adaptation. These factors include personal motivation and attitudes toward the learning of a foreign language, personality factors and situation factors. With respect to attitudes to learning a second language, Gardner and colleagues in a series of studies in Canada have identified "integrativeness," referring to an individual's attitudes toward the other language community, and openness to other cultural groups in general, and a willingness and interest in engaging in social interactions with members of the other language community, to be important for second-language acquisition (Gardner, 1985, 2000; Gardner and Clément, 1990; Masgoret and Gardner, 2003).

Cognitive perspectives

Whereas the affective and behavioral approaches to acculturation are respectively concerned with stress and emotional feelings, and with skills in dealing with everyday encounters and behavioral changes, the cognitive position (stemming from social cognition – see Chapter 4) is concerned with how people perceive and think about themselves and others in the face of intercultural encounters. The cognitive aspect is present during the appraisal process noted in the discussion of acculturative stress above. However, cognitive aspects mostly refer to how people process information about their own group (ingroup) and about other groups (outgroups), including how people categorize one another and how people identify with these categories.

When individuals and groups enter into an acculturation situation, they are faced with the questions "Who am I?" and "Which group do I belong to?" (Berry, 2007b). These two questions form the basis of one of the influential theoretical positions within the cognitive approaches: social identity theory (Tajfel, 1978, 1982; Tajfel and Turner, 1986). The theory is largely concerned with why and how individuals identify with, and behave as part of, social groups (Jasinskaja-Lahti, Liebkind and Solheim, 2009; Liebkind, 2006; Liebkind and Jasinskaja-Lahti, in press; Verkuyten, 2005b, in press). Tajfel and Turner (1986) argued that individuals need to belong to a group in order to secure a firm sense of well-being. Humans have the tendency to put others and themselves into categories, and this helps us to associate (i.e., identify) with certain groups and not others. Moreover, human beings have the tendency to positively evaluate the group to which they belong, and this enhances their self-image.

Within the context of acculturation, social identity theory is concerned with how groups and individuals define their identity in relation to the members of their own ethnic group (i.e., ethnic identity) on the one hand, and to the larger society within which they are acculturating on the other (i.e., national identity; Phinney, 1990). Phinney (1993) has developed a comprehensive (developmental) theory regarding how ethnic and national identities develop, the stages individuals pass through (Phinney, 1989) as well as scales for assessing the ethnic and national identities (Phinney, 1993; Phinney and Ong, 2007). Phinney and her colleagues (Phinney, Lochner and Murphy, 1990) have also examined how ethnic and national identities may be linked to psychological adaptation.

Early research conceptualized ethnic and national identities at opposite ends of a continuum where the strengthening of one (e.g., ethnic identity) resulted in the weakening of the other (i.e., national identity). Stated in another way, one could not have strong ethnic and national identity at the same time. Current research regards ethnic and national identities as two independent dimensions where it is possible to have strong identification with both dimensions (bicultural identity or integrated) or weak identification with both identities (marginal) (Phinney, 1990). Alternatively, it is possible to identify strongly on ethnic identity and weakly on national identity (separated or ethnically embedded) and vice versa, strongly on national identity and weakly on ethnic identification (assimilated). This conceptualization parallels that of the bi-dimensional approach to acculturation noted above (see also "Dimensions of acculturation").

One line of research in this theoretical perspective is the Bicultural Identity Integration (BII) spearheaded by Benet-Martínez. BII is a framework for investigating individual differences in bicultural identity organization, where the focus is on biculturals' subjective perceptions of how much their dual cultural identities intersect or overlap. BII aims to capture the degree to which biculturals perceive their mainstream and ethnic cultural identities as compatible and integrated vs. oppositional and difficult to integrate (Benet-Martínez, Leu, Lee and Morris, 2002). Benet-Martínez and Haritatos point out that "Individuals high on BII tend to see themselves as part of a 'hyphenated culture' (or even part of a combined, 'third,' emerging culture) and find it easy to integrate both cultures in their everyday lives" (2005, p. 1019). The two forms of biculturalism described here have respectively been referred to as alternating and blended biculturalism (LaFromboise et al., 1993; Phinney and Devich-Navarro, 1997). Benet-Martínez and her colleagues have found that the two ways in which biculturals experience their identity are related to distinct personalities, and to contextual factors (Benet-Martínez, Lee and Leu, 2006). Individuals who see their two identities as separate are driven by dispositional factors such as cultural isolation and are low in openness; in contrast, individuals who manage to blend the two identities may be low on neuroticism (Benet-Martínez and Haritatos, 2005).

Linking this line of research to personality, Benet-Martínez and her colleagues have also explored whether bilinguals have two personalities. In a series of studies, Ramírez-Esparza, Gosling, Benet-Martínez, Potter and Pennebaker (2004) found personality differences between US-American and Mexican monolinguals. These differences in personality were further explored in English–Spanish bilinguals in Mexico and in the US. The study showed that bilinguals were more extraverted, agreeable and conscientious in English than Spanish, and these differences were consistent with the personality displayed in each culture.

Developmental perspectives

With few exceptions (e.g., Motti-Stefanidi *et al.*, in press), many of the developmental perspectives to date lack clear theoretical positions, and are just strands of ideas highlighting the importance of including developmental issues in acculturation. Children and youth from immigrant families undergo major developmental changes at the same time as they are undergoing acculturation, such that acculturation and developmental changes confound each other, and it becomes difficult to disentangle the two kinds of changes from each other (Oppedal, 2006; Phinney, 2006).

In spite of these difficulties, Huntsinger and Jose (2006) in a longitudinal study with sixty European American and sixty second-generation Chinese American youths attempted to disentangle acculturation from developmental processes. They examined personality variables at two time points: at middle childhood (12 years old) and at adolescence (17 years old). They found that while the two groups substantially differed in their personality at Time 1, when they were 12 years old, by the age of 17 – Time 2 – there were hardly any differences between them. They demonstrated how these changes were related to psychosocial adjustment and academic achievement. For example, anxiety was the only Time 1 personality factor that predicted unique variance at Time 2 for both groups. Personality factors such as extraversion at Time 1 showed different predictions for depression, self-esteem and academic achievement among the two groups. Such findings indicate how complex the relationship between acculturation and development can be.

One area that may help to isolate acculturation influences from developmental changes may be through the examination of cultural transmission (see the enculturation and socialization section in Chapter 2) in different acculturation contexts and across acculturating groups. Such studies have been reported by Phalet and Schönpflug (2001) and by Vedder and colleagues (Vedder, Berry, Sabatier and Sam, 2009). It should be emphasized that neither study was designed with the intention of disentangling acculturation from development changes; however, they are referred to here to illustrate a possible research direction.

Because of the difficulties in isolating acculturation from development (Motti-Stefanidi *et al.*, in press; Sam, 2006a) researchers have to date identified developmental issues such as cultural identity (Phinney, 1990), development of self (Kağitçibaşi, 2007; Kwak, 2003), family relationships (Fuligni, Yip and Tseng, 2002; Stuart, Ward, Jose and Narayanan, in press) and peer relations (Fandrem, Strohmeier and Roland, 2009) that may become complicated by acculturation experiences during normal developmental changes. One exception to this trend is the work of Phinney (1990), who has proposed a developmental theory of how youths with immigrant background develop ethnic and national identity as part of their acculturation.

In recent years some researchers (e.g., García Coll, Lamberty, Jenkins, McAdoo, Crnic, Wasik and Vázquez Garcia, 1996; Oppedal, 2006; Motti-Stefanidi *et al.*, in press; Sam, 2006a) have tried to link these different aspects into an integrated model inspired by various developmental theories such as systems theory (e.g., Lerner, 2006) and ecological models (e.g., Bronfenbrenner and Morris, 2006).

The recurring question in developmental studies on acculturation is whether immigrant children and youth should be viewed as regular children, similar to their national peers when it comes to how they deal with developmental tasks, or whether they are special in that their acculturation experiences may impact on how they resolve developmental tasks. Based on a comparative study of almost 8,000 ethnocultural youths in thirteen western countries including Australia, Canada, Germany, Finland and the United States, Phinney and Vedder (2006) examined the universality of intergenerational discrepancies in family values. One conclusion from the study is that intergenerational family discrepancies may be a normal developmental process common to immigrant and national families alike. However, the study also found larger discrepancies in immigrant families with respect to family relationship values (such as obligations); the suggestion is that acculturation processes may be contributing to these discrepancies.

Personality and individual factors

One of the notions behind psychological acculturation as a concept is the recognition that individuals differ in the extent to which they engage in the acculturation process; nevertheless research findings highlighting the link between individual and personal factors (broadly defined as personality) and acculturation are mixed (Kosic, 2006). Personal characteristics as portrayed here are some of the moderating factors arising during acculturation described in the acculturative stress model, that is, the affective perspectives. Research on acculturation and personality usually examines a single or a number of personality characteristics or abilities to see their effect on stress reduction in the adaptation process (see the Internet for one such example; Additional Topics, Chapter 13). Similarly, research has focussed on www.cambridge.org/berry

whether there are some individual characteristics that enhance or hamper cultural learning (from the behavioral perspectives approach). For this line of research, see the section on intercultural personality in Chapter 15.

Relatively few studies have succeeded in demonstrating the role of personality traits in cross-cultural adaptation (Ward, 1996), and these have generally documented low explained variance from personality variables. One reason for the lack of unequivocal support for personality's role in cross-cultural adaptation is a problem with measurement and prediction of "adjustment" and adaptation. Cross-cultural adjustment has been examined in different ways ranging from health indicators such as depression, intercultural relationships (e.g., friendship patterns) with members of the national society, feelings of acceptance, academic achievement and job performance with life, making it difficult to establish the predictive ability of personality (Ward and Chang, 1997); this is a situation which calls for a meta-analytic examination (see Mol, Born, Willemsen and Van der Molen, 2005). On the other side of the problem is precisely what constitutes personality trait. Equally problematic in establishing the contribution of personality in cross-cultural adaptation is the general lack of research on "person–situation" interaction. This situation led Searle and Ward (1990) to propose the cultural-fit hypothesis. These researchers highlighted the significance of the person–situation interaction and suggested that the "fit" between the personal characteristics and norms in the new cultural setting could be a better predictor of immigrants' adaptation than personality per se. Ward and Chang (1997) found support for the "cultural-fit hypothesis" when they demonstrated that US-Americans living in Singapore were more extrovert than Singaporeans and consequently experienced frustration or rejection in response to their persistent attempts to initiate and sustain social relations with the locals.

Acculturation processes

In the previous section, by examining the ABCs of acculturation we looked at what changes occur during acculturation. In addition, we also looked at some (ontogentic) developmental issues and personal factors involved in acculturation. In this section, we will look at how changes may come about. Much of research in this area comes from the work of Berry (1974, 2006a), in his acculturation strategies model.

Acculturation strategies

In this section, we turn our attention to the question of whether there are variations in how individuals acculturate. Berry (1974) proposed a model of acculturation strategies on the assumption that the way in which individuals acculturate depends on how they simultaneously deal with two fundamental issues. The first

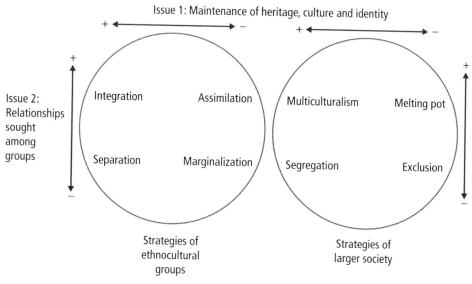

Figure 13.2 Acculturation strategies in ethnocultural groups and the larger society (from Berry, 2001a).

of these two issues is the extent to which acculturating individuals regard maintenance of their cultural heritage important or not (i.e., cultural maintenance). The
second issue is concerned with the extent to which individuals regard contact with
members of other cultural groups and participating in the new society to be important or not (i.e., contact and participation). When orientations to these two issues
intersect, Berry (1974) proposed four different **acculturation strategies** termed
assimilation, integration, separation and **marginalization**. These strategies are
depicted in the lefthand side of Figure 13.2

Assimilation is the strategy when individuals do not wish to maintain the identity of their heritage culture, seek close interaction with other cultures, and adopt the
cultural values, norms and traditions of the new society. When individuals place
a high value on holding onto their original culture, and at the same time avoid
interaction with members of the new society, the Separation strategy is defined.
When there is an interest in maintaining one's original culture, while also having daily interactions with other groups, this is called Integration. The strategy of
Marginalization arises when there is little possibility or a lack of interest in cultural
maintenance (often for reasons of enforced cultural loss), as well as little interest in
having relations with others (often for reasons of exclusion or discrimination).

The four strategies are neither static, nor end-outcomes in themselves. They
can change depending on situational factors (e.g., in the wake of the 9/11 attacks
in the US, Muslims had to renegotiate their identities – see Sirin and Fine, 2007).
The righthand side of Figure 13.2 illustrates the parallel concepts that are often
employed when describing the public attitudes and public policies in the larger
society. This side of the figure will be discussed in Chapter 14.

Using cluster analysis, Berry and his colleagues (Berry, Phinney, Sam and Vedder, 2006) found four **acculturation profiles**, which reflect the different ways in which young people orient themselves to five intercultural issues: their acculturation strategies; cultural identities; language use and proficiency; peer relationships; and family relationship values. The sample for this analysis included over 4,000 immigrant youths in thirteen different countries, and involved over thirty different ethnic groups (see Internet, Additional Topics, Chapter 13). The profiles give support to the original four acculturation strategies: the National, Ethnic, Integration and Diffuse profiles generally correspond to the assimilation, separation, integration and marginalization strategies. However, the profiles go beyond them in their inclusion of attitudes, identities, language, social behaviors and values.

Much research has been devoted to the relative preference for the different acculturation strategies (Van Oudenhoven, Prins and Buunk, 1998) and how acculturation strategies may impact on adaptation outcome (Castro, 2003). Regarding preferences for acculturation strategies, numerous studies have been undertaken in different countries and with different kinds of acculturating groups. With some few exceptions, integration is the most preferred strategy, and marginalization is the least (Berry, 2003). Relative preference for assimilation and separation seems to vary with respect to the ethnic group and the society of settlement, and also situational domains. In the Berry *et al.* (2006) study, the researchers found that among all the immigrants combined, integration was the most preferred strategy. However, for the combined Turkish samples (N = 714) separation appeared to be the most preferred strategy (40.3%). In contrast, Vietnamese (N = 718) seemed to prefer assimilation (25.6%) nearly as much as integration (33.1%), and these preferences were related to whether the Vietnamese resided in a "settler society" (i.e., a society that has a long history of settling people, such as Australia, Canada or the USA), or one of recent immigration (e.g., Finland and Norway).

Acculturation strategies as presented above assume that acculturating individuals and groups have the freedom to choose how they want to engage in intercultural relations. This, of course, is not always the case (Berry, 1974). The kinds of attitudes members of the larger society have toward immigrants, or the kinds of settlement policies the larger society has toward acculturating groups, can influence the adopted strategy. The expectation of the larger society (i.e., acculturation expectations) toward how a group should acculturate has been the basis of theoretical models such as the Interactive Acculturation Model (IAM) of Bourhis and his colleagues (Bourhis, Moise, Perreault and Senecal, 1997). The IAM model has been useful in making predictions about acculturation preferences of Japanese–US-American worker relationships with great success (Komisarof, 2009).

Extending IAM, and arguing that differences exist between what immigrants or acculturating groups do in terms of chosen acculturation strategies (real plane) and the strategies they prefer (ideal plane), Navas and her colleagues have developed the Relative Acculturation Expanded Model (RAEM) (Navas, García, Sánchez, Rojas, Pumares and Fernández, 2005). This reasoning is in line with the discrepancy between attitudes and behaviors (see Fishbein and Ajzen, 2010). Navas and her colleagues also point to the fact that preferred strategies (i.e., on the ideal plane) and the actual chosen strategy (real plane) vary with respect to the sphere of life (e.g., work, family and religious beliefs). The REAM has been extended to incorporate acculturation expectations of members of the larger society (see Bourhis *et al.*, 1997) to predict areas of agreement and disagreement in the acculturation of Maghrebians and Spaniards in Spain (Navas, Rojas, García and Pumares, 2007).

Dimensions of acculturation

Until the 1970s much research on ways of acculturating assumed that one's level of acculturation could be understood using a single dimension (one-dimensional view), varying from a preference for fully remaining as a member of one's heritage culture, through to becoming a full member of the dominant society. The existence of two independent dimensions proposed by Berry (1974, 1980) has been verified by a number of studies (e.g., Ryder, Alden and Paulhus, 2000).

Although there is support for the existence of two dimensions, controversy has been brewing regarding the operationalization of the two underlying dimensions (i.e., the degree to which people wish to maintain their heritage cultures and identities, and the degree to which people participate with others in the larger society). Some researchers (e.g., Liebkind, 2001; Snauwaert, Soenens, Vanbeselaere and Boen, 2003) have noted that the second dimension has been operationalized in different ways, including identification with the larger society (e.g., Hutnik, 1986, 1991), adoption of the national culture (e.g., Donà and Berry, 1994; Nguyen, Messe and Stollak, 1999; Sayegh and Lasry, 1993) and adapting to the larger society (e.g., Arends-Tóth and Van de Vijver, 2006).

Whereas many studies have operationalized the second issue in one specific way, some studies have compared the different operationalizations (Arends-Tóth and Van de Vijver, 2007; Playford and Safdar, 2007) yielding very different results. For instance, in two separate studies among two groups of immigrants of Moroccan and Turkish descent in Belgium, Snauwaert *et al.* (2003) operationalized the second issue in three different ways: as contact, adoption and identification. In line with these hypotheses, these conceptualizations yielded substantially different distributions of participants in terms of their acculturation strategies (i.e., integration, assimilation, separation and marginalization). Whereas integration was the most popular strategy according to the contact conceptualization, separation was the most popular one when the second issue was conceptualized as adoption and identification.

In part to deal with such discrepancies in findings, Berry *et al.* (2006) examined how young people orient themselves to five intercultural issues: their acculturation strategies; cultural identities; language use and proficiency; peer relationships; and family relationship values. As was previously pointed out (see the previous section), the researchers identified four acculturation profiles in their analysis, and they concluded that the integration profile remains the most common way to acculturate when the operationalization is expanded to acculturation variables beyond that of attitudes. See the Internet for a summary of the four acculturation profiles (Additional Topics, Chapter 13).

Acculturation outcomes

A core question to acculturation research is what are the consequences of acculturation? One view on human behavior is that it entails adaptations to ecological and cultural contexts. If this is the case, it should follow that behavioral problems may arise when an individual who has been born and raised (socialized) in one cultural context moves to another cultural context. This question also can be stated as *how well* do people adapt to acculturation demands? A closely related question is whether there is a relationship between *how* people acculturate and *how well* they adapt.

When discussing *how well* people adapt during acculturation, the interest is in the long-term outcome of acculturation (Berry *et al.*, 1989). Adaptation is not synonymous with acculturation, but follows from the change. Adaptation in the context of acculturation has been defined variously, including health status, communication competence, self-awareness, stress reduction, feelings of acceptance and culturally skilled behaviors (see Mendenhall and Oddou, 1985; Ward, 1996). We begin this discussion by drawing on the distinction between psychological and sociocultural adaptation.

Psychological and sociocultural adaptation

The distinction between psychological and sociocultural adaptation proposed by Ward and colleagues (e.g., Searle and Ward, 1990; Ward, 1996, 2001) gives us two forms of adaptation that have dominated acculturation research. Simply stated, these two forms of adaptation respectively deal with "feeling well" and "doing well" (Van de Vijver and Phalet, 2004). Psychological adaptation in this case refers to an individual's satisfaction and overall emotional or psychological well-being. Studies interested in psychological adaptation have often focussed on mental health outcomes such as (lack of) depression and anxiety, and are based on the affective approach to acculturation (Berry, 2006a). Sociocultural adaptation refers to how successfully the individual acquires the appropriate cultural skills in living effectively in the new sociocultural milieu. Studies of sociocultural adaptation have usually focussed on the absence of behavior problems, and on school achievement, and social competence; these studies commonly use the B (behavior) approach to acculturation. The two forms of adaptation are interrelated: dealing successfully with problems and positive interactions with members of the larger national society culture are both likely to improve one's feelings of well-being and satisfaction; similarly, it is easier to accomplish tasks and develop positive interpersonal relations if one is feeling good and accepted.

In a meta-analysis involving sixty-seven independent samples (N = 10,286 participants), Wilson (2009) examined the effect sizes of three different groups of predictor variables on sociocultural adaptation. Effect size correlations with sociocultural adaptation ranged from small to medium with respect to demographic factors (e.g., previous overseas experience and duration of sojourn) and interpersonal variables (e.g., discrepancy in expectations, language and personality) to medium-to-large effects for intercultural variables (e.g., cultural empathy and perceived discrimination).

Depending on the group of acculturating people being examined, these two forms of adaptation and in particular that of sociocultural adaptation can be expanded to include school adaptation for young people, who need to adjust, and succeed in the school, and work adaptation for adults, who have to adjust to work and occupational challenges that may be different from what they are used to. With respect to young people, Motti-Stefanidi and her colleagues (in press) have suggested that much of their sociocultural adaptation in reality is concerned with dealing with developmental tasks they face.

Do acculturating groups adapt equally well, better or more poorly than a reference group? The basis for comparisons is an important issue when discussing the adaptation of people undergoing acculturation. Should acculturating people be compared with (1) non-acculturating members of their own ethnic group; (2) other acculturating groups in the new society; or (3) with members of the new and larger society? Or, should they be assessed against a psychometrically and standardized instrument measuring adaptation? All three reference groups for comparison and a standardized instrument should ideally be utilized simultaneously. But, quite often, information on the comparison reference groups is not available, nor does the standardized instrument provide unbiased scores. Considering the different groups that could be used in making comparisons, it is perhaps not surprising that research findings in terms of how well acculturating groups adapt are mixed. Some studies have found good adaptation outcomes (both psychological and sociocultural) with some acculturating groups doing either better or equally well as their national peers in the society of residence (Ali, 2002; Berry et al., 2006; Escobar, Nervi and Gara, 2000; Motti-Stefanidi, Pavlopoulos, Obradovic and Masten, 2008). However, other studies have found poor adaptation outcomes (Alegría et al., 2008; Frisbie, Cho and Hummer, 2001).

Beyond different reference groups being used when comparing the adaptation of immigrant groups, mixed findings have also arisen because of differences in operationalization of acculturation itself, and the adaptation outcome of interest (see Koneru, Weisman de Mamani, Flynn and Betancourt, 2007, for a review). For instance, studies have focussed on satisfaction with life (Neto, 2001); self-esteem (Nesdale and Mak, 2003); antisocial behaviors (Murad, Joung, van Lenthe, Bengi-Arslan and Crijnen, 2003) and school adjustment (Suárez-Orozco, Suárez-Orozco and Todorova, 2008). Moreover, adaptation is dependent on several moderating factors, including immigration policies, and acculturation expectations of the society of settlement.

Although much attention has been directed to psychological and sociocultural adaptation, some research has found links between acculturation and physical health (Schulpen, 1996), such as different forms of cancer (Abraído-Lanza, Chao and Gates, 2008; Hyman, 2001) and cardiovascular diseases (Kliewer, 1992; Maskarinec and Noh, 2004). However, rather than acculturation resulting in poor physical health, many studies seem to suggest that immigrants have better physical health, when compared with their non-migrating peers in the society of emigration (see Kliewer, 1992). It appears that with increasing acculturation, health status "migrates" toward the national norm; this has been referred to as the "convergence hypothesis" (Sam, 2006b). Closely linked to this observation is what has become known as the "**immigrant paradox**" (García Coll *et al.*, in press). Its most important aspect is the counterintuitive finding that immigrants show better adaptation outcomes than their national peers; in addition, first-generation immigrants are found to report better adaptation than their second-generation peers (Sam, Vedder, Liebkind, Neto and Virta, 2008; Sam, Vedder, Ward and Horenczyk, 2006).

School adjustment

Schools and other educational settings constitute the main acculturation context for immigrant children and youths. They can be viewed as a miniature society of settlement; schools represent and introduce the new culture to immigrant children. School adjustment can be seen as a primary task, and as a highly important outcome, of the cultural transition process. Accordingly school adjustment is seen as one major acculturation outcome for immigrant children and youth. Immigrant children, just like their parents, constitute a heterogeneous group in terms of ethnicity, nationality and immigration history. Similarly, they have diverse backgrounds (ranging from debilitating factors like poor SES/socioeconomic status, prejudice and discrimination to remarkable strengths like high parental aspirations and close family ties). This makes it difficult to make generalizations about antecedent factors in school adjustment.

Within many immigrant communities the importance attributed to school adjustment is particularly high (Horenczyk and Tatar, in press; Vedder and Horenczyk,

2006). However, there is no doubt that many immigrant children struggle to succeed academically in the school system of the larger society (Suárez-Orozco, Pimentel and Martin, 2009) and this is manifested in poor school grades, and high rates of school dropout (Nusche, 2009). This is contrary to the number of studies that show that immigrant children generally have positive attitudes to school (Berry *et al.*, 2006; Suárez-Orozco and Suárez-Orozco, 1995), have high school aspirations (Fuligni, 1997, 1998) and are optimistic about their academic future (Phalet and Andriessen, 2003). In a study by Andriessen, Phalet and Lens (2006), these researchers showed that school achievement may not simply be a matter of having high school aspirations, but the perception of the importance of school work and future career. Specifically, Andriessen and her colleagues examined the motivational benefits of perceived instrumentality (defined as perception of the importance of school work for future successful life) and internally regulated future goals among adolescents of Dutch, Moroccan and Turkish descent in Dutch high schools. They found that positively perceived instrumentality for future goals increased task motivation and indirectly increased adaptive learning for all three groups of the sample. On a different note, it has been found in the United States that length of residence may be related to poor academic performance and academic aspirations (i.e., the immigrant paradox) (see, e.g., Fuligni, 1997, 1998). This decline in academic achievement among immigrant youth has also been linked to a number of debilitating factors within the school (e.g., perception of school violence) and at home (e.g., family conflicts and parents' educational background) (Suárez-Orozco, Pimentel and Martin, 2009). In sum, school adjustment and academic achievement of immigrant youth is a more complex phenomenon than personal aspirations and school milieu.

Work adaptation

Work adaptation refers to competent performance, the successful accomplishment of work goals and organizational commitment to a local unit (Aycan, 1997). For immigrants and other acculturating individuals, work adaptation is not limited to doing well at the workplace, and meeting the organizational goals successfully. It also encompasses being employed in the occupational sector where one has been educated and trained, and, frequently, the unfortunate event of being unemployed. It is common that acculturating individuals experience downward mobility in occupation (Hayfron, 2006) brought about by lack of recognition of previous education and training, lack of culturally appropriate skills for the job and various forms of cultural barriers and discrimination. In addition, acculturating individuals with the same qualification and experience may also be discriminated against in their wages, even after several years on the labor force of the new society (Laryea and Hayfron, 2005). Downward mobility and loss of occupational status for the immigrant can jeopardize the overall adaptation (Aycan and Berry, 1996). Indeed, studies have shown that better-adapted acculturating individuals also report being more satisfied with their employment conditions. (See also the section on sojourners and sojourner effectiveness in Chapter 15 for more discussion on work adaptation of expatriates.)

Recently studies have been carried out on the relationship between acculturation strategies, ethnic and national identification and labor success among immigrants into Germany (see Constant and Zimmermann, 2008; Zimmermann, Zimmermann and Constant, 2007). In one study Constant and Zimmermann (2008) argued that ethnic identity can affect the attachment to the host country, and performance of immigrants in its labor market, beyond human capital and ethnic origin characteristics. Estimates for immigrants in Germany showed that ethnic identity is important for the decision to work and significantly and differentially affects the labor force participation of men and women. While women with integrated identity were more likely to work than assimilated women, this pattern did not hold true for migrant men.

To answer the question whether there is a relationship between how people acculturate and how well they adapt, we refer once more to the thirteen-country comparative study on ethnocultural youth. In this study Berry et al. (2006) found that irrespective of the society of settlement, those with an integration profile had the best psychological and sociocultural adaptation outcomes, while those with a diffuse profile had the worst. In between, those with an ethnic profile had moderately good psychological adaptation but poorer sociocultural adaptation, while those with a national profile had moderately poor psychological adaptation and slightly negative sociocultural adaptation. For some ethnic groups, such as Turks, the ethnic profile is psychologically, but not socioculturally, adaptive in non-settler societies (such as Germany and Norway), although on the whole the integration profile appeared to be the best way to acculturate. Phinney and her colleagues have also found that identification with both the heritage society and the national society (i.e., acculturation involving integration) is predictive of higher self-esteem (Phinney, Cantu and Kurtz, 1997; Phinney and Chavira, 1992). In addition, Chen, Benet-Martínez and Bond (2008) have found that Chinese immigrants high in terms of bicultural integration also had the highest level of psychological well-being. In short, there appears to be a link between how people choose to acculturate, and how well they adapt.

Methodological issues

Acculturation research has come under some criticisms in recent years (e.g., Chirkov, 2009; Rudmin, 2003), and most of the criticisms have been on methodological grounds, such as how constructs should be conceptualized and operationalized. In addition, some critics (e.g., Chirkov, 2009) have expressed the view that culture and acculturation should be understood using more social constructivist approaches and qualitative methods. Here, we highlight two methodological issues of concern, beginning with assessment of acculturation and then design of acculturation research.

Assessment of acculturation

Using the model in Figure 13.1 as our point of departure, we recommend that all elements in the model need to be assessed in all acculturation research (Berry, 2006b). These are: (1) the cultural (group) as well as (2) psychological (individual) features of the two groups in contact, both (3) prior to contact and (4) resulting from contact. Research on acculturation at the group level should begin by examining some of the core cultural phenomena that are brought to the contact setting by each of the original cultures as well as those cultural features that change following contact; these examinations require the use of ethnographic methods (see Chapter 10, the section on "Ethnography"). These may include political (e.g., policies regarding settlement), economic and demographic, as well as cultural changes (e.g., new language, and traditions). In addition to features brought to the acculturation setting by the two original cultural groups, it is important to consider the factors determining the nature of their interaction, such as cultural distance (e.g., Ward *et al.*, 2001). This refers to how similar or different the two groups are on cultural dimensions such as language, religion and values. It is important to stress here that the group-level phenomena to be examined are largely cultural in nature, and as such the use of ethnographic methods may be an appropriate approach. Unfortunately, studies that assess this aspect of acculturation are rare, and therefore making inferences about the role of culture, and cultural differences, in acculturation outcomes is problematic.

At the individual level of acculturation, assessment should include factors such as personality characteristics and abilities that existed prior to the contact, and changes in these following contact, including changes in attitudes, behaviors and identities in both groups. It is also important to assess the acculturation strategies and levels of psychological and sociocultural adaptation in both groups.

Arends-Tóth and Van de Vijver (2006, pp. 147–154) have identified six issues that acculturation researchers need to deal with when designing their study. These issues are, however, not exclusive to acculturation research. They recommend:

1. Explicitly stating the goal of the study, the rationale for including acculturation measures and the choice of acculturation variables. It is important that there are explicit measures for acculturation, rather than using proxies such as length of residence, or generational status.

2. Clearly identifying the aspects of acculturation (e.g., knowledge, behavior, values and attitudes) to be studied. These different areas do not change uniformly, resulting in lowered reliability of scales.
3. Providing a rationale for the research methodology selected, such as survey, case study, observation or experimental approach. A triangulation of methods or mixed methods may be ideal. Much acculturation research has utilized the survey method, making it difficult to establish causality; experimental studies are very much lacking.
4. Justifying the choice of a theoretical model and measurement method for assessing acculturation strategies (e.g., use of one, two or four statement instruments, use of priming or survey approach; see below).
5. Justifying the choice of life domains and situations to be dealt with in the items. This could be social relations and affiliations, daily activities and cultural traditions. Language use and proficiency is often used as an indicator of acculturation. But this may best be thought of as a (sociocultural) outcome.
6. Justifying the choice of item wording and language. People undergoing acculturation may not be very fluent in the national language; hence short and straightforward sentences devoid of colloquial expression are preferable. Moreover, it should be determined whether the instrument should be presented in the national, ethnic or an international language, or participants be given the choice of different languages. Since language is an indicator of acculturation outcome, it needs to be controlled for in statistical analyses.

Measuring acculturation strategies

Earlier in the chapter, we made reference to differences in results depending on how the two underlying issues of acculturation strategies are operationalized. In many studies, both attitudes (i.e., preferences for ways of acculturating) and behaviors (e.g., language knowledge and use, friendship choice), as well as cultural identities, have been assessed. The term "strategies" is intended to refer to a pattern beyond attitudes alone. As noted above, these different psychological aspects of acculturation form a pattern (or profile) in some studies. Rudmin (2003, 2009; Rudmin and Ahmadzadeh, 2001) has criticized how the four strategies of assimilation, integration, separation and marginalization have been assessed, and these criticisms have been responded to (Berry, 2009; Berry and Sam, 2003). Arends-Tóth and Van de Vijver (2006) have identified three main approaches in which acculturation strategies have been assessed, and have referred to these as the one-, two- and four-statement methods. Briefly, whereas the "one-statement method" typically involves a one-dimensional, bipolar scale ranging from maintaining the heritage culture at one pole to adopting the national culture at the other pole, the

"2-statement method" entails assessing acculturation strategies using two separate scales: one representing orientations toward the mainstream culture and the other representing orientations toward the heritage culture. The "4-statement method" is also based on the bi-dimensional model of acculturation. Here, orientations toward each of the four acculturation strategies are discussed in separate items. A more detailed description of the different methods, their advantages, limitation and studies that have used them can be found on the Internet (Additional Topics, Chapter 13; see also Arends-Tóth and Van de Vijver, 2006).

Design of acculturation studies

Methods for studying acculturation vary; they range from observation and case studies to self-report. The method chosen depends to some extent on which aspect of acculturation (i.e., acculturation conditions, orientations or strategies and acculturation outcomes) is being examined. In the previous section, we looked at issues to be borne in mind when studying acculturation, which aspects of acculturation should be studied, as well as how to measure acculturation strategies in particular. In this subsection, we look at some specific acculturation research designs.

Cross-sectional and longitudinal designs

Acculturation is a process which takes place over time, and results in changes both in the culture and in the individual. As a process, change can best be understood using longitudinal designs. This is not to suggest that cross-sectional designs are useless. Much of what we know of acculturation today comes from cross-sectional studies. Still, longitudinal studies are very much needed.

Culture change, as well as individual change, can only be noted and assessed when groups and sets of individuals are compared over time. While this is ideal, in practice such comparisons are not practicable in most acculturation research settings. Instead, a more usual practice is that many of the cultural features are identified from other sources (e.g., earlier ethnographic accounts) or partially reconstructed from reports of the older members of the community, who have had less acculturation experience. Similarly, individual change should ideally be assessed in longitudinal research, although such designs are often plagued with problems of "subject mortality" through death or out-migration (Berry, 2006b).

A common alternative to longitudinal research is cross-sectional research in which a time-related variable (e.g., length of residence, generational status or proportion of time spent in new society is employed). Such variables are used as acculturation proxies. An assumption here is that acculturation is a cumulative process over time, but this assumption may not always be valid. Nevertheless, some research (e.g., Berry et al., 2006) has found systematic and interpretable differences in acculturation strategies according the length of time that the immigrant had lived in their new society. Preference for integration was higher, and for marginalization lower, in cohorts that had lived longer in the new society.

Experimental studies

Much of acculturation research is interested in understanding factors and conditions that affect or bring about change, or can account for an outcome. To be able to account for the outcome, extraneous and confounding factors have to be excluded, or controlled for in our analyses. To achieve this, experimental studies are most ideal (see the section on internal and external context in Chapter 12). Although there are several forms of experimental studies, one form that is very much needed in acculturation research is priming. This type of study involves experimentally manipulating the mind-sets of participants and measuring the resulting changes in behavior (Matsumoto and Yoo, 2006). In one priming study, Hong and her colleagues used US-American and Chinese iconic images (e.g., the US Capitol and Chinese Great Wall) to stimulate American and Chinese mind-sets among bicultural Chinese Americans in order to examine attribution errors (Hong, Morris, Chiu and Benet-Martínez, 2000). Maddux and his colleagues (Leung and Chiu, in press; Leung, Maddux, Galinsky and Chiu, 2008; Maddux and Galinsky, 2009) also used the priming method to demonstrate a link between intercultural experience (e.g., time spent living abroad) and creative thinking. In one study, the researchers showed that priming foreign living experiences temporarily enhanced creative tendencies for participants who had previously lived abroad. In another study, they showed that the degree to which individuals had adapted to different cultures while living abroad mediated the link between foreign living experience and creativity.

Comparative studies

While it is important to seek general principles that relate acculturation experiences to acculturation outcomes, many acculturation studies examine one acculturating group settled into one society. The findings from such studies cannot be generalized beyond the group(s) and the societies where the study has taken place. Moreover, most acculturation research has been conducted in just a few western societies (e.g., Australia, Canada, Europe, USA), while most acculturation is taking place in other parts of the world (e.g., China, India, African and South American societies). Although it is important to know about acculturation phenomena in one group in one society, there is the risk that such limited research findings will be generalized beyond the setting in which they were obtained (Berry, 2006b). Hence, comparative studies of acculturation have long been advocated (e.g., Berry *et al.*, 1987), but few have been accomplished until now. One ambitious comparative study is the thirteen-country analysis by Berry and his colleagues (Berry *et al.*, 2006). This study has brought research closer to identifying some universal features of acculturation. For instance, the study showed that the kind of society in which individuals reside (i.e., settler vs. non-settler society) affects the way the individual chooses to acculturate, in addition to how well they adapt. But more importantly, irrespective of which society the individual resides in, the most successful acculturation strategy was found to be integration.

Conclusions

Psychology of acculturation is a young area within the broad field of cross-cultural psychology. Nevertheless, it is the fastest-growing area as evidenced by changes in the published articles in journals (Brouwers, Van Hemert, Breugelmans and Van de Vijver, 2004; Lonner, 2004). The interest in and growth of acculturation psychology undoubtedly is in response to unprecedented increase in worldwide migration and globalization (Sam and Berry, 2006). As a growing field, the issues being addressed and emphasized are still in flux. As we conclude this chapter, we highlight four issues that may influence the future direction of the field, namely domain, context, process and generalization.

In the original definition of acculturation (Redfield *et al.*, 1936), acculturation was defined as taking place in both (or all) cultural groups and individuals that are in contact. One current issue in acculturation research is whether acculturative change should be examined only among the non-dominant populations or among all groups in society. In some studies of the acculturation expectations held by dominant groups (e.g., Arends-Tóth and Van de Vijver, 2007) there is a clear distinction between public and private domains of cultural maintenance and change. The expectations are that immigrant and ethnocultural groups can retain their cultures, but do so in family and heritage community contexts. However, in some societies (Australia, Canada and the European Union), public policy clearly articulates that acculturation is a process of change in all groups. For example, the EU (2005) "Common Basic Principles on Integration," policy states that: "Integration is a dynamic, two-way process of mutual accommodation by all immigrants and residents of Member States. Integration is a dynamic, long-term, and continuous two-way process of mutual accommodation, not a static outcome. It demands the participation not only of immigrants and their descendants but of every resident." This vision of acculturation and adaptation as a mutual process corresponds well with the original definition. However, it appears that many in the larger receiving societies do not accept this vision (see the subsection on multiculturalism in Chapter 14). This issue may well be the most important one for acculturation researchers to monitor in future studies.

The issue of context deals with acculturating conditions, that is, under what conditions is the acculturation taking place. This calls for a detailed understanding of the acculturating groups, and of individuals in these groups. Although acculturation involves at least two groups and their individual members, research seems to have focussed almost exclusively on the non-dominant group. Moreover, the condition prior to the acculturation of the non-dominant group has also been neglected in acculturation studies. The importance of the context has been demonstrated clearly (Birman, Trickett and Buchanan, 2005; Nguyen, Messe and Stollak, 1999). Nevertheless, contextual information needed for the proper understanding of the process has only been given cursory attention in psychological acculturation research, and in cases where this vital information is available, it is often placed in an appendix, and not well linked to acculturation process or outcome variables.

Acculturation entails a process of change for which longitudinal studies are invaluable. However, the cost and time involved in longitudinal studies have led to a relative lack of them. The need for longitudinal studies will among others help disentangle the confounding of development and acculturation.

One goal of cross-cultural psychology is to achieve some degree of generalization. That is, we seek to identify those psychological processes and outcomes that are culture-specific and those that are culture-general. In the absence of comparative studies, we are very much limited in making generalizations, and even more so in identifying universal features of acculturation. To date, most comparative studies of acculturation have involved at best two or three countries and about the same number of ethnocultural groups. More large-scale comparative studies are needed.

As the world goes through globalization, and our lives become increasingly intertwined with distant people and economies, there are two issues relevant to acculturation. The first is whether globalization will bring about cultural and psychological homogenization in a process of assimilation leading to a "melting pot," or will breed resistance to such an outcome. The second question is whether individuals will develop a global identity without having to physically live next to other cultural groups, or being physically annexed or colonized by another country. With respect to the first issue, it has been argued (Berry, 2008) that all four acculturation strategies are evident in response to globalized contact: homogenization and assimilation are not inevitable. Regarding the second issue, precisely how this global identity develops, and how it affects psychological adjustment is less understood (Chen et al., 2008) and this will undoubtedly attract a lot of research attention. In addition, the recent economic recess may result in repatriation of some labor and economic migrants into their country of origin, and these changes may stimulate another line of research (Tartakovsky, 2008; Yijälä and Jasinskaja-Lahti, 2010). In contemporary societies the meeting between cultures has taken different forms, including virtual. How these new realities impact on acculturation is an area lacking in research.

KEY TERMS

acculturation • acculturation profiles • acculturation strategies • acculturative stress • adaptation (to acculturation) • assimilation • cultural identity • immigrant paradox • integration • larger society • marginalization • psychological acculturation • separation

FURTHER READING

Berry, J. W., Phinney, J. S., Sam, D. L., and Vedder, P. (eds.) (2006). *Immigrant youth in cultural transition: Acculturation, identity and adaptation across national contexts.* Mahwah, N.Y.: Erlbaum.

This book is an empirical report of a comparative study of the acculturation of immigrant adolescents, their national peers and their parents in thirteen countries. The book provides both empirical evidence of how immigrant youth acculturate, how well they adapt and the link between acculturation and adaptation. Moreover, the book provides a basis for policy formulation. For a summary of this book see *Applied Psychology: An International Review*, 2006, 303–332.

Jasinskaja-Lahti, I., and Mähönen, T. A. (2009). *Identities, intergroup relations and acculturation: The cornerstones of intercultural encounters.* Helsinki: Helsinki University Press.

This fifteen-chapter edited book focusses on identity, intergroup relationships and acculturation as a dynamic process. The book also presents methodological solutions for capturing the acculturation as a process.

Sam, D. L., and Berry, J. W. (eds). (2006). *The Cambridge handbook of acculturation psychology.* Cambridge: Cambridge University Press.

This 31-chapter edited book provides an extensive overview of different aspects of acculturation, including theoretical, empirical and contextual factors.

Ward, C., Bochner, S., and Furnham, A. (2001). *The psychology of culture shock.* Hove: Routledge.

This is a second edition of a book first published by the last two authors on the acculturation of different acculturating groups. Although the book is almost ten years old, and a new edition is currently underway (by the first author), it is still a very up-to-date book that provides good insights into different aspects of how individuals deal with new cultures.

14 Intercultural relations

CONTENTS

This chapter seeks to portray comparative research and applications in the field of intercultural relations. It begins with an examination of the concept of **intercultural strategies**, which is parallel to that of acculturation strategies introduced in Chapter 13. One of these strategies (multiculturalism) is both contested theoretically and examined empirically; some of these ideas and findings are then presented. The chapter continues with a presentation of some core theories and concepts, and illustrates them with selected research and applications across cultures.

The study of intercultural relations can be viewed as a core part of cross-cultural psychology. It shares with the subfield of acculturation a focus on psychological phenomena that result from contact among cultural groups and their individual members. And like acculturation, intercultural relations research examines the ways in which people work out their lives while living together in culturally plural societies (Brewer, 2007; Sam and Berry, 2006; Ward, 2008). The various kinds of groups that share social space in plural societies have been described in Chapter 13 (including immigrants, refugees, ethnocultural groups, sojouners and indigenous peoples). However, somewhat different from acculturation, intercultural relations phenomena can take place without firsthand contact; they can be rooted in awareness from prior historical contact or from contemporary telecommunications. Thus, such basic intercultural processes as stereotypes, attitudes and prejudice can be examined among people who do not have direct contact with others, since individual beliefs and attitudes may derive from collective phenomena in a person's cultural community, rather than from firsthand contact. So, as for all domains of cross-cultural psychology, we need to take these background cultural contexts into account in order to understand individual psychological phenomena.

As was discussed in Chapter 13, acculturation involves two basic issues: the continuity or loss of people's culture and behavior, and the nature of the contact between cultural groups. In the present chapter, we focus more on the second of these two issues, and on the relationships that ensue. We limit our examination to the relationships that take place between cultural groups within culturally plural societies, rather than internationally between societies.

Intercultural strategies

As noted, the concept of intercultural strategies (Berry, 1997) is parallel to that of acculturation strategies presented in Chapter 13. As we saw, these strategies consist of two components: attitudes and behaviors (i.e., both the preferences and actual practices) that are exhibited in day-to-day intercultural encounters. Of particular importance in considering these intercultural strategies is their mutual or reciprocal nature. While this was also true for acculturation strategies (where these strategies exist in both the dominant and non-dominant cultural groups), in intercultural strategies the phenomena of interest are relationships, which require examination in all groups in contact. Hence, both the left and right sides of Figure 13.2 need equal attention in any intercultural research and applications. As we also saw, the integration strategy for ethnocultural groups corresponds to a national policy of multiculturalism. The ideologies and policies of the dominant group and the preferences of non-dominant peoples are both core features in understanding the process and outcomes of intercultural relations in plural societies (see Berry, 2004; Bourhis *et al.*, 1997; Navas *et al.*, 2007). With the use of this framework, comparisons of intercultural strategies can be made between individuals and their groups, and between non-dominant peoples and the larger society. As in all cross-cultural research, these policies and individual preferences need to be understood in their historical, economic and geopolitical contexts.

The intercultural strategies of both the dominant and non-dominant ethnocultural groups can be examined at three levels: national, institutional and individual. Figure 14.1 shows the three levels for each side of the intercultural relationships. On the right are the views held by the various non-dominant cultural groups. On the left are the views held by the dominant larger society. There are three levels, with the most encompassing (the national society or cultural groups) at the top; at the bottom are the least encompassing (the individual); and in between are various social groupings (called institutions), which can include governmental agencies, educational or health systems, or workplaces.

At the first level (on the left side), we can examine national policies articulated by the larger plural society. For example, the Canadian and Australian national policies of multiculturalism promote both heritage cultural maintenance, and full and equitable participation in the larger society by all groups (Berry, 1984; Watts and Smolicz, 1997). Similarly, the European Union (2005) has adopted a set of "Common Basic Principles for Immigrant Integration Policy in the EU." It states that: "Integration is a dynamic, two-way process of mutual accommodation by all immigrants and residents of Member States." That is, both the dominant and non-dominant groups need to engage in a process of change; not all changes are expected to be carried out by immigrants or other non-dominant cultural groups. In China and India as well, public policies also seek to support the rights of cultural communities to maintain their heritages, and to support their rights to participate in the larger society. Some elements of these policies will be presented in more detail in the section on multiculturalism below (see also Westin, Bastos, Dahinden and Góis, 2009).

Levels	Dominant Mainstream Larger society	Non-dominant Minority group Cultural group
National	National policies	Group goals
Institutional	Uniform or plural	Diversity and equity
Individual	Multicultural ideology	Acculturation strategies

Figure 14.1 Levels of application of intercultural strategies in dominant and non-dominant groups in plural societies.

At this first level (on the right side of Figure 14.1), many ethnocultural groups also express their preferences in formal statements: some seek integration into the larger society (e.g., Maori in New Zealand), while some others seek separation (e.g., the Scottish National Party or Parti Québécois in Canada, who seek independence for their national groups).

At the bottom (individual) level, we can assess the attitudes that individuals in the larger society hold toward these four intercultural strategies, using the concept of multicultural ideology (see below). Furthermore, for members of various non-dominant cultural groups, we have already noted (in Chapter 13) that there are important variations in individual acculturation strategies.

At the middle (institutional) level, competing visions rooted in these alternative intercultural strategies confront and even conflict with each other daily. The dominant larger society may opt for uniform programs and standards (based on their own cultural views) in such core institutions as education, health, justice and defense (as in France and Germany; European Monitoring Centre on Racism and Xenophobia, 2008). In contrast, non-dominant cultural groups often seek the joint goals of diversity and equity. This involves, first, the recognition of the group's cultural uniqueness and specific needs, and, second, having their group needs met with the same level of understanding, acceptance and support as those of the dominant group. The goals of diversity and equity correspond closely to the integration and multiculturalism strategies (combining cultural maintenance with inclusive participation), whereas the push for uniformity resembles the assimilation and melting pot approach (see Berry, 1997).

Multiculturalism

As we have noted in Chapter 13, all contemporary societies are culturally plural; however, this notion needs to be distinguished from the term "multicultural," as used in Figure 13.2. The distinction is that while all societies are culturally plural, only some societies like it that way. These latter ones are multicultural in the sense that they: (1) seek to maintain and enhance their diversity (rather than trying to reduce or eliminate it); and (2) seek to encourage full and equitable participation in the daily life and institutions of the larger society (rather than placing barriers to such participation). There is perhaps no issue currently more debated in plural societies than the question of how to understand and manage this cultural diversity (Adams, 2007; Kymlicka, 2007; Moghaddam, 2008).

In many parts of the world, there is an evolving meaning for the concepts of integration and multiculturalism (Estonian Integration Foundation, 2007; Glazer, 1997; Van de Vijver, Breugelmans and Schalk-Soekar, 2008). One meaning of multiculturalism corresponds to the integration orientation as noted in Figure 13.2; this is the meaning for the concepts used in this chapter. However, for some, multiculturalism implies primarily the maintenance of many cultures in a society, without much participation or sharing. In this meaning, multiculturalism comes closer to separation than to integration, because it "carries the risk of accentuating cultural differences ... and exacerbates the 'us–them' type of thinking" (Kağtçibaşi, 1997, p. 44). Similarly, Brewer has seen this meaning of multiculturalism as leading to group distinctions that become "fault lines for conflict and separatism" (1997, p. 208). For others, multiculturalism and integration are perceived as temporary way stations on the route to assimilation (Hamberger, 2009).

Of course, the term "multiculturalism" can have any number of meanings; however, in most contemporary plural societies it conveys a sense of balance within a shared framework for living together. As phrased by Watts and Smolicz (1997, p. 52): "Multiculturalism presupposes the existence of an overarching framework of shared values that acts as a linchpin in a multi-ethnic state – a framework that is flexible and responsive to the various cultures and ethnic groups that compose the nation." This overarching framework was termed the larger society in Figure 13.2.

Multiculturalism policies

In Figure 13.2, multiculturalism was identified as the orientation that accepts *both* the maintenance of cultural characteristics and identities of all cultural groups, *and* the equitable contact among, and participation of all, groups in the larger plural society. This understanding of the term, linking it to the two issues involved in acculturation, was proposed (Berry, 1984) as a way to provide a psychological basis for understanding and evaluating Canadian multiculturalism policy. In Canada, as in most immigrant-receiving countries, early policies favored the assimilation of immigrants in the pursuit of the melting pot. However, this gradually changed, leading to the view that assimilation had not worked anywhere in the world, and that it was impracticable as a general policy. In 1971 the Canadian Federal Government announced a national multiculturalism policy that was intended to "break down discriminatory attitudes and cultural jealousies. National unity, if it is to mean anything in the deeply personal sense, must be founded on confidence in one's own individual identity; out of this can grow respect for that of others and a willingness to share ideas, attitudes and assumptions" (Government of Canada, 1971, p. 3).

The fundamental goal of the policy is to improve intercultural relations, and to enhance mutual acceptance among all ethnocultural groups. This goal is to be approached through three program components. One is the cultural component of the policy, which is to be achieved by providing support and encouragement for cultural maintenance and development among all cultural groups. This component parallels the first issue in the strategies framework, which deals with the maintenance of heritage cultures and identities. Second is the social component, which promotes the sharing of cultural expressions by providing opportunities for intergoup contact, and the removal of barriers to full participation in the larger society. This component parallels the second issue in the strategies framework, which deals with contact with other ethnocultural groups. The last program – the intercultural communication component – represents the bilingual reality of the larger society of Canada, and promotes the learning of one or both Official Languages (English and French) as a means for all ethnocultural groups to interact with each other and to participate in national life.

The European Union (2005) integration policy corresponds to the meaning of multiculturalism used here, in that it promotes both the rights to cultural maintenance and full participation by all cultural groups. One article accepts the right to cultural maintenance: "The practice of diverse cultures and religions is guaranteed under the Charter of Fundamental Rights and must be safeguarded, unless practices conflict with other inviolable European rights or with national law." Another principle promotes full participation: "Frequent interaction between immigrants and Member States citizens is a fundamental mechanism for integration." Thus, these two principles of the EU policy resemble the Canadian policy in fundamental ways, and correspond to the usage of the concepts of integration and multiculturalism used in this chapter. These core ideas are represented in the two equally important emphases: the maintenance of heritage cultures and identities and the full and equitable participation of all cultural groups in the life of the larger society. Pursuing the first without the second leads to segregation; however, emphasizing the second without the first leads to a melting pot. Together, and in balance with each other, it should be possible to achieve multiculturalism, and avoid exclusion. However, in some societies (as noted above) there is often a common misunderstanding that multiculturalism means only the presence of many independent cultural communities in a society, without their equitable participation and incorporation (see Joppke, 1996).

Research on the perception, meaning and public acceptance of multiculturalism as a concept and policy began with the work by Berry, Kalin and Taylor (1977) in Canada, and has continued in a number of countries (e.g., in the Netherlands by Breugelmans and Van de Vijver, 2004, and Van de Vijver, Breugelmans and Schalk-Soekar, 2008; and in New Zealand by Ward and Masgoret, 2009). There are two core concepts relating to the psychological examination of multiculturalism: multicultural ideology, and the multiculturalism hypothesis.

Multicultural ideology

The concept of multicultural ideology refers to the general acceptance of a multicultural way of living together in a plural society (Berry et al., 1977, pp. 131–134).

The first studies (Berry *et al.*, 1977; Berry and Kalin, 1995) employed national samples in Canada to examine the perception of the meaning of, and attitudes toward, such a multiculturalism policy and programs. There are three elements to this ideology. In addition to the two elements already discussed with respect to the strategies framework (cultural maintenance and equitable participation by all groups) there is a third feature to multicultural ideology: the acceptance by the dominant group that they also need to change in order to achieve some mutual accommodation.

In these studies, these three components combined to become a broad ideological orientation toward how they believe individuals and groups should accommodate each other in the larger society. Items were developed that assessed these views, phrased both positively and negatively. Positive items included: "Canada would be a better place if members of ethnic groups would keep their own way of life alive" (cultural maintenance); and "There is a lot that Canadians can gain from friendly relations with immigrants" (contact). Negative items included: "If members of ethnic groups want to keep their own culture, they should keep it to themselves, and not bother the rest of us" (expressing segregation, and negativity with respect to contact). Items also expressed the basic ideas that cultural diversity is a resource and is something to be valued by a society.

Results generally supported the construct validity of the multicultural ideology scale (e.g., Berry *et al.*, 1977; Berry and Kalin, 1995); internal consistency of the scale is high (alpha .80), and it forms part of a complex set of relationships with other conceptually similar scales (negatively with ethnocentrism, and positively with ethnic tolerance and attitudes toward immigration). However, conceptually multicultural ideology is explicitly related more to the idea that diversity is a resource for a society, and that all groups, including the dominant ones, need to adapt to each other in order for there to be harmonious intercultural relations in culturally diverse groups.

Results also showed that a large majority of Canadians endorsed multicultural ideology as the way for groups to relate to each other. In the first national survey, 63.9 percent of respondents were on the positive side of the scale, and this rose to 69.3 percent in the second survey. Overall, we can say that Canadians support this way of living together by a large and growing margin; we can also say that there public opinion rather happily coincides with public policy (Adams, 2007). In the Netherlands, Breugelmans, Van de Vijver and Schalk-Soekar (2009) found that the level of support for multiculturalism has remained stable in recent years, despite some public claims regarding the demise of support for multiculturalism. However, support in the Netherlands is higher for the second component (the removal of barriers to participation, and the reduction of discrimination) than for the first component (support for cultural maintenance and its expression, particularly in the public domain).

Thus, there is a need to monitor not only public attitudes in general, but also with respect to components of multiculturalism policy.

Analyses indicated that, rather than there being four distinct intercultural strategies in dominant groups, the items scaled into a unidimensional construct, with preferences for multiculturalism anchoring one end of the dimension, and items from the other three orientations anchoring the other end. This structure of multicultural attitudes has been confirmed by others (e.g., Arends-Tóth and Van de Vijver, 2003; Breugelmans and Van de Vijver, 2004; Breugelmans, Van de Vijver and Schalk-Soekar, 2009). This unidimensional structure may well be due to the high endorsement rate of multiculturalism items and the low endorsement rate for the alternatives. This is because when attitudes are very positive for one way of viewing intercultural relationships, and there is a common rejection of the other three ways, a unilinear structure is likely to result.

More recent examinations of multiculturalism have been carried out in the Netherlands (Van de Vijver, Breugelmans and Schalk-Soekar, 2008). They defined the concept as "the acceptance of and support for the plural nature of a society among mainstreamers and immigrant groups" (2008, p. 93). Using a scale to assess multicultural attitudes (based on the earlier multicultural ideology scale), they found that multiculturalism is "a multifaceted, unifactorial attitude with a good cross-cultural equivalence" (2008, p. 93). As in much social attitude research, an individual's level of education was positively related to support for multiculturalism. They also provided evidence of stability over time in these attitudes in the Netherlands; this is in contrast to a gradual increase in support found in Canada (Adams, 2007; Kymlicka, 2007) over the years since its inception.

One feature of research findings in the Netherlands is that there is a difference between the public and private domains of life in which an individual or cultural community can express their cultural maintenance. In much of this research, it was found that it is acceptable to express one's heritage culture in the family and in the community, but that it should not be expressed in the public domain, such as in educational or work institutions. This view is opposed to the basic principles outlined by the European Union, where the process is identified as one of mutual accommodation.

An international comparison of attitudes toward multiculturalism (Leong and Ward, 2006) used information from the Eurobarometer (2000) survey of fifteen countries. Scales assessed seven attitudes, including "blaming minorities," "multicultural optimism" and "cultural assimilation." They used an average of these scale scores, and related them to a number of other variables (including socioeconomic indicators, and Hofstede's and Schwartz's values; see Chapter 4, section on values). Higher socioeconomic levels were associated with greater support for multiculturalism, and some values (e.g., Schwartz's humanitarianism/egalitarianism) were also positively related. In contrast other values (e.g., Schwartz's conservatism, and Hofstede's collectivism) were negatively related to the acceptance of multiculturalism.

Multiculturalism hypothesis

Following from the Canadian policy, Berry *et al.* (1977, p. 192) proposed the multiculturalism hypothesis. This is expressed in the policy statement as the belief that confidence in one's identity will lead to sharing, respect for others and the reduction of discriminatory attitudes. In a nutshell, the Canadian policy (Heritage Canada, 1999, p. 2) asserts that: "Multiculturalism ensures that all citizens can keep their identities, can take pride in their ancestry and have a sense of belonging. Acceptance gives Canadians a feeling of security and self-confidence making them open to and accepting of diverse cultures."

Three varieties of the multiculturalism hypothesis have been distinguished by Moghaddam (2008). The first, as just discussed, refers to the relationship between ingroup confidence/security and the acceptance of other groups. The second concerns the relationship between ingroup affiliation and outgroup rejection. Here, the hypothesis is that there is no necessary relationship between the strength of ingroup associations and rejection of outgroups. As Brewer noted, "ingroup love is not a precursor of outgroup hate" (1999, p. 430). The third variety of the multiculturalism hypothesis concerns differential endorsement of multiculturalism by dominant and non-dominant ethnocultural groups. For example, "when minority groups endorse assimilation rather than multiculturalism, they are supporting their own 'melting away'. When majority groups endorse assimilation, they are more likely endorsing their own survival" (Moghaddam, 2008, p. 153). Hence, the multiculturalism hypothesis needs to distinguish between the views of dominant and non-dominant groups.

The multiculturalism hypothesis has been examined empirically in a number of studies in different countries (Berry, 2006c; Berry *et al.*, 1977; Phinney, Jacoby and Silva, 2007; Verkuyten, 2005a). In Canada, Berry *et al.* (1977) considered that this confidence involves a sense of security; conversely it is manifested as a sense of threat to one's cultural group. The multiculturalism hypothesis is that such a sense of security in one's identity will be a psychological precondition for the acceptance of those who are culturally different. Conversely, when their identity is threatened, people will reject others, whether they are members of other ethnocultural groups or immigrants to the society.

In two national surveys in Canada (Berry and Kalin, 2000; Berry *et al.*, 1977; reviewed by Berry, 2006c), measures of cultural security and economic security were created with respect to extant diversity, and the continuing flow of immigration. In more recent studies (Berry, 2006c) in Canada, we have found that three measures of security (cultural, economic and personal) are positively related to each other, and to the acceptance of multiculturalism, of immigrants and of a number of specific ethnocultural and immigrant groups. We thus conclude that the multiculturalism hypothesis has received support from research in Canada.

In the USA, Phinney *et al.* (2007) carried out two studies to examine the relationship between ethnic identities and attitudes toward cultural groups in a large sample of university students from different ethnocultural groups. The first study showed that Asian and Latino Americans who had an "achieved" (i.e., a secure) identity reported significantly more positive intergroup attitudes than those with a "diffuse" (i.e., unsecured) cultural identity. In their second study, using qualitative methods with adolescents from five ethnic groups, they assessed ethnic identity and attitudes. Again results "showed that ethnic identity achieved adolescents, compared to diffuse adolescents, gave responses indicating greater awareness and understanding of intergroup relations. Overall, the results provide evidence that a secure ethnic identity is associated with positive intergroup attitudes and mature intercultural thinking" (Phinney *et al.*, 2007, p. 478).

Research in New Zealand by Ward and Masgoret (2009) employed a large national sample to examine relationships between identity security, multicultural ideology and attitudes toward immigrants. The model obtained revealed significant relationships among these variables: "a strong Multicultural Ideology, high levels of Contact, and low levels of Intergroup Threat relate directly to positive Attitudes toward Immigrants, and these attitudes in turn strongly relate to the endorsement of immigration policies concerning migrant numbers and source" (2009, p. 234).

Research in the Netherlands by Verkuyten (2005a) was also intended to examine the multiculturalism hypothesis. In a series of studies, Verkuyten employed samples of Turkish-Dutch and Dutch adolescents and university students, and assessed the endorsement of multiculturalism (using the concept of multicultural ideology), the cultural identities and evaluations of ingroup and outgroup. He found that the Turkish-Dutch participants endorse multiculturalism more than the Dutch samples (which is consistent with research findings in Canada with non-dominant and dominant groups; Berry and Kalin, 2000). With respect to cultural identities, Verkuyten found that for Dutch participants, acceptance of multiculturalism was associated with a lower ingroup identification and a higher outgroup evaluation. However, for Turkish-Dutch participants, greater acceptance of multiculturalism was associated with higher ingroup identification and more positive ingroup evaluation.

In seeking to evaluate the multiculturalism hypothesis, Verkuyten did not assess identity security. Instead he assessed the strength of ingroup identity and own-group evaluation. These were assessed by scales seeking how much an individual identified with their ingroup, and how positively they evaluated it. This confusion between security of identity and strength of identity (and positive ingroup evaluation) was addressed by Berry (1984), where it was argued that they are not at all the same concepts. In ethnocentrism theory (see below) a strong ethnic identity and positive evaluation of the ingroup are known to be related to outgroup rejection, whereas the multiculturalism hypothesis proposes that a high level of identity security is related to outgroup acceptance. As argued by Berry (1984, pp. 363–364):

we need to distinguish between two forms of "confidence". If we mean simply "own group glorification", or "strongly positive ingroup attitudes", then ethnocentrism theory … predicts an opposite relationship. Indeed, in the national survey conducted by Berry *et al.* (1977) the more positively one rated one's own group, the more negatively they rated all other groups … However, the multiculturalism policy does not intend to develop confidence by own-group glorification. If we render the notion of confidence as a "sense of security"… then there is evidence of a positive relation with ethnic tolerance.

Parallel research on the relationship between security and outgroup acceptance has been carried out using the integrated threat hypothesis (see, e.g., Riek, Mania and Gaertner, 2006; Stephan, Renfro, Esses, Stephan and Martin, 2005). This hypothesis argues that a sense of threat to a person's identity (the converse of a secure cultural identity) will lead to rejection of the group that is the source of threat, and in some cases to an enhanced ethnic identity (called reactive identity). Much of this research on threat has been examined in a meta-analysis by Riek *et al.* (2006). Different types of threats have been studied, including realistic threat (e.g., due to real group conflict over resources), symbolic threat (e.g., conflicting values and beliefs) and intergroup anxiety (e.g., uncertainty about how to relate to the outgroup). Using a sample of ninety-five published studies, they found significant correlations (ranging from +.42 to +.46 for the various forms of threat) between threat and outgroup attitudes. They also found that the status of the group moderated these relationships: for outgroups with low status (e.g., ethnic minorities) anxiety had a stronger relationship with negative outgroup attitudes than when outgroups were of relatively high status. In general, they concluded that "the results of the meta-analysis indicate that intergroup threat has an important relationship with outgroup attitudes. As people perceive more intergroup competition, more value violations, higher levels of intergroup anxiety, more group esteem threats, and endorse more negative stereotypes, negative attitudes toward outgroups increase" (Riek *et al.*, 2006, p. 345).

We conclude that since first being introduced, the multiculturalism hypothesis has largely been supported. Various feelings of security and threat appear to be part of the psychological underpinnings of the acceptance of multiculturalism. Whether phrased in positive terms (security is a prerequisite for tolerance of others and the acceptance of diversity), or in negative terms (threats to, or anxiety about, one's cultural identity and cultural rights underpin prejudice), there is little doubt that there are intimate links between being accepted by others and accepting others. However, when the hypothesis is examined using other feelings (such as positive ingroup evaluation or strength of ethnic identity) rather than identity security or confidence, the opposite (ethnocentric) relationship is found.

Central theories

Contact theory

It has long been proposed that contact among ethnocultural groups in plural societies can lead to more positive intercultural relations (Allport, 1954). The basic idea is that contact and sharing among groups will promote mutual acceptance. However, the hypothesis requires that certain conditions need to be present in the contact setting: equal status between groups; sharing some common goals; some degree of cooperation; and support by authorities, laws and norms.

According to the original formulation (Allport, 1954, p. 278): "Prejudice ... may be reduced by equal status contact between majority and minority groups in the pursuit of common goals. The effect is greatly enhanced if this contact is sanctioned by institutional supports (i.e., by law, custom or local atmosphere), and provided it is of a sort that leads to the perception of common interests and common humanity between members of the two groups." Numerous overviews of this hypothesis (Pettigrew, 2008; Pettigrew and Tropp, 2006a, 2008; Pettigrew, Christ, Wagner and Stellmacher, 2007) have revealed a complex pattern of relationships between contact and attitudes. For example, Pettigrew and Tropp (2006, 2008) carried out meta-analyses of hundreds of studies of the contact hypothesis, which came from many countries and many diverse settings (schools, work, experiments). Their findings provide general support for the contact hypothesis in that intergroup contact does generally relate negatively to prejudice in both dominant and non-dominant samples: "Overall, results from the meta-analysis reveal that greater levels of intergroup contact are typically associated with lower levels of prejudice" (Pettigrew and Tropp, 2006a, p. 267). This effect was stronger where there were structured programs that incorporated the four conditions outlined by Allport than when these conditions were not present. In their second examination, Pettigrew and Tropp (2006a, p. 271) note that these conditions may not be necessary for the hypothesis to work: "integroup contact typically leads to positive outcomes even when no intergroup friendships were reported, and in the absence of Allport's proposed conditions."

The most recent meta-analysis (Pettigrew and Tropp, 2008) examined the role of three mediating variables in the relationship between contact and prejudice reduction: enhancing knowledge about the outgroup; reducing anxiety about intergroup contact; and increasing empathy and perspective taking. They found that all three mediators had effects. However, the mediational value of increased knowledge was less strong than anxiety reduction and empathy.

One important question is whether direct contact is a prerequisite for contact theory to be supported. To address this question, Pettigrew, Christ, Wagner and Stellmacher (2007) drew a large sample of adults from an ongoing study of prejudice in Germany. Direct contact was assessed by a question about the number of personal friends a respondent had who were foreigners in Germany; indirect contact was assessed by a question about the number of one's own friends having foreign friends. Prejudice was measured by two scales: one asking about foreigners in general, and one about Muslims in particular. In addition, a scale was used to assess the role of both personal and collective perceived threat. They found a correlation (+.62) between having foreign friends and having friends who had foreign friends. For both the direct and indirect measures, there were negative correlations with both prejudice measures (ranging from –. 30 to –.34). Moreover, the two forms of contact appear to reinforce each other: respondents with both forms of contact had more positive attitudes than those with only one or none. In a structural equation model to examine the role of perceived threat, they found that having foreign friends reduces both individual and collective threat. However, indirect contact through a German friend who had a foreign friend had a major effect on diminishing collective threat, while there was only a small effect on individual threat. They concluded that indirect contact is effective in reducing prejudice against foreigners. They interpreted their overall results within a normative framework: that is, they consider that there are clusters of individuals who accept foreigners as friends, for which there are norms of tolerance for foreigners.

In general, many authors (e.g., Crisp and Abrams, 2008; Kenworthy, Turner, Hewstone and Voci, 2006; Ward, 2004) conclude that contact theory is widely supported, and that there are likely to be positive consequences from increased intercultural contact.

Ethnocentrism theory

The distinctions among three kinds of groups in plural societies were outlined by Sumner (1906). These are: ingroups (groups a person belongs to, and whose norms are accepted); outgroups (those a person does not belong to, and whose norms are rejected); and positive reference groups (groups a person does not belong to, but whose norms are accepted). In plural societies, it is important to recognize this third type of group, rather than simply considering only relationships between ingroups and outgroups. This is because for some non-dominant groups, the dominant group may serve as either as an outgroup, or as a positive reference group. It is probable that the dominant society is seen as a positive reference group for those seeking to integrate or assimilate, while it is likely seen as an outgroup by those seeking to separate or marginalize. Some evidence of this was found by Berry *et al.* (1977), where both dominant cultural groups (English and French) were evaluated positively by most ethnocultural groups, usually only slightly less positively than their ingroup evaluation.

The patterns of attitudes among these three kinds of groups are addressed by ethnocentrism theory (Sumner, 1906). LeVine and Campbell (1972) proposed that ethnocentrism is a social and psychological universal. Reviewing the research they concluded that all cultural groups assess themselves in more positive terms than they assess outgroups. As noted above, one possible way of thinking about ethnocentrism is in opposition to the multiculturalism hypothesis: in ethnocentrism, the more positively persons evaluate their ingroup, the more negatively they evaluate outgroups. However, Brewer (2007) has examined this ingroup bias, and has argued that such ingroup favoritism is not necessarily associated with outgroup derogation.

This is the position taken by Berry et al. (1977), when they found evidence for ethnocentrism in Canada. In plural societies, ethnocentrism can be examined using the mutual attitudes of ethnocultural groups. In the first national survey (Berry and Kalin, 1979; Berry et al., 1977), they obtained ratings of eight groups (e.g., English-, French-, Chinese Canadians, plus "immigrants in general") on eight evaluative adjectives (e.g., "important," "clean," "interesting"), and created an overall evaluation of each group. In the second national survey (Berry and Kalin, 1995; Kalin and Berry, 1996), they assessed "comfort levels" when being around members of fourteen ethnocultural groups (same groups as in first survey, plus others, e.g., Arabs, Sikhs). In both surveys, there is clear evidence that each group holds more positive evaluations of their own group than of other groups. On the basis of these findings, they concluded that ethnocentrism is present in all ethnocultural groups, but they also found that some groups appear to be more ethnocentric than other groups. In keeping with our concept of universalism, these findings contribute to accepting ethnocentrism as a psychological universal: ethnocentrism is a widely shared phenomenon; but it varies in expression across ethnocultural groups.

Key concepts

In this section, we examine some of the key notions and processes that have served as the basis for much intercultural research and applications (Berry, 2004). Following the conventional distinction in psychology between cognition, evaluation and behavior (see, for example, Ward, 2004), intercultural relations research distinguishes between the processes of stereotype (largely cognitive), attitudes and prejudice (mainly evaluative) and discrimination (engaging in behavior). Figure 14.2 provides an overview of these distinctions, as well as identifying a set of processes within them. As for all cross-cultural psychology, we need to examine the cultural (including historical, economic and political) contexts that underlie the psychological processes that are portrayed. While the arrows in the figure are drawn from these background contexts to the psychological phenomena,

GROUP FACTORS

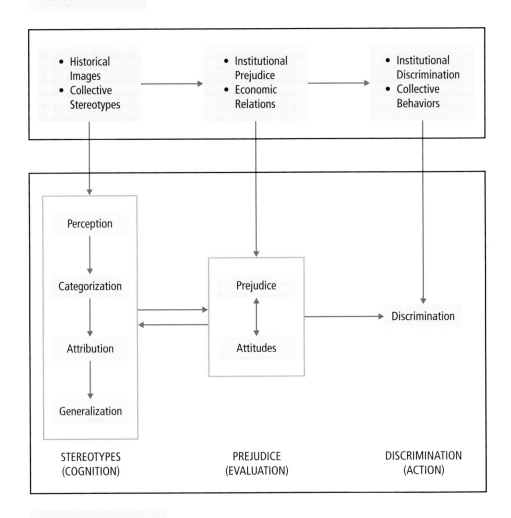

INDIVIDUAL PROCESSES

Figure 14.2 Central concepts in intercultural relations at group and individual levels.

it is also possible that some actions on the part of individuals (such as reactions to prejudice and discrimination) could lead to changes in the intercultural contexts.

These contexts are the essential underpinnings of all intercultural psychological processes and behaviors. An influential group of social psychologists (Allport, Allport, Brown, Cantril, Doob and English, 1939) early argued for this joint perspective: psychological concepts and principles are not sufficient; prejudice also needs to be understood "in terms of their economic, political and historical backgrounds"

(Allport *et al.*, p. 169). Pettigrew (2006) has identified these two distinct traditions of examining intercultural relations: one is essentially psychological and focusses on individual and intergroup processes (micro); the other is cultural and structural and focusses on societal-level factors such as prior history of relationships (macro). He also argues for the need to combine these two research levels, noting that they should be seen as complementary rather than as conflicting.

Stereotypes

If we look upon stereotypes simply as cognitive categories which are necessary to bring order to diversity (Hamilton, 1981; Jost and Hamilton, 2005), then stereotypes may be useful psychological tools to have available in plural societies. The argument is that in order to keep track of the numerous groups around them, people develop and share these generalizations as a normal psychological process. While stereotypes were earlier thought to be problematic in themselves, these acts of categorization are in essence benign; the problem lies in the overgeneralizations and the often negative evaluations (attitudes and discrimination) which are directed toward members of the categories. Thus, while stereotypes which are inaccurate or which carry negative evaluations are problematic, they can also make us aware of, and keep readily available, information which is important to have handy in day-to-day multicultural interactions. These arguments have been elaborated by Taylor, who has examined some of the "socially desirable" aspects of stereotyping in plural societies. These exist in "situations where intergroup stereotypes reflect mutual attraction, even though the members of each group maintain, through stereotypes, their own ethnic distinctiveness" (Taylor, 1981, p. 164). This situation, where a desire for positive relations *and* group distinctiveness both exist, we have identified earlier as the integration and multicultural mode of intercultural relations in plural societies.

As shown in Figure 14.2, stereotyping is rooted in the historical images and collective social representations of a group. At the psychological level, stereotyping begins with the perception of similarities and differences among a set of objects. These various observations are then subjected to an act of categorization, whereby the complexity of the stimuli is reduced to a smaller number of sets (Kosic and Phalet, 2006). The observed similarities then become attributed to members of the category; and the observed differences then become the basis for differentiating the categories. Finally, generalizations are made, so that all members of a category are believed to share in the same basic attributes of the group, resulting in loss of individuality. In essence, stereotypes are consensus views about the shared characteristic of a particular social category.

A core issue is whether stereotypes reflect reality in any way. Because they overgeneralize and deny individuality, they are clearly inaccurate representations of every person in a group. But, is there any evidence that some qualities that are attributed to members reflect some reality? One approach to this question has been made by Campbell (1967) when addressing this "kernel of truth" issue. He proposed that the greater the real cultural differences between two groups of people, then the more likely these differences will appear in their mutual stereotypes. In a study in East Africa (Brewer and Campbell, 1976) with 1,500 participants belonging to thirty different cultural groups, they found some evidence for the "mirror image" phenomenon. For example, if two groups are in conflict, each sees itself as "peaceful" and the other as "warlike"; and these stereotypes are reciprocated. Thus, there is some convergence of evidence for the validity of stereotypes in intergroup relations. However, it is probably the case that their usefulness is outweighed by their problems of overgeneralization.

Much recent work has been carried out using a stereotype content model (Fiske, Cuddy, Glick and Xu, 2002). This model distinguishes between two dimensions of stereotypes: competence and warmth. When these two dimensions are crossed, four variations appear in the content of group stereotypes: high competence and high warmth are associated with "admiration"; high competence and low warmth with "envy"; low competence and low warmth with "contempt"; and low competence and high warmth with "paternalism." When applied to the perception of immigrant and other kinds of groups by US-American university students (Lee and Fiske, 2006), four clusters of groups appear in this two-dimensional space. Low competence and warmth are assigned to homeless and poor people, and to undocumented migrants; high competence and low warmth are assigned to rich people, professionals and to immigrants from East Asia; high competence and warmth are assigned to college students, third-generation immigrants and immigrants from Europe and Canada; while medium competence and high warmth are assigned to housewives, elderly people and immigrants from Italy and Ireland. From these studies, it is clear that at least two dimensions are required to distinguish the stereotypes that are held of various groups.

Prejudice

Turning to the evaluation of groups in intercultural relations, there are two distinguishable but related concepts: general ethnic prejudice and ethnic attitudes toward specific groups. As for stereotypes, we need to understand the historical and cultural roots of these evaluations. There are often economic factors at work as well; we may derogate those we seek to exploit. And those with whom we have been in conflict are often viewed negatively, even generations after the conflict has ended (Liu and Hilton, 2005).

A central concept in intercultural relations is that of ethnic prejudice. A comprehensive survey of prejudice (Dovidio, Glick and Rudman, 2005) was published on the fiftieth anniversary of the classic volume by Allport (1954). The study of ethnic prejudice has burgeoned in the past fifty years, but much of it has been carried out in a single society, rather than across cultures. Some exceptions to this observation are the pan-European studies of prejudice using the 1997 and 2000 Eurobarometer surveys (Jackson, Brown, Brown and Marks, 2001; Leong and Ward, 2006), and Green (2007), who used data from the 2003 European Social Survey.

Jackson *et al.* (2001) sought evidence of predictors of prejudice toward immigrants among approximately 15,000 respondents in fifteen Western European countries. Using a sample of 890 respondents who were self-identified as part of the dominant group, they assessed self- and group-interest, racism and perceived threat, permitting a further examination of the multiculturalism hypothesis. Attitudes toward immigrants included the view that immigrants should be sent back to their countries of origin; self-interest was assessed by scales including family income; and perceived threat was examined by a scale of items such as "The presence of people from minority groups is a cause of insecurity." In regression analyses, perceived threat explained the largest proportion in the variance in negative attitudes toward immigrants.

A second study using data from Eurobarometer (Leong and Ward, 2006) examined the role of national values (using both the Hofstede and Schwartz country-level values). It also employed some socioeconomic variables (such as GNP and unemployment) as predictors of attitudes. These attitudes were assessed by scales of Blame (e.g., "non-European immigrants tend to abuse the system of social welfare"); Policies (e.g., accepting the creation of organizations to bring people of different origins together); Disturbance (e.g., personally finding the presence of people of another nationality disturbing in one's daily life); Multiculturalism (e.g., "this country's diversity in terms of race, religion and culture adds to its strengths"); and Assimilation (e.g., "In order to become fully accepted members of this country, people from non-European backgrounds must give up their own culture"). They found that the national values as mastery, masculinity, power distance, uncertainty avoidance and collectivism were negatively related to national attitudes toward multiculturalism and immigrants. The economic indicators also predicted these attitudes: countries that were more affluent tended to have higher support for policies promoting intercultural contact. However, the other economic factors had little relationship. Overall, Leong and Ward (2006) concluded that values have a substantial role in the level of support for multiculturalism and for immigrants and immigration.

In an analysis of data from the 2003 European Social Survey, Green (2007) found three distinct clusters of persons that varied according to their attitudes toward immigrants in Europe. Items posed questions about categorical entry criteria (such as skin color and religion) and individual expulsion criteria (such as criminal history, unemployment). One group was designated as lenient gatekeepers (23% of sample), who opposed all criteria. A second group was termed strict gatekeepers (36%), who favored all criteria. A third group, called individualistic gatekeepers (41%), favored individual criteria but opposed categorical criteria. Individual membership in these three types of gatekeeper groups was predicted by years of education, age, contact with immigrants and another form of prejudice (homophobia). Countries also varied in their cluster membership: Sweden, Norway and Denmark were in the lenient gatekeeper cluster; Poland, Portugal, Greece and Hungary were strict gatekeepers; and Switzerland, Germany and the Netherlands were individualist gatekeepers. Green notes that these distinctions appear to have a geographical distribution (they are Northern, Eastern/Southern and Western Europe countries respectively) and suggests that the history of labor-needs policies and resources may explain these country differences.

The most researched forms of prejudice have been with respect to immigrants (e.g., Leong, 2008) and "race." In much recent research, a distinction has been made between old-fashioned and new (or modern) racism (Vala, 2009). This distinction is rooted in the finding that many individuals are now reluctant to openly express racist attitudes, and seek to express racism indirectly. This change has been accompanied by a shift from a focus on the biological basis of group differentiation to a cultural basis, and even to non-specific expressions of inferiority and superiority (e.g., in research on social dominance orientation; Sidanius and Pratto, 1999). In this research, non-group-specific items are used (e.g., "Some people are just inferior to others") to elicit generalized prejudice.

In the USA, research on racism has been dominated by the examination of prejudice against peoples of African origin (Pettigrew, 2009). In much of Europe, research has tended to use the concept of xenophobia and is focussed on people of Muslim faith or Arab origin (Westin, Bastos, Dahinden and Góis, 2009). An example of this interest is research in the Netherlands by González, Verkuyten, Weesie and Poppe (2008). They examined prejudice toward Muslims (as well as acceptance of multiculturalism) among a large sample of Dutch adolescents, using a set of predictors that assessed both realistic and symbolic threat, contact, stereotypes and ingroup identification. They found that about half the respondents had negative feelings regarding Muslims, and that symbolic threat (but not realistic threat) and stereotypes predicted these negative attitudes. In a complex analysis, the relationship between ingroup identification and prejudice was mediated by symbolic threat, and contact and acceptance of multiculturalism predicted prejudice. The authors concluded that

These findings are in line with previous research in the Netherlands (Verkuyten, 2005a) and with Berry's (2006c) argument that multiculturalism can provide confidence, trust, and security among everyone living in pluralistic societies ... Multiculturalism seems to provide a general ideological view about the importance of cultural diversity that not only reduces a sense of group threat but also emphasizes that people should be recognized and valued in their group identity, and that there should be social equality and equal opportunities. (Gonzalez *et al.*, 2008, p. 680)

A fundamental feature of plural societies is that a complex pattern of interethnic attitudes is likely to exist between ingroup and outgroup members. A basic argument is that there should be consideration of reciprocal attitudes (in a two-group case) or of the matrix of ethnic attitudes among all interacting groups in a plural society, rather than a focus on just what the dominant group thinks about or how it evaluates various non-dominant groups. As noted above, the first study to take this approach was that of Brewer and Campbell (1976) in East Africa, who studied the mutual stereotypes of fifty cultural groups; they also studied their mutual attitudes. Subsequently, Berry and Kalin (1979) drew data from a national survey (Berry *et al.*, 1977) and extracted attitudes toward the five most numerous ethnic groups in the sample. The data in the five-by-five matrix have each group's own group rating on the diagonal, while the two halves of the matrix contain the particular pairs of intergroup ratings. Three questions may be asked of such a matrix: First, does the ethnocentric tendency to rate one's own group relatively highly hold for all groups? Second, does the tendency to rate all other groups in a consistent hierarchy also hold? And third, is there a balanced relationship (Heider, 1958) among the mutual attitudes held by a pair of groups? The answers to these three questions are all positive.

Discrimination

A concrete outcome to these various cognitive and evaluative processes is the level of discrimination to be found in plural societies. There is substantial evidence to support the important role of discrimination in various psychological phenomena, including acculturation strategies (e.g., Berry *et al.*, 2006) and adaptation (e.g., Jasinskaja-Lahti, Liebkind, Jaakkola and Reuter, 2006). Critics of multiculturalism as a general policy often claim that it has, as its real motive, the wish "to keep people in their place" by more easily identifying them as different and perhaps of lower value in society. In terms of the two issues at the base of the intercultural strategies framework, it is indeed possible that culturally distinct peoples are encouraged by a larger society to maintain their differences in order to exclude them from day-to-day participation in the economic, political and educational life of the society. The danger has been recognized by many observers of multiculturalism, and has been identified by Jayasuriya (1990) as the possibility of one's "life style" limiting one's "life chances" in Australian society.

Note that discrimination is used here to refer not only to acts of forceful exclusion (such as in segregation and exclusion), but also to forceful inclusion (as in assimilation into the melting pot). Only in the multicultural way of organizing intercultural relations, when a society is open to and accepting of the wishes of an individual or group, and where individuals are free to choose their preferred degrees of cultural maintenance and participation in the larger society, do we consider there to be no discrimination.

Conclusions

The domain of intercultural relations is inherently concerned with both culture and social behavior. However, only recently has the field come to be cross-cultural in the sense that these relationships are examined in multiple cultural settings. Just as for acculturation research, where most studies are "one shot" (i.e., the examination of one group acculturating in one society), intercultural relations research has often been similarly "one shot" (the examination of relations in one society). Moreover, as for acculturation research, most intercultural relations studies are not carried out globally, nor in societies where the most problematic intercultural relations are manifested (such as in China, India and Russia). Clearly, in order to achieve some general understanding of the theories and principles outlined in this chapter, comparative research is required. Given the moderate universalist position adopted in this text, we believe that some general principles may well emerge from such comparative research. Already, ethnocentrism and contact theories appear to have been established as a psychological universal. There is a need for a parallel examination of the concepts reviewed here, including the multiculturalism hypothesis. If these are widely supported, there may well be a basis for pursuing the goal of international accommodation and peace through equal status contact and mutual security.

KEY TERMS

attitudes (ethnic) • contact hypothesis • discrimination • ethnocentrism ethnocultural group • ingroup • intercultural strategies • multicultural ideology multiculturalism • multiculturalism hypothesis • outgroup • plural society • positive reference group • prejudice (ethnic) • security • stereotype (ethnic) • threat • tolerance • xenophobia

FURTHER READING

Dovidio, P., Glick, A., and Rudman, A. (eds.) (2005). *On the nature of prejudice: Fifty years after Allport*. Oxford: Blackwell.

An essential review of research on one of the most influential theories in intercultural relations.

Pettigrew, T. (2008). Future directions for intergroup contact theory and research. *International Journal of Intercultural Relations*, 32, 187–189.

A thoughtful look forward to where contact theory could contribute to the improvement of intercultural relations.

Smith, P., Bond, M. H., and Kağitçibaşi, C. (2006). *Understanding social psychology across cultures: Living and working in a changing world.* London: Sage.

A comprehensive overview of many domains of social behavior, including insights into intercultural relations.

Ward, C. (2004). Psychological theories of culture contact and their implications for intercultural training and interventions. In D. Landis, J. M. Bennett and M. J. Bennett (eds.), *Handbook of intercultural training* (pp. 185–216). Thousand Oaks, Calif.: Sage.

An overview and evaluation of the psychological aspects of intercultural contact research.

Ward, C., and Leong, C.-H. (2006). Intercultural relations in plural societies. In D. Sam and J. W. Berry (eds.), *The Cambridge handbook of acculturation psychology* (pp. 484–503). Cambridge: Cambridge University Press.

A presentation of the main features of intercultural relations in plural societies.

15 | Intercultural communication and training

CONTENTS

With growing migration, globalization and internationalization comes an increased need for an understanding of intercultural communication, as well as the use of this information for training people in order to make them more competent in dealing with intercultural issues. The field is very diverse, with publications from a wide variety of scientific and applied disciplines. For example, there is research in linguistics (especially sociolinguistics), sociology, cultural anthropology and cross-cultural psychology. Much of this variety can be surveyed in a handbook edited by Landis, Bennett and Bennett (2004). In this chapter, we mainly focus on the psychological aspects of intercultural communication and training, and point out important issues and studies from a psychological perspective.

This chapter contains three main sections, each representing a distinct area of intercultural communication and training. The first, on intercultural communication, describes the attempts of researchers to delineate which elements of communication are the sources of communication problems during intercultural encounters. This section is somewhat more theoretical than later sections because the main questions focus on the nature of intercultural communication rather than on the application of this knowledge. The second section concerns sojourners, those people who stay in another culture mostly for purposes of work or study (e.g., international exchange students). This is a special group of acculturating people that has already been discussed in Chapter 13. In addition to the usual acculturation issues that were described in that chapter, there are a number of specific aspects in the acculturation of sojourners that are described here. The final section is on intercultural competency and training. The growing number of intercultural contacts and the concomitant number of failures and problems in such contacts has spurred researchers to develop training programs to increase people's intercultural effectiveness. We present an overview of the different types of training that are available and of the evidence for their effectiveness. One further topic (intercultural negotiation) can be found on the Internet (Additional Topics, Chapter 15).

www.cambridge.org/berry

This chapter differs somewhat from many other discussions on intercultural communication in the sense that it deals mainly with temporary settlers and visitors to another country. More permanent forms of intergroup contact and acculturation were dealt with in Chapters 13 and 14. In addition, much of the intercultural communication literature emphasizes the significance of intercultural contacts for personal development and growth (notably of sojourners from western societies; Jandt, 2007; Ting-Toomey, 2005a). This is an important topic, but it is usually not considered to form part of cross-cultural psychology, so it is not discussed in detail here.

Intercultural communication

Intercultural communication problems

In the chapters of Part I we have argued that modes of social, linguistic and cognitive functioning and the underlying processes are by and large shared across cultures. This similarity makes it possible for people from different cultural and linguistic backgrounds to communicate with each other, at least in principle. However, when employing a distinction between process, competence and performance (see the section on generalization in Chapter 1), a similarity in underlying processes does not imply that their manifestations in actual communication patterns are also the same. Because of variations in these manifestations, a number of failures of communication can occur. Moreover, it is important to distinguish between failures of communication that are obvious and more subtle errors that go unnoticed.

Both linguistic and non-linguistic forms of communication play a role in intercultural communication. Most important is language, which is a highly culture-specific medium. If two people do not share a common language their interactions are severely restricted. Less obvious are communication difficulties when command of a common language is less than perfect. Variations in pronunciation and usage of English have long been a point of concern in air traffic control (Ruffell Smith, 1975).

Prosodic aspects of language, which include emphasis (pitch, loudness) and intonation contours, also occasionally can lead to misunderstandings. A classic example comes from the work of Gumperz (1982). Indian and Pakistani women working in a staff cafeteria in Britain were seen as surly and uncooperative. Gumperz observed that the few words they said could be interpreted negatively. When serving out food a British assistant would say "gravy?" with a rising intonation. The Indian and Pakistani women would use the same word, but pronounce it with a falling intonation. To the people they served this sounded like a statement of fact that under the circumstances was redundant and sometimes rude. Listening to taped sequences the migrant women at first could not hear any differences. After some training they began to recognize the point. During the training it also became clear to the women why attitudes toward them had often been negative, and they regained confidence in their ability to learn.

It is likely that there are commonalities across cultures in pragmatic aspects of language, such as the taking of turns in conversations, exchange of compliments, politeness and an indirect versus a direct style of communication (for a summary see Blum-Kulka, House and Kasper, 1988). At the same time, there is evidence for cross-cultural differences. For example, considering linguistic as well as non-linguistic cues, Ambady, Koo, Lee and Rosenthal (1996) found that politeness among Koreans was influenced more by relational cues than among US-Americans. Also, Barnlund and Araki (1985) found Japanese to be less direct in paying compliments and more modest in expressing them verbally than US-Americans.

In Chapter 7 (p. 161) research on connotative and denotative meaning of words was discussed. Although there appears to be substantial evidence for similarity in connotative meanings across languages, there is also evidence of some differences; these can easily lead to misunderstandings. In the same chapter research on non-verbal communication in the form of emotion expression in the face or in the tone of voice was also discussed (see p. 172). We have seen that even if emotions are similar across cultures, the rules about which emotion can be shown, and in which situation, may vary across cultures (display rules).

Another aspect of non-verbal or bodily communication is the use of gestures. The notion of gestures as a universal, albeit rudimentary, form of communication gained some popularity (e.g., Kendon, 1984). However, like linguistic utterances, the meaning of a specific gesture can differ strongly across cultures. For example, Morris, Collett, Marsh and O'Shaughnessy (1979) found that common well-defined gestures can have a different meaning in various regions of Europe; and even within countries they are not always used with the same meaning. Ekman and his co-workers (e.g., Ekman, 1982; Ekman and Friesen, 1969) distinguished various categories of gestures, such as adaptors (or body manipulators), regulators, illustrators and emblems. Adaptors, like scratching one's nose, developed from movements connected with bodily needs or interpersonal contacts. In the course of development they can become fragmented and lose their function. Scratching one's nose when deep in thought can be a remnant of nose picking. Child training includes the modification of adaptors, especially those that are considered improper in the presence of others. Regulators are head and arm gestures or body postures that play a role in taking turns in listening and speaking in conversations between two or more interactants. They are often made without explicit awareness, so they can lead to misunderstandings between people from different cultures. Illustrators are directly tied to speech; they serve to underline or depict what is being said and are related to features of the language.

Emblems have a cognitive meaning by themselves that is usually familiar to members of a culture. They are meant to communicate this meaning and normally there is a verbal equivalent; the research by Morris *et al.* (1979) was based on emblems. Emblems are most prone to cross-cultural differences in meaning because they are strongly tied to specific concepts. However, some emblems may still be understood even when the perceiver has no knowledge of the culture of the sender. The arm gesture "come to me" is likely to be understood worldwide but a fist with an outstretched finger to indicate a gun offers no basis for recognition for someone who has no prior knowledge of guns. Ekman and Friesen (1969) made a distinction between referential emblems, where the distance between the form of a gesture and the referent (what is being depicted) is small, and conventional emblems, where this difference is large and dependent on prior cultural knowledge. Poortinga, Schoots and Van de Koppel (1993) found that Dutch students could not only give the meaning of referential emblems generated by persons from China and Kurdistan, but also reported that most of these gestures were present in their own culture. This suggests that there is a repertoire of referential emblems common to at least a broad range of cultures. However, the rate of recognition for conventional emblems varied; a few, like some emblems depicting a Chinese character for a numeral, were interpreted correctly below chance level in a multiple-choice test. Most reports focus on differences. For example, Pika, Nikolada and Marentette (2009) analyzed for three western groups (English and French Canadians and Germans) how finger gestures are being used to signal numbers. The most important difference observed was that the German respondents used the thumb and the Canadians the index finger to signal the number 1.

Related to gestures are body position and personal space. Most of the research is of a less recent date and has been summarized by Altman and Chemers (1980). The notion of personal space is based on the idea that every person is surrounded by a private sphere. When somebody comes and stands too close to us this is experienced as an intrusion. The anthropologist Hall (1966) was the first to draw attention to cross-cultural differences in personal space. He noted that Arabs, Southern Europeans and Latin Americans stand close together when talking. They tend to touch each other and even breathe in each other's faces, while people of Northern European descent keep a much greater physical distance. Hall postulated a dimension ranging from high-contact to low-contact cultures. Sussman and Rosenfeld (1982) found that Japanese students in the USA were seated further apart than students from Venezuela when talking in their own languages. When speaking English this difference disappeared: students from Japan and Venezuela were then seated at a similar distance as observed for students from the USA. This suggests that cross-cultural differences tend to be situation-specific.

The literature on sources of intercultural communication problems suggests that most problems emerge from situation-specific differences in customs and meaning (see the discussion on cultural conventions in the section on psychological organization of cross-cultural differences in Chapter 12). Unlike research on psychological preferences, such as values in Chapter 4, there appear to be no underlying dimensions of cross-cultural differences. It is not known how often and how seriously intercultural encounters are disrupted by an insufficient comprehension of prosodic and pragmatic aspects of language, or by errors of non-verbal communication. Unfamiliarity with social rules and customs certainly adds to the ignorance and consequent ineptness of a stranger. It seems that most of the evident misunderstandings tend to arise out of concrete conventions in everyday social situations that a stranger misinterprets or is unaware of. Triandis (1975) reports the example of the Greek villager inviting someone to dinner and mentioning that he is welcome "any time." For a US-American this amounts to a non-invitation; the vagueness of the time makes it noncommittal. However, the Greek villager means to convey literally that his guest will be welcome at any time.

Theories of intercultural communication

Most studies on sources of intercultural communication problems tend to focus on specific problems in specific situations or modalities of communication. We suggested that various problems have little in common with each other; and we did not postulate any theoretical dimension or model to organize them. However, various more theoretical approaches to intercultural communication have been developed that do attempt to provide such an organization. These are discussed in this subsection.

Theories of intercultural communication try to provide explanations for communication difficulties in terms of broad sociocultural factors (Gudykunst, 2005a;

Gudykunst and Mody, 2002). According to Gudykunst, Lee, Nishida and Ogawa (2005) there are three ways in which culture can be included in communication theory. First, culture can be integrated explicitly into the theory. Second, theories can seek to explain cultural variations in communication. Third, theories can seek to explain communication patterns between individuals from different cultures when they are interacting.

An example of the first kind of theory is speech code theory (Philipsen, 1997; Philipsen, Coutu and Covarrubias, 2005), which is built around a series of propositions. One postulate is that each culture is characterized by a distinctive speech code: "A speech code is a system of socially-constructed symbols and meanings, premises, and rules pertaining to communicative conduct" (Philipsen, 1997, p. 126). This formulation indicates that the theory has intersubjectivist (see Chapter 10, p. 226) and social constructionist leanings (see Chapter 12, p. 283), with an emphasis on meanings as communicative acts in which cultures differ from each other. This is further emphasized in another proposition that a speech code implies a culturally distinctive psychology and rhetoric. Thus, speech is the central feature in terms of which everything else, including individual and social behavior, can be explained. Philipsen *et al.* (2005) admit that most of the propositions of the theory cannot be tested directly, but they argue that there is an accumulation of indirect empirical evidence that is consistent with the theory.

The second type of theory often refers to value dimensions such as individualism–collectivism for the explanation of cultural variations (Gudykunst *et al.*, 2005). Although value dimensions were not formulated originally as communication theories, they can be seen as frameworks for understanding cross-cultural differences in communication. For example, more egalitarian versus more socially dominant patterns of communication relate to Hofstede's power distance dimension (Hofstede, 1980).

Another dimension refers to variation between low-context and high-context cultures (Hall, 1976). For example, Ting-Toomey's face-negotiation theory (e.g., Ting-Toomey, 1985, 2005b) has two foci: "face" (reflecting a sense of identity and self-worth in relations with others) and conflict-handling. Conflict situations are seen as emotional and as face-threatening. In terms of differentiation between countries, the distinction between low-context and high-context cultures more or less parallels the distinction between low-contact and high-contact cultures. Within high-context cultures much of the information in communication processes is shared by the sender and receiver of a message or is present in the context. Within low-context cultures, much of the information is made explicit in the transmitted message. Most western countries can be qualified as low-context cultures, while Japan, Korea and Vietnam are high-context cultures. In more recent writings individualism–collectivism, and the distinction between the interdependent and the independent construal of the self have become the main parameters for categorizing cultures (Ting-Toomey, 2005b). In empirical studies some support for these distinctions has been found (e.g., Oetzel and Ting-Toomey, 2003).

As an example of the third kind of theory Gudykunst *et al.* (2005) refer to Gudykunst's (e.g., 1993, 2005b, 2005c) Anxiety/Uncertainty Management (AUM) Theory. The idea is that in order to enable effective communication, both anxiety and uncertainty need to be managed and maintained at a certain level (not too high and not too low). There is cross-cultural variation in these management processes, mainly along the lines of the individualism–collectivism dimension. Part of the overall AUM theorizing deals with intercultural adaptation of sojourners. The latter are seen as strangers to the cultures they are visiting. A defining feature is that they tend to perceive their interactions with locals "as a series of crises" (Gudykunst, 2005b, p. 421). Uncertainty management and anxiety management to deal with people and situations in the host society are seen as antecedent to intercultural adjustment. Self-concept or self-esteem, motivation to interact with members of the host culture and reactions to them are conceptualized in detail in an elaborate set of theoretical axioms for which we refer to Gudykunst's (e.g., 2005a, b) writings.

There is a noticeable difference between the studies on the sources of intercultural communication problems described in the previous section and the theories of intercultural communication in this section. Whereas much empirical research seems to point to communication problems being rather situation-specific, most theories tend to invoke broad cultural dimensions to describe communication differences. A central question is what type of explanation – a situation-specific or a general, dimensional explanation – best fits intercultural communication problems. Take as an example the casting down of one's eyes when interacting with a superior, which is found in some countries, instead of maintaining eye contact, found in other countries. This difference could be seen as the expression of local conventions that are highly situation-dependent (people do not cast down their eyes in every situation), but also as an instance of the power distance dimension (Hofstede, 1980, 2001). The latter explanation clearly involves more general assumptions about the nature of cross-cultural differences than does an explanation in terms of conventions or customs.

Sojourners

Chapter 13 already discussed the status of sojourners, or expatriates, as a special group of people who have to deal with acculturation processes (see Bochner, 2006; Ward, Bochner and Furnham, 2001). As noted above, much research on sojourners is closely linked with an intercultural communication and training perspective. So-journers generally expect that they will only reside in another country or culture for a limited amount of time (e.g., the duration of their contract or course of study) and they tend to have institutional support from their employer or university, even up to regular "Skype" meetings via Internet with the home organization. Therefore, the acculturation issues that they are presented with are weighted differently than those for more permanent migrants. A certain kind of acculturation is always necessary, but the knowledge of an eventual return to their culture of origin leads to an emphasis on the acquisition of sociocultural skills and less on questions of changing identity or other behaviors (Berry, in press b). In addition, because most sojourner visits to another country are planned beforehand, there is a stronger emphasis on selection, preparation and training in order to facilitate intercultural efficiency. As we shall see later in this chapter, preparation is often focussed more on the acquisition of linguistic proficiency than of cultural proficiency.

Sojourner adjustment

The origin of the term "culture shock" is credited to the anthropologist Oberg (1960), who used it to indicate the difficulties that arise from exposure to an unfamiliar environment. Oberg referred to the strain of making new adaptations, a sense of loss, confusion about one's role and feelings of anxiety. In the AUM theory of Gudykunst (2005a, b) we have seen that the interactions with strangers are referred to as a series of crises. Guthrie (1966) mentioned the frustration of subtle cultural differences that impede social interactions. In an extensive project with foreign students from 139 nations studying in eleven countries, a quarter reported feelings of depression (Klineberg and Hull, 1979). The extent to which difficulties are experienced is not the same for all sojourners. Major variables include the distance between home culture and host culture, the type of involvement, the duration of contact and the status of the visitor in the host country (as subordinates, managers, students; see Bochner, 1982, 2006).

There has been debate over how the adjustment of sojourners to the new culture over the course of time is shaped (Ward *et al.*, 2001). This adjustment has sometimes been said to follow a U-shaped curve. Sojourners initially have few problems; they are enthusiastic and fascinated by new experiences. After some time, feelings of frustration, loneliness and anxiety take over. Still later, as the sojourner learns to cope, well-being increases again. The U-curve has been extended to a double U, or W, curve to include a period of adjustment after the return of sojourners to their homeland (see Brein and David, 1971). At first there is the thrill of being back in the known environment and of meeting family and friends. Then disappointments occur because some of the more positive aspects of the life abroad are lost. Finally, after some time readjustment follows.

Despite the intuitive appeal the U-curve and W-curve have not stood up well to empirical scrutiny. An overview of research by Ward *et al.* (2001, 2004) has shown that some individuals follow such patterns, but many others do not. The stress of acculturation experienced by many sojourners can decrease rather than increase over time (e.g., Ward and Kennedy, 1994). The utility of U-curves and W-curves can be questioned because of the many uncertainties concerning the precise form and the time period over which non-linear changes occur (see Furnham and Bochner, 1986).

At a mundane level there is little doubt that newcomers to a culture have problems because they are unfamiliar (and often not at ease) with the prevalent rules, social norms and other cultural conventions. Gradually sojourners will acquire the knowledge and skills they need in order to handle social encounters competently. One study which shows this clearly was reported by Ward, Okura, Kennedy and Kojima (1999). They conducted a longitudinal study with Japanese students in New Zealand, who completed questionnaires assessing psychological and sociocultural adaptation at various times in the course of a year. Ward, Okura *et al.* found that adjustment problems were greatest at the beginning and decreased over time.

Intercultural personality

Despite the recognition that individuals may differ in the extent to which they engage in the acculturation process, clear results on personality and acculturation have not yet been obtained (Kosic, 2006). Research has largely examined different aspects of personal characteristics of the individual (broadly defined as personality) and how these characteristics may enhance or hinder adaptation. One goal of this line of research has been to identify an "overseas type" who could readily adjust to a new cultural environment by focussing on how certain characteristics of the individual (e.g., ethnocentric tendencies) affected adjustment (see Church, 1982, for review). Research on acculturation and personality has usually examined one or more personality characteristics or cognitive abilities to see their effect on stress reduction in the adaptation process.

Of numerous studies few have succeeded in demonstrating convincingly the role of personality traits in cross-cultural adaptation (e.g., Bakker, Van Oudenhoven and Van der Zee, 2004; Valentine, 2001; Ward, Chang and Lopez-Nerney, 1999; Ward, Leong and Low, 2004). In an early study among Canadians working abroad, Kealey (1989) found that personality traits were poor predictors of a diverse set of fourteen outcome variables. When standard personality traits are used (e.g., the "Big Five," the EPQ; see Chapter 5, the section on other trait dimensions) they do not seem to predict intercultural adjustment over and above more specific skills (Matsumoto, LeRoux, Bernhard and Gray, 2004). A few other studies have found some support for the predictive role of personality traits, although effects were rather modest (e.g., Mak and Tran, 2001). A meta-analysis of thirty empirical studies on the prediction of expatriate job performance found that predictive validities of the Big Five for sojourners were similar to those reported for domestic employees (Mol, Born, Willemsen and Van der Molen, 2005). Extraversion, emotional stability, agreeableness and conscientiousness were predictive of expatriate job performance; openness was not. There may also be an indirect effect of general personality traits in the sense that they facilitate or hinder the development of specific skills such as emotion regulation or critical thinking, which in turn predict intercultural adjustment (Matsumoto, LeRoux, Robles and Campos, 2007).

A recurring problem in studies on the role of personality in cross-cultural adaptation is that "adjustment" is an ill-defined construct. In Chapter 13 we already mentioned that cross-cultural adjustment has been examined in different ways (e.g., mental health indicators, interactions with members of the national society, feelings of acceptance, school achievement, job performance and satisfaction with life). We also pointed out that this makes it difficult to establish the predictive ability of personality (Ward and Chang, 1997). Mol, Born and Van der Molen (2005) have argued that adjustment should be seen as – at most – a mediating variable between predictors and expatriate effectiveness. They propose the development of more adequate sampling of expatriate job performance in order to test the predictive power of skills, conditions and personality types.

One way forward in personality studies of sojourners may be the inclusion of "person–situation" interactions. The "fit" between the personal characteristics and norms in the new cultural setting could be a better predictor of immigrants' adaptation than personality per se (i.e., the cultural-fit hypothesis; Searle and Ward, 1990). Ward and Chang (1997) showed that US-Americans living in Singapore were more extrovert than Singaporeans and consequently experienced frustration or rejection in response to their attempts to initiate and sustain social relations with the locals. Whereas extraversion was not directly related to psychological well-being, those sojourners who perceived the host-society norms as less discrepant with their norms had a lower level of psychological distress and depression. However, Ward, Leong and Low (2004) reported a study among students and expatriates from Australia and Singapore that did not support the cultural-fit hypothesis. Neuroticism and extraversion were related to psychological and sociocultural adaptation in both sojourning samples.

Another way forward may be to develop more specific instruments geared at assessing only those aspects of personality that are most relevant to sojourner performance. One example is the Intercultural Adjustment Potential Scale – an instrument that is specifically geared toward predicting intercultural adjustment (Matsumoto et al., 2001). This scale measures traits, such as emotion regulation, openness, flexibility and critical thinking, that are more relevant to intercultural competency than are general traits such as the Big Five. Matsumoto et al. (2007) reported that the ICAPS predicted intercultural adjustment over and above traditional personality scales in a sample of international students in the USA. The Multicultural Personality Questionnaire is another example of an instrument that has been specifically developed to measure traits that are relevant to people working in international and multicultural environments (Van der Zee and Van Oudenhoven, 2000, 2001). It measures cultural empathy, open-mindedness, social initiative, emotional stability and flexibility – a number of traits that are related to the Big Five but more specifically geared toward predicting intercultural effectiveness. There are some results indicating that the traits measured by this scale are related to psychological and social well-being in a foreign environment (Van Oudenhoven and Van der Zee, 2002).

All in all, the evidence on personal factors being important in the success of sojourners is relatively scant. Many practitioners take the view that a focus on conditions and skills seems to be more fruitful for understanding the causes of sojourner success and well-being than a focus on trait-like dimensions. Skills and conditions have the additional advantage that they can be better targeted by means of interventions such as intercultural competency training which are discussed in the next section. However, there is still a strong appeal to looking for personal qualities that can predict sojourner success. One of the most recent additions to this tradition is that of "cultural intelligence," which can be found in Box 15.1.

Intercultural competence

Until now, this chapter has mainly focussed on the sources of intercultural communication problems and on the antecedents of sojourner adjustment and well-being. There is another, though partly overlapping, field of research that is more directly geared at intercultural competence (Deardorff, 2009). Theory development in intercultural competence is reminiscent of that in the field of intercultural communication (discussed earlier in this chapter). Both fields are characterized by conceptual schemes bringing together high-order inclusive concepts. An overview of such schemes on intercultural competence has been given by Spitzberg and Chagnon (2009).

A more applied question is how intercultural communication and work performance of sojourners may be enhanced by means of interventions. There are many training modules for intercultural competence; most have been developed for application in a business context. One characteristic of the field of intercultural competence training is that it has been driven by pragmatic demands. Empirical research on intercultural competence started in the 1960s among Peace Corps volunteers from the USA, when there was an increased need to deal with the problems arising from intercultural contact and communication.

Perhaps as a result of its practical orientation, empirical tests of the effectiveness of training have tended to trail behind the development of new training (Van de Vijver and Breugelmans, 2008; Van de Vijver and Leung, 2009). In this section, we will mainly focus on research on sojourner effectiveness and on the types of training that are available and on the evidence that has been gathered with respect to their effectiveness.

Sojourner effectiveness

Research on the effectiveness and competence of sojourners has mainly focussed on three types of variables: external conditions, skills and personality (Van de Vijver and Breugelmans, 2008). Of these the first two are more important for intervention studies (external conditions can be adjusted and skills can be trained), whereas the third variable is more important for selection (which type of sojourner is more likely to be successful?). Kealey, Protheroe, MacDonald and Vulpe (2005) have emphasized the necessity to take both environmental and personal qualities into account with respect to the success of overseas sojourns. They conclude that interpersonal skills and cultural knowledge, as well as the organization of the project and the environmental context (regulations in the host country, economic factors) are all important.

An example of the importance of external conditions is given by the landmark study by Torbiörn (1982) with 800 Swedish expatriates. He obtained data from approximately thirty persons (business men and their wives) in each of twenty-six countries by means of a postal survey. He found that only 8 percent of the respondents reported being unhappy, which was a low percentage. Much larger percentages have been mentioned, notably by Tung (1981), who found lack of success in up to 30 percent of US managers, although in subsequent surveys this figure was much lower (Tung, 1998; Harzing, 1995).

Torbiörn also found no evidence that accompanying spouses were more frequently unhappy than the workers. However, he strongly confirmed that one cannot have a successful sojourn when one's family is unhappy. Perhaps the most salient result of Torbiörn's study was that having friends among the nationals of the host country, rather than having contacts only with fellow expatriates, is an important determinant of satisfaction. Initially those who only mix with expatriates may have more positive experiences, but in the long run personal friendships with members of the host society are very important for the sojourner. This is a consistent finding also with other groups of expatriates, including students (Klineberg and Hull, 1979) and technical advisors (Kealey, 1989).

Not all studies have found external factors to be equally important. Sinangil and Ones (1997) collected data from 220 expatriates working in Turkey as well as from a national co-worker of each expatriate. A factor analysis showed five factors of which job knowledge and motivation was the most important for a successful assignment in the eyes of host nationals, while relational skills came second. The family situation emerged only as the fifth factor; in the light of Torbiörn's findings, its effects are likely to be underestimated by host-country nationals. However, their ratings did

Box 15.1 **CQ (cultural intelligence)**

According to Earley and Ang (2003, p. 59) cultural intelligence refers to "*a person's capability to adapt effectively to new cultural contexts*" (italics in the original). They draw parallels with existing definitions of general intelligence, which is often described as the ability to adapt to one's environment. A culturally intelligent person will acquire new behaviors as they are needed to meet demands. Earley and Ang distinguish four facets: a general or metacognitive; a cognitive; a motivational; and a behavioral. Each of these is further subdivided into various elements, portraying cultural intelligence as a multifaceted concept. CQ has become a popular concept in only a few years.

In the *Handbook of cultural intelligence* Ang and Van Dyne (2008) have brought together both conceptual analyses and empirical data on CQ. In a summarizing chapter, Gelfand, Imai and Fehr (2008, p. 376) hail CQ as offering the promise "to revolutionize and transform the cultural competence literature." The concept is said to offer: (1) parsimony, since it focusses on a small number of facets; (2) theoretical synthesis and coherence, since four facets have been brought together in a unified construct; (3) theoretical precision; (4) the identification of missing cultural competencies that have received less attention so far; (5) connecting research across disciplinary borders; and (6) links between cultural competencies and the intelligence literature.

What is there to sustain such strong claims? CQ is assessed with an instrument (the CQS) consisting of twenty items that were selected from a larger item pool (Van Dyne, Ang and Koh, 2008). This scale has four subscales to represent the four facts mentioned, with four to six items each. The items ask for self-report ratings on seven-point response scales. Items within subscales have similar formulations. For example, the six items in the cognitive scale all start with "I know" (e.g., "I know the rules for expressing non-verbal behaviors in other cultures"); items for other facets start mainly with "I change" (behavioral facet), or "I enjoy" (motivational facet). The four facets were found to result in a four-factor structure across samples from Singapore and the USA, a finding replicated in other studies (e.g., Shannon and Begley, 2008). Van Dyne *et al.* (2008) also examined method variance by comparing self-ratings of MBA students in the USA with the ratings by a peer from their class. The two sets of ratings showed correlations from .37 to .54 for the four-facet scales – a promising finding.

The theoretical analyses in Ang and Van Dyne (2008) mainly merge CQ with other concepts. For example, Sternberg (2008) draws parallels between the research he and his colleagues conducted on indigenous skills and CQ as "practical intelligence flexibly applied across cultural settings" (2008, p. 314). Leung and Li (2008) suggest that CQ may be a proximal cause of intercultural effectiveness while social axioms (see the section on values in Chapter 4) are distal causes. Berry and Ward (2006) argue that CQ is very similar to two existing psychological domains that have an established place in cross-cultural psychology: general intelligence and acculturation. As seen in Chapter 6, the cross-cultural use of general intelligence has been attended by many conceptual and empirical problems. Berry and Ward argue that these

Box 15.1 continued

difficulties also attend the concept and measurement of CQ, and have not been taken into account. With respect to the field of acculturation (discussed in Chapter 13), they argue that there is little value added by CQ over and above the concepts and findings already available in the existing acculturation literature.

The empirical research reported in Ang and Van Dyne (2008) is mainly of two kinds: studies in which the CQS was administered, and studies linking other evidence to the CQ concept or its facets. A study of the latter type is that by Janssens and Cappellen (2008), who found comments in a set of interviews with managers which they interpreted retrospectively as in line with the distinctions of CQ. Scores on the CQS are at the basis of the chapter by Shannon and Begley (2008). In an international sample of business students studying in Ireland they found a correlation of not more than $r = .16$ between an overall CQ score and the peer-rated question: "Can this person deal effectively in multicultural contexts?" Given the low proportion of variance explained by this correlation, it comes as a surprise that the authors see this as a positive finding (because of its statistical significance). Still there are only a few chapters in which a failure to find positive evidence is reported. This was the case in a test by Ward and Fischer (2008) of a model involving motivational CQ.

Probably the strongest positive finding is reported by Tarique and Takeuchi (2008). In a sample of 212 students in New York coming from many countries they found a correlation for metacognitive CQ of $r = .61$ with "the number of international non-work experiences." In other words, students who had visited more countries tended to have higher CQS scores.

Recently Van de Vijver and Breugelmans (2008, p. 119) complained that "the effectiveness of very few procedures has been unequivocally demonstrated while for most training procedures validity data are conspicuously absent." The research reported in Ang and Van Dyne (2008) tries to overcome this shortcoming for the CQS, although studies on predictive validity with job performance criteria are still lacking. Two questions that remain are whether the findings are sufficient to warrant the application of the CQS and whether the CQS is a better predictor of intercultural effectiveness than other scales, which usually have a considerably larger number of items and a more limited theoretical scope, such as the Multicultural Personality Questionnaire (Van der Zee and Van Oudenhoven, 2000, 2001) or the Intercultural Development Inventory (Hammer and Bennett, 2002; Hammer, Bennett and Wiseman, 2003).

In summary, there appear to be various ways in which you can read this Box. At one extreme you can be taken aback by the large discrepancy between the conceptual hype and the limited evidence of empirical validity. At the other extreme you may see CQ as a revolutionary conceptualization and the CQS as a creative operationalization in the field of intercultural communication about which several researchers have great expectations. In other words, you will have to answer the question: does this new emperor have solid clothes or is he (still) essentially naked?

correlate with expatriates' adjustment and intentions to stay, showing that factors of skills and motivation are important for job performance, independent of culture.

Intercultural skills can be targeted by interventions and training procedures (Bhawuk, Landis and Lo, 2006). As we will see in the next section, many training modules have been devised to increase sojourners' skills in intercultural communication and adjustment. The literature on this topic is quite large, but there is still little research on the actual effectiveness of these training programs. Some of the most frequently mentioned skills in intercultural effectiveness are the capacity for feeling empathy for people from other cultures (sometimes referred to as sensitivity), emotional stability, flexibility in dealing with stress following from intercultural encounters, and language competence (e.g., Arthur and Bennett, 1995; Gudykunst, 1998; Hammer, Gudykunst and Wiseman, 1978). Kealey (1995) listed three categories of skills: adaptation skills, including flexibility and stress tolerance, but also conditions such as marital stability; cross-cultural skills, including realism and involvement in culture; and partnership skills, including openness to others and initiative. Many of these skills resemble some of the personality characteristics that have been proposed to make a sojourner effective (see previous section). The main reason to see them as skills or rather personality characteristics seems to be the extent to which researchers think that they can be targeted by intercultural training.

In an analysis of a large set of subjective measures of intercultural effectiveness and life satisfaction among seventy US business people working in China, Cui and Van den Berg (1991) found evidence for a distinction between communication competence, cultural empathy and communication behavior aspects of intercultural effectiveness. Van der Zee and Van Oudenhoven (2000, 2001) distinguished between five skills: cultural empathy, open-mindedness, social initiative, emotional stability and flexibility. However, the extent to which training programs aimed at improving these skills also improve sojourner adjustment, effectiveness and well-being is still not very clear (Van de Vijver and Breugelmans, 2008).

In recent years, cultural distance has come to the fore as a predictor of sojourner adjustment. A larger perceived cultural distance is negatively related to psychological and sociocultural adjustment of sojourners (Ward and Searle, 1991). Redmond (2000) studied 644 international students at a US-American university, where he operationalized cultural distance as differences between country of origin and the USA on the four Hofstede dimensions (Hofstede, 1980). Of course, such operationalization implies that students match the cultural characteristics of their country in a similar fashion as the respondents of the Hofstede questionnaire. Redmond found that relations between intercultural skills (e.g., adaptation, communication effectiveness and social decentering) and the experience and handling of stress were different for students coming from cultures with a large distance from the USA than for students coming from cultures with a small distance from the USA. Similarly, Galchenko and Van de Vijver (2007) found that perceived cultural distance reported by the respondents was a more powerful predictor of accultura-tion outcomes than were acculturation styles and personality among international students in Russia. Intercultural distance has not been found to be predictive in every study. For example, Berry *et al.* (2006) found no evidence among youth of a relationship between cultural distance (using differences on the four Hofstede value dimensions) and either the experience of discrimination or an orientation to the society of settlement. This may have to do with the fact that this study was not about sojourners but rather ethnic youth settled in various countries.

Intercultural training

If sojourners have to learn how to function in a host culture, it makes sense to prepare them beforehand. This reasoning is the basis of intercultural training (Bhawuk, Landis and Lo, 2006). In their intercultural training model, they seek to integrate aspects of the acculturation framework of Berry (2004) and the intercul-tural training framework of Landis and Bhawuk (2004). This model incorporates a number of key background variables drawn from previous training research and applications, including: goal centrality, past intercultural experiences, per-ceived cultural differences, intercultural sensitivity and acculturation strategies. The outcome is a set of variables including: behavioral intentions, reinforcement from the dominant culture (such as public and institutional policies and practices), behavioral rehearsal and learning, and eventually intercultural behaviors. One key assertion is that there needs to be matching between the acculturation strategies of both cultural parties, and that these in turn need to be matched with intercultural training approaches.

Most of the training programs that exist in North America and Western Europe are meant to prepare prospective expatriates for living and working in another cul-ture, although the adjustment of expatriates to western countries occasionally also has been addressed (e.g., Herfst, Van Oudenhoven and Timmerman, 2008). Some programs last for weeks or even months; the duration of others is a matter of a few hours. The longer programs usually include an intensive course in the language of the host country. Beyond language, much of the content of these programs is inspired by ideas and knowledge from intercultural communication literature. De-scriptions of various techniques can be found in Brislin and Yoshida (1994).

There have been various attempts to create some order in the diversity of avail-able techniques. Elaborate schemes have been proposed (Fowler and Blohm, 2004), but a convenient and simple scheme was presented by Gudykunst and Hammer (1983; Gudykunst, Guzley and Hammer, 1996). They proposed a classification with two major distinctions, namely didactic versus experiential, and culture-general versus culture-specific. The scheme can be presented as a figure with four quad-rants (see Figure 15.1).

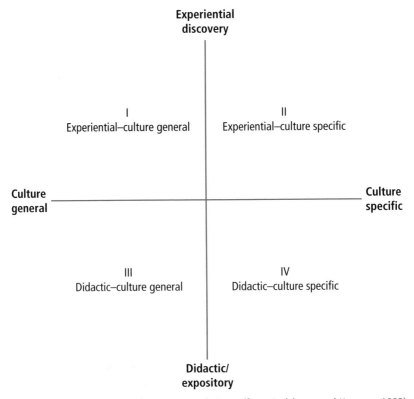

Figure 15.1 A classification scheme for training techniques (from Gudykunst and Hammer, 1983).

In the first quadrant, training methods are placed in which personal experiences of the trainees are considered important to help them recognize how their stereotypes and attitudes affect their behavior. These methods presumably improve communication competence in any culture. To this quadrant belong techniques that emphasize direct experience with people from various other cultures. This is realized in intercultural workshops with participants of various cultural origins, where one learns to become more aware of the ways in which one's own cultural background and values influence perceptions and interactions with others. A second kind of program entails sensitivity training and T-group sessions. The objectives of this kind of training, widely practiced in the 1960s and 1970s, are an increase in self-awareness and personal growth; a person with self-knowledge presumably can also understand others, independent of their culture.

A third kind of technique is the culture-general simulation game. There exists a large number of these games, mostly based on similar principles. Imaginary "cultures" with contrasting values are specified in brief descriptions. The group of trainees is divided over the cultures; the subgroups receive one of the descriptions and have to familiarize themselves with it. Then follows some kind of interaction (e.g., bargaining for trade or a treaty). The games are designed so that the interactions are problematic and are likely to fail. At the end of the simulation there is a debriefing during which the reasons for the difficulties are discussed. Many of the games have been developed by training institutes for their own use and have not been published. A classic example is a game called BAFA-BAFA (Shirts, 1973). An objection to such games is that norms and customs are created which would not be found in any real society. Since evaluations of most of such games have not been published it is unclear whether or not they improve intercultural effectiveness.

There are two important training techniques that belong to the second quadrant. First, there are techniques that involve real bicultural contacts. They can take the form of a sensitivity training on an existing international conflict with members of the nations concerned in attendance. Such programs can be problematic, because of the strong identification of participants with the views of their own group. The second group of methods is that of international workshops in which participants from two countries together discuss critical incidents in interactions between people from their respective cultures.

The bottom half of Figure 15.1 refers to didactic programs, where trainees are taught by instruction. To the left quadrant (on culture-general didactic methods) belong traditional academic courses in cross-cultural psychology or intercultural communication. Gudykunst, Guzley and Hammer (1996) also mention here videotapes, and "culture-general assimilators" – a technique described below. Language courses are the most important form of didactic culture-specific training (the lower right quadrant of Fig. 15.1). In addition, there is a variety of briefings (area orientations) about the country trainees are going to visit, including information concerning the economic and political situation, problems that an expatriate is likely to face, and major customs and attitudes, much of which information can be found on the Internet.

The technique that has been developed most systematically for intercultural training is the culture assimilator, also called the "intercultural sensitizer." First constructed by Fiedler, Mitchell and Triandis (1971), culture assimilators consist of a large number of short episodes describing interactions between people belonging to two different cultures – the target culture and the trainee's culture. Usually a series of critical incidents is described, such as interactions in which something goes wrong. Each episode is followed by four or five possible reasons for the communication failure. The trainee has to choose the correct answer. In the ideal case there is one interpretation that is typically selected by members of the target culture. The other three or four are based on attributions likely to be made by members of the trainee's culture. After their choice the trainees are given feedback why their answer was correct or incorrect. In a good assimilator this feedback contains much culturally relevant information.

Most culture assimilators have been constructed for US-Americans who are trained for an assignment abroad (Albert, 1983; Cushner and Landis, 1996), but the technique has been recommended elsewhere (e.g., Herfst *et al.*, 2008; Thomas and Wagner, 1999). Initially all culture assimilators were culture-specific, but Brislin, Cushner, Cherrie and Yong (1986) have constructed a culture-general assimilator that should increase the effectiveness of trainees independent of their cultural background and the culture they intend to visit. In Box 15.2 one of the 100 items of this instrument is presented. When taken at face value, non-westerners may find the topics and the concerns of the items rather "US-American." Nevertheless, this is a first step toward multicultural assimilators. In another approach, Bhawuk (1998) developed culture assimilators on the basis of Hofstede's individualism–collectivism dimension (1980, 2001). He obtained some evidence suggesting that these so-called culture theory-based assimilators might work better in intercultural training than culture-specific or culture-general assimilators.

The construction and validation of an assimilator is a tedious effort. It requires the collection of a large number of incidents. For each of these, likely attributions about the causes of miscommunication have to be found. The correct answer has to be identified. The items have to be validated by checking whether the distributions of answers by individuals from various cultures indeed are different (i.e., whether the attributions are indeed non-isomorphic). Feedback information has to be written for each answer explaining why it is correct or incorrect. Finally, evidence has to be collected on the validity of the instrument: does the administration of an assimilator help to improve intercultural effectiveness (e.g., Albert, 1983; Cushner, 1989; Herfst *et al.*, 2008)?

Many intercultural communication training programs tend to focus on internal psychological characteristics (whether in the form of traits or meanings) and how these are different cross-culturally. These programs help to appreciate that people in other groups may look at things in a way that differs from what we find in our own cultural environment. Often an additional aspect is emphasized, namely the role of stereotypes and ethnocentric views (discussed in Chapter 14). A further emphasis in training follows from a diversified view on behavior–culture relationships as has been advocated in this book. For example, in an ecocultural perspective the most important dimensions of cross-cultural differences include the actual economic conditions in which different people in the world are living.

Generally, a weak point of intercultural training programs is the lack of evaluation of their effects. Often a brief questionnaire is administered at the end of training, but this indicates more whether the trainees liked the program than whether it was effective. Blake, Heslin and Curtis (1996) have described how a proper evaluation study should be conducted, but they could hardly refer to evaluation studies that met these standards. Similarly, Mol, Born and Van der Molen (2005) underscore the importance of assessing intercultural effectiveness in terms of job performance criteria, rather than through indirect measures such as subjective evaluations. They

Box 15.2   **A culture assimilator item**

The following item has been abbreviated from Brislin, Cushner, Cherrie and Yong (1986, pp. 212–213, 223).

The Eager Teacher: Upon graduating college with a degree in English education with a Spanish minor, Rick Meyers accepted a position teaching English in a fairly large and progressive coeducational school in Merida, Mexico, capital city of the state of Yucatán. He had met the language director earlier that year while on a spring recess tour of Mexico and felt quite comfortable with him.

Eager to start the new school year off right, Rick spent a considerable amount of time in preparation of lessons and materials and in extra-help sessions with students. It seemed as if he was always doing something school related, often spending his lunch, free periods and after-school hours with small groups of students.

Although his relationships with the students were growing, after the first few weeks, Rick noticed that his fellow teachers seemed cold and removed. He was seldom invited to after-school and weekend get-togethers or sought out during free times at school. Not sure what to make of this, Rick kept more and more to himself, feeling increasingly lonely and rejected.

What is the major issue of concern for Rick?

1. It is not common or acceptable for teachers in Mexico to show so much personal attention to students.
2. Rick has not spent the requisite amount of social time with his fellow workers.
3. The other teachers were resentful as Rick was seen as someone special and was given attention by most of the students.
4. Rick expected to be perceived as an expert. When this was not the case, he was disappointed that his talents were not utilized by all.

Rationales for the alternative explanations

After respondents have thought about the answers and made a choice, they are referred to another page of the book where a rationale is given for each of the four alternatives. (It has been found that subjects usually not only read the text with their own answer, but go over all the alternatives.) The following explanations are given for the item you just read:

1. While our validation sample suggested this as a possibility, one of the writer's first-hand experiences demonstrates otherwise. Especially in the larger and more progressive schools, contact between teachers and students is quite frequent and in many ways expected. Please choose again.

Box 15.2 continued

2. This is the best answer. Although skillful in his teaching and quite successful on the job, Rick's participation with other staff has been minimal. In many places, the degree of one's socializing with others is of critical importance. Although contrary to most Americans' desire to perform the task efficiently and well, attention must also be paid to social norms and expectations with colleagues to ensure success in the workplace.

3. There is no indication in the story that the students were responding to anything more than Rick's genuine offer of time and assistance. There is a better response. Please try again.

4. Although this may result in problems for some people in some situations, there is no indication that this is an issue for Rick. There is a better answer. Please choose again.

argue that assessments of objective criteria are hardly found. In our view this defines a major challenge for the further development of intercultural training.

For a long time the term "intercultural communication training" mainly referred to programs for special target groups, preparing for assignments outside the trainees' home country. However, there has been a growing awareness that in a world that becomes a global village and in multicultural societies, education on cultural matters should be part of the school curriculum. Brislin and Horvath (1997, p. 345) wrote: "Many of the goals of training and education are the same: increased awareness of cultural differences, increased knowledge, movement beyond stereotypes, introduction to emotional confrontations, coverage of different behaviors that meet similar everyday goals, and so forth." It can be argued that much of this education should be part of learning foreign languages (Krumm, 1997). According to Bennett, Bennett and Allen (1999) language learning and intercultural learning can be combined so that linguistic competence and intercultural competence develop in parallel. This trend is further elaborated by Dana and Allen (2008), who discuss the need for transitions in the education and training of psychologists to better address diversity in the increasingly complex societies in which they render their services.

Conclusions

Intercultural communication and training is an area of increasing relevance as people from different cultures and societies meet and interact more and more frequently. In this chapter we first pointed out various difficulties in communication across cultural boundaries that go beyond mutually unintelligible languages. We saw that there are many instances of differences at the level of performance in processes that are found across cultures (e.g., prosodic and pragmatic aspects of language, gestures and personal space). We also saw that most instances of cross-cultural miscommunication tend to have very specific causes and that there was limited evidence of broad dimensions of cross-cultural differences. We then turned to theories of intercultural communication. We saw that these theories tend to be formulated at a high level of abstraction, focussing on one or a few major cultural dimensions (e.g., individualism–collectivism) as discussed extensively elsewhere in this textbook. This contrasts with the findings on intercultural miscommunications.

The second section discussed research on sojourner adjustment and intercultural personality. We looked at evidence for the role of specific skills, of external conditions and, notably, of sojourner personality. There was quite some agreement among researchers about which skills, conditions or personality traits should contribute, but the empirical support was rather mixed. A number of promising factors were identified (e.g., contact with hosts, cultural distance) but also a number of challenges, such as the need to develop a clear notion of "adjustment" in order to test ideas about which factors contribute most.

The first question addressed in the final section was to what extent personal qualities of the sojourner, knowledge of the host culture and prior experience in various cultures contribute to a successful sojourn. The second subsection discussed attempts to develop interventions and training programs aimed at making intercultural sojourners perform better. Training programs were distinguished along two dimensions: didactic versus experiential approaches and culture-general versus culture-specific approaches. Various promising training programs were discussed (e.g., the culture assimilator).

Throughout this chapter we saw that researchers tend to prefer theories that explain cross-cultural differences in terms of a few broad cultural dimensions. In particular, individualism–collectivism is used by many authors as an explanation of a large array of differences. However, we have also seen that most differences which are found tend to be very situation-specific or domain-specific. This discrepancy between theory and empirical evidence may be one of the reasons that some areas in intercultural communication and training struggle with the lack of a solid empirical basis. There are some other challenges, such as the need to clearly define sojourner effectiveness and that many studies and observations on samples have been done in relatively few cultures, with hardly any critical research seeking discriminant validity (see Chapter 12, p. 273).

Nevertheless, research on intercultural communication and training clearly is a very important area of application in cross-cultural psychology. There is a growing demand for knowledge and interventions in this domain. We feel that detailed analyses of intercultural communication problems, sojourner performance and the potential to prepare people for functioning in different cultural contexts could be one of the major contributions of cross-cultural psychology. However, we also feel that in order to achieve this it is necessary to develop more critical tests of ideas and to refrain from making broad generalizations.

KEY TERMS

culture assimilator • intercultural communication • intercultural training • intercultural competence • sojourners

FURTHER READING

Brislin, R., and Horvath, A.-M. (1997). Cross-cultural training and multicultural education. In J. W. Berry, M. H. Segall and C. Kağitçibaşi (eds.), *Handbook of cross-cultural psychology, Vol. III, Social and behavioral applications* (2nd edn., pp. 327–369). Boston: Allyn & Bacon.

A review chapter that addresses not only the more traditional field of training for sojourners, but also student education.

Carr, S. (ed.) (2010). *The psychology of mobility in a global era.* New York: Springer.

A set of essays on the relationships between increasing international mobility and global social and psychological change.

Landis, D., Bennett, M., and Bennett, J. M. (2004). *Handbook of intercultural training* (3rd edn.). Thousand Oaks, Calif.: Sage.

An extensive collection of chapters addressing a range of issues in intercultural training.

Ward, C., Bochner, S., and Furnham, A. (2001). *The psychology of culture shock* (2nd edn.). Hove: Routledge.

A thorough and integrative overview of research on the way sojourners adapt to living in other cultures.

16 | Work and organizations

CONTENTS

Cross-cultural research on work and organizations is a large and active field that cannot be represented in scope and depth within a single chapter. We have selected topics with a clear history of cross-cultural psychological research. Several other topics could have been included (e.g., Bhagat and Steers, 2009; Gelfand, Erez and Aycan, 2007; Smith, Peterson and Thomas, 2008). Still, this chapter should provide you with an overview of major topics in cross-cultural research on work and organizations.

This chapter is organized in a hierarchical fashion from countries via organizations to individual-level variables. The first section discusses structural characteristics of organizations as they are found in various societies. The second section deals with organizational culture, which is based on the presumption that a work organization can be conceived of as a culture, on a smaller scale but otherwise in a similar sense as a societal culture. Next to organizational culture a more psychological concept is mentioned, namely organizational climate. The third section deals with values, a widely studied topic not only in cross-cultural organizational research, but also in the business and management literature. Although values are essentially psychological characteristics of individuals, much research has also dealt with values at the levels of countries (see Chapter 4), and work organizations. The fourth section focusses on managers, who are central to the functioning of work organizations. Two frequently researched aspects of managerial functioning are reviewed: leadership and decision making. The final section describes two topics dealing with employees at large: motivation and job satisfaction.

Organizational structure

An important characteristic of complex organizations is the distribution of tasks. Not every employee has the same responsibilities and the same kind of work. The total body of work that has to be performed is assigned to different divisions and subdivisions creating an organizational structure. The question posed most often is whether and to what extent organizations in different countries have similar structures. This has been mainly studied from an institutional-level perspective in organizational sociology and organization science, but structure also has implications for the individual functioning of employees.

In the 1970s and early 1980s the importance of political factors was emphasized. For example, an international research group called Industrial Democracy in Europe (IDE, 1981) studied whether state regulations and legislation were related to organizational structure and behavior, particularly as far as workers' participation was concerned. The study was carried out in eleven (mainly Western) European countries and Israel. It was found that participation, especially at the collective level through labor unions, was indeed influenced by the extent to which regulations concerning participation were entrenched in the law. According to the IDE group their results indicated that democracy in industries is influenced by sociopolitical factors rather than by requirements of a technological or structural nature.

Political variables are often confounded with other cultural variables like values, beliefs and customs. This confounding was emphasized in an orientation that has had a significant impact on the discussion of the role of cultural factors in organizations, namely the contingency approach. In organizational theory the structure of an organization is assumed to be contingent upon variables such as the size (number of employees), technology, resources and the history of the organization. In a broader sense contingency variables also include the environment in which the organization is functioning such as the form of government of the country and the level of education of the workforce.

One form of contingency theory, reminiscent of a strict universalist perspective outlined in Chapter 12, was the "culture-free hypothesis." According to this hypothesis situational demands are the sole determinants of organizational change; so theories about organizations have validity independent of the culture in which an organization is functioning. Effects of cultural variables, if any, are suppressed by the much stronger effects of technology. Consequently, the relationships between structural or contextual variables should be invariant across cultures (e.g., Miller, 1987). Organizations in countries at approximately the same level of industrial development should show strong similarities. The idea that technological development should have a homogenizing effect on organizations is known as the "convergence hypothesis" (Ronen, 1986). Support for this hypothesis came from a group of researchers working in Britain: the Aston group (Pugh and Hinings, 1976). They found that the number of employees influenced the structure of an organization, but that technological changes had little effect (Pheysey, 1993).

However, in some international comparative studies, with companies of similar size operating in the same branch of industry, major differences were reported. This led Maurice (1979) to adopt a more relativist position, claiming that cross-national comparisons within the contingency approach are no more than extensions of studies within a single country. One might say that the convergence approach, according to Maurice's views, is based on imposed etics (see Box 1.2). He maintains that a society's culture is part of the essence of an organization, which cannot be understood without reference to the culture in which it is situated. At a more pragmatic level, multinational companies seeking to implement uniform organizational structures globally have faced serious challenges (Bartlett and Ghoshal, 1998).

The discussion on convergence continues to influence more recent analyses. Galán and Sánchez-Bueno (2009) studied whether political and economic events, such as privatization, opening of the domestic market and joining the European Community, led to changes in the strategies of companies in Spain. In a survey including 100 of the largest Spanish corporations they found convergence of structure (diversification and use of divisions) with other European economies. They interpreted these findings as consistent with universalistic predictions of evolvement toward a common form. Another study among thirty industrial companies in Sudan was more supportive of the ideas of the Aston group (Mohamed, 2007). Size of a company (number of employees) was a major factor in standardization and formalization. In contrast, technology (assessed in terms of automatization and mass-production) only showed moderate effects.

On the other hand, Steers, Nardon and Sanchez-Runde (2009) compared "typical" organizations in eight countries (China, Japan, France, Germany, Malaysia, Mexico, Nigeria, USA) and concluded that while there is considerable variation within countries, national trends can be identified. They argued that comparisons across cultures carried out with sufficient precision can provide information regarding why companies in various parts of the world are often organized on the basis of different principles. In their analysis they not only referred to aspects that are company-controlled, such as hierarchical structures, but also independent agencies, such as financial and legal services, labor unions, and supply and demand chains.

Steers *et al.* (2009) presented charts for a typical company in these various countries, including its surrounding agencies. These charts are quite different in appearance. US companies are characterized by top–down decision making, reliance on outside service companies and flexibility in the workforce (employees are easily laid off). Common in German companies is a supervisory board that oversees the activities of the management board (i.e., the top managers who are responsible for strategy and operations of the company). In Germany another factor is the work council representing employees and unions; such councils are entrenched in the law and have representation in the supervisory board of companies. The typical, family-owned company in China has little formal structure, with seniority being an important consideration; the management style tends to be paternalistic. Relationships with members of the extended family, suppliers and distributors reflect traditional Chinese cultural concepts, such as *guanxi* and *mientzu*. *Guanxi* implies a strong personal relationship and good connections based on mutual trust and exchange of favors. *Mientzu*, or "face," refers to the dignity and the prestige that someone commands and is entitled to receive.

The classifications by Steers *et al.* (2009) are based both on the literature about organizational structure and values, and on extensive professional experience. They provide a descriptive account, reflecting a qualitative rather than a quantitative orientation. When comparing research such as that by Galán and Sánchez-Bueno (2009) and Mohamed (2007) with that of Steers *et al.* (2009) it is difficult to escape the idea that the choice of method of analysis is related to reported outcomes, with the more descriptive and qualitative studies revealing stronger cultural contrasts.

While convergence may occur at the level of organizational structure and technology (macro-level variables), this does not exclude the possibility that individual attitudes and values (micro-level variables) could remain culturally distinct. Drenth and colleagues (Drenth and Den Hartog, 1999; Drenth and Groenendijk, 1997) saw little reason to assume strong cultural influences on structural characteristics. Cultural variables may have little to do with how an organization is structured, but they may have much to do with how it is functioning. In their view, a structural variable such as formalization (i.e., the presence of formal rules and procedures) is subject to few cultural prescriptions, but the extent to which employees adhere to the rules will differ between cultures. Similarly, in respect of centrality of decision making there can be large differences between cultures in the actual influence of lower echelons, even if structurally the strategic decision-making power is mostly in the hands of top executives everywhere.

We can conclude that there have been several ideas about how culture does or does not influence organizational structures, but that the empirical evidence for these ideas is mixed. Opinions differ along two main dimensions. First is the role of culture, for which two contrasting viewpoints exist (corresponding to universalism and relativism described in Chapter 12). Second is the contrast between institutional level and individual level. Organizational structure is primarily a concept from organizational sociology and tends to be defined at the institutional level. Among psychologists (e.g., Drenth and Groenendijk, 1997) there is a tendency to emphasize the importance of organizational processes and individual behavior. The effects of culture may well be stronger at the latter than at the former level.

Organizational culture

Culture is traditionally defined at the level of societies and it encompasses many spheres of life. Organizational culture is defined at the level of organizations. The underlying assumption is that organizations differ from each other not only in production techniques, marketing and the attitudes of their employees, but also in deep-rooted beliefs, meaning and values. Deal and Kennedy (1982) wrote about the "inner values," "rituals" and "heroes" of an organization as determinants of its success. Heroes are significant figures, such as the company founder or other senior executives with a large influence. The concept of organizational culture was based on the observation that organizations in some countries have a much better performance record than those in others. In particular, Japanese industries showed a rapid rate of development from the 1950s through the 1980s. This success was largely ascribed to social policies and management practices in Japanese culture (e.g., Ouchi, 1981), rather than to the long working hours of the Japanese workforce.

Qualitative research methods have been recommended to capture the essence of an organization's culture. Early on an analogy with ethnographic research was already suggested (e.g., Allaire and Firsirotu, 1984; Frost, Moore, Louis, Lundberg and Martin, 1985), including "thick description" as advocated by Geertz (1973). An influential author with a background in psychology has been Schein (1985, 2004), who distinguished three levels in organizations' cultures: (1) observable behaviors and artifacts; (2) values and (3) unconscious basic assumptions about relations to the environment, and the nature of reality. According to Schein: "Perhaps the most intriguing aspect of culture as a concept is that it points us to phenomena that are below the surface, that are powerful in their impact but invisible and to a considerable degree unconscious" (2004, p. 8). Schein refers to the "feel" of an organization and recommends the use of less objective methods, such as interviewing, ad hoc observation (without standardized schedules) and group discussion. Qualitative studies have provided numerous organizational variables that can be linked to organizational culture (e.g., Ashkanasy, Wilderom and Peterson, 2000a).

The volume of empirical research based on more quantitative methods is smaller but still extensive. A landmark study on twenty organizations in Denmark and the Netherlands was reported by Hofstede, Neuijen, Ohayv and Sanders (1990). First, interview data (guided by a checklist) were collected from key informants. Then an extensive questionnaire was administered to a stratified sample in each organization. Finally, the findings were checked in feedback discussions. Employee values were found to differ more according to demographic variables (such as nationality, age and education) than to organization membership. The main differences between organizations were found in daily practices as they were perceived by the employees. The core of an organization's culture appeared to lie more in shared practices than in shared values. Hofstede *et al.* argued that cultural values are acquired fairly early in life and are difficult to change later on. In contrast, organizational practices are learned later in life at the workplace. In Chapter 12 we included a section on the psychological organization of cross-cultural differences, mentioning a range of possible interpretations of cross-cultural differences. In the present research by Hofstede *et al.* (1990) organizational culture showed up as a set of conventions or practices. Hofstede and his colleagues even pointed out that the use of the same term at both levels could be misleading; still, they did not abandon the term organizational culture.

Comprehensive notions of organizational culture continue to be used in quantitative studies (Ashkanasy *et al.*, 2000a). For example, a distinction was made by Van Muijen, Koopman and De Witte (1996) between two levels of organizational culture. At the first level are visible and tangible manifestations (like buildings, rules, technology) and at the second level are values and norms on which behaviors are based. Studies by Hofstede *et al.* (1990) and Van Muijen *et al.* (1996) made use of the typical methodology of quantitative research: questionnaires and surveys. An overview of instruments can be found in Ashkanasy, Broadfoot and Falkus (2000). Most address several dimensions, such as leadership, innovation, planning and communication, and these have become the targets of further research.

A distinction is often made between organizational climate and organizational culture. James *et al.* (2008) refer to organizational climate as the aggregate measures of employees' perceptions of the work environment on their well-being. When employees agree on the impact of their work environment, this shared opinion refers to organizational climate. James *et al.* emphasize that climate remains a property of the individual employees, while organizational culture, which includes normative beliefs and values, refers to characteristics of organizations as systems. The distinction between individual and system is seen as the key to set climate and culture apart. Other authors argue that climate and culture are not strongly differentiated (e.g., Ashkanasy, Wilderom and Peterson, 2000b; Schneider, 2000), a viewpoint which seems to make sense since scales to assess climate and culture often look similar (Ashkanasy, Broadfoot *et al.*, 2000). The central issue is the distinction between individual-level and culture-level analysis. Do survey data collected on individuals after aggregation to the culture level reflect culture-level characteristics that are the same as the individual (unaggregated) psychological characteristics? Organization researchers have started to address this question, which we discussed in the section on distinguishing between the culture level and the individual level in Chapter 12 (e.g., Fischer, 2008; Smith and Fischer, 2008).

Caution is needed in drawing parallels between cultures as characteristics of national or ethnic populations and the characteristics of the employees of organizations. Apart from the difficulty of distinguishing between individual and institutional level there is the problem that the scattered findings make it difficult to gain a coherent picture of the extent to which organizations differ in culture, and what the implications are. An additional difficulty is that organizational cultures do not really meet the two criteria which we mentioned in Chapter 1 in the section on sampling for identifying separate cultures, namely differentiation and permanence. These criteria are undermined in so far as employees can switch relatively easily and successfully between employers, and work organizations are much more dynamic than nations in accepting innovations and in merging with other organizations. In summary, despite its widespread use, organizational culture remains a somewhat fuzzy concept.

Work values

Hofstede's study (1980) on work-related values in national subsidiaries of IBM marked the beginning of an important tradition of research in cross-cultural psychology. In the 1990s this work became the most frequently cited source from the cross-cultural literature, with references not only in psychology but also in cultural anthropology and intercultural communication. Moreover, the Hofstede dimensions have been used most extensively in organizational and management research. There has been a proliferation of studies both at individual and country level, with little integration of findings (e.g., Kirkman, Lowe and Gibson, 2006; Tsui, Nifadkar and Ou, 2007). For this reason we will add some further comments on Hofstede's study, in addition to those made in Chapter 4.

Data were collected in two rounds, around 1968 and around 1972. Seven different levels of occupation were distinguished ranging from managers to administrative personnel. Altogether there were more than 116,000 respondents in twenty languages. The survey instrument included some 160 questions of which 63, mainly pertaining to values, were used in the cross-cultural analysis of values. In the section on values in Chapter 4 this work was discussed because of its relevance for social psychology. There we saw that Hofstede identified four dimensions, namely power distance, uncertainty avoidance, individualism–collectivism and masculinity–femininity. For the present chapter it is important to consider that these dimensions were derived from country-level scores obtained through aggregation of individual item scores with national samples. The uncertainty avoidance and power distance indices, with three items each, were obtained through "eclectic analysis" (Hofstede, 1980, pp. 76–77). The indices for individualism and masculinity resulted from a factor analysis of twenty-two (later fourteen) items enquiring about the importance of various work goals. A meaningful distinction between countries could only be obtained with factor analysis on a data matrix of work goals by countries. After some readjustments thirty-two items provided a three-factor solution explaining 49 percent of the variance at country level. The first factor was a combination of individualism and power distance (with reversed sign), the second factor represented masculinity and the third factor corresponded to uncertainty avoidance. For conceptual reasons Hofstede maintained a distinction between the two dimensions of individualism and power distance that together constituted the first factor. He justified this with the argument that the correlations between the two dimensions ($r = -.67$) virtually disappeared if variance due to national wealth was controlled for.[1]

An extensive search for convergent evidence led to numerous supportive arguments for each of the dimensions (Hofstede, 1980). For example, subordinates in low power distance countries negatively evaluated close supervision and preferred consultative decision making. The strongest predictor of the power distance indices across forty countries was geographical latitude. Hofstede explained this relationship as arising from the higher need for technology in enhancing human survival in colder countries. He did not postulate a direct causal relationship between environmental temperature and the power distance index, but saw the climatic factors at the beginning of a causal chain that through a long process of adaptation has led to cross-cultural differences in social structure. Another example is the high correlation ($r = .82$) between individualism and economic wealth (per capita GNP). In countries low on individualism, conformity is liked, and autonomy is rated as less important, while in countries with high individualism, variety is sought and security is seen as less important.

In Chapter 4 several concerns were raised about dimensions like those of Hofstede (1980). For organizational research the most serious is that there are numerous studies which did not find patterns and correlations expected on the basis of Hofstede's analysis (e.g., Ellis, 1988; Fernandez, Carlson, Stepina and Nicholson, 1997; Fijneman *et al.*, 1996). It is always possible that these studies suffered from inadequacies, but that can hardly be said of explicit attempts at replication. An attempt by Hoppe (1990, reported in Smith and Schwartz, 1997) to replicate Hofstede's four factors in samples

---

[1] If it is considered that at least part of the remaining variance must represent error; there may not be much variance left to be explained in terms of the two separate dimensions.

of managers from seventeen countries was not successful. Poor replication results for two of the factors (uncertainty avoidance and masculinity) were also reported in Merritt (2000) and in Spector, Cooper, Sparks *et al.* (2001).

Merritt's findings deserve more attention as they were based on a large project. She administered an 82-item questionnaire, including most of the items from Hofstede's original work value survey, to over 9,000 airline pilots in nineteen countries. The correlations between the four indices reported by Hofstede (1980) and the country scores of the pilots were $r = .74$ (power distance), $r = .16$ (masculinity), $r = .48$ (individualism) and $r = .25$ (uncertainty avoidance). Thus, power distance and individualism were substantially replicated, but the replication failed for the other two dimensions, although Merritt tried to reconstruct scales for the failed dimensions.

Value dimensions are attractive. They allow both managers and researchers to transcend "culture" as a fuzzy notion, providing a "mapping of the nations of the world" (Smith and Schwartz, 1997; Nardon and Steers, 2009). One way to build such maps is with cluster analysis, a method used by Hofstede (1980). After some modifications of the outcome (on the basis of historical arguments), eight clusters remained: more developed Latin, less developed Latin, more developed Asian, less developed Asian, Near Eastern, Germanic, Anglo and Nordic, while Japan formed an additional cultural area on its own. These clusters, as well as those found in studies of motivational and attitudinal variables, tend to group countries by geographical proximity (e.g., Ronen, 1986).

Another use of value dimensions is the search for correlates. A major purpose of these dimensions in relation to organizations is to provide potential explanations of variations in other aspects of work-related phenomena. Of the hundreds of studies in the literature we mention one. Smith, Peterson, Schwartz and colleagues (2002; Smith, Bond and Kağitçibaşi, 2006) in a study with data from forty-seven countries examined sources of guidance that managers rely on. Managers are required to deal with a large number of events that happen in the work context; the question was where they are looking for guidance on how to address events. Eight sources of guidance were specified (e.g., formal rules and procedures, subordinates, superior) for each of eight events (e.g., filling a vacancy, a subordinate doing poor work). Smith *et al.* used country scores on value questionnaires to look for correlates of the guidance scores that they obtained in their samples. Hofstede's country scores on power distance and related value dimensions could explain a substantial proportion of the variance between countries in reliance on superiors and on formal rules. However, the value dimensions explained hardly any of the variance in reliance on co-workers, warning against the attribution of too much significance to values as an explanation of cross-cultural differences.

Many studies take the distinction between individualist and collectivist societies, and sometimes those on other dimensions, for granted (e.g., Kirkman *et al.*, 2006; Klassen, 2004). According to Lonner (in press), students of culture and behavior, including cultural anthropologists and biologists, tend to think in universalistic terms and to pursue universal dimensions. Values have become the most important way in the literature to represent cultural variability and are unlikely to lose this position in cross-cultural organizational psychology within the foreseeable future. However, it seems likely that next to the dimensions of Hofstede (1980, 2001), other sets of dimensions, like those we mentioned in Chapter 4 (see, e.g., Inglehart, 1997; Inglehart and Baker, 2000; Schwartz, 1992, 1994b, 2006), will be receiving more attention in the organizational literature.

Managerial behavior

In this section we move to the behavior of individuals within the organization. The management and administration of an organization can be seen as an institutional activity which is the task of managers. We have selected two topics, leadership styles and decision making. References to other aspects can be found, for example, in Aditya, House and Kerr (2000), and in Smith *et al.* (2008).

Leadership styles

A good leader influences employees to pursue the goals of the organization, but this can be done in different ways and managers differ in leadership styles. In the earlier US-American literature two behavior categories emerged as typical for effective leaders, namely consideration and initiating structure (see Wexley and Yukl, 1984). Consideration has to do with the concern and support of the leader for subordinates. Initiating structure refers to the definition and structuring by leaders of the various roles and tasks to be performed by themselves and other employees. Blake and Mouton (1964) expressed these dimensions as "concern for people" and "concern for production," while Likert (1967) distinguished between "exploitative" (or authoritative) and "participative" behavior. Cross-cultural variations of these categories have been described by J. B. P. Sinha (1980, 2008) for India and by Misumi (1985) for Japan.

Misumi's PM leadership theory distinguishes two main functions in a group: one is contributing to the group's goal achievement and problem-solving (Performance, or P), and the other is promoting the group's self-preservation and strengthening the group processes (Maintenance, or M). Both the P and the M function play a role in any leadership process. Misumi's theory leads to a typology with four basic types: namely PM, Pm, pM and pm leadership (a capital indicates a high value on a dimension, and a small letter a low value). Misumi saw his typology as an extension of (classical) western theories which often emphasized two orthogonal dimensions for performance and maintenance. For Misumi his dimensions can be augmenting one another. He expected that the PM theory would have universal validity because the morphology and dynamics of leadership elsewhere should be similar to those in Japan. Studies that supported these expectations were summarized by Smith and Peterson (1988). Data from Britain, Hong Kong, the USA and Japan showed positive correlations between subordinates' ratings of their work situation and ratings on P and M scales for their supervisors.

J. B. P. Sinha (1980, 1984) defined for India the concept of the "nurturant-task leader." This management style has two components: concern for the task and a nurturant orientation toward subordinates. The nurturant-task leader creates a climate of purposiveness and maintains a high level of productivity. But he also shows care and affection for the well-being of subordinates and is committed to their professional growth. The nurturant-task leadership style is flexible and as a subordinate needs less guidance and direction it should change gradually to a more participative style. Sinha proposed a continuum from authoritarian (which often is seen as related to the task-oriented leadership style in the US literature) to participative, with nurturant-task leadership in the middle. Participative management was considered the ideal, but as only feasible under certain social conditions often not (yet) present in India.

More recently, Sinha (2008) has referred to "nurturant task-participative" (NT-P) leadership, emphasizing the participative nature of nurturant-task leadership. It is a style suitable for dependent subordinates who accept the superiority of the leader. Even when in India subordinates grow to more independence and confidence in dealing with their tasks, they continue to respect the superior and to look for inspiration and mentorship.

Nurturant-task leadership is reminiscent of paternalism – a leadership style in which the superior tends to act like a father, providing guidance and protection to the subordinate, but expecting loyalty and obedience in return. In a ten-country study with measures of four dimensions (paternalism, power distance, loyalty to community, fatalism) Aycan, Kanungo, Mendonca, Deller, Stahl and Kurshid (2000) found that of these four paternalism explained most variance. The highest country scores were found for India, Turkey and China, while the lowest scores were observed for Germany and Israel. Cheng, Chou, Wu, Huang and Farh (2004) found that in China paternalism, which is a prevalent leadership style, had a significant and unique effect on subordinate responses compared to western transformational leadership. This suggests that usual western dimensions of leadership may need to be supplemented with other dimensions.

In the meantime there has also been a shift in western thinking from models in which exchange relations were emphasized (referred to as "transactional" leadership) to transformational leadership or charismatic leadership, and, more generally, to a broader role of affect in organizational behavior (e.g., Barsade, Brief and Spataro, 2003). Charismatic leaders are perceived as dynamic, inspirational and supporting their subordinates' development (transformation). They are also credited with emotional appeal to followers and power over them. Charismatic leadership is seen as a universally effective style (Bass, 1997) and was an important dimension in the most extensive cross-cultural leadership study to date, the GLOBE project.

The GLOBE (Global Leadership and Organizational Behavioral Effectiveness) research program, initiated by House, collected data on values and managerial practices from 17,000 managers in 951 organizations located in 62 countries (House, Hanges, Javidan, Dorfman and Gupta, 2004). The project built on and extended previous work, notably that of Hofstede (1980, 2001). The GLOBE team developed items and scales on the basis of existing literature; co-investigators from a range of countries were consulted on the formulation and relevance of items. There were 112 leadership items covering 21 subscales from which, with the help of factor analysis, 6 global dimensions were derived: charismatic leadership (visionary, inspirational), team-oriented leadership (collaborative, team building), participative leadership (involving others), humane-oriented leadership (supportive and considerate of others), autonomous leadership (acting independently, large distance to subordinates) and self-protective leadership (self-centered, bureaucratic, elitist).

Nine dimensions of culture were distinguished, covered by seventy-eight items. A strong point of the project is that not a single rating but a differentiated set of ratings was obtained, namely of matters "as they are" (practices) and "as they should be" (values). Respondents were also asked to rate how most other people in their nation would respond (typicality ratings). The nine dimensions of culture are: future orientation, gender egalitarianism, assertiveness, humane orientation, ingroup collectivism, institutional collectivism, performance orientation, power concentration (corresponding to Hofstede's concept of power distance) and uncertainty avoidance. The approximate meaning of most of these attributes is clear from their names. (Institutional collectivism refers to the collective distribution of resources and rewards; ingroup collectivism reflects pride, loyalty and cohesiveness toward one's organization or family; humane orientation refers to fairness, altruism, generosity and kindness to others.)

The most interesting question in the GLOBE project was where good leadership is invariant across cultures and where important differences are found. Two leadership styles – charismatic leadership and team-oriented leadership – were strongly endorsed in all regions of the world. For other styles more cross-cultural differences were found; for example, participative leadership received higher scores in Germanic Europe but lower scores in the Middle East, and the score for self-protective leadership was considerably higher in Southern Asia than in the Nordic countries.

Other questions in the GLOBE project pertained to the relationships between attributes of societies and leadership styles and behaviors. In general it was found that cultural values rather than practices were related to leadership dimensions; according to House *et al.* (2004) this is because both represent preferred end-states. Also, organizational cultures were found to resemble the societies in which the organizations are located. For all nine dimensions, nation-level practices were a significant predictor of organization-level practices, explaining from 21 to 47 percent of the variance (Brodbeck *et al.*, 2004)

The most unexpected major finding in the GLOBE project was a strong negative correlation on most dimensions between scores on questions about matters "as they are" (practices) and question on matters "as they should be" (values). For Hofstede (2006) this was a major reason to challenge the operationalization of values and the items used in the GLOBE project. Javidan, House, Dorfman, Hanges and Sully de Luque (2006; see also Smith, 2006) argued in reply that people may not behave in certain ways because they hold particular views; rather they may hold views on what should be, based on what they see happening. If in a society practices are much in line with a value, the increment desired for that practice appears to be less than in societies with a low score for that practice. Along similar lines Van Maseland and Van Hoorn (2009) have argued that survey instruments insufficiently distinguish between the importance of a value and the question of to what extent that value is being satisfied by a given state of affairs. This discussion strikes at the heart of the meaning of value dimensions, calling for more research on the relationship between practices and values.

A somewhat related trend is to ask for local theories and data rather than for the fit of local data to external (western) theories. In such a context Dickson, Den Hartog and Castaño (2009) positively comment on the work of J. B. P. Sinha (2008) in India. Thus, at the same time as dimensions of values and leadership appear to be stronger than ever before, organization researchers appear to be struggling with the question of how they contribute to the understanding of cross-cultural differences.

Decision making

One of the primary tasks of managers is to make decisions on issues that arise in the domain for which they bear responsibility. Much cross-cultural research on decision making has not specifically focussed on organizational setting, but will be referred to here because of its importance in the functioning of managers. Research varies from descriptive accounts to models in which probabilities of outcomes of imaginary bets are manipulated.

Much of the earlier cross-cultural research on decision making has been summarized by Wright (1985). He discussed research within organizational settings as well as experimental research. In descriptive studies based on impressions and clinical-style interviews (e.g., Abegglen, 1958) differences emerged that could be explained in terms of cultural factors. In studies with more systematic data collection (e.g., Pascale, 1978) there was a tendency toward striking similarities. Wright concluded that the picture was still unclear. At the time, the most extensively studied topic in the organization literature was the superiority of Japanese over American organizational efficiency. This has been attributed to a more consultative or participatory style of decision making that finds its expression in the *ringi* process, whereby plans are drafted at the lower levels of an organization and employees are encouraged to develop their own ideas into a plan. A draft plan is circulated among the departments involved and can be changed repeatedly in the process. It gradually moves up the chain of command for approval. In this way the knowledge and experience of many employees is used and consensus is promoted. The *ringi* system is a bottom–up procedure of decision making that is supposed to lead to more involvement of employees with the organization and to a sense of commitment to the success of plans because everyone shares the responsibility. However, it also has weaknesses, such as the long time it can take for a plan to get through a bureaucracy and the large amount of paperwork which results from it (Misumi, 1984).

Steers *et al.* (2009) refer to the Japanese way as consultative decision making. They postulate another mode: centralized decision making as characteristic of "Anglo" countries (USA, Australia, etc.). Here management is doing the problem analysis, possibly with advice from outside experts, and providing the solution. Implementation is hampered because workers tend to experience as a threat decisions for which they do not see the rationale. In a third mode, collaborative decision making, typical for Germany, the problem analysis and decisions are discussed by management with representatives from work councils and unions. The implementation of decisions is facilitated since workers' representatives had a say.

Wright (1985; Wright and Phillips, 1980; Wright, Phillips and Wisudha, 1983) reported a consistent difference in probabilistic thinking between western (mainly British) and South-East Asian samples, including Malaysians, Indonesians and Chinese. In their studies Wright and colleagues asked participants to answer a question and then to indicate how confident they were about the correctness of their opinion. Respondents were usually overconfident, but Asians more so. But a speculation by Wright that the Japanese would be non-probabilistic thinkers was not confirmed by Yates *et al.* (1989). In a later report Yates, Lee, Shinotsuka, Patalano and Sieck (1998) concluded that substantial differences in judgment accuracy exist between Japanese, Chinese and US-American respondents, if the information on which the decision has to be based is provided to the respondent. If the decision maker has to acquire that information actively from specified sources, the results suggest that differences largely disappear.

In their review Weber and Hsee (2000; Hsee and Weber, 1999) described several factor analytic studies of judgments of real-life risks (like hazardous technologies) that showed the same two factors, namely dread (catastrophic potential and lack of control) and risk of the unknown (unobservable and possible long-term harm).

In studies in which Chinese respondents were compared with westerners (mainly US-Americans) Chinese showed a higher preparedness to make risky investment choices, which was ascribed to the cushioning effects of Chinese social networks in the case of catastrophic outcomes. Weber and Hsee (2000) plead in their review for theory-based research with multiple methods and differentiation according to domain. Their recommendations appear to be quite similar to the notion of limited generalizability of cross-cultural differences discussed in Chapter 12 in the section on psychological organization of such differences.

As in other areas of cross-cultural research, the extent to which differences are reported appears to depend at least to some extent on the research method. Evidence based on case analyses and interpretations of the literature (rather than meta-analyses in which effect size is the main entry) tends to point toward major differences. In an article offering conceptual distinctions, Sagie and Aycan (2003) argued that participation in decision making can have different meanings across cultures. They postulated that participation varies across cultures along two dimensions: individualism–collectivism and power distance. Ignoring the high correlation found by Hofstede (1980) they use low and high positions on these dimensions as the basis for a two-by-two table describing four styles of participation in decision making. Low individualism and high power distance lead to a paternalistic style in which senior employees participate in principle on all, but in reality on very few, issues. This style is frequently observed in industrializing countries such as India, Korea, Turkey and Mexico. Another style, with high individualism and low power distance, is associated with face-to-face participation of a superior with subordinates on the basis of their expertise and experience; the participation is about tactical issues related to work rather than about strategic issues which are decided at the top level. The face-to-face style is associated with self-managing teams found in western industrialized countries. According to Sagie and Aycan not all countries fit their two-by-two scheme. For example, the tensions between authority and participation typical in western countries are not found in Japan, because of the solidarity between labor and management.

After reviewing the cross-cultural literature on decision making, Yates *et al.* (2002) raised an exciting question, namely what the implications of differences are where the judgments of one group amount systematically to better decisions than those of another group. They consider it likely that precedents set by the experience of others and oneself lead to strategies in which the outcomes of probabilistic thinking, and thus differences as mentioned in this section, could become rather irrelevant. In other words, actual decisions are likely to depend on a host of factors and not only on assessment of probabilities. However, in international interactions (e.g., international teams) a lack of awareness of differences in decision-making customs could easily become a hindrance. Yates *et al.* point out that awareness and understanding of the reasons for variations could help to avoid such negative effects.

Psychological variables in the work context

There are many aspects of individual organizational behavior that have been studied in cultural context, like job attitudes, commitment to the organization and trust (e.g., Bhagat and Steers, 2009; Gelfand *et al.*, 2007). In this section we focus on two, namely work motivation and job satisfaction. Box 16.1 discusses personnel selection, a topic typical of professional psychology, but relatively rarely dealt with in the cross-cultural literature on organizations.

Motivation

Among the motivation (or need) theories that have inspired cross-cultural researchers the most prominent are those of McClelland (1961) and Maslow (1954). The basic argument in McClelland's work is that economic development cannot be explained without reference to social and psychological variables. He was struck by the apparent role which achievement motivation (a motivation to get ahead) plays in the process of national development. Like other researchers at that time, he hardly paid attention to the role of education and the opportunities that a given ecocultural context offers individuals for development; these issues have only been emphasized in more recent analyses (e.g., Sen, 2000).

Maslow (1954) has proposed a hierarchy with six levels of needs that people are motivated to satisfy. Lower-level needs have to be satisfied, at least to some extent, before higher levels can be addressed. Maslow's distinctions served as the basis for the first major international survey of work motivation conducted by Haire, Ghiselli and Porter (1966). They slightly modified Maslow's scheme and investigated the following needs: security, social, esteem, autonomy and self-actualization. Haire and colleagues obtained data from ad hoc samples of at least some 200 managers in fourteen countries, – nine from Europe, plus the USA, Argentina, Chile, India and Japan. Of the various needs, self-actualization was rated as the most important in all countries, followed in most countries by the need for autonomy (i.e., the opportunity to think and act independently). Between-country differences in the relative importance of needs from Maslow's hierarchy were relatively small; but relatively large differences were found in the degree to which needs were satisfied. In all countries, the two needs rated most important were the least satisfied. The most satisfied managers (on all needs combined) came from Japan and the cluster of Nordic European countries. Managers from developing countries (which formed a separate cluster in this study) and from Latin European countries were the most dissatisfied.

In addition to research on the general needs and motives that are satisfied by work there have also been studies of the activity of working and the outcomes of work. The analysis of the meaning of working has a long history in social philosophy

Box 16.1 Selection and placement with culturally diverse applicants

The use of tests affects the lives of more people than any other professional activity of psychologists. The potential merit of properly standardized tests as predictors of future job performance is beyond question. For personnel selection meta-analyses have produced strong evidence of predictive validity and utility; a company is likely to enhance productivity when hiring suitable employees, and tests of intelligence (or general mental ability) and work sample tests tend to be the most valid predictors (e.g., Schmidt and Hunter, 1998).

Frequently employees have to be recruited from a culturally diverse pool of applicants. This is the case in countries with a culturally heterogeneous population (due to immigration or ethnic diversity). It is also more and more common that applicants for a job live in different countries. Cultural diversity raises issues of selection fairness. It has been argued in several chapters that score distributions on psychological measures, including intelligence tests, are likely to differ across cultures. Needless to say, members of lower-scoring groups have a lower probability of being hired.

Fairness has several meanings (e.g., AERA, 1999; Camilli, 2006). Some of these focus on the assessment instruments and the assessment procedure, such as the requirement of equitable treatment in administration conditions for all applicants, or the opportunity for applicants to familiarize themselves with the type of task that will be administered (test training). Fairness can also refer to perceptions of applicants. For example, in the selection of carpenters a reading test in the dominant language of a country may be seen as discriminating against migrants, even when the purpose is to screen for the skill to deal with manuals and written instructions.

A fairly common meaning equates fairness with equal group outcomes. A condition for fairness in this sense is that the proportion of passing scores should be the same in identifiable groups (e.g., ethnic groups, men and women). A test or procedure that does not meet this condition is said to have an "adverse effect" for the lower-scoring group. A rule of thumb is that a test (or selection procedure) has an adverse effect if the ratio of passing scores (or hiring) between groups falls below 4:5.

Among psychometricians fairness of an instrument mostly refers to the absence of predictive bias: the same test-criterion regression function should apply to different groups. This is a tricky requirement. If there are differences in score distributions between groups, different regression functions apply and it has long been known that no decision rule can be formulated under which there is complete absence of prediction bias for members of the different groups across the range of scores (Petersen and Novick, 1976). However, when score distributions and validity coefficients are so similar that there is limited adverse effect, decision rules can be formulated that hardly deviate from the ideal. The more serious issues with fairness are with instruments and selection strategies.

Box 16.1 continued

To enhance fairness the equivalence of instruments has to be optimized. There is a substantial volume of research on how to identify cultural bias in tests (establishing lack of equivalence) at both item and test score levels. In Chapters 1 and 12 we have mentioned analysis of equivalence, including item bias. An important set of guidelines on the adaptation of tests across cultures has been prepared by the International Test Commission (www.intestcom.org/guidelines; for further references see Bartram, 2008; Gregoire and Hambleton, 2009).

Selection strategies are meant to diminish adverse effects. It is important to note that not all differences may be the result of test bias. Assessment may reflect valid ("real") differences between groups in terms of job performance, for example due to quality of education, or command of the main language. There is not a single answer to the question of how resulting issues of fairness should be dealt with. One way to clarify this is by distinguishing three primary stakeholders in selection decisions.

1. *The individual applicant.* It is in the interest of each individual applicant to be given a job in which s/he can maximize his or her potential. This amounts to a "placement" decision – that is, each applicant is hired and given the most suitable position for that person. This happens (ideally) in educational systems where all pupils are placed in the type of school that best matches their capabilities.
2. *The employer.* In a labor market with more applicants than positions typically there is maximization of employer interests/utility. The most promising applicant tends to be hired – that is, the person with the highest scores. If the assertion about utility in the first paragraph of this box is correct, this selection strategy makes sense for an employer seeking to maximize economic benefit.
3. *Society at large.* Here utility considerations include both sociopolitical factors (notably integration of minorities) and economic factors (productivity).

The professional responsibility of psychologists and human resources managers who deal with personnel hiring and promotion is not limited to the second point, but includes societal interests (see especially Messick, 1995). If a broader social responsibility is accepted, parameters in a fairness equation should include factors like rates of unemployment in designated groups, estimated organizational benefits of selection (Schmidt and Hunter, 1998), economic costs of loss of productivity through hiring less qualified employees, and compensation for (prior) disadvantages of individuals/groups in education.

Such an approach is difficult and cumbersome and requires negotiation between stakeholders (trade union to represent workers' interests, and representatives of employers, minority groups and the government). Ideally interactions should lead to some consensus on selection strategies balancing various interests, for example in the form of quota hiring (minimum percentages of hiring from designated groups).

Box 16.1 continued

The complexities of selection in culturally diverse settings can be illustrated with the case of South Africa, where unfair selection is outlawed in the Employment Equity Act (e.g., Theron, 2007). There is a legacy of large disadvantaged groups from Apartheid times and official recognition of eleven languages. It is deemed fair that applicants are entitled to use their mother tongue during selection, but there is not a single psychometric instrument that has been standardized for all language groups (Meiring, Van de Vijver, Rothmann and Barrick, 2005). Political power and a part of the economic power is in the hands of a small black elite, but in industry and commerce most senior jobs continue to be occupied by members of the white minority and selection procedures contribute to a perpetuation of this imbalance. At the same time, any drastic disruption of current practice may result in great economic costs, as shown by the economic downturn in Zimbabwe between 1995 and 2010, where agricultural production collapsed after farms had been taken from white owners to compensate for previous injustices.

and more recently in the social sciences. Most famous is Weber's (1905/1976) treatise on the rise of capitalism as a result of Protestant religious dogma and work ethic. This widely endorsed theory postulated that the Protestant religion is associated with high achievement motivation which serves as the antecedent leading to industrial development in Western Europe. In a rare early empirical test Munroe and Munroe (1986a) compared achievement motivation in two samples of Abaluyia in western Kenya. One sample consisted of secondary school students whose families had been converted to Protestantism a few generations ago, and the other sample, of respondents who adhered to the traditional (animistic) religion. Of several variables pertaining to achievement motivation, some were found to be in line with Weber's hypothesis. The authors note that effects were small and that for each supportive finding there were several non-supportive results. The most elaborate study on the meaning of working did not support Weber's theory. This study reported by the Meaning of Working International Research team (MOW, 1987) is described in Box 16.2. Perhaps the most convincing criticism of Weber's thesis is an analysis of historical data from Germany in which a higher level of education of Protestants has been shown to explain differences in economic prosperity which Weber attributed to religion (Becker and Woessmann, 2009).

Questions were later raised about Maslow's need hierarchy and the extent to which such findings as mentioned also apply to employees with low incomes. Sanchez-Runde, Lee and Steers (2009) point out that research in less industrialized nations and with low-earning workers is rare; however, there are indications that need for job

Box 16.2 **The meaning of working**

Here we report on a classic project with, in our opinion, interesting and significant outcomes about cross-cultural differences. The leading concept in this project was work centrality. This was defined as "a general belief about the value of working in one's life" (MOW, 1987, p. 17). To assess this concept respondents were asked directly how important working was for them, and also how important it was in relation to other life roles (leisure, community life, religion and family). The importance of working was best illustrated by two findings. Eighty-six percent of all participants indicated that they would continue to work even if they had sufficient money to live in comfort for the rest of their lives. The second finding was that working was second in importance among the five life roles; only family was rated higher.

The MOW study was based on a complex model with work centrality as the core. Societal norms are intermediate, and valued working outcomes and preferred working goals form a peripheral layer. To the model were further added antecedents and consequents of work centrality. Social norms (which can show cross-cultural differences) were seen as the basis for normative evaluations about work. A distinction was made between entitlements (the right to meaningful and interesting work) and obligations (the duty to contribute to society by working).

The study involved respondents from eight countries listed here from high to low in the order in which working was considered important: Japan, (now former) Yugoslavia, Israel, USA, Belgium, the Netherlands, (West) Germany and Britain. Two kinds of samples were drawn in each country: a national sample (N = 450 or more) that was taken as representative for the country and various target groups (N = 90 approximately). These target groups were homogeneous with respect to demographic or work-related characteristics, such as age or occupation. In Yugoslavia there was no national sample; for this country estimates were derived from the results of the target groups.

The importance of working varied between occupations, with the highest scores for professionals and the lowest for temporary workers. Skilled workers and the unemployed had medium scores on centrality of working. Except in Belgium and the USA women scored significantly lower than men, with the most noticeable gender difference in Japan. Differences between countries were about 1.5 times larger than between occupational groups. The Japanese had by far the highest score, a finding expected by the MOW team; the score was lowest in Britain. The second lowest position of Germany and the second highest position of the Yugoslavs were considered surprising. A tentative explanation for this pattern suggested by the MOW team was that the centrality of working is a non-linear function of the length of time since industrialization. The West European countries, with Britain in the lead, have the

Box 16.2 continued

oldest history in this respect; Japan and Yugoslavia have only more recently become industrialized.

Meaningful differences were found for both the entitlements and the obligations aspect of societal norms. On the entitlements side the USA scored low and the Netherlands, Belgium and Germany high. The Netherlands were low on obligations; Yugoslavia and Israel scored high. Of particular interest is the balance between these two variables, that is, between the right to work and one's duty to do so. In Japan, Britain, Yugoslavia and Israel these two variables were approximately balanced. In the USA there was more endorsement of duties than of rights. In the remaining three countries – the Netherlands, Germany and Belgium – entitlements were more emphasized than obligations. The MOW team believed (on intuitive grounds) that a balance between rights and duties would seem the most preferable state of affairs. Going a step further, one could speculate that an overemphasis on rights when it was coupled with a low work centrality (as in the Netherlands) might adversely affect the level of economic activity of a nation in the long run.

security among these large working populations is more important than the pursuit of self-actualization. All in all, findings on work motivation seem to suggest that actual working conditions can help explain cross-cultural differences, a viewpoint that is supported by research on job satisfaction, to which we shall turn now.

Job satisfaction

For decades age and position have been found consistently to be correlates of job satisfaction of individual employees in many countries (Berry, Poortinga, Segall and Dasen, 1992). In more recent research with larger samples and more countries these findings have been largely replicated, but with further specifications that could be identified through the use of multilevel analysis (see the analysis sections of Chapters 1, 12). Hui, Au and Fock (2004) reanalyzed data from the World Values Survey (WVS) with large samples from thirty-three countries. Age, income, life freedom (i.e., control over the way your life turns out) and job autonomy (i.e., freedom to make decisions in the job) were significant predictors of job satisfaction at the individual level. The individual-level data of the WVS were combined with country-level indicators of power distance (Hofstede, 1980) and national wealth. At this level power distance turned out to be a significant predictor of job satisfaction. In addition, Hui *et al.* found a cross-level interaction: power distance moderates the relationship between job autonomy and job satisfaction. In countries with high power distance the effect of job autonomy essentially is taken away so that this variable hardly has a positive effect on job satisfaction.

In another study, which involved 129,000 employees, 51 percent blue-collar and 49 percent white-collar workers, of a single international company in forty-one countries, Huang and Van de Vliert (2004) again showed at the individual level that job satisfaction was highly correlated with hierarchical position in the organization. They used a multilevel model in which, at the individual level, job status (or job level) was taken as a predictor of job satisfaction. The authors expected that this relationship would be moderated by the country-level characteristic of individualism. Multilevel analysis confirmed that in countries scoring high on an index of individualism, job level was positively correlated with job satisfaction, but not in countries with a low score on the individualism index. In this analysis differences in individualism were controlled for national income, so that affluence cannot explain the findings. Huang and Van de Vliert also found that the opportunity to use one's skills is a correlate of job satisfaction. When there is limited opportunity to apply one's abilities, as can be the case in countries with low scores on individualism, white-collar workers were found to be less satisfied with their jobs than blue-collar workers.

In a related study Huang and Van de Vliert (2003) used a similar multilevel model, but with intrinsic job characteristics (challenge, recognition and autonomy) and extrinsic job characteristics (pay, job security and working conditions) as predictors of satisfaction. Here the moderating effects of four country-level indices were examined: individualism, power distance, national wealth and social security. The most notable findings were that the link between intrinsic job characteristics and job satisfaction is stronger in richer and more individualistic countries, and in countries with better governmental social welfare programs and low power distance. Also, in countries with good social welfare and low power distance intrinsic job characteristics tended to be related to satisfaction, while in countries without these conditions this relationship tended to be absent.

The studies by Hui *et al.* (2004) and Huang and Van der Vliert (2003, 2004) show for job satisfaction how more precise results can emerge when country level and individual level are clearly distinguished. They represent a new trend in culture-comparative research. Multilevel analysis is becoming increasingly popular in organizational research, and various interactions between levels have been reported already (e.g., Smith and Fischer, 2008). More research with further differentiation between levels (countries, organizations, divisions, work teams) is to be expected (Fischer, 2008).

In this section we have focussed on job satisfaction. We would like to note that related topics exist, notably "organization commitment" and "organizational citizenship" (Wasti, 2008; Farh, Hackett and Chen, 2008). In part these topics reflect a shift in orientation, inspired by the perception that in East Asian organizations employees tend to be highly committed and proactive. Such a broadening of concepts was also mentioned in respect of leadership styles; it underlines the importance of incorporating indigenous insights from various cultural regions in cross-cultural psychology.

Conclusions

. . . .

Bhagat and McQuaid (1982) were of the opinion that the state of the art in cross-cultural work and organization psychology left much to be desired. Later Bhagat, Kedia, Crawford and Kaplan (1990) were more positive. Although they noted a lack of theoretical and methodological rigor, they saw progress in so far as the applicability of western findings elsewhere was questioned and theories were introduced to account for findings. Bhagat (2009) espoused a positive view of the field, noting a further trend toward theoretically and methodologically more rigorous studies, linking cultures, organizations and work. Such a positive view is shared by many researchers in cross-cultural organizational psychology. There has been advancement in knowledge and the scope for application is enormous, especially due to continuing globalization. Probably the most critical questions raised nowadays are about the relevance of the available knowledge to address concrete problems in everyday work contexts.

In the discussion of topics, the general direction across the sections in this chapter has been from broad cultural variables to more specific individual variables. In the first section we discussed the role of national culture in shaping organizational structure, and how cultural variables may play a lesser role in how organizations are structured and a stronger role in how employees are functioning. We then turned to organizational culture – a concept that has gained great popularity among organization researchers and consultants alike. We expressed reservations because the culture concept as used in this book differs in scope from the notion of organization culture. Moreover, the more subjective aspects of organizational culture, accessible only with qualitative methods, continue to raise concerns about validity.

The value dimensions that were discussed in the third section are bridging across levels; they are seen both as cultural (in the sense of national cultures) and as individual attributes. This is a particularly rich domain of research in terms of the number of studies conducted and the widely shared opinion that value differences can help explain international differences in organizational and work variables.

In the area of managerial behavior the most central topic of research is leadership. We mentioned research on leadership styles from Japan and India that also appeared to be applicable outside these countries. We also referred to the most extensive cross-cultural study of leadership styles and values to date, the GLOBE project, of which perhaps the most salient finding has been that charismatic leadership works across a wide range of industrialed and industrializing countries. A short overview of decision making has drawn attention to thematic issues that have come up in several chapters, namely the finding of sizable cross-cultural differences and the question of their generalizability.

In the final section we addressed cross-cultural research on work motivation and job satisfaction drawing both on older research and on modern studies that made use of multilevel analyses to refine results. With the introduction of larger studies and better designs more consistent findings can be anticipated that will justify cross-cultural organizational psychology as an active area of research, driven by the awareness that an understanding of diversity in cultural background is an important condition for the success of organizations in a time of globalization.

KEY TERMS

contingency theory • decision making (by managers) • job satisfaction • leadership styles • motivation (work-related) • organizational culture • organizational structure • work-related values

FURTHER READING

Bhagat, R. S., and Steers, R. M. (eds.) (2009). *The Cambridge handbook of culture, organizations, and work.* Cambridge: Cambridge University Press.

This volume provides a broad overview of the state of the art in the field of work and organization psychology.

Gelfand, M. J., Erez, M., and Aycan, Z. (2007). Cross-cultural organizational behavior. *Annual Review of Psychology*, 58, 479–514.

The article briefly reviews a wide range of factors in organizational behavior.

Hofstede, G. (2001). *Culture's consequences: International differences in work related values* (2nd edn.). Beverly Hills: Sage.

The "classic" work in which the origin of Hofstede's value dimensions are described and embedded in a rich overview of the literature. (The original edition was published in 1980.)

House, R. J., Hanges, P. J., Javidan, M., Dorfman, P. W., and Gupta, V. (eds.) (2004). *Culture, leadership and organizations: The GLOBE study of 62 societies.* Thousand Oaks, Calif.: Sage.

This volume reports on the most extensive cross-cultural leadership study to date, with measures of values and (perceptions of) leadership styles.

Smith, P. B., Peterson, M. F., and Thomas, D. C. (eds.) (2008). *The handbook of cross-cultural management research.* Los Angeles: Sage.

This handbook deals with a large set of topics in cross-cultural management research. It is a rich source, also because of the extensive list of references.

17 | Health

CONTENTS

This chapter focusses on health in relation to cultural context. It begins with an introduction to some conceptual issues including some definitions of central terms, how health problems can be compared, and a brief overview over how culture and health may be related. The chapter also examines possible links between culture and mental illness (psychopathologies), and how different societies attempt to relieve mental health suffering and problems (psychotherapies). The chapter also focusses on positive mental health, health behavior from the point of view of the United Nations Millennium Development Goals and how ecology and population may be related to health.

Health has been defined by the World Health Organization (WHO) as "a state of complete physical, mental and social well-being, and not just the absence of disease or infirmity" (WHO, 1948). However, studies have shown that the very concept of health differs across cultures (Helman, 2008). From a western point of view, health is often conceptualized in a biomedical model, where health is seen in terms of disease. Disease in turn is seen as originating from a specific and identifiable cause within, or arriving from outside, the body. Views from other cultures regard health as an imbalance either between negative (*yin*) and positive (*yang*) forces as in the case of Chinese medicine, or elemental ingredients (*bhutas*) and waste products from food (*vayu, pitta* and *kaph*) in Indian Ayurvedic medicine. Similarly, Galenic-Islamic medicine is based on humoral theory, where illness arises from excesses or deficiencies of the humors (Tseng, 2001). The model of health that is adopted invariably determines what is healthy and the treatment approaches.

In the past few decades there has been a change in the way people think about health: in the unanimous acceptance of the Alma Ata Declaration of "Health For All by the Year 2000" (WHO, 1978) and in the "Ottawa Charter on Health Promotion" (WHO, 1986), there has been a shift away from curing disease once it has occurred to the prevention of disease (through public health measures such as primary health care), and even more fundamentally to the promotion of health (through such factors as appropriate diet and exercise, and the avoidance of unhealthy substances). This shift in emphasis has positioned health at the center of national development policy (Brundtland, 2005), where governments are accountable for the health of their people (Kickbusch, 2003). Central to health policy is governments' responsibility for providing their people with the opportunity to lead socially and economically productive lives. At the start of the twenty-first century, there seems to be an even more radical shift from disease prevention to "capacity building for health" as a societal goal (Breslow, 1999).

With respect to disease prevention, one major effort has been an emphasis on reducing risks. The WHO has identified a number of risk factors: underweight/overweight; unsafe sex; high blood pressure; tobacco and alcohol consumption; unsafe water, sanitation and hygiene; iron deficiency; indoor smoke from solid fuels; high cholesterol; and obesity. Together, these risks account for more than one-third of all deaths worldwide (WHO, 2002). In many developing countries, at least 30 percent of all deaths result from fewer than five of these risks. Many of these risks can be reduced or eliminated by simply changing one's life style and behavior.

Clearly psychology has a basic role to play here, using established techniques and programs for behavior change. Hence, with this shift in goals, there has been a shift in approach as well, away from an exclusively high-technology biological-oriented strategy, to one that recognizes the potential role of the social and behavioral sciences in the health area (MacLachlan, 2006). It should be pointed out at the outset that the social and behavioral science role is not limited solely to *mental* health: the approach taken here is that psychology and cross-cultural psychology are just as relevant for *physical* and *social* health issues. This position is one that is shared with the WHO (1982, p. 4), which explicitly indicates that: "**psychosocial factors** have been increasingly recognized as key factors in the success of health and social actions. If actions are to be effective in the prevention of diseases and in the promotion of health and well being, they must be based on an understanding of culture, tradition, beliefs and patterns of family interaction."

Some specific ways in which cross-cultural psychology can contribute to such understanding are through the study of the shared and customary health activities of a cultural group, and then examine the health beliefs (what health is), attitudes and values (the importance attached to health) and the actual health-related behaviors of individuals. This dual-level approach to health considers both the cultural and the individual levels to be worthy of study, using anthropological and psychological techniques, and then linking the two levels. See Berry and Sam (2007) for a framework for understanding the link between health and cultural contexts.

Some definitions and conceptualizations

In medical anthropology and medical sociology, a distinction is often made among disease, illness and sickness to respectively denote medical, personal and social aspects of human ailment (Caplan, McCartney and Sisti, 2004; Hofmann, 2002). Disease is a health problem that consists of a physiological malfunction that results in an actual or potential reduction in physical capacities and/or a reduced life expectancy (Twaddle, 1994). It is the outward, clinical manifestation of physical malfunction or infection. Illness is the human experience and perceptions of the malfunction. It is a subjectively interpreted undesirable state of health, and consists of subjective feeling states of inadequate bodily functioning. How individuals perceive, experience and cope with disease is based on our explanations of sickness.

Sickness is the society's way of making sense of and dealing with the individual perception of malfunctioning (illness); and the underlying pathology (disease) (Kleinman, Eisenberg and Good, 2006). In short, sickness is illness *plus* disease.

The distinction among disease, illness and sickness points to the fact that it is possible to be ill (subjectively) without disease (objectively; i.e., in the absence of any pathological condition). It is equally possible to have a disease (i.e., show a pathological condition), but not be ill. These two situations can help to explain cross-cultural differences in health and health help-seeking behavior, such as individual health behavior, and treatment compliance behavior.

Parallel to the distinction between disease and illness is the distinction between curing and healing. Curing entails the elimination of disease from the body, and healing is an act that leads to the subjective perception of feeling well, or the improvement of the ailing body. In effect, one can be cured of a disease, but the person may not feel healed, and vice versa: the person feels healed, but the disease may not be cured (i.e., the disease or pathology eliminated). This distinction may explain the current status of HIV/AIDS, whereas of today, people cannot be cured of HIV infection, but they may have the feelings of being healed.

Cross-cultural psychology is not only concerned with the health of individuals, but also that of the cultural group to which the individual belongs; this is because population-level factors invariably impinge on the individual. At the population level, health indicators, such as child mortality and life expectancy, may be an indicator of the health of the society at a given time (Lindstrand, Bergström, Rosling *et al.*, 2006). Such indicators may help explain the health of individuals in a society. In the 1990s the WHO and the World Bank in collaboration with the Harvard School of Public Health introduced the concept of Global Burden of Disease (GBD) (Lopez, Mathers, Ezzati, Jamison and Murray, 2006). The GBD is a comprehensive regional and global assessment of mortality and disability from 107 diseases and injuries and 10 risk factors. The number of diseases, injuries and risk factors used in the initial GBD assessments in the 1990s has increased. In concrete terms, burden of disease is the gap between present health status and an ideal situation where everyone lives into old age[1] free of disease and disability. Premature death, disability and exposure to certain risk factors that contribute to illness can contribute toward the gap. Central to the notion of burden of disease is the Disability Adjusted Life Years (DALY), which is the unit of measurement of the overall burden of disease. Specifically, it is a combination of the total Years of Life Lost (YLL) (because of premature death) and the number of Years one Lives with Disability (YLD): (DALY = YLL + YLD). Although one DALY is equivalent to one year of healthy life lost, GBD is often expressed in terms of proportion (%) of DALY. GBD makes it possible to compare the magnitude of different health

---

[1] Life expectancies in Japan are used as the norm, because of the generally longer life expectancies in that country.

problems (globally and regionally), and how much they contribute to overall global or regional health problems.

About 14 percent of GBD has been attributed to mental disorders, mostly due to depression, schizophrenia and other common mental disorders, alcohol-use and substance-use disorders. The other 86 percent of GBD is attributed to physical health such as cardiovascular diseases, infectious diseases, such as HIV/AIDS and malaria, and non-communicable diseases such as cancer. The burden of disease varies by age, gender, culture and region. It also changes with time. Later in the chapter, as we look at some specific diseases, we will indicate how much burden the disease carries.

Psychopathologies across cultures

At the start of the twentieth century, Emil Kraepelin, credited as the father of modern psychiatry, observed that some patients he encountered during a lecture tour in Asia and North America failed to express their illness with the prototypical symptoms characteristic of his German and Northern Europe patients. He proposed the establishment of *Vergleichende Psychiatrie* or Comparative Psychiatry as a subdiscipline in psychiatry to study cultural differences in psychopathology. From the time Kraepelin proposed this, the field of psychopathology has progressed, albeit slowly, under different names including ethnopsychiatry, cultural psychiatry, transcultural psychiatry, culture and psychopathology, and cultural clinical psychology. The field is largely concerned with abnormal behaviors; however, it is a difficult area to comprehend, partly because of the specialist nature of the topic, and the fact that much of mental illness is difficult to objectively verify: people's feelings and thoughts are private and subjective (Angel and Williams, 2000), and these can be more complicated when thoughts and emotions get distorted through disease and illness.

By "abnormal behaviors and states" psychologists and psychiatrists usually mean those features of an individual's behavior or experience that have been classified as an "illness" or a "disorder" (not just "eccentricities"), and are judged as strange or bizarre by others who interact with the individual in daily life. They also go well beyond the more usual difficulties that are caused by stressful situations, which vary across cultures (Sewell, 2008). In this chapter, we use the term "mental disorder" synonymously with the terms "mental illness," "abnormal behavior" and "psychopathology." While more formal definitions are provided in the psychiatric literature, the everyday definition referring to unusual and strange behavior allows us to designate the domain with which we are concerned.

A listing of major mental disorders as found in the *International Statistical Classification of Diseases and Related Health Problems 10th Revision Version for*

Box 17.1 **A classification of mental disorders**

To facilitate the international reporting of psychiatric illness, the World Health Organization (1997c) has developed an *International Statistical Classification of Diseases and Related Health Problems 10th Revision Version for 2007* (ICD-10).[2]
Below are the main categories and their codes.

1. [F00–F09] *Organic Mental Disorders:* such as Alzheimer's disease, and dementia (due to such organic factors as Huntington's and Parkinson's disease).
2. [F10–F19] *Mental Disorders Due to Psychoactive Substance Use:* such as alcohol, tobacco, cannabis, sedatives, cocaine and hallucinogens.
3. [F20–F29] *Schizophrenia and Delusional Disorders:* such as paranoia, catatonic schizophrenia and delusions.
4. [F30–F39] *Affective Disorders:* such as manic and depressive mood disorders.
5. [F40–F49] *Neurotic Disorders:* such as phobia, anxiety, obsession, amnesia, multiple personality, hypochondriasis and neurasthenia (fatigue syndrome).
6. [F50–F59] *Physiological Dysfunction:* such as anorexia, obesity, insomnia, sleep walking and sexual dysfunctions (lack of desire, enjoyment or response).
7. [F60–F69] *Personality Disorders:* such as impulsive, dependent personality, problems of gender identity, pathological gambling, fire-setting and stealing; also included are abnormalities of sexual preference (fetishism, exhibitionism, voyeurism, paedophilia, but *not* homosexuality).
8. [F70–F79] *Mental Retardation:* such as arrested mental development (low IQ).
9. [F80–F89] *Developmental Disorders:* such as language, aphasia, and reading problems, autism and hyperkinesis.
10. [F90–F98] *Childhood Disorders:* such as sibling rivalry, tics, bedwetting and stuttering.
11. [F99] Unspecified mental disorders.

The categories of mental disorders as reported in the DSM-IV-TR are different from those reported in the ICD-10. For instance, Neurotic Disorders [F40–F49] are coded separately as Anxiety Disorders and Somatoform Disorders in the DSM-IV.

2007 – ICD-10 (WHO, 2007c) is provided in Box 17.1. A more complete description of each category is available in most textbooks of abnormal psychology (e.g., Comer, 2009; Kring, Davison, Neale and Johnson, 2006). In addition to the ICD-10, there are the *Diagnostic and Statistical Manual of Mental Disorders*, 4th edition (with revised text) (DSM-IV-TR; American Psychiatric Association, 2000), and the

---

[2] See www.who.int/classifications/icd/en/bluebook.pdf (retrieved July 29, 2010). The manual is currently undergoing revision.

Chinese Classification of Mental Disorders, 3rd Edition (CCMD-3; Chinese Society of Psychiatry, 2001). There are both minor and major differences in these various classification systems in terms of names, categories and criteria for making a specific diagnosis. For instance, neurasthenia, one of the most common disorders in China, is not listed in the DSM-IV. It is listed in the ICD-10, but was absent in some earlier editions of the ICD. Whereas the DSM-IV suggests that a full-fledge schizophrenia diagnosis should be made after the symptoms have persisted for at least 6 months, the ICD-10 suggests 12 months.

Biases in the classification system of mental disorders

A major problem in psychopathology is that there are many different ways in which mental disorders can be classified, with no one way necessarily more valid or better than the others (Thakker, Ward and Strongman, 1999). As noted earlier, the experience of mental disorder itself is highly subjective (Angel and Williams, 2000), and making sense of it depends in part on how articulate the person is in expressing his or her feelings and thoughts and the manner in which the behavioral aspects expressed are acceptable or unacceptable in the society in question. Equally problematic is developing a reliable classification system, because mental disorders become prevalent at particular times and/or fade away with time. One such example is homosexuality, which in many western countries has been regarded as a normal behavior, after the governing body of the APA voted to remove it from the category of psychopathology in 1973. Meanwhile, in some countries like Uganda, not only is homosexuality an abnormal behavior, but it is also a criminal offence (Candia, 2009). The classification systems themselves are affected by changes in professional knowledge and advances in medical and psychological science. For instance, Internet addiction is currently not a recognized disorder, but there are plans to include it in the next edition of the diagnostic manual published by the APA. Concomitant to professional knowledge are social factors such as political ideology, patterns of clinical practice and the legal and medical system with particular reference to health insurance, all of which can influence the classification system. Against this background, a universal classification system is difficult to achieve.

Nevertheless, the DSM-IV tries to portray itself as such (Draguns and Tanaka-Matsumi, 2003; Widiger and Clark, 2000), despite its failure to incorporate into the current edition the many recommendations on cultural factors (see López and Guarnaccia, 2000; Mezzich, Kleinman, Fabrega and Parron, 1996). The implicit assumption of the DSM-IV is that its diagnostic categories represent (extreme) universal disorders (Thakker and Ward, 1998). This is predominantly the western illness perspective: the biomedical model of mental illness. As Thakker and Ward succinctly put it, the biomedical model views mental illness to be "fundamentally biological in origin, and, given the common physiology of Homo sapiens worldwide, psychopathology [is] essentially homogeneous, with only superficial variation in presentation across peoples" (1998, p. 502). This view is what we have termed "extreme universalism." On the other hand, the CCMD-3 admits to the influence of Chinese culture (e.g., *gi-gong* – exercise of vital energy – a Chinese healing system based on trance) in the development of its nosologies. This is in spite of every effort made in both CCMD-2-R and CCMD-3 to be aligned with the ICD-10, one which is devoid of culture (Chen, 2002). By assuming an extreme universalist stance, classification manuals such as the DSM-IV have become biased against mental disorders that have not found their way into the manual. This may include such disorders as neurasthenia (found in the CCMD-3, and ICD-10), and the so-called culture-bound syndromes (found in the appendix of the DSM-IV, but not listed in the ICD-10).

Irrespective of differences and biases in the manuals, it is now acknowledged that the different disorders found in the manuals account for substantial personal, social and economic loss. More importantly, however, is that neuropsychiatric conditions account for as much as a third (31.7% YLD) of all years lived with disability, including 1.4 percent of all deaths and 1.1 percent of years of life lost (YLL, in 1990) (WHO, 2005). Nevertheless, Prince and his colleagues have argued that the global burden of mental disorders may have been grossly underestimated because of lack of appreciation for the link between mental disorders and other health conditions (Prince, Patel, Saxena, Maj, Maselko, Phillips and Rahman, 2007). The WHO (2005) has for instance indicated that there is "no health without mental health" because mental disorder increases one's risks to both communicable and non-communicable diseases and vice versa. In addition, the stigma associated with mental disorder makes it difficult for people to seek medical attention (Thornicroft, 2008).

One important theoretical issue regarding psychopathology cross-culturally is whether these phenomena are (1) invariant across cultures in their origin and expression (i.e., extreme universals), or (2) present in some form in all cultures, but subject to cultural influence on factors such as the onset and expression (i.e., moderate universals), or rather (3) unique to some cultures, and understandable only in terms of that culture (culturally relative). This third view is the essence of ethnopsychiatry and is part of the move to understand "indigenous psychologies" of abnormal behavior. Later in the chapter, we will look at some specific mental illnesses in the discussion of psychopathology and whether their expression is invariant across cultures. But before then, we will look at the prevalence of some common mental illnesses, and the suggested link between culture and psychopathology.

Prevalence of some mental health disorders across countries

One way to determine whether psychopathology is universal or culturally relative is the prevalence of the problem across cultural settings. Similar prevalence rates across countries and cultural societies may be an indication that psychopathology is universal. Differences in prevalence rates may mean that psychopathology is either relative, or moderately universal (i.e., culture is implicated in one form or the other). A preliminary indication of possible moderate universal psychopathology comes from the WHO study conducted in fourteen sites including Ankara in Turkey, Berlin in Germany, and Verona in Italy (Goldberg and Lecrubier, 1995; Üstün and Sartorius, 1995). This study used three different ways to reach a diagnosis (a short screening instrument; a detailed structured interview; and clinical diagnosis by the physician) among patients attending a primary care health facility. The prevalence of some of the disorders examined can be found on page 22 of *The World Health Report 2001* (WHO, 2001); the study found differences in prevalence rates across the board. For instance, the prevalence rate for Current Depression was 29.5 percent in Santiago, Chile, while the rate was just 2.3 percent in Nagasaki, Japan, and 11.6 percent in Ankara, Turkey. The prevalence rate for Generalized Anxiety in Ankara was 0.9 percent whereas the rate was 22.6 percent in Rio de Janierio.

One conclusion we may reach on the basis of difference in prevalence rates in countries is that psychopathology, at least based on diagnosis, appears to be present in all the societies, indicating some form of the universality of psychopathology. The huge differences in prevalence imply that what qualifies as psychopathology, and how this is expressed, may be different from society to society, suggesting some form of moderate universalism. It is possible that the relatively low Generalized Anxiety among outpatients in Ankara, for instance, is "compensated" for by the relatively high Current Depression among the patients there. There is much evidence to suggest that there is high co-morbidity (i.e., co-occurrences), with huge overlaps between disorders (Lowe, Spitzer, Williams, Mussell, Shellberg and Kroemge, 2008). Another possibility is that categories of diagnoses identified in the primary care unit reflect a particular external cultural point of view (i.e., an imposed etic) with respect to psychopathology. This latter point of view comes from the critique that there are biases in the classification of mental disorders (Widiger and Clark, 2000). This is due to a large extent to the imposition of western nosologies and illness categories on other cultural groups. This phenomenon has been referred to as the "category fallacy" by Kleinman (1977), who suggests that psychiatric categories and practices are bound to the cultural context of professional psychiatric theory and practice. This fallacy may occur in the situation where researchers and clinicians impute the illness categories of their culture to other cultures (an imposed etic). A possible example of this is classifying neurasthenia (in China) as depression as found in western societies, or *Tajin Kyofuaho* (in Japan) as social phobia.

The link between culture and psychopathology

Tseng (2007) has suggested that there may be six different ways that culture can impact on psychopathology, and these have further been linked to different culture-bound syndromes. The six different ways are: "pathogenic" effect (i.e., conditions where cultural beliefs induce stress and anxiety, and lead to the development of a disorder); "pathoselective" effect (i.e., conditions where culture chooses a unique, albeit pathological, pattern of dealing with stress); "pathoplastic" (i.e., culture modifying the manifestation); "pathoelaboration" (i.e., culture elaborating disorders into a unique nature); "pathofacilitating" (i.e., culture promoting the frequency of a disorder); and "pathoreactive" (i.e., culture shaping response to the clinical condition). A more detailed description of these six ways can be found on the Internet (Additional Topics, Chapter 17). In a literature review, Kirmayer and Sartorius (2007) also indicated that through cultural explanatory models, individuals make causal attributions that affect their physiology which then gives rise to culture-specific varieties of disorders such as panic disorder, hypochondriacal worry and medically unexplained symptoms.

To illustrate the link between culture and psychopathology, and whether the expression of psychopathology is invariant across cultures, we will now look at three specific psychopathological conditions (i.e., organic disorders, schizophrenia and depression), together with the broad area of culture bound syndromes.

Organic mental disorders

These are disorders with demonstrable pathology or aetiology, or which arise directly from a medical disorder (i.e., disease). These are in contrast to all other mental disorders that are referred to as functional disorder. Prior to the 1970s, psychiatry distinguished between organic and functional disorders, with an implicit assumption that only the former were disorders of the brain, and were biological (Walker and Tessner, 2008). This distinction is, however, criticized on the grounds that all mental disorders have biological, environmental (i.e., social and cultural) and psychological bases. Nevertheless, the position has still remained that organic disorders have clearly identifiable biological conditions. Two major organic disorders are "dementia" and "delirium." Other organic disorders are mental disorders that are caused by an identifiable medical condition such as neuro-syphilis arising from syphilis. Currently, DSM-IV has two separate categories: one for dementia and delirium, and the other is "mental disorders due to general medical condition." In the previous edition (DSM-III), these were organized as organic disorders, as was also the case in ICD-10, and the CCMD-3. The change from DSM-III (American Psychiatric Association, 1980) to DSM-IV is another example of change over time due to ideology, mentioned earlier.

Because of their strong biological base, organic disorders are the most likely candidates for supporting an extreme universalist position. Organic disorders by definition do not have room for pathogenic and pathoplastic cultural effects; however, this position is just based on a logical possibility. There is little research available that would substantiate it, and those studies that are available suggest that cultural factors, such as unique life style collectively shared by a group of people, may indirectly affect the occurrence, rates and forms of expression (Tseng, 2001).

Disorders of schizophrenia

Although it is now commonly acknowledged that schizophrenia is not a single disorder but a group of disorders that may be heterogeneous (Jenkins and Barrett, 2004), in this chapter we classify them under the single rubric of schizophrenia. The signs of the disorder are disordered thinking, disorganized speech, hallucinations, delusions and disorganized motor behavior such as catatonia, withdrawal or blunting of emotional expression (Jenkins and Barratt, 2004). In spite of its low incidence rate (15.2 new cases per 100,000; McGrath et al., 2004) and consistently low lifetime prevalence (4.0 per 1,000 population; Saha et al., 2006) schizophrenia is the most debilitating mental disorder in the world (Stompe and Friedman, 2007), accounting for 1.1 percent of the total DALY, and 2.8 percent of total years lost to disability.

The consistent low prevalence rates have been used as one reason to propose that there is a biological base and that this might be inherited (Cannon, 2005; Siegert, 2001). In addition, patients undergoing pharmacological treatments have shown improvements (Adams et al., 2000), suggesting a biological base of the disorder. These findings lend support to the extreme universality position (Jarskog, Miyamoto and Lieberman, 2007; Miyamoto et al., 2005). However, the precise biological markers are difficult to identify, and how drug therapy works remains unclear. In major survey studies a large number of potential genetic variations (alleles) have been identified as possible factors, but no clear patterns have emerged (Ross and Margolis, 2009). A further complication is that the diagnosis of schizophrenia has a considerable margin of uncertainty; it cannot even be excluded that more than a single illness will lead to the appearance of schizophrenic symptoms (International Schizophrenia Consortium, 2009; Stefansson et al., 2009).

Using a variety of indicators, schizophrenia has been identified in several societies since the beginning of the twentieth century (Draguns and Tanaka-Matsumi, 2003). These studies point to a possible role of cultural factors in this disorder, where certain cultural experiences appear to precipitate its onset and prognosis (Kulhara and Chakrabarti, 2001). There is evidence that cultural practices (in definitions and diagnostic preferences) may affect the apparent prevalence, and this may partially account for minor differences in rates across cultures. This subtle interaction between "true" rates in schizophrenia in different societies and variations in diagnostic procedures led to the initiation of a series of comparative studies on schizophrenia and other psychoses across different populations in the 1960s. In the course of three decades, the WHO has conducted three major studies on the course and outcome of schizophrenia in twenty research centers in seventeen countries including Colombia, Czech Republic, Denmark, India, Nigeria, Taiwan, UK and the USA (see Leff, Sartorious, Jablensky, Korten and Ernberg, 1992; WHO, 1973, 1979a). Features of the studies included simultaneous case finding and data collection, use of standardized instruments, trained project psychiatrists and multiple follow-up assessments. The studies have generated a rich amount of information on over 2,000 cases of schizophrenia and related disorders.

Although the WHO studies suggest a "core of common symptoms" including social and emotional withdrawal, delusions and flat affect, substantial differences in profiles were found from study center to study center. For example, US schizophrenics differed from Danish and Nigerian on symptoms of lack of insight and auditory hallucinations (fewer of both) while Nigerians had more frequent "other hallucinations" (i.e., visual and tactile) than the other two groups. Other studies have also shown that the contents of delusions varied, where delusions of grandeur are rarely found in village community samples (Stompe et al., 1999). Similarly, religious delusions and delusional guilt are primarily found in Christian traditions, and rarely in Islamic, Hindu or Buddhist societies (Stompe et al., 1999, 2006). While the paranoid subtype of schizophrenia is the most common form of the disorder in all the countries in WHO studies, except for Nigeria (where schizoaffective was most diagnosed), the rate of catatonic subtype was very similar in all sites. In one study, however, Murphy (1982) concluded that the cationic subtype is rare among Europe-Americans. The difference between Murphy's finding and the WHO studies has been suggested to be due to the inclusion criteria for the WHO studies (Stompe et al., 1999). Given the "common core" (and the partial reduction of variation in diagnosis when common instruments are employed) it has been concluded by the authors of the original (WHO) studies, and by reviewers alike, that schizophrenia is best understood as a moderate universal disorder, one that is recognizably present in all cultures, but that it appears to respond to different cultural experiences in prevalence rates and modes of expression.

Another important finding of the WHO studies was the follow-up assessment of prognosis of the disorder, defined as the percentage of the patients characterized by psychosis. The finding was that patients from developing countries showed better outcomes compared with their peers in developed countries (Jablensky, 2007). While several other studies have confirmed the better prognosis of schizophrenia for patients in developing countries (e.g., Hopper and Wanderling, 2000; Thara, 2004), there is a lack of knowledge of the exact sociocultural factors that account for the better outcome among patients in developing countries.

Before embracing the notion of a moderate universalism conclusion fully, some cautionary points need to be made: first, the studies involved instruments, concepts and researchers who were mostly western-oriented, and, second, the patient populations are not a representative sample of world cultural variation (and were to some extent themselves acculturated to western life). Kleinman has criticized the inclusion and exclusion criteria in the WHO studies on the grounds that "similarity was an artefact of the methodology" (1988, p. 19). Differences in prognosis have also been questioned on the grounds that so-called schizophrenic patients in developing countries may be suffering from reactive psychotic episode rather than the classic schizophrenia (Kleinman, 1988). It is not uncommon that some infections and parasitic diseases such as trypanosomiasis, which are common in Africa, may mimic schizophrenia. Newer analyses of the WHO data, however, have dismissed the claim of patients in developing countries as suffering from something else (Jablensky, 2007), and have concluded that schizophrenic disorders in non-western populations can reliably be distinguished from acute transient psychoses. The conclusion is that schizophrenia is a universal disorder, found in all known societies; however, the subtypes, contents of delusions and hallucinations, and the prognosis of the disorder may vary across-cultures.

Another purpose of the WHO studies on schizophrenia was to investigate the role of stressful life events occurring a couple of weeks before the onset of the schizophrenia episodes (Day *et al.*, 1987). While the centers in developed countries identified a number of stressful events in the area of personal, family/household livelihood, these were not found in the developing countries. Tanaka-Matsumi and Draguns (1997) believe that this may be due to cultural differences in what may constitute stressors in different societies. Other studies have found support for the link between stress and the onset of schizophrenia (Corcoran, Walker, Huot, Mittal, Tessner, Kestler and Malaspina, 2003) and its relapse. In a one-year follow-up study analyses indicated stressful life events made a significant cumulative contribution over time to relapse (Hirsch *et al.*, 1996). Moreover, a link has been found between schizophrenia and more subtle everyday factors such as daily hassles (Norman and Malla, 1993). One form of daily hassles – expressed emotion (EE), which refers to family members' negative emotional reactions to patients – may be relevant as a stressor in psychosis relapse in schizophrenia. Schizophrenia patients returning to families with high criticism and emotional involvement levels have about 50 percent chance of relapse, compared with 15 percent in patients returning to low-EE families (Butzlaff and Hooley, 1998; Corcoran *et al.*, 2003; Vaughn and Leff, 1976). A problem with the link between stress and schizophrenia is causality and its direction. Indeed the bi-directionality of the patient–family interaction has been proposed by some researchers (Barrowclough and Parle, 1997).

Depression

Whereas the western construct of depression was previously thought to be absent in non-western societies (Bebbington and Copper, 2007), this disorder is currently acknowledged to be present in all societies and affects members of all cultural and ethnic groups (while the way the disorder is expressed and managed differs from society to society [Kleinman, 2004]). Furthermore, developments in drug therapy have been argued to give support to causal theory claims that depression is caused by neurotransmitter deficiencies and, therefore, has a biological base. The use of brain imaging to identify biomarkers and endophenotypes has also been helpful in identifying regions of the brain involved in depressive disorders (Peterson *et al.*, 2009). In spite of this, efforts to pinpoint the specific pathways to the development of the disorder remain elusive. In contrast, the huge differences in prevalence and incidence rates across societies suggest some form of cultural influence.

While not as debilitating as schizophrenia, depression is one of the commonest mental health problems in the world. In addition to the disorder's relatively high life-time prevalence rate (around 2–15%), it is also associated with substantial disability. The estimates in 2000 of burden of disease rated depression as the fourth leading cause of disease burden, and accounted for 4.4 percent of DALY. The disease is also responsible for the greatest proportion of disease burden attributable to non-fatal health outcomes, accounting for close to 12 percent total years lived with disability, globally (Moussavi, Chatterji, Verdes, Tandon, Patel and Üstün, 2007). Projections indicate that depression will climb to the second position in terms of overall burden of disease, accounting for 5.7 percent of DALY (Murray and Lopez, 1997).

Based on the World Mental Health Survey (2010) initiative involving twenty-eight surveys with a total sample size of over 154,000 (1,300 to 36,000 per survey), the 12-month prevalence rate of depression ranged from 1.0 percent (in Nigeria) to 10.3 percent (in the US) (see Kessler and Üstün, 2008). Depression is also 1.5 to 3 times more common among women than men (Gorman, 2006). Differences in comparative rates in depression have been suggested as being due to research artifacts, such as a select sample (i.e., involving people visiting a primary health care unit), and to differential use of the depression diagnosis by psychiatrists. Bebbington and Copper (2007) have suggested that these differences in rates could also be due to variations in pathways to care, the health care system in the country and attitudes toward physicians.

Regarding differential use of depression diagnosis across cultures by psychiatrists, analyses suggest that the answer is probably "no," that there is no such thing as differential diagnosis (Draguns and Tanaka-Matsumi, 2003). However, the local cultural meaning of "being depressed" varies widely according to the patient's language and the differentiation of emotional terminology in a language (Kleinman and Kleinman, 2007; Okello and Musisi, 2006). It has also been suggested that the English word "depressed" has no equivalent in some languages, such as among American Indians and in some South Asian groups (Manson, 1995). The Yoruba in Nigeria have been found to have a very low prevalence rate of depression (ca. 2.3% life long; and 1.0% 12-month prevalence rate; Gureje *et al.*, 2006).

This low prevalence rate may be due to the suggestion that Yorubas have only one word for depression, anxiety and anger (Abusah, 1993). While this does *not* mean that Yorubas do not experience depressed states as described in western literature, it suggests that westerners may have difficulties identifying this disorder among Yorubas (Thakker and Ward, 1998). Specifically, unsophisticated physicians may wrongly diagnose anxiety in place of depression among members of this group.

The WHO (1983) conducted a cross-cultural study investigating the diagnosis and classification of depression in four countries (Canada, Iran, Japan and Switzerland) similar to the one on schizophrenia. The goal was to examine whether a standardized instrument – Schedule for Standardized Assessment of Depressive Disorder (SADD) – could adequately be used by psychiatrists to diagnose the disorder. The total sample was 573, and the SADD examined thirty-nine symptoms of depression, using open-ended questions. Several core symptoms were identified (i.e., symptoms found in more than 76% of the patients). These included a sad mood, and a lack of energy, interest and enjoyment. These symptoms were often accompanied by emotional changes (e.g., feelings of guilt, anger and anxiety), physical changes (e.g., sleep disturbance, tiredness and loss of appetite, weight and strength), behavioral changes (e.g., crying, withdrawal and agitation) and changes in self-evaluation (i.e., low self-esteem, pessimism and feelings of hopelessness and worthlessness); severe depression may be accompanied by suicidal tendencies. These symptoms are often regarded to be the core, and found in most of the countries that took part in the studies. Of interest are symptoms such as somatic complaints and guilt feelings that are found to be less prevalent in some countries but are more in others. Such differences have also been seen as a demonstration of cultural factors in depression. The experience of a physical symptom such as a headache, rather than psychological one like sadness (Lai and Surood, 2008) has generated a number of heated debates regarding the universality of depression. The experiences of these physical or bodily symptoms are thought to be related to an underlying psychological disorder. These symptoms are relatively less common in western societies, but more so in non-western societies (Mukherji, 1995). The presence or absence of somatization as one way of dividing western and non-western peoples in their expression of depression has been contested (Gray-Little, 2009). Al-Issa (1995) and Chen (1995) have suggested that the apparent high rates of somatization in non-westerners may be a consequence of the disapproval of strong expression of negative emotions. In many of these countries, open expression of emotions in any form is socially unacceptable. Therefore, directing these emotional feelings into bodily complaints is more legitimate (Mukherji, 1995).

A question requiring attention is whether somatization (broadly classified as "somatoform disorders" in DSM-IV) is a particular cultural group's way of expressing depressive disorders, or a separate form of disorder. This issue is demonstrated in Kleinman's observation that the largest percentage (i.e., 93%) of patients who had been diagnosed in China as suffering from neurasthenia *(shenjing shuairuo* in Chinese) – a disorder characterized by bodily weakness, fatigue, tiredness, headaches and dizziness – could also be classified as suffering from depressive disorder. Neurasthenia to a large extent looks like a somatoform disorder (see Kleinman and Kleinman, 2007). Tanaka-Matsumi and Draguns (1997) have suggested that a distinction needs to be made between "spontaneous" expression of somatic complaints, and "elicited" expression of symptoms such as dysphoria. According to this distinction, non-westerners spontaneously report bodily complaints when they come into contact with health professionals, but through careful interviewing, these non-western patients may be elicited to report on their emotional problems. Tseng (2001) adds that the spontaneous bodily symptoms non-westerners report are simply a prelude to underlying emotional problems.

Despite variations, most observers (e.g., Draguns and Tamaka-Matsumi, 2003) believe that, as in the case of schizophrenia, there is a "common core" of symptoms of depression that allows the disorder to be recognized in all cultures. Depression thus qualifies as a moderate universal, but like all other universals at the present time, the western bias in research approach and in the populations studied may well have affected the conceptualization and descriptions.

Culture-bound syndromes

Culture-bound syndromes are patterns of behavior considered to be abnormal or psychopathological, and are found only in a particular cultural group. While culture-bound syndromes are the most readily recognized psychological problems when reference is made to links between culture and mental illness, they are the disorders that receive least treatment in the general psychiatric, clinical and abnormal psychology textbooks. Often, they are set aside thus putting them at risk of being dismissed as irrelevant, and not worthy of serious consideration. Neither DSM-III-R (American Psychiatric Association, 1987) nor ICD-9 (WHO, 1997b) makes reference to culture-bound syndromes. DSM-IV has a section on culture-bound syndromes, but these have been placed in an appendix, and do not follow the normal categories used by the DSM-IV. It appears that culture-bound syndromes cover all mental disorders that are not normally found in western psychiatric and clinical psychology textbooks.

Culture-relative studies of psychopathology abound in the literature; there is apparently nothing more intriguing in this field than discovering another apparently unique way of "being mad"! The rich reports of "culture-bound syndromes" have fueled the extreme relativist position and have led to the claim that there are unique, local forms of psychosis, not known outside of a particular culture. A sample of these conditions is on the Internet (additional Topics, Chapter 17) to give a sense of their special and interesting qualities.

Culture-bound syndromes have been referred to by various names including psychogenic psychoses, ethnic psychoses, ethnic neuroses, hysteric psychoses, exotic psychoses, culture-reactive syndromes and culture-related specific syndromes (Simons and Hughes, 1993). Each culture-bound syndrome is a collection of signs and symptoms which are restricted to a limited number of cultures primarily by reason of certain psychosocial features. A question often raised is whether these syndromes are local expressions of some universal disorders already known and classified, or whether they are culturally unique (Bhugra, Sumathipala and Siribaddana, 2007). This issue may be illustrated with the case of Dhat syndrome (Additional Topics, Chapter 17).

www.cambridge.org/berry

A point made earlier was that culture impacts on every kind of psychopathology to some extent, whether it is predominantly biological or psychological in nature. Thus, one can question why some disorders are classified as culture-bound and others not. Unless the cultural impact is very significant, a disorder may not qualify as a culture-bound syndrome. Tseng (2007) has suggested that the different ways in which culture may be linked to psychopathology can be used as a basis to classify culture-bound syndromes (see Additional Topics, Chapter 17). According to Tseng, pathogenic effect is an essential and sufficient condition for defining culture-bound syndromes; similarly, pathoselective effect is another essential and sufficient condition. Pathoplastic, pathoelaboration and pathofacilitating may contribute to the development of psychopathology, but they are not in themselves sufficient for the development of a culture-bound disorder. Pathoreactive is not a sufficient condition for culture-bound syndrome. This is a secondary effect, taking the form of labeling. The six cultural effects are not culturally exclusive. They act in multiple ways.

www.cambridge.org/berry

What can be said about the universality of psychopathology? Aboud (1998) has divided the answer to this general question into various components. First, all cultures appear to have separate categories for normal and abnormal behavior. Second, common symptoms are widespread across cultures, but there can be differences in expression, sometimes in the form of culture-bound syndromes. Third, how these symptoms are classified appears to vary, even though there is widespread international use of ICD-10 and DSM-IV. Finally, the course and outcome of mental disorders are often culturally variable, but with only occasional culturally unique features. It should be clear that most of this evidence points in the direction of a moderate universalist position. On the one hand, there appears to be important cultural patterning of those disorders that are most evidently biologically rooted (making the extreme universalist position untenable). On the other hand, initial attempts to discover some "common core" of symptoms of the major psychoses across cultures, and to identify underlying categorizing principles for the apparently culture-bound syndromes, have both yielded some success. Nevertheless, such a conclusion must be a tentative one, awaiting further research from points of view, and samples, that are less clearly rooted in a single (western) cultural tradition.

Psychotherapy

Just as there are cultural factors involved in the development and display of psychopathology, so, too, are there cultural factors involved in the process of attempting to alleviate these problems, through a process referred to as psychotherapy (Tseng, 2004). Psychotherapy is a general term that is employed to refer to any practice that involves a patient and a healer in a personal relationship, with the goal of alleviating the patient's suffering due to a psychological problem or disorder. This definition, however, does not take culture into consideration. Draguns has provided a cultural perspective definition of psychotherapy as "a procedure that is sociocultural in its ends and interpersonal in its means, it occurs between two or more individuals and is embedded in a broader, less visible, but no less real cultural context of shared social learning, store of meanings, symbols, and implicit assumptions concerning the nature of social living" (1975, p. 273). We share Draguns' view where we regard psychotherapy as a special practice involving a designated healer (or therapist) and an identified client (or patient), with the particular purpose of solving a problem from which the client is suffering or promoting the client's mental health. The practice may take various forms, and the fundamental orientation may be supernatural, natural, biomedical, sociophilosophical or psychological (Tseng, 2001). We also see psychotherapy as entailing a triangular relationship between the client, the therapist and the society. Usually, cultural beliefs and practices prevalent in a society enter into the psychotherapeutic process, because they form part of both the therapist's and patient's definitions and understandings of the problem.

Within the therapeutic setting, we can distinguish between indigenous and cross-cultural psychotherapies. In contemporary societies of globalization and migration, we can add multicultural psychotherapy. In the case of indigenous psychotherapy, and other health interventions, all three elements (i.e., client, therapist and society) share a common culture, since there is no intercultural situation involved. Indigenous psychotherapies are thus often referred to as culture-embedded in the cultural system in which they were developed, and often are difficult to transport to a different cultural setting. In the case of cross-cultural psychotherapy (across international borders; e.g., Tantam, 2007), and intercultural counseling (across ethnocultural groups within a country; e.g., Cuéllar and Paniagua, 2000), serious misunderstandings may result. This is because western-based theory and method are frequently used to examine and assist persons of other cultures. Multicultural psychotherapies, on the other hand, go a step further than ordinary cross-cultural psychotherapies in the sense that they employ culturally sensitive and culturally appropriate psychotherapeutic methods taking into consideration the cultural and ethnic backgrounds of the therapist and client and the acculturating context (Tanaka-Matsumi, 2008). Central to multicultural psychotherapy is cultural adaptation of empirically supported psychotherapy. This entails "the incorporation of culture-relevant and culture-sensitive information into the practice of psychotherapy with diverse clients" (Tanaka-Matsumi, 2008, p. 178).

Indigenous psychotherapies

Indigenous psychotherapies can be found in virtually all societies. Sometimes they are used in conjunction with western psychiatry, sometimes alone. While these psychotherapies function as healing methods for problems, often they are considered by neither the therapist nor the clients as psychotherapy for emotional disorders. On the contrary, they are seen as religious ceremonies or healing exercises related to supernatural or natural powers (Castillo, 2001; Mpofu, Peltzer and Bojuwoye, in press). From a mental health point of view, indigenous healing practices produce psychotherapeutic effects, and may be thought of as "folk psychotherapy" (Tseng, 2001). Because they are an inherent part of the triangle of cultural relationships discussed above, they are often effective. However, they may work for reasons other than this match or fit with the patients' beliefs (Simwaka, Peltzer and Banda, 2007). Jilek (1993) has noted that indigenous healers are often more accessible to those needing help, they also tend to accept the patients' descriptions of their problems, and they are often empathetic and charismatic, leading to the establishment of a trusting and potentially more effective healing relationship.

In western industrialized societies, psychotherapy has taken different forms, and is based on various theoretical positions in psychology (e.g., learning theory, Gestalt theory, humanist theory). Currently, cognitive-behavioral is the leading theoretical preference in many western countries (Hays, 2006). We regard these as *indigenous* therapies of the West, but do not dwell on them, even though they are the most frequent basis for cross-cultural psychotherapy. Instead, we will identify some indigenous therapies that have been developed in non-western cultures.

Indigenous or folk healing methods actually cover a wide range of practices. If the healing practice is closely linked to religion, it may be called "religious healing practice" or a "healing ceremony." If this involves the mediation of spirits, it may be called "shamanism" or "divination" or "fortune-telling." Under each of these, different forms of practices have been identified (see Winkelman, 1992, for a discussion).

Among the range of these indigenous psychotherapies are those rooted in Japanese culture and thought: *Morita* therapy (Morita, 1998), and *Naikan* therapy (Tanaka-Matsumi, 1979). According to Murase (1982, p. 317), both of these therapies are "revivalistic, and oriented towards a rediscovery of the core values of Japanese society." These core values are *amae* and *sunao*, and are related to *Morita* and *Naikan* respectively, although both values are thought to enter, to some extent, into both therapies. A more detailed description of *Morita* and *Naikan* therapies can be found on the Internet (Additional Topics, Chapter 17).

Morita therapy was developed in Japan by the psychiatrist Morita (1874–1938) during the 1920s, about the same time that Freud developed psychoanalysis in Austria, to treat psychoneurotic problems. It is based upon isolation and rest, rather than verbal interactions. Broadly, the therapy involves a behavioral structured program aimed at encouraging an outward look to life and increased social functioning (He and Li, 2007).

Naikan therapy was developed by Japanese Buddhist Ishin Yoshimoto (1916–1988) as a short-term structural treatment for marital and familial conflicts, interpersonal relationship issues, depression and anxiety, self-esteem issues, behavioral disorders and addictive behaviors (Sheikh and Sheikh, 1989). The overall goal of the therapy is for the patient to increase his or her awareness of self as well as accept without becoming judgmental (Maeshiro, 2009). The term *Naikan* comes from the Japanese *Nai* ("inside") and *kan* ("looking"). A poetic translation is "seeing oneself with the mind's eye." It is a structured method of self-reflection that helps individuals understand themselves, their relationships and the fundamental nature of human existence.

Voodoo is a synthesis of African, Roman Catholic and local beliefs and practices into a folk religion that has served to give the people of Haiti a sense of unique identity. It has also served the purpose of healing (among others), thus exhibiting the not uncommon link between religion and medicine found in many parts of the world. One of the most spectacular features of *voodoo* is ritual possession trance, in which saints (*loa*) enter into and "possess" the practitioner, who can either be a believer (with no special psychological problem), a patient or a priest/doctor who seeks to heal.

Many varieties of possession have been identified by Tseng (2001) and Winkelman (1992), including the patient being possessed by harmful spirits of a dead person, the patient being possessed by protecting spirits, and the voodoo priest being possessed by spirits that assist in the diagnosis and cure of the patient. Thus, in *voodoo* healing there is an intimate matrix of relationships involving not just a patient and a therapist, but a patient-believer, a therapist-priest and a variety of good and evil spirits, all set in a complex medico-religious belief system; this system in turn is rooted in a culture contact (acculturation) situation that led to its development, and set the stage for its widespread acceptance in the population.

What are we to make of (non-western) indigenous psychotherapies? Are they merely local superstitions that have no value, or perhaps only work to the extent that superstitious people believe in them? Or do they each have a status with respect to their sociocultural systems that parallels, for example, that of Freudian psychoanalysis in some western societies? For some critics, both sets of practices may be dismissed as mere superstitions that work to some extent because, and only because, people believe they will work (as a placebo effect). Without "scientific foundations" or "proof" they could be dismissed easily by skeptics. However, Lo and Fung (2003) point out that most indigenous psychotherapies do work, at least as well as those employed in western psychotherapy. For instance, Kitanishi, Fujimoto and Toyohara (1992) and He and Li (2007) have found good prognosis among patients who were treated with *Morita* therapy. Similarly, Qie and Xue (2003) have found good prognosis among patients who have undergone *Naikan* therapy. Thus, these indigenous therapies cannot be dismissed as lacking in effectiveness. Moreover, a wide range of such (non-western) indigenous psychotherapies (or their derivatives) are now being accepted into western medical thought, as supplementary to other psychotherapeutic practices (Jilek, 1988). Perhaps *all* of these practices are effective to some extent precisely because clients believe in them, and are accepted as part of one's all-encompassing cultural belief system. This belief permits the "mobilization of endogenous resources" (Prince, 1980, p. 297) as well as involving the family and the community, leading to relief for the sufferer. It may matter little what these beliefs and resources are, as long as they are accepted by the patient (Gielen, Draguns and Fish, 2008; Gielen, Fish and Draguns, 2004).

Cross-cultural psychotherapy

The foregoing conclusion raises a question: to what extent does cross-cultural psychotherapy work? That is, can medical beliefs and practices from one culture be effective in the healing process in another culture? To answer this question, it may be useful to consider the extreme universalism, moderate universalism and relativist positions. In the discussion of indigenous psychotherapies, we noted the existence of culturally unique ideas and practices that were part of a larger complex of cultural beliefs and values; and the claim in the literature is that they may have a positive effect in their local settings. A common dimension to all of these approaches – the mobilization of one's own resources through medico-religious practices that one believes in – seems to be a central thread. Thus, it would be a reasonable, but tentative, conclusion that there may be some underlying universal basis for the healing process. A common core to psychotherapeutic practices may exist, but with different historical and cultural roots, and with highly varied cultural expressions. Approaching the issue from the extreme universalist position, attempts to employ Freudian psychoanalytic theory and practice in non-western cultures is one example: are psychoanalytic formulations etic principles of human development and psychopathology? While psychoanalysts believe this to be the case (Fenichel, 1955), using the technique beyond the western educated elite limits its verification (Prince, 1980). If this claim is correct, then we can dismiss the cross-cultural use of psychoanalytic theory as a candidate for an extreme universal approach to psychotherapy, and possibly its local use as an indigenous one. One may attempt cultural adaptations of various psychotherapies, which by so doing shifts one from an extreme universalist position to at least a moderate universalist one (see Christopher, 2001; Lo and Fung, 2003).

In an effort to determine the effectiveness of culturally adapted psychotherapies, Griner and Smith (2006) meta-analyzed seventy-six studies involving a sample of over 25,000 participants. All the studies included a comparison of a culturally adapted psychological intervention to a "traditional" intervention. Results indicated "an overall positive effect of culturally adapted mental health interventions. Across all 76 studies the random effects weighted average effect size was $d = .45$, and across 62 studies with experimental or quasi-experimental designs, it was $d = .40$. Average effect sizes across many potential moderating variables ... typically ranged from $d = .30$ to $d = .60$" (Griner and Smith, 2006, p. 541). These results show that culturally adapted psychotherapies may be moderately universal in their effectiveness.

Multicultural psychotherapies

As was pointed out, a central aspect of multicultural psychotherapy is the cultural adaptation of psychotherapeutic methods that have been proven scientifically to be effective. A number of guiding questions can be found in the multicultural literature on how to achieve cultural adaptation of a particular therapy (see Tanaka-Matsumi 2008 for a discussion of various guiding steps). One important step is therapists and counselors being aware of their own ethnic views and biases, and how these might interact with those of the client to impede the therapeutic process. One such effort is ADDRESSING (Hays, 2001), which is an acronym that therapists can use to generate hypotheses about a client's beliefs, values, emotional expression, health belief system and symptoms presentation. ADDRESSING – which stands for Age; Developmental and acquired Disabilities; Religion and spirituality; Ethnicity; Socioeconomic status; Sexual orientation; Indigenous heritage; National origin; and Gender – is designed to prompt the therapist to address each of the letters. In addition, through functional analysis of cognitive and behavioral therapies, it is possible to adapt the therapy to suit the needs of people of diverse ethnic backgrounds. Functional analysis entails the identification of antecedents (A), the behaviors (B) and their consequences (C). The goal of functional analysis is the "identification of important, controllable, causal functional relationships applicable to a specified set of target behaviours for an individual client" (Haynes and O'Brien, 1990, p. 654). Once the target behavior is identified, "the task is to monitor the occurrence of the target behaviour and its antecedent events and situations, and the target behaviour's consequences" (Tanaka-Matsumi, 2008, p. 187), including the response of others within the social settings of the client.

Positive mental health

The last two sections of this chapter have looked at mental health problems and how societies try to alleviate these problems. In this section, we turn to the more positive aspects of mental health, in line with the current conception of health by the WHO (Kok, 2007; Seligman, 2008). In keeping with its role as a promoter of health worldwide, the WHO initiated a long-term project on quality of life (Skevington, Lotfy and O'Connell, 2004; WHOQOL, 1995). The aim was to develop an international cross-culturally comparable quality of life assessment instrument. It assesses the individual's perceptions in the context of their culture and value systems, and their personal goals, standards and concerns. The key question of the project is "what makes for a good or satisfying life?" The concept of QOL is widely used across disciplines including economics, ecology, law, political science and social welfare, and health psychology. While the concept is shared, the findings do not always correlate. For example, it is often noted that increase in income is not necessarily related to subjective (psychological) well-being (Diener and Seligman, 2009; Kahneman and Krueger, 2006), or to health outcomes more generally (Diener and Biswas-Diener, 2002), a phenomenon which has become known as the Easterlin paradox in economics. This paradox "suggests that there is no link between the level of economic development of a society and the overall happiness of its members" (Stevenson and Wolfers, 2008, p. 1).

The concept of QOL is also multidimensional, a feature that stems from its multi-disciplinary use. However, two basic dimensions have emerged: one representing objective factors in the cultural environment, and the other representing subjective appraisals and reactions to them. These two sets of factors have been termed "socio-environmental" and "personal" by Fernández-Ballesteros et al. (2001). Included in the first set are environmental quality, financial conditions, social support, and in the second set are life satisfaction, health, functional abilities and leisure activities. In this distinction we see similarity to the field of cross-cultural psychology, where we attempt to link contextual variables to psychological variables. Overall, QOL has been defined as the product "of the dynamic interaction between external conditions of an individual's life and the internal perceptions of those conditions" (Browne et al., 1994, p. 235). In psychology the measurement of QOL has usually focussed on the subjective aspects, while estimates of the more objective conditions have been drawn from accounts given by the other disciplines.

At the core of the more personal facets of QOL is the notion of subjective well-being (SWB), defined as a person's cognitive and affective evaluation of his or her life (Diener, Lucus and Oishi, 2002). More specifically, it refers to life satisfaction and the balance between positive and negative affect in one's life. Cross-cultural studies of SWB have been carried out for over half a century, in several countries, where studies show that most people are *pretty* happy, but there are differences across cultures with respect to what makes them happy (Biswas-Diener, Vittersø and Diener, 2005; Eid and Larsen, 2008). Generally, the research shows that for most people around the world, positive affect predominates over negative affect (Dolan, Peasgood and White, 2008). These studies also seem to suggest that individual happiness, and that of a nation, are somewhat constant. Happiness, according to earlier research, did not change in the face of rising prosperity or adverse misfortunes. Individuals invariably returned to their base line happiness level after a period on a "hedonic treadmill" (Biswas-Diener, 2008; Inglehart, Foa, Peterson and Welzel, 2008).

In a series of international surveys (from 1981 to 2007), the World Values Survey found, contrary to the contention that happiness is relatively stable, that the overall level of happiness of most of the countries involved in the studies has changed, that is, people have become happier (Ingelhart *et al.*, 2008). This increase in happiness was found to be related to economic development, democratization and increasing social tolerance, which give people the perception of free choice. Moreover, these studies have also shown that it is not in the richest or the most economically developed countries that the people are happiest. While Denmark is presently the happiest nation, with Puerto Rico and Colombia respectively occupying the second and third positions, Armenia and Zimbabwe occupy the last two positions. The USA – the wealthiest nation – occupies sixteenth position.

Regarding the relationship between wealth and SWB, Diener and Biswas-Diener (2002, p. 119) summarized the following relationship:

1. There are large correlations between the wealth of nations and the mean reports of SWB in them; 2. There are mostly small correlations between income and SWB within nations, although these correlations appear to be larger in poor nations, and the risk of unhappiness is much higher for poor people; 3. Economic growth in the last decades in most economically developed societies has been accompanied by little rise in SWB, and increases in individual income lead to variable outcomes; and 4. People who prize material goals more than other values tend to be substantially less happy, unless they are rich.

Diener (1996) suggested that while SWB correlates positively with wealth (purchasing power) *across* nations (+.62), it is not the *level* of income, but recent *increases* in income that may predict SWB better *within* nations. This suggests that individuals may adapt to their economic circumstances, and respond more to changes in them than to their long-term financial situation. It is likely that there may be no single relationship that holds up across cultures: different factors may account for SWB in different cultures.

Drawing on methods that have been effective in enhancing mental health, psychology has in recent years been interested in improving our understanding of how, why and under what conditions positive emotions, positive character and the institutions that enable them flourish (Gable and Haidt, 2005; Seligman, 2002; Seligman, Steen, Park and Peterson, 2005). This new interest is also concerned with shifting psychology's overemphasis on human suffering and disorder to a more balanced understanding of human beings and their well-being. One effort within the positive psychology movement is the search for positive qualities among human beings, and how these may be related to life satisfaction. Peterson and his colleagues (Park, Peterson and Seligman, 2004; Peterson and Seligman, 2004; Peterson, Park and Seligman, 2005a and b) have identified twenty-four character strengths highly endorsed among adults in over fifty different countries. These strengths included kindness, fairness, authenticity, gratitude and open-mindedness. The correlations of the rankings across nations are strong, usually ranging in the .80s. The researchers suggest that the results point to some form of universal human nature and/or the character requirements minimally needed for a viable society. In addition, these strengths have been found to be associated with life satisfaction: the higher a given character strength in terms of rank, the more life satisfaction the individual reports (Park, Peterson and Seligman, 2004).

Health behavior

At the beginning of this chapter we noted that cultural factors (including many behavioral, social and environmental factors) play an important role in health generally, not just in mental health. At this point we turn more explicitly to these relationships, focussing as much on the promotion of health and the prevention of disease, as on the curative aspects. Before we go further, we want to highlight the distinction between health promotion and disease prevention. These two terms are often used together, and sometimes as synonyms. Disease prevention is concerned first and foremost with reducing the burden of chronic disease and infectious diseases by preventing their development in the first place. This may be through the reduction or elimination of risk factors, or an early intervention in order to hinder a disease from taking a serious turn (Heggenhougen, 2008). Health promotion is more concerned with how individuals' choices may enhance their health by providing and sustaining healthy living through policies at both the societal level and in private sectors.

The focus on health promotion and disease prevention has created a role for social and behavioral scientists in the development and implementation of public health programmes. For example, campaigns for the reduction of substance abuse and of drinking while driving, and the advocacy of low-fat diets and exercise, are clearly activities in which social psychologists' expertise in attitude change, and clinical psychologists' expertise in behavior modification could have a major part (Seligman, Steen, Park and Peterson, 2005). In spite of the huge potential social scientists have in developing disease prevention and health promotion programs, current efforts to implement specific programs are slow (Mittlemark, 2009). For the rest of this section, we will highlight a few specific cases of health promotion measures, taking as our point of departure three of the Millennium Development Goals (MDG) of the United Nations (United Nations, 2001) (see also the section on national development in Chapter 18). The MDGs are eight developmental goals, deemed to be the developmental challenges of our present time, and were adopted by 189 countries and ratified by the United Nations, and are to be achieved by 2015. For our purpose, the goals of interest are: to eradicate extreme poverty and hunger; to reduce child mortality; and to combat HIV/AIDS, malaria and other diseases. These three goals are closely linked to the other five developmental goals, and effort to achieve one will have important implications for the others. Because of the close links between the target goals, we will address them under the following subheadings: poverty, hunger and malnutrition; infant and child survival; HIV/AIDS; and malaria.

Poverty, hunger and malnutrition

Poverty is associated with inadequate food, and hunger is the most extreme form of poverty, where individuals are not able to meet the basic needs of food (Bread for the World Institute, 2010). Other than starvation and famine, which affect billions of the world population, famished individuals have to battle chronic under-nourishment and micronutrients deficiencies (referred to as hidden hunger; e.g., vitamin A, iron, iodine and zinc), which may result in stunted growth, poor cognitive development with a negative cascading effect on school failure, heightened vulnerability to diseases and infections (Dalmiya and Schultnik, 2003; Grantham-McGregor, Cheung, Cueto, Glewwe, Richter, Strupp et al., 2007). These problems are particularly prevalent in low-income countries. On the other side of the poverty scale is the so-called nutrition transition, seen in several low- and middle-income countries. This is a shift from a diet dominated by starchy low-fat and high-fiber food items, combined with labor-intensive daily life, to a diet high in fat and sugar combined with a sedentary life style (Lindstrand et al., 2006). This shift leads from hunger to obesity. About 40 percent of the world's population are presently suffering from hunger or obesity, with about equal proportion in the two categories of nutritional problems. This has created a "double burden of disease" from both under- and overnutrition.

Biologically, the human body can cope fairly well with short periodic food scarcity, but not with continuous long periods of abundant food. The human body is not physiologically prepared for overconsumption. This calls for new behaviors to reduce overconsumption in the presence of abundant food, especially fat- and sugar-rich diets. Consequences of obesity on psychological development is an area where there is little research. But obesity has been linked to other serious health problems such as diabetes and cardiovascular conditions. It is difficult to estimate the DALY lost due to over- and undernutrition. This is because these situations in themselves are not diseases, but causes of diseases. In the last part of this section, we will look at undernutrition, rather than overnutrition, as it relates to malnutrition, because undernutrition affects people who are at an economic disadvantage, with limited access to medical help. This is an area where changes in life style may be one way to deal with the problem.

The purpose of research on malnutrition and health behavior is to seek a better understanding of the links between biological and psychological aspects of human development (Aboud, 1998; Dasen, Inhelder, Lavallee and Retschitzky, 1978). The theories in this respect have changed drastically over a very short time: in the early 1970s, the predominant hypothesis was of a simple effect of reduced food intake on the number of brain cells, while now it is recognized that we are dealing with a very complex model of multiple interactions (Grantham-McGregor *et al.*, 2007). The ultimate and applied purpose of such research is to better understand the causes of malnutrition that go well beyond lack of food, but also diarrheal disease (Black *et al.*, 2008), and the mechanisms of its effects on psychological development, in order to be able to prevent malnutrition altogether, or at least minimize its ill effects. Since malnutrition occurs in a complex ecological, economic, social and cultural system, the solution is rarely as simple as providing more food, even though that may well have to be the first and most urgent measure (Gibson, 2006). Both longitudinal and cross-sectional studies have shown that improving the diets of pregnant women, infants and toddlers can prevent stunting (Engle *et al.*, 2007). Similarly, supplementation of food during the second and third years of life improved the cognitive development of children (Li, Barnhart, Stein and Martorell, 2001).

Infant and child survival

Closely linked to psychological developmental problems arising from poverty and malnutrition is the problem of infant mortality. In 2002, the global infant mortality rate was 56 per 1,000 live births. This rate ranged from 3 to 165 deaths per 1,000, with the highest rates in sub-Saharan Africa. Globally, an estimated 7.5 million children die annually during their first life of year. Infant mortality is normally divided into "neonatal" (i.e., the period between birth and the first month of life) and "post-neonatal" (i.e., the period between the first month and the first year of life) mortality. "Childhood" mortality refers to mortality during the first five years of life. Childhood mortality is currently estimated to be 82 per 1,000 births. It was estimated in 2001 that 10.4 million children died before they reached the age of 5 (Linstrand *et al.*, 2006). Here too, the highest mortality rates ca. 175 deaths per 1,000 births is in sub-Saharan Africa.

Harkness, Wyon and Super (1988) have identified "child survival" (a more positive orientation than "child mortality") as one area where behavioral sciences have made a positive impact in reducing the burden of disease. One specific approach aimed at improving survival rates throughout the world has been the "GOBI strategy" initiated by UNICEF. GOBI initially focussed on four techniques (Gatrell, 2002):

1. Growth monitoring to identify early cases of growth failure and malnutrition.
2. Oral rehydration therapy for infants and children with severe diarrhea in order to reduce the high rate of mortality from fluid loss.
3. Breastfeeding promotion, for the direct nutritional and immunologic benefits as well as the indirect reduction of contamination from unsanitary bottle feeding.
4. Immunization against major infectious diseases of childhood.

While initial results have been impressive, there have also been some evident failures, and social-behavioral analysis of these problems has been instructive. For example, merely knowing about the nature and causes of a child health problem (e.g., diarrhea) is apparently not sufficient to correct the problem. An educated woman may be in a better position to understand that this might be due to an infection from the food. Thus, ever since Caldwell's (1979) seminal paper on the importance of maternal education in child survival, efforts were made throughout the 1980s to delineate the role of maternal education in child survival. Rather than discuss the various pathways, the original GOBI has now been expanded into GOBI-FFF to include three kinds of support for women (Cash, Keusch and Lamstein, 1987), where FFF stands for Female education, Family spacing and Food supplements. Studies have shown that maternal education among other things has resulted in women beginning to have children at a later age, to have fewer children (partly because they begin late), and lower maternal mortality among educated women; thus children are not left as orphans. In addition, educated women are also found to space births, either through empowerment by taking control over their lives or by making use of contraceptives.

Sexually transmitted diseases and HIV/AIDS

The worldwide concern with the HIV/AIDS epidemic has stimulated much research by cross-cultural psychologists on sexual and reproductive health (Wellings *et al.*,

2006) and health education (Pick, Givaudan and Poortinga, 2003; Pick, Poortinga and Givaudan, 2003). In 2007 around 33 million people were living with HIV/ AIDS, and 2.7 million people were newly infected with the virus. Since the 1980s, when the disease became known, about 25 million people have died of it. Being infected with HIV and dying from AIDS are unevenly distributed geographically. While the epidemics are declining in some countries, they are thriving in some other parts of the world. Over 90 percent of HIV infected people live in developing countries (UNAIDS, 2008).

The virus is transmitted in three ways: by unprotected heterosexual intercourse (accounting for around 70% of infections), and male (but not female) homosexual relations (around 10%); by blood (infected needles, and transfusions, accounting for 5–10%); and from mother to child during pregnancy, delivery or breastfeeding (around 10% of all cases, but these constitute 90% of all child cases). While a drop in sexually transmitted diseases was noted in the mid-1980s, since 1995 there has been a gradual and sustained overall increase of 57 percent (Hedge, 2007, p. 875), with rates ranging from a 15 percent increase in first herpes attack through a 139 percent increase in gonorrhea, a 196 percent increase in chlamydia and a 1,058 percent increase in syphilis (Hedge, 2007). Although other STDs make up about 1 percent of DALY, this is overshadowed by the 6.0 percent DALY HIV/AIDS makes. Moreover, unlike the other STDs, which have several effective medical treatments, there are currently no known medicines that can cure or prevent HIV infections, notwithstanding the fact that anti-retroviral therapy has prolonged the life expectancy of HIV-infected people in high-income countries by up to a decade. Consequently, considerable attention has been devoted to prevention; this is why behavioral and social sciences have been so prominent in this field (Piot, Bartos, Larson, Zewdie and Man, 2008).

One approach has been to emphasize the ABCs of prevention: Abstinence; Be true to your lover; Condom use. However, there are both psychological and cultural issues in such a prevention program, including the roles of men and women, norms regarding sexual behavior, attitudes toward condom use, communication media and norms about open discussion of sexual relations. Most HIV-prevention programs have employed an approach known as KAP (i.e., Knowledge, Attitudes, Practices; Toovey, Jamieson and Holloway, 2004) to understand how a population was oriented to health problems. For example: (K) "How does one get AIDS?"; (A) "Do you think you can be infected by HIV?"; (P) "Did you use condom during your last sexual intercourse?" On the basis of this initial stocktaking a prevention program, emphasizing K, A or P, may be initiated. For example, if knowledge were widely present, and attitudes were appropriate (i.e., to reduce risk), then a program could deal directly with changing behavior. However, if either the necessary knowledge or attitudes were not in place, then the program would need to start earlier in the KAP sequence. Such programs can also target specific populations, such as adolescents, married couples, or sex workers and their clients, or even health care providers depending on survey results (Pick, Givuadan, Sirkin and Orgeta, 2007).

Malaria

Nearly half of the world's population from over ninety countries lives with the risk of malaria (Carter, 2007). It is estimated that annually, there are between 300 million and 500 million clinical cases of malaria, and 1.3 million deaths, the majority in developing countries (WHO, 2002). This estimate is possibly only a fraction of the actual incidence of the disease as there is often non- or underreporting of it. Even so, malaria accounts for nearly 3 percent of DALY (WHO, 2008). Malaria is transmitted by a parasite, *plasmodium*, of which there are four kinds. The seriousness of the sickness depends on the type of *plasmodium* with which one is infected. The parasite or *plasmodium* requires mosquitoes as a host, and mosquitoes require stagnant water as a breeding environment. Thus, preventive work should aim at eliminating mosquitoes, or preventing mosquitoes from biting. In addition, prophylactics can be taken to prevent infestation with the parasite from developing into full-fledged malaria. Once malaria is diagnosed, medical treatment may be required. Malaria attacks are more common in pregnant women than other adults, because pregnancy decreases a woman's immunity. The disease can also be more devastating for children. Adults living in endemic areas with exposure to repeated malaria infection since birth generally attain a degree of immunity from severe disease. Conversely, travelers from non-endemic areas are highly susceptible (Carter, 2007). Children recovering from severe forms of the disease were previously considered to attain full recovery, but new evidence suggests that severe malaria may be associated with persisting neurological and cognitive impairments in survivors (Carter, Ross, Neville, Obiero, Katana, Mung'ala-Odera, Lees and Newton, 2005).

Treatment of individuals with quinine or other drugs such as Chloroquine (the "cure" orientation) has been the most common attack on the disease, although some individual "prevention" measures are widely used as well (e.g., the use of impregnated mosquito nets). New, more effective drugs for individual treatment, and the development of insecticides (notably, DDT) for mosquito control, have made it possible since the 1950s to mount a worldwide campaign to eradicate the disease. In spite of the effectiveness of insecticides, other problems have arisen. Insecticides have proven to be harmful to humans and to the environment. The parasite has also developed resistance to many of the drug treatments, making them less effective. While previous efforts to eradicate the disease failed, some health advocates and NGOs such as the Gates Foundation have started discussing ways to completely eliminate the disease (Roberts and Enserink, 2007). One immediate aim is to halve the burden of the disease by 2010 through the "Roll back malaria" action (Editorial, 2001).

While some regions have became virtually malaria-free, there has been a recent large-scale resurgence of the disease due to a growing resistance of mosquitoes and parasites to chemical treatment (both insecticides and drugs; Bray, Martin, Tilley, Ward, Kirk and Fidock, 2005; Gregson and Plowe, 2006). Alternative approaches to controlling the disease, employing social and behavioral techniques, have been advocated (Panter-Brick, Clarke, Lomas, Pinder and Lindsey, 2006). In the Panter-Brick *et al.* (2006), a social ecology model was used in rural Gambia. Such a model contextualizes behavior within social and physical settings, while focussing on the interplay between human actors and external factors shaping their agency. Specifically, this perspective "examines transactions among people within their social and physical settings, over time and across several levels of analysis: personal, familial, cultural and institutional" (Panter-Brick *et al.*, 2006, pp. 2811–2812). Linking this perspective to malaria prevention, the researchers found in the first phase of the project that there is a high utilization of mosquito nets among the residents of the rural community, which had a long history of net use; however, due to poverty and the cost of new nets, the nets in use were old, and had holes. Thus, the prevention program aimed at encouraging the residents to repair (at low cost) nets with holes. This was done in a culturally appealing way (through songs) and the use of strategically placed posters to remind people of the content of the songs, indicating the importance and cost-effectiveness of repairing the nets.

Ecology, population and health

A persistent theme in this book has been that ecology, culture and behavior are intimately and continuously connected. In Chapters 1 and 10, culture was defined both as adaptive to and as changing the ecosystem; behavior was portrayed as both being influenced by and influencing culture; and the ecosystem was seen as both affecting and being affected by individual behavior (see Figure 1.1). In the past few decades, there has been a growing awareness of these relationships as they impact on health, both societal and individual (McMichael, 2002; Pimentel *et al.*, 2007). The key links in these relationships have been identified as population increase (Erhlich and Erhlich, 1997; Townsend, 2003), and social inequality (e.g., Farmer, 2005) both affecting the level and distribution of health resources and the potential for development (McMichael, 2002). In the rest of this chapter, we will briefly look at two issues: fertility behavior and health consequences.

Fertility behavior

Current interest in the global human population emanates from the early 1950s (Lindstrand *et al.*, 2006), where among other things it was projected that the world's population could grow to between 10.8 and 27 billion by the year 2150, with most of the growth taking place in developing countries. In the late 1960s Ehrlich (1968) published the book *The population bomb*, in which he argued that at the rate the population was growing the world could face lack of food and raw materials. He was wrong in this pessimistic assessment of the world: human beings have been innovative enough to produce enough food, with new technology, as well as to curb the growth of the world's population. Currently, it is estimated at 6.8 billion, with the 7 billion mark expected to be reached in July 2012. Global population projections have not been so dramatic to warrant their inclusion in the UN's MDG.

In spite of this there has been renewed interest in population changes (see APA, 2003; Trommsdorff, Kim and Nauck, 2005, for special issues of journals focussing on this topic), as population growth can affect the environment and the fight to overcome poverty. Globally, the population growth rate has declined from 2.0 percent in the 1960s to 1.5 percent in the early 2000s. The total fertility rate of six children per woman in 1960 has fallen to 2.8 in 2002. While the current fertility rate is above the 2.1 "replacement level of fertility," in some regions of the world, particularly sub-Saharan Africa (e.g., Mali and Niger) fertility rates are 7.3; and in some European and Asian countries (e.g., Italy, 1.3; and Japan, 1.2) fertility rates are well below the global mean (Nation Master, 2008), let alone the replacement level. The crux of the current interest is with the falling fertility rates in western countries and aging population; these countries may have problems sustaining their economies and ever growing social welfare programs (Caldwell, Caldwell and McDonald, 2002). At the same time, the growing populations of developing countries could result in poverty, food scarcities and changes in their ecosystems (Townsend, 2003). This imbalance in global population growth could also set in motion migration push and pull factors with their attendant acculturation and intercultural relations challenges (see Chapters 13 and 14).

Are there social and behavioral factors that might help to explain these dramatic trends, and, if so, can these same factors be employed to help control the increase? At the outset, the role of a number of other factors needs to be acknowledged: improved health care including curative and preventative measures and improved nutrition have both changed the pattern of infant survival and longevity. The decline in disease has come about through combined biomedical and behavioral science interventions. The decline in fertility is also a product of both these sciences, with the medical sciences providing fertility control technology, and the behavioral sciences playing a major role in research and promotion of their use (e.g., the use of KAP programs, outlined in the previous section). In this section we examine some other social and psychological factors.

Early research by Fawcett (1973) highlighted a wide variety of factors, including the value of children to parents, family structure (including forms of marriage), knowledge and use of birth control technology, values and beliefs regarding abortion, and ability to plan for the future. These factors (and other, non-psychological social variables) have begun to be considered as part of large systems, in which demographic, political, social, cultural and psychological variables interact to affect population growth.

One psychological variable in these studies are reasons adults give for having children. The question of why people have children has been the focus of two major international collaborative studies called the "Value of Children Study." The first study (see Kağitçibaşi, 1984) was initiated in the late 1960s and included nine countries (Germany, Indonesia, Korea, Philippines, Singapore, Taiwan, Thailand, Turkey and the USA). The second study was undertaken more than three decades later (Nauck and Klaus, 2007; Trommsdorff, Kim and Nauch, 2005) as a replication of the first, but was expanded to look into intergenerational relations. The second study included three generations of women: adolescents, their mothers and grandmothers. In addition to the original participating countries, two sub-Saharan African countries – Ghana and South Africa – were included.

A basic approach taken in the study was that the "values attributed to children are conceptualized as intervening between antecedent background and social psychological variables, and consequent fertility-related outcome" (Kağitçibaşi, 1984, see also Kağitçibaşi, 1996). Two issues are of interest here: one is the reasons given for wanting children, and the other is the qualities one would like to see in one's children. These studies found that there may be three reasons why people choose to have children (Kağitçibaşi, 2007): economic/utilitarian, psychological/emotional and social/normative values. The economic/utilitarian values refer to children's material benefits both while they are young and also when they grow up to be adults. The latter takes the form of old-age security for parents; the former has to do with children's contribution to household economy and household chores. The psychological value of the child has to do with the emotional feeling of joy, fun, companionship, pride and parents' sense of accomplishment from having children. Finally, the social/normative value refers to the social acceptance people enjoy when they have children, such as the status bestowed upon a man or a woman for being a father or a mother respectively. While some of the original research findings have been replicated (see Kağitçibaşi and Ataca, 2005), questions have been raised about some other findings, such as whether the three values can really be identified in all the societies studied (Sam, Amponsah and Hetland, 2008; Sam, Peltzer and Mayer, 2005). Nevertheless, this knowledge can be used in curtailing fertility rates in places where it is still very high.

Health consequences

Increasing populations challenge resources and resource distribution in a society. The recognition of this fact is the main reason for national policy reforms that attempt to shorten the period between the advent of increased life span, and the time when reduced fertility is achieved (the "demographic transition"). For example, the "one child family" initiative in China (Jing and Zhang, 1998) has recognized that, as in all ecological thinking, one change is intimately linked with many other changes: economic growth requires a young and active population, but too many children undermine per capita wealth; one child per family (especially when she is a girl) interferes with traditional Chinese family and social values, but enhances per capita wealth, and so on.

Health outcomes are also part of this ecological system, as demonstrated by the discipline of epidemiology for more than a century. Population increases are usually accompanied by industrialization, which in turn creates pollutants, stress, hypertension and a variety of diseases (lung, heart, cancer). These "webs of causation" are now well-documented for many diseases (Kawachi and Subramanian, 2005). At the same time, population growth and industrialization increase per capita wealth, which in turn allows for advances in medical research and health care. However, one of the most startling aspects of this relationship is that it is not the *average* (per capita) wealth, but the *equitable distribution* of that wealth (and of associated health services) that predicts general health status and longevity (Farmer, 2005; Marmot and Wilkinson, 2005). This finding is one reason why it is not the wealthiest nations that top the United Nations Human Development Index, but those that are moderately wealthy and have more egalitarian systems of distributing that wealth (See UNDP, 2009). These inequalities in the distribution of health resources exist not only across social classes, and across regions within countries, but even more so across countries. International variation in the support for health is vast, with the least support going to those peoples who need it the most (Farmer, 2005).

These relationships between broad sets of variables, however, tell us little about what underlies the link between socioeconomic status and health. Chamberlain (1997) argues that studies of the experiences of individuals and families are essential if we are to discover why poverty and health are linked. His research shows how a number of factors intermix in this relationship, including contact with health professionals, the meaning and value of health, and various health practices (diet, exercise, substance use).

Conclusions

This chapter has focussed on the role of culture in a number of health issues, ranging from negative aspects of health (e.g., psychopathology), through positive health (in the area of quality of life) to the prevention and promotion of better health (as in the case of, e.g., HIV/AIDS and malnutrition). Situating this chapter in the applied area of the book is to emphasize how cultural knowledge can be used to improve the health of an individual and to enhance public health. The approach taken here also highlights the contribution of social and behavioral sciences to health promotion and prevention strategies. At the core of the MDG is not just economic development, but the aim to achieve better health for individuals and reduce public health problems.

The applications of cross-cultural psychology to improve health undoubtedly must proceed cautiously, and with a concern for validation in each cultural setting. Some important successes have been achieved (e.g., Pick and Sirkin, 2010, where sex education is used as a basis from which to fight poverty). However, the health beliefs, attitudes and behaviors in many societies are deeply rooted in their cultures, making them more difficult to understand, and less susceptible to programs of cross-cultural change. Culturally adapting a psychotherapeutic method, for instance, or using culturally compelling and not merely culturally appropriate methods will go a long way in our fight against health problems.

KEY TERMS

culture-bound syndromes • depression • Disability Adjusted Life Years • disease global burden of disease (GBD) • health (definition) • illness • malnutrition prevention (health) • promotion (health) • psychopathology • psychosocial factors psychotherapy • quality of life • schizophrenia • sexually transmitted disease sickness • subjective well-being

FURTHER READING

Ayers, S., Baum, A., McManus, C., Newman, S., Wallston, K., Weinman, J., and West, R. (eds.) (2007). *The Cambridge handbook of psychology, health and medicine*. Cambridge: Cambridge University Press.

This handbook has ca. 250 short chapters and covers most topics in the area of health, medicine and psychology. Most of the topics are not addressed from a cultural perspective, but from one of current knowledge of specific health issues. The book can be regarded as a reference for academics, various health care professionals (including nurses, psychologists) on various health-related issues.

Bhugra, B., and Bhui, K. (eds.) (2007). *Textbook of cultural psychiatry*. Cambridge: Cambridge University Press.

This edited textbook provides a framework for the provision of mental health care in a multicultural/multiracial society and global economy. The book describes cultural psychiatry in diverse societies and includes practical examples and case studies.

Helman, C. (ed.) (2008). *Medical anthropology*. Surrey: Ashgate.

This edited book includes key papers outlining the history, concepts, research findings and controversies in the area of medical anthropology, the cross-cultural study of health, illness and medical care. Among the topics covered are transcultural psychiatry, food and nutrition, traditional healers, childbirth and bereavement and the applications of medical anthropology to international health issues, such as the HIV/AIDS pandemic, malaria prevention and family.

MacLachlan, M. (2006). *Culture and health: A critical perspective towards global health*. Chichester: Wiley.

This book gives an informative and integrative discussion on how culture interacts with health, illness and rehabilitation, and how this knowledge can be used for health promotion.

Tseng, W.-S. (2001). *Handbook of cultural psychiatry*. San Diego: Academic Press.

This fifty-chapter handbook provides a comprehensive review of various aspects of mental illness from a (cross-)cultural perspective. The book focusses on the history of the field of cultural psychiatry, key concepts, emic and etic views on the theories, diagnosis, expression, treatment and prognosis of most of the disorders in current diagnostic manuals as well as those not there, such as culture-bound syndromes.

18 | Culturally informed and appropriate psychology

CONTENTS

In this chapter we examine the relationship between the science and practice of psychology as it has developed in the western world, and the need for a culturally informed, relevant and appropriate psychology for all the world's peoples. Psychological knowledge in the west (hereafter referred to as **western psychology**) is often of little relevance to the majority world (a term used, for example, by Kağitçibaşi, 2007, in preference to "developing" or "Third" World). We accept and applaud the goal of advancing the development of a global psychology, one that is both valid and useful for all cultural populations. There are a number of possible paths toward this goal, including: an examination of the impact of the presence of western psychology on the psychology done in other societies; the development of indigenous psychologies in many distinct societies; and the pulling together of all of these psychologies into a universal psychology that is global in scope.

This move toward an international perspective has been increasingly important in recent years, including for the history of psychology (Brock, 2006), for the teaching of psychology (Karandashev and McCarthy, 2006) and for the practice of psychology (Stevens and Gielen, 2007). The theoretical basis for considering the possibility of actually achieving a global psychology is the position of moderate universalism espoused in this text: if it is the case that basic psychological processes are shared features of all people, then there is an opportunity to draw together concepts and findings from different cultures.

We begin with an examination of the impact of western psychology on the rest of the world, taking into account the availability of, and the demand for, the flow of this knowledge and profession. Then we turn our attention to the concept and development of indigenous psychologies in many parts of the world. Finally, we consider the possible usefulness of psychological knowledge gained in these ways for human and national development as it applies to societies and countries.

Culturally informed psychology

As we have seen throughout this book, cross-cultural psychology seeks to develop an understanding of human behavior that is intimately linked to the cultural contexts in which it has developed and is now displayed. In this chapter, we examine two features of this project: understanding the current international domination by a psychology that has remained largely uninformed by culture; and the search for a psychology that is rooted in the cultural traditions of societies around the world.

Impact of western psychology

It is apparent to everyone involved in psychology internationally that the discipline and the profession are overwhelmingly rooted in, and practiced in, western industrialized societies (Pawlik and Rosenzweig, 2000). The rest of the world has often assumed the roles of "consumers" or "subjects"; psychology is "sold to" or "tried out on" other peoples. The evidence for this state of affairs has been clearly presented by Adair, Coehlo and Luna (2002), Adair and Kağitçibaşi (1995), Allwood and Berry (2006) and Cole (2006). For example, Cole (2006, p. 905) has noted that the leadership of international psychology, particularly the International Union of Psychological Science, has "remained firmly in Euro-American hands. These countries dominate participation and management of the congress to this day, despite the fact that psychologists from approximately 100 countries currently participate (Rosenzweig, Holtzman, Sabourin and Belanger, 2000)."

This imbalance could be problematic for the majority world, since there may be a serious mismatch between what is available in western psychology and what is needed by the majority world (Moghaddam, Erneling, Montero and Lee, 2007). This is because while western psychology is just one of the many indigenous psychologies (Allwood, 1998), it has taken on the role and status of *the* psychology. In the face of the dominance of western psychology, the term "indigenous psychology" has (inappropriately) come to be used mainly to refer to those psychologies that reflect the traditions, beliefs and ideologies of the majority world. If the move toward a global or international psychology is simply a continuation of this international distribution to, and acceptance of, western psychology by the majority world, the change is not likely to be one that enhances our understanding of all the world's peoples, nor of much use to them.

Part of the answer to the problems of imbalance and dominance is the development of a psychology that is both sensitive to cultural variation in all societies, and is global in scope; and so one might take the emergence of cross-cultural psychology as an important move in the right direction. While this is partly true, it is also the case that cross-cultural psychology has been guilty of using the majority world as a kind of natural laboratory and has been known to exploit its human resources in various other ways (Drenth, 2004; Warwick, 1980). As noted in Chapter 10 for cultural anthropology, much early fieldwork was "extractive" (Gasché, 1992), simply taking information out of a cultural group. For Warwick, "[f]rom the choice of topic to the publication and dissemination of the findings, cross-cultural research is inescapably bound up with politics" (1980, p. 323); the cross-cultural work may involve differences in goals, differences in power and differences in intended use (even to the extent of misuse) of the results. To deal with these problems, Watkins and Shulman (2008; see below) have advocated a "psychology of liberation," by which psychologists in the majority world take charge of their own research and professional agendas.

This export and import of psychology has led to psychology being done in other countries, without much regard for local cultural circumstances or needs, and is part of the general process known as globalization. However, Berry (2008) has argued that assimilation is not the only outcome of globalization, by which all the cultures of the world become homogeneous, and resemble the dominant western world. In keeping with the intercultural strategies framework (see Figure 13.1), the alternatives of rejecting and reacting to these outside influences are common, as are novel or innovative ways of living with multiple cultural influences. A special journal issue on globalization has examined evidence for many of these alternative ways of dealing with this phenomenon (Kim and Bhawuk, 2008).

One attempt to deal with these ethical problems has been made by Gauthier (2008) by formulating a "Universal Declaration of Ethical Principles for Psychologists." An outline of the main goals and principles of this declaration is presented in Box 18.1.

It is also possible to attempt to address these problems by employing some distinctions that have been made in cross-cultural psychology. We start with the observation that psychology can be exported and imported "as is" (from western cultures to other countries). This represents a kind of "scientific assimilation," and

Box 18.1 **Universal Declaration of Ethical Principles for Psychologists**

The Universal Declaration of Ethical Principles for Psychologists (UDEPP) was developed "to articulate principles and values that provide a common moral framework for psychologists throughout the world, and that can be used as a moral justification and guide for the development of differing standards as appropriate for differing cultural contexts" (International Union of Psychological Science, 2008). The project was jointly sponsored by the International Union of Psychological Science, the International Association of Applied Psychology and the International Association for Cross-Cultural Psychology. Members of a working committee were drawn from all of the inhabited continents, and chaired by Janel Gauthier of Canada. The UDEPP is based on an examination of existing codes from many countries, and numerous historical and contemporary views on ethics generally; comparisons were made and commonalities were extracted from them.

The UDEPP is intended as an ethical and moral guide for psychologists to use as a template to direct the development of codes of ethics in different societies. As stated,

> The *Universal Declaration* describes those ethical principles that are based on shared human values. It reaffirms the commitment of the psychology community to help build a better world where peace, freedom, responsibility, justice, humanity, and morality prevail ... [It] ... articulates principles and related values that are general and aspirational rather than specific and prescriptive. Application of the principles and values to the development of specific standards of conduct will vary across cultures, and must occur locally or regionally in order to ensure their relevance to local or regional culture, customs, beliefs, and laws.

Among its principles are:

1. Respect for the Dignity of Persons and Peoples
   "Respect for dignity recognizes the inherent worth of all human beings, regardless of perceived or real differences in social status, ethnic origin, gender, capacities, or other such characteristics. This inherent worth means that all human beings are worthy of equal moral consideration."
2. Competent Caring for the Well-Being of Persons and Peoples
   "Competent caring for the well-being of persons and peoples involves working for their benefit and, above all, doing no harm. It includes maximizing benefits, minimizing potential harm, and offsetting or correcting harm."
3. Integrity
   "Integrity is vital to the advancement of scientific knowledge and to the maintenance of public confidence in the discipline of psychology. Integrity is based on

Box 18.1 continued

honesty, and on truthful, open and accurate communications. It includes recognizing, monitoring, and managing potential biases, multiple relationships, and other conflicts of interest that could result in harm and exploitation of persons or peoples."

4. Professional and Scientific Responsibilities to Society

"As a science and a profession, it has responsibilities to society. These responsibilities include contributing to the knowledge about human behavior and to persons' understanding of themselves and others, and using such knowledge to improve the condition of individuals, families, groups, communities, and society."

The concept of universality in the UDEPP is consistent with the use of the concept as used in this text. It is a document that accepts basic principles as common to all human interaction; it proposes that differential cultural experiences will generate variability in the development of these principles; and the culturally defined professional and research roles of psychologists will further differentiate the expression of these principles in the relevant setting. By so doing, the Declaration avoids the twin dangers of overprescribing or constraining (strong universalism), or overtolerating variations (relativism) in the worldwide practice of psychology.

has been referred to as psychology being done *in* a particular culture (Berry, 1978). Second, there are the parallel processes of developing indigenous psychologies locally, or adapting imported ones by indigenizing them: this we refer to as a psychology *of* a particular culture. Third, there are attempts to integrate all available psychologies into a *universal* psychology.

Early on, Lagmay (1984, p. 31) argued that the entry of western (mainly US-American) psychology was a case of "cultural diffusion," and was part of a more general flow of cultural elements that included language, educational and legal systems, and the media. The overall impact of this fifty-year period of American colonization was that "Western Science and cultural concepts became part of the educated speech and thinking of all who went through the schools ... the language of research, interpretation and construction in the social sciences in the Philippines ... has been definitely American and Western" (1984, p. 32). Such export and import of western psychology is not likely to constitute an "appropriate psychology" for developing countries (Moghaddam and Taylor, 1986). More recently, Pe-Pua (2006) for the Philippines, Diaz-Loving and colleagues (2008) for Mexico, Diaz-Loving (2005) for Latin America more generally, and Nsamenang (2008) and Super and Harkness (2008) for Africa have all analyzed how western psychology has, in various ways, changed aspects of their respective societies.

In an empirical examination of the adoption of western psychology in the Arab-speaking world, Zebian, Alamuddin, Maalouf and Chatila (2007) have used content analysis of research published in English in the Arab-speaking world over the past fifty years. They examined "the citing of local research ... the degree to which researchers acknowledge and address local research and human development needs ... an awareness of culturally significant processes and constructs ... [and] show a critical awareness of the applicability and transferability of existing methods, concepts and theories ... and the degree to which research contributes to a greater understanding of individual functioning in the local context" (Zebian *et al.*, 2007, pp. 91–92). They concluded that the "researchers do not engage in culturally sensitive research practices, and that these levels have not significantly changed with time" (2007, p. 112). Much of the problem was related to the adoption of concepts, measures and methods from western psychology, with at most translation and the substitution of some words.

For sub-Saharan Africa (Nsamenang, 1995, 2008) has identified the problem succinctly: "Psychology is an ethnocentric science, cultivated mainly in the developed world and then exported to sub-Saharan Africa" (1995, p. 729). While considerable evidence points to this conclusion (e.g., Carr and MacLachlan, 1998) the question arises: how can there be export without there being a willingness to import? That is, there must be a "demand side" that corresponds to the "supply side" of this flow (Berry, 2001b). While, in principle, it is possible for the majority world to turn its back on western psychology (as many now advocate for a whole range of products and services that are available through globalization; see Laird, 2009), there is an obvious imbalance in the relative power (political, economic) of the two sides.

In this situation, psychologists in the majority world face a dilemma when they are called upon to explain or interpret the behavior of people to themselves. In opinion surveys, assessment for educational and work selection, and in clinical practice, psychologists are often in a position to be influential, both with the public at large and with key decision makers in government and other institutions. We may ask: if their training, values and technology are rooted in western psychological science, and are minimally informed by local cultural and psychological knowledge, what likelihood is there that this influence will be culturally appropriate? Unless this likelihood is substantial, psychologists in developing countries may end up playing the role of inadvertent acculturators. Such training may be all the more unsuitable when it is so specialized (focussed on local western topics) that the psychologist is ill-equipped to deal with broader issues, set in complex local cultural contexts (Moghaddam, 1989). The alternative to working with an imported psychology is to attempt to develop one locally.

Such alternatives have indeed been described. According to Carr and MacLachlan (1998), when faced with the dominant western psychology, one can first try "to assimilate into the mainstream ... by replicating Western studies in developing countries." However, second, when faced with the irrelevance of such work, some psychologists moved to a search for "positive aspects of cultural attributes." Third, that is replaced by an approach that "involves transcending both the conformity of stage 1 and the anti-conformity of stage 2, and assessing social reality independently of the 'need' for comparison with other cultures" (Carr and MacLachlan, 1998, p. 13). This last way of dealing with the problem has generated the burgeoning field of indigenous psychologies (Adair and Diaz-Loving, 1999; Allwood and Berry, 2006; Kim and Berry, 1993; Kim, Yang and Hwang, 2006; D. Sinha, 1997). Some of these "alternative psychologies" and strategies to implement them have been presented by Moghaddam *et al.* (2007). Many of these alternatives have taken the form of indigenous psychologies, where western psychology is rejected and replaced by more culturally appropriate ways of examining and interpreting human behavior.

How should we evaluate the impact of western psychology on the lives of peoples in the majority world? On the one hand, psychology is only a small part of western thought, and may not have direct and widespread impact on a functioning culture or its individual members. On the other, psychology may be part of a broader package of acculturative influences that affect many of the core institutions (education, work, religion) through which all or most people pass in the course of their development. While substantial acculturation may indeed take place, it can take different forms; moreover, it may be difficult to specify the particular contribution of psychology to this process.

Indigenous psychologies

By indigenous psychologies is meant "a set of approaches to understanding human behavior within the cultural contexts in which they have developed and are currently displayed. They can also be seen as attempts to root psychological research in the conceptual systems that are indigenous to a culture, including the philosophical, theological, and scientific ideas that are part of the historical and contemporary lives of people and their institutions" (Allwood and Berry, 2006, p. 243). This notion can be linked to a number of others, including ethnopsychology (cf. the discussion of ethnoscience in the section on cognitive anthropology in Chapter 10), and common sense or naive psychology (as proposed by Heider, 1958). The roots of indigenous psychologies lie in the intellectual tradition of *Geisteswissenschaften* (cultural sciences) rather than the *Naturwissenschaften* (natural sciences; see Kim and Berry, 1993).

This contrast between the cultural and natural sciences approaches has been emphasized by Kim and Park (2006). They argue that there is a need for a "transactional approach" in psychological research, in which human beings are considered as agents in determining their own actions, and in which the transactions (situated in relationships between individuals) are the important unit of activity to be understood rather than the individual. More generally, Kim *et al.* (2006) seek to blur the lines between the indigenous psychology approach and that of cultural psychology, claiming that these two approaches stand in contrast to cross-cultural psychology, which they consider to be exclusively wedded to the natural sciences approach. This position has also been advocated by Boski (2006). This view of the similarity of indigenous psychology to cultural psychology, and their relationship with the culture-comparative approach, reminds us of the need to better understand the overall links between all three schools of research linking culture and psychology, as discussed in Chapters 1 and 12. These relationships were the focus of a special issue of the *Asian Journal of Social Psychology* (Hwang and Yang, 2000). Our view, as expressed in Chapter 1, is that all three approaches can be incorporated in the larger field of cross-cultural psychology (see also Berry, 2000).

An international project examining the current state of indigenous psychologies was carried out by Allwood and Berry (2006). They posed four questions to fifteen leading indigenous psychologists in twelve societies. These questions were to describe: the (1) history of indigenous psychologies globally and (2) in their own society; and (3) the important characteristics of indigenous psychologies globally and (4) in their own society. An analysis of the responses revealed a number of common characteristics. First were some positive qualities, including the widespread recognition of the importance of the historical and philosophical notions in their cultures, and the contemporary characteristics of their societies, in achieving a relevant indigenous psychology. Moreover, the view was widely shared that indigenous psychologies could advance psychology in two ways: they serve to create a more valid and useful local psychology; and they serve as contributions in the pursuit of a global psychology, through the use of the comparative "cross-indigenous" method. Second were three negative qualities. Indigenous psychologies are: seen as a post-colonial reaction to the dominance of concepts, methods and findings of western psychology; a recognition that these imported psychologies could not usually be applied to the development needs of their societies; and a source of reaction to their work on indigenous psychology by local and international colleagues, where doing indigenous psychological research was claimed to be undermining their careers. A number of differences in views about indigenous psychologies were also discerned: some viewed the dominance of US-American psychology as the main problem, while others also saw it in European psychology; and the importance of religion as a source of insight into indigenous psychology varied across respondents.

The most important difference found was the contrasting views that may be described as "indigenous versus indigenizing." Is the starting point in developing indigenous psychologies to be rooted exclusively in their own history, society and culture? Or is it in the importation followed by the modification of western psychology? This issue was raised by D. Sinha (1997), who saw these paths as complementary. The process of indigenization was the route; this could be by way of the examination of local cultural themes, or by drawing on western psychology. The product was the attainment of indigenous psychologies and eventually the achievement of a universal or global psychology.

Sinha had previously identified the transfer of western psychology to India "as part of the general process of Modernization" (1986, p. 10), characterizing it as "completely isolated from the Indian tradition, and alien to the local intellectual soil" (1986, p. 11), leading to endless "repetitions of foreign studies" (1986, p. 33). These importations have been characterized by others as "Yankee doodling" or just playing around with western psychology. Historically, Sinha notes four phases, beginning with a pre-independence period during which Indian psychology "remained tied to the apron strings of the West, and did not display any sign of maturing" (1986, p. 36). Then came a period of post-independence expansion in which there was a burgeoning of research, but not so much for policy and action as for academic prestige. The third period was one of problem-oriented research during which concerns for breaking the dependency were joined with those for more applied research. Finally came the period of indigenization, in which the imported western psychology underwent a process of cultural transformation to become more informed by Indian social and cultural traditions, and relevant to Indian economic and political needs.

Sinha (1997) has presented a systematic account of this process in many parts of the majority world. His main position is composed of two complementary assertions. First is the need to embed every psychology in a specific cultural context. Second is the need to establish the universality of the empirical basis and principles of psychology. In his view, "indigenization is considered to be a vital step towards a universal psychology" (D. Sinha, 1997, p. 131; cf. Berry and Kim, 1993; Yang, 2000), and corresponds to the universalistic approach taken in this book. As noted above, his second position is to insist on the distinction between the product (indigenous psychology), and the process of indigenization. The first refers to a psychology with four attributes: it is psychological knowledge that is not external or imported; it is evidenced by the daily activities of people (rather than in experiments or tests); it is behavior that is understood in terms of local frames of reference; and it is composed of knowledge that is relevant to the life of a cultural population. In contrast, indigenization is a process of transforming the borrowed, transplanted or imposed psychology in order to better suit the needs of a cultural population.

However, some researchers, e.g., Adair, argue that "the goal of an indigenous psychology [is] ... the transformation of the imported discipline into a mature, self-sustaining scientific discipline addressing the needs of the country and culture"

(2004, p. 115). This requires the development of psychological institutions, both in the universities and in the professional practice of psychology. This is clearly an approach that takes only the indigenizing route toward the achievement of indigenous psychologies, starting with the importation of western psychology. Adair outlines four stages in this process: importation, implantation, indigenization and autochthonization (2004, p. 118). Importation begins with taking western psychology into the curriculum or research activity; this can be by way of local scholars returning after being trained abroad, or the use of foreign textbooks. Implantation occurs when the imported psychology becomes widely accepted as a normal part of what is done in the psychology department or clinic. Indigenization occurs when western psychology begins to be criticized or challenged for its lack of relevance to the needs of society. Autochthonization occurs when a critical mass of scholars come to accept that there is a need for writing textbooks and doing research that are relevant to local cultural themes and needs. This transformation process may or may not lead to an indigenous psychology being developed; the lingering influence of early exposure to western psychology and the continuing need to play the "international career game" may inhibit the development of an indigenous psychology that is fundamentally rooted in the local society and culture.

A number of books have been published that provide overviews of psychological research within particular societies, advancing toward the goal of attaining indigenous psychologies. Foremost among these are Rao, Paranjpe and Dalal (2008) for India, Diaz-Loving and colleagues (2008) for Mexico, Zinchenko and Petrenko (2008) for Russia and Ahmed and Gielen (1998) for the Arabic-speaking world. The Indian handbook is a monumental undertaking (see Box 18.2) covering both indigenous topics and those that extend western psychological concepts and empirical research into the Indian context.

We consider here three examples of the development of an indigenous psychology from cultural foundations: in Mexico, in the Philippines and in Taiwan. First is the work of Diaz-Guerrero (1975, 1982, 1993; see Diaz-Loving and Lozano, 2009, for an overview of this body of work). Diaz-Guerrero developed a Mexican psychology rooted in "historico-sociocultural premises." He defined these as "a set of culturally significant statements that are held by a majority of persons in a culture" (1975, p. xx). In Mexico these themes include affiliative obedience, machismo, respect, protection of women, and virginity. Of particular importance is abnegation (Diaz-Guerrero, 2000): the tendency to self-sacrifice or abase oneself before more powerful others. It is the opposite of self-assertion. In his research, Diaz-Guerrero found three elements to abnegation: sacrificing oneself for one's family; social amiability; and a wish to please. These characteristics may derive from the long colonial history of Mexico, and continue as an aspect of their contemporary relationship with a dominant neighbor. For Diaz-Guerrero (2000, p. 83), "Mexican culture is one of love, and the American one is a culture of power." He

Box 18.2 *Handbook of Indian psychology*
(Rao, Paranjpe and Dalal, 2008)

India has one of the world's oldest established religio-philosophical systems of thought (along with that of China and the Greco-Roman region). Expectations about the content of an Indian psychology would include such topics as the study of consciousness, meditation, yoga, spirituality and health, and approaches to human conduct from Buddhism, Hinduism and Jainism. These topics are portrayed by a set of high-level scholars educated and practiced in India and around the world.

In the view of Rao, the senior editor of the *Handbook*, the field of Indian psychology extends well beyond the topics mentioned. He notes that "Indian psychology is a complex subject variously viewed as esoteric and spiritual, philosophical and speculative, practical and ritualistic, and of course, as we believe, a systematic and scientific understanding of human nature. There is truth in all these characterisations" (2008, p. xvii). Rao expresses his vision of what Indian psychology is and could be. He begins by a critique of much of contemporary "psychology in India" as mere replication of western studies of western concepts. He is also somewhat concerned that Indian psychology has become something akin to a "psychology of the Indian people," attempting to identify what Indian peoples are like. His own view is that "Indian psychology is indigenous psychology in that it is a psychology derived from indigenous thought systems and therefore clearly best suited to address India specific psychological issues and problems" (2008, p. 3).

However, like many scholars working in indigenous psychology, he prefers to see these culture-specific endeavors as contributions to a wider, global psychology: Indian psychology "is more than indigenous psychology for the reason that it offers fruitful psychological models and theories, though derived from classical Indian thought, that hold pan human interest" (2008, p. 3). One reason for this universal perspective is his assertions that "Indian psychology does not exclude anything that is currently studied in psychology, but includes a great deal more" (2008, p. 8). If only we could claim the same inclusiveness and range of interests for western psychology!

Following this introductory chapter by Rao on the character and scope of Indian psychology, the volume is organized into three general parts devoted to "Systems and Schools," "Topics and Themes" and "Applications and Implications." The first part is largely concerned with broad cultural and theological influences on Indian psychology. However, conspicuous by its absence is a treatment of the Islamic contribution. The second part includes topics that are typical of western psychological approaches, including motivation, personality, cognition, emotion and consciousness, all cast within an Indian cultural perspective. In the third part, authors seek to apply specific knowledge from these domains of Indian psychology to areas of practice such as meditation and health, and organizational effectiveness.

Box 18.2 continued

This volume presents an exceedingly rich set of materials. If similar volumes could be developed for the other major cultural perspectives in the contemporary world, such as the East Asian, the Islamic, the sub-Saharan African and the indigenous peoples of the Pacific, Australia and the Americas, we would be well on the way to achieving more truly universal psychology.

even postulates that such a disposition may be "found in all traditional societies" (2000, p. 85). In such relationships between colonized and colonial societies, it may simply be functional to abnegate.

The second example comprises the writings produced by Enriquez (1981, 1993). His work has been continued by Pe-Pua (2006) and Protacio-De Castro (2006). Enriquez has consistently criticized western influences on Filipino intellectual life. His alternative was to develop a *Sikolohiyang Pilipino* that is rooted in local culture and history. It emphasizes four areas of concern:

1) identity and national consciousness, specifically looking at the social sciences as the study of man and *diwa* [consciousness and meaning], or the indigenous conception and definition of the psyche, as a focus of social psychological research; 2) social awareness and involvement as dictated by an objective analysis of social issues and problems; 3) national and ethnic cultures and languages including the study of early or traditional psychology, called *kinagisnang sikolohiya*; and 4) bases and application of indigenous psychology in health practices, agriculture, art, mass media, religion, etc. but also including the psychology of behavior and human abilities as demonstrated in Western psychology and found applicable to the Philippine setting. (Enriquez, 1989, p. 21)

The indigenous psychology movement has three primary areas of protest: it is against a psychology that perpetuates the colonial status of the Filipino mind; it is against the imposition on a majority world country of psychologies developed in and appropriate to industrialized countries; and it is against a psychology used for the exploitation of the masses.

For Enriquez, "[t]he new consciousness, labeled *Sikolohiyang Pilipino* reflecting Filipino psychological knowledge, has emerged through the use of the local language as a tool for the identification and rediscovery of indigenous concepts and as an appropriate medium for the delineation and articulation of Philippine realities together with the development of a scientific literature which embodies the psychology of the Filipino people" (Enriquez, 1989, p. 21). In his most comprehensive exposition, Enriquez (1993) portrayed *Sikolohiyang Pilipino* as the outcome of a long history of discrimination and resistance. He proposed two counteracting processes (indigenizing from without, and from within), the first being stimulated by (reaction to) the western world (cf. "export"), and the second being stimulated by a fundamental interest in Filipino culture (cf. refusal to "import"). Enriquez went beyond explicating indigenous concepts, to indigenous methods, proposing that "asking around," interacting with people in their "natural habitat," and establishing and maintaining empathy are three ways of doing research on Filipino psychology that are culturally appropriate. While it is difficult for a non-Filipino to comprehend some of the cultural meanings, it is relatively easy to understand both the underlying sentiments and the long-term implications of these views for a psychology of the Philippines.

A third body of research has been produced in this case in Taiwan by Yang and his colleagues (Yang, 1999, 2000, 2006; Hwang, 2005) in pursuit of a Chinese indigenous psychology. The work of Yang has focussed on three domains of psychological life that he considers most relevant in Chinese culture. These are: Chinese familism; Chinese traditionalism and modernity; and the self in Chinese culture. In the first domain, he has developed concepts and measures of the cognitive, affective and intentional features of the intense interconnectedness among individuals within the Chinese family. Cognitive features include harmony, solidarity, wealth and fame. Affective components include feelings of family unity, belongingness, love, responsibility and safety. Intentional components include interdependence, forbearance, modesty, conformity, respect for seniority and ingroup favoritism. He found this concept of familism to be relevant to life outside the conventional family, extending to work and other settings outside.

In the second domain, he conceptualized and assessed Chinese traditionalism and modernism as two independent dimensions, but found that they usually coexisted (rather than being a source of psychological conflict). Traditionalism includes submission to authority, filial piety, ancestral worship, endurance, fatalism and male dominance. Chinese modernism includes egalitarianism, open-mindedness, self-reliance, assertiveness, hedonism and gender equality. In the third domain, he drew upon traditional Chinese distinctions between two orientations: individual and social. The individual-oriented self is characterized by strong autonomy and weak homonomy; the social-oriented self consists of weak autonomy and strong homonymy. The social orientation is further differentiated into four kinds of relationships: horizontal, vertical, with family and with others. Empirical work revealed that these various Chinese selves emerged in factor analytic studies with Chinese students and adults. This conceptual and empirical work has established a solid foundation for a Chinese indigenous psychology.

This program has been examined and analyzed by Gabrenya, Kung and Chen (2006), who refer to it as a movement to make sense of psychological phenomena in Chinese cultures that lie beyond the conventional purview of western psychology. They examine the growth of this movement in terms of a number of issues, including: the cultural relevance of topics; methodological appropriateness;

ideological relevance; and the language of research (English or Chinese). Sampling a group of over 100 Taiwanese psychologists (divided into four subgroups), they enquired about the importance of these issues. There were variations in the level of support for the movement: those with graduate training overseas were less supportive, as were experimental psychologists; those locally trained and in the social and clinical areas were more supportive. These divisions appear to be linked to the insider–outsider debate (similar to the emic–etic approaches) in the social sciences; that is, do you "have to be one to know one?"

A common criticism of indigenization is that there will be a proliferation of psychologies: if every population had its own psychology, an infinite regress to an individual psychology (for a population of one) is possible; or if not so minute, then regress to provincial, city or village psychologies is envisaged. In addition to the problem of proliferation, Poortinga (1999) has argued that the indigenization of psychology places too much emphasis on differences in behavior found across cultures. Much of the field has hardly paid attention to the discovery of psychological similarities, particularly the common processes and functions that underlie surface behavioral variation. In his view "those who argue for a culturalist interpretation of behavior have the obligation not only to show how (much) behavior differs per cultural population, but also how (much) it is the same" (Poortinga, 1999, p. 430). Poortinga (2004) has also expressed a concern for the assumption that cultural insiders have a better knowledge of psychological phenomena than cultural outsiders. Here we are reminded of Pike's (1967) metaphor of the dual emic–etic approach as binoculars: both insider and outsider points of view provide perspective on a phenomenon (see Box 1.2).

Our view is that a balance has to be found (Berry, 2000; Dasen and Mishra, 2000; Poortinga, 1997). On the one hand, it does not make sense to ignore the achievements of (a mainly) western psychology, and to reinvent the wheel in each culture. On the other hand, the ethnocentrism of western psychology makes it necessary to take other viewpoints on human behavior into account. One of the goals of cross-cultural psychology is the eventual development of a universal psychology that incorporates all indigenous (including western) psychologies. We will never know whether all diverse data and cultural points of view have been incorporated into the eventual universal psychology, but we should at least cast our net as widely as possible, in order to gather all the relevant information that is available.

Culturally appropriate psychology

How can psychology move from the issues of the dominance of western psychology, and the emergence of indigenous psychologies, to a position of actually applying our concepts and knowledge to the betterment of humankind? In order to move in such a direction, some consensus is required on what is meant by "development."

The UN made an attempt to articulate the goals of national development in 2001, with the title "UN Millennium Project." They proposed a set of eight goals: eradicate extreme poverty and hunger; achieve universal primary education; promote gender equality and empower women; reduce child mortality; improve maternal health; combat HIV/AIDS, malaria, and other diseases; ensure environmental sustainability; and develop a global partnership for development.

It is clear that many of these domains constitute problems at the present time. It should also be clear that they all have psychological dimensions, including the need to engage in attitude and value change. Some of these psychological underpinnings are now being addressed by researchers in the majority world as well as in the "minority" world, including cross-cultural psychologists from many countries.

National development

In Chapter 13 we addressed the issue of acculturation and change at both the population and individual levels; we distinguished between features of the two cultures in contact, and how they contributed to both cultural and psychological change. Within this framework, we can locate national development as change at the population level (using economic, political and social indicators) and at the individual level (such as abilities, attitudes, values, motives). For these changes to constitute development, they need to be in the direction of some valued end-state that can be articulated by groups or individuals involved in the process (see Box 18.3). This definition of development fits generally into those views that have been expressed in the psychological literature since the 1970s (see D. Sinha, 1997, for a review).

However, criticism of such a definition also abounds in the literature. For example, Rist and Sabelli (1986) have questioned the very notion of development, particularly its universality. Referring to development as one of the western world's favorite myths, they systematically attack most of the accepted truths about development held by western "developers." They assert that not every culture has a concept for "development," and that if there is, it may not be at all like the one in the developer's program. However, if the procedures outlined in Box 18.3 are followed, misunderstandings about development should be discovered prior to the commencement of development programs. The very existence (or non-existence) of and important variations in the meaning of development should be revealed early in psychologically oriented research, and appropriate decisions can be made on these bases.

The concept of development and the consequences of development aid have been examined and challenged in recent years by psychologists (e.g., MacLachlan,

Box 18.3 **Psychology and development**

The potential contribution of psychology to research and application in the area of national development is rather large, despite the criticisms noted by social scientists. If we define development as the process of individuals and groups moving from some present state to some more valued end-state (rather than in terms of some general notion of progress), then psychology can contribute in the following ways:

1. *Understanding the present state.* This is the obvious starting point for development, and many psychological constructs are relevant to its description: *skills* (cognitive, technical, social, etc.); *attitudes* to change; *personality characteristics* that may assist or prevent change; *values* concerning maintaining the past (or present) state of affairs; and *interests* in various change alternatives That is, constructing a "psychological profile," or a study of the distribution of psychological characteristics in a population, should provide an understanding of the human resources upon which development may take place (Allen *et al.*, 2007). Of course, there are political factors (such as the social organization and distribution of these resources), and economic factors (such as natural resources) that must enter into this present-state description, but psychology does have something to contribute to the overall understanding of the current situation.

2. *Understanding the valued end-state.* In addition to the global goals articulated by the UN (2001), psychological research can draw out the local or indigenous meanings of a concept; this approach is one possible contribution of psychology to the study of national development. What, in fact, are the meanings assigned to "development" in various societies? Is it always associated with increased urbanization, industrialization and organization (as the western notion of "development" implies), or are there important cultural variations such as promoting peace, contentment and harmony, and reducing human suffering? The valued end-state can also be studied by psychologists employing the conventional notions of *aspirations*, *needs*, *values* and *preferences*. In short, "what do people want (if anything) out of life?" is a question that psychology can help to answer.

3. *Understanding the process of change.* How do people get from the present state to the future valued end-state? In addition to the human and material resources mentioned earlier, people have *capabilities* (Sen, 2005) and other psychological resources such as *motives*, *drives* and *coping mechanisms*, all of which have an established place in psychology. Examining these dynamic factors, including the possibility of increasing their level and effectiveness of their organization in a population is an important potential contribution of psychology to national development.

Box 18.3 continued

4. *Design, implementation and evaluation of development programs*. Psychologists have usually enjoyed a solid training in research methods on human behavior. Cultural variations in behavior have usually been ignored. As a result of ignoring this cultural factor, many development programs have ended in failure. A psychology background can also be of immense help in a development team that is attempting to understand whether a particular development program is having its intended effects. In such areas, both qualitative and quantitative methods, such as observation, interviewing, sampling, the use of control groups and the statistical evaluation of change over time (including an informed choice between longitudinal and cross-sectional designs), psychology has a significant contribution to make.

McAuliffe and Carr, 2010) as well as by economists and other social scientists (e.g., Maathai, 2009; Moyo, 2009; Sen, 2005). MacLachlan *et al.* (2010) present a devastating critique of international aid programs that are intended to enhance national development. Drawing on four core psychological principles (social dominance, perceptions of justice, cultural identity and learning), they argue that the lack of equity in international aid programs, the perception of injustice in their delivery, the challenge to indigenous cultural identities and the lack of learning from past failures make international aid ineffective, even destructive.

Maathai (2009) argues that African nations and peoples have become accustomed to development aid, and have lost their cultural identities, motivation and sense of common purpose; these have been replaced by passive inertia and demoralization. The result is endemic poverty, corruption and civil wars. The way out of these problems is not more aid from western societies, but new leadership that needs to come from within African societies themselves. That is, Africa requires an indigenous effort to deal with these consequences of international development initiatives. Similarly, Moyo (2009) argues that foreign aid has harmed Africa. Her view is that development assistance to African governments has fostered dependency, encouraged corruption and promoted poor governance and poverty. Since foreign aid helps perpetuate the cycle of poverty and hinders economic growth in Africa, it should be phased out. Both these characterizations of the effects of development aid in Africa point to a pattern of psychological qualities resembling the abnegation that was identified for Mexico by Diaz-Guerrero (2000).

Sen (2005) outlines his concept of "capabilities," defined as a person's capacity and freedom to choose and to act. Capabilities are not simply what people are able to do, but their freedom to do what they want to do. Sen distinguishes between capabilities, on the one hand, and both commodities (e.g., resources) and functionings (e.g., activities that lead to a sense of well-being), on the other. The former are a characteristic of the social and political conditions in which a person lives, while the latter depend on personal characteristics of the individual. Pick and Sirkin (2010; see the conclusions of Chapter 17, this volume) describe a set of intervention programs in Mexico and other Latin American countries that are directed at increasing agency and empowerment, and that amount to implementation of several of Sen's ideas.

For all of these critics, there are obvious psychological underpinnings to world, and to the issues confronting individuals. The link between their descriptions of the current situation in the majority world is thus a matter ripe for examination by cross-cultural psychologists. However, there appears to be no systematic research on this relationship as yet by psychologists.

However, a collaborative role for psychology has been elaborated by Zaman and Zaman (1994). They argue that psychology does have a role to play (along with other disciplines), but that the psychology that is employed has to be culturally appropriate. They propose three concepts that would be of use in Pakistan for development purposes. All three involve a joint focus on the individual and on the sociocultural context. For them, there are the following obviously relevant constructs: the first is individual and affective feelings for efficacy; the second is to attend more to feelings of helplessness; and the third is to consider human agency as a basic factor in development programs.

Despite these limitations, a role for psychology has also been claimed and articulated by Moghaddam, Branchi, Daniels, Apter and Harré (1999). They too call for an appropriate psychology, one that recognizes cultural differences, but also power differences between the West and the majority world. When the psychology is inappropriate and the power differentials great, then there would be either or both resistance to, or/and failure of the development program.

A liberation psychology movement (Watkins and Shulman, 2008) has taken up some of these criticisms and extended them to many domains of relevance to the majority world. In their critique of western psychology, Watkins and Shulman (2008, p. 1) state as their purpose to "rethink the goals and practices of psychology in an age of disruptive globalization." Following the work of Esteva (1992), who challenges the very notion of development, they argue (2008, p. 34) that the term "development" simply reminds people of "what they are not," leading people to become "enslaved to other peoples' dreams," rather than pursue their own. One alternative they propose is to engage in a genuine development that is a "transition from less human to more human conditions for each and every person." Another alternative is to engage in "counter development" that rejects the idea of unlimited progress, and replaces it with humility and austerity. In terms of the relationships between globalization and acculturation proposed by Berry (2008), rather than being assimilated into the acceptance of the vision of development as advocated by western-dominated development agencies, there is a rejection of them and a return to indigenous ways that resemble the separation strategy. And in some ways, these alternatives also resemble the abnegation that was identified by Diaz-Guerrero (1993).

A major contribution to this debate has been made by Kağitçibaşi. In her view, human development requires theoretical and empirical work at both the individual and cultural levels (Kağitçibaşi, 2007; Kağitçibaşi and Poortinga, 2000). This requires collaboration in research and application between psychologists and others in the field. In particular, she links the two meanings of development (ontogenetic and societal), arguing that without programs for optimal human (ontogenetic) development, there can be little hope of human (societal or national) development. While critical of some earlier forays by psychologists into the field (especially those who used the concept of "modernization," or their individualistic stance; Kağitçibaşi, 2007), she nevertheless advocates the relevance of psychology to a whole range of development issues, including early childhood education, health, the role of family (especially the empowerment and training of mothers) and more generally the quality of social, cultural and economic life.

Poortinga (2009) has advocated the culturally sensitive transfer of intervention programs across cultures. He draws upon the distinctions among adoption, adaptation and assembly (concepts that were originally developed for the transfer of psychological tests across cultures). In terms introduced in Box 1.2, adoption refers to the use of a program that stays close to the original (cf. an imposed etic). Adaptation refers to the alteration of aspects of the program that have not worked well (cf. an emic). Assembly refers to the development of an entirely new program, based on the earlier steps in this sequence (cf. a derived etic).

The role of psychology in studying and promoting national development has been advocated particularly in India, where the journal entitled *Psychology and Developing Societies* is edited. This journal publishes articles devoted to a range of issues related to national development, including leadership, locally appropriate assessment and practice. Apart from D. Sinha (1990), whose work has been mentioned earlier in this chapter, J. B. P. Sinha (1970, 1980, 1984) has also contributed to the study of national development. His approach is an integrative one, in which psychology is seen as a "partner in development," both with other disciplines, and between psychologists from industrialized and developing countries. He has traced the evolving meaning of "development," and along with this change, the evolution of the roles played by psychologists. In the 1950s national development was generally "taken as being synonymous to economic development, which was naturally the domain of economists ... however ... economic development of the newly independent nations did not obey the rational formula of saving, investment, and growth, because of the interfering effects of the socio-cultural features of the traditional societies" (J. B. P. Sinha, 1984, p. 169). A volume examining the contribution of J. B. P. Sinha (Pandey, Sinha and Sinha, 2010) underscores his contributions to the study of national development. In this body of work, we can observe one of the important contributions of cross-cultural psychology: knowledge and points of view gained from working in other cultures can give a much needed perspective, and can provide alternative modes of action for western psychological research and application. To be of most value, cross-cultural psychology should be the two-way street exemplified in this discussion of national development.

Conclusions

The application of cross-cultural psychology to problem-solving in diverse cultures has been the central theme of Part III of this book. In principle, the discipline is poised to be of use in a number of domains (acculturation, intergroup relations, work organizations, communication and health). However, in this chapter we have attempted to establish some conceptual and practical features and limits to this enterprise. In particular, the need to make sure that the science and the problem are matched is paramount. Armed with basic knowledge from Part I of this book, and with methodological and theoretical tools from Part II, we believe that matching *is* possible. To accomplish this, however, working partnerships and two-way exchanges of psychological knowledge are required.

KEY TERMS

appropriate psychology • dependency • globalization • ethnopsychology • indigenization • national development • western psychology

FURTHER READING

Allwood, C. M., and Berry, J. W. (eds.) (2006). Origins and development of indigenous psychologies: An international analysis. Special issue, *International Journal of Psychology*, 41, no. 4.

An analysis of a survey of the views of indigenous psychologists, with some empirical papers to illustrate the themes.

Cole, M. (2006). Internationalism in psychology: We need it now more than ever. *American Psychologist*, 61, 904–917.

A personal account of his journey through international psychology, with important observations on how to balance the field.

Hwang, K. K., and Yang, C. F. (eds.) (2000). Indigenous, cultural and cross-cultural psychologies. Special Issue, *Asian Journal of Social Psychology*, 3.

This includes papers providing a comparison of three approaches to understanding culture–behavior relationships.

Kağitçibaşi, C. (2007). *Family, self and human development across cultures* (2nd edn.). Mahwah, N.J.: Lawrence Erlbaum Associates.

This book was mentioned in Further Reading in Chapter 3, but is also relevant for the perspective the author provides on the role of psychology in the majority world.

Kim, U., and Berry, J. W. (eds.) (1993). *Indigenous psychologies: Research and experience in cultural context.* Newbury Park, Calif.: Sage.

A collection of original chapters by authors from various countries portraying their ideas and findings about psychologies that are indigenous to their cultures.

Kim, U., Yang, K.-S., and Hwang, K.-K. (eds.) (2006). *Indigenous and cultural psychology: Understanding people in context.* New York: Springer.

A compendium of recent papers on views about, and empirical studies of, indigenous psychologies around the world.

Kim, Y. Y., and Bhawuk, D. (eds.) (2008). Globalization and diversity. Special issue, *International Journal of Intercultural Relations*, 33.

A set of papers examining various aspects of globalization, especially those that entail psychological processes and impacts.

Nsamenang, B. (ed.) (2008). Culture and human development. Special issue, *International Journal of Psychology*, 43, no. 2.

A set of papers dealing with developmental issues in various societies.

Stevens, M., and Gielen, U. (eds.) (2007). *Toward a global psychology: Theory, research and pedagogy.* Mahwah, N.J.: Lawrence Erlbaum Associates.

An overview of the movement to internationalize the discipline of psychology.

Epilogue

The reader will have realized that this book offers a selective presentation of a diverse field. Necessarily many important points of view, empirical research studies and programs of application have not been mentioned, never mind given substantive treatment. Our attention, however, has not been random, but was guided by major themes and debates on the relationship between behavior and culture.

We have also taken the position that psychological processes are shared, species-wide characteristics. These common psychological qualities are nurtured, and shaped by enculturation and socialization, sometimes further affected by acculturation, and ultimately expressed as overt human behaviors. While set on course by these transmission processes relatively early in life, behaviors continue to be guided in later life by direct influence from ecological, cultural and sociopolitical factors. In short, we have considered culture, in its broadest sense, to be a major source of human behavioral diversity producing variations on underlying themes. It is the common qualities that make comparisons possible, and the variations that make comparisons interesting.

Our enterprise has some clearly articulated goals, and it is reasonable to ask whether the field of cross-cultural psychology generally, and this book in particular, has met them. In our view, one of the goals, as expressed in Chapter 1, has *not* been achieved: we are nowhere close to producing a universal psychology through the comprehensive integration of results of comparative psychological studies. However, we have taken some important steps toward this goal, both in terms of demonstrating how human psychological functioning is similar across cultures and how important differences in behavior repertoire emerge. Chapters 2 to 9 review empirical studies in various fields of cross-cultural psychology, showing ample evidence of both panhuman psychological qualities, and variation in the development and overt display of these qualities across cultures.

In Part II of the book, we considered three areas of thinking and research that define the terrain within which cross-cultural psychology has largely operated: culture, biology, and method and theory. This section of the book essentially provides an interpretive frame for the materials reviewed earlier, by linking them to cognate disciplines and to fundamental issues of comparative science. By so doing, we have intended to lift the whole of the first section above the level of description to the level of possible (and alternative) interpretations. Central to this was the distinction between various forms of relativism and universalism as ways of thinking about the often subtle and complex interplay between psychological similarities and differences across cultures. While we have opted for a moderate universalist stance, it is possible that future advances in the biological and cultural sciences will reinforce allegiance to strong universalism or to relativism, at least for some parts of the whole range of behavior.

Cross-cultural psychological findings can be assessed not only against disciplinary, methodological and theoretical criteria, but also against practical criteria in the world of day-to-day problems. In Part III, again selectively, we considered areas of real concern to many people in many parts of the world. Using the findings, tools and ideas drawn from basic research in cross-cultural psychology, we explored how a cross-cultural approach can begin to make a difference. In a rapidly changing and increasingly interconnected and globalized world, concerns about acculturation and intercultural relations, about work, communication, health and national development, have all come into the foreground and have stimulated many to direct their research toward these issues. Answers are partial, and much remains to be done, but the evidence we have marshaled points, we believe, to a central and important role for cross-cultural psychology in helping to deal with some of the major problems facing the world.

Scientific analysis does not exist in a vacuum; it ultimately has to be justified in terms of its demonstrated contribution, or prospect for future contribution, to human well-being. We realize that this is a tall order, and that the very definition of "human well-being" can be the topic of elaborate discussion. However, cross-cultural psychology has the pretension to look across the boundaries of one's own culture, and from a global perspective the differences in well-being between societies are so striking that a debate on finer points soon becomes hypocritical. Despite globalization (which has been mainly profitable to those that control the means of production and distribution), the major divide between rich and poor societies in the world continues to exist, and cannot be ignored. This raises the question of what the specific expertise is of cross-cultural psychologists to ameliorate the situation. Looking at the history of psychology it is evident that its theoretical foundations are not very strong. Even the success of theories by giants like Freud, Piaget and Vygotsky has been short-lived, and many of their ideas have not stood up to later critical analysis.

Can we then pretend that in cross-cultural psychology there is a fund of knowledge that is ready for use to improve the situation, particularly of the poor in this world? We think that this is the case, if one is prepared to look for a balance between scientific restraint (using only well-tested knowledge) and the acceptance of risks, because existing needs have to be addressed here and now. In many areas of application, there will always be a question about how to achieve the optimal balance between using only well-established knowledge, and the need to act decisively to address important and pressing needs.

Of course, cross-cultural researchers are not just seekers of knowledge: they are inevitably part of an intercultural process, in which many factors other than obtaining information play a role. In some of the chapters we have touched upon political and ethical issues that are usually present: why is the research being done, whose interests will it serve and with whom will the information be shared? While formerly extractive, cross-cultural researchers now begin to recognize that the interests of the population investigated are part of their responsibility. Instead of merely studying a group, one should join them in analyzing matters that they consider of importance. This definitely holds as far as interventions are concerned. In fact, intervention programs should be constructed to meet the needs of a population and with the explicit input of that population in the definition of needs to be addressed by a program and in its objectives.

We have also shown that collaboration should not only include "cultural partners" but should extend to "disciplinary partners" as well. Cross-cultural psychology is essentially an "interdiscipline," drawing not only on psychology, but also on other social, biological and ecological sciences. This is an important scientific niche to occupy, since human problems (and hence the possibility of achieving human well-being) are obviously not uniquely psychological. Many contemporary issues have arisen because of social and political changes such as (de)colonization and globalization (sometimes verging on neocolonization). These contribute to migrant and refugee movements, economic and political inequalities, and to epidemics of psychological, social and physical problems (including racism, ethnic conflict and war, and the spread of HIV/ AIDS). All of these problems have evident psychological and cultural dimensions. However, we need to take care that our central concern with cultural *influences* on behavior does not lead us to an exclusive focus on cultural *differences* in behavior. Such an emphasis was present earlier in our discipline, and may have sometimes fed into prejudice and intercultural hostility. Hence in this book we have also emphasized the existence of both cultural similarities and of ongoing cultural change.

To live up to its promise the field of cross-cultural psychology will require three major changes: the development of persistent and collaborative work on particular topics; the incorporation of psychologists from *all* societies into this enterprise; and the convincing of our students and colleagues to accept the view that culture is indeed one of the most important contributors to human behavior. If this book stimulates any of these changes, then we will consider ourselves to be rewarded.

Key Terms

Absolute orientation: Horizontal spatial orientation with a frame of reference that is absolute, i.e., independent of one's location and orientation.

Absolutism: A theoretical position that considers human behavior as not essentially influenced by culture, and that studies behavior without taking a person's culture into account.

Acculturation: Changes in a cultural group or individuals as a result of contact with another cultural group (see also psychological acculturation).

Acculturation profiles: These are groups of individuals that differ in their acculturation strategies. These profiles are derived using cluster analyses, grouping together individuals who tend to share similar acculturation attitudes, cultural identities, language use and proficiency, peer relations and family relation values.

Acculturation strategies: The way that individuals and ethnocultural groups orient themselves to the process of acculturation. Four strategies are: assimilation, integration, separation and marginalization.

Acculturative stress: A negative psychological reaction to the experiences of acculturation, often characterized by anxiety, depression and a variety of psychosomatic problems.

Adaptation (to acculturation): The process of dealing with the experiences of acculturation; a distinction is often made between psychological adaptation (feelings of personal well-being and self-esteem) and sociocultural adaptation (competence in dealing with life in the larger society).

Adaptation (biological): Changes in the genetic make-up of a population through natural selection in reaction to demands of the environment.

Adaptation (social): Changes in the behavior repertoire of a person or group in reaction to demands of the ecological or social environment.

Affective meaning: The connotative or emotional meaning which a word has in addition to its denotative or referential meaning.

Aggregation: Scores obtained at a lower level (e.g., individual level) in a multilevel design are combined to be used as an index at a higher level (e.g., culture level).

Allele: Variation of a single gene; alleles form the most important basis for individual differences within a species.

Amae: A concept from Japan referring to a form of passive love or dependence that finds its origin in the relationship of the infant with its mother.

Analogy: Similarities in traits between species that have evolved independently from each other, due to similar environmental demands (see also homology).

Antecedents of emotions: Situations that tend to lead to the emergence of certain emotions.

Anthropology: A scientific discipline that seeks to understand human societies in all their variety, and in various domains (cultural, social, biological and psychological).

Appropriate psychology: A psychology that is conceptually and practically attuned to the needs of a society or cultural group.

Assimilation: The acculturation strategy in which people do not wish to maintain their own culture, and seek to participate in the larger society.

Attachment: The bonding between a mother and her young child during the first year of life, thought by many developmental psychologists to have consequences through the entire life span.

Attitudes (ethnic): Positive or negative evaluations of individuals (or groups) because of their membership in a cultural or ethnocultural group.

Basic color terms: A set of words for major colors to which, according to some authors, all languages evolve.

Basic emotions: Emotional states that presumably can be identified universally, often with reference to characteristic patterns of facial musculature.

Big Five dimensions of personality: Five dimensions that tend to be seen as enduring dispositions, likely to be biologically anchored, and that together cover the main ways in which individual persons differ from each other in personality.

Biological transmission: See genetic transmission.

Child training: Practices that are used by parents, and others, to ensure that cultural transmission takes place.

Cognitive anthropology: A subdiscipline of anthropology that seeks to understand the relationship between culture and the cognitive life of the group.

Cognitive styles: A conception of cognitive activity that emphasizes the way in which cognitive processes are organized and used, rather than the level of development of cognitive abilities.

Color categorization: The way in which the colors of the visible spectrum are categorized by means of color names.

Componential approach: The approach that uses multiple emotion components (e.g., appraisals, physiological symptoms, action tendencies) as indicators of emotions instead of only a single indicator.

Contact hypothesis: The proposition that contact between cultural and ethnocultural groups, and their members, will lead to more positive intercultural attitudes.

Contextualized cognition: A conception of cognitive activity that emphasizes the development and use of cognitive processes in relation to specific cultural contexts and practices.

Contingency theory (with respect to organizations): A group of theories addressing the questions how, and how much, organizational structure is contingent upon (i.e., the consequence of) various kinds of contextual variables (cultural, political, technological, etc.).

Convention (also: cultural practice, cultural rule): Explicitly or implicitly accepted agreement among the members of a group as to what is appropriate in some social interaction or in some field of activity.

Convergent validity: Evidence for validity derived from findings of the presence of relationships between variables in accordance with theoretical expectations.

Cross-cultural psychology (definition): Cross-cultural psychology is the study of: similarities and differences in individual psychological functioning in various cultural and ethnocultural groups; the relationships between psychological variables and sociocultural, ecological and biological variables; and of ongoing changes in these variables.

Cross-ethnicity effect (in face recognition): The tendency that individuals from groups with different facial features from their own group tend to look more alike to them.

Cultunit: The set of people who belong to a cultural group. For the purpose of research a culture may be defined on the basis of a limited set of variables (e.g., speaking a certain language, employment in a certain organization, membership of a youth club).

Cultural bias: Cross-cultural differences that are not related to the trait or concept presumably measured by an instrument (or by some other method), and that tend to distort the interpretation of these differences.

Cultural evolution: A view that cultures have changed over time in adaptation to their ecosystems and other influences.

Cultural identity: How individuals think and feel about themselves in relation to the cultural or ethnocultural groups with which they are associated.

Cultural psychology: A theoretical approach that sees culture and behavior as essentially inseparable; and that is closely linked to cultural relativism and psychological anthropology.

Cultural relativism: A view that cultures should be understood in their own terms, rather than being judged by the standards of other groups (see also ethnocentrism).

Cultural transmission: Processes by which cultural features of a population are transferred to its individual members (see also enculturation and socialization).

Cultural universals: Those cultural features that are present in all societies in some form, such as language, family and technology.

Culture: The shared way of life of a group of people, including their artifacts (such as social institutions, and technology, i.e., external culture), and their symbols (such as communications and myths, i.e., internal culture).

Culture-as-a-system: Conceptualization of culture in which all its aspects are considered to be interrelated (to form a "system").

Culture assimilator: A series of short episodes describing incidents in the interaction between persons belonging to different cultures; intended for teaching intercultural communication.

Culture-bound syndromes: Patterns of behavior that are said to occur only in a particular cultural group and that are considered to be abnormal or psychopathological.

Culture-comparative research: A research tradition in which similarities and differences in behavior are studied across cultures.

Culture-specific emotion concepts: Emotion concepts that can only be found within a single cultural or linguistic community.

Decision making (by managers): Decisions and processes of decision making in work organizations influenced by cultural variables related to styles of leadership and risk assessment.

Definition of cross-cultural psychology: See cross-cultural psychology (definition).

Dependency: A state of affairs in which a group or individual is habitually dependent on others. It is usually applied to individuals and nation states that have been long-term recipients of international aid.

Depression: A psychological illness characterized by sadness, a lack of energy and of interest and enjoyment of life.

Depth cues in pictures: Aspects of pictures that lead to a sensation of depth in observers (including overlap of depicted objects, size at which various objects are represented, position of objects, etc.).

Developmental niche: A system in which the physical environment, sociocultural customs of childrearing, and psychological conceptions (beliefs, etc.) of parents interact with the developing child.

Disability Adjusted Life Years (DALY): The unit of measurement of the overall global burden of disease (GBD). Specifically, it is a combination of the total Years of Life Lost (YLL) (because of premature death) and the number of Years one Lives with Disability (YLD): (DALY = YLL + YLD). One (1) DALY is equivalent to one year of healthy life lost.

Disaggregation: A score at a higher level (e.g., a country) in a multilevel design is used as an equal index for elements (e.g., individuals) at a lower level.

Discrimination: The act of treating persons differently because of their membership in a cultural or ethnocultural group.

Discriminant validity: Evidence for validity derived from findings of the absence of relationships between variables in accordance with theoretical expectations.

Disease: The outward, clinical manifestation of physical malfunction or infection of the body with respect to health.

Display rules: Cultural norms regarding the control and expression of emotions in various situations.

Dual inheritance model: A model postulating a cultural inheritance system that is based on social learning and that cannot be reduced to the genetic inheritance system.

Ecocultural framework: A conceptual approach to understanding similarities and differences in human behavior across cultures in terms of individual and group adaptation to ecological and sociopolitical contexts.

Ego-referenced orientation: Horizontal spatial orientation with a frame of reference that is dependent on one's own location and orientation.

Emic approach: The study of behavior within one culture, often emphasizing culture-specific aspects.

Emotion components: Various aspects by which one emotional state can be distinguished from another, including facial expression, appraisal and antecedents of emotions.

Enculturation: A form of cultural transmission by which a society transmits its culture and behavior to its members by surrounding developing members with appropriate models.

Equivalence: A condition for interpreting psychological data obtained from different cultures in the same way (also referred to as comparability of data); data can have structural equivalence (measuring cross-culturally the same trait), metric equivalence (measuring the same trait on scales with the same metric) and full-score equivalence (measuring the same trait on the same scale).

Ethnocentrism: A point of view that accepts one's own group's standards as the best, and judges all other groups in relation to them.

Ethnocultural group: A group living in a plural society that is derived from a heritage cultural group, but which has changed as a result of acculturation in the larger society.

Ethnographic archives: A collection of ethnographic reports about various cultures, brought together into a form that can be used for comparative research (see also Human Relations Area Files).

Ethnography: The branch of cultural anthropology that seeks to describe and understand the features of one particular cultural group.

Ethnology: The branch of cultural anthropology that seeks to understand the basic feature of cultures in general, including social structures, language and technology. It differs from ethnography, which seeks to understand particular cultures.

Ethnopsychology: A perspective on human behavior that is rooted in a particular cultural worldview (see also indigenous psychologies).

Ethnoscience: The various branches of the scientific knowledge that exists in particular cultures (such as ethnobiology, ethnopharmocology).

Ethology: The study by biologists of animal behavior in natural environments.

Etic approach: The comparative study of behavior across cultures, often assuming some form of universality of the psychological underpinnings of behavior.

Everyday cognition: An approach to the study of cognition that seeks to understand how individuals engage in cognitive activity in their everyday lives.

Evolutionary psychology: A school of psychology based on the evolutionary thinking of ethology and sociobiology.

Expatriates: See sojourners.

External culture: See culture, external and internal.

Extraversion: A personality dimension ranging from sociable and outgoing (extraverted) to quiet and passive (introverted).

Fitness (biological): The probability of survival and reproduction of an organism.

Flynn effect: The phenomenon of rising mean cultural group or national scores in general intelligence over time.

g: The symbol used to designate general intelligence based on the general factor that is often present in the analysis of performance on intelligence tests.

Gene: A segment of DNA that can be recognized by its specific locus and function; the gene is the functional unit of genetic material.

General intelligence: A unified view of the level of cognitive functioning of an individual person, derived from the positive correlations found between scores on a wide range of cognitive tests (especially intelligence batteries) (see also g).

Generalization: The extension of an interpretation or inference to a larger set or domain than the one on which data have been obtained.

Generativity: The need to be needed. It includes commitments that go beyond oneself and that benefit larger groups, including family, friends or society.

Genetic transmission (also biological transmission): The transfer of genetic information from parents to their children. Each individual can be seen as representing a specific selection of genetic properties from the pool of genetic information present in the population.

Global burden of disease (GBD): The gap between present health status and an ideal situation where everyone lives into old age.

Globalization: The process of change that results in increasing interconnections (e.g., economic, political) among individuals, cultural groups or nation states.

Grandmother hypothesis: The assumption that menopause, which is rarely found in species other than humans, is an adaptation, enabling older women to invest in (care for) grandchildren rather than in new babies of their own.

Gross National Product (GNP): The market value of all goods and services produced in one year by labour and property supplied by the residents of a country.

Handicap principle: Seemingly useless or harmful traits (handicaps), evolved just because they signal their expensiveness and thus the high fitness quality of the bearer of this trait (e.g., the male peacock's tail).

Health: A state of complete physical, mental and social well-being, and not merely the absence of disease or infirmity.

Holocultural approach: A research method based on ethnographic archives that includes many societies in a single comparative study.

Homology: A homologous trait is any characteristic of organisms which is inherited from a common ancestor. Homology integrates humans in the array of other primate species, all descending from a common ancestor (see also analogy).

Human Relations Area Files (HRAF): An ethnographic archive of information about many of the world's societies organized by cultural topic.

Illness: The human experience and perceptions of a health malfunction. It is a subjectively interpreted undesirable state of health.

Immigrant paradox: The counterintuitive finding that immigrants often tend to show better adaptation outcomes than their national peers in spite of poorer socioeconomic status. The term is also used to refer to research findings where first-generation immigrants show better adaptation outcomes than their second- and later-generation peers.

Implicit motivation: Motives, including affiliation, achievement and power, that are built on early developmental (prelinguistic) experiences and that are later reflected in people's imaginations.

Inclusive fitness: The sum of the individual fitness outcomes resulting from their own procreation (Darwinian fitness); also from the procreation of relatives with whom the individual shares genes (see also kin selection).

Independent self and interdependent self: Two ways of viewing oneself; namely as a separate, autonomous individual seeking independence from others, or as an individual inherently linked to others. (A similar distinction is between separated self and relational self.)

Indigenization: The transformation through which an imported psychology becomes a more culturally appropriate psychology.

Indigenous conceptualizations (of intelligence): An approach to the study of cognition in a cultural group that seeks to understand how individuals construe and act out their cognitive life within their own cultural terms.

Indigenous personality concepts: Concepts that originated in non-western cultures and are rooted in local views of human functioning (note that most concepts originate from western indigenous views).

Indigenous psychologies: A body of theory and empirical research emphasizing the local development and application of psychology in various cultures.

Individualism and collectivism: A distinction between the tendencies to be primarily concerned with oneself, or with one's group.

Inference: The interpretation of data in terms of some domain of behavior or trait to which the data are thought to pertain (see also levels of inference).

Ingroup: A group to which an individual belongs, such as an ethnocultural or social group.

Integration: The acculturation strategy in which people wish to maintain their cultural heritage, and seek to participate in the larger society.

Intercultural communication: Exchange of information (verbally or non-verbally) between members of different cultural populations.

Intercultural communication training: Preparation of prospective sojourners for assignments outside their home country by means of various kinds of training programs.

Intercultural competence: The competence of a person to interact adequately with others from a different cultural background; often considered as not only consisting of certain skills and knowledge, but also of more general personality traits.

Intercultural strategies: A set of strategies used by members of a plural society to engage in intercultural relations. These include: melting pot, multiculturalism, segregation and exclusion (see also acculturation strategies).

Internal culture: See culture, external and internal.

Job satisfaction: The extent to which workers are pleased (or displeased) with their work.

Kin selection: According to this conception, individuals' social behaviors will vary in line with the degree of genetic relatedness among group members.

Larger society: A term used to refer to the overall social composition and arrangements in a culturally plural society, including its government, and its economic, educational and legal institutions. It differs from the concept of "mainstream" which refers mainly to the dominant society.

Leadership styles: Different ways in which leaders (notably managers in industrial organizations) influence the performance of subordinates. Often a dimension is distinguished with concern for employees and concern for productivity as endpoints.

Levels of inference (or generalization): Levels pertaining to the width or inclusiveness of behavioral domains and psychological traits in terms of which data are interpreted.

Life span development: Covers not only the period from birth to maturity, but also continues through maturity to eventual demise.

Linguistic relativity (also Whorfian hypothesis): The idea that there are important relationships between characteristics of a language and the ways of thinking found in speakers of that language.

Literacy: The knowledge and use of language in reading and writing.

Locus of control: A tendency to consider what happens to oneself either as a consequence of one's own actions (internal control) or as contingent upon forces beyond one's control, such as other persons (external control).

Majority world: The countries in which the majority of the world population is living. The term is strongly associated with economic poverty and low educational opportunities.

Malnutrition: A state resulting from insufficient food intake, and indicated by low weight and height in relation to age.

Marginalization: The acculturation strategy in which people do not maintain their cultural heritage, and also do not participate in the larger society.

Menarche: First menstrual period.

Mixed methods: Research methods in which qualitative methodology and quantitative methodology are combined.

Motivation (work-related): The complex of motives (or drives) and needs that presumably make people perform at work.

Multicultural ideology: A positive orientation of individuals to cultural diversity in plural societies, involving the acceptance of ethnocultural groups and their participation in the larger society.

Multiculturalism: A term used to refer to both the existence of, and a policy supporting the presence of, many ethnocultural groups living together in the larger society. The policy supports both the maintenance of diverse ethnocultural groups, and the equal participation of these groups in the larger society.

Multiculturalism hypothesis: The hypothesis that when an individual or cultural group is secure in their own cultural identity they will be able to accept those who are different from themselves. Conversely, when they are threatened, they will reject those who are different.

Multilevel analysis: Research in which elements at one level are nested in another level; the interactions between the levels are considered explicitly in the analysis (see also levels of analysis).

National character: A (small) set of personality traits that are considered salient or frequently occurring in a nation.

National development: A process of change in psychological, social, economic and political features that leads a society toward achieving its own goals.

Natural selection: The evolutionary process of natural selection that has three steps: reproduction, variance and selection.

Neuroticism (or emotionality): A personality dimension ranging from instability (e.g., "moody," "touchy") to stability (even-tempered).

Ontogenetic development: The systematic changes in the behavior of an individual person across the life span.

Organizational culture: Deep-rooted beliefs, meanings and values that are shared by the members of an organization, in distinction from other organizations. Sometimes the emphasis is more on practices prevalent in an organization, or on variables such as production techniques and attitudes of employees (the term "organizational climate" is also used, especially in the latter sense).

Organizational structure: The distribution of tasks in an organization. The total body of work that has to be performed is assigned to different divisions and subdivisions and ultimately to work groups and individuals with different tasks.

Outgroup: A group to which an individual does not belong, and whose norms are rejected.

Paradigm: A metatheoretical, often philosophical, position on the nature of the phenomena studied in a science and the ways they can be studied.

Parent–offspring conflict: Conflict of interest regarding the parental investment in an offspring.

Parental ethnotheories (also called parental beliefs, implicit developmental theories): A set of cultural beliefs and practices held by parents regarding the proper way to raise a child (see also child training).

Parental investment: Any investment by the parent in an individual offspring that decreases the parent's ability to invest in other offspring.

Personality traits: Characteristics of individual persons that are consistent over time and across situations, and through which they distinguish themselves from others.

Pleiotropy: The variety of effects that one gene can have on the development of an organism.

Plural society: A society in which a number of ethnocultural groups live together within a shared political and economic framework.

Positive reference group: A group to which an individual does not belong, and whose norms are accepted or admired.

Prejudice (ethnic): A general negative orientation toward a cultural or ethnocultural group other than one's own (see also ethnocentrism).

Prevention (health): Taking steps to avoid health problems before they appear, often through public education and public health programs.

Priming: The activation of mental representations that then serve as interpretive frames in the processing of subsequent information; in cross-cultural research this often involves activation of cultural characteristics such as values or self-construals.

Promotion (health): Advocating and supporting the achievement of health through public education and public health programs.

Psychological acculturation: Changes in the psychological features of persons as a result of their contact with another cultural group (see also acculturation).

Psychological anthropology (formerly known as culture-and-personality): A subdiscipline of anthropology that seeks to use and apply psychological concepts and methods to the understanding of cultural groups.

Psychopathology: A psychological illness that is considered by the community or experts to be reflected in strange or bizarre behavior.

Psychosocial factors (health): Features (other than biophysical) of the ecological and sociopolitical environments that contribute to the attainment (or loss) of health.

Psychotherapy: Practices that involve a patient and a healer in a personal relationship whose goal is to relieve the patient's suffering.

Qualitative approaches: Research methodology with an emphasis on the understanding of processes and meanings; often these cannot be experimentally or psychometrically examined or measured in terms of quantity, amount, etc.

Quality of life (QOL): A concept that emphasizes positive aspects of a person's life, in particular those that contribute to life satisfaction.

Quantitative approaches: Research methodology in which the measurement (in terms of quantity, amount or frequency) of the phenomena that are being examined is emphasized.

Quasi-experiment: An experimental study in which the researcher has less than full control over experimental conditions.

Reciprocal altruism: The evolution of cooperation in genetically unrelated individuals by alternating altruistic acts.

Relativism: A theoretical position that assumes human behavior is strongly influenced by culture, and that it can only be studied by taking a person's culture into account.

Schizophrenia: A psychological illness characterized by lack of insight, hallucinations and reduced affect.

Security: The sense that an individual or cultural group has that their cultural or economic position in society is secure, and not being threatened by others (see also threat).

Senescence: Biological changes of an organism as it ages after maturity.

Sensitive period: Refers to rapid learning of certain skills that takes place during a "critical" time period in development. Learning before or after this period tends to be much slower.

Sensory stimuli: Stimuli that solicit processes in the sensory organs (eye, ear, etc.), but are presumed to involve few other psychological functions, such as perception and cognition.

Separation: The acculturation strategy in which people wish to maintain their cultural heritage, and seek to avoid participation in the larger society.

Sexually transmitted disease: Any disease that is contracted by means of sexual relations.

Sickness: A society's way of making sense of and dealing with an individual's perception of malfunctioning (illness); and the underlying pathology (disease). Sickness, in short, is illness *plus* disease.

Social axioms: People's general beliefs about how the world functions.

Social representations: A system of values, ideas and beliefs that are shared by a group of people; they are used to organize the social world and communication among group members.

Socialization: A form of cultural transmission by which a society deliberately shapes the behavior of its developing members through instruction.

Sociobiology: The explanation of social behavior, including that of the human species, in terms of principles of evolutionary biology.

Sojourners (also called expatriates): Persons who live in another country for a certain period, varying from a number of weeks to a few years, and who have frequent interactions with local inhabitants for purposes of work or study.

Spatial orientation: The way persons locate objects and themselves in space; especially with respect to the question of whether they use their own position for indications of direction (ego-referenced orientation) or have a preference for absolute or geocentric spatial coordinates.

Stereotypes (ethnic): Shared beliefs about the characteristics thought to be typical of members of a cultural or ethnocultural group.

Subjective culture: How members of a culture view themselves and how they evaluate their way of life.

Subjective well-being: A person's cognitive and affective appraisal of his or her life.

Theory of mind: The tendency to ascribe mental states to oneself and to others; theories of mind are used to understand other people's behaviors and psychological states and those of oneself.

Threat: The sense that an individual or cultural group has that their cultural or economic position is society is being threatened, in particular by other cultural groups (see also security).

Tight–loose: A dimension contrasting societies that are tightly structured and expect conformity from their members, with those that are more loosely knit and allow greater individual variability.

Tolerance: The acceptance of individuals or cultural groups. The opposite of prejudice.

Transfer of tests: The use of tests with members of cultural populations other than the one for which they were originally designed.

Ubuntu: A mode of individual functioning considered characteristic for people in southern Africa.

Universalism: A theoretical position that considers basic psychological processes to be shared characteristics of all people, and culture as influencing their development and display.

Universality: Psychological concepts, or relationships between concepts, are universal if they appear suitable for the description of the behavior of people in any culture.

Universals in language: Characteristics thought to be found in all human languages.

Validity: The degree to which findings and interpretations have been shown to approximate a presumed state of affairs in reality, independent of the prior beliefs of scientists.

Values: Conceptions of what is desirable, which influence the selection of means and ends of actions.

Visual illusions: Systematic distortions in the visual perception of the objective reality as it presents itself to the perceiver (usually studied with simple figures, such as the Müller–Lyer, known to lead to such distortions).

Western psychology: The large body of scientific knowledge and practice that is based in the western (Euro-American) cultural region.

Whorf's hypothesis: See linguistic relativity.

Work-related values: Desired states and outcomes (see values) derived from cross-cultural studies in organizations, usually presented as value dimensions (e.g., individualism–collectivism, power distance).

Xenophobia: The fear or dislike of the unknown or foreign; it is often used as a synonym for prejudice.

Bibliography

Abegglen, J. C. (1958). *The Japanese factory*. Glencoe, Ill.: The Free Press.

Aberle, D. F., Cohen, A. K., Davis, A., Levy, M., and Sutton, F. X. (1950). Functional prerequisites of society. *Ethics*, 60, 100–111.

Aboud, F. (1998). *Health psychology in global perspective*. Thousand Oaks, Calif.: Sage.

Aboud, F., and Alemu, T. (1995). Nutritional status, maternal responsiveness and mental development of Ethiopian children. *Social Science and Medicine*, 41, 725–732.

Abraído-Lanza, A. F., Chao, M. T., and Gates, C. Y. (2008). Acculturation and cancer screening among Latinas: Results from the National Health Interview Survey. *Annals of Behavioural Medicine*, 29, 22–28.

Abu-Lughod, L. (1991). Writing against culture. In R. Fox (ed.), *Recapturing anthropology* (pp. 137–162). Santa Fe, N.Mex.: School of American Research.

Abusah, P. (1993). Multi-cultural influences in case management: Transcultural psychiatry. *Mental Health in Australia*, 5, 67–75.

Adair, J. (2004). On the indigenization and authochthonization of the discipline of psychology. In B. Setiadi, A. Supratiknya, W. J. Lonner and Y. H. Poortinga (eds.), *Ongoing themes in psychology and culture* (pp. 115–129). Yogakarta: International Asociation for Cross-Cultural Psychology.

Adair, J. G. (2006). Creating indigenous psychologies: Insights from empirical social studies of the science of psychology. In U. Kim, K.-S. Yang and K.-K. Hwang (eds.), *Indigenous and cultural psychology: Understanding people in context* (pp. 467–487). New York: Springer.

Adair, J., and Diaz-Loving, R. (1999). Indigenous psychologies: The meaning of the concept and its assessment. *Applied Psychology*, 48, 397–402.

Adair, J., and Kağitçibaşi, C. (eds.) (1995). National development of psychology: Factors facilitating and impeding progress in developing countries. Special issue, *International Journal of Psychology*, 30, 6.

Adair, J., Coelho, A., and Luna, J. (2002). How international is international psychology? *International Journal of Psychology*, 37, 160–170.

Adamopoulos, J. (2008). On the entanglement of culture and individual behavior. In F. J. R. Van de Vijver, D. A. van Hemert and Y. H. Poortinga (eds.), *Individuals and cultures in multilevel analysis* (pp. 27–62). Mahwah, N.J.: Erlbaum.

Adams, C., Wilson, P., Gilbody, S., Bagnall, A.-M., and Lewis, R. (2000). Drug treatments for schizophrenia. *Quality in Health Care*, 9, 73–79.

Adams, M. (2007). *Unlikely utopia: The surprising triumph of Canadian pluralism*. Toronto: Viking.

Aditya, R. N., House, R. J., and Kerr, S. (2000). Theory and practice of leadership: Into the new millennium. In C. L. Cooper and E. A. Locke (eds.), *Industrial and organizational psychology: Linking theory with practice* (pp. 130–167). Oxford: Blackwell.

AERA (1999). American Educational Research Association, American Psychological Association, and National Council for Measurement in Education. *Standards for educational and psychological testing.* Washington, DC: American Educational Research Association.

Ager, A. (ed.) (1999). *Refugees: Perspectives on the experience of forced migration.* London: Cassell.

Ahmed, R. A., and Gielen, U. (eds.) (1998). *Psychology in the Arab countries.* Cairo: Menoufia Press.

Ainsworth, M. D. S. (1967). *Infancy in Uganda: Infant care and the growth of love.* Baltimore: Johns Hopkins University Press.

Ainsworth, M. D. S., Blehar, M. C., Waters, E., and Wall, S. (1978). *Patterns of attachment: A psychological study of the strange situation.* Hillsdale, N.J.: Erlbaum.

Ajzen, I., and Fishbein, M. (1977). Attitude–behavior relations: A theoretical analysis and review of empirical research. *Psychological Bulletin*, 84, 888–918.

Alasuutari, P. (1995). *Researching culture: Qualitative method and cultural studies.* London: Sage.

Albas, D. C., McCluskey, K. W., and Albas, C. A. (1976). Perception of the emotional content of speech. *Journal of Cross-Cultural Psychology*, 7, 481–490.

Albert, R. D. (1983). The intercultural sensitizer or cultural assimilator: A cognitive approach. In D. Landis and R. W. Brislin (eds.), *Handbook of intercultural training, Vol. II* (pp. 186–217). New York: Pergamon.

Alegría, M., Canino, G., Shrout, P. E., Woo, M., Duan, N., Vila, D., Torres, M., Chen, C., and Meng, X.-L. (2008). Prevalence of mental illness in immigrant and non-immigrant U.S. Latino groups. *American Journal of Psychiatry*, 165, 359–369.

Alexander, R. D. (1987). *The biology of moral systems.* New York: Aldine de Gruyter.

Alexander, R. D. (1990). Epigenetic rules and Darwininian algorithms – The adaptive study of learning and development. *Ethology and Sociobiology*, 11, 241–303.

Al-Issa, I. (ed.) (1995). *Handbook of culture and mental illness.* Madison, Wisc.: International University Press.

Al-Issa, I., and Tousignant, M. (eds.) (1997). *Ethnicity, immigration and psychopathology.* New York: Plenum.

Ali, J. (2002). Mental health of Canada's immigrants. Supplement to mental health Reports, Volume 13, Statistics Canada. Retrieved May 19, 2009, from www. statcan.gc.ca/cgi-bin/af-fdr.cgi?l=eng&loc=http://www.statcan.gc.ca/pub/82-003-s/2002001/pdf/82-003-s2002006-eng.pdf&t=Mental health of Canada's immigrants

Allaire, Y., and Firsirotu, M. E. (1984). Theories of organizational culture. *Organization Studies*, 5, 193–226.

Allen, J., Vaage, A. B., and Hauff, E. (2006). Refugees and asylum seekers in societies. In D. L. Sam and J. W. Berry (eds.), *The Cambridge handbook of acculturation psychology* (pp. 198–217). Cambridge: Cambridge University Press.

Allen, M., Ng, S., Ikeda, K., Jawan, J., Sufi, A., Wilson, M., and Yang, K.-S. (2007). Two decades of change in cultural values and economic development in eight East Asian and Pacific Island nations. *Journal of Cross-Cultural Psychology*, 38, 247–269.

Allik, J. (2005). Personality dimensions across cultures. *Journal of Personality Disorders*, 19, 212–232.

Allik, J., and McCrae, R. R. (2004). Toward a geography of personality traits: Patterns of profiles across 36 cultures. *Journal of Cross-Cultural Psychology*, 35, 13–28.

Allik, J., and Realo, A. (1996). The hierarchical nature of individualism and collectivism. *Culture & Psychology*, 2, 109–117.

Allik, J., Mõttus, R., and Realo, A. (in press). Does national character reflect mean personality traits when both are measured by the same instrument? *Journal of Research in Personality*, 44.

Allison, A. C. (1964). Polymorphism and natural selection in human populations. *Cold Spring Harbor Symposium in Quantitative Biology*, 24, 137–149.

Allport, F., Allport, G., Brown, J., Cantril, H., Doob, L., and English, H. (1939). Resolution and manifestoes of scientists. *Science*, 89, 166–169.

Allport, G. W. (1954). *The nature of prejudice*. Reading, Mass.: Addison-Wesley.

Allport, G. W. (1961). *The individual and his religion*. New York: Macmillan.

Allport, G. W., and Ross, J. M. (1967). Personal religious orientation and prejudice. *Journal of Personality and Social Psychology*, 5, 432–443.

Allport, G. W., Vernon, P. E., and Lindzey, G. (1960). *A study of values*. Boston: Houghton Mifflin.

Allwood, C. (1998). The creation and nature of indigenized psychologies from the perspective of the anthropology of knowledge. *Knowledge and Society*, 11, 153–172.

Allwood, C. M., and Berry, J. W. (2006). Origins and development of indigenous psychologies: An international analysis. *International Journal of Psychology*, 41, 241–268.

Altman, I., and Chemers, M. M. (1980). Cultural aspects of environment–behavior relationships. In H. C. Triandis and R. W. Brislin (eds.), *Handbook of cross-cultural psychology, Vol. V* (pp. 335–394). Boston: Allyn & Bacon.

Ambady, N., and Bharucha, J. (2009). Culture and the brain. *Current Directions in Psychological Science*, 18, 342–345.

Ambady, N., Koo, J., Lee, F., and Rosenthal, R. (1996). More than words: Linguistic and nonlinguistic politeness two cultures. *Journal of Personality and Social Psychology*, 70, 996–1011.

American Psychiatric Association (APA) (1987). Diagnostic and statistical manual of mental disorders (revised 3rd edn.). Washington, DC: American Psychiatric Association.

American Psychiatric Association (APA) (1980). Diagnostic and statistical manual of mental disorders (3rd edn.). Washington, DC: American Psychiatric Association.

American Psychiatric Association (2000). *Diagnostic and statistical manual of mental disorders* (4th edn.). Washington, DC: American Psychiatric Association.

Amir, Y., and Sharon, I. (1987). Are social psychological laws cross-culturally valid? *Journal of Cross-Cultural Psychology*, 18, 383–470.

Anastasi, A. (1982). *Psychological testing* (6th edn.). New York: Macmillan.

Andriessen, I., Phalet, K., and Lens, W. (2006). Future goal setting, task motivation, and learning of minority and non-minority students in Dutch schools. *British Journal of Educational Psychology*, 76, 827–850.

Ang, S., and Van Dyne, L. (eds.) (2008). *Handbook of cultural intelligence: Theory, measurement, and applications.* New York: Sharpe.

Angel, R. J., and Williams, K. (2000). Cultural models of health and illness. In I. Cuellar and F. R. Paniagua (eds.), *Handbook of multicultural mental health* (pp. 25–44). San Diego: Academic Press.

APA (2003). International perspectives: Population and reproduction. Special Issue, *American Psychologist*, 58, 193–234.

APA (2008). Members say no to psychologist involvement in interrogations in unlawful detention settings. *Monitor on Psychology*, 30, 10.

Aptekar, L., and Stöcklin, D. (1997). Children in particularly difficult circumstances. In J. W. Berry, P. R. Dasen and T. S. Saraswathi (eds.), *Handbook of cross-cultural psychology*, Vol. II, *Basic processes and human development* (pp. 377–412). Boston: Allyn & Bacon.

Archer, J. (1992). *Ethology and human development.* New York: Harvester Wheatsheaf.

Arends-Tóth, J., and Van de Vijver, F. (2003). Multiculturalism and acculturation: Views of Dutch and Turkish-Dutch. *European Journal of Social Psychology*, 33, 249–266.

Arends-Tóth, J., and Van de Vijver, F. J. R. (2006). Assessment of psychological acculturation. In D. L. Sam and J. W. Berry (eds.), *The Cambridge handbook of acculturation psychology* (pp. 142–160). Cambridge: Cambridge University Press.

Arends-Tóth, J., and Van de Vijver, F. J. R. (2007). Acculturation attitudes: A comparison of measurement methods. *Journal of Applied Social Psychology*, 7, 1462–1488.

Argyle, M. (1969). *Social interaction.* London: Methuen.

Ariès, P. (1960). *L'enfant et la vie familiale sous l'Ancien Régime* [Child and family life in the Old Order]. Paris: Éditions du Seuil.

Armstrong, R. E., Rubin, E. V., Stewart, M., and Kuntner, L. (1970). *Susceptibility to the Müller–Lyer, Sander parallelogram, and Ames Distorted Room illusions as a function of age, sex and retinal pigmentation among urban Midwestern groups.* Research report. Northwestern University, Department of Psychology.

Arnett, J. (1995). Broad and narrow socialization: The family in the context of cultural theory. *Journal of Marriage and the Family*, 57, 617–628.

Arnett, J. (1999). Adolescent storm and stress, reconsidered. *American Psychologist*, 54, 317–326.

Arnold, M. B. (1960). *Emotion and personality*. New York: Columbia University Press.

Arrow, H., and Burns, K. L. (2004). Self-organizing culture: How norms emerge in small groups. In M. Schaller and C. Crandall (eds.), *The psychological foundations of culture* (pp. 171–199). Mahwah, N.J.: Erlbaum.

Arthur, W., and Bennett, W. (1995). The international assignee: The relative importance of factors perceived to contribute to success. *Personnel Psychology*, 48, 99–113.

Asch, S. E. (1956). *Studies in independence and conformity*. Psychological Monographs, 70 (Whole No. 416), 1–70.

Ashkanasy, N. M., Broadfoot, L. E., and Falkus, S. (2000). Questionnaire measures of organizational culture. In N. M. Ashkanasy, C. P. M. Wilderom and M. F. Peterson (eds.), *Handbook of organizational culture and climate* (pp. 131–146). Thousand Oaks, Calif.: Sage.

Ashkanasy, N. M., Wilderom, C. P. M., and Peterson, M. F. (eds.) (2000a). *Handbook of organizational culture and climate*. Thousand Oaks, Calif.: Sage.

Ashkanasy, N. M., Wilderom, C. P. M., and Peterson, M. F. (2000b). Introduction. In N. M. Ashkanasy, C. P. M. Wilderom and M. F. Peterson (eds.), *Handbook of organizational culture and climate* (pp. 1–18). Thousand Oaks, Calif.: Sage.

Atran, S. (1998). Folk biology and the anthropology of science: Cognitive universals and cultural particulars. *Behavioral and Brain Sciences*, 21, 547–609.

Atran, S. (2007). Religion's social and cognitive landscape. In S. Kitayama and D. Cohen (eds.), *Handbook of cultural psychology* (pp. 437–453). New York: Guildford Press.

Atran, S., and Medin, D. (2008). *The native mind and the cultural construction of nature*. Cambridge, Mass.: The MIT Press.

Atran, S., and Norenzayan, A. (2004). Religion's evolutionary landscape: Counterintuition, commitment, compassion, communion. *Behavioral and Brain Sciences*, 27, 713–770.

Au, T. K. (1983). Chinese and English counterfactuals: The Sapir–Whorf hypothesis revisited. *Cognition*, 15, 155–187.

Au, T. K. (1984). Counterfactuals: In reply to Alfred Bloom. *Cognition*, 17, 289–302.

Austad, S. N. (1997). Postreproductive survival. In K. W. Wachter and C. E. Finch (eds.), *Between Zeus and the salmon: The biodemography of longevity* (pp. 161–174). Washington, DC: National Academy Press.

Averill, J. R. (1974). An analysis of psychophysiological symbolism and its influence on theories of emotion. *Journal for the Theory of Social Behaviour*, 4, 147–190.

Ayabe-Kanamura, S., Schicker, I., Laska, M., Hudson, R., Distel, H., Kobayakawa, T., and Saito, S. (1998). Differences in perception of everyday odors: A Japanese-German cross-cultural study. *Chemical Senses*, 23, 31–38.

Aycan, Z. (1997). Expatriate adjustment as a multifaceted phenomenon: Individual and organizational level predictors. *The International Journal of Human Resource Management*, 8, 434–456.

Aycan, Z., and Berry, J. W. (1996). Impact of employment-related experiences on immigrants' psychological well-being and adaptation to Canada. *Canadian Journal of Behavioural Science*, 28, 240–251.

Aycan, Z., Kanungo, R. N., Mendonca, M., Yu, K., Deller, J., Stahl, G., and Kurshid, A. (2000). Impact of culture on human resource management practices: A ten-country comparison. *Applied Psychology: An International Review*, 49, 192–220.

Ayers, S., Baum, A., McManus, C., Newman, S., Wallston, K., Weinman, J., and West, R. (eds.) (2007). *The Cambridge handbook of psychology, health and medicine.* Cambridge: Cambridge University Press.

Bakker, W., Van Oudenhoven, J. P., and Van Der Zee, K. I. (2004). Attachment styles, personality, and Dutch emigrants' intercultural adjustment. *European Journal of Personality*, 18, 387–404.

Baldassare, M., and Feller, S. (1975). Cultural variations in personal space: Theory, methods, and evidence. *Ethos*, 3, 481–503.

Baltes, P. (1997). On the incomplete architecture of human ontogeny. *American Psychologist*, 52, 366–380.

Baltes, P. B., Lindenberger, U., and Staudinger, U. M. (2006). Life span theory in developmental psychology. In W. Damon and R. M. Lerner (eds.), *Handbook of child psychology, Vol. I, Theoretical models of human development* (6th edn., pp. 569–664). New York: Wiley.

Bandura, A. (1969). *Principles of behavior modification.* Oxford: Holt, Rinehart & Winston.

Bandura, A. (1977). *Social learning theory.* Englewood Cliffs, N.J.: Prentice-Hall.

Bandura, A. (1997). *Self-efficacy: The exercise of control.* New York: Freeman.

Barnlund, D. C., and Araki, S. (1985). Intercultural encounters: The management of compliments. *Journal of Cross-Cultural Psychology*, 16, 9–26.

Baron, R. M., and Kenny, D. A. (1986). The moderator–mediator variable distinction in social psychological research: Conceptual, strategic, and statistical considerations. *Journal of Personality and Social Psychology*, 51, 1173–1182.

Barr, R. G., Konner, M., Bakeman, R., and Adamson, L. (1991). Crying in !Kung San infants: A test of the cultural specificity hypothesis. *Developmental Medicine and Child Neurology*, 33, 601–610.

Barrett, K. C. (2006). Solving the emotion paradox: Categorizations and the experience of emotion. *Personality and Social Psychology Bulletin*, 10, 20–46.

Barrett, L. F., Lindquist, K., and Gendron, M. (2007). Language as a context for emotion perception. *Trends in Cognitive Sciences*, 11, 327–332.

Barrett, L. F., Mesquita, B., Ochsner, K. N., and Gross, J. J. (2007). The experience of emotion. *Annual Review of Psychology*, 58, 373–403.

Barrett, P. T., Petrides, K. V., Eysenck, S. B. G., and Eysenck, H. J. (1998). The Eysenck Personality Questionnaire: An examination of the factorial similarity of P, E, N, and L across 34 countries. *Personality and Individual Differences*, 25, 805–819.

Barrowclough, C., and Parle, M. (1997). Appraisal, psychological adjustment, and expressed emotion in relatives of patients suffering from schizophrenia. *British Journal of Psychiatry*, 171, 26–30.

Barry, H. (1980). Description and uses of the Human Relations Area Files. In H. C. Triandis and J. W. Berry (eds.), *Handbook of cross-cultural psychology, Vol. II, Methodology* (pp. 445–78). Boston: Allyn & Bacon.

Barry, H., and Schlegel, A. (eds.) (1980). *Cross-cultural samples and codes.* Pittsburgh: University of Pittsburgh Press.

Barry, H., Bacon, M., and Child, I. (1957). A cross-cultural survey of some sex differences in socialization. *Journal of Abnormal and Social Psychology*, 55, 327–332.

Barry, H., Child, I., and Bacon, M. (1959). Relation of child training to subsistence economy. *American Anthropologist*, 61, 51–63.

Barsade, S. G., Brief, A. P., and Spataro, S. E. (2003). The affective revolution in organizational behavior: The emergence of a paradigm. In J. Greenberg (ed.), *Organizational behavior* (2nd edn., pp. 3–52). Mahwah, N.J.: Erlbaum.

Barth, F. (2002). An anthropology of knowledge. *Current Anthropology*, 43, 1–18.

Bartlett, C. A., and Ghoshal, S. (1998). *Managing across borders: The transnational solution* (2nd edn.). Boston: Harvard Business School.

Bartram, D. (2008). Introduction to the special issue on global norming. *International Journal of Testing*, 8, 303.

Bass, B. M. (1997). Does the transactional-transformational leadership paradigm transcend organizational and national boundaries? *American Psychologist*, 52, 130–139.

Baumeister, R. F. (2005). *The cultural animal.* New York: Oxford University Press.

Bayley, N. (1969). *Bayley scales of infant development.* New York: Psychological Corporation.

Bebbington, P., and Copper, C. (2007). Affective disorders. In D. Bhugra and K. Bhui (eds.), *Textbook of cultural psychiatry* (pp. 224–241). Cambridge: Cambridge University Press.

Becker, S. O., and Woessmann, L. (2009). Was Weber wrong? A human capital theory of Protestant economic history. *Quarterly Journal of Economics*, 124, 531–596.

Bedford, O. (1994). Guilt and shame in American and Chinese culture. Unpublished Ph.D. dissertation, University of Colorado.

Beh, H. G., and Diamond, M. (2000). An emerging ethical and medical dilemma: Should physicians perform sex assignment on infants with ambiguous genitalia? *Michigan Journal of Gender & Law*, 7, 1–63.

Belsky, J., Steinberg, L., and Draper, P. (1991). Childhood experience, interpersonal development, and reproductive strategy: An evolutionary theory of socialization. *Child Development*, 62, 647–670.

Bender, M., and Chasiotis, A. (2010). Number of siblings in childhood explains cultural variance in autobiographical memory in Cameroon, PR China, and Germany. *Journal of Cross-Cultural Psychology*, 41, 1–20.

Benedict, R. (1934). *Patterns of culture.* New York: Mentor.

Benet-Martínez, V., and Haritatos, J. (2005). Bicultural identity integration (BII): Components and psychological antecedents. *Journal of Personality*, 73, 1015–1050.

Benet-Martínez, V., Lee, F., and Leu, J. (2006). Biculturalism and cognitive complexity: Expertise in cultural representations. *Journal of Cross-Cultural Psychology*, 37, 386–407.

Benet-Martínez, V., Leu, J., Lee, F., and Morris, M. (2002). Negotiating biculturalism: Cultural frame-switching in biculturals with oppositional vs. compatible cultural identities. *Journal of Cross-Cultural Psychology*, 33, 492–516.

Bennett, J. M., Bennett, M. J., and Allen, W. (1999). Developing intercultural competence in the language classroom. In R. M. Paige, D. M. Lange and Y. A. Yershova (eds.), *Culture as the core: Integrating culture into the language curriculum*. CARLA Working Paper #15, 13–45. Minnesota: University of Minnesota.

Bennett, J. W. (1999). Classical anthropology. *American Anthropologist*, 100, 951–956.

Berk, L. (2003). *Development through the lifespan* (3rd edn.). New York: Pearson.

Berlin, B., and Kay, P. (1969). *Basic color terms: Their universality and evolution*. Berkeley: University of California Press.

Berlyne, D. E. (1980). Psychological aesthetics. In H. C. Triandis and W. J. Lonner (eds.), *Handbook of cross-cultural psychology*, Vol. III (pp. 323–361). Boston: Allyn & Bacon.

Bernard, H. (ed.) (1998). *Handbook of methods in cultural anthropology*. Walnut Creek, Calif.: AltaMira Press.

Bernard, R. (2002). *Research methods in anthropology*. Walnut Creek, Calif.: AltaMira Press.

Bernhard, G. (1988). *Primates in the classroom: An evolutionary perspective on children's learning*. Amherst: University of Massachusetts Press.

Berry, J. W. (1966). Temne and Eskimo perceptual skills. *International Journal of Psychology*, 1, 207–229.

Berry, J. W. (1967). Independence and conformity in subsistence-level societies. *Journal of Personality and Social Psychology*, 7, 415–418.

Berry, J. W. (1969). On cross-cultural comparability. *International Journal of Psychology*, 4, 119–128.

Berry, J. W. (1971). Müller–Lyer susceptibility: Culture, ecology or race? *International Journal of Psychology*, 6, 193–197.

Berry, J. W. (1974). Psychological aspects of cultural pluralism. *Topics in Culture Learning*, 2, 17–22.

Berry, J. W. (1976). *Human ecology and cognitive style: Comparative studies in cultural and psychological adaptation*. New York: Sage/Halsted.

Berry, J. W. (1978). Social psychology: Comparative, societal and universal. *Canadian Psychological Review*, 19, 93–104.

Berry, J. W. (1979). A cultural ecology of social behaviour. In L. Berkowitz (ed.), *Advances in experimental social psychology*, Vol. XII (pp. 177–206). New York: Academic Press.

Berry, J. W. (1980). Acculturation as varieties of adaptation. In A. Padilla (ed.), *Acculturation: Theory, models and some new findings* (pp. 9–25). Boulder, Colo.: Westview.

Berry, J. W. (1984). Multicultural policy in Canada: A social psychological analysis. *Canadian Journal of Behavioural Sciences*, 16, 353–370.

Berry, J. W. (1989). Imposed etics-emics-derived etics: The operationalization of a compelling idea. *International Journal of Psychology*, 24, 721–735.

Berry, J. W. (1990). Psychology of acculturation. In J. Berman (ed.), *Cross-cultural perspectives: Nebraska Symposium on motivation, Vol. XXXVII* (pp. 201–234). Lincoln, Nebr.: University of Nebraska Press.

Berry, J. W. (1994). Ecology of individualism–collectivism. In U. Kim, H. C. Triandis, C. Kağitçibaşi, S-C. Choi and G. Yoon (eds.), *Individualism and collectivism: Theory, method and applications* (pp. 77–84). Thousand Oaks, Calif.: Sage.

Berry, J. W. (1997). Immigration, acculturation and adaptation. *Applied Psychology: An International Review*, 46, 5–68.

Berry, J. W. (2000). Cross-cultural psychology: A symbiosis of cultural and comparative approaches. *Asian Journal of Social Psychology*, 3, 197–205.

Berry, J. W. (2001a). A psychology of immigration. *Journal of Social Issues*, 57, 615–631.

Berry, J. W. (2001b). Interamerican or Unter-American? Trafficking in international psychology. Invited address. Interamerican Society of Psychology. Santiago, July.

Berry, J. W. (2003). Conceptual approaches to acculturation. In K. Chun, P. Balls Organista and G. Marín (eds.), *Acculturation: Advances in theory, measurement and applied research* (pp. 17–37). Washington, DC: APA Press.

Berry, J. W. (2004). Fundamental psychological processes in intercultural relations. In D. Landis and J. Bennett (eds.), *Handbook of intercultural research and training* (3rd edn., pp. 166–184). Thousand Oaks, Calif.: Sage.

Berry, J. W. (2006a). Stress perspectives on acculturation. In D. L. Sam and J. W. Berry (eds.), *The Cambridge handbook of acculturation psychology* (pp. 43–57). Cambridge: Cambridge University Press.

Berry, J. W. (2006b). Design of acculturation studies. In D. L. Sam and J. W. Berry (eds.), *The Cambridge handbook of acculturation psychology* (pp. 129–141). Cambridge: Cambridge University Press.

Berry, J. W. (2006c). Attitudes towards immigrants and ethnocultural groups in Canada. *International Journal of Intercultural Relations*, 30, 719–734.

Berry, J. W. (2007a). Socialization. In J. Grusec and P. Hastings (eds.), *Handbook of socialization* (pp. 543–558). New York: Guilford Press.

Berry, J. W. (2007b). Acculturation and identity. In D. Bhugra and K. Bhui (eds.), *Textbook of cultural psychiatry* (pp. 169–178). Cambridge: Cambridge University Press.

Berry, J. W. (2007c). Integration: A cultural and psychological perspective. In Estonian Integration Foundation (eds.), *The meaning of integration* (pp.124–141). Tallinn: Estonian Integration Foundation.

Berry, J. W. (2008). Globalization and acculturation. *International Journal of Intercultural Relations*, 32, 328–336.

Berry, J. W. (2009). A critique of critical acculturation. *International Journal of Intercultural Relations*, 33, 361–371.

Berry, J. W. (2010). Mobility and acculturation. In S. Carr (ed.), *The psychology of mobility in a global era* (pp. 193–210). New York: Springer.

Berry, J. W. (in press). The ecocultural framework: A stocktaking. In F. J. R. Van de Vijver, A. Chasiotis and S. M. Breugelmans (eds.), *Fundamental questions in cross-cultural psychology*. Cambridge: Cambridge University Press.

Berry, J. W., and Bennett, J. A. (1989). Syllabic literacy and cognitive performance among the Cree. *International Journal of Psychology*, 24, 429–450.

Berry, J. W., and Bennett, J. A. (2002). Cree conceptions of cognitive competence. *International Journal of Psychology*, 27, 1–16.

Berry, J. W., and Cavalli-Sforza, L. L. (1986). Cultural and genetic influence on Inuit art. Unpublished report to the Social Science and Humanities Research Council of Canada.

Berry, J. W., and Irvine, S. H. (1986). Bricolage: Savages do it daily. In R. Sternberg and R. Wagner (eds.), *Practical intelligence: Nature and origins of competence in the everyday world* (pp. 271–306). New York: Cambridge University Press.

Berry, J. W., and Kalin, R. (1979). Reciprocity of inter-ethnic attitudes in a multicultural society. *International Journal of Intercultural Relations*, 3, 99–112.

Berry, J. W., and Kalin, R. (1995). Multicultural and ethnic attitudes in Canada: Overview of the 1991 survey. *Canadian Journal of Behavioural Science*, 27, 301–320.

Berry, J. W., and Kalin, R. (2000). Multicultural policy and social psychology: The Canadian experience. In S. Renshon and J. Duckitt (eds.), *Political psychology in cross-cultural perspective* (pp. 263–284). New York: Macmillan.

Berry, J. W., and Kim, U. (1993). The way ahead: From indigenous psychologies to a universal psychology. In U. Kim and J. W. Berry (eds.), *Indigenous psychologies* (pp. 277–280). Newbury Park: Sage.

Berry, J. W., and Sam, D. L. (2003). Accuracy in scientific discourse. *Scandinavian Journal of Psychology*, 44, 65–68.

Berry, J. W., and Sam, D. L. (2007). Culture and ethnic factors in health. In S. Ayers., A. Baum, C. McManus, S. Newman, K. Wallston, J. Weinman and R. West (eds.), *The Cambridge handbook of psychology, health and medicine* (pp. 64–79). Cambridge: Cambridge University Press.

Berry, J. W., and Triandis, H. C. (2006). Culture. In K. Pawlik and G. d'Ydewalle (eds.), *Psychological concepts: An international and historical perspective* (pp. 47–62). Hove: Psychology Press.

Berry, J. W., and Ward, C. (2006). Cultural intelligence: A critique. *Group & Organization Management*, 31, 64–77.

Berry, J. W., Bennett, J., Denny, P., and Mishra, R. (2000). Ecology, culture, and cognitive processing. Paper presented to Congress of International Association for Cross-Cultural Psychology, Pultusk, Poland.

Berry, J. W., Irvine, S. H., and Hunt, E. B. (eds.) (1988). *Indigenous cognition: Functioning in cultural context.* Dordrecht: Nijhoff.

Berry, J. W., Kalin, R., and Taylor, D. (1977). *Multiculturalism and ethnic attitudes in Canada.* Ottawa: Supply and Services.

Berry, J. W., Kim, U., Minde, T., and Mok, D. (1987). Comparative studies of acculturative stress. *International Migration Review,* 21, 491–511.

Berry, J. W., Phinney, J. S., Sam, D. L., and Vedder, P. (eds.) (2006). *Immigrant youth in cultural transition: Acculturation, identity, and adaptation across national contexts.* Mahwah, N.J.: Erlbaum.

Berry, J. W., Poortinga, Y. H., Segall, M. H., and Dasen, P. R. (1992). *Cross-cultural psychology: Research and applications.* Cambridge: Cambridge University Press.

Berry, J. W., Poortinga, Y. H., Segall, M. H., and Dasen, P. R. (2002). *Cross-cultural psychology: Research and applications* (2nd edn.). Cambridge: Cambridge University Press.

Berry, J. W., Kim, U., Power, S., Young, M., and Bujaki, M. (1989). Acculturation attitudes in plural societies. *Applied Psychology: An International Review,* 38, 185–206.

Berry, J. W., Poortinga, Y. H., Pandey, J., Dasen, P. R., Saraswathi, T. S., Segall, M. H., and Kağitçibaşi, C. (eds.) (1997). *Handbook of cross-cultural psychology* (2nd edn., Vols. I–III). Boston: Allyn & Bacon.

Berry, J. W., Van de Koppel, J. M. H., Sénéchal, C., Annis, R. C., Bahuchet, S., Cavalli-Sforza, L. L., and Witkin, H. A. (1986). *On the edge of the forest: Cultural adaptation and cognitive development in Central Africa.* Lisse: Swets & Zeitlinger.

Bertino, M., Beauchamp, G. K., and Jen, K. C. (1983). Rated taste perception in two cultural groups. *Chemical Senses,* 8, 3–15.

Best, D. L. (2010). Gender. In M. H. Bornstein (ed.), *Handbook of cultural developmental science* (pp. 209–222). New York: Taylor & Francis.

Best, D. L., and Williams, J. E. (1993). Cross-cultural viewpoint. In A. E. Beall and J. Sternberg (eds.), *Perspectives on the psychology of gender* (pp. 215–248). New York: Guilford Press.

Beveridge, W. M. (1935). Racial differences in phenomenal regression. *British Journal of Psychology,* 26, 59–62.

Beveridge, W. M. (1940). Some differences in racial perception. *British Journal of Psychology,* 30, 57–64.

Bhagat, R. S. (2009). Culture, work and organizations: A future agenda. In R. S. Bhagat and R. M. Steers (eds.), *The Cambridge handbook of culture, organizations, and work* (pp. 519–525). Cambridge: Cambridge University Press.

Bhagat, R. S., and McQuaid, S. J. (1982). Role of subjective culture in organizations: A review and directions for future research. *Journal of Applied Psychology (Monograph),* 67, 653–685.

Bhagat, R. S., and Steers, R. M. (eds.) (2009). *The Cambridge handbook of culture, organizations, and work.* Cambridge: Cambridge University Press.

Bhagat, R. S., Kedia, B. L., Crawford, S. E., and Kaplan, M. R. (1990). Cross-cultural issues in organizational psychology: Emergent trends and directions for research in the 1990's. In C. L. Cooper and I. T. Robertson (eds.), *International review of industrial and organizational psychology* (pp. 59–99). New York: Wiley.

Bhawuk, D. P. S. (1998). The role of culture-theory in cross-cultural training: A multimethod study of culture-specific, culture general, and culture theory-based assimilators. *Journal of Cross-Cultural Psychology*, 29, 630–655.

Bhawuk, D. P. S., Landis, D., and Lo, K. D. (2006). Intercultural training. In D. L. Sam and J. W. Berry (eds.), *The Cambridge handbook of acculturation psychology* (pp. 504–524). Cambridge: Cambridge University Press.

Bhugra, B., and Bh.ui, K. (eds.) (2007). *Textbook of cultural psychiatry*. Cambridge: Cambridge University Press.

Bhugra, D., Sumathipala, A., and Siribaddana, S. (2007). Culture-bound syndromes: A re-visitation. In D. Bhugra and K. Bhui (eds.), *Textbook of cultural psychiatry* (pp. 141–156). Cambridge: Cambridge University Press.

Biederman, I., Yue, X., and Davidoff, J. (2009). Representation of shape in individuals from a culture with minimal exposure to regular simple artifacts: Sensitivity to nonaccidental versus metric properties. *Psychological Science*, 20, 1437–1442.

Birch, J. (1997). Efficiency of the Ishihara test for identifying red–green colour deficiency. *Ophthalmic and Physiological Optics*, 17, 403–408.

Birdwhistell, R. L. (1970). *Kinesics and context*. Philadelphia: University of Philadelphia Press.

Birg, H. (1995). *World population projections for the 21st century – Theoretical interpretations and quantitative simulations*. New York: St. Martin's Press.

Birman, D., and Trickett, E. J. (2001). Cultural transitions in first-generation immigrants: Acculturation of Soviet Jewish refugee adolescents and parents. *Journal of Cross-Cultural Psychology*, 32, 456–477.

Birman, D., Trickett, E. J., and Buchanan, R. M. (2005). A tale of two cities: Replication of study on the acculturation and adaptation of immigrant adolescents from the Former Soviet Union in different community context. *American Journal of Community Psychology*, 35, 83–101.

Bischof-Köhler, D. (1991). The development of empathy in infants. In M. E. Lamb and H. Keller (eds.), *Infant development: Perspectives from German speaking countries* (pp. 245–273). Hillsdale, N.J.: Erlbaum.

Bischof-Köhler, D. (1998). Zusammenhänge zwischen kognitiver, motivationaler und emotionaler Entwicklung in der frühen Kindheit und im Vorschulalter [Correlations between cognitive, motivational and emotional development in early childhood and preschool age]. In H. Keller (ed.), *Lehrbuch Entwicklungspsychologie* [Textbook developmental psychology] (pp. 325–377). Bern: Huber.

Biswas-Diener, R. M. (2008). Material wealth and subjective well-being. In M. Eid and R. J. Larsen (eds.), *The science of subjective well-being* (pp. 307–322). New York: Guilford Press.

Biswas-Diener, R. M., Vittersø, J., and Diener, E. (2005). Most people are pretty happy, but there is cultural variation: The Inughuit, The Amish, and The Maasai. *Journal of Happiness Studies*, 6, 205–226.

Bjorklund, D. F. (1997). The role of immaturity in human development. *Psychological Bulletin*, 122, 153–169.

Bjorklund, D. F., and Pellegrini, A. D. (2002). *The origins of human nature: Evolutionary developmental psychology*. Washington, DC: American Psychological Association.

Black, R. E., Allen, L. H., Bhutta, Z. A., Caulfield, L. E., De Onis, M., Ezzati, M., Mathers, C., and Rivera, J. (2008). Maternal and child undernutrition: Global and regional exposures and health consequences. *The Lancet*, 371, 243–260.

Blake, B. F., Heslin, R., and Curtis, S. C. (1996). Measuring impacts of cross-cultural training. In D. Landis and R. S. Bhagat (eds.), *Handbook of intercultural training* (2nd edn., pp. 61–80). Thousand Oaks, Calif.: Sage.

Blake, R. R., and Mouton, J. S. (1964). *The managerial grid*. Houston: Gulf Publishing.

Blakemore, S.-J., and Choudhury, S. (2006). Development of the adolescent brain: Implications for executive function and social cognition. *Journal of Child Psychology and Psychiatry*, 47, 296–312.

Bleichrodt, N., Drenth, P. J. D., and Querido, A. (1980). Effects of iodine deficiency on mental and psychomotor abilities. *American Journal of Physical Anthropology*, 53, 55–67.

Bloom, A. (1981). *The linguistic shaping of thought: A study in the impact of language on thinking in China and the West*. Hillsdale, N.J.: Erlbaum.

Blum-Kulka, S., House, J., and Kasper, G. (1988). Investigating cross-cultural pragmatics: An introductory overview. In S. Blum-Kulka, J. House and G. Kasper (eds.), *Cross-cultural pragmatics: Requests and apologies* (pp. 1–34). Norwood, N.J.: Ablex.

Boas, F. (1911). *The mind of primitive man*. New York: Macmillan.

Bochner, S. (1972). Problems in culture learning. In S. Bochner and P. Wicks (eds.), *Overseas students in Australia* (pp. 65–81). Sydney: University of New South Wales Press.

Bochner, S. (ed.) (1982). *Cultures in contact: Studies in cross-cultural interaction*. Oxford: Pergamon.

Bochner, S. (1986). Observational methods. In W. J. Lonner and J. W. Berry (eds.), *Field methods in cross-cultural research* (pp. 165–201). London: Sage.

Bochner, S. (2006). Sojourners. In D. L. Sam and J. W. Berry (eds.), *The Cambridge handbook of acculturation psychology* (pp. 181–197). Cambridge: Cambridge University Press.

Bock, P. K. (1999). *Rethinking psychological anthropology* (2nd edn.). Prospect Heights, Ill.: Waveland Press.

Boesch, C. (1991). Teaching among wild chimpanzees. *Animal Behavior*, 41, 530–532.

Boesch, C. (1993). Aspects of transmission in wild chimpanzees. In K. Gibson and T. Ingold (eds.), *Tools, language and cognition in human evolution* (pp. 171–183). Cambridge: Cambridge University Press.

Boesch, C. (1995). Innovation in wild chimpanzees (Pan troglodytes). *International Journal of Primatology*, 16, 1–16.

Boesch, E. E. (1986). Science, culture and development. In M. Gottstein and G. Link (eds.), *Cultural development, science and technology in Sub-Saharan Africa* (pp. 19–29). Berlin: German Foundation for International Development.

Boesch, E. E. (1991). *Symbolic action theory and cultural psychology.* Heidelberg: Springer.

Boesch, E. E. (2002). The myth of lurking chaos. In H. Keller, Y. H. Poortinga and A. Schölmerich (eds.), *Biology, culture and development: Integrating diverse perspectives* (pp. 116–135). Cambridge: Cambridge University Press.

Bogin, B. (1999). *Patterns of human growth* (2nd edn.). Cambridge: Cambridge University Press.

Bohnemeyer, J. (1998a). *Time relations in discourse: Evidence from a comparative approach to Yukatek Maya.* Wageningen: Ponsen & Looijen.

Bohnemeyer, J. (1998b). Temporal reference from a radical pragmatics perspective: Why Yucatec do not need to express "after" and "before." *Cognitive Linguistics*, 9, 239–282.

Boldt, E. D. (1978). Structural tightness and cross-cultural research. *Journal of Cross-Cultural Psychology*, 9, 151–165.

Bolhuis, J. J., and Wynne, C. D. L. (2009). Can evolution explain how minds work? *Nature*, 458, 832–833.

Bollen, K. A. (2002). Latent variables in psychology and the social sciences. *Annual Review of Psychology*, 53, 605–634.

Bond, M. H. (ed.) (1988). *The cross-cultural challenge to social psychology.* Newbury Park, Calif.: Sage.

Bond, M. H. (1991). Chinese values and health: A cultural investigation. *Psychology & Health*, 5, 137–152.

Bond, M. H., and Van de Vijver, F. J. R. (in press). Making scientific sense of cultural differences in psychological outcomes: Unpacking the magnum mysterium. In D. Matsumoto and F. Van de Vijver (eds.), *Cross-cultural Research Methods.* Cambridge: Cambridge University Press.

Bond, M. H., Leung, K., Au, A. *et al.* (2004). Culture-level dimensions of Social Axioms and their correlates across 41 cultures. *Journal of Cross-Cultural Psychology*, 35, 548–570.

Bond, R., and Smith, P. B. (1996). Culture and conformity: A meta-analysis of studies using Asch's (1952b, 1965) line judgment task. *Psychological Bulletin*, 119, 111–137.

Bornstein, H. (1997). Selective vision. *Behavioral and Brain Sciences*, 20, 180–181.

Bornstein, M. H. (1973). Colour vision and colour naming: A psychophysiological hypothesis of cultural differences. *Psychological Bulletin*, 80, 257–285.

Bornstein, M. H. (1994). Cross-cultural perspectives on parenting. In G. d'Ydewalle, P. Eelen and P. Bertelson (eds.), *International perspectives on psychological science, Vol. II* (pp. 359–369). Hove: Erlbaum.

Bornstein, M. H. (ed.) (1991). *Cultural approaches to parenting.* Hillsdale, N.J.: Erlbaum.

Bornstein, M. H. (ed.) (2010). *Handbook of cultural developmental science.* New York: Taylor & Francis.

Bornstein, M. H., and Lansford, J. (2010). Parenting. In M. H. Bornstein (ed.), *Handbook of cultural developmental science* (pp. 259–278). New York: Taylor & Francis.

Bornstein, M. H., Kessen, W. H., and Weiskopf, S. (1976). The categories of hue in infancy. *Science*, 191, 201–202.

Bornstein, M. H., Tal, J., Rahn, C., Galperín, C. Z., Pêcheux, M.-G., Lamour, M., Toda, S., Azuma, H., Ogino, M., and Tamis-LeMonda, C. S. (1992). Functional analysis of the contents of maternal speech to infants of 5 and 13 months in four cultures: Argentina, France, Japan and the United States. *Developmental Psychology*, 28, 593–603.

Boroditsky, L., Schmidt, L. A., and Phillips, W. (2003). Sex, syntax and semantics. In D. Gentner and S. Goldin-Meadow (eds.), *Language in mind: Advances in the study of language and thought* (pp. 61–79). Cambridge, Mass.: The MIT Press.

Boski, P. (2006). Humanism-materialism: Centuries-long Polish cultural origins and 20 years of research in cultural psychology. In U. Kim, K.-S. Yang and K.-K. Hwang (eds.), *Indigenous and cultural psychology: Understanding people in context* (pp. 373–402). New York: Springer.

Bouchard, T., Lykken, D., McGue, M., Segal, N., and Tellegen, A. (1990). Sources of human psychological differences: The Minnesota study of twins reared apart. *Science*, 212, 1055–1059.

Boucher, J. D., and Carlson, G. E. (1980). Recognition of facial expression in three cultures. *Journal of Cross-Cultural Psychology*, 11, 263–280.

Bourdieu, P. (1998). *Practical reason: On the theory of action.* Stanford: Stanford University Press.

Bourhis, R., Moise, C., Perreault, S., and Senecal, S. (1997). Towards an interactive acculturation model: A social psychological approach. *International Journal of Psychology*, 32, 369–386.

Bouvy, A.-M., Van de Vijver, F. J. R., Boski, P., Schmitz, P., and Krewer, B. (1994). Introduction. In A.-M. Bouvy, F. J. R. Van de Vijver, P. Boski and P. Schmitz (eds.), *Journeys into cross-cultural psychology* (pp. 1–6). Lisse: Swets & Zeitlinger.

Bowerman, M. (1996). The origins of children's spatial semantic categories: Cognitive versus linguistic determinants. In J. J. Gumperz and S. C. Levinson (eds.), *Rethinking linguistic relativity* (pp. 145–202). Cambridge: Cambridge University Press.

Bowerman, M., and Choi, S. (2001). Shaping meanings for language. In M. Bowerman and C. Levinson (eds.), *Language acquisition and conceptual development* (pp. 475–511). Cambridge: Cambridge University Press.

Bowlby, J. (1969). *Attachment and loss, Vol. I, Attachment.* New York: Basic Books.

Bowles, S., Choi, J.-K., and Hopfensitz, A. (2003). The co-evolution of individual behaviors and social institutions. *Journal of Theoretical Biology*, 223, 135–147.

Boyd, R., and Richerson, P. J. (1985). *Culture and the evolutionary process*. Chicago: The University of Chicago Press.

Boyd, R., and Richerson, P. J. (2005). *The origin and evolution of cultures*. New York: Oxford University Press.

Boyd, R., Gintis, H., Bowles, S., and Richerson, P. J. (2003). The evolution of altruistic punishment. *Proceedings of the National Academy of Sciences of the United States of America*, 100, 3531–3535.

Brandt, M. E., and Boucher, J. D. (1985). Judgements of emotions from antecedent situations in three cultures. In I. Reyes Lagunes and Y. H. Poortinga (eds.), *From a different perspective: Studies of behaviour across cultures* (pp. 348–362). Lisse: Swets & Zeitlinger.

Bray, P. G., Martin, R. E., Tilley, L., Ward, S. A., Kirk, K., and Fidock, D. A. (2005). Defining the role of PfCRT in Plasmodium falciparum chloroquine resistance. *Molecular Microbiology*, 56, 323–333.

Brazelton, T. B. (1973). *Neonatal behavioural assessment scale*. London: National Spastics Society.

Bread for the World Institute. (2010). The hungry report 2010: A just and sustainable recovery. Washington, DC: Bread for the World Institute. Retrieved July 30, 2010, from www.hungerreport.org/2010/

Brein, M., and David, K. H. (1971). Intercultural communication and the adjustment of the sojourner. *Psychological Bulletin*, 76, 215–230.

Breland, K., and Breland, M. (1961). The misbehaviour of organisms. *American Psychologist*, 16, 681–684.

Breslow, L. (1999). From disease prevention to health promotion. *Journal of the American Medical Association*, 281, 1030–1033.

Bresnahan, M. J., Levine, T. R., Shearman, S. M., Lee, S. Y., Park, C.-Y., and Kiyomiya, T. (2005). A multimethod multitrait validity assessment of self-construal in Japan, Korea, and the United States. *Human Communication Research*, 31, 33–59.

Breugelmans, S. M. (in press). The relationship between individual and culture. In F. J. R. Van de Vijver, A. Chasiotis and S. M. Breugelmans (eds.), *Fundamental questions in cross-cultural psychology*. Cambridge: Cambridge University Press.

Breugelmans, S. M., and Poortinga, Y. H. (2006). Emotion without a word: Shame and guilt with Rarámuri Indians and rural Javanese. *Journal of Personality and Social Psychology*, 91, 1111–1122.

Breugelmans, S. M., and Van de Vijver, F. (2004). Antecedents and components of majority attitudes towards multiculturalism in the Netherlands. *Applied Psychology: An International Review*, 53, 400–422.

Breugelmans, S. M., Van de Vijver, F., and Schalk-Soekar, S. (2009). Stability of majority attitudes toward multiculturalism in the Netherlands between 1999 and 2007. *Applied Psychology: An International Review*, 58, 653–671.

Breugelmans, S. M., Poortinga, Y. H., Ambadar, Z., Setiadi, B., Vaca, J. B., and Widiyanto, P. (2005). Body sensations associated with emotions in Rarámuri Indians, rural Javanese, and three student samples. *Emotion*, 5, 166–174.

Brewer, M. (1997). The social psychology of intergroup relations: Can research inform practice? *Journal of Social Issues*, 53, 197–211.

Brewer, M. (1999). The psychology of prejudice: Ingroup love or outgroup hate? *Journal of Social Issues*, 55, 429–444.

Brewer, M. (2007). The importance of being we: Human nature and intergroup relations. *American Psychologist*, 62, 728–738.

Brewer, M., and Campbell, D. T. (1976). *Ethnocentrism and intergroup attitudes: East African evidence*. London: Sage.

Brewer, M., and Yuki, M. (2007). Culture and social identity. In S. Kitayama and D. Cohen (eds.), *Handbook of cultural psychology* (pp. 307–322). New York: Guilford Press.

Bril, B. (1989). Die kulturvergleichende Perspektive: Entwicklung und Kultur [The cross-cultural perspective: Development and culture]. In H. Keller (ed.), *Handbuch der Kleinkindforschung* (1. Aufl., S. 71–88) [Handbook of research in early childhood]. Heidelberg: Springer.

Bril, B., and Sabatier, C. (1986). The cultural context of motor development: Postural manipulations in the daily life of Bambara babies (Mali). *International Journal of Behavioural Development*, 9, 439–453.

Brislin, R. W. (1974). The Ponzo illusion: Additional cues, age, orientation and culture. *Journal of Cross-Cultural Psychology*, 5, 139–161.

Brislin, R. W. (2009). Theory, critical incidents and the preparation for intercultural experiences. In R. Wyer, C. Chiu and Y. Hong (eds.), *Understanding culture: Theory, research and application* (pp. 379–392). Hove: Psychology Press.

Brislin, R. W., and Horvath, A.-M. (1997). Cross-cultural training and multicultural education. In J. W. Berry, M. H. Segall and C. Kağitçibaşi (eds.), *Handbook of cross-cultural psychology, Vol. III, Social behavior and applications* (2nd edn., pp. 327–369). Boston: Allyn & Bacon.

Brislin, R. W., and Keating, C. (1976). Cross-cultural differences in the perception of a three-dimensional Ponzo illusion. *Journal of Cross-Cultural Psychology*, 7, 397–411.

Brislin, R. W., Lonner, W. J., and Thorndike, R. M. (1973). *Cross-cultural research methods*. New York: Wiley.

Brislin, R. W., Cushner, K., Cherrie, C., and Yong, M. (1986). *Intercultural interactions: A practical guide*. Beverly Hills: Sage.

Brock, A. (ed.) (2006). *Internationalizing the history of psychology*. New York: New York University Press.

Brodbeck, F. C., Hanges, P. J., Dickson, M. W., Gupta, V., and Dorfman, P. W. (2004). Societal culture and industrial sector influences on organizational culture. In R. J. House, P. J. Hanges, M. Javidan, P. W. Dorfman and V. Gupta (eds.), *Culture, leadership and organizations: The GLOBE study of 62 societies* (pp. 654–668). Thousand Oaks, Calif.: Sage.

Bronfenbrenner, U. (1979). *The ecology of human development*. Cambridge, Mass.: Harvard University Press.

Bronfenbrenner, U., and Morris, P. A. (2006). The bioecological model of human development. In R. M. Lerner (ed.), *Handbook of Child Psychology, Vol. I,*

Theoretical models of human development (6th edn., pp. 793–828). Hoboken, N.J.: Wiley.

Broodryk, J. (2002). *Ubuntu: Life lessons from Africa*. Pretoria: National Library.

Brosnan, S. F., Newton-Fisher, N. E., and Van Vugt, N. (2009). A melding of the minds: When primatology meets personality and social psychology. *Personality and Social Psychology Review*, 13, 129–147.

Brouwers, S., Van de Vijver, F., and Van Hemert, D. (2009). Variation in Raven's Progressive Matrices scores across time and place. *Learning and Individual Differences*, 19, 330–338.

Brouwers, S., Van Hemert, D., Breugelmans, S. M., Van de Vijver, F. (2004). A historical analysis of empirical studies published in the *Journal of Cross-Cultural Psychology* 1970–2004. *Journal of Cross-Cultural Psychology*, 35, 251–262.

Brown, D. E. (1991). *Human universals*. New York: McGraw-Hill.

Brown, R. W., and Lenneberg, E. H. (1954). A study of language and cognition. *Journal of Abnormal and Social Psychology*, 49, 454–462.

Browne, J. P., O'Boyle, C. A., McGee, H. M., Joyce, C. R. B., MacDonald, N. J., O'Malley, K., and Hiltbrunner, B. (1994). Individual quality of life in the healthy elderly. *Quality of Life Research*, 3, 235–244.

Brundtland, G. H. (2005). Right to health: The Anna Lindh Lecture of 2005. Retrieved June 15, 2009, from www.rwi.lu.se/publicseminars/annalindh/al05.shtml

Bruner, J. S. (1990). *Acts of meaning*. Cambridge, Mass.: Harvard University Press.

Brunet, O., and Lézine, I. (1951/1971 [3rd edn.]). *Le développement psychologique de la première enfance* [Psychological development in infancy]. Paris: PUF.

Brunswik, E. (1956). *Perception and the representative design of psychological experiments*. Berkeley: University of California Press.

Bshary, R., Grutter, A. S., Willener, A. S. T., and Leimar, O. (2008). Pairs of cooperating cleaner fish provide better service quality than singletons. *Nature*, 455, 964–967.

Buchan, N. R., Croson, R. T. A., and Dawes, R. M. (2002). Swift neighbors and persistent strangers: A cross-cultural investigation of trust and reciprocity in social exchange. *American Journal of Sociology*, 108, 168–206.

Buckle, L., Gallup, G. G., and Rodd, Z. A. (1996). Marriage as a reproductive contract: Patterns of marriage, divorce, and remarriage. *Ethology and Sociobiology*, 17, 363–377.

Burman, E. (2007). Between orientalism and normalization: Cross-cultural lessons from Japan for a critical history of psychology. *History of Psychology*, 10, 179–198.

Burnstein, E., Crandall, C., and Kitayama, S. (1994). Some neo-Darwinian decision rules for altruism: Weighing cues for inclusive fitness as a function of the biological importance of the decision. *Journal of Personality and Social Psychology*, 67, 773–789.

Buss, D. M. (1989). Sex differences in human mate preferences: Evolutionary hypotheses tested in 37 cultures. *Behavioral and Brain Sciences*, 12, 1–49.

Buss, D. M., Abbott, M., Angleitner, A. *et al.* (1990). International preference in selecting mates: A study of 37 cultures. *Journal of Cross-Cultural Psychology*, 21, 5–47.

Buss, D. M., Haselton, M. G., Shackelford, T. K., Bleske, A. L., and Wakefield, J. C. (1998). Adaptations, exaptations and spandrels. *American Psychologist, 53,* 533–548.

Butzlaff, R. L., and Hooley, J. (1998). Expressed emotion and psychiatric relapse. *Archives of General Psychiatry, 55,* 547–552.

Byrne, B. M. (2006). *Structural equation modeling with EQS: Basic concepts, applications and programming* (2nd edn.). Mahwah, N.J.: Erlbaum.

Byrne, B. M. (2010). *Structural equation modeling with AMOS: Basic concepts, applications and programming* (2nd edn.). New York: Routledge.

Caldwell, J. C. (1979). Education as a factor in mortality decline: An examination of Nigerian data. *Population Studies, 33,* 395–413.

Caldwell, J. C., Caldwell, P., and McDonald, P. (2002). Policy responses to low fertility and its consequences: A global survey. *Journal of Population Research, 19,* 1–12.

Camerer, C. F. (2003). *Behavioral game theory: Experiments on strategic interaction.* Princeton: Princeton University Press.

Camilli, G. (2006). Test fairness. In R. L. Brennan (ed.), *Educational measurement* (4th edn., pp. 221–256). Washington, DC: American Council on Education.

Campbell, D.T. (1967). Stereotypes and the perception of group differences. *American Psychologist, 22,* 812–829.

Campbell, D. T. (1969). Reforms as experiments. *American Psychologist, 24,* 409–429.

Campbell, D. T. (1970). Natural selection as an epistemological model. In R. Naroll and R. Cohen (eds.), *A handbook of method in cultural anthropology* (pp. 51–85). New York: Natural History Press.

Campbell, D. T. (1975). On the conflicts between biological and social evolution and between psychology and moral tradition. *American Psychologist, 30,* 1103–1126.

Campbell, D. T., and Fiske, D. W. (1959). Convergent and discriminant validation by the multitrait-multimethod matrix. *Psychological Bulletin, 56,* 81–105.

Candia, S. (2009). *Government defends need to legislate on homosexuality.* Retrieved December 29, 2009, from www.gayrightsuganda.org/

Cann, R. L., Stoneking, M., and Wilson, A. C. (1987). Mitochondrial DNA and human evolution. *Nature, 325,* 31–36.

Cannon, T. (2005). The inheritance of intermediate phenotypes in schizophrenia. *Current Opinion in Psychiatry, 18,* 135–140.

Caplan, A. L., McCartney, J. J., and Sisti, D. A. (eds.) (2004). *Health, disease and illness: Concepts in medicine.* Georgetown: Georgetown University Press.

Carlson, S. M., and Moses, L. J. (2001). Individual differences in inhibitory control and children's theory of mind. *Child Development, 72,* 1032–1053.

Carr, S. (ed.) (2010). *The psychology of mobility in a global era.* New York: Springer.

Carr, S., and MacLachlan, M. (1998). Psychology in developing countries: Reassessing its impact. *Psychology and Developing Societies, 10,* 1–20.

Carr, S. C., and Sloan, T. S. (eds.) (2003). *Poverty and psychology.* New York: Kluwer.

Carroll, J. B. (1993). *Human cognitive abilities: A survey of factor-analytic studies.* Cambridge: Cambridge University Press.

Carroll, J. B., and Casagrande, J. B. (1958). The function of language classifications in behavior. In E. Maccoby, T. Newcomb and E. L. Hartley (eds.), *Readings in social psychology* (3rd edn., pp. 18–31). New York: Holt, Rinehart & Winston.

Carter, J. A. (2007). Malaria. In S. Ayers, A. Baum, C. McManus, S. Newman, K. Wallston, J. Weinman and R. West (eds.), *The Cambridge handbook of psychology, health and medicine* (pp. 64–79). Cambridge: Cambridge University Press.

Carter, J. A., Ross, A. J., Neville, B. J. R., Obiero, E., Katana, K., Mung'ala-Odera, V., Lees, J. A., and Newton, C. R. J. C. (2005). Developmental impairments following severe falciparum malaria in children. *Tropical Medicine and International Health*, 10, 3–10.

Cash, R., Keusch, G., and Lamstein, J. (1987). *Child survival: The UNICEF GOBI-FFF program.* Beckenham: Croom Helm.

Castillo, R. J. (2001). Lessons from folk healing practices. In W.-S. Tseng and J. Stretzer (eds.), *Culture and psychotherapy: A guide to clinical practice* (pp. 81–101). Washington, DC: American Psychiatric Press.

Castro, V. S. (2003). *Acculturation and psychological adaptation.* Westport, Conn.: Greenwood Press.

Cavalli-Sforza, L. L., and Feldman, M. (1981). *Cultural transmission and evolution: A quantitative approach.* Princeton: Princeton University Press.

Cawte, J. (1972). *Cruel, poor and brutal nations.* Honolulu: Hawaii University Press.

Ceci, S. J., and Williams, W. (eds.) (1999). *The nature–nurture debate.* Oxford: Blackwell.

Celano, M. P., and Tyler, F. B. (1991). Behavioral acculturation among Vietnamese refugees in the United States. *Journal of Social Psychology*, 131, 373–385.

Chamberlain, K. (1997). Socioeconomic health differentials: From structure to experience. *Journal of Health Psychology*, 2, 399–412.

Chao, R. K. (1995). Chinese and European American cultural models of the self reflected in mother's childrearing beliefs. *Ethos*, 23, 328–354.

Chasiotis, A. (1999). *Kindheit und Lebenslauf: Untersuchungen zur evolutionären Psychologie der Lebensspanne* [Childhood and life course: Investigations into the evolutionary psychology of the life-span]. Bern: Huber.

Chasiotis, A. (2010). Developmental psychology without dualistic illusions: Why we need evolutionary biology to understand developmental psychology. In U. Frey, B. Störmer and K. Willführ (eds.), *Homo novus – A human without illusions* (pp. 147–160). Berlin: Springer.

Chasiotis, A. (in press). An epigenetic view on culture: What evolutionary developmental psychology has to offer for cross-cultural psychology. In S. M. Breugelmans, A. Chasiotis and F. J. R. Van de Vijver (eds.), *Fundamental questions in Cross-Cultural Psychology.* Cambridge: Cambridge University Press.

Chasiotis, A., and Hofer, J. (2003). Die Messung impliziter Motive in Deutschland, Costa Rica und Kamerun [The measurement of implicit motives in Germany, Costa Rica, and Cameroon]. Research report to the German Research Foundation (DFG).

Chasiotis, A., Hofer, J., and Campos, D. (2006). When does liking children lead to parenthood? Younger siblings, implicit prosocial power motivation, and explicit love for children predict parenthood across cultures. *Journal of Cultural and Evolutionary Psychology*, 4, 95–123.

Chasiotis, A., Keller, H., and Scheffer, D. (2003). Birth order, age at menarche, and intergenerational context continuity: A comparison of female somatic development in West and East Germany. *North American Journal of Psychology*, 5, 153–170.

Chasiotis, A., Bender, M., Kiessling, F., and Hofer, J. (2010). The emergence of the independent self: Autobiographical memory as a mediator of false belief understanding and motive orientation in Cameroonian and German preschoolers. *Journal of Cross-Cultural Psychology*, 41, 368–390.

Chasiotis, A., Kiessling, F., Hofer, J., and Campos, D. (2006). Theory of mind and inhibitory control in three cultures: Conflict inhibition predicts false belief understanding in Germany, Costa Rica, and Cameroon. *International Journal of Behavioral Development*, 30, 192–204.

Chasiotis, A., Kiessling, F., Winter, V., and Hofer, J. (2006). Sensory motor inhibition as a prerequisite for theory of mind – A comparison of clinical and normal preschoolers differing in sensory motor abilities. *International Journal of Behavioral Development*, 30, 178–190.

Chasiotis, A., Scheffer, D., Restemeier, R., and Keller, H. (1998). Intergenerational context discontinuity affects the onset of puberty: A comparison of parent–child dyads in West and East Germany. *Human Nature*, 9, 321–339.

Chen, D. (1995). Cultural and psychological influences on mental health issues for Chinese Americans. In L. L. Adler and B. R. Mukherji (eds.), *Spirit vs. scalpel: Traditional healing and modern psychotherapy* (pp. 185–196). Westport, Conn.: Bergin & Garvey.

Chen, S. X., Benet-Martínez, V., and Bond, M. (2008). Bicultural identity, biculturalism, and psychological adjustment in multicultural societies: Immigration-based and globalization-based acculturation. *Journal of Personality*, 76, 803–838.

Chen, S. X., Bond, M. H., Chan, B., Tang, D., and Buchtel, E. E. (2009). Behavioral manifestations of modesty. *Journal of Cross-Cultural Psychology*, 40, 603–626.

Chen, Y.-F. (2002). Chinese classification of mental disorders (CCMD-3): Towards integration on international classification. *Psychopathology*, 35, 171–175.

Cheney, D., and Seyfarth, R. (1999). *How monkeys see the world.* Chicago: The University of Chicago Press.

Cheng, B.-S., Chou, L.-F., Wu, T.-Y., Huang, M.-P., Farh, J.-L. (2004). Paternalistic leadership and subordinate responses: Establishing a leadership model in Chinese organizations. *Asian Journal of Social Psychology*, 7, 89–117.

Cheung, F. M. (2004). Use of Western and indigenously developed personality tests in Asia. *Applied Psychology: An International Review*, 53, 173–191.

Cheung, F. M., and Leung, K. (1998). Indigenous personality measures: Chinese examples. *Journal of Cross-Cultural Psychology*, 29, 233–248.

Cheung, F. M., Fan, W., Cheung, S. F., and Leung, K. (2008). Standardization of the Cross-cultural [Chinese] Personality Assessment Inventory for adolescents in Hong Kong: A combined emic-etic approach to personality assessment. *Acta Psychologica Sinica*, 40, 839–852.

Cheung, F. M., Leung, K., Zang, J. X., Sun, H. F., Gan, Y. Q., Song, W. Z., and Xie, D. (2001). Indigenous Chinese personality constructs: Is the Five-Factor Model complete? *Journal of Cross-Cultural Psychology*, 32, 407–433.

Cheung, G. W., and Rensvold, R. B. (2002). Evaluating goodness-of-fit indexes for testing measurement equivalence. *Structural Equation Modeling*, 9, 233–255.

Chiao, J. Y., and Ambady, N. (2007). Cultural neuroscience: Parsing universality and diversity. In S. Kitayama and D. Cohen (eds.), *Handbook of cultural psychology* (pp. 615–644). New York: Guildford Press.

Child, I. L. (1954). Socialization. In G. Lindzey (ed.), *Handbook of social psychology*, *Vol. II* (pp. 655–692). Cambridge, Mass.: Addison-Wesley.

Childs, C. P., and Greenfield, P. M. (1980). Informal modes of learning and teaching: The case of Zinacanteco weaving. In N. Warren (ed.), *Studies in cross-cultural psychology*, *Vol. II* (pp. 269–316). London: Academic Press.

Chinese Culture Connection (1987). Chinese values and the search for culture-free dimensions of culture. *Journal of Cross-Cultural Psychology*, 18, 143–164.

Chinese Society of Psychiatry (2001). The third edition of The Chinese classification and diagnostic criteria of mental disorders (in Chinese). Jinan: Shandong Science and Technology Press.

Chirkov, V. I. (2009). Critical psychology of acculturation: What do we study and how do we study it, when we investigate acculturation? *International Journal of Intercultural Relations*, 33, 94–105.

Chisholm, J. S. (1993). Death, hope, and sex: Life-history theory and the development of reproductive strategies. *Current Anthropology*, 34, 1–24.

Chiu, C.-Y., and Kim, Y.-H. (in press). Rethinking culture and the self: Some basic principles and their implications. In F. J. R. Van de Vijver, A. Chasiotis and S. M. Breugelmans (eds.), *Fundamental questions of cross-cultural psychology*. Cambridge: Cambridge University Press.

Choi, I., Nisbett, R., and Norenzayan, A. (1999). Causal attribution across cultures: Variation and universality. *Psychological Bulletin*, 125, 47–63.

Choi, S., and Bowerman, M. (2001). Learning to express motion events in English and Korean: The influence of language-specific lexicalization patterns. *Cognition*, 41, 83–121.

Chomsky, N. (1965). *Aspects of a theory of syntax*. Cambridge, Mass.: The MIT Press.

Chomsky, N. (1980). *Rules and representations*. Oxford: Blackwell.

Chomsky, N. (2000). *New horizons in the study of language*. Cambridge: Cambridge University Press.

Chrea, C., Ferdenzi, C., Valentin, D., and Abdi, H. (2007). Revisiting the relation between language and cognition: A cross-cultural study with odors. *Behaviour, Brain & Cognition*, 22 (2).

Chrea, C., Valentin, D., Sulmont-Rossé, C., Nguyen, D. H., and Abdi, H. (2005). Semantic, typicality and odor representation: A cross-cultural study. *Chemical Senses*, 30, 37–49.

Christopher, J. C. (2001). Culture and psychotherapy: Toward a hermeneutic approach. *Psychotherapy*, 38, 115–128.

Chua, H. F., Boland, J. E., and Nisbett, R. E. (2005). Cultural variation in eye movements during scene perception. *Proceedings of the National Academy of Sciences*, 102, 12629–12633.

Church, A. T. (1982). Sojourner adjustment. *Psychological Bulletin*, 91, 540–572.

Church, A. T. (2000). Culture and personality: Toward an integrated cultural trait psychology. *Journal of Personality*, 68, 651–703.

Church, A. T. (2009). Prospects for an integrated trait and cultural psychology. *European Journal of Personality*, 23, 153–182.

Church, A. T., Katigbak, M. S., Ortiz, F. A., Del Prado, A. M., Vargas-Flores, J., Ibáñez-Reyes, J., Reyes, J. A. S., Pe-Pua, R., and Cabrera, H. F. (2005). Investigating implicit trait theories across cultures. *Journal of Cross-Cultural Psychology*, 36, 476–496.

Cissé, Y. (1973). Signes graphiques, representations, concepts et tests relatifs à la personne chez les Malinka et les Bambasa du Mali [Graphic signs, representations, concepts and tests relative to personality among the Malinka and the Bambasa of Mali]. In Colloques Internationaux, *Le notion de Personne en Afrique Noir* [The idea of the person in black Africa]. Paris: Editions du CNRS.

Cohen, R. (1970). Entry into the field. In R. Naroll and R. Cohen (eds.), *Handbook of method in cultural anthropology* (pp. 220–245). New York: Natural History Press.

Cole, M. (1975). An ethnographic psychology of cognition. In R. W. Brislin, S. Bochner and W. Lonner (eds.), *Cross-cultural perspectives on learning* (pp. 157–175). Beverly Hills: Sage.

Cole, M. (1988). Cross-cultural research in the sociohistorical tradition. *Human Development*, 31, 137–157.

Cole, M. (1992a). Culture in development. In M. H. Bornstein and M. Lamb (eds.), *Developmental psychology: An advanced textbook* (3rd edn., pp. 731–789). Hillsdale, N.J.: Erlbaum.

Cole, M. (1992b). Context, modularity and the cultural constitution of development. In L. Winegar and J. Valsiner (eds.), *Childrens' development within social contexts*, *Vol. II* (pp. 5–31). Hillsdale, N.J.: Erlbaum.

Cole, M. (1996). *Cultural psychology: A once and future discipline*. Cambridge, Mass.: Belknap.

Cole, M. (2006). Internationalism in psychology: We need it now more than ever. *American Psychologist*, 61, 904–917.

Cole, M., and Cole, S. R. (2004). *The development of children* (5th edn.). New York: Freeman.

Cole, M., and Engeström Y. (2007). Cultural-historical approaches to designing for development. In J. Valsiner and A. Rosa (eds.), *The Cambridge handbook of sociocultural psychology* (pp. 484–507). Cambridge: Cambridge University Press.

Cole, M., and Scribner, S. (1977). Developmental theories applied to cross-cultural cognitive research. *Annals of the New York Academy of Sciences*, 285, 366–373.

Cole, M., Gay, J., Glick, J., and Sharp, D. (1971). *The cultural context of learning and thinking*. New York: Basic Books.

Collins, W., Maccoby, E., Steinberg, L., Hetherington, E., and Bornstein, M. (2000). Contemporary research on parenting: The case of nature and nurture. *American Psychologist*, 55, 218–232.

Comer, R. J. (2009). *Abnormal psychology* (6th edn.). New York: Worth Publishers.

Constant, A. F., and Zimmermann, K. F. (2008). Measuring ethnic identity and its impact on economic behaviour. *Journal of the European Economic Association*, 6, 424–433.

Corcoran, C., Walker, E., Huot, R., Mittal, V., Tessner, K., Kestler, L., and Malaspina, D. (2003). The stress cascade and schizophrenia: Etiology and onset. *Schizophrenia Bulletin*, 29, 671–692.

Corsaro, W., and Johannesen, B. (2007). The creation of new cultures in peer interaction. In J. Valsiner and A. Rosa (eds.), *The Cambridge handbook of sociocultural psychology* (pp. 444–459). Cambridge: Cambridge University Press.

Costa, P. T., Jr., and McCrae, R. R. (1992). *Revised NEO Personality Inventory (NEO-PI-R) and NEO Five Factor Inventory (NEO-FFM) professional manual*. Odessa, Fla.: Psychological Assessment Resources.

Costa, P. T., Jr., and McCrae, R. R. (1994). "Set like plaster": Evidence for the stability of adult personality. In T. Heatherington and J. Weinberger (eds.), *Can personality change?* (pp. 21–140). Washington, DC: American Psychological Association.

Costello, E. J., and Angold, A. (2006). Developmental epidemiology. In D. Cicchetti and D. J. Cohen (eds.), *Developmental psychopathology* (2nd edn., pp. 41–75). New York: Wiley.

Cousins, S. (1989). Culture and selfhood in Japan and the U.S. *Journal of Personality and Social Psychology*, 56, 124–131.

Creswell, J. W. (2009). *Research design: Qualitative, quantitative, and mixed methods approaches* (3rd edn.). Thousand Oaks, Calif.: Sage.

Crisp, R. J., and Abrams, D. (2008). Improving intergroup attitudes and reducing stereotype threat: An integrated contact model. *European Review of Social Psychology*, 19, 242–284.

Cronbach, L. J., Gleser, G. C., Nanda, H., and Rajaratnam, N. (1972). *The dependability of behavioral measurements*. New York: Wiley.

Cronk, L. (1994). Evolutionary theories of morality and the manipulative use of signals. *Zygon*, 29, 81–101.

Cuéllar, I., and Paniagua, F. R. (eds.) (2000). *Handbook of multicultural mental health*. San Diego: Academic Press.

Cuéllar, I., Harris, L. C., and Jasso, R. (1980). An acculturation scale for Mexican American normal and clinical populations. *Hispanic Journal of Behavioral Sciences*, 2, 199–217.

Cui, G., and Van den Berg, S. (1991). Testing the construct validity of intercultural effectiveness. *International Journal of Intercultural Relations*, 15, 227–241.

Cushner, K. (1989). Assessing the impact of a culture-general assimilator. *International Journal of Intercultural Relations*, 13, 125–146.

Cushner, K., and Landis, D. (1996). The intercultural sensitizer. In D. Landis and R. S. Bhagat (eds.), *Handbook of intercultural training* (2nd edn., pp. 185–202). Thousand Oaks, Calif.: Sage.

D'Andrade, R. (1995). *The development of cognitive anthropology.* Cambridge: Cambridge University Press.

Dalmiya, N., and Schultnik, W. (2003). Combating hidden hunger: The role of international agencies. *Food Nutrition Bulletin*, 24, 569–577.

Daly, M., and Wilson, M. (1983). *Evolution and behavior* (2nd edn.). Boston: Willard Grant Press.

Daly, M., and Wilson, M. (1988). *Homicide.* New York: Aldine.

Dana, R. H., and Allen, J. (eds.) (2008). *Cultural competency training in a global society.* New York: Springer.

Dansereau, F., Alutto, J. A., and Yammarino, F. J. (1984). *Theory-testing in organizational behavior: The "variant" approach.* Englewood Cliffs, N.J.: Prentice Hall.

Darwin, C. (1859). *The origin of species by means of natural selection.* London: Murray.

Darwin, C. (1871). *The descent of man, and selection in relation to sex.* London: Murray.

Darwin, C. (1872/1998). *The expression of the emotions in man and animals* (3rd edn.). London: HarperCollins.

Dasen, P. R. (1984). The cross-cultural study of intelligence: Piaget and the Baoulé. *International Journal of Psychology*, 19, 407–434.

Dasen, P. R. (1999). Représentations sociales de l'adolescence: une perspective interculturelle [Social representations of adolescents: An intercultural perspective]. In B. Bril, P. R. Dasen, C. Sabatier and B. Krewer (eds.), *Propos sur l'enfant et l'adolescent: Quels enfants pour quelles cultures?* [Remarks on children and adolescents: Which children for which cultures?] (pp. 319–338). Paris: L'Harmattan.

Dasen, P. R. (2000). Rapid social change and the turmoil of adolescence: A cross-cultural perspective. *International Journal of Group Tensions*, 29, 17–50.

Dasen, P. R., and Akkari, A. (eds.) (2008). *Educational theories and practices from the majority world.* New Delhi: Sage.

Dasen, P. R., and Mishra, R. C. (2000). Cross-cultural views on human development in the third millennium. *International Journal of Behavioral Development*, 24, 428–434.

Dasen, P. R., and Mishra, R. C. (2010). *Development of geocentric spatial language and cognition: An ecocultural perspective.* Cambridge: Cambridge University Press.

Dasen, P. R., Inhelder, B., Lavallee, M., and Retschitzky, J. (1978). *Naissance de l'intelligence chez l'enfant Baoulé de Côte d'Ivoire* [The birth of intelligence among Baoulé children in the Ivory Coast]. Berne: Hans Huber.

Davis, C. M., and Carlson, J. A. (1970). A cross-cultural study of the strength of the Müller–Lyer illusion as a function of attentional factors. *Journal of Personality and Social Psychology*, 16, 403–410.

Dawkins, R. (1976). *The selfish gene.* New York: Oxford University Press.

Dawkins, R. (1979). Defining sociobiology. *Nature*, 280, 427–428.

Day, R., Nielsen, J. A., Korten, A., *et al.* (1987). Stressful life events preceding the acute onset of schizophrenia: A cross-national study from the World Health Organization. *Culture, Medicine and Psychiatry*, 11, 123–205.

De Raad, B., and Peabody, D. (2005). Cross-culturally recurrent personality factors: Analyses of three factors. *European Journal of Personality*, 19, 451–474.

De Raad, B., Barelds, D. P. H., Levert, E., *et al.* (2010). Only three factors of personality description are fully replicable across languages: A comparison of 14 trait taxonomies. *Journal of Personality and Social Psychology*, 98, 160–173.

De Waal, F. B. M. (2009). Darwin's last laugh. *Nature*, 460, 175.

Deal, T. E., and Kennedy, A. A. (1982). *Corporate cultures: The rites and rituals of corporate life.* Reading, Mass.: Addison-Wesley.

Deardorff, D. K. (ed.) (2009). *The SAGE handbook of intercultural competence.* Thousand Oaks, Calif.: Sage.

Dennett, D. (1995). *Darwin's dangerous idea: Evolution and the meanings of life.* New York: Simon & Schuster.

Denzin, N. K., and Giardina, M. D. (eds.) (2006). *Qualitative inquiry and the conservative challenge.* Walnut Creek, Calif.: Left Coast Press.

Denzin, N. K., and Lincoln, Y. S. (eds.) (2000). *Handbook of qualitative research* (2nd edn.). Thousand Oaks, Calif.: Sage.

Denzin, N. K., and Lincoln, Y. S. (2005a). Introduction: The discipline and practice of qualitative research. In N. K. Denzin and Y. Lincoln (eds.), *The Sage Handbook of qualitative research* (3rd edn., pp. 1–32). Thousand Oaks, Calif.: Sage.

Denzin, N. K., and Lincoln, Y. S. (eds.) (2005b). *The Sage Handbook of qualitative research* (3rd edn.). Thousand Oaks, Calif.: Sage.

Deregowski J. B. (1968). Difficulties in pictorial depth perception in Africa. *British Journal of Psychology*, 59, 195–204.

Deregowski, J. B. (1980). *Illusions, patterns and pictures: A cross-cultural perspective.* London: Academic Press.

Deregowski, J. B. (1989). Real space and represented space: Cross-cultural perspectives. *Behavioral and Brain Sciences*, 12, 51–74.

Deregowski, J. B., and Bentley, A. M. (1986). Perception of pictorial space by Bushmen. *International Journal of Psychology*, 21, 743–752.

Deregowski, J. B., and Parker, D. M. (1994). The perception of spatial structure with oblique viewing, an explanation for Byzantine perspective? *Perception*, 23, 5–13.

Deregowski, J. B., and Serpell, R. (1971). Performance on a sorting task: A cross-cultural experiment. *International Journal of Psychology*, 6, 273–281.

Deregowski, J. B., Muldrow, E. S., and Muldrow, W. F. (1972). Pictorial recognition in a remote Ethiopian population. *Perception*, 1, 417–425.

Dettwyler, K. A. (1995). A time to wean. In P. Stuart-Macadam and K. Dettwyler (eds.), *Breast feeding: Biocultural perspectives* (pp. 39–73). Hawthorne, N.Y.: Aldine de Gruyter.

Devereux, G., and Loeb, E. M. (1943). Antagonistic acculturation. *American Sociological Review*, 8, 133–147.

Dezutter, J., Soenens, B., and Hutsebaut, D. (2006). Religiosity and mental health: A further exploration of the relative importance of religious behaviors vs. religious attitudes. *Personality and Individual Differences*, 40, 807–818.

Diamond, M. (1997). Sexual identity and sexual orientation in children with traumatized or ambiguous genitalia. *Journal of Sex Research*, 34, 199–222.

Diaz-Guerrero, R. (1975). *Psychology of the Mexican: Culture and personality.* Austin: University of Texas Press.

Diaz-Guerrero, R. (1982). The psychology of the historic-sociocultural premise. *Spanish Language Psychology*, 2, 382–410.

Diaz-Guerrero, R. (1993). A Mexican ethnopsychology. In U. Kim and J. W. Berry (eds.), *Indigenous psychologies: Experience and research in cultural context.* Newbury Park, Calif.: Sage.

Diaz-Guerrero, R. (2000). Is abnegation a basic experiential trait in traditional societies? The case of Mexico. In J. W. Berry, R. C. Mishra and R. C. Tripathi (eds.), *Psychology in human and social development: Lessons from diverse cultures* (pp. 68–85). Delhi: Sage.

Diaz-Loving, R. (2005). Emergence and contributions of a Latin American indigenous social psychology. *International Journal of Psychology*, 40, 213–227.

Diaz-Loving, R., and Lozano, I. (2009). Rogelio Diaz-Guerrero: A legacy of psychological creation and research. In A. Gari and K. Mylonas (eds.), *Quod erat demonstratum* (pp. 45–54). Athens: Pedio.

Diaz-Loving, R., Rivera Aragón, S., Reyes Lagunes, I., Rocha Sánchez, T., Reidl Martínez, L., Sánchez Aragón, R., *et al.* (2008). *Etnopsicología Mexicana: Siguiendo la huella teórica y empírica de Diaz-Guerrero.* Mexico City: Trillas.

Dickinson, D. L. (2000). Ultimatum decision-making: A test of reciprocal kindness. *Theory and Decision*, 48, 151–177.

Dickson, M. W., Den Hartog, D. N., and Castaño, N. (2009). Understanding leadership across cultures. In R. S. Bhagat and R. M. Steers (eds.), *The Cambridge handbook of culture, organizations, and work* (pp. 219–244). Cambridge: Cambridge University Press.

Diener, E. (1996). Subjective well-being in cross-cultural perspective. In H. Grad, A. Blanco and J. Georgas (eds.), *Key issues in cross-cultural psychology* (pp. 319–330). Lisse: Swets & Zeitlinger.

Diener, E., and Biswas-Diener, R. (2002). Will money increase subjective well-being? A literature review and guide to needed research. *Social Indicators Research*, 57, 119–169.

Diener, E., and Seligman, M. E. P. (2009). Beyond money: Towards an economy of well-being. In E. Diener (ed.), *The science of well-being: The collected works of Ed Diener* (pp. 201–265). Social Indicators Research Series 3. Dordrecht: Springer.

Diener, E., Diener, M., and Diener, C. (1995). Factors predicting subjective well-being of nations. *Journal of Personality and Social Psychology*, 69, 851–864.

Diener, E., Lucas, R. E., and Oishi, S. (2002). Subjective well-being: The science of happiness and life satisfaction. In C. R. Snyder and S. J. Lopez (eds.), *Handbook of positive psychology* (pp. 63–73). Oxford: Oxford University Press.

Dissanayake, E. (1992). *Homo aestheticus: Where art comes from and why.* New York: The Free Press.

Distel, H., Ayabe-Kanamura, S., Martínez-Gómez, M., Schicker, I., Kobayakawa, T., Saito, S., and Hudson, R. (1999). Perception of everyday odors: Correlation between intensity, familiarity and strength of hedonic judgment. *Chemical Senses,* 24, 191–199.

Dobzhansky, T., Ayala, F. J., Stebbins, G. L., and Valentine, J. W. (1977). *Evolution.* San Francisco: Freeman.

Doi, T. (1973). *The anatomy of dependence.* Tokyo: Kodansha International.

Doi, T. (1984). Psychotherapy: A cross-cultural perspective from Japan. In P. Pedersen, N. Sartorius and A. Marsella (eds.), *Mental health services: The cross-cultural context* (pp. 267–279). London: Sage Publishers.

Dolan, P., Peasgood, T., and White, M. (2008). Do we really know what makes us happy? A review of the economic literature on the factors associated with subjective well-being. *Journal of Economic Psychology,* 29, 94–122.

Donà, G., and Ackermann, L. (2006). Refugees in camps. In D. L. Sam and J. W. Berry (eds.), *The Cambridge handbook of acculturation psychology* (pp. 218–232). Cambridge: Cambridge University Press.

Donà, G., and Berry, J.W. (1994). Acculturation attitudes and acculturative stress of Central American refugees in Canada. *International Journal of Psychology,* 29, 57–70.

Doty, R. L. (1986). Cross-cultural studies of taste and smell perception. In D. Duvall, D. Muller-Schwarze and R. Silverstein (eds.), *Clinical signals in vertebrates, Vol. IV.* New York: Plenum.

Doty, R. L. (2001). Olfaction. *Annual Review of Psychology,* 52, 423–452.

Dougherty, J. W., and Keller, C. (1982). Task autonomy: A practical approach to knowledge structure. *American Ethnologist,* 9, 763–774.

Dovidio, J., Glick, P., and Rudman, A. (eds.) (2005). *On the nature of prejudice: Fifty years after Allport.* Oxford: Blackwell.

Draguns, J. G. (1975). Resocialization into culture: The complexities of taking a worldwide view of psychotherapy. In R. W. Brislin, S. Bochner and W. J. Lonner (eds.), *Cross-cultural perspectives on learning* (pp. 273–289). Beverly Hills: Sage.

Draguns, J. G. (1982). Methodology in cross-cultural psychopathology. In I. Al-Issa (ed.), *Culture and psychopathology* (pp. 33–70). Baltimore: University Park Press.

Draguns, J. G., and Tanaka-Matsumi, J. (2003). Assessment of psychopathology across and within cultures: Issues and findings. *Behaviour Research and Therapy,* 41, 755–775.

Draper, P., and Harpending, H. (1988). A sociobiological perspective on human reproductive strategies. In K. B. MacDonald (ed.), *Sociobiological perspectives on human development* (pp. 340–372). New York: Springer.

Drenth, P. J. D. (2004). Ethics and social responsibility. In C. Spielberger (ed.), *Encyclopedia of applied psychology* (pp. 841–844). Amsterdam: Elsevier.

Drenth, P. J. D., and Den Hartog, D. H. (1999). Culture and organizational differences. In W. J. Lonner, D. L. Dinnel, D. K. Forgays and S. A. Hayes (eds.), *Merging past, present, and future in cross-cultural psychology* (pp. 489–502). Lisse: Swets & Zeitlinger.

Drenth, P. J. D., and Groenendijk, B. (1997). Organisatiepsychologie in cross-cultureel perspectief [Organizational psychology in cross-cultural perspective]. In P. J. D. Drenth, H. Thierry and C. J. de Wolff (eds.), *Nieuw handboek arbeids- en organisatiepsychologie, Vol. II* [New handbook of work and organization psychology] (pp. 1407–1451). Houten: Bohn.

Ducci, L., Arcuri, L. W., Georgis, T., and Sineshaw, T. (1982). Emotion recognition in Ethiopia. *Journal of Cross-Cultural Psychology*, 13, 340–351.

Dunbar, R. I. M. (1995). Neocortex size and group size in primates: A test of the hypothesis. *Journal of Human Evolution*, 28, 287–296.

Dunbar, R. I. M. (1996). *The trouble with science.* Cambridge, Mass.: Harvard University Press.

Dunbar, R. I. M., and Barrett, L. (2007). *Oxford handbook of evolutionary psychology.* Oxford: Oxford University Press.

Dunbar, R., and Spoors, M. (1995). Social networks, support cliques, and kinship. *Human Nature*, 6, 273–290.

Duncan, H. F., Gourlay, N., and Hudson, W. (1973). *A study of pictorial perception among Bantu and White primary school children in South Africa.* Johannesburg: Witwatersrand University Press.

Durham, W. H. (1982). Interactions of genetic and cultural evolution: Models and examples. *Human Ecology*, 10, 289–323.

Durkheim, E. (1915). *The elementary forms of the religious life.* London: George Allen & Unwin Ltd.

Duveen, G. (2007). Culture and social representations. In J. Valsiner and A. Rosa (eds.), *The Cambridge handbook of sociocultural psychology* (pp. 543–559). Cambridge: Cambridge University Press.

Dwairy, M. (2006). *Counseling and psychotherapy with Arabs and Muslims: A culturally sensitive approach.* New York: Teachers College Press.

Dyal, J. A. (1984). Cross-cultural research with the locus of control construct. In H. M. Lefcourt (ed.), *Research with the locus of control construct, Vol. III* (pp. 209–306). New York: Academic Press.

Dziurawiec, S., and Deregowski, J. B. (1986). Construction errors as a key to perceptual difficulties encountered in reading technical drawings. *Ergonomics*, 29, 1203–1212.

Eagly, A. H., and Wood, W. (1999). The origins of sex differences in human behavior: Evolved dispositions versus social roles. *American Psychologist*, 54, 408–423.

Earley, P. C., and Ang, S. (2003). *Cultural intelligence: Individual interactions across cultures.* Stanford: Stanford University Press.

Eckensberger, L. (1972). The necessity of a theory for applied cross-cultural research. In L. J. Cronbach and P. J. D. Drenth (eds.), *Mental tests and cultural adaptation* (pp. 99–107). The Hague: Mouton.

Eckensberger, L. H. (1979). A metamethodological evaluation of psychological theories from a cross-cultural perspective. In L. Eckensberger, W. Lonner and Y. H. Poortinga (eds.), *Cross-cultural contributions to psychology* (pp. 255–275). Lisse: Swets & Zeitlinger.

Eckensberger, L. H. (1996). Agency, action, and culture: Three basic concepts for cross-cultural psychology. In J. Pandey, D. Sinha and D. P. S. Bhawuk (eds.), *Asian contributions to cross-cultural psychology* (pp. 72–102). New Delhi: Sage.

Eckensberger, L. H. (2002). Paradigms revisited: From incommensurability to respected complementarity. In H. Keller, Y. H. Poortinga and A. Schölmerich (eds.), *Biology, culture, and development: Perspectives in Ontogenetic Development* (pp. 341–383). Cambridge: Cambridge University Press.

Eckensberger, L. H., and Plath, I. (2002). Soziale Kognition [Social cognition]. In W. Schneider and B. Sodian (eds.), *Kognitive Entwicklung* [Cognitive development] (Enzyklopedie der Psychologie, CV Bd 2, pp. 409–493). Göttingen: Hogrefe.

Edelman, R. J., and Iwawaki, S. (1987). Self-reported expression and the consequences of embarrassment in the United Kingdom and Japan. *Psychologia*, 30, 205–216.

Editorial. (2001). Global campaign to eradicate malaria. *British Journal of Medicine*, 322, 1191–1192.

Edwards, C., and Weisner, T. (eds.) (2010). The contribution of John and Beatrice Whiting. Special Issue, *Journal of Cross-cultural Psychology*, 41, 483–632.

Ehrlich, P. R. (1968). *The population bomb.* New York: Ballantine Books.

Ehrlich, P. R., and Ehrlich, A. H. (1997). The population explosion: Why we should care and what we should do about it. *Environmental Law*, 27.

Eibl-Eibesfeldt, I. (1979). Human ethology: Concepts and implications for the sciences of man. *Behavioral and Brain Sciences*, 2, 1–57.

Eibl-Eibesfeldt, I. (1989). *Human ethology.* New York: Aldine de Gruyter.

Eid, M., and Larsen, R. J. (eds.) (2008). *The science of subjective well-being.* New York: Guildford Press.

Eimas, P. D. (1975). Auditory and phonetic coding of the cues for speech. Discrimination of the [r-l] distinctions by young infants. *Perception and Psychophysics*, 18, 341–347.

Ekman, P. (1973). Cross-cultural studies of facial expression. In P. Ekman (ed.), *Darwin and facial expression* (pp. 169–222). New York: Academic Press.

Ekman, P. (1980). *The face of man.* New York: Garland Press.

Ekman, P. (1992). Are there basic emotions? *Psychological Review*, 99, 550–553.

Ekman, P. (1994). Strong evidence for universals in facial expression: A reply to Russell's mistaken critique. *Psychological Bulletin*, 115, 268–287.

Ekman, P. (ed.) (1982). *Emotion in the human face* (2nd edn.). Cambridge: Cambridge University Press.

Ekman, P., and Friesen, W. V. (1969). The repertoire of nonverbal behavior: categories, origins, usage and coding. *Semiotica*, 1, 49–98.

Ekman, P., and Friesen, W. V. (1971). Constants across cultures in the face and emotion. *Journal of Personality and Social Psychology*, 17, 124–129.

Ekman, P., and Friesen, W. V. (1986). A new pancultural expression of emotion. *Motivation and Emotion*, 10, 159–168.

Ekman, P., Friesen, W., O'Sullivan, M., *et al.* (1987). Universals and cultural differences in the judgments of facial expressions of emotion. *Journal of Personality and Social Psychology*, 53, 712–717.

Ekstrand, L. H., and Ekstrand, G. (1986). Developing the emic/etic concepts for cross-cultural research. In L. H. Ekstrand (ed.), *Ethnic minorities and immigrants in a cross-cultural perspective* (pp. 52–66). Lisse: Swets & Zeitlinger.

Elfenbein, H. A., and Ambady, N. (2002). On the universality and cultural specificity of emotion recognition: A meta-analysis. *Psychological Bulletin*, 128, 203–235.

Elias, N., and Blanton, J. (1987). Dimensions of ethnic identity in Israeli Jewish families living in the United States. *Psychological Reports*, 60, 367–375.

Ellis, B. (1988). Hofstede's culture dimensions and Rokeach's values: How reliable is the relationship? In J. W. Berry and R. C. Annis (eds.), *Ethnic psychology: Research and practice with immigrants, refugees, native peoples, ethnic groups, and sojourners* (pp. 266–274). Lisse: Swets & Zeitlinger.

Ellis, B. J. (2004). Timing of pubertal maturation in girls: An integrated life history approach. *Psychological Bulletin*, 130, 920–958.

Ellis, H. D., Deregowski, J. B., and Shephard, J. W. (1975). Description of white and black faces by white and black subjects. *International Journal of Psychology*, 10, 119–123.

Ember, C., and Ember, M. (2009). *Cross-cultural research methods* (2nd edn.). Lanham, Md.: AltaMira.

Ember, M., Ember, C., and Peregrine, P. (2007). *Cultural anthropology* (12th edn.). New York: Prentice Hall.

Engle, P. L., Black, M. M., Behmann, J. R., Cabral de Mello., M., Gertler, P. J., Kapiriri, L., Martorell, R., and Eming Young, M. (2007). Strategies to avoid the loss of developmental potential in more than 200 million children in the developing world. *The Lancet*, 369, 229–242.

Engeström, Y. (ed.) (2005). *Putting activity theory to work: Contributions from developmental work research*. Berlin: Lehmanns Media.

Enriquez, V. G. (1981). *Decolonizing the Filipino psyche*. Quezon City: Psychology Research and Training House.

Enriquez, V. G. (1989). *Indigenous psychology and national consciousness*. Tokyo: Institute for the Study of Languages and Cultures of Asia and Africa.

Enriquez, V. G. (ed.) (1990). *Indigenous psychologies*. Quezon City: Psychology Research and Training House.

Enriquez, V. G. (1993). Developing a Filipino psychology. In U. Kim and J. W. Berry (eds.), *Indigenous psychologies: Research and experience in cultural context* (pp. 152–169). Newbury Park, Calif.: Sage.

Erikson, E. (1968). *Identity: Youth and crisis*. New York: Norton.

Escobar, J. I., Nervi, C. H., and Gara, M. A. (2000). Immigration and mental health: Mexican Americans in the United States. *Harvard Review of Psychiatry*, 8, 64–72.

Esteva, G. (1992). Development. In W. Sachs (ed.), *The development dictionary* (pp. 6–25). London: Zed Books.

Estonian Integration Foundation (eds.) (2007). *The meaning of integration*. Tallinn: Estonian Integration Foundation.

Eurobarometer (2000). *Attitudes toward minority groups in the European Union: A special analysis of the Eurobarometer 2000 opinion poll on behalf of the European Union Monitoring Centre on racism and Xenophobia*. Eurobarometer Opinion Poll. Retrieved January 12, 2006, from http://europa.eu.int/comm/ public opinion/indexen.htm

European Monitoring Centre on Racism and Xenophobia (2008). Migrants' experiences of racism and xenophobia in 12 EU Member States. Retrieved July 30, 2010, from www.libertysecurity.org/auteur655.html

European Union (2005). *Common basic principles for immigrant integration policy in the EU*. Retrieved July 30, 2010, from www.enaro.eu/dsip/download/eu-Common-Basic-Principles.pdf

Evans, N., and Levinson, S. C. (2009). The myth of language universals: Language diversity and its importance for cognitive science. *Behavioral and Brain Sciences*, 32, 429–448.

Eysenck, H. J., and Eysenck, S. B. G. (1975). *Manual of the Eysenck Personality Questionnaire*. San Diego: Hodder & Stoughton.

Fandrem, H., Strohmeier, D., and Roland, E. (2009). Bullying and victimization among Norwegian and immigrant adolescents in Norway: The role of proactive and reactive aggressiveness. *Journal of Early Adolescence*, 29, 898–923.

Farh, L. J.-L., Hacket, R. D., and Chen, Z. (2008). Organizational citizenship behavior in global context. In P. B. Smith, M. F. Peterson and D. C. Thomas (eds.), *The handbook of cross-cultural management research* (pp. 165–184). Los Angeles: Sage.

Farmer, P. (2005). *Pathologies of power: Health, human rights and new war on the poor*. Berkeley: University of California Press.

Fawcett, J. T. (ed.) (1973). *Psychological perspectives on population*. New York: Basic Books.

Feather, N. (1975). *Values in education and society*. New York: The Free Press.

Fehr, E., and Fischbacher, U. (2003). The nature of human altruism. *Nature*, 425, 785–791.

Fehr, E., and Fischbacher, U. (2004). Third party punishment and social norms. *Evolution and Human Behavior*, 25, 63–87.

Feldman-Barrett, L., Mesquita, B., Ochsner, K. N., and Gross, J. J. (2007). The experience of emotion. *Annual Review of Psychology*, 58, 373–403.

Fenichel, O. (1955). *The psychoanalytic theory of neurosis*. London: Routledge & Paul Kegan.

Ferguson, G. (1956). On transfer and the abilities of man. *Canadian Journal of Psychology*, 10, 121–131.

Fernald, A. (1989). Intonation and communicative intent: Is the melody the message? *Child Development*, 60, 1497–1510.

Fernald, A. (1992). Human maternal vocalizations to infants as biologically relevant signals: An evolutionary perspective. In J. H. Barkow, L. Cosmides and J. Tooby (eds.), *The adapted mind: Evolutionary psychology and the generation of culture* (pp. 391–428). New York: Oxford University Press.

Fernandez, D. R., Carlson, D. S., Stepina, L. P., and Nicholson, J. D. (1997). Hofstede's country classification 25 years later. *Journal of Social Psychology*, 137, 43–54.

Fernández-Ballesteros, R., Zamarrón, M. D., and Ruíz, M. A. (2001). The contribution of socio-demographic and psychosocial factors to life satisfaction. *Ageing & Society*, 21, 25–43.

Fiedler, F. E., Mitchell, T., and Triandis, H. C. (1971). The culture assimilator: An approach to cross-cultural training. *Journal of Applied Psychology*, 55, 95–102.

Figueredo, A. J., Corral-Verdugo, V., Frías-Armenta, M., Bachar, K. J., White, J., McNeill, P. L., Kirsner, B., and Del PilarCastell-Ruiz, I. (2001). Blood, solidarity, status, and honor: The sexual balance of power and spousal abuse in Sonora, Mexico. *Evolution and Human Behavior*, 22, 295–328.

Fijneman, Y., Willemsen, M., and Poortinga, Y. H. in cooperation with Erelcin, F. G., Georgas, J., Hui, H. C., Leung, K., and Malpass, R. S. (1996). Individualism-collectivism: An empirical study of a conceptual issue. *Journal of Cross-Cultural Psychology*, 27, 381–402.

Fischbacher, U., Gächter, S., and Fehr, E. (2001). Are people conditionally cooperative? Evidence from a public goods experiment. *Economic Letters*, 71, 397–404.

Fischer, R. (2008). Multilevel approaches in organizational settings: Opportunities, challenges and implications for cross-cultural research. In F. J. R. Van de Vijver, D. A. van Hemert and Y. H. Poortinga (eds.), *Individuals and cultures in multi-level analyisis* (pp. 173–196). Mahwah, N.J.: Erlbaum.

Fischer, R. (in press). About chicken and eggs: Four methods for investigating culture–behaviour links. In F. J. R. Van de Vijver, A. Chasiotis and S. M. Breugelmans (eds.), *Fundamental questions in cross-cultural psychology*. Cambridge: Cambridge University Press.

Fischer, R., and Schwartz, S. H. (in press). Whence value priorities? Individual, cultural, and social sources of variation. *Journal of Cross-Cultural Psychology*.

Fischer, R., Ferreira, M. C., Assmar, E., *et al.* (2009). Individualism-collectivism as descriptive norms. *Journal of Cross-Cultural Psychology*, 40, 187–213.

Fischer, R., Vauclair, C. M., Fontaine, J. R. J., Schwartz, S. H. (2010). Are individual-level and country-level value structures different? Testing Hofstede's legacy with the Schwartz Value Survey. *Journal of Cross-Cultural Psychology*, 41, 135–151.

Fish, J. M. (2000). What anthropology can do for psychology: Facing physics envy, ethnocentrism, and a belief in race. *American Anthropologist*, 102, 552–563.

Fishbein, M., and Ajzen, I. (2010). *Predicting and changing behaviour: The reasoned action approach*. NewYork: Psychology Press.

Fishman, J. (1960). A systematization of the Whorfian hypothesis. *Behavioral Science*, 5, 323–338.

Fiske, A. P. (1991). *Structures of social life: The four elementary forms of human relations*. New York: The Free Press.

Fiske, A. P. (2002). Using individualism and collectivism to compare cultures – a critique of the validity and measurement of the constructs: Comment on Oyserman *et al*. *Psychological Bulletin*, 128, 78–88.

Fiske, A., Kitayama, S., Markus, H., and Nisbett, R. (1998). The cultural matrix of social psychology. In D. Gilbert, S. Fiske and G. Lindzey (eds.), *Handbook of social psychology* (pp. 915–981). New York: McGraw-Hill.

Fiske, D. W. (1971). *Measuring the concepts of personality*. Chicago: Aldine.

Fiske, S. T., Cuddy, A. J., Glick, P., and Xu, J. (2002). A model of (often mixed) stereotype content: Competence and warmth respectively follow from perceived status and competition. *Journal of Personality and Social Psychology*, 82, 878–902.

Fivush, R., and Fromhoff, F. A. (1988). Style and structure in mother–child conversations about the past. *Discourse Processes*, 11, 337–355.

Flatz, G., and Rotthauwe, H. W. (1977). The human lactase polymorphism: Physiology and genetics of lactose absorption and malabsorption. *Progress in Medical Genetics*, 2, 205–249.

Flynn, J. R. (1987). Massive IQ gains in 14 nations: What IQ tests really measure. *Psychological Bulletin*, 101, 171–191.

Flynn, J. R. (1999). Searching for justice: The discovery of IQ gains over time. *American Psychologist*, 54, 5–20.

Flynn, J. R. (2007). *What is intelligence? Beyond the Flynn effect*. Cambridge: Cambridge University Press.

Fontaine, J. R. J. (2005). Equivalence. In K. Kempf-Leonard (ed.), *Encyclopedia of social measurement, Vol. I* (pp. 803–813). New York: Academic Press.

Fontaine, J. R. J. (in press). A fourfold conceptual framework for cultural and cross-cultural psychology: Relativism, construct universalism, repertoire universalism, and absolutism. In F. J. R. Van de Vijver, A. Chasiotis and S. M. Breugelmans (eds.), *Fundamental questions in cross-cultural psychology*. Cambridge: Cambridge University Press.

Fontaine, J. R. J., Poortinga, Y. H., Setiadi, B., and Markam, S. S. (2002). Cognitive structure of emotion terms in Indonesia and the Netherlands. *Cognition & Emotion*, 16, 61–86.

Fontaine, J. R. J., Scherer, K. R., Roesch, E. R., and Ellsworth, P. (2007). The world of emotions is not two-dimensional. *Psychological Science*, 18, 1050–1057.

Fontaine, J. R. J., Luyten, P., De Boeck, P., Corveleyn, J., Fernandez, M., Herrera, D., Ittzés, A., and Tomcsányi, T. (2006). Untying the Gordian knot of guilt and shame: The structure of guilt and shame reactions based on situation and person variation in Belgium, Hungary, and Peru. *Journal of Cross-Cultural Psychology*, 37, 273–292.

Forrest, B., and Gross, P. R. (2004). *Creationism's Trojan horse: The wedge of intelligent design*. Oxford: Oxford University Press.

Fournier, M., Schurmans, M.-N., and Dasen, P. R. (1999). Représentations sociales de l'intelligence: effets de l'utilisation de langues différentes [Social representations of intelligence: The effects of using different languages]. In B. Bril, P. R. Dasen, C. Sabatier and B. Krewer (eds.), *Propos sur l'enfant et l'adolescent: quels enfants pour quelles cultures?* [Remarks on children and adolescents: Which children for which cultures?] (pp. 279–296). Paris: L'Harmattan.

Fowler, S. M., and Blohm, J. M. (2004). An analysis of methods for intercultural training. In D. Landis, J. M. Bennett and M. J. Bennett (eds.), *Handbook of intercultural training* (3rd edn., pp. 37–84). Thousand Oaks, Calif.: Sage.

Fox, N. A. (1995). Of the way we were: Adult memories about attachment experiences and their role in determining infant–parent relationships: A commentary on Van Ijzendoorn (1995). *Psychological Bulletin*, 117, 404–410.

Frank, H., Harvey, O. J., and Verdun, K. (2000). American responses to five categories of shame in Chinese culture: A preliminary cross-cultural construct validation. *Personality and Individual Differences*, 28, 887–896.

Frazer, J. G. (1890/1995). *The golden bough*. London: Touchstone.

Freeman, D. (1983). *Margaret Mead and Samoa: The Making and unmaking of an anthropological myth*. Cambridge, Mass.: Harvard University Press.

Freud, S. (1928). *Totem and taboo: Resemblances between the psychic lives of savages and neurotics*. New York: Dodd.

Freud, S. (1938). *An outline of psychoanalysis*. London: Hogarth.

Frijda, N. H., Kuipers, P., and Ter Schure, E. (1989). Relations among emotion, appraisal, and emotional action readiness. *Journal of Personality and Social Psychology*, 57, 212–228.

Frijda, N. H., Markam, S. S., Sato, K., and Wiers, R. (1995). Emotions and emotion words. In J. A. Russell, A. J. R. Manstead, J. C. Wellenkamp and J. M. Fernandez-Dols (eds.), *Everyday conceptions of emotions: An introduction to the psychology, anthropology, and linguistics of emotions* (pp. 121–143). Dordrecht: Kluwer Academic.

Frisbie, W. P., Cho, Y., and Hummer, R. A. (2001). Immigration and the health of Asian and Pacific Islander Adults in the United States. *American Journal of Epidemiology*, 153, 372–380.

Frost, P. J., Moore, L. F., Louis, M. R., Lundberg, C. C., and Martin, J. (eds.) (1985). *Organizational culture*. Beverly Hills: Sage.

Fuligni, A. J. (1997). The academic achievement of adolescents from immigrant families: The roles of family background, attitudes, and behavior. *Child Development*, 68, 351–363.

Fuligni, A. J. (1998). The adjustment of children from immigrant families. *Current Directions in Psychological Science*, 7, 99–103.

Fuligni, A. J., Yip, T., and Tseng, V. (2002). The impact of family obligation on the daily activities and psychological well-being of Chinese Americans. *Child Development*, 73, 302–314.

Furnham, A., and Bochner, S. (1986). *Culture shock: Psychological reactions to unfamiliar environments*. London: Methuen.

Gable, S. L., and Haidt, J. (2005). What (and why) is positive psychology? *Review of General Psychology*, 9, 103–110.

Gabrenya, W., Kung, M.-C., and Chen, L.-Y. (2006). Understanding the Taiwan indigenous psychology movement: A sociology of science approach. *Journal of Cross-Cultural Psychology*, 37, 597–622.

Gabrenya, W. K., Jr., Wang, Y. E., and Latané, B. (1985). Cross-cultural differences in social loafing on an optimizing task: Chinese and Americans. *Journal of Cross-cultural Psychology*, 16, 223–264.

Galán, J. I., and Sánchez-Bueno, M. J. (2009). Strategy and structure in context: Universalism versus institutional effects. *Organization Studies*, 30, 609–627.

Galchenko, I., and Van de Vijver, F. J. R. (2007). The role of perceived cultural distance in the acculturation of exchange students in Russia. *International Journal of Intercultural Relations*, 31, 181–197.

Gallois, C., Franklyn-Stokes, A., Giles, H., and Coupland, N. (1988). Communication accommodation theory and intercultural encounters: Intergroup and interpersonal considerations. In Y. Y. Kim and W. B. Gudykunst (eds.), *International and intercultural communication annual, Vol. XII, Theories in intercultural communication* (pp. 157–185). Newbury Park, Calif.: Sage.

Gann, P. H., Hennekens, C. H., Ma, J., Longcope, C., and Stampfer, M. J. (1996). Prospective study of sex hormone levels and risk of prostate cancer. *Journal of the National Cancer Institute*, 88, 1118–1126.

Garcia, J., and Koelling, R. A. (1966). Relation of cue to consequence in avoidance learning. *Psychonomic Science*, 4, 123–124.

García Coll, C. T., Lamberty, G., Jenkins, R., McAdoo, H. P., Crnic, K., Wasik, B. H., and Vázquez García, H. (1996). An integrative model for the study of developmental competencies in minority children. *Child Development*, 67, 1891–1914.

García Coll, C., Patton, F., Marks, A., Dimitrova, R., Yang, H., Suarez-Aviles, G., and Batchelor, A. (in press). Who succeeds and why: Developmental and contextual considerations. In A. Masten, D. Hernandez and K. Liebkind (eds.), *Capitalizing on migration: The potential of immigrant youth*. Cambridge: Cambridge University Press.

Gardner, R. C. (1985). *Social psychology and second language learning: The role of attitudes and motivation*. London: Edward Arnold.

Gardner, R. C. (2000). Correlation, causation, motivation, and second language acquisition. *Canadian Psychology*, 41, 10–24.

Gardner, R. C., and Clément, R. (1990). Social psychological perspectives on second language acquisition. In H. Giles and W. P. Robinson (eds.), *Handbook of language and social psychology* (pp. 495–515). London: Wiley.

Gasché, J. (1992). A propos d'une expérience d'éducation bilingue au Perou: L'indigénisation d'un programme; sa critique de l'anthropologie [On an experience of bilingual education in Peru: The indigenisation of a programme; its critique of anthropology]. *Journal de la Société Suisse de Américanistes*, 53–4, 131–142.

Gatewood, J. B. (1985). Actions speak louder than words. In J. W. D. Dougherty (ed.), *Directions in cognitive anthropology*. Chicago: University of Illinois Press.

Gatrell, A. C. (2002). *Geographies of health: An introduction.* Oxford: Blackwell.

Gauthier, J. (2008). Universal Declaration of Ethical Principles for Psychologists. International Union of Psychological Science. Retrieved August 1, 2010, from www.am.org/iupsys/resources/ethics/univdecl2008.html

Geber, M., and Dean, M. F. (1957). The state of development of newborn African children. *The Lancet*, 272, 1216–1219.

Geertz, C. (1973). *The interpretation of cultures.* New York: Basic Books.

Geertz, C. (1984). From the native's point of view: On the nature of anthropological understanding. In R. A. Shweder and R. A. LeVine (eds.), *Culture theory: Essays on mind, self, and emotion* (pp. 123–136). New York: Cambridge University Press.

Geertz, H. (1959). The vocabulary of emotion: A study of Javanese socialization processes. *Psychiatry*, 22, 225–237.

Gelfand, M. J., Erez, M., and Aycan, Z. (2007). Cross-cultural organizational behavior. *Annual Review of Psychology*, 58, 479–514.

Gelfand, M. J., Imai, I., and Fehr, R. (2008). Thinking intelligently about cultural intelligence: The road ahead. In S. Ang and L. van Dyne (eds.), *Handbook of cultural intelligence: Theory, measurement, and applications* (pp. 375–387). New York: Sharpe.

Gelfand, M. J., Nishii, L., and Raver, J. (2006). On the nature and importance of cultural tightness-looseness. *Journal of Applied Psychology*, 91, 1225–1244.

Gelman, R. (1998). Domain specificity in cognitive development: Universals and nonuniversals. In M. Sabourin, F. Craik and M. Robert (eds.), *Advances in Psychological Science, Vol. II, Biological and cognitive aspects* (pp. 557–579). Hove: Psychology Press.

Gelman, S. A. (2003). *The essential child: Origins of essentialism in everyday thought.* Oxford: Oxford University Press.

Gentner, D., and Goldin-Meadow, S. (2003). Whither Whorf. In D. Gentner and S. Goldin-Meadow (eds.), *Language in mind: Advances in the study of language and thought* (pp. 3–14). Cambridge, Mass.: The MIT Press.

Georgas, J., Van de Vijver, F., and Berry, J. W. (2004). The ecocultural framework, ecosocial indices and psychological variables in cross-cultural research. *Journal of Cross-Cultural Psychology*, 35, 74–96.

Georgas, J., Weiss, L., Van de Vijver, F., and Saklofske, D. (2003). *Culture and children's intelligence.* San Diego: Academic Press.

Georgas, J., Berry, J. W., Van de Vijver, F., Kağitçibaşi, C., and Poortinga, Y. (eds.) (2006). *Families across cultures: A 30-nation psychological study.* Cambridge: Cambridge University Press.

Gergely, G., Bekkering, H., and Kiraly, I. (2002). Rational imitation in preverbal infants. *Nature*, 415, 755.

Gergely, G., Nadasdy, Z., Csibra, G., and Biro, S. (1995). Taking the intentional stage at 12 months of age. *Cognition*, 56, 165–193.

Gergen, M. M., and Gergen, K. J. (2000). Qualitative inquiry: Tensions and transformations. In N. K. Denzin and Y. Lincoln (eds.), *Handbook of qualitative research* (2nd edn., pp. 1025–1046). Thousand Oaks, Calif.: Sage.

Gesell, A. (1940). *The first five years of life: A guide to the study of the preschool child (Part I).* New York: Harper.

Gesell, A., and Amatruda, C. (1947). *Developmental diagnosis.* New York: Harper Bros.

Gibbons, J. L. (2000). Adolescence in international and cross-cultural perspective: An introduction. *International Journal of Group Tensions*, 29, 3–16.

Gibson, J. J. (1966). *The senses considered as perceptual systems.* Boston: Houghton Mifflin.

Gibson, R. S. (2006). Zinc: The missing link in combating micronutrient malnutrition in developing countries. *Proceedings of the Nutrition Society*, 65, 51–60.

Gielen, U. P., Draguns, J. G., and Fish, J. M. (eds.) (2008). *Principles of multicultural counseling and therapy.* New York: Routledge.

Gielen, U. P., Fish, J. M., and Draguns, J. G. (eds.) (2004). *Handbook of culture, therapy, and healing.* Mahwah, N.J.: Lawrence Erlbaum Publishers.

Gintis, H., Smith, E. A., and Bowles, S. (2001). Costly signaling and cooperation. *Journal of Theoretical Biology*, 213, 103–119.

Girndt, T., and Poortinga, Y. H. (1997). Interculturele communicatie: Conventies en misverstanden [Intercultural communication: Conventions and misunderstandings]. *De Psycholoog*, 32, 299–304.

Gladwin, T. (1970). *East is a big bird: Navigation and logic on Puluwat atoll.* Cambridge, Mass.: Harvard University Press.

Glazer, N. (1997). *We are all multiculturalists now.* Cambridge, Mass.: Harvard University Press.

Goldberg, D. P., and Lecrubier, Y. (1995). Form and frequency of mental disorders across centres. In T. B. Üstün and N. Sartorius (eds.), *Mental illness in general health care: An international study* (pp. 323–334). Chichester: Wiley.

Goldin-Meadow, S., and Mylander, C. (1998). Spontaneous sign systems created by deaf children in two cultures. *Nature*, 391, 279–281.

González, K. V., Verkuyten, M., Weesie, J., and Poppe, E. (2008). Prejudice towards Muslims in the Netherlands: Testing integrated threat theory. *British Journal of Social Psychology*, 47, 667–685.

Goodall, J. (1986). *The chimpanzees of Gombe.* Cambridge, Mass.: Belknap.

Goodenough, W. (1956). Componential analysis and the study of meaning. *Language*, 32, 195–216.

Goodenough, W. (1980). Ethnographic field techniques. In H. C. Triandis and J. W. Berry (eds.), *Handbook of cross-cultural psychology, Vol. II, Methodology* (2nd edn.). Boston: Allyn & Bacon.

Goodenough, W. H. (1996). Culture. In D. Levinson and M. Ember (eds.), *Encyclopedia of cultural anthropology, Vol. I* (pp. 291–299). New York: Henry Holt.

Goody, J., and Watt, I. (1968). The consequences of literacy. In J. Goody (ed.), *Literacy in traditional societies* (pp. 27–68). New York: Cambridge University Press.

Gordon, M. M. (1964). *Assimilation in American life: The role of race, religion and national origins.* New York: Oxford University Press.

Gorman, J. L. (2006). Gender differences in depression and response to psychotropic medication. *Gender Medicine*, 3, 93–109

Gorsuch, L. R. (1988). Psychology of religion. *Annual Review of Psychology*, 39, 201–221.

Goswami, U. (2008). *Cognitive development*. New York: Psychology Press.

Gottlieb, G. (1998). Normally occurring environmental and behavioral influences on gene activity: From central dogma to probabilistic epigenesis. *Psychological Review*, 105, 792–802.

Gottlieb, G., Wahlsten, D., and Lickliter, R. (1998). The significance of biology for human development: A developmental psychobiological system view. In W. Damon (Chief Ed.) and R. M. Lerner (Vol. Ed.), *Handbook of child psychology, Vol. I, Theoretical models of human development* (5th edn., pp. 233–273). New York: Wiley.

Gould, J. L., and Marler, P. (1987). Learning by instinct. *Scientific American*, 256, 1, 62–73.

Gould, S. J. (1991). Exaptation: A crucial tool for evolutionary psychology. *Journal of Social Issues*, 47, 43–65.

Gould, S. J., and Lewontin, R. C. (1979). The spandrels of San Marco and the Panglossian paradigm: A critique of the adaptationist programme. *Proceedings of the Royal Society of London* (Series B), 205, 581–598.

Government of Canada (1971). *Policy statement to House of Commons on multiculturalism*. Ottawa: Government of Canada.

Grantham-McGregor, S., Cheung, Y. B., Cueto, S., Glewwe, P., Richter, L., and Strupp, B., *et al.* (2007). Child development in developing countries: Developmental potential in the first 5 years for children in developing countries. *The Lancet*, 359, 60–70.

Graves, T. D. (1967). Psychological acculturation in a tri-ethnic community. *Southwestern Journal of Anthropology*, 23, 337–350.

Gray-Little, B. (2009). The assessment of psychopathology in racial and ethnic minorities. In J. N. Butcher (ed.), *Oxford handbook of personality assessment* (pp. 396–414). Oxford: Oxford University Press.

Green, E. (2007). Guarding the gates of Europe: A typological analysis of immigration attitudes across 21 countries. *International Journal of Psychology*, 42, 365–379.

Greenberg, J. H. (1957). The nature and uses of linguistic typologies. *International Journal of American Linguistics*, 23, 68–77.

Greenfield, P. M. (1997). Culture as process: Empirical methods for cultural psychology. In J. W. Berry, Y. H. Poortinga and J. Pandey (eds.), *Handbook of cross-cultural psychology, Vol. 1, Theory and method* (2nd edn., pp. 301–346). Boston: Allyn & Bacon.

Greenfield, P. M. (2000). What psychology can do for anthropology, or why anthropology took postmodernism on the chin. *American Anthropologist*, 102, 564–576.

Greenfield, P. M. (2004). *Weaving generations together*. Santa Fe, N.Mex.: School of American Research Press.

Greenfield, P. M., and Lave, J. (1982). Cognitive aspects of informal education. In D. Wagner and H. Stevenson (eds.), *Cultural perspectives on child development* (pp. 181–207). San Francisco: Freeman.

Greenfield, P. M., Maynard, A. E., and Childs, C. P. (2003). Historical change, cultural learning, and cognitive representation in Zinacantec Maya children. *Cognitive Development*, 18, 455–487.

Greenfield, P. M., Keller, H., Fuligni, A., and Maynard, A. (2003). Cultural pathways through universal development. *Annual Review of Psychology*, 54, 461–490.

Gregoire, J., and Hambleton, R. K. (2009). Advances in test adaptation research: A special issue. *International Journal of Testing*, 9, 75–77.

Gregson, A., and Plowe, C. V. (2006). Mechanisms of resistance of malaria parasites to Antifolates. *Pharmacological Review*, 57, 117–145.

Greve, W., and Bjorklund, D. (2009). The Nestor effect: Extending evolutionary developmental psychology to a lifespan perspective. *Developmental Review*, 29, 163–179.

Griesel, R. D., Richter, L. M., and Belciug, M. (1990). Electroencephalography and performance in a poorly nourished South African population. *South African Medical Journal*, 78, 539–543.

Griffiths, R. (1970). *The abilities of young children: A comprehensive system of mental measurement for the first 8 years of life.* London: Young & Son.

Griner, D., and Smith, T. B. (2006). Culturally adapted mental health interventions: A meta-analytic review. *Psychotherapy: Theory, Research, Practice, Training*, 43, 531–548.

Gross, P. R., Levitt, N., and Lewis, M. W. (eds.) (1996). *The flight from science and reason.* Annals of the New York Academy of Sciences, Vol. 775. New York: The New York Academy of Sciences.

Guanzon-Lapeña, Ma. M., Church, A. T., Carlota, A. J., and Katigbak, M. S. (1998). Indigenous personality measures: Philippine examples. *Journal of Cross-Cultural Psychology*, 29, 249–270.

Guba, E. G., and Lincoln, Y. S. (1994). Competing paradigms in qualitative research. In N. K. Denzin and Y. S. Lincoln (eds.), *Handbook of qualitative research* (pp. 105–117). Thousand Oaks, Calif.: Sage.

Gudykunst, W. B. (1993). Toward a theory of effective interpersonal and intergroup communication: An anxiety/uncertainty management (AUM) perspective. In R. L. Wiseman and J. Koester (eds.), *Intercultural communication competence* (pp. 33–71). Thousand Oaks, Calif.: Sage.

Gudykunst, W. B. (1995). Anxiety/Uncertainty Management (AUM) theory: Current status. In R. L. Wiseman (ed.), *Intercultural communication theory* (pp. 8–58). Thousand Oaks, Calif.: Sage.

Gudykunst, W. B. (1998). *Bridging differences: Effective intergroup communication* (3rd edn.). Thousand Oaks, Calif.: Sage.

Gudykunst, W. B. (ed.) (2005a). *Theorizing about intercultural communication.* Thousand Oaks, Calif.: Sage.

Gudykunst, W. B. (2005b). An anxiety/uncertainty management (AUM) theory of effective communication. In W. B. Gudykunst (ed.), *Theorizing about intercultural communication* (pp. 281–322). Thousand Oaks, Calif.: Sage.

Gudykunst, W. B. (2005c). An anxiety/uncertainty management (AUM) theory of strangers' intercultural adjustment. In W. B. Gudykunst (ed.), *Theorizing about intercultural communication* (pp. 419–457). Thousand Oaks, Calif.: Sage.

Gudykunst, W. B., and Hammer, M. R. (1983). Basic training design: Approaches to intercultural training. In D. Landis and R. W. Brislin (eds.), *Handbook of intercultural training*, Vol. I (pp. 118–154). New York: Pergamon.

Gudykunst, W. B., and Kim, Y. Y. (1984). *Communicating with strangers: An approach to intercultural communication*. New York: Random House.

Gudykunst, W. B. and Lee, C. M. (2003). Assessing the validity of self-construal scales: A response to Levine *et al. Human Communication Research*, 29, 253–274.

Gudykunst, W. B., and Mody, B. (eds.) (2002). *Handbook of international and intercultural communication*. Thousand Oaks, Calif.: Sage.

Gudykunst, W. B., Guzley, R. M., and Hammer, M. R. (1996). Designing intercultural training. In D. Landis and R. S. Bhagat (eds.), *Handbook of intercultural training* (2nd edn., pp. 61–80). Thousand Oaks, Calif.: Sage.

Gudykunst, W. B., Lee, C. M., Nishida, T., and Ogawa, N. (2005). Theorizing about intercultural communication: Introduction. In W. B. Gudykunst (ed.), *Theorizing about intercultural communication* (pp. 3–32). Thousand Oaks, Calif.: Sage.

Gumperz, J. J. (1982). *Discourse strategies*. Cambridge: Cambridge University Press.

Gureje, O., Lasebikan, V. O., Kola, L., and Makanjuola, V. A. (2006). Lifetime and 12-month prevalence of mental disorders in the Nigeria survey of mental health and well-being. *Journal of Psychiatry*, 188, 465–471.

Guthrie, G. M. (1966). Cultural preparation for the Philippines. In R. B. Textor (ed.), *Cultural frontiers of the Peace Corps*. Cambridge, Mass.: The MIT Press.

Hagen, M. A., and Jones, R. K. (1978). Cultural effects on pictorial perception: How many words is one picture really worth? In R. D. Walk and H. L. Pick (eds.), *Perception and experience* (pp. 171–209). New York: Plenum.

Haidt, J., and Keltner, D. (1999). Culture and facial expression: Open-ended methods find more expressions and a gradient of recognition. *Cognition & Emotion*, 13, 225–266.

Haire, M., Ghiselli, E. E., and Porter, L. W. (1966). *Managerial thinking: An international study*. New York: Wiley.

Hall, E. T. (1966). *The hidden dimension*. New York: Doubleday.

Hall, E. T. (1976). *Beyond culture*. Garden City, N.Y.: Anchor Press.

Hamberger, A. (2009). Immigrant integration: Acculturation and social identity. *International Journal of Identity and Migration Studies*, 3, 2–21.

Hamilton, D. L. (ed.) (1981). *Cognitive processes in stereotyping and intergroup behavior*. Hillsdale, N.J.: Erlbaum.

Hamilton, W. D. (1964). The genetical evolution of social behavior, I, II. *Journal of Theoretical Biology*, 7, 1–52.

Hammer, M. R., and Bennett, M. J. (2002). *The Intercultural Development Inventory (IDI) manual*. Portland, Oreg.: Intercultural Communication Institute.

Hammer, M. R., Bennett, M. J., and Wiseman, R. (2003). Measuring intercultural sensitivity: The Intercultural Development Inventory. *International Journal of Intercultural Relations*, 27, 421–443.

Hammer, M. R., Gudykunst, W. B., and Wiseman, R. L. (1978). Dimensions of intercultural effectiveness: An exploratory study. *International Journal of Intercultural Relations*, 2, 382–393.

Hammersley, M. (2008). *Questioning qualitative inquiry*. Los Angeles: Sage.

Hardin, C. L., and Maffi, L. (eds.) (1997). *Color categories in thought and language*. Cambridge: Cambridge University Press.

Hardy, J. L., Frederick, C. M., Kay, P., and Werner, J. S. (2005). Color naming, lens aging, and grue: What the optics of the aging eye can teach us about color language. *Psychological Science*, 16, 321–327.

Harkness, S., and Super, C. H. (eds.) (1995). *Parents' cultural belief systems: Their origins, expressions, and consequences*. New York: Guilford Press.

Harkness, S., Wyon, J., and Super, C. (1988). The relevance of behavioural sciences to disease prevention and control in developing countries. In P. Dasen, J. W. Berry and N. Sartorius (eds.), *Cross-cultural psychology and health: Towards applications* (pp. 239–255). London: Sage.

Harlow, H. F. (1958). The nature of love. *American Psychologist*, 13, 673–685.

Harlow, H. F., and Harlow, M. K. (1962). Social deprivation in monkeys. *Scientific American*, 207, 136–146.

Harris, P. R., and Moran, R. T. (1991). *Managing cultural differences*. Houston: Golf.

Harzing, A. W. K. (1995). The persistent myth of high expatriate failure rates. *The International Journal of Human Resource Management*, 6, 457–474.

Harzing, A.W. K. (2006). Response styles in cross-national mail survey research: A 26-country study. *International Journal of Cross-Cultural Management*, 6, 243–266.

Hauser, M. D., Chomsky, N. A., and Fitch, W. T. (2002). The faculty of language: What is it, who has it, and how did it evolve? *Science*, 298, 1569–1579.

Hawkes, K., and Blurton Jones, N. (2005). Human age structures, paleodemography, and the grandmother hypothesis. In E. Voland, A. Chasiotis and W. Schiefenhövel (eds.), *Grandmotherhood: The evolutionary significance of the second half of female life* (pp. 118–140). New Brunswick, N.J.: Rutgers University Press.

Hayfron, J. E. (2006). Immigrants in the labour market. In D. L. Sam and J. W. Berry (eds.), *The Cambridge handbook of acculturation psychology* (pp. 439–451). Cambridge: Cambridge University Press.

Haynes, S. H., and O'Brien, W. H. (1990). Functional analysis in behavior therapy. *Clinical Psychology Review*, 10, 649–668.

Haynes, S. H., and O'Brien, W. H. (2000). *Principles of behavioral assessment: A functional approach to psychological assessment.* New York: Plenum/Kluwer Press.

Hays, P. A. (2001). *Addressing cultural complexities in practice: A framework for clinicians and counsellors.* Washington, DC: American Psychological Association.

Hays, P. A. (2006). Introduction: Developing culturally responsive cognitive-behavioral therapies. In P. A. Hays and G. Y. Iwamasa (eds.), *Culturally responsive cognitive-behavioral therapy: Assessment, practice, and supervision* (pp. 3–19). Washington, DC: American Psychological Association.

He, Y., and Li, C. (2007). Morita therapy for schizophrenia. *Cochrane Database of Systematic Reviews* Issue 1. Art. No.: CD006346. DOI: 10.1002/14651858. CD006346.

Hebb, D. O. (1949). *The organization of behavior.* New York: Wiley.

Hedden, T., Ketay, S., Aron, A., Markus, H. R., and Gabriel, J. D. E. (2009). Cultural influences on neural substrates of attentional control. *Psychological Science*, 19, 12–17.

Hedge, B. (2007). Sexually transmitted disease. In S. Ayers, A. Baum, C. McManus, S. Newman., K. Wallston, J. Weinman and R. West (eds.), *The Cambridge handbook of psychology, health and medicine* (pp. 875–877). Cambridge: Cambridge University Press.

Hedges, L. V., and Olkin, I. (1985). *Statistical methods for meta-analysis.* Orlando, Fla.: Academic Press.

Heggenhougen, K. (ed.) (2008). *International encyclopedia of public health.* Amsterdam: Elsevier.

Heider, F. (1958). *The psychology of interpersonal relations.* New York: Wiley.

Heine, S. J. (2005). Where is the evidence for pancultural self-enhancement? A reply to Sedikides, Gaertner, and Toguchi. *Journal of Personality and Social Psychology*, 89, 531–538.

Heine, S. J. (2008). *Cultural psychology.* New York: Norton.

Heine, S. J., and Buchtel, E. E. (2009). Personality: The universal and the culturally specific. *Annual Review of Psychology*, 60, 369–394.

Heine, S. J., Buchtel, E. E., and Norenzayan, A. (2008). What do cross-national comparisons of personality traits tell us? The case of conscientiousness. *Psychological Science*, 19, 309–313.

Heine, S. J., Kitayama, S., and Hamamura, T. (2007). Which studies test whether self-enhancement is pancultural? Reply to Sedikides, Gaertner, and Vevea, 2007. *Asian Journal of Social Psychology*, 10, 198–200.

Heine, S. J., Lehman, D. R., Markus, H. R., and Kitayama, S. (1999). Is there a universal need for positive self-regard? *Psychological Review*, 106, 766–794.

Heine, S. J., Lehman, D. R., Peng, K., and Greenholtz, J. (2002). What's wrong with cross-cultural comparisons of subjective Likert scales? The reference-group effect. *Journal of Personality and Social Psychology*, 82, 903–918.

Helman, C. (ed.) (2008). *Medical anthropology.* Surrey: Ashgate.

Helms-Lorenz, M., Van de Vijver, F., and Poortinga, Y. H. (2003). Cross-cultural differences in cognitive performance and Spearman's hypothesis: g or c? *Intelligence*, 31, 9–29.

Henrich, J. (2001). In search of Homo economicus: Behavioral experiments in 15 small-scale societies. *American Economic Review*, 91, 73–78.

Henrich, J., and McElreath, R. (2007). Dual-inheritance theory: The evolution of human cultural capacities and cultural evolution. In R. I. M. Dunbar and L. Barrett (eds.), *Oxford handbook of evolutionary psychology* (pp. 555–570). Oxford: Oxford University Press.

Henrich, J., Boyd, R., Bowles, S., Camerer, C., Fehr, E., and Gintis, H. (eds.) (2004). *Foundations of human sociality*. Oxford: Oxford University Press.

Henrich, J., Boyd, R., Bowles, S., Gintis, H., Fehr, E., and Camerer, C. (eds.) (2004). *Foundations of human sociality: Ethnography and experiments in 15 small-scale societies*. Oxford: Oxford University Press.

Henrich, J., Boyd, R., Bowles, S., *et al.* (2005). "Economic man" in cross-cultural perspective: Behavioral experiments in 15 small-scale societies. *Behavioral and Brain Sciences*, 28, 795–815.

Herfst, S. L., Van Oudenhoven, J. P., and Timmerman, M. E. (2008). Intercultural effectiveness training in three western immigrant countries: A cross-cultural evaluation of critical incidents. *International Journal of Intercultural Relations*, 32, 67–80.

Heritage Canada (1999). *Annual report*. Ottawa: Government of Canada.

Herrnstein, R. J., and Murray, C. (1994). *The bell curve: Intelligence and class structure in American life*. New York: The Free Press.

Herskovits, M. J. (1948). *Man and his works: The science of cultural anthropology*. New York: Knopf.

Hespos, S. J., and Spelke, E. S. (2004). Conceptual precursors to language. *Nature*, 430, 453–456.

Hewlett, B. S. (1991). *Intimate fathers: The nature and context of Aka Pygmy paternal infant care*. Ann Arbor: University of Michigan Press.

Hill, K. (2002). Altruistic cooperation during foraging by the Ache, and the evolved human predisposition to cooperate. *Human Nature*, 13, 105–128.

Hill, K., and Hurtado, A. M. (1996). *Ache life history: The ecology and demography of a foraging people*. New York: Aldine.

Hinde, R. A. (1974). *Biological bases of human social behaviour*. New York: McGraw-Hill.

Hinde, R. A. (1982). *Ethology: Its nature and relations with other sciences*. Oxford: Oxford University Press.

Hirsch, S., Bowen, J., Emami, J., Cramer, P., Jolley, A., Haw, C., and Dickinson, M. (1996). One year prospective study of the effect of life events and medication in the aetiology of schizophrenic relapse. *British Journal of Psychiatry*, 168, 49–56.

Hirschfeld, L. A., and Gelman, S. A. (eds.) (1994). *Mapping the mind: Domain specificity in cognition and culture*. New York: Cambridge University Press.

Ho, D. Y. F. (1996). Filial piety and its psychological consequences. In M. H. Bond (ed.), *Handbook of Chinese psychology* (pp. 155–165). Hong Kong: Oxford University Press.

Ho, D. Y. F., Peng, S., Lai, A. C., and Chan, S. F. (2001). Indigenization and beyond: Methodological relationalism in the study of personality across cultural traditions. *Journal of Personality*, 69, 925–953.

Hofer, J., Busch, H., Chasiotis, A., Kärtner, J., and Campos, D. (2008). Concern for generativity and its relation to implicit pro-social power motivation, generative goals, and satisfaction with life: A cross-cultural investigation. *Journal of Personality*, 76, 1–30.

Hofmann, B. (1992). On the triad disease, illness and sickness. *Journal of Medicine and Philosophy*, 27, 651–673.

Hofstede, G. (1980). *Culture's consequences: International differences in work-related values*. Beverly Hills: Sage.

Hofstede, G. (1983). The cultural relativity of organizational practices and theories. *Journal of International Business Studies*, 14, 75–89.

Hofstede, G. (1991). *Cultures and organizations: Software of the mind*. London: McGraw-Hill.

Hofstede, G. (2001). *Culture's consequences: Comparing values, behaviors, institutions, and organizations across nations* (2nd edn.). Thousand Oaks, Calif.: Sage.

Hofstede, G. (2006). What did GLOBE really measure? Researchers' minds versus respondents' minds. *Journal of International Business Studies*, 37, 882–896.

Hofstede, G., and McCrae, R. R. (2004). Personality and culture revisited: Linking traits and dimensions of culture. *Cross-Cultural Research*, 38, 52–88.

Hofstede, G., Neuijen, B., Ohayv, D. D., and Sanders, G. (1990). Measuring organizational cultures: A qualitative/quantitative study across twenty cases. *Administrative Science Quarterly*, 35, 286–316.

Holden, G. W., and Vittrup, B. (2009). *Religion*. In M. H. Bornstein (ed.), *Handbook of developmental science* (pp. 279–295). New York: Psychology Press.

Holland P. W., and Wainer, H. (eds.) (1993). *Differential item functioning*. Hillsdale, N.J.: Erlbaum.

Hong, Y. (2009). A dynamic constructivist approach to culture: Moving from describing culture to explaining culture. In R. Wyer, C. Chiu and Y. Hong (eds.), *Understanding culture: Theory, research, and application* (pp. 3–23). Hove: Psychology Press.

Hong, Y., Morris, M., Chiu, C., and Benet-Martínez, V. (2000). Multicultural minds: A dynamic constructivist approach to culture and cognition. *American Psychologist*, 55, 709–720.

Hoorens, V., and Poortinga, Y. (2000). Behavior in social context. In K. Pawlik and M. Rosenzweig (eds.), *International handbook of psychology* (pp. 40–63). London: Sage.

Hopkins, B. (1977). Considerations of comparability of measures in cross-cultural studies of early infancy from a study on the development of black and white infants in Britain. In Y. H. Poortinga (ed.), *Basic problems in cross-cultural psychology* (pp. 36–46). Lisse: Swets & Zeitlinger.

Hopkins, B., and Westra, T. (1990). Motor development, maternal expectations, and the role of handling. *Infant Behavior and Development*, 13, 117–122.

Hoppe, M. H. (1990). A comparative study of country elites: International differences in work-related values and learning and their implications for management training development. Unpublished Ph.D. dissertation, University of North Carolina.

Hopper, K., and Wanderling, J. (2000). Revisiting the developed versus developing country distinction in course and outcome in schizophrenia: Results from ISoS, the WHO collaborative follow-up project. *Schizophrenia Bulletin*, 26, 835–846.

Horenczyk, G., and Tatar, M. (in press). Conceptualizing the school acculturative context: School, class, and the immigrant student. In A. Masten, D. Hernández and K. Liebkind (eds.), *Capitalizing on immigration: The potential of immigrant youth*. Cambridge: Cambridge University Press.

Horton, R. (1993). *Patterns of thought in Africa and the West: Essays on magic, religion and science*. Cambridge: Cambridge University Press.

House, R. J., Hanges, P. J., Javidan, M., Dorfman, P. W., and Gupta, V. (2004). *Culture, leadership and organizations: The GLOBE study of 62 societies*. Thousand Oaks, Calif.: Sage.

Hox, J. J. (2002). *Multilevel analysis: Techniques and applications*. Mahwah, N.J.: Erlbaum.

Hrdy, S. B. (1999). *Mother nature: A history of mothers, infants, and natural selection*. New York: Pantheon.

Hrdy, S. B. (2005). Cooperative breeders with an ace in the hole. In E. Voland, A. Chasiotis and W. Schiefenhövel (eds.), *Grandmotherhood: The evolutionary significance of the second half of female life* (pp. 295–317). New Brunswick, N.J.: Rutgers University Press.

Hsee, C. K., and Weber, E. U. (1999). Cross-national differences in risk preference and lay predictions. *Journal of Behavioral Decision Making*, 12, 165–179.

Hsu, F. L. K. (1972). *Psychological anthropology* (new edn.). Oxford: Schenkman.

Hsu, F. L. K. (1985). The self in cultural cross-cultural perspective. In A. G. Marsella, G. de Vos and F. L. K. Hsu (eds.), *Culture and self* (pp. 24–55). London: Tavistock.

Huang, X., and Van de Vliert, E. (2003). Where intrinsic job satisfaction fails to work: National moderators of intrinsic motivation. *Journal of Organizational Behavior*, 24, 159–179.

Huang, X., and Van de Vliert, E. (2004). Job level and national culture as joint roots of job satisfaction. *Applied Psychology: An International Review*, 53, 329–348.

Huberman, A. M., and Miles, M. B. (1994). Data management and analysis methods. In N. K. Denzin and Y. S. Lincoln (eds.), *Handbook of qualitative research* (2nd edn., pp. 428–444). Thousand Oaks, Calif.: Sage.

Hudson, W. (1960). Pictorial depth perception in sub-cultural groups in Africa. *Journal of Social Psychology*, 52, 183–208.

Hudson, W. (1967). The study of the problem of pictorial perception among unacculturated groups. *International Journal of Psychology*, 2, 89–107.

Hui, H. (1982). Locus of control: A review of cross-cultural research. *International Journal of Intercultural Relations*, 6, 301–323.

Hui, M. K., Au, K., and Fock, H. (2004). Empowerment effects across cultures. *Journal of International Business Studies*, 35, 46–60.

Humphreys, L. G. (1985). Race differences and the Spearman hypothesis. *Intelligence*, 9, 275–283.

Hunt, E., and Agnoli, F. (1991). The Whorfian hypothesis: A cognitive psychology perspective. *Psychological Review*, 98, 377–389.

Hunt, R. (2007). *Beyond relativism: Rethinking comparability in cultural anthropology*. Walnut Creek, Calif.: AltaMira Press.

Huntsinger, C. S., and Jose, P. E. (2006). A longitudinal investigation of personality and social adjustment among Chinese American and European American adolescents. *Child Development*, 77, 1309–1324.

Hupka, R. B., Zaleski, Z., Otto, J., Reidl, L., and Tarabrina, N. V. (1996). Anger, envy, fear, and jealousy as felt in the body: A five-nation study. *Cross-Cultural Research*, 30, 243–264.

Hutnik, N. (1986). Patterns of ethnic minority identification and models of social adaptation. *Ethnic and Racial Studies*, 9, 150–167.

Hutnik, N. (1991). *Ethnic minority identity: A social psychological perspective*. Oxford: Clarendon Press.

Hwang, K.-K. (2001). The deep structure of confucianism: A social psychological approach. *Asian Philosophy*, 11, 179–204.

Hwang, K.-K. (2004). The epistemological goal of indigenous psychology: The perspective of constructive realism. In B. Setiadi, A. Supratiknya, W. J. Lonner and Y. H. Poortinga (eds.), *Ongoing themes in psychology and culture* (pp. 169–185). Yogakarta: International Association for Cross-Cultural Psychology.

Hwang, K.-K. (2005). A philosophical reflection on the epistemology and methodology of indigenous psychologies. *Asian Journal of Social Psychology*, 8, 5–18.

Hwang, K.-K. (2006). Constructive realism and Confucian realtionalism. In U. Kim, K.-S. Yang, and K.-K. Hwang (eds.), *Indigenous and cultural psychology: Understanding people in context* (pp. 73–108). New York: Springer.

Hwang, K.-K., and Yang, C.-F. (eds.) (2000). Indigenous, cultural and cross-cultural psychologies. Special issue, *Asian Journal of Social Psychology*, 3, 183–293.

Hyman, I. (2001). Immigration and health. Health Policy Working Paper Series. Ottawa: Health Canada. Retrieved June 12, 2009 from www.hc-sc.gc.ca/iacb-dgiac/arad-draa/english/rmdd/wpapers/immigration01.html

IDE (Industrial Democracy in Europe International Research Group) (1981). *Industrial democracy in Europe*. Oxford: Clarendon Press.

Imperato-McGinley, J., Peterson, R. E., Gautier, T., and Sturla, E. (1979). Androgens and the evolution of the male gender identity among male pseudohermaphrodites with 5a-reductase deficiency. *New England Journal of Medicine*, 300, 1233–1237.

Ingelhart, R., Foa, R., Peterson, C., and Welzel, C. (2008). Development, freedom, and rising happiness: A global perspective (1981–2007). *Perspectives on Psychological Science*, 3, 264–285.

Inglehart, R. (1997). *Modernization and postmodernization: Cultural, economic and political change in 43 societies*. Princeton: Princeton University Press.

Inglehart, R. (2000). *Modernization and postmodernization: Cultural, economic, and political change in 43 societies* (2nd edn.). Princeton: Princeton University Press.

Inglehart, R., and Baker, W. E. (2000). Modernization, cultural change, and the persistence of traditional values. *American Sociological Review*, 65, 19–51.

Ingman, M., Kaessmann, H., Pääbo, S., and Gullensten, U. (2000). Mitochondrial genome variation and the origins of modern humans. *Nature*, 408, 708–712.

International Schizophrenia Consortium (2009). Common polygenic variation contributes to risk of schizophrenia and bipolar disorder. *Nature*, 460, 748–752.

International Union of Psychological Science (2008). Universal Declaration of Ethical Principles for Psychologists. Montreal: IUPsyS. Retrieved August 13, 2010 from www.am.org/iupsys/resources/ethics/univdecl2008.html

Irvine, S. H. (1979). The place of factor analysis in cross-cultural methodology, and its contribution to cognitive theory. In L. Eckensberger, W. Lonner and Y. H. Poortinga (eds.), *Cross-cultural contributions to psychology* (pp. 300–341). Lisse: Swets & Zeitlinger.

Irvine, S. H., and Berry, J. W. (1988). The abilities of mankind: A reevaluation. In S. Irvine and J. W. Berry (eds.), *Human abilities in cultural context* (pp. 3–59). New York: Cambridge University Press.

Ishii, R., Yamaguchi, S., and O'Mahony, M. (1992). Measures of taste discriminability for sweet, salty and umami stimuli: Japanese versus Americans. *Chemical Senses*, 17, 365–380.

Jablensky, A. (2007). Schizophrenia and related psychoses. In D. Bhugra and K. Bhui (eds.), *Textbook of cultural psychiatry* (pp. 207–233). Cambridge: Cambridge University Press.

Jackson, J. S., Brown, K., Brown, T., and Marks, B. (2001). Contemporary immigration policy orientations among dominant group members in Western Europe. *Journal of Social Issues*, 57, 431–456.

Jahoda, G. (1954). A note on Ashanti names and their relationship to personality. *British Journal of Psychology*, 45, 192–195.

Jahoda, G. (1971). Retinal pigmentation, illusion susceptibility and space perception. *International Journal of Psychology*, 6, 199–208.

Jahoda, G. (1975). Retinal pigmentation and space perception: A failure to replicate. *International Journal of Psychology*, 97, 133–134.

Jahoda, G. (1979). A cross-cultural perspective on experimental social psychology. *Personality and Social Psychology Bulletin*, 5, 142–148.

Jahoda, G. (1980). Theoretical and systematic approaches in cross-cultural psychology. In H. C. Triandis and W. W. Lambert (eds.), *Handbook of cross-cultural psychology, Vol. I, Perspectives* (pp. 69–141). Boston: Allyn & Bacon.

Jahoda, G. (1982). *Psychology and anthropology: A psychological perspective.* London: Academic.

Jahoda, G. (1986). Nature, culture and social psychology. *European Journal of Social Psychology*, 16, 17–30.

Jahoda, G. (1990). Variables, systems, and the problem of explanation. In F. J. R. Van de Vijver and G. J. M. Hutschemaekers (eds.), *The investigation of culture* (pp. 115–130). Tilburg: Tilburg University Press.

Jahoda, G. (1992). *Crossroads between culture and mind.* New York: Harvester Wheatsheaf.

Jahoda, G. (in press). Past and present of cross-cultural psychology. In F. J. R. Van de Vijver, A. Chasiotis and S. M. Breugelmans (eds.), *Fundamental questions in cross-cultural psychology.* Cambridge: Cambridge University Press.

Jahoda, G., and Krewer, B. (1997). History of cross-cultural and cultural psychology. In J. W. Berry, Y. H. Poortinga and J. Pandey (eds.), *Handbook of cross-cultural psychology, Vol. 1, Theory & Method* (2nd edn., pp. 1–42). Boston: Allyn & Bacon.

Jahoda, G., and Stacey, B. (1970). Susceptibility of geometrical illusions according to culture and professional training. *Perception and Psychophysics*, 7, 179–184.

Jahoda, G., Cheyne, W. M., Deregowski, J. B., Sinha, D., and Collingbourne, R. (1976). Utilization of pictorial information in classroom learning: A cross-cultural study. *AV Communication Review*, 24, 295–315.

James, L. R., Choi, C. C., Ko, C.-H. E., McNeil, P. K., Minton, M. K., Wright, M. A., and Kim, K. (2008). Organizational and psychological climate: A review of theory and research. *European Journal of Work and Organizational Psychology*, 17, 5–32.

James, W. (1884). What is an emotion? *Mind*, 9, 188–205.

Jandt, F. (2007). *An introduction to intercultural communication* (5th edn.). Thousand Oaks, Calif.: Sage.

Janssens, M., and Cappellen, T. (2008). Contextualizing cultural intelligence: The case of global managers. In S. Ang and L. van Dyne (eds.), *Handbook of cultural intelligence: Theory, measurement, and applications* (pp. 159–173). New York: Sharpe.

Jarskog, F., Miyamoto, S., Lieberman, J. A. (2007). Schizophrenia: New pathological insights and therapies. *Annual Review of Medicine*, 58, 49–61.

Jasinskaja-Lahti, I., and Mähönen, T. A. (2009). *Identities, intergroup relations and acculturation: The cornerstones of intercultural encounters.* Helsinki: Helsinki University Press.

Jasinskaja-Lahti, I., Liebkind, K., Solheim, E. (2009). To identify or not to identify? National dis-identification as an alternative reaction to perceived ethnic discrimination. *Applied Psychology: An International Review*, 58, 105–128.

Jasinskaja-Lahti, I., Liebkind, K., Jaakkola, M., and Reuter, A. (2006). Perceived discrimination, social support networks, and psychological well-being among three immigrant groups. *Journal of Cross-Cultural Psychology*, 37, 293–311.

Javidan, M., House, R. J., Dorfman, P. W., Hanges, P. J., and Sully de Luque, M. (2006). Conceptualizing and measuring cultures and their consequences: A comparative review of GLOBE's and Hofstede's approaches. *Journal of International Business Studies*, 37, 897–914.

Jayasuriya, L. (1990). Rethinking Australian muticulturalism: Towards a new paradigm. *The Australian Quarterly*, 62, 12–22.

Jenkins, J. H., and Barratt, R. J. (2004). Introduction. In J. H. Jenkins and R. J. Barratt (eds.), *Schizophrenia, culture, and subjectivity: The edge of experience*. Cambridge: Cambridge University Press.

Jensen, A. R. (1982). Reaction time and psychometric g. In H. J. Eysenck (ed.), *A model for intelligence* (pp. 93–132). Berlin: Springer Verlag.

Jensen, A. R. (1985). The nature of Black–White difference on various psychometric tests: Spearman's hypothesis. *Behavioral and Brain Sciences*, 8, 193–263.

Jensen, A. R. (1998). *The g factor: The science of mental ability*. Westport, Conn.: Praeger.

Ji, C., and Suh, K. (2008). Doctrinal faith and religious orientations in right-wing authoritarianism: A pilot study of American and Korean protestant college students. *Journal of Psychology and Christianity*, 27, 253–265.

Ji, L.-J., Peng, K., and Nisbett, R. (2000). Culture, control and perception of relationships in the environment. *Journal of Personality and Social Psychology*, 78, 943–955.

Jilek, N. G. (1988). *Indian healing: Shamanic ceremonialism in the Pacific Northwest*. Vancouver: Hancock House.

Jilek, W. (1993). Traditional medicine relevant to psychiatry. In N. Sartorious, G. de Giromano, G. Andrews, G. A. German and L. Eisenberg (eds.), *Treatment of mental disorders: Review of effectiveness* (pp. 341–390). Washington, DC: American Psychiatric Press.

Jing, Q., and Zhang, H. (1998). China's reform and challenges for psychology. In J. Adair, D. Belanger and K. Dion (eds.), *Advances in psychological science, Vol. I, social, personal and cultural aspects* (pp. 271–291). Hove: Psychology Press.

Jodelet, D. (2002). Les représentations sociales dans le champs de la culture [Social representations in the cultural field]. *Social Science Information*, 41, 111–133.

Johnstone, R. (1976). The concept of the "marginal man": A refinement of the term. *Australian and New Zealand Journal of Science*, 12, 145–147.

Joppke, C. (1996). Multiculturalism and immigration: A comparison of the United States, Germany, and Great Britain. *Theory and Society*, 25, 449–500.

Jost, J., and Hamilton, D. (2005). Stereotypes in our culture. In J. Dovidio, P. Glick and A. Rudman (eds.), *On the nature of prejudice: Fifty years after Allport* (pp. 208–224). Oxford: Blackwell.

Kagan, J. (2007). *What is emotion?* New Haven: Yale University Press.

Kağitçibaşi, C. (1982). *The changing value of children in Turkey*. Honolulu, HI: East–West Population Institute.

Kağitçibaşi, C. (1984). Socialization in a traditional society: A challenge to psychology. *International Journal of Psychology*, 19, 145–157.

Kağitçibaşi, C. (1990). Family and socialization in cross-cultural perspective: A model of change. In J. Berman (ed.), *Cross-cultural perspectives: Nebraska Symposium on Motivation, 1989* (pp. 135–200). Lincoln: University of Nebraska Press.

Kağitçibaşi, C. (1994). A critical appraisal of individualism and collectivism: Toward a new formulation. In U. Kim, H. C. Triandis, C. Kağitçibaşi, S.-C. Choi and G. Yoon (eds.), *Individualism and collectivism* (pp. 52–65). Thousand Oaks, Calif.: Sage.

Kağitçibaşi, C. (1996). *Family and human development across cultures: A view from the other side*. Hillsdale, N.J.: Erlbaum.

Kağitçibaşi, C. (1997a). Individualism and collectivism. In J. W. Berry, M. H. Segall and C. Kağitçibaşi (eds.), *Handbook of cross-cultural psychology, Vol. III, Social behavior and applications* (pp. 1–49). Boston: Allyn & Bacon.

Kağitçibaşi, C. (1997b). Whither multiculturalism? *Applied Psychology: An International Review*, 46, 44–49.

Kağitçibaşi, C. (2005). Autonomy and relatedness in cultural context: Implications for self and family. *Journal of Cross-Cultural Psychology*, 36, 403–422.

Kağitçibaşi, C. (2007). *Families, self and human development across cultures: Theory and applications* (2nd edn.). Mahwah, N.J.: Lawrence Erlbaum Associates.

Kağitçibaşi, C., and Ataca, B. (2005). Value of children and family change: A three-decade portrait from Turkey. *Applied Psychology: An International Review*, 54, 317–337.

Kağitçibaşi, C., and Poortinga, Y. H. (2000). Cross-cultural psychology: Issues and overarching themes. *Journal of Cross-Cultural Psychology*, 31, 129–147.

Kahneman, D., and Krueger, A. B. (2006). Developments in the measurement of subjective well-being. *Journal of Economic Perspectives*, 20, 3–24.

Kalin, R., and Berry, J. W. (1996). Interethnic attitudes in Canada: Ethnocentrism, consensual hierarchy and reciprocity. *Canadian Journal of Behavioural Science*, 28, 253–261.

Kalmus, H. (1969). Ethnic differences in sensory perception. *Journal of Biosocial Science*, Supplement 1, 81–90.

Kang, S.-M. (2006). Measurement of acculturation, scale format, and language competence: Their implication for adjustment. *Journal of Cross-Cultural Psychology*, 37, 660–693.

Kaniasty, K., and Norris, F. (1995). Mobilization and deterioration of social support following natural disasters. *Contemporary Directions in Psychological Science*, 4, 94–98.

Kaplan, H., Hill, J., Lancaster, J., and Hurtado, A. M. (2000). A theory of human life history evolution: Diet, intelligence, and longevity. *Evolutionary Anthropology*, 9, 156–185.

Kappeler, P. M., and Pereira, M. E. (eds.) (2003). *Primate life history and socioecology.* Chicago: The University of Chicago Press.

Kappeler, P. M., and Van Schaik, C. P. (eds.) (2004). *Sexual selection in primates: New and comparative perspectives.* Cambridge: Cambridge University Press.

Karandashev, V., and McCarthy, S. (eds.) (2006). International practices in the teaching of psychology. Special issue, *International Journal of Psychology*, 41, 1–71.

Karasz, A., and Singelis, T. M. (2009). Qualitative and mixed metods research in cross-cultural psychology. *Journal of Cross-Cultural Psychology*, 40, 909–916.

Kardiner, A., and Linton, R. (1945). *The individual and his society.* New York: Columbia University Press.

Kärtner, J., Keller, H., and Yovzi, R. D. (2010). Mother–infant interaction during the first 3 months: The emergence of culture-specific contingency patterns. *Child Development*, 81, 540–554.

Kashima, Y. (2005). Is culture a problem for social psychology? *Asian Journal of Social Psychology*, 8, 19–38.

Kashima, Y., and Triandis, H. C. (1986). The self-serving bias in attributions as a coping strategy. *Journal of Cross-Cultural Psychology*, 17, 83–97.

Kaufmann, J. (1996). *Conference diplomacy* (3rd edn.). London: Macmillan.

Kawachi, I., and Subramanian, S. V. (2005). Health demography. In D. L. Poston and M. Micklin (eds.), *Handbook of population* (pp. 787–808). New York: Kluwer Academic/Plenum.

Kay, P., and Maffi, L. (1999). Color appearance and the emergence and evolution of basic color lexicons. *American Anthropologist*, 101, 743–760.

Kay, P., and McDaniel, C. K. (1978). The linguistic significance of the meanings of basic color terms. *Language*, 54, 610–646.

Kay, P., Berlin, B., Maffi, L., and Merrifield, W. R. (2003). *The World Color Survey.* Stanford, Calif.: Center for the Study of Language and Information.

Kazarian, S., and Evans, D. (eds.) (1998). *Cultural clinical psychology: Theory, research and practice.* New York: Oxford University Press.

Kealey, D. J. (1989). A study of cross-cultural effectiveness: Theoretical issues, practical applications. *Intercultural Journal of Intercultural Relations*, 13, 387–428.

Kealey, D. J. (1996). The challenge of international personnel selection. In D. Landis and R. S. Bhagat (eds.), *Handbook of intercultural training* (2nd edn., pp 81–105). Thousand Oaks, Calif.: Sage.

Kealey, D. J., and Ruben, B. D. (1983). Cross-cultural personnel selection criteria, issues and methods. In D. Landis and R. W. Brislin (eds.), *Handbook of intercultural training, Vol. I* (pp. 155–175). New York: Pergamon.

Kealey, D. J., Protheroe, D. R., MacDonald, D., and Vulpe, T. (2005). Re-examining the role of training in contributing to international project success: A literature review and a new model training program. *International Journal of Intercultural Relations*, 29, 339–353.

Kearins, J. M. (1981). Visual-spatial memory in Australian aboriginal children of desert regions. *Cognitive Psychology*, 13, 434–460.

Keller, H. (1980). *Beobachtung, Beschreibung und Interpretation von Eltern-Kind-Interaktionen im ersten Lebensjahr. Beobachtungsmanual fuer die ersten vier Lebensmonate* [Observation, description and interpretation of parent–child interactions in the first year of life. Observation manual for the first four months of life]. Unpublished manuscript, Institute of Psychology, Technical University of Darmstadt, Germany.

Keller, H. (2007). *Cultures of infancy*. Mahwah, N.J.: Erlbaum.

Keller, H., and Chasiotis, A. (2007). Maternal investment. In C. A. Salmon and T. K. Shackelford (eds.), *Family relationships: An evolutionary perspective* (pp. 91–114). New York: Oxford University Press.

Keller, H., Chasiotis, A., and Runde, B. (1992). Intuitive parenting programs in German, US-American, and Greek parents of 3-month-old infants. *Journal of Cross-Cultural Psychology*, 23, 510–520.

Keller, H., Poortinga, Y. H., and Schölmerich, A. (2002). *Between culture and biology: Perspectives on ontogenetic development*. Cambridge: Cambridge University Press.

Keller, H., Schölmerich, A., and Eibl-Eibesfeldt, I. (1988). Communication patterns in adult–infant interactions in western and non-western cultures. *Journal of Cross-Cultural Psychology*, 19, 427–445.

Keller, H., Yovsi, R. D., and Voelker, S. (2002). The role of motor stimulation in parental ethnotheories: The case of Cameroonian Nso and German women. *Journal of Cross-Cultural Psychology*, 33, 398–414.

Keller, H., Kärtner, J., Borke, J., Yovzi, R., and Kleis, A. (2005). Parenting styles and the development of the categorical self: A longitudinal study on mirror self-recognition in Cameroonian Nso and German families. *International Journal of Behavioral Development*, 34, 496–504.

Keller, H., Lohaus, A., Völker, S., Cappenberg, M., and Chasiotis, A. (1999). Temporal contingency as a measure of interactional quality. *Child Development*, 70, 474–485.

Keller, H., Otto, H., Lamm, B., Yovsi, R. D., and Kärtner, J. (2008). The timing of verbal/vocal communications between mothers and their infants: A longitudinal cross-cultural comparison. *Infant Behavior & Development*, 31, 217–226.

Keller, H., Lohaus, A., Kuensemueller, P., Abels, M., Yovsi, R. D., and Völker, S. (2004). The bio-culture of parenting: Evidence from five cultural communities. *Parenting: Science and Practice*, 4, 25–50.

Kendon, A. (1984). Did gestures escape the curse at the confusion of Babel? In A. Wolfgang (ed.), *Nonverbal behavior: Perspectives, applications, intercultural insights* (pp. 75–114). Lewiston, N.Y.: Hogrefe.

Kenrick, D. T., and Keefe, R. C. (1992). Age preferences reflect sex differences in human reproductive strategies. *Behavioral and Brain Sciences*, 15, 75–133.

Kenworthy, J., Turner, R., Hewstone, M., and Voci, A. (2006). Intergroup contact: When does it work and why? In J. Dovidio, P. Glick and A. Rudman (eds.),

On the nature of prejudice: Fifty years after Allport (pp. 278–292). Oxford: Blackwell.

Kessen, W. (1979). The American child and other cultural inventions. *American Psychologist*, 34, 815–820.

Kessler, R. C., and Üstün, T. B. (eds.) (2008). *The WHO world mental health surveys: Global perspectives on the epidemiology of mental disorders.* Cambridge: Cambridge University Press.

Kettlewell, H. B. D. (1959). Darwin's missing evidence. *Scientific American*, 200, 3, 48–53.

Kickbusch, I. (2003). The contributions of the World Health Organization to a new public health and health promotion. *American Journal of Public Health*, 9, 383–388.

Kilbride, P. L. (1980). Sensorimotor behavior of Baganda and Samia infants: A controlled comparison. *Journal of Cross-Cultural Psychology*, 11, 131–152.

Kim, C., Laroche, M., and Tomiuk, M. A. (2001). A measure of acculturation for Italian Canadians: Scale development and construct validation. *International Journal of Intercultural Research*, 25, 607–637.

Kim, H., and Markus, H. R. (1999). Deviance or uniqueness, harmony or conformity? A cultural analysis. *Journal of Personality and Social Psychology*, 77, 785–800.

Kim, M. S., and Raja, N. S. (2003). When testing lacks validity. *Human Communication Research*, 29, 275–290.

Kim, U. (2001). Culture, science, and indigenous psychologies: An integrated analysis. In D. Matsumoto (ed.), *Handbook of culture and psychology* (pp. 51–76). Oxford: Oxford University Press.

Kim, U., and Berry, J. W. (eds.) (1993). *Indigenous psychologies: Research and experience in cultural context.* Newbury Park, Calif.: Sage.

Kim, U., and Park, Y.-S. (2006). The scientific foundations of indigenous and cultural psychology: The transactional approach. In U. Kim, K.-S. Yang and K.-K. Hwang (eds.), *Indigenous and cultural psychology: Understanding people in context* (pp. 27–48). New York: Springer.

Kim, U., Park, Y.-S., and Park, D. (2000). The challenge of cross-cultural psychology: The role of indigenous psychologies. *Journal of Cross-Cultural Psychology*, 31, 63–75.

Kim, U., Yang, K.-S., and Hwang, K.-K. (eds.) (2006). *Indigenous and cultural psychology: Understanding people in context.* New York: Springer.

Kim, U., Triandis, H. C., Kağıtçıbaşı, C., Choi, S.-C., and Yoon, G. (eds.) (1994). *Individualism and collectivism: Theory, method and application.* Thousand Oaks, Calif.: Sage.

Kim, Y. H., Chiu, C. Y., Peng, S. Q., Cai, H. J., and Tov, W. (2010). Explaining East-West differences in the likelihood of making favorable self-evaluations: The role of evaluation apprehension and directness of expression. *Journal of Cross-Cultural Psychology*, 41, 62–75.

Kim, Y. Y., and Bhawuk, D. (eds.) (2008). Globalization and diversity. Special issue, *International Journal of Intercultural research*, 33, 301–368.

Kirkman, B. L., Lowe, K. B., and Gibson, C. B. (2006). A quarter century of culture's consequences: A review of empirical research incorporating Hofstede's cultural values framework. *Journal of International Business Studies*, 37, 285–320.

Kirmayer, L. J., and Sartorius, N. (2007). Cultural models and somatic syndromes. *Psychosomatic Medicine*, 69, 832–840.

Kita, S. (2009). Cross-cultural variation of speech accompanying gesture. *Language and Cognitive Processes*, 24, 145–167.

Kitanishi, K., Fujimoto, H., Toyohara, T. (1992). Treatment results and objects in Morita therapy institute between 20 years. *Morita-ryohoshitsu-kiyo* [Bulletin of Morita Clinical Therapy], 14, 2–7.

Kitayama, S., and Cohen, D. (eds.) (2007). *Handbook of cultural psychology*. New York: Guildford Press.

Kitayama, S., and Markus, H. R. (1994). Introduction to cultural psychology and emotion research. In S. Kitayama and H. R. Markus (eds.), *Emotion and culture: Empirical studies of mutual influence* (pp. 1–22). Washington, DC: American Psychological Association.

Kitayama, S., Duffy, S., and Uchida, U. (2007). Self as cultural mode of being. In S. Kitayama and D. Cohen (eds.), *Handbook of cultural psychology* (pp. 136–174). New York: Guilford Press.

Kitayama, S., Markus, H. R., and Kurokawa, M. (2000). Culture, emotion and well-being: Good feelings in Japan and the United States. *Emotion and Motivation*, 14, 93–124.

Kitayama, S., Duffy, S., Kawamura, T., and Larsen, J. T. (2003). Perceiving an object and its context in different cultures: A cultural look at New Look. *Psychological Science*, 14, 201–206.

Kitayama, S., Markus, H. R., Matsumoto, H., and Norasakkunit, V. (1997). Individual and collective processes in the construction of the self: Self-enhancement in the United States and self-criticism in Japan. *Journal of Personality and Social Psychology*, 72, 1245–1267.

Klassen, R. M. (2004). Optimism and realism: A review of self-efficacy from a cross-cultural perspective. *International Journal of Psychology*, 39, 205–230.

Klein, R. C., Weller, S. C., Zeissig, R., Richards, F. O., and Ruebush II, T. K. (1995). Knowledge, beliefs, and practices in relation to malaria transmission and vector control in Guatemala. *American Journal of Tropical and Medical Hygiene*, 52, 383–388.

Kleinman, A. (1977). Depression, somatisation and the "new cross-cultural psychiatry." *Social Science and Medicine*, 11, 3–9.

Kleinman, A. (1988). *Rethinking psychiatry: From cultural category to personal experience*. New York: The Free Press.

Kleinman, A. (2004). Culture and depression. *The New England Journal of Medicine*, 351, 951–953.

Kleinman, A., and Kleinman, J. (2007). Somatization: The interconnections in Chinese society among culture, depressive experiences and the meanings of pain. In M. Lock and J. Farquhar (eds.), *Beyond the body proper: Reading the anthropology of material life* (pp. 468–473). Durham, N.C.: Duke University Press.

Kleinman, A., Eisenberg, L., and Good, B. (2006). Culture, illness, and care: Clinical lessons from anthropologic and cross-cultural research. *FOCUS: The Journal of Life Long Learning in psychiatry*, 4, 140–149.

Kleiwer, E. V. (1992). Epidemiology of diseases among migrants. *International Migration Quartely Review*, 30, 141–165.

Klineberg, O. (1940). *Social psychology.* New York: Henry Holt.

Klineberg, O., and Hull, W. F. (1979). *At a foreign university: An international study of adaptation and coping.* New York: Praeger.

Kloos, P. (1988). *Door het oog van de anthropoloog* [Through the eyes of the anthropologist]. Muiderberg: Coutinho.

Kluckhohn, C. (1951). Values and value orientations in the theory of action. In T. Parsons and E. Shils (eds.), *Toward a general theory of action.* Cambridge, Mass.: Harvard University Press.

Kluckhohn, F., and Strodtbeck, C. (1961). *Variations in value orientations.* Evanston, Ill.: Row, Peterson.

Kochanska, G., and Thompson, R. A. (1997). The emergence and development of conscience in toddlerhood and early childhood. In J. E. Grusec and L. Kuczynski (eds.), *Parenting and children's internalization of values: A handbook of contemporary theory* (pp. 53–77). New York: Wiley.

Kok, G. (2007). Health promotion. In S. Ayers, A. Baum, C. McManus, S. Newman, K. Wallston, J. Weinman and R. West (eds.), *The Cambridge handbook of psychology, health and medicine* (pp. 355–359). Cambridge: Cambridge University Press.

Komisarof, A. (2009). Testing a modified Interactive Acculturation Model in Japan: American–Japanese coworker relations. *International Journal of Intercultural Relations*, 33, 399–418.

Koneru, V. K., Weisman de Mamani, A. G., Flynn, P. M., and Betancourt, H. (2007). Acculturation and mental health: Current findings and recommendations for future research. *Applied and Preventive Psychology*, 12, 76–96.

Konner, M. (1981). Evolution of human behavior development. In R. H. Munroe, R. L. Munroe and B. B. Whiting (eds.), *Handbook of cross-cultural human development* (pp. 3–51). New York: Garland.

Konner, M. (2007). Evolutionary foundations of cultural psychology. In M. Kitayama and D. Cohen (eds.), *Handbook of cultural psychology* (pp. 77–105). New York: Guilford Press.

Kosic, A. (2006). Personality and individual factors in acculturation. In D. L. Sam and J. W. Berry (eds.), *The Cambridge handbook of acculturation psychology* (pp. 113–128). Cambridge: Cambridge University Press.

Kosic, A., and Phalet, K. (2006). Ethnic categorization of immigrants: The role of prejudice, perceived acculturation strategies and group size. *International Journal of Intercultural Relations*, 30, 769–782.

Kosic, A., Kruglanski, A. W., Pierro, A., and Mannetti, L. (2004). The social cognition of immigrants' acculturation: Effects of the need for closure and the reference group at entry. *Journal of Personality and Social Psychology*, 86, 796–813.

Kövecses, Z. (2000). *Metaphor and emotion: Language, culture, and body in human feeling*. Cambridge: Cambridge University Press.

Kozhevnikov, M. (2007). Cognitive styles in the context of modern psychology: Toward an integrated framework of cognitive style. *Psychological Bulletin*, 133, 464–481.

Kraepelin, E. (1974). Comparative psychiatry. In S. R. Hirsch and M. Shepherd (eds.), *Themes and variations in European Psychiatry* (pp. 3–6). Bristol: Wiley. (Original work published 1904 in *Zentralblatt für Nervenheilkunde und Psychiatrie*, 15, 433–437.)

Kring, A. M., Davison, G. C., Neale, J. M., and Johnson, S. L. (2006). *Abnormal psychology* (10th edn.). New York: Wiley.

Kroeber, A. L. (1917). The superorganic. *American Anthropologist*, 19, 163–213.

Kroeber, A. L., and Kluckhohn, C. (1952). *Culture: A critical review of concepts and definitions*. Cambridge, Mass.: Peabody Museum, Vol. 47, no. 1.

Kruger, D. J. (2001). Psychological aspects of adaptations for kin directed altruistic helping behaviors. *Social Behavior and Personality*, 29, 323–331.

Krumm, H. J. (1997). Der Erwerb und die Vermittlung von Fremdsprachen [Acquiring and transmitting foreign languages]. In F. E. Weinert (ed.), *Psychologie des Unterrichts und der Schule* [Psychology of teaching and the school] (pp. 503–534). Göttingen: Hogrefe.

Kuhn, M. H., and McPartland, T. S. (1954). An empirical investigation of self-attitudes. *American Sociological Review*, 19, 68–76.

Kuhn, T. S. (1962). *The structure of scientific revolutions*. Chicago: The University of Chicago Press.

Kulhara, P., and Chakrabarti, S. (2001). Culture and schizophrenia and other psychotic disorders. *Psychiatric Clinics of North America*, 24, 449–464.

Kumagai, H. A., and Kumagai, A. K. (1986). The hidden "I" in Amae: "Passive love" and Japanese social construction. *Ethos*, 14, 305–319.

Kuwano, S., Namba, S., and Schick, A. (1986). A cross-cultural study on noise problems. In A. Schick, H. Höge and G. Lazarus-Mainka (eds.), *Contributions to psychological acoustics* (pp. 370–395). Oldenburg: Universität Oldenburg.

Kvernmo, S. (2006). Indigenous peoples. In D. L. Sam and J. W. Berry (eds.), *The Cambridge handbook of acculturation psychology* (pp. 233–250). Cambridge: Cambridge University Press.

Kwak, K. (2003). Adolescents and their parents: A review of intergenerational family relations for immigrant and non-immigrant families. *Human Development*, 46, 115–136.

Kymlicka, W. (2007). *Multicultural odysseys: Navigating the new international politics of diversity*. Oxford: Oxford University Press.

LaFromboise, T., Coleman, H., and Gerton, J. (1993). Psychological impact of biculturalism: Evidence and theory. *Psychological Bulletin*, 114, 395–412.

Lagmay, A. (1984). Western psychology in the Philippines: Impact and response. *International Journal of Psychology*, 19, 31–44.

Lai, D. W. L., and Surood, S. (2008). Socio-cultural variations in depressive symptoms of aging in South Asian Canadians. *Asian Journal of Gerontology and Geriatrics*, 3, 84–91.

Laird, G. (2009). *The price of a bargain: The quest for cheap and the death of globalization.* Toronto: McClelland & Stewart.

Lakatos, I. (1974). Falsification and the methodology of scientific research programmes. In I. Lakatos and A. Musgrave (eds.), *Criticism and the growth of knowledge* (pp. 91–196). Cambridge: Cambridge University Press.

Laland, K. N., Odling-Smee, J., and Feldman, M. W. (2000). Niche construction, biological evolution, and cultural change. *Behavioral and Brain Sciences*, 23, 131–146.

Lamb, M. (ed.) (1986). *The father's role: Applied perspectives.* New York: Wiley.

Lamb, M., and Sutton-Smith, B. (eds.) (1982). *Sibling relationships: Their nature and significance across the lifespan.* Hillsdale, N.J.: Erlbaum.

Landers, C. (1989). A psychobiological study of infant development in South India. In J. K. Nugent, B. M. Lester and T. B. Brazelton (eds.), *The cultural context of infancy* (pp. 169–207). Norwood: Ablex.

Landis, D., and Bhawuk, D. (2004). Synthesizing theory building and practice in intercultural training. In D. Landis, J. M. Bennett and M. J. Bennett (eds.), *Handbook of intercultural training* (3rd edn., pp. 451–466). Thousand Oaks, Calif.: Sage.

Landis, D., Bennett, J. M., and Bennett, M. J. (eds.) (2004). *Handbook of intercultural training* (3rd edn.). Thousand Oaks, Calif.: Sage.

Lange, C. G. (1885). *Om Sindsbevoegelser: Et psykofysiologiske Studie* [The Emotions: A psycho-physiological study]. Copenhagen: Kronar.

Lantz, D., and Stefflre, V. (1964). Language and cognition revisited. *Journal of Abnormal and Social Psychology*, 69, 472–481.

Laroche, M., Kim, C., and Hui, M. K. (1997). A comparative investigation of dimensional structures of acculturation for Italian Canadians and Greek Canadians. *Journal of Social Psychology*, 137, 317–331.

Larson, J. (1999). The conceptualization of health. *Medical Care Research and Review*, 56, 123–136.

Laryea, S. A., and Hayfron, J. E. (2005). African immigrants and the labour market: Exploring career opportunities, earning differentials and job satisfaction. In W. T. Tettey and K. P. Puplampu (eds.), *The African diaspora in Canada: Negotiating identity and belonging* (pp. 113–131). Calgary: Univesity of Calgary Press.

Lave, J., and Wenger, E. (1991). *Situated learning: Legitimate peripheral participation.* Cambridge: Cambridge University Press.

Lawrence, R. A. (1994). *Breastfeeding: A guide for the medical profession* (4th edn.). St. Louis: Mosby.

Lay, C., Fairlie, P., Jackson, S., Ricci, T., Eisenberg, J., Sato, T., Teeaar, A., and Melamud, A. (1998). Domain-specific allocentrism-idiocentrism. *Journal of Cross-Cultural Psychology*, 29, 434–460.

Lazarus, R. S., and Folkman, S. (1984). *Stress, appraisal and coping.* New York: Springer.

LCHC (Laboratory of Comparative Human Cognition) (1982). Culture and intelligence. In R. Sternberg (ed.), *Handbook of human intelligence* (pp. 642–719). New York: Cambridge University Press.

LCHC (Laboratory of Comparative Human Cognition) (1983). Culture and cognitive development. In P. H. Mussen and W. Kessen (eds.), *Handbook of child psychology, Vol. I* (pp. 295–356). New York: Wiley.

Lee, N. Y. L., and Johnson-Laird, P. N. (2006). Are there cross-cultural differences in reasoning? *Proceedings of the 28th Annual Meeting of the Cognitive Science Society*, 459–464.

Lee, R. D. (2003). Rethinking the evolutionary theory of aging: Transfers, not births, shape senescence in social species. *Proceedings of the National Academy of Science*, 100, 9637–9642.

Lee, T., and Fiske, S. (2006). Not an outgroup, not yet an ingroup: Immigrants in the Stereotype Content model. *International Journal of Intercultural Relations*, 30, 751–768.

Leenen, I., Givaudan, M., Pick, S., Venguer, T., Vera, J., and Poortinga, Y. H. (2008). Effectiveness of a Mexican health education program in a poverty-stricken rural area of Guatemala. *Journal of Cross-Cultural Psychology*, 39, 198–214.

Leff, J., Sartorious, N., Jablensky, A., Korten, A., and Ernberg, G. (1992). International pilot study of schizophrenia: Five-year follow-up findings. *Psychological Medicine*, 22, 131–145.

Leibowitz, H. W., Brislin, R., Perlmutrer, L., and Hennessey, R. (1969). Ponzo perspective illusion as a manifestation of space perception. *Science*, 166, 1174–1176.

Lenneberg, E. H. (1953). Cognition in linguistics. *Language*, 29, 463–471.

Lenneberg, E. H. (1967). *Biological foundations of language.* New York: Wiley.

Leong, C.-H. (2008). A multilevel research framework for the analyses of attitudes toward immigrants. *International Journal* of Intercultural Relations, 32, 115–129.

Leong, C.-H., and Ward, C. (2006). Cultural values and attitudes towards immigrants and immigration: The case of the Eurobarometer survey on racism and xenophobia. *International Journal of Intercultural Relations*, 30, 769–810.

Lerner, R. M. (2006). Developmental science, developmental systems, and contemporary theories. In R. M. Lerner (ed.), *Handbook of child psychology, Vol. I, Theoretical models of human development* (pp. 1–17). Hoboken, N.J.: Wiley.

Leung, A. K., Maddux, W. W., Galinsky, A. D., and Chui, C. (2008). Multicultural experience enhances creativity: The when and how. *American Psychologist*, 63, 169–181.

Leung, A. K., and Chiu, C. (in press). Multicultural experience, idea receptiveness, and creativity. *Journal of Cross-Cultural Psychology.*

Leung, K., and Bond, M. H. (2004). Social axioms: A model for social beliefs in multicultural perspective. *Advances in experimental social psychology, Vol. XXXVI* (pp. 119–197). San Diego: Academic Press.

Leung, K., and Li, F. (2008). Social axioms and cultural intelligence: Working across boundaries. In S. Ang and L. Van Dyne (eds.), *Handbook of cultural intelligence: Theory, measurement, and applications* (pp. 332–341). Sharpe: New York.

Leung, K., and Van de Vijver, F. J. R. (2008). Strategies for strengthening causal inferences in cross cultural research: The consilience approach. *International Journal of Cross-Cultural Management*, 8, 145–169.

Levenson, R. W., Ekman, P., Heider, K., and Friesen, W. V. (1992). Emotion and autonomic nervous system activity in the Minangkabau of West-Sumatra. *Journal of Personality and Social Psychology*, 62, 972–988.

Lévi-Strauss, C. (1962). *La pensée sauvage*. Paris: Plon.

Lévi-Strauss, C. (1966). *The savage mind*. London: Weidenfeld & Nicolson.

LeVine, R. A. (1990). Infant environments in psychoanalysis: A cross-cultural view. In J. W. Stigler, R. A. Shweder and G. Herdt (eds.), *Cultural psychology: Essays on comparative human development* (pp. 454–474). Cambridge: Cambridge University Press.

LeVine, R. A., and Campbell, D. T. (1972). *Ethnocentrism*. New York: Wiley.

Levine, R.V., and Norenzayan, A. (1999). The pace of life in 31 countries. *Journal of Cross-Cultural Psychology*, 30, 178–205.

Levine, T. R., Bresnahan, M. J., Park, H. S., Lapinsky, M. K., Wittenbaum, G. M., Shearman, S. M., Lee, S. Y., Chung, D., and Ohashi, R. (2003). Self-construal scales lack validity. *Human Communication Research*, 29, 210–252.

Levinson, D. J. (1978). *The seasons of a man's life*. New York: Knopf.

Levinson, D. J. (1996). *The seasons of a woman's life*. New York: Knopf.

Levinson, S. C. (1998). Studying spatial conceptualization across cultures: Anthropology and cognitive science. *Ethos*, 26, 7–24.

Levinson, S. C. (2000). Yélî Dnye and the theory of basic colors. *Journal of Linguistic Anthropology*, 10, 1–53.

Levinson, S. C. (2003). *Space in language and cognition*. Cambridge: Cambridge University Press.

Levy, R. I. (1984). The emotions in comparative perspective. In K. R. Scherer and P. Ekman (eds.), *Approaches to emotion* (pp. 397–412). Hillsdale, N.J.: Erlbaum.

Lévy-Bruhl, L. (1910). *Les fonctions mentales dans les societes inferieures* [*Mental functions in primitive societies*]. Paris: Alcan.

Lewis, J. R., and Ozaki, R. (2009). Amae and Mardy: A comparison of two emotion terms. *Journal of Cross-Cultural Psychology*, 40, 917–934.

Lewis, O. (1966). *La vida*. New York: Random House.

Lewontin, R. C. (1978). Adaptation. *Scientific American*, 239, 3, 156–169.

Li, H., Barnhart, H. X., Stein, A. D., and Martorell, R. (2001). Effects of early childhood supplementation on the educational achievement of women. *Pediatrics*, 112, 1156–1162.

Li, J. C., Dunning, D., and Malpass, R. S. (1998). Cross-racial identification among European-Americans: Basketball fandom and the contact hypothesis. *Paper presented at the biennial meeting of the American Psychology-Law Society*, Redondo Beach, Calif., March.

Li, P., and Gleitman, L. (2002). Turning the tables: Language and spatial reasoning. *Cognition*, 83, 265–294.

Liebkind, K. (2001). Acculturation. In R. Brown and S. Gaertner (eds.), *Blackwell handbook of social psychology, Vol. IV* (pp. 386–406). Oxford: Blackwell.

Liebkind, K. (2006). Ethnic identity and acculturation. In D. L. Sam and J. W. Berry (eds.), *The Cambridge handbook of acculturation psychology* (pp. 78–96). Cambridge: Cambridge University Press.

Liebkind, K., and Jasinskaja-Lahti, I. (in press). Specifying social psychological adaptation of immigrant youth: Integroup attitudes, interactions and identity. In A. Masten, D. Hernandez and K. Liebkind (eds.), *Capitalizing on immigration: The potential of immigrant youth*. Cambridge: Cambridge University Press.

Liepke, C., Adermann, K., Raida, M., Mägert, H.-J., Forssmann, W.-G., and Zucht, H.-D. (2002). Human milk provides peptides highly stimulating the growth of bifidobacteria. *European Journal of Biochemistry*, 269, 712–718.

Likert, R. (1967). *The human organization: Its management and values*. New York: McGraw-Hill.

Lillard, A. (1998). Ethnopsychologies: Cultural variations in theories of mind. *Psychological Bulletin*, 123, 3–32.

Lin, E. J.-L., and Church, A. T. (2004). Are indigenous Chinese personality dimensions culture-specific? *Journal of Cross-Cultural Psychology*, 35, 586–605.

Lincoln, Y., and Guba, E. G. (2000). Paradigmatic controversies, contradictions, and emerging conflicts. In N. K. Denzin and Y. Lincoln (eds.), *Handbook of qualitative research* (2nd edn., pp. 163–188). Thousand Oaks, Calif.: Sage.

Lindholm, C. (2007). *Culture and identity: The history, theory, and practice of psychological anthropology*. New York: Cambridge University Press.

Lindsey, D. T., and Brown, A. M. (2002). Color naming and the phototoxic effects of sunlight on the eye. *Psychological Science*, 13, 506–512.

Lindsey, D. T., and Brown, A. M. (2004). Sunlight and "blue": The prevalence of poor lexical discrimination within the "grue" range. *Psychological Science*, 15, 291–294.

Lindstrand, A., Bergström, S., Rosling, H., Rubenson, B., Stenson, B., and Tylleskär, T. (2006). *Global health: An introductory textbook*. Lund: Studentlitertur.

Linton, R. (1936). *The study of man*. New York: Appleton-Century-Crofts.

Linton, R. (1949). The distinctive aspects of acculturation. In R. Linton (ed.), *Acculturation in seven American Indian tribes* (pp. 501–520). New York: Appleton-Century.

Liu, J., and Hilton, D. (2005). How the past weighs on the present: Social representations of history and their role in identity politics. *British Journal of Social Psychology*, 44, 1–21.

Liu, L. A. (1985). Reasoning counterfactually in Chinese: Are there any obstacles? *Cognition*, 21, 239–270.

Lo, H.-T., and Fung, K. P. (2003). Culturally competent psychotherapy. *Canadian Journal of Psychiatry*, 48, 161–170.

Lomax, A., and Berkowitz, N. (1972). The evolutionary taxonomy of culture. *Science*, 177, 228–239.

Longabaugh, R. (1980). The systematic observation of behavior in naturalistic settings. In H. C. Triandis and J. W. Berry (eds.), *Handbook of cross-cultural psychology*, *Vol. I, Perspectives* (pp. 57–126). Boston: Allyn & Bacon.

Lonner, W. J. (1980). The search for psychological universals. In H. C. Triandis and W. W. Lambert (eds.), *Handbook of cross-cultural psychology, Vol. I, Perspectives* (pp. 143–204). Boston: Allyn & Bacon.

Lonner, W. J. (2004). JCCP at 35: Commitment, continuity and creative adaptation. *Journal of Cross-Cultural Psychology*, 35, 123–136.

Lonner, W. J. (in press). The continuing challenge of discovering psychological "order" across cultures. In F. J. R. Van de Vijver, A. Chasiotis and S. M. Breugelmans (eds.), *Fundamental questions in cross-cultural psychology*. Cambridge: Cambridge University Press.

Lonner, W. J., and Berry, J. W. (eds.) (1986). *Field methods in cross-cultural research*. London: Sage.

Lonner. W. J., and Adamopoulos, J. (1997). Culture as antecedent to behavior. In J. W. Berry, Y. H. Poortinga and J. Pandey (eds.), *Handbook of cross-cultural psychology, Vol. I, Theory and method* (2nd edn., pp. 43–83). Boston: Allyn & Bacon.

López, A. D., Mathers, C. D., Ezzati, M., Jamison, D. T., and Murray, C. J. L. (eds.) (2006). *Global burden of disease and risk factors*. New York: Oxford University Press.

López, S. R., and Guarnaccia, P. J. J. (2000). Cultural psychopathology: Uncovering the social world of mental illness. *Annual Review of Psychology*, 51, 571–598.

Lorenz, K. (1965). *Evolution and modification of behavior*. Chicago: The University of Chicago Press.

Low, B. S. (1989). Cross-cultural patterns in the training of children: An evolutionary perspective. *Journal of Comparative Psychology*, 103, 311–319.

Lowe, B., Spitzer, R. L., Williams, J. B. W., Mussell, M., Shellberg, D., and Kroemge, K. (2008). Depression, anxiety and somatization in primary care: Syndrome overlap and functional impairment. *General Hospital Psychiatry*, 30, 191–199.

Lucas, R. E., and Diener, E. (2008). Can we learn about national differences in happiness from individual responses? A multilevel approach. In F. J. R. Van de Vijver, D. A. van Hemert and Y. H. Poortinga (eds.), *Individuals and cultures in multilevel analysis* (pp. 221–246). Mahwah, N.J.: Erlbaum.

Lucy, J. A., and Shweder, R. A. (1979). Whorf and his critics: Linguistic and nonlinguistic influences on color memory. *American Anthropologist*, 81, 581–615.

Lumsden, C. J., and Wilson, E. O. (1981). *Genes, mind and culture: The coevolutionary process*. Cambridge, Mass.: Harvard University Press.

Luria, A. R. (1971). Towards the problem of the historical nature of psychological processes. *International Journal of Psychology*, 6, 259–272.

Luria, A. R. (1976). *Cognitive development: Its cultural and social foundations.* Cambridge, Mass.: Harvard University Press.

Lutz, C. (1988). *Unnatural emotions: Everyday sentiments on a Micronesian atoll and their challenge to western theory.* Chicago: The University of Chicago Press.

Lynn, R. (2006). *Race differences in intelligence: An evolutionary analysis.* Augusta, Ga.: Washington Summit Publishers.

Lynn, R., and Vanhanen, T. (2002). *IQ and the wealth of nations.* Westport, Conn.: Praeger.

Maass, A., Karasawa, M., Politi, F., and Suga, S. (2006). Do verbs and adjectives play different roles in different cultures? A cross-linguistic analysis of person representation. *Journal of Personality and Social Psychology*, 90, 734–750.

Maathai, W. (2009). *The challenge for Africa: A new vision.* London: Heinemann.

Maccoby, E. E. (1984). Middle childhood in the context of the family. In W. A. Collins (ed.), *Development during middle childhood: The years from 6–10* (pp. 184–239). Washington, DC: National Academy Press.

Maccoby, E. E. (1998). *The two sexes: Growing up apart, coming together.* Cambridge, Mass.: Belknap Press.

MacDonald, K. (1998). Evolution, culture and the five-factor model. *Journal of Cross-Cultural Psychology*, 29, 119–149.

MacDonald, K. B. (1988). *Social and personality development: An evolutionary synthesis.* New York: Springer.

MacDonald, K. B. (1992). Warmth as a developmental construct: An evolutionary analysis. *Child Development*, 63, 753–773.

MacLachlan, M. (2006). *Culture and health: A critical perspective towards global health.* Chichester: Wiley.

MacLachlan, M., McAuliffe, E., and Carr, S. (2010). *The aid triangle: Recognizing the human dynamics of dominance, justice and identity.* London: Zed Books.

MacLin, O. H., Malpass, R. S., and Honaker, S. (2001). Racial categorization of faces: The ambiguous race face effect. *Psychology, Public Policy and Law*, 7, 98–118.

Maddux, W. W., and Galinsky, A. D. (2009). Cultural borders and mental barriers: The relationship between living abroad and creativity. *Journal of Personality and Social Psychology*, 96, 1047–1061.

Maeda, F., and Nathan, J. H. (1999). Understanding *taijin kyofusho* through its treatment, Morita therapy. *Journal of Psychosomatic Research*, 46, 525–550.

Maeshiro, T. (2009). Naikan Therapy in Japan: Introspection as a way of healing. Introduction to Naikan Therapy. *World Cultural Psychiatry Review*, 4, 33–38.

Main, J., and Solomon, J. (1990). Procedures for identifying infants as disorganized/disoriented during the Ainsworth Strange Situation. In T. M. Greenberg, D. Cicchetti and E. M. Cummings (eds.), *Attachment in the preschool years: Theory, research and intervention* (pp. 121–160). Chicago: The University of Chicago Press.

Main, M., Kaplan, N., and Cassidy, J. (1985). Security in infancy, childhood and adulthood: A move to the level of representation. In I. Bretherton and

E. Waters (eds.), *Growing points of attachment theory and research, Vols. I–II* (pp. 66–106). Chicago: The University of Chicago Press.

Majid, A., Boster. J. S., and Bowerman, M. (2008). The cross-linguistic categorization of everyday events: A study of cutting and breaking. *Cognition*, 109, 235–250.

Majid, A., Bowerman, M., Kita, S., Haun, D. B. M., and Levinson, S. C. (2004). Can language restructure cognition? The case for space. *Trends in Cognitive Sciences*, 8, 108–114.

Mak, A., and Tran, C. (2001). Big Five personality and cultural relocation in Vietnamese Australian students' intercultural self-efficacy. *International Journal of Intercultural Relations*, 25, 181–201.

Malinowski, B. (1922). *Argonauts of the Western Pacific*. New York: Dutton.

Malinowski, B. (1944). *A scientific theory of culture*. Chapel Hill, N.C.: University of North Carolina Press.

Malpass, R. S. (1996). Face recognition at the interface of psychology, law and culture. In H. Grad, A. Blanco and J. Georgas (eds.), *Key issues in cross-cultural psychology* (pp. 7–21). Lisse: Swets & Zeitlinger.

Malpass, R. S., and Kravitz, J. (1969). Recognition for faces of own and other races. *Journal of Personality and Social Psychology*, 13, 333–334.

Mange, E. J., and Mange, A. P. (1999). *Basic human genetics* (2nd edn.). Sunderland, Mass.: Sinauer.

Mann, J. (1992). Nurturance or negligence: Maternal psychology and behavioral preference among preterm twins. In J. Barkow, L. Cosmides and J. Tooby (eds.), *The adapted mind: Evolutionary psychology and the generation of culture* (pp. 367–390). New York: Oxford University Press.

Manson, S. M. (1995). Culture and major depression: Current challenges in the diagnosis of mood disorders. *Psychiatric Clinics of North America*, 18, 487–501.

Marcia, J. E. (1980). Identity in adolescence. In J. Adelson (ed.), *Handbook of adolescent psychology* (pp. 159–187). New York: Wiley.

Marcoen, A. (1995). Filial maturity of middle-aged adults in the context of parent care: Model and measures. *Journal of Adult Development*, 2, 125–136.

Marcoen, A., Grommen, R., and Van Ranst, N. (eds.) (2006). *Als de schaduwen langer worden* [When the shadows become longer]. Leuven: Lanoo.

Markon, K. E., Krueger, R. F., and Watson, D. (2005). Delineating the structure of normal and abnormal personality: An integrative hierarchical approach. *Journal of Personality and Social Psychology*, 88, 139–157.

Markus, H. R., and Hamedani, M. G. (2007). Sociocultural psychology: The dynamic interdependence among self system and social systems. In S. Kitayama and D. Cohen (eds.), *Handbook of cultural psychology* (pp. 3–39). New York: Guildford Press.

Markus, H. R., and Kitayama, S. (1991). Culture and the self: Implications for cognition, emotion and motivation. *Psychological Review*, 98, 244–253.

Markus, H. R., and Kitayama, S. (1994). The cultural shaping of emotion: A conceptual framework. In S. Kitayama and H. R. Markus (eds.), *Emotion and culture: Empirical studies of mutual influence* (pp. 339–351). Washington, DC: American Psychological Association.

Markus, H. R., and Kitayama, S. (1998). The cultural psychology of personality. *Journal of Cross-Cultural Psychology*, 29, 63–87.

Marmot, M., and Wilkinson, R. G. (eds.) (2005). *Social determinants of health.* Oxford: Oxford University Press.

Maseland, R., and Van Hoorn, A. (2009). Explaining the negative correlation between values and practices: A note on the Hofstede-GLOBE debate. *Journal of International Business Studies*, 40, 527–532.

Masgoret, A.-M., and Gardner, R. C. (2003). Attitudes, motivation, and second language learning: A meta-analysis of studies conducted by Gardner and associates. *Language Learning*, 53, 167–211.

Masgoret, A.-M., and Ward, C. (2006). The cultural learning approach to acculturation. In D. L. Sam and J. W. Berry (eds.), *The Cambridge handbook of acculturation psychology* (pp. 58–77). Cambridge: Cambridge University Press.

Maskarinec, G., and Noh, J. J. (2004). The effect of migration on cancer incidence among Japanese in Hawaii. *Ethnicity & Disease*, 14, 431–439.

Maslow, A. H. (1954). *Motivation and personality.* New York: Harper.

Masuda, T., Ellsworth, P.C., Mesquita, B., Leu, J., Tanida, S., Van de Veerdonk, E. (2008). Placing the face in context: Cultural differences in the perception of facial emotion. *Journal of Personality and Social Psychology*, 94, 365–381.

Matsumoto, D. (1996). *Culture and psychology.* Pacific Grove, Calif.: Brooks/Cole.

Matsumoto, D. (1999). Culture and self: An empirical assessment of Markus and Kitayama's theory of independent and interdependent self-construals. *Asian Journal of Social Psychology*, 2, 289–310.

Matsumoto, D. (2006). Culture and cultural worldviews: Do verbal descriptions about culture reflect anything other than verbal descriptions about culture? *Culture & Psychology*, 12, 33–62.

Matsumoto, D., and Van de Vijver, F. J. R. (eds.) (in press). *Cross-cultural research methods in psychology.* Cambridge: Cambridge University Press.

Matsumoto, D., and Yoo, S. H. (2006). Towards a new generation of cross-cultural research. *Perspectives on Psychological Science*, 1, 234–250.

Matsumoto, D., Nezlek, J., and Koopmann, B. (2007). Evidence for universality in phenomenological emotion response system coherence. *Emotion*, 7, 57–67.

Matsumoto, D., LeRoux, J. A., Bernhard, R., and Gray, H. (2004). Personality and behavioral correlates of intercultural adjustment potential. *International Journal of Intercultural Relations*, 28, 281–309.

Matsumoto, D., LeRoux, J. A., Robles, Y., and Campos, G. (2007). The intercultural adjustment potential scale (ICAPS) predicts adjustment above and beyond personality and general intelligence. *International Journal of Intercultural Relations*, 31, 747–759.

Matsumoto, D., LeRoux, J. A., Ratzlaff, C., Tatani, H., Uchida, H., Kim, C., and Araki, S. (2001). Development and validation of a measure of intercultural adjustment potential in Japanese sojourners: The Intercultural Adjustment Potential Scale (ICAPS). *International Journal of Intercultural Relations*, 25, 483–510.

Matsumoto, D., Yoo, S. H., Fontaine, J., *et al.* (2008). Mapping expressive differences around the world: The relationship between emotional display rules and individualism v. collectivism. *Journal of Cross-Cultural Psychology*, 39, 55–74.

Maurice, M. (1979). For a study of the "societal effect": Universality and specificity in organization research. In C. J. Lammers and D. J. Hickson (eds.), *Organizations alike and unlike* (pp. 42–60). London: Routledge & Kegan Paul.

Mauro, R., Sato, K., and Tucker, J. (1992). The role of appraisal in human emotions: A cross-cultural study. *Journal of Personality and Social Psychology*, 62, 301–317.

Maxwell, J. (1992). Understanding and validity in qualitative research. *Harvard Educational Review*, 62, 279–300.

Maynard Smith, J. (1982). *Evolution and the theory of games.* Cambridge: Cambridge University Press.

Mayr, E. (1983). How to carry out the adaptationist program. *American Naturalist*, 121, 324–334.

Mayr, E. (1984). *The growth of evolutionary thought.* Cambridge, Mass.: Harvard University Press.

Mayr, E. (1997). *This is biology.* Cambridge, Mass.: Harvard University Press.

Mbigi, L. (1997). *Ubuntu: The African dream in management.* Randburg: Knowledge Resources.

McAdams, D.P. (2001a). The psychology of life stories. *Review of General Psychology*, 5, 100–122.

McAdams, D. P. (2001b). Generativity in midlife. In M. E. Lachman (ed.), *Handbook of midlife development* (pp. 395–443). New York: Wiley.

McClelland, D. C. (1961). *The achieving society.* Princeton: Van Nostrand.

McCluskey, K., Albas, D., Niemi, R., Cuevas, C., and Ferrer, C. (1975). Cross-cultural differences in the perception of the emotional content of speech. *Developmental Psychology*, 11, 551–555.

McCrae, R. R. (2002). NEO-PI-R data from 36 cultures: Further intercultural comparisons. In R. R. McCrae and J. Allik (eds.), *The five-factor model of personality across cultures* (pp. 105–125). New York: Kluwer.

McCrae, R. R. (2009). Personality profiles of cultures: Patterns of ethos. *European Journal of Personality*, 23, 205–227.

McCrae, R. R., and Allik, J. (eds.) (2002). *The five-factor model of personality across cultures.* New York: Kluwer.

McCrae, R. R., and Costa, P. T., Jr. (1996). Toward a new generation of personality theories: Theoretical contexts for the Five-Factor Model. In J. S. Wiggins (ed.), *The five-factor model of personality: Theoretical perspectives* (pp. 51–87). New York: Guilford Press.

McCrae, R. R., and Costa, P. T., Jr. (2008). The five-factor theory of personality. In O. P. John, R. W. Robins and L. A. Pervin (eds.), *Handbook of personality: Theory and research* (3rd edn., pp. 159–181). New York: Guilford Press.

McCrae, R. R., and Terracciano, A. (2006). National character and personality. *Current Directions in Psychological Science*, 15, 156–161.

McCrae, R. R., and Terracciano, A. (2008). The five-factor model and its correlates in individuals and cultures. In F. J. R. Van de Vijver, D. A. van Hemert and Y. H. Poortinga (eds.), *Multilevel analyses of individuals and cultures* (pp. 249–283). Mahwah, N.J.: Erlbaum.

McCrae, R. R., Terracciano, A., Realo, A., and Allik, J. (2007). Climatic warmth and national wealth: Some culture-level determinants of national character stereotypes. *European Journal of Personality*, 21, 953–976.

McCrae, R. R., Costa, P. T., Jr., Del Pilar, G. H., Rolland, J.-P., and Parker, W. D. (1998). Cross-cultural assessment of the five-factor model: The Revised NEO Personality Inventory. *Journal of Cross-Cultural Psychology*, 29, 171–188.

McCrae, R. R., Terracciano, A., and 78 Members of the Personality Profiles of Cultures Project (2005a). Universal features of personality traits from the observer's perspective: Data from 50 cultures. *Journal of Personality and Social Psychology*, 88, 547–561.

McCrae, R. R., Terracciano, A., and 79 Members of the Personality Profiles of Cultures Project (2005b). Personality profiles of cultures: Aggregate personality traits. *Journal of Personality and Social Psychology*, 89, 407–425.

McDonough, L., Choi, S., and Mandler, J. M. (2003). Understanding spatial relations: Flexible infants, lexical adults. *Cognitive Psychology*, 46, 229–259.

McElreath, R., and Henrich, J. (2007). Modeling cultural evolution. In R. I. M. Dunbar and L. Barrett (eds.), *Oxford handbook of evolutionary psychology* (pp. 571–585). Oxford: Oxford University Press.

McGrath, J., Saha, S., Welham, J., El Saadil, O., MacCauley, C., and Chant, D. (2004). A systematic review of the incidence of schizophrenia: The distribution of rates and the influence of sex, urbanicity, migrant status and methodology. *BMC Medicine*, 2. Retrieved from www.biomedcentral.com/1741-7015/2/13

McGrath, R. E., and Goldberg, L. R. (2006). How to measure national stereotypes? *Science*, 311, 776–777.

McGrew, W. C. (1992). *Chimpanzee material culture*. Cambridge: Cambridge University Press.

McLuhan, M. (1971). *The Gutenberg galaxy: The making of typographic man*. London: Routledge and Kegan Paul.

McMichael, A. J. (2002). Population, environment, disease, and survival: Past patterns, uncertain futures. *The Lancet*, 359, 1145–1148.

McNett, C. (1970). A settlement pattern scale of cultural complexity. In R. Naroll and R. Cohen (eds.), *A handbook of method in cultural anthropology* (pp. 872–886). New York: Natural History Press.

Mead, M. (1928). *Coming of age in Samoa: A psychological study of primitive youth for Western civilization*. New York: Morrow Quill Paperbacks.

Medin, D. L., and Atran, S. (2004). The native mind: Biological categorization and reasoning in development and across cultures. *Psychological Review*, 111, 960–983.

Medin, D. L., Unsworth, S. J., and Hirschfeld, L. (2007). Culture, categorization, and reasoning. In S. Kitayama and D. Cohen (eds.), *Handbook of cultural psychology* (pp. 615–644). New York: Guildford Press.

Meiring, D., Van de Vijver, F. J. R., Rothmann, S., and Barrick, M. R. (2005). Construct, item, and method bias of cognitive and personality tests in South Africa. *South African Journal of Industrial Psychology*, 31, 1–8.

Meissner, C. A., and Brigham, J. C. (2001). Thirty years of investigating the own-race bias in memory for faces: A meta-analytic review. *Psychology, Public Policy and Law*, 7, 3–35.

Mendenhall, M., and Oddou, G. (1985). The dimensions of expatriate acculturation. *Academy of Management Review*, 10, 39–47.

Mendoza-Denton, R., and Mischel, W. (2007). Integrating system approaches to culture and personality: The cultural cognitive-affective processing system. In S. Kitayama and D. Cohen (eds.), *Handbook of cultural psychology* (pp. 175–195). New York: Guilford Press.

Mendoza-Denton, R., Ayduk, O. N., Shoda, Y., and Mischel, W. (1997). Cognitive-affective processing system analysis of reactions to the O. J. Simpson criminal trial verdict. *Journal of Social Issues*, 53, 563–581.

Menon, U., and Shweder, R. A. (1994). Kali's tongue: Cultural psychology and the power of shame in Orissa, India. In S. Kitayama and H. R. Markus (eds.), *Emotion and culture* (pp. 241–284). Washington, DC: APA Press.

Mergler, N. L., and Goldstein, M. D. (1983). Why are there old people? Senescence as biological and cultural preparedness for the transmission of information. *Human Development*, 26, 72–90.

Merritt, A. (2000). Culture in the cockpit: Do Hofstede's dimensions replicate. *Journal of Cross-Cultural Psychology*, 31, 283–301.

Mesquida, C. G., and Wiener, N. I. (1996). Human collective aggression: A behavioral ecology perspective. *Ethology and Sociobiology*, 17, 247–262.

Mesquida, C. G., and Wiener, N. I. (1999). Male age composition and severity of conflicts. *Politics and the Life Sciences*, 18, 181–189.

Mesquita, B., and Frijda, N. H. (1992). Cultural variations in emotions: A review. *Psychological Bulletin*, 112, 179–204.

Mesquita, B., and Karasawa, M. (2002). Different emotional lives. *Cognition & Emotion*, 16, 127–141.

Mesquita, B., Frijda, N. H., and Scherer, K. R. (1997). Culture and emotion. In J. W. Berry, P. R. Dasen and T. S. Saraswathi (eds.), *Handbook of cross-cultural psychology, Vol. II, Basic processes and human development* (2nd edn., pp. 255–297). Boston: Allyn & Bacon.

Messick, S. (1995). Validity of psychological assessment. *American Psychologist*, 50, 741–749.

Mezzich, J. E., Kleinman, A., Fabrega, H., and Parron, D. E. (eds.) (1996). *Culture and psychiatric diagnosis: A DSM-IV perspective*. Washington, DC: APA Press Inc.

Michotte, A. (1954). *La perception de la causalité* [The perception of causality]. Leuven: Publications Universitaires de Louvain.

Milinski, M., Semmann, D., and Krambeck, H. J. (2002). Reputations help solve the "tragedy of the commons." *Nature*, 415, 424–426.

Milinski, M., Semmann, D., Bakker, T., and Krambeck, H. J. (2001). Cooperation through indirect reciprocity: Image scoring or standing strategy? *Proceedings of the Royal Society of London, Series B-Biological Sciences*, 268, 2495–2501.

Miller, G. (2000). *The mating mind: How sexual choice shaped the evolution of human nature.* New York: Random House.

Miller, G. A. (1987). Meta-analysis and the culture-free hypothesis. *Organization Studies*, 8, 309–325.

Miller, J. G. (1984). Culture and the development of everyday social explanation. *Journal of Personality and Social Psychology*, 46, 961–978.

Miller, W. R., and Thoresen, C. E. (2003). Spirituality, religion and health: An emerging research field. *American Psychologist*, 58, 24–35.

Mischel, W. (1968). *Personality and assessment.* New York: Wiley.

Mischel, W. (1973). Toward a cognitive social learning reconceptualization of personality. *Psychological Review*, 80, 252–283.

Mischel, W. (1990). Personality dispositions revisited and revised: A view after three decades. In L. A. Pervin (ed.), *Handbook of personality: Theory and research* (pp. 111–134). New York: Guilford Press.

Mischel, W., and Shoda, Y. (1995). A cognitive-affective system theory of personality: Reconceptualizing situations, dispositions, dynamics, and invariance in personality structure. *Psychological Review*, 102, 246–268.

Mishra, R. C. (1997). Cognition and cognitive development. In J. W. Berry, P. R. Dasen and T. S. Saraswathi (eds.), *Handbook of cross-cultural psychology, Vol. II, Basic processes and human development* (pp. 143–176). Boston: Allyn & Bacon.

Mishra, R. C., and Berry, J. W. (2008). Cultural adaptations and cognitive processes of tribal children in Chotanagpur. In N. Srinivasan, A. K. Gupta and J. Pandey (eds.), *Advances in cognitive science* (pp. 289–301). New Delhi: Sage.

Mishra, R. C., Dasen, P. R., and Niraula, S. (2003). Ecology, language, and performance. *International Journal of Psychology*, 38, 366–383.

Mishra, R. C., Singh, S., and Dasen, P. R. (2009). Geocentric dead reckoning in Sanskrit- and Hindi-medium school children. *Culture & Psychology*, 15, 386–408.

Mishra, R. C., Sinha, D., and Berry, J. W. (1996). *Ecology, acculturation and adaptation: A study of Adivasi in Bihar.* New Delhi: Sage.

Misumi, J. (1984). Decision-making in Japanese groups and organizations. In B. Wilpert and A. Sorge (eds.), *International perspectives on organizational democracy, Vol. II* (pp. 525–539). Chichester: Wiley.

Misumi, J. (1985). *The behavioral science of leadership.* Ann Arbor, Mich.: University of Michigan Press.

Mittlemark, M. B. (2009). Editorial. *Global Health Promotion*, 16, 3–4.

Miyamoto, S., Duncan, G. E., Marx, C. E., and Lieberman, J. A. (2005). Treatments for schizophrenia: A critical review of pharmacology and mechanisms of action of psychotic drugs. *Molecular Psychiatry*, 10, 79–104.

Miyamoto, Y., Nisbett, R., and Masuda, T. (2006). Culture and the physical environment. *Psychological Science,* 17, 113–119.

Mkhize, N. (2004). Psychology: An African perspective. Chapter 4 in K. Ratele, N. Duncan, D. Hook, N. Mkhize, P. Kiguwa and A. Collins (eds.), *Self, community and psychology* (pp. 1–29). Cape Town: UCT Press.

Moghaddam, F. (1989). Specialization and despecialization in psychology: Divergent processes in the three worlds. *International Journal of Psychology,* 24, 103–116.

Moghaddam, F. (2008). *Multiculturalism and intergroup relations.* Washington, DC: APA Books.

Moghaddam, F., and Taylor, D. M. (1986). What constitutes an "appropriate psychology" for the developing world? *International Journal of Psychology,* 21, 253–267.

Moghaddam, F., Erneling, C., Montero, M., and Lee, N. (2007). Toward a conceptual foundation for a global psychology. In M. Stevens and U. Gielen (eds.), *Toward a global psychology: Theory, research and pedagogy* (pp. 179–206). Mahwah, N.J.: Erlbaum.

Moghaddam, F., Branchi, C., Daniels, K., Apter, M., and Harré, R. (1999). Psychology and national development. *Psychology and Developing Societies,* 11, 119–141.

Mohamed, H. E. (2007). Structure–context alignment: Evidence from a developing country (Sudan). *Cross-Cultural Management: An International Journal,* 14, 23–42.

Mol, S. T., Born, M. Ph., and Van der Molen, H. T. (2005). Developing criteria for expatriate effectiveness: Time to jump off the adjustment bandwagon. *International Journal of Intercultural Relations,* 29, 339–353.

Mol, S. T., Born, M. Ph., Willemsen, M. E., and Van der Molen, H. T. (2005). Predicting expatriate job performance for selection purposes: A quantitative review. *Journal of Cross-Cultural Psychology,* 36, 1–31.

Monk, C. S., McClure, E. B., Nelson, E. E., Zarahn, E., Bilder, R. M., Leibenluft, E., Charney, D. S., Ernst, M., and Pine, D. S. (2003). Adolescent immaturity in attention-related brain engagement to emotional facial expressions. *NeuroImage,* 20, 420–428.

Moore, C., and Mathews, H. (eds.) (2001). *The psychology of cultural experience.* Cambridge: Cambridge University Press.

Morita, S. (1974). The therapeutic result of special treatment for shinkeishitsu. In T. Kora (ed.), *Morita Shomazenshu, Vol. III* (pp. 67–71). Tokyo: Hakuyosha.

Morita, S. (1998). *Morita therapy and the true nature of anxiety based disorders.* Albany: State University of New York Press.

Morris, D., Collett, P., Marsh, P., and O'Shaughnessy, M. (1979). *Gestures: Their origin and distribution.* London: Jonathan Cape.

Morris, M., and Peng, K. (1994). Culture and cause: American and Chinese attributions for social and physical events. *Journal of Personality and Social Psychology,* 67, 949–971.

Moscovici, S. (1972). Society and theory in social psychology. In J. Israel and H. Tajfel (eds.), *The context of social psychology* (pp. 17–68). London: Academic Press.

Moscovici, S. (1982). The phenomenon of social representations. In R. M. Farr and S. Moscovici (eds.), *Social representations* (pp. 3–70). Cambridge: Cambridge University Press.

Motti-Stefanidi, F., Berry, J. W., Chryssochoou, X., Sam, D. L., and Phinney, J. S. (in press). Positive immigrant youth in context: Developmental, acculturation and social psychological perspectives. In A. Masten, D. Hernandez and K. Liebkind (eds.), *Capitalizing on immigration: The potential of immigrant youth.* Cambridge: Cambridge University Press.

Motti-Stefanidi, F., Pavlopoulos, V., Obradovic, J., and Masten, A. S. (2008). Acculturation and adaptation of immigrants in Greek urban schools. *International Journal of Psychology*, 43, 45–58.

Moussavi, S., Chatterji, S., Verdes, E., Tandon, A., Patel, V., and Üstün, B. (2007). Depression, chronic diseases, and decrements in health: Results from the World Health Surveys. *The Lancet*, 370, 851–858.

MOW (Meaning of Working International Research Team) (1987). *The meaning of working.* London: Academic Press.

Moyo, D. (2009). *Dead aid: Why aid is not working and how there is a better way for Africa.* London: Penguin.

Mpofu, E., Peltzer, K., and Bojuwoye, O. (in press). Indigenous healing practices in sub-Saharan Africa. In E. Mpofu (ed.), *Counselling people of African ancestry.* New York: Cambridge University Press.

Mukherji, B. R. (1995). Cross-cultural issues in illness and wellness: Implications for depression. *Journal of Social Distress and the Homeless*, 4, 203–217.

Munroe, R. H., and Munroe, R. L. (1994). Field observations of behavior as a cross-cultural method. In P. K. Bock (ed.), *Handbook of psychological anthropology* (pp. 255–77). Westport, Conn.: Greenwood.

Munroe, R. L., and Gauvain, M. (2009). The cross-cultural study of children's learning and socialization: A short history. In D. F. Lancy, J. Bock and S. Gaskins (eds.), *The Anthropology of learning in childhood* (pp. 35–63). Lanham, Md.: AltaMira.

Munroe, R. L., and Munroe, R. H. (1975). *Cross-cultural human development.* Monterey, Calif.: Brooks/Cole.

Munroe, R. L., and Munroe, R. H. (1986a). Weber's Protestant ethic revisited: An African case. *Journal of Psychology*, 120, 447–456.

Munroe, R. L., and Munroe, R. H. (1986b). Field work in cross-cultural psychology. In W. J. Lonner and J. W. Berry (eds.), *Field methods in cross-cultural research* (pp. 111–136). London: Sage.

Munroe, R. L., and Munroe, R. H. (1997). A comparative anthropological perspective. In J. W. Berry, Y. H. Poortinga and J. Pandey (eds.), *Handbook of cross-cultural psychology, Vol. I, Theory and method* (2nd edn., pp. 171–213). Boston: Allyn & Bacon.

Murad, S. D., Joung. I. M., Van Lenthe, F. J., Bengi-Arslan, L., and Crijnen, A. A. (2003). Predictors of self-reported problem behaviours in Turkish immigrant and Dutch adolescents in the Netherlands. *Journal of Child Psychology and Psychiatry*, 44, 412–423.

Muramoto, Y. (2003). An indirect self-enhancement in relationships among Japanese. *Journal of Cross-Cultural Psychology*, 34, 552–566.

Murase, T. (1982). Sunao: A central value in Japanese psychotherapy. In A. Marsella and G. White (eds.), *Cultural conceptions of mental health and therapy* (pp. 317–329). Dordrecht: Reidel.

Murdock, G. P. (1937). Comparative data on the division of labor by sex. *Social Forces*, 15, 551–553.

Murdock, G. P. (1949). *Social structure*. New York: Macmillan.

Murdock, G. P. (1967). *Ethnographic atlas*. Pittsburgh: University of Pittsburgh Press.

Murdock, G. P. (1975). *Outline of world cultures (5th edn.)*. New Haven, Conn.: Human Relations Area Files.

Murdock, G. P., Ford, C. S., Hudson, A. E., Kennedy, R., Simmons, L. W., and Whiting, J. W. M. (2008). *Outline of cultural materials* (5th edn.). New Haven, Conn.: Human Relations Area Files Press.

Murphy, H. B. M. (1982). Culture and schizophrenia. In I. Al-Issa (ed.), *Culture and psychopathology* (pp. 221- 249). Baltimore: University Park Press.

Murray, C. J. L., and Lopez, A. D. (2007). Alternative projections of mortality and disability by cause 1990–2020: Global Burden of Disease Study. *The Lancet*, 349, 1498–1504.

Muthén, B. O. (1994). Multilevel covariance structure analysis. *Sociological Methods & Research*, 22, 376–398.

Naidu, R. K. (1983). A developing program of stress research. *Paper presented at the seminar on Stress, Anxiety and Mental Health*. Allahabad, Dec.

Nardon, L., and Steers, R. M. (2009). The culture theory jungle: Divergence and convergence in models of national culture. In R. S. Bhagat and R. M. Steers (eds.), *The Cambridge handbook of culture, organizations, and work* (pp. 3–22). Cambridge: Cambridge University Press.

Naroll, R. (1970a). What have we learned from cross-cultural surveys? *American Anthropologist*, 72, 1227–1288.

Naroll, R. (1970b). The culture bearing unit in cross-cultural surveys. In R. Naroll and R. Cohen (eds.), *Handbook of method in cultural anthropology* (pp. 721–65). New York: Natural History Press.

Naroll, R. (1970c). Galton's problem. In R. Naroll and R. Cohen (eds.), *Handbook of method in cultural anthropology* (pp. 974–989). New York: Natural History Press.

Naroll, R., and Cohen, R. (eds.) (1970). *Handbook of method in cultural anthropology*. New York: Natural History Press.

Naroll, R., Michik, G., and Naroll, F. (1980). Holocultural research methods. In H. C. Triandis and J. W. Berry (eds.), *Handbook of cross-cultural psychology, Vol. II, Methodology* (pp. 479–521). Boston: Allyn & Bacon.

Nation Master (2008). People Statistics: Fertility rate by country. Retrieved November 20, 2009 from www.nationmaster.com/graph/peo_tot_fer_rat-people-total-fertility-rate&date=2008

Nauck, B. (2008). Acculturation. In F. J. R. Van de Vijver, D. A. Van Hemert and Y. H. Poortinga (eds.), *Multilevel analysis of individuals and cultures* (pp. 379–410). Mahwah, N.J.: Erlbaum.

Nauck, B., and Klaus, D. (2007). The varying value of children: Empirical results from eleven societies in Asia, Africa and Europe. *Current Sociology*, 55, 487–503.

Navas, M., Rojas, A. J., García, M., and Pumares, P. (2007). Acculturation strategies and attitudes according to the Relative Acculturation Extended Model (RAEM): The perspectives of natives versus immigrants. *International Journal of Intercultural Relations*, 31, 67–86.

Navas, M., García, M. C., Sánchez, J., Rojas, A. J., Pumares, P., and Fernández, J. S. (2005). Relative Acculturation Extended Model: New contributions with regard to the study of acculturation. *International Journal of Intercultural Relations*, 29, 21–37.

Neisser, U., Boodoo, G., Bouchard, T. J., Boykin, W. A., Brody, N., Ceci, C. J., Halpern, D. F., Loehlin, J. C., Perloff, R., Sternberg, R. J., and Urbina, S. (1996). Intelligence: Knowns and unknowns. *American Psychologist*, 51, 77–101.

Nelson, E. A. S., Schiefenhövel, W., and Haimerl, F. (2000). Child care practices in nonindustrialized societies. *Pediatrics*, 105, e75.

Nesdale, D., and Mak, A. S. (2003). Ethnic identification, self-esteem and immigrant psychological health. *International Journal of Intercultural Relations*, 27, 23–40.

Neto, F. (2001). Satisfaction with life among adolescents from immigrant families in Portugal. *Journal of Youth and Adolescence*, 30, 53–67.

Neyer, F. J., and Lang, F. R. (2003). Blood is thicker than water: Kinship orientation across the life span. *Journal of Personality and Social Psychology*, 84, 310–321.

Nguyen, H. H., Messe, L. A., and Stollak, G. E. (1999). Toward a more complex understanding of acculturation and adjustment: Cultural involvements and psychosocial functioning in Vietnamese youth. *Journal of Cross-Cultural Psychology*, 30, 5–31.

Nicholas, L. J., and Cooper, S. (2001). *The status of psychology in South Africa.* Pretoria: Report for the Foundation for Research Development.

Niiya, Y., Ellsworth, P. C., Yamaguchi, S. (2006). Amae in Japan and the United States: An exploration of a "culturally unique" emotion. *Emotion*, 6, 279–295.

Nisbett, R. E. (2003). *The geography of thought: How Asians and Westerners think differently . . . and why.* New York: The Free Press.

Nisbett, R. E. (2006). Cognition and perception: East and West. In Q. Jing, M. Rosenzweig, G. d'Ydewale, H. Zhang, H.-C. Chen and K. Zhang (eds.), *Progress in psychological science around the world: Social and applied issues* (pp. 209–228). Hove: Psychology Press.

Nisbett, R. E. (2007). A psychological perspective: Cultural psychology – past, present, and future. In S. Kitayama and D. Cohen (eds.), *Handbook of cultural psychology* (pp. 837–844). New York: Guildford Press.

Nisbett, R. E., and Cohen, D. (1996). *Culture of honor: The psychology of violence in the South.* Boulder, Colo.: Westview Press.

Nisbett, R., Peng, G., Choi, I., and Norenzayan, A. (2001). Culture and systems of thought: Holistic vs analytic cognition. *Psychological Review*, 108, 291–310.

Norasakkunkit, V., and Kalick, M.S. (2002). Culture, ethnicity, and emotional distress measures: The role of self-construal and self-enhancement. *Journal of Cross-Cultural Psychology*, 33, 56–70.

Norenzayan, A., Choi, I., and Peng, K. (2007). Perception and cognition. In S. Kitayama and Cohen, D. (eds.), *Handbook of cultural psychology* (pp. 569–594). New York: Guilford Press.

Norman, R. M., and Malla, A. K. (1993). Stressful life events and schizophrenia. I: A review of the research. *British Journal of Psychiatry*, 162, 161–166.

Norman, W. T. (1963). Toward an adequate taxonomy of personality: Replicated factor structure in peer nomination personality ratings. *Journal of Abnormal and Social Psychology*, 66, 574–583.

Nosaka, A., and Chasiotis, A. (2005). Exploring the variation in intergenerational relationships among Germans and Turkish immigrants: An evolutionary perspective on behaviour in a modern social setting. In E. Voland, A. Chasiotis and W. Schiefenhövel (eds.), *Grandmotherhood: The evolutionary significance of the second half of female life* (pp. 256–276). New Brunswick, N.J.: Rutgers University Press.

Nowak, M. A., and Sigmund, K. (1998). Evolution of indirect reciprocity by image scoring. *Nature*, 393, 573–577.

Nsamenang, A. B. (1992). *Human development in cultural context: A third world perspective*. Newbury Park, Calif.: Sage.

Nsamenang, A. B. (1995). Factors influencing the development of psychology in sub-Saharan Africa. *International Journal of Psychology*, 30, 729–738.

Nsamenang, A. B. (2001). Perspective africaine sur le développement social: Implications pour la recherche développementale interculturelle [African perspective on social development: Implications for developmental cross-cultural research]. In C. Sabatier and P. R. Dasen (eds.), *Contextes, cultures, développement et éducation: Autres enfants, autres écoles* [Contexts, cultures, development and education: Other children, other schools]. Paris: L'Harmattan.

Nsamenang, A. B., and Lo-Oh, J. L. (2010). Afrique noir. In M. H. Bornstein (ed.), *Handbook of cultural developmental science* (pp. 383–407). New York: Taylor & Francis.

Nsamenang, B. (ed.) (2008). Culture and human development. Special Issue, *International Journal of Psychology*, 43, 2, 73–113.

Nuechterlein, K. H., Dawson, M. E., Ventura, J., Gitlin, M., Subotnik, K. L., Snyder, K. S., Mintz, J., and Bartzokis, G. (1994). The vulnerability/stress model of schizophrenic relapse: A longitudinal study. *Acta Psychiatrica Scandinavica*, 89, 58–64.

Numbers, R. L. (2006). *The Creationists: From scientific creationism to intelligent design* (expanded edn.). Cambridge, Mass.: Harvard University Press.

Nursey-Bray, P. F. (1970). Négritude and the McLuhan thesis. *African Quarterly*, 10, 237–250.

Nusche, D. (2009). What works in migrant education? A review of evidence and policy options. *OECD Education Working Papers, No. 22*. Paris: OECD Publishing.

Oberg, K. (1960). Cultural shock: Adjustment to new cultural environments. *Practical Anthropology*, 7, 177–182.

Odling-Smee, F. J., Laland, K. N., and Feldman, M. W. (2003). *Niche construction: The neglected process in evolution*. Princeton: Princeton University Press.

Oetzel, J., and Ting-Toomey, S. (2003). Face concerns in interpersonal conflict: A cross-cultural empirical test of the face-negotiation theory. *Communications Research Reports*, 20, 105–155.

Oishi, S., and Roth, D. P. (2009). The role of self-reports in culture and personality research: It is too early to give up on self-reports. *Journal of Research in Personality*, 43, 107–109.

Okello, E. S., and Musisi, S. (2006). Depression as a clan illness (eByekika): An indigenous model of psychotic depression among the Baganda of Uganda. *World Cultural Psychiatric Research Review*, 1, 60–72.

Oliver, R. A. C. (1932). The musical talents of natives in East Africa. *British Journal of Psychology*, 22, 333–343.

Oliver, R. A. C. (1933). The adaptation of intelligence tests to tropical Africa, I, II. *Overseas Education*, 4, 186–191; 5, 8–13.

O'Mahony, M., and Ishii, R. (1986). A comparison of English and Japanese taste languages: Taste descriptive methodology, codability and the umami taste. *British Journal of Psychology*, 77, 161–174.

Onishi, K. H., and Baillargeon, R. (2005). Do 15-month-old infants understand false beliefs? *Science*, 308, 255–258.

Oppedal, B. (2006). Development and acculturation. In D. L. Sam and J. W. Berry (eds.), *The Cambridge handbook of acculturation psychology* (pp. 97–112). Cambridge: Cambridge University Press.

Osgood, C. E. (1977). Objective cross-national indicators of subjective culture. In Y. H. Poortinga (ed.), *Basic problems of cross-cultural psychology* (pp. 200–235). Lisse: Swets & Zeitlinger.

Osgood, C. E. (1979). From yang and yin to and or but in cross-cultural perspective. *International Journal of Psychology*, 14, 1–35.

Osgood, C. E. (1980). *Lectures on language performance*. New York: Springer Verlag.

Osgood, C. E., May, W. H., and Miron, M. S. (1975). *Cross-cultural universals of affective meaning*. Urbana, Ill.: University of Illinois Press.

Osgood, C. E., Suci, G. J., and Tannenbaum, P. H. (1957). *The measurement of meaning*. Urbana: University of Illinois Press.

Ouchi, W. G. (1981). *Theory Z: How American business can meet the Japanese challenge*. Reading, Mass.: Addison-Wesley.

Overman, E. S. (ed.) (1988). *Methodology and epistemology for social science: Selected papers of Donald T. Campbell*. Chicago: University of Chicago Press.

Oyama, S. (2000a). *Evolution's eye: A systems view of the biology–culture divide.* Durham, N.C.: Duke University Press.

Oyama, S. (2000b). *The ontogeny of information: Developmental systems and evolution* (2nd edn.). Durham, N.C.: Duke University Press.

Oyserman, D., and Lee, S. W. S. (2008). Does culture influence what and how we think? Effects of priming. *Psychological Bulletin*, 134, 311–342.

Oyserman, D., and Sorensen, N. (2009). Understanding cultural syndrome effects on what and how we think: A situated cognition model. In R. Wyer, C. Chiu and Y. Hong (eds.), *Understanding culture: Theory, research and application* (pp. 25–52). Hove: Psychology Press.

Oyserman, D., Coon, H. M., and Kemmelmeier, M. (2002). Rethinking individualism and collectivism: Evaluation of theoretical assumptions and meta-analyses. *Psychological Bulletin*, 128, 3–72.

Oyserman, D., Sorensen, N., Reber, R., and Chen, S. X. (2009). Connecting and separating mind-sets: Culture as situated cognition. *Journal of Personality and Social Psychology*, 97, 217–235.

Padilla, A. M. (ed.) (1995). *Hispanic psychology: Critical issues in theory and research.* Thousand Oaks, Calif.: Sage.

Pande, N., and Naidu, R. K. (1992). Anasakti and health: A study of non-attachment. *Psychology and Developing Societies*, 4, 91–104.

Pandey, J., Sinha, T. N., and Sinha, A. K. (eds.) (2010). *Dialogue for development: Essays in honour of J. B. P. Sinha.* New Delhi: Concept Publishers.

Panter-Brick, C., Clarke, S., Lomas, H., Pinder, M., and Lindsey, S. W. (2006). Culturally compelling strategies for behaviour change: A social ecology model and case study in malaria prevention. *Social Science & Medicine*, 62, 2810–2825.

Papoušek, H., and Papoušek, M. (1987). Intuitive parenting: A dialectic counterpart to the infant's integrative competence. In J. D. Osofsky (ed.), *Handbook of infant development* (pp. 669–720). New York: Wiley.

Papoušek, H., and Papoušek, M. (1991). Innate and cultural guidance of infants' integrative competencies: China, the United States, and Germany. In M. H. Bornstein (ed.), *Cultural approaches to parenting* (pp. 23–44). Hillsdale, N.J.: Erlbaum.

Paramei, G. V. (2005). Singing the Russian blues: An argument for culturally basic color terms. *Cross-Cultural Research*, 39, 10–34.

Paranjpe, A. C. (1984). *Theoretical psychology: The meeting of East and West.* New York: Plenum.

Paranjpe, A. C. (1998). *Self and identity in modern psychology and Indian thought.* New York: Plenum.

Park, N., Peterson, C., and Seligman, M. E. P. (2004). Strengths of character and well-being. *Journal of Social and Clinical Psychology*, 23, 603–619.

Park, N., Peterson, C., and Seligman, M. E. P. (2006). Character strengths in fifty-four nations and the fifty US states. *The Journal of Positive Psychology*, 1, 118–129.

Pascale, R. T. (1978). Communication and decision making across cultures: Japanese and American comparisons. *Administrative Science Quarterly*, 23, 91–110.

Pavot, W., and Diener, E. (1993). Review of the Satisfaction with Life Scale. *Psychological Assessment*, 5, 1964–1972.

Pawlik, K., and d'Ydewalle, G. (eds.) (2006). *Psychological concepts: An international and historical perspective*. Hove: Psychology Press.

Pawlik, K., and Rosenzweig, M. (eds.) (2000). *International handbook of psychology*. London: Sage.

Peabody, D. (1967). Trait inferences: Evaluative and descriptive aspects. *Journal of Personality and Social Psychology Monographs*, 7 (Whole No. 644).

Peabody, D. (1985). *National characteristics*. Cambridge: Cambridge University Press.

Peccei, J. S. (2005). Menopause: Adaptation and epiphenomenon. In E. Voland, A. Chasiotis and W. Schiefenhövel (eds.), *Grandmotherhood: The evolutionary significance of the second half of female life* (pp. 38–58). New Brunswick, N.J.: Rutgers University Press.

Peeters, H. (1988). Vijf eeuwen gezin in Nederland [Five centuries of nuclear family in the Netherlands]. In H. Peeters, L. Dresen-Coenders and T. Brandenberg (eds.), *Vijf eeuwen gezinsleven* [Five centuries of family life] (pp. 11–30). Nijmegen: SUN.

Pellicano, E. (2007). Links between theory of mind and executive function in young children with autism: Clues to developmental primacy. *Developmental Psychology*, 43, 974–990.

Pelto, P. (1968). The difference between "tight" and "loose" societies. *Transaction*, April, 37–40.

Pelto, P. J., and Pelto, G. H. (1981). *Anthropological research*. Cambridge: Cambridge University Press.

Peng, K., and Nisbett, R. (1999). Culture, dialectics and reasoning about contradiction. *American Psychologist*, 54, 741–754.

Peng, K., Nisbett, R., and Wong, N. (1997). Validity problems comparing values across cultures, and possible solutions. *Psychological Methods*, 2, 329–344.

Penn, D. C., Holyak, K. J., and Povinelli, D. J. (2008). Darwin's mistake: Explaining the discontinuity between human and nonhuman minds. *Behavioral and Brain Sciences*, 31, 109–178.

Pe-Pua, R. (2006). From decolonising psychology to the development of a cross-indigenous perspective in methodology: The Philippine experience. In U. Kim, K.-S. Yang and K.-K. Hwang (eds.), *Indigenous and cultural psychology: Understanding people in context* (pp. 109–137). New York: Springer.

Petersen, A. C. (1988). Adolescent development. *Annual Review of Psychology*, 39, 583–607.

Petersen, N. S., and Novick, M. R. (1976). An evaluation of some models of culture-fair selection. *Journal of Educational Measurement*, 13, 3–29.

Peterson, B. S., Warner, V., Bansal, R., Zhu, H., Hao, X., Liu, J., Durkin, K., Adams, P. B., Wickramaratne, P., and Weissman, M. M. (2009). Cortical thinning in persons at increased familial risk for major depression. *Proceedings of the National Academy of Sciences*, 106, 6273–6278.

Peterson, C., and Seligman, M. E. P. (2004). *Character strengths and virtues: A handbook and classification*. Washington, DC: American Psychological Association.

Peterson, C., Park, N., and Seligman, M. E. P. (2005a). Assessment of character strengths. In G. P. Koocher, J. C. Norcross and S. S. Hill III (eds.), *Psychologists' desk reference* (2nd edn., pp. 93–98). New York: Oxford University Press.

Peterson, C., Park, N., and Seligman, M. E. P. (2005b). Orientations to happiness and life satisfaction: The full life versus the empty life. *Journal of Happiness Studies*, 6, 25–41.

Peterson, M. F., and Ruiz-Quintanilla, S. A. (2003). Cultural socialization as a source of intrinsic work motivation. *Group & Organization Management*, 28, 188–216.

Pettigrew, T. (2006). A two-level approach to anti-immigrant prejudice and discrimination. In R. Mahalingam (ed.), *Cultural psychology of immigrants* (pp. 95–112). Mahwah, N.J.: Erlbaum.

Pettigrew, T. (2008). Future directions for intergroup contact theory and research. *International Journal of Intercultural Relations*, 32, 187–189.

Pettigrew, T. (2009). Probing the complexity of intergroup prejudice. *International Journal of Psychology*, 44, 40–42.

Pettigrew, T., and Tropp, L. (2000). Does intergroup contact reduce prejudice? Recent meta-analytic findings. In S. Oskamp (ed.), *Reducing prejudice and discrimination* (pp. 93–114). Mahwah, N.J.: Erlbaum.

Pettigrew, T., and Tropp, L. (2006a). Allport's intergroup contact hypothesis. In J. Dovidio, P. Glick and A. Rudman (eds.), *On the nature of prejudice: Fifty years after Allport* (pp. 262–277). Oxford: Blackwell.

Pettigrew, T., and Tropp, L. (2006b). A meta-analytic test of intergroup contact theory. *Journal of Personality and Social Psychology*, 90, 751–783.

Pettigrew, T., and Tropp, L. (2008). How does intergroup contact reduce prejudice? Meta-analytic tests of three mediators. *European Journal of Social Psychology*, 38, 922–934.

Pettigrew, T., Christ, O., Wagner, U., and Stellmacher, J. (2007). Direct and indirect intergroup contact effects on prejudice: A normative interpretation. *International Journal of Intercultural Relations*, 31, 411–425.

Pfeiffer, W. (1982). Cultural-bound syndromes. In I. Al-Issa (ed.), *Culture and psychopathology*. Baltimore: University Park Press.

Phalet, K., and Andriessen, I. (2003). Acculturation and educational attainment: Towards a contextual approach of minority school achievement. In L. Hagendoorn, J. Veenman and W. Vollebergh (eds.), *Integrating immigrants in the Netherlands* (pp. 145–172). Aldershot: Ashgate.

Phalet, K., and Schönpflug, U. (2001). Intergenerational transmission of collectivism and achievement values in two acculturation contexts: The case of Turkish families in Germany and Turkish and Moroccan families in the Netherlands. *Journal of Cross-Cultural Psychology*, 32, 189–201.

Pham, T. B., and Harris, R. J. (2001). Acculturation strategies among Vietnamese-Americans. *International Journal of Intercultural Relations*, 25, 279–300.

Pheysey, D. C. (1993). *Organizational cultures: Types and transformations.* London: Routledge.

Philipsen, G. (1997). A theory of speech codes. In G. Philipsen and T. L. Albrecht (eds.), *Developing communication theories* (pp. 119–156). Albany: State University of New York Press.

Philipsen, G., Coutu, L. M., and Covarrubias, P. (2005). Speech code theory: Restatement, revisions and response to criticisms. In W. B. Gudykunst (ed.), *Theorizing about intercultural communication* (pp. 55–68). Thousand Oaks, Calif.: Sage.

Phinney, J. S. (1989). Stages of ethnic identity development in minority group adolescents. *The Journal of Early Adolescence*, 9, 34–49.

Phinney, J. S. (1990). Ethnic identity in adolescents and adults: A review of research. *Psychological Bulletin*, 108, 499–514.

Phinney, J. S. (1992). The Multi-group Ethnic Identity Measure: A new scale for use with diverse groups. *Journal of Adolescent Research*, 7, 156–176.

Phinney, J. S. (1993). A three-stage model of ethnic identity development. In M. Bernal and G. Knight (eds.), *Ethnic identity: Formation and transmission among Hispanics and other minorities* (pp. 61–79). Albany: State University of New York Press.

Phinney, J. S. (2006). Acculturation is not an independent variable: Approaches to studying acculturation as a complex process. In M. H. Bornstein and L. R. Cote (eds.), *Acculturation and parent–child relationships: Measurement and development* (pp. 79–95). Mahwah, N.J.: Erlbaum.

Phinney, J. S., and Chavira, V. (1992). Ethnic identity and self-esteem: An exploratory longitudinal study. *Journal of Adolescence*, 15, 271–281.

Phinney, J. S., and Devich-Navarro, M. (1997). Variations in bicultural identification among African American and Mexican American adolescents. *Journal of Research on Adolescence*, 7, 3–32.

Phinney, J. S., and Ong, A. (2007). Conceptualization of ethnic identity: Current status and future directions. *Journal of Counselling Psychology*, 54, 271–281.

Phinney, J. S., and Vedder, P. (2006). Family relationship values of adolescents and parents: Intergenerational discrepancies and adaptation, In J. W. Berry, J. S. Phinney, D. L. Sam and P. Vedder (eds.), *Immigrant youth in cultural transitions: Acculturation, identity, and adaptation across national contexts* (pp. 167–184). Mahwah, N.J.: Erlbaum.

Phinney, J. S., Cantu, C., and Kurtz, D. (1997). Ethnic and American identity as predictors of self-esteem among African American, Latino, and White adolescents. *Journal of Youth and Adolescence*, 26, 165–185.

Phinney, J. S., Jacoby, B., and Silva, C. (2007). Positive intergroup attitudes: The role of ethnic identity. *International Journal of Behavioral Development*, 31, 478–490.

Phinney, J. S., Lochner, B.T., and Murphy, R. (1990). Ethnic identity development and psychological adjustment in adolescence. In A. R. Stiffman and L. E. Davis (eds.),

Ethnic issues in adolescent mental health (pp. 53–72). Thousand Oaks, Calif.: Sage.

Piaget, J. (1970a). *The science of education and the psychology of the child.* New York: Grossman.

Piaget, J. (1970b). Piaget's Theory. In P. H. Mussen (ed.), *Carmichael's manual of child psychology* (3rd edn., pp. 703–732). New York: Wiley.

Piaget, J. (1975). La psychogenèse des connaissances et sa signification epistémologique [Psychogenesis of knowledge and its epistemological meaning]. In M. Piatelli-Palmarini (ed.), *Théories du langage, théories de l'apprentissage* [Theories of language, theories of teaching]. Paris: Editions du Seuil.

Pick, S., and Sirkin, J. (2010). *Breaking the cycle of poverty: The human basis for sustainable development.* New York: Oxford University Press.

Pick, S., Givaudan, M., and Poortinga, Y. H. (2003). Sexuality and life skills education: A multistrategy intervention in Mexico. *American Psychologist*, 58, 230–234.

Pick, S., Poortinga, Y. H., and Givaudan, M. (2003). Integrating intervention theory and strategy in culture-sensitive health promotion programs. *Professional Psychology: Research and Practice*, 34, 422–429.

Pick, S., Givaudan, M., Sirkin, J., and Ortega, I. (2007). Communication as a protective factor: Evaluation of a life skills HIV/AIDS prevention program for Mexican elementary-school students. *AIDS Education and Prevention*, 19, 408–421.

Piedmont, R. L., and Leach, M. M. (2002). Cross-cultural generalizability of the Spiritual Transcendence Scale in India: Spirituality as a universal aspect of human experience. *American Behavioral Scientist*, 45, 1888–1901.

Pika, S., Nikolada, E., and Marentette, P. (2009). How to order a beer: Cultural differences in the use of conventional gestures for numbers. *Journal of Cross-Cultural Psychology*, 40, 70–80.

Pike, K. L. (1967). *Language in relation to a unified theory of the structure of human behavior.* The Hague: Mouton.

Pimentel, D., Cooperstein, S., Randell, H., Filiberto, D., Sorrentino, S., Kaye, B., Nicklin, C., Yagi, J., Brian, J., O'Hern, J., Habas, A., and Weinstein, C. (2007). Ecology of increasing diseases: Population growth and environmental degradation. *Human Ecology*, 35, 653–668.

Pinker, S., and Bloom, P. (1990). Natural language and natural selection. *Behavioral and Brain Science*, 13, 707–726.

Piot, P., Bartos, M., Larson, H., Zewdie, D., and Mane, P. (2008). Coming to terms with complexity: A call to action for HIV prevention. *The Lancet*, 372, 845–859.

Playford, K., and Safdar, S. (2007). Various conceptualizations of acculturation and the prediction of international students' adaptations. In A. Chybicka and M. Kazmierczak (eds.), *Appreciating diversity: Cultural and gender issues* (pp. 37–66). Cracow: Impuls.

Plomin, R., and De Fries, J. (1998). The genetics of cognitive abilities and disabilities. *Scientific American*, May, 62–69.

Plotkin, H. C., and Odling-Smee, F. J. (1981). A multiple-level model of evolution and its implications for sociobiology. *Behavioral and Brain Sciences*, 4, 225–268.

Pollack, R. H. (1963). Contour detectability thresholds as a function of chronological age. *Perceptual and Motor Skills*, 17, 411–417.

Pollack, R. H., and Silvar, S. D. (1967). Magnitude of the Müller–Lyer illusion in children as a function of pigmentation of the Fundus oculi. *Psychonomic Science*, 8, 83–84.

Poortinga, Y. H. (1971). Cross-cultural comparison of maximum performance tests: Some methodological aspects and some experiments. *Psychologia Africana*, Monograph Supplement, No. 6.

Poortinga, Y. H. (1972). A comparison of African and European students in simple auditory and visual tasks. In L. J. Cronbach and P. J. D. Drenth (eds.), *Mental tests and cultural adaptation* (pp. 349–354). The Hague: Mouton.

Poortinga, Y. H. (1985). Empirical evidence of bias in choice reaction time experiments. *Behavioral and Brain Sciences*, 8, 236–237.

Poortinga, Y. H. (1989). Equivalence of cross-cultural data: An overview of basic issues. *International Journal of Psychology*, 24, 737–756.

Poortinga, Y. H. (1992). Towards a conceptualization of culture for psychology. In S. Iwawaki, Y. Kashima and K. Leung (eds.), *Innovations in cross-cultural psychology* (pp. 3–17). Lisse: Swets & Zeitlinger.

Poortinga, Y. H. (1995). The use of tests across cultures. In T. Oakland and R. K. Hambleton (eds.), *International perspectives on academic assessment* (pp. 187–206). Boston: Kluwer.

Poortinga, Y. H. (1997). Towards convergence? In J. W. Berry, Y. H. Poortinga and J. Pandey (eds.), *Handbook of cross-cultural psychology, Vol. I, Theory and Method* (2nd edn., pp. 347–387). Boston: Allyn & Bacon.

Poortinga, Y. H. (1999). Do differences in behaviour imply a need for different psychologies? *Applied Psychology*, 48, 419–432.

Poortinga, Y. H. (2003). Coherence of culture and generalizability of data: Two questionable assumptions in cross-cultural psychology. In J. Berman and J. Berman (eds.), *Cross-cultural differences in perspectives on the self*, Vol. 49 of the Nebraska Symposium on Motivation (pp. 257–305). Lincoln, Nebr.: University of Nebraska Press.

Poortinga, Y. H. (2004). Is cultural imposition less of an issue with indigenous psychologies? In B. Setiadi, A. Supratiknya, W. Lonner and Y. Poortinga (eds.), *Ongoing themes on psychology and culture* (pp. 187–199). Yogyakarta: Kanisius.

Poortinga, Y. H. (2009). Adapting intervention programs for use across societies: Between valid transfer and cultural imposition. In S. Bekman and A. Aksu-Koc (eds.), *Perspectives on development, family and culture* (pp. 301–313). Cambridge: Cambridge University Press.

Poortinga, Y. H., and Foden, B. I. M. (1975). A comparative study of curiosity in black and white South African students. *Psychologia Africana*, Monograph Supplement, No. 8.

Poortinga, Y. H., and Soudijn, K. (2002). Behavior–culture relationships and ontogenetic development. In H. Keller, Y. H. Poortinga and A. Schölmerich (eds.), *Biology, culture and development: Integrating diverse perspectives* (pp. 320–340). Cambridge: Cambridge University Press.

Poortinga, Y. H., and Van de Vijver, F. J. R. (1987). Explaining cross-cultural differences: Bias analysis and beyond. *Journal of Cross-Cultural Psychology*, 18, 259–282.

Poortinga, Y. H., and Van de Vijver, F. J. R. (1997). Is there no cross-cultural evidence in colour categories of psychological laws, only of cultural rules? *Behavioral and Brain Sciences*, 20, 205–206.

Poortinga, Y. H., and Van de Vijver, F. J. R. (2004). Cultures and cognition: Performance differences and invariant structures. In R. Sternberg and E. Grigorenko (eds.), *Culture and competence: Contexts of life success* (pp. 139–162). Washington, DC: APA Press.

Poortinga, Y. H., and Van Hemert, D. A. (2001). Personality and culture: Demarcating between the common and the unique. *Journal of Personality*, 69, 1033–1060.

Poortinga, Y. H., Schoots, N. H., and Van de Koppel, J. M. H. (1993). The understanding of Chinese and Kurdish emblematic gestures by Dutch subjects. *International Journal of Psychology*, 28, 31–44.

Poortinga, Y. H., Van de Vijver, F. J. R., and Van Hemert, D. A. (2002). Cross-cultural equivalence of the Big Five: A tentative interpretation of the evidence. In R. R. McCrae and J. Allik (eds.), *The five-factor model of personality across cultures* (pp. 271–293). New York: Kluwer.

Popper, K. R. (1959). *The logic of scientific discovery*. New York: Basic Books.

Popper, K. R. (1963). *Conjectures and refutations*. London: Routledge & Kegan Paul.

Porteus, S. D. (1937). *Primitive intelligence and environment*. New York: Macmillan.

Posner, M. I. (1978). *Chronometric explorations of mind*. Hillsdale, N.J.: Erlbaum.

Post, R. H. (1962). Population differences in red and green color vision deficiency: A review, and a query on selection relaxation. *Eugenics Quarterly*, 9, 131–146.

Post, R. H. (1971). Possible cases of relaxed selection in civilized populations. *Human Genetics*, 13, 253–284.

Powell, L. H., Shahabi, L., and Thoresen, C. (2003). Religion and spirituality: Links to physical health. *American Psychologist*, 58, 36–52.

Premack, D., and Woodruff, G. (1978). Does a chimpanzee have a theory of mind? *Behavioral and Brain Sciences*, 4, 515–526.

Prince, M., Patel, M., Saxena, S., Maj, M., Maselko, J., Phillips, M. R., and Rahman, A. (2007). No health without mental health. *The Lancet*, 370, 859–877.

Prince, R. (1980). Variations in psychotherapeutic procedures. In H. C. Triandis and J. Draguns (eds.), *Handbook of cross-cultural psychology, Vol. VI, Psychopathology* (pp. 291–349). Boston: Allyn & Bacon.

Protacio-De Castro, E. (2006). The case of the Philippines. Special Issue on Indigenous Psychologies, *International Journal of Psychology*, 41, 252–254.

Przeworski, A., and Teune, H. (1970). *The logic of comparative social inquiry*. New York: Wiley.

Pugh, D. S., and Hinings, C. R. (eds.) (1976). *Organizational structure: Extensions and replications*. London: Saxon House.

Pullum, G. K. (1989). The great Eskimo vocabulary hoax. *Natural Language and Linguistic Theory*, 7, 275–281.

Qie, F., and Xue, L. (2003). Application of Naikan therapy in China. *Psychiatria et Neurology Japonica*, 105, 982–987.

Raihani, N. J., Grutter, A. S., and Bshary, R. (2010). Punishers Benefit From Third-Party Punishment in Fish. *Science*, 327, 171.

Ramadan, A., and Gielen, U. (eds.) (1998). *Psychology in the Arab countries*. Cairo: Menoufla Press.

Ramírez-Esparza, N., Gosling, S., Benet-Martínez, V., Potter, J., and Pennebaker, J. (2006). Do bilinguals have two personalities? A special case of cultural frame-switching. *Journal of Research in Personality*, 40, 99–120.

Rao, K. R., Paranjpe, A., and Dalal, A. (eds.) (2008). *Handbook of Indian psychology*. New Delhi: Cambridge University Press.

Ratner, C. (2002). *Cultural psychology: Theory and method*. New York: Kluwer.

Raudenbush, S. W., and Bryk, A. S. (2002). *Hierarchical linear models* (2nd edn.). Newbury Park, Calif.: Sage.

Ray, V. F. (1952). Techniques and problems in the study of human color perception. *South Western Journal of Anthropology*, 8, 251–259.

Raybeck, D. (2005). The case for complementarities. *Cross-Cultural Research*, 39, 235–251.

Rayner, K., Castelhano, M., and Yang, J. (2009). Eye movements when looking at unusual/weird scenes: Are there cultural differences? *Journal of Experimental Psychology Learning, Memory, and Cognition*, 35, 254–259.

Realo, A., Allik, J., Lönnquiest, J.-E., Verkasalo, M., Kwialowska, A., Kööts, L., Kütt, M., Barkauskiene, R., Laurinavicius, A., Karpinski, K., Kolyshko, A., Sebre, S., and Renge, V. (2009). Mechanisms of the national character stereotype: How people in six neighbouring countries of Russia describe themselves and the typical Russian. *European Journal of Personality*, 23, 229–249.

Rebelsky, F. (1967). Infancy in two cultures. *Nederlands Tijdschrift voor de Psychologie*, 22, 379–387.

Redfield, R., Linton, R., and Herskovits, M. J. (1936). Memorandum on the study of acculturation. *American Anthropologist*, 38, 149–152.

Redmond, M. V. (2000). Cultural distance as a mediating factor between stress and intercultural communication competence. *International Journal of Intercultural Relations*, 24, 151–159.

Reese, E., Haden, C. A., and Fivush, R. (1993). Mother–child conversations about the past: Relationships of style and memory over time. *Cognitive Development*, 8, 403–430.

Reichard, U. H. (2003). Monogamy: Past and present. In U. H. Reichard and C. Boesch (eds.), *Monogamy: Mating strategies and partnerships in birds, humans, and other mammals* (pp. 3–25). Cambridge: Cambridge University Press.

Reichardt, C. S., and Rallis, S. F. (1994). Qualitative and quantitative inquiries are not incompatible: A call for a new partnership. In C. S. Reichardt and S. F. Rallis (eds.), *The qualitative-quantitative debate: New perspectives* (pp. 85–91). San Francisco: Jossey-Bass.

Relethford, J. H. (1997). *The human species: An introduction to biological anthropology* (3rd edn.). Mountain View, Calif.: Mayfield.

Rentfrow, P. J., Gosling, S. D., and Potter, J. (2008). A theory of the emergence, persistence, and expression of geographic variation in personality characteristics. *Perspectives on Psychological Science*, 3, 339–369.

Reuning, H., and Wortley, W. (1973). Psychological studies of the Bushmen. *Psychologia Africana*, Monograph Supplement, No. 7.

Reynolds, V., and Tanner, R. (1995). *The socioecology of religion*. New York: Oxford University Press.

Reynolds, V., Falger, V., and Vine, I. (eds.) (1987). *The sociobiology of ethnocentrism*. London: Croom Helm.

Rhee, E., Uleman, J. S., and Lee, H. K. (1996). Variations in collectivism and individualism by ingroup and culture: Confirmatory factor analyses. *Journal of Personality and Social Psychology*, 71, 1037–1054.

Rhee, E., Uleman, J., Hoon, L., and Roman, R. (1995). Spontaneous self-descriptions and ethnic identities in individualistic and collectivistic cultures. *Journal of Personality and Social Psychology*, 69, 142–152.

Richerson, P. J., and Boyd, R. (2005). *Not by genes alone: How culture transformed human evolution*. Chicago: The University of Chicago Press.

Riek, B., Mania, E., and Gaertner, S. (2006). Intergroup threat and outgroup attitudes: A meta-analytic review. *Personality and Social Psychology Review*, 10, 336–353.

Rimé, B., and Giovanni, D. (1986). The physiological patterns of reported emotional states. In K. R. Scherer, H. G. Wallbott and A. B. Summerfield (eds.), *Experiencing emotion: A cross-cultural study* (pp. 84–97). Cambridge: Cambridge University Press.

Rist, G., and Sabelli, F. (eds.) (1986). *Il était une fois le développement* [Once upon a time there was development]. Lausanne: Editions d'en Bas.

Rivers, W. H. R. (1901). Vision. In *Physiology and psychology, Part I*. Reports of the Cambridge Anthropological Expedition to Torres Straits (Vol. II). Cambridge: Cambridge University Press.

Rivers, W. H. R. (1924). *Social organization*. London: Kegan Paul, Trench, Trubner & Co.

Robbins, R. (2006). *Cultural anthropology: A problem-based approach*. Belmont, Calif.: Thomson.

Roberson, D., Davies, I., and Davidoff, J. (2000). Color categories are not universal: Replications and new evidence from a stone-age culture. *Journal of Experimental Psychology: General*, 129, 369–398.

Roberson, D., Davidoff, J., Davies, I. R. L., and Shapiro, L. R. (2004). The development of color categories in two languages: A longitudinal study. *Journal of Experimental Psychology: General*, 133, 554–571.

Roberts, G., and Sherratt, T. N. (1998). Development of cooperative relationships through increasing investment. *Nature*, 394, 175–179.

Roberts, L., and Enserink, M. (2007). Malaria: Did they really say . . . eradication? *Science*, 318, 1544–1545.

Rogoff, B. (1990). *Apprenticeship in thinking: Cognitive development in social context*. New York: Oxford University Press.

Rogoff, B. (2003). *The cultural nature of human development*. Oxford: Oxford University Press.

Rogoff, B., and Gauvain, M. (1984). The cognitive consequences of specific experiences: Weaving vs. schooling among the Navajo. *Journal of Cross-Cultural Psychology*, 15, 453–475.

Rogoff, B., Mistry, J., Göncü, A., and Mosier, C. (1993). Guided participation in cultural activity by toddlers and caregivers. *Monographs of the Society for Research in Child Development*, 58, 8 (No. 236).

Rokeach, M. (1973). *The nature of human values*. New York: The Free Press.

Romney, A., and D'Andrade, R. (1964). Cognitive aspects of English kin terms. *American Anthropologist*, 66, 146–170.

Romney, A. K., and Moore, C. (1998). Toward a theory of culture as shared cognitive structures. *Ethos*, 26, 314–337.

Ronen, S. (1986). *Comparative and multinational management*. New York: Wiley.

Rosaldo, M. (1980). *Knowledge and passion: Ilongot notions of self and social life*. Cambridge: Cambridge University Press.

Rosch (Heider), E. (1972). Universals in color naming and memory. *Journal of Experimental Psychology*, 93, 10–20.

Rosch (Heider), E. (1977). Human categorization. In N. Warren (ed.), *Studies in cross-cultural psychology*, Vol. 1 (pp. 1–49). London: Academic Press.

Rosch, E. (1978). Principles of categorization. In E. Rosch and B. B. Lloyd (eds.), *Cognition and categorization* (pp. 27–48). Hillsdale, N.J.: Erlbaum.

Rosch, E., and Mervis, C. B. (1975). Family resemblance: Studies in the internal structure of categories. *Cognitive Psychology*, 7, 573–605.

Roseman, I. J., Wiest, C., and Swartz, T. S. (1994). Phenomenology, behaviors, and goals differentiate discrete emotions. *Journal of Personality and Social Psychology*, 67, 206–221.

Rosenberger, N. R. (ed.) (1994). *Japanese sense of self*. Cambridge: Cambridge University Press.

Rosenzweig, M. R., Holtzman, W., Sabourin, M., and Belanger, D. (2000). *History of the International Union of Psychological Science (IUPsyS)*. Hove: Psychology Press.

Ross, C. A., and Margolis, R. L. (2009). Schizophrenia: A point of disruption. *Nature*, 458, 976–977.

Ross, N. (2004). *Culture and cognition: Implications for theory and method*. Thousand Oaks, Calif.: Sage.

Rothbaum, F., Kakinuma, M., Nagaoka, R., and Azuma, H. (2007). Attachment and AMAE: Parent–child closeness in the United States and Japan. *Journal of Cross-Cultural Psychology*, 38, 465–486.

Rotter, J. B. (1954). *Social learning and clinical psychology.* Englewood Cliffs, N.J.: Prentice Hall.

Rotter, J. B. (1966). *Generalized expectancies for internal versus external control of reinforcement.* Psychological Monographs, 80 (Whole no. 609).

Royal Anthropological Institute (1951). *Notes and queries on anthropology* (6th edn.). London: Routledge.

Rozin, P. (2007). Food and eating. In S. Kitayama and D. Cohen (eds.), *Handbook of cultural psychology* (pp. 391–416). New York: Guildford Press.

Rubin, D. C., Wetzler, S. E., and Nebes, R. D. (1986). Autobiographical memory across the adult lifespan. In D. C. Rubin (ed.), *Autobiographical memory* (pp. 202–221). Cambridge: Cambridge University Press.

Rudmin, F. W. (2003). Critical history of the acculturation psychology of assimilation, separation, integration and marginalization. *Review of General Psychology*, 7, 3–37.

Rudmin, F. W. (2009). Constructs, measurements and models of acculturation and acculturative stress. *International Journal of Intercultural Relations*, 33, 106–123.

Rudmin, F. W., and Ahmadzadeh, V. (2001). Psychometric critique of acculturation psychology: The case of Iranian migrants in Norway. *Scandinavian Journal of Psychology*, 42, 41–56.

Ruffell Smith, H. (1975). Some problems of voice communication for international aviation. In A. Chapanis (ed.), *Ethnic variables in human factors engineering* (pp. 225–230). Baltimore: Johns Hopkins University Press.

Ruffman, T., Perner, J., Naito, M., Parkin, L., and Clements, W. (1998). Older (but not younger) siblings facilitate false belief understanding. *Developmental Psychology*, 34, 161–174.

Rushton, J. P. (2000). *Race, evolution and behavior.* Port Huron: Charles Darwin Research Institute.

Russell, J. A. (1980). A circumplex model of affect. *Journal of Personality and Social Psychology*, 39, 1161–1178.

Russell, J. A. (1983). Pancultural aspects of the human conceptual organization of emotions. *Journal of Personality and Social Psychology*, 45, 1281–1288.

Russell, J. A. (1991). Culture and the categorisation of emotions. *Psychological Bulletin*, 110, 426–450.

Russell, J. A. (1994). Is there universal recognition of emotion from facial expression? A review of cross-cultural studies. *Psychological Bulletin*, 115, 102–141.

Russell, J. A. (1995). Facial expressions of emotion: What lies beyond minimal universality? *Psychological Bulletin*, 118, 379–391.

Russell, J. A., Lewicka, M., and Niit, T. (1989). A cross-cultural study of a circumplex model of affect, *Journal of Personality and Social Psychology*, 57, 848–856.

Russell, P. A., Deregowski, J. B., and Kinnear, P. R. (1997). Perception and aesthetics. In J. W. Berry, P. R. Dasen and T. S. Saraswathi (eds.), *Handbook of cross-cultural psychology, Vol. II, Basic processes and human development* (2nd edn., pp. 107–142). Boston: Allyn & Bacon.

Russon, A. E. (2002). Comparative developmental perspectives on culture: The great apes. In H. Keller, Y. H. Poortinga and A. Schölmerich (eds.), *Biology, culture and development: Integrating diverse perspectives* (pp. 30–56). Cambridge: Cambridge University Press.

Ruzgis, P. (1994). Culture and intelligence: Cross-cultural investigation of implicit theories of intelligence. *Voprosy-Psikhologii*, 1, 142–146.

Ryder, A., Alden, L., and Paulhus, D. (2000). Is acculturation undimensional or bidimensional? A head-to-head comparison in the prediction of personality, self-identity and adjustment. *Journal of Personality and Social Psychology*, 79, 49–65.

Sabatier, C. (1999). Adolescents issus de l'immigration: les clichés à l'épreuve des faits [Adolescents of immigrant origin: Cliches and facts]. In B. Bril, P. R. Dasen, C. Sabatier and B. Krewer (eds.), *Propos sur l'enfant et l'adolescent: quels enfants pour quelles cultures?* [Remarks on children and adolescents: Which children for which cultures?] (pp. 357–382). Paris: L'Harmattan.

Sabatier, C., and Berry, J. W. (2008). The role of family acculturation, parental style, and perceived discrimination in the adaptation of second-generation immigrant youth in France and Canada. *European Journal of Developmental Psychology*, 5, 159–185.

Sabbagh, M. A., Xu, F., Carlson, S. M., Moses, S. J., and Lee, K. (2006). The development of executive functioning and theory of mind: A comparison of Chinese and U.S. preschoolers. *Psychological Science*, 17, 74–81.

Sabini, J., and Silver, M. (2005). Why emotion names and experiences don't neatly pair. *Psychological Inquiry*, 16, 1–10.

Safdar, S., Lewis, J. R., and Daneshpour, M. (2006). Social axioms in Iran and Canada: Intercultural contact, coping and adjustment. *Asian Journal of Social Psychology*, 9, 123–131.

Sagie, A., and Aycan, Z. (2003). A cross-cultural analysis of participative decision-making in organizations. *Human Relations*, 56, 453–473.

Saha, S., Welham, J., Chat, D., and McGrath, J. (2006). Incidence of schizophrenia does not vary with economic status of the country: Evidence from a systematic review. *Social Psychiatry and Psychiatric Epidemiology*, 4, 338–340.

Sahlins, M. (1976). Colors and cultures. *Semiotica*, 16, 1–22.

Sahlins, M. (1977). *The use and abuse of biology*. London: Tavistock Publications.

Sahlins, M., and Service, E. (eds.) (1960). *Evolution and culture*. Ann Arbor, Mich.: University of Michigan Press.

Sam, D. L. (1995). Acculturation attitudes among young immigrants as a function of perceived parental attitudes towards cultural change. *Journal of Early Adolescence*, 15, 238–258.

Sam, D. L. (2002). Psychometric properties of acculturation strategies: A structural equation modelling perspective. Symposium paper presented at the XVIth International Congress of the International Association for Cross-cultural Psychology. Indonesia, July 15–19.

Sam, D. L. (2006a). Adaptation of children and adolescents with immigrant background: Acculturation or development? In M. H. Bornstein and L. Cote (eds.), *Acculturation and parent–child relationship: Measurement and development* (pp. 97–111). Mahwah, N.J.: Erlbaum.

Sam, D. L. (2006b). Acculturation and health. In D. L. Sam and J. W. Berry (eds.), *The Cambridge handbook of acculturation psychology* (pp. 452–468). Cambridge: Cambridge University Press.

Sam, D. L., Amponsah, B., and Hetland, J. (2008). Values of children among sub-Saharan African women: The case of Ghanaian women. *Journal of Psychology in Africa*, 18, 521–530.

Sam, D. L., and Berry, J. W. (eds). (2006). *The Cambridge handbook of acculturation psychology*. Cambridge: Cambridge University Press.

Sam, D. L., and Berry, J. W. (2010). Acculturation: When individuals and groups of different cultural backgrounds meet. *Perspectives on Psychological Science*, 5, 472–481.

Sam, D. L., Peltzer, K., and Mayer, B. (2005). The changing values of children and preferences regarding family size in South Africa. *Applied Psychology: An International Review*, 54, 355–377.

Sam, D. L., Vedder, P., Ward, C., and Horenczyk, G. (2006). Psychological and sociocultural adaptation of immigrant youth. In J. W. Berry, J. S. Phinney, D. L. Sam and P. Vedder (eds.), *Immigrant youth in cultural transitions: Acculturation, identity, and adaptation across national contexts* (pp. 117–141). Mahwah, N.J.: Erlbaum.

Sam, D. L., Vedder, P., Liebkind, K., Neto, F., and Virta, E. (2008). Migration, acculturation and the paradox of adaptation in Europe. *European Journal of Developmental Psychology*, 5, 138–158.

Sanchez, J. I., and Fernandez, D. M. (1993). Acculturative stress among Hispanics: A bidimensional model of ethnic identification. *Journal of Applied Social Psychology*, 23, 654–668.

Sanchez-Runde, C., Lee, S. M., and Steers, R. M. (2009). Cultural drivers of work behavior: Personal values, motivation and job attitudes. In R. S. Bhagat and R. M. Steers (eds.), *The Cambridge handbook of culture, organizations, and work* (pp. 305–333). Cambridge: Cambridge University Press.

Santa, I. L., and Baker, L. (1975). Linguistic influences on visual learning. *Memory and Cognition*, 3, 445–450.

Sarantakos, S. (2005). *Social research* (3rd edn.). Basingstoke: Palgrave Macmillan.

Saraswathi, T. S. (1999). Adult–child continuity in India: Is adolescence a myth or an emerging reality? In T. S. Saraswathi (ed.), *Culture, socialization and human development: Theory, research and applications in India* (pp. 213–232). New Delhi: Sage.

Saucier, G., and Goldberg, L. R. (2001). Lexical studies of indigenous personality factors: Premises, products, and prospects. *Journal of Personality*, 69, 847–879.

Saunders, B., and Van Brakel, J. (eds.) (2002). *Theories, technologies, instrumentalities of culture*. Lanham, Md.: University Press of America.

Saunders, B. A. C., and Van Brakel, J. (1997). Are there non-trivial constraints on colour categorizations? *Behavioral and Brain Sciences*, 20, 167–179.

Saxe, G. B. (1981). Body parts as numerals: A developmental analysis of numeration among remote Oksapmin village populations in Papua New Guinea. *Child Development*, 52, 302–316.

Saxe, G. B., and Moylan, T. (1982). The development of measurement operations among the Oksapmin of Papua New Guinea. *Child Development*, 53, 1242–1248.

Sayegh, L., and Lasry, J. (1993). Immigrants' adaptation in Canada: Assimilation, acculturation, and orthogonal cultural identification. *Canadian Psychology*, 24, 98–109.

Schachter, S., and Singer, J. E. (1962). Cognitive, social, and physiological determinants of emotional state. *Psychological Review*, 69, 379–399.

Schaffer, D. R., and Kipp, K. (2007). *Developmental Psychology: Childhood and adolescence* (8th edn.). Belmont, Calif.: Wadsworth.

Schaller, M., and Crandall, C. (eds.) (2004). *The psychological foundations of culture*. Mahwah, N.J.: Erlbaum.

Schaller, M., Conway, L. C., and Crandall, C. S. (2004). The psychological foundations of culture: An introduction. In M. Schaller and C. S. Crandall (eds.), *The psychological foundations of culture* (pp. 3–12). Mahwah, N.J.: Erlbaum.

Schein, E. H. (1985). *Organizational culture and leadership*. San Francisco: Jossey-Bass.

Schein, E. H. (2004). *Organizational culture and leadership* (3rd edn.). San Francisco: Jossey-Bass.

Scheper-Hughes, N. (1995). *Death without weeping*. Berkeley: University of California Press.

Scherer, K. R. (1997). Profiles of emotion-antecedent appraisal: Testing theoretical predictions across cultures. *Cognition & Emotion*, 11, 113–150.

Scherer, K. R. (2005). What are emotions? And how can they be measured? *Social Science Information*, 44, 693–727.

Scherer, K. R., and Wallbott, H. G. (1994). Evidence for universality and cultural variation of differential emotion response patterning. *Journal of Personality and Social Psychology*, 66, 310–328.

Scherer, K. R., Wallbott, H. G., and Summerfield, A. B. (eds.) (1986). *Experiencing emotion: A cross-cultural study*. Cambridge: Cambridge University Press.

Schiefenhövel, W. (1988). *Geburtsverhalten und reproduktiver Strategien der Eipo: Ergebnisse humanethologischer und ethnomedizinischer Untersuchungen im zentralen Bergland von Irian Jaya (West-Neuguinea), Indonesien* [Birth behavior and reproductive strategies of the Eipo: Results of human-ethological and ethnomedical investigations in the central mountain country of Irian Jaya (west New Guinea), Indonesia]. Berlin: Reimer.

Schlegel, A., and Barry, H. (1986). The cultural consequences of female contribution to subsistence. *American Anthropologist*, 88, 142–150.

Schlegel, A., and Barry, H. (1991). *Adolescence: An anthropological enquiry*. New York: The Free Press.

Schliemann, A., Carraher, D., and Ceci, S. (1997). Everyday cognition. In J. W. Berry, P. R. Dasen and T. S. Saraswathi (eds.), *Handbook of cross-cultural psychology, Vol. II, Basic processes and human development* (2nd edn., pp. 177–216). Boston: Allyn & Bacon.

Schmidt, F. L., and Hunter, J. E. (1998). The validity and utility of selection methods in personnel psychology: Practical and theoretical implications of 85 years of research findings. *Psychological Bulletin*, 124, 262–274.

Schmitt, D. (2003). Universal sex differences in the desire for sexual variety: Tests from 52 nations, 6 continents, and 13 islands. *Journal of Personality and Social Psychology*, 85, 85–104.

Schmitt, D. (2005). Sociosexuality from Argentina to Zimbabwe: A 48-nation study of sex, culture, and strategies of human mating. *Behavioral and Brain Sciences*, 28, 247–311.

Schmitt, D. P., Allik, J., McCrae, R. R., Benet-Martínez, V., Alcalay, L., Ault, L., *et al.* (2007). The geographic distribution of Big Five personality traits: Patterns and profiles of human self description across 56 nations. *Journal of Cross-Cultural Psychology*, 38, 173–212.

Schneider, B. (2000). The psychological life of organizations. In N. M. Ashkanasy, C. P. M. Wilderom and M. F. Peterson (eds.), *Handbook of organizational culture and climate* (pp. xvii–xxi). Thousand Oaks, Calif.: Sage.

Schönpflug, U. (ed.) (2009). *Cultural transmission: Developmental, psychological, social and methodological perspectives*. Cambridge: Cambridge University Press.

Schönpflug, W. (1993). Applied psychology: Newcomer with a long tradition. *Applied Psychology: An International Review*, 42, 5–66.

Schulpen, T. W. J. (1996). Migration and child health: The Dutch experience. *European Journal of Pediatrics*, 155, 351–356.

Schwartz, S. H. (1992). Universals in the content and structure of values: Theoretical advances and empirical tests in 20 countries. In M. Zanna (ed.), *Advances in experimental social psychology, Vol. XXV* (pp. 1–65). Orlando, Fla.: Academic Press.

Schwartz, S. H. (1994a). Are there universal aspects in the structure and contents of human values? *Journal of Social Issues*, 50, 19–45.

Schwartz, S. H. (1994b). Beyond individualism and collectivism: New cultural dimensions of values. In U. Kim, H. C. Triandis, C. Kağitçibaşi, S. C. Choi and G. Yoon (eds.), *Individualism and collectivism: Theory, method and applications* (pp. 85–119). Thousand Oaks, Calif.: Sage.

Schwartz, S. H. (2004). Mapping and interpreting cultural differences around the world. In H. Vinken, J. Soeters and P. Ester (eds.), *Comparing cultures: Dimensions of culture in a comparative perspective* (pp. 43–73). Leiden: Brill.

Schwartz, S. H. (2006). A theory of cultural value orientations: Explication and applications. *Comparative Sociology*, 5, 136–182.

Schwartz, S. H. (in press). Values: Cultural and individual. In F. J. R. Van de Vijver, A. Chasiotis and S. M. Breugelmans (eds.), *Fundamental questions in cross-cultural psychology.* Cambridge: Cambridge University Press.

Schwartz, S. H., and Bilsky, W. (1990). Toward a theory of the universal content and structure of values: Extensions and cross-cultural replications. *Journal of Personality and Social Psychology*, 58, 878–891.

Schwartz, S. H., and Boehnke, K. (2004). Evaluating the structure of human values with confirmatory factor analysis. *Journal of Research in Personality*, 38, 230–255.

Schwartz, S. H., and Sagiv, L. (1995). Identifying culture specifics in the content and structure of values. *Journal of Cross-Cultural Psychology*, 26, 92–116.

Schwartz, S. H., Melech, G., Lehmann, A., Burgess, S., Harris, M., and Owens, V. (2001). Extending the cross-cultural validity of the theory of basic human values with a different method of measurement. *Journal of Cross-Cultural Psychology*, 32, 519–542.

Scribner, S. (1979). Modes of thinking and ways of speaking: Culture and logic reconsidered. In R. O. Freedle (ed.), *New directions in discourse processing* (pp. 223–243). Norwood, N.J.: Ablex.

Scribner, S., and Cole, M. (1981). *The psychology of literacy.* Cambridge, Mass.: Harvard University Press.

Searle, W., and Ward, C. (1990). The prediction of psychological and sociocultural adjustment during cross-cultural transitions. *International Journal of Intercultural Relations*, 14, 449–464.

Sedikides, C., Gaertner, L., and Toguchi, Y. (2003). Pancultural self-enhancement. *Journal of Personality and Social Psychology*, 84, 60–70.

Sedikides, C., Gaertner, L., and Vevea, J. L. (2005). Pancultural self-enhancement reloaded: A meta-analytic reply to Heine (2005). *Journal of Personality and Social Psychology*, 89, 539–551.

Sedikides, C., Gaertner, L., and Vevea, J. L. (2007). Inclusion of theory-relevant moderators yield the same conclusions as Sedikides, Gaertner, and Vevea (2005): A meta-analytical reply to Heine, Kitayama, and Hamamura (2007). *Asian Journal of Social Psychology*, 2, 59–67.

Segall, M. H. (1984). More than we need to know about culture, but are afraid not to ask. *Journal of Cross-Cultural Psychology*, 15, 153–162.

Segall, M. H., Campbell, D. T., and Herskovits, K. J. (1966). *The influence of culture on visual perception.* Indianapolis: Bobbs-Merrill.

Segall, M. H., Dasen, P. R., Berry, J. W., and Poortinga, Y. H. (1999). *Human behavior in global perspective: An introduction to cross-cultural psychology* (rev. 2nd edn.). Boston: Allyn & Bacon.

Segalowitz, N. S. (1980). Issues in the cross-cultural study of bilingual development. In H. C. Triandis and A. Heron (eds.), *Handbook of cross-cultural psychology, Vol. IV, Developmental psychology* (pp. 55–92). Boston: Allyn & Bacon.

Selig, J. P., Card, N. A., and Little, T. D. (2008). Latent structural equation modeling in cross-cultural research: Multigroup and multilevel approaches. In F. J. R. Van de Vijver, D. A. Van Hemert and Y. H. Poortinga (eds.), *Individuals and cultures in multilevel analysis* (pp. 93–119). Mahwah, N.J.: Erlbaum.

Seligman, M. E. P. (2002). Positive psychology, positive prevention and positive therapy. In C. R. Snyder and S. J. Lopez (eds.), *Handbook of positive psychology* (pp. 3–9). Oxford: Oxford University Press.

Seligman, M. E. P. (2008). Positive health. *Applied Psychology: An International Review*, 57, 3–18.

Seligman, M. E. P., Steen, T. A., Park, N., and Peterson, C. (2005). Positive psychology progress: Empirical validation and of interventions. *American Psychologist*, 60, 410–421.

Semin, G. (2009). Language, culture and cognition: How do they interact? In R. Wyer, C. Chiu and Y. Hong (eds.), *Understanding culture: Theory, research and application* (pp. 259–270). Hove: Psychology Press.

Semin, G. R., and Fiedler, K. (1988). The cognitive functions of linguistic categories in describing persons: Social cognition and language. *Journal of Personality and Social Psychology*, 54, 558–568.

Semin, G., and Zwier, S. (1997). Social cognition. In J. W. Berry, M. H. Segall and C. Kağitçibaşi (eds.), *Handbook of cross-cultural psychology, Vol. III, Social behavior and applications* (pp. 51–75). Boston: Allyn & Bacon.

Sen, A. (1995). *Inequality reexamined.* Boston: Harvard University Press.

Sen, A. (2000). *Development as freedom.* Oxford: Oxford University Press.

Sen, A. (2005). Human rights and capabilities. *Journal of Human Development*, 6, 151–166.

Serpell, R. (1993). *The significance of schooling: Life journeys in an African society.* Cambridge: Cambridge University Press.

Serpell, R., and Deregowski, J. B. (1980). The skill of pictorial perception: An interpretation of cross-cultural evidence. *International Journal of Psychology*, 15, 145–180.

Setiono, K., and Sudradjat, N. W. (2008). A Moslem-oriented approach for teaching psychology. Poster presentation at the Third International Conference on the Teaching of Psychology, St. Petersburg, July 12–16.

Sewell. H. (2008). *Working with ethnicity, race and culture in mental health: A handbook for practitioners.* London: Kingsley.

Shadish, W. R. (2000). The empirical program of quasi-experimentation. In L. Brickman (ed.), *Research design, Donald Campbell's legacy, Vol. 2* (pp. 13–35). Thousand Oaks, Calif.: Sage.

Shadish, W. R., Cook, T. D., and Campbell, D. T. (2002). *Experimental and quasi-experimental designs for generalized causal inference.* Boston: Houghton Mifflin.

Shannon, L. M., and Begley, T. M. (2008). Antecedents of the four-factor model of cultural intelligence. In S. Ang and L. van Dyne (eds.), *Handbook of cultural intelligence: Theory, measurement, and applications* (pp. 41–55). New York: Sharpe.

Sheikh, A., and Sheikh, K. S. (eds.) (1989). *Eastern and western approaches to healing: Ancient wisdom and modern knowledge.* New York: Wiley.

Shepher, J. (1983). *Incest. A biosocial view*. New York: Academic Press.

Shirts, R. G. (1973). *BAFA BAFA: A cross-cultural simulation*. Delmar, Calif.: Simile II.

Shostak, M. (1981/2000). *Nisa – The Life and Words of a !Kung Woman*. Cambridge, Mass.: Harvard University Press.

Shuey, A. (1958). *The testing of Negro intelligence*. New York: Social Science Press.

Shweder, R. A. (1984). Anthropology's romantic rebellion against the enlightenment, or there's more to think than reason and evidence. In R. A. Shweder and R. A. LeVine (eds.), *Culture theory: Essays on mind, self and emotion* (pp. 27–66). Cambridge: Cambridge University Press.

Shweder, R. A. (1990). Cultural psychology – What is it? In J. W. Stigler, R. A. Shweder and G. Herdt (eds.), *Cultural psychology: Essays on comparative human development* (pp. 1–43). Cambridge: Cambridge University Press.

Shweder, R. A. (1991). *Thinking through cultures: Expeditions in cultural psychology*. Cambridge, Mass.: Harvard University Press.

Shweder, R. A. (2007). An anthropological perspective. In S. Kitayama and D. Cohen (eds.), *Handbook of cultural psychology* (pp. 821–844). New York: Guilford Press.

Shweder, R. A., and Bourne, E. J. (1984). Does the concept of the person vary cross-culturally? In R. A. Shweder and R. LeVine (eds.), *Culture theory* (pp. 158–199). New York: Cambridge University Press.

Siantz, M. L. d. L. (1997). Factors that impact developmental outcomes. In A. Booth, A. C. Crouter and N. Landale (eds.), *Immigration and the family: Research and policy on US immigrants* (pp. 149–161). Mahwah, N.J.: Erlbaum.

Sidanius, J., and Pratto, F. (1999). *Social dominance: An intergroup theory of social hierarchy and oppression*. Cambridge: Cambridge University Press.

Siegert, R. (2001). Culture, cognition and schizophrenia. In J. F. Schumaker and R. Ward (eds.), *Cultural cognition and psychopathology* (pp. 171–189). Westport, Conn.: Praeger.

Sigel, I. E., McGillicuddy-De Lisi, A., and Goodnow, J. J. (eds.) (1992). *Parental belief systems: The psychological consequences for children* (2nd edn.). Hillsdale, N.J.: Erlbaum.

Silvar, S. D., and Pollack, R. H. (1967). Racial differences in pigmentation of the Fundus oculi. *Psychonomic Science*, 7, 159–160.

Simons, R. C., and Hughes, C. C. (1993). Culture bound syndromes. In A. C. Gaw (ed.), *Culture, ethnicity and mental illness* (pp. 75–93). Washington, DC: American Psychiatric Press.

Simons, R., and Hughes, C. C. (eds.) (1985). *The culture-bound syndromes*. Dordrecht: Reidel.

Simwaka, A., Peltzer, K., and Banda, D. (2007). Indigenous healing in Malawi. *Journal of Psychology in Africa*, 17, 155–162.

Sinaiko, H. W. (1975). Verbal factors in human engineering: Some cultural and psychological data. In A. Chapanis (ed.), *Ethnic variables in human engineering* (pp. 159–177). Baltimore: Johns Hopkins University Press.

Sinangil, H. K., and Ones, D. S. (1997). Empirical investigations of the host country perspective in expatriate managment. *New Approaches to Employee Managment,* 4, 173–205.

Singelis, T. M., Triandis, H. C., Bhawuk, D. P. S., and Gelfand, M. J. (1995). Horizontal and vertical dimensions of individualism and collectivism: A theoretical and measurement refinement. *Cross-Cultural Research,* 29, 240–275.

Singh, G. (1985). Dhat syndrome revisited. *Indian Journal of Psychiatry,* 11, 119–122.

Singleton, R. A., and Straits, B. C. (2005). *Approaches to social research* (4th edn.). New York: Oxford University Press.

Sinha, D. (1984). Towards partnership for relevant research in the Third World. *International Journal of Psychology,* 19, 169–177.

Sinha, D. (1986). *Psychology in a Third World country: The Indian experience.* New Delhi: Sage.

Sinha, D. (1990). Interventions for development out of poverty. In R. W. Brislin (ed.), *Applied cross-cultural psychology* (pp. 77–97). Newbury Park, Calif.: Sage.

Sinha, D. (1997). Indigenizing psychology. In J. W. Berry, Y. H. Poortinga and J. Pandey (eds.), *Handbook of cross-cultural psychology, Vol. I, Theory and method* (2nd edn., pp. 129–169). Boston: Allyn & Bacon.

Sinha, J. B. P. (1970). *Development through behaviour modification.* Bombay: Allied Publishers.

Sinha, J. B. P. (1980). *The nurturant-task leader.* New Delhi: Concept Publishing House.

Sinha, J. B. P. (1984). A model of effective leadership styles in India. *International Studies of Management and Organization,* 14, 86–98.

Sinha, J. B. P. (2008). *Culture and organizational behaviour.* New Delhi: Sage.

Sireci, S. G. (in press). Evaluating test and survey items for bias across languages and cultures. In D. Matsumoto and F. J. R. van de Vijver (eds.), *Cross-cultural research methods in psychology.* Cambridge: Cambridge University Press.

Sirin, S. R., and Fine, M. (2007). Hyphenated-selves: Muslim American youth negotiating identities on the fault lines of global conflicts. *Applied Developmental Science,* 11, 151–163.

Skevington, S. M., Lotfy, M., and O'Connell, K. A. (2004). The World Health Organization's WHOQOL-BREF quality of life assessment: Psychometric properties and results of the international field trial. A Report from the WHOQOL Group. *Quality of Life Research,* 13, 299–310.

Skinner. B. F. (1957). *Verbal behavior.* New York: Appleton-Century-Crofts.

Smith, E. A., Bliege Bird, R., and Bird, D. W. (2003). The benefits of costly signaling: Meriam turtle hunters. *Behavioral Ecology,* 14, 116–126.

Smith, J. A., Harré, R., and Van Langenhove, L. (eds.) (1995). *Rethinking methods in psychology.* London: Sage.

Smith, P. B. (2004). Acquiescent response bias as an aspect of cultural communication style. *Journal of Cross-Cultural Psychology,* 35, 50–61.

Smith, P. B. (2006). When elephants fight, the grass gets trampled: The GLOBE and Hofstede projects. *Journal of International Business Studies*, 37, 915–921.

Smith, P. B., and Fischer, R. (2008). Acquiescence, extreme response bias and culture: A multilevel analysis. In F. J. R. Van de Vijver, D. A. Van Hemert and Y. H. Poortinga (eds.), *Individuals and cultures in multilevel analysis* (pp. 283–312). Mahwah, N.J.: Erlbaum.

Smith, P. B., and Peterson, M. F. (1988). *Leadership, organizations and culture: An event management model*. London: Sage.

Smith, P. B., and Schwartz, S. H. (1997). Values. In J. W. Berry, M. H. Segall and C. Kağitçibaşi (eds.), *Handbook of cross-cultural psychology, Vol. III, Social behavior and applications* (pp. 77–118). Boston: Allyn & Bacon.

Smith, P. B., Bond, M. H., and Kağitçibaşi, C. (2006). *Understanding social psychology across cultures: Living and working in a changing world*. London: Sage.

Smith, P. B., Peterson, M. F., and Thomas, D. C. (2008). *The handbook of cross-cultural management research*. Los Angeles: Sage.

Smith, P. B., Trompenaars, F., and Dugan, S. (1995). The Rotter locus of control scale in 43 countries: A test of cultural relativity. *International Journal of Psychology*, 30, 377–400.

Smith, P. B., Peterson, M. F., Ahmad, A. H., *et al.* (2002). Demographic effects on the use of vertical sources of guidance by managers in widely different cultural contexts. *International Journal of Cross-Cultural Management*, 5, 1–26.

Snauwaert, B., Soenens, B., Vanbeselaere, N., and Boen, F. (2003). When integration does not necessarily imply integration: Different conceptualizations of acculturation orientations lead to different classifications. *Journal of Cross-Cultural Psychology*, 34, 231–239.

Snow, M. E., Jacklin, C. N., and Maccoby, E. E. (1983). Sex-of-child differences in father–child interaction at one year of age. *Child Development*, 54, 227–252.

Snustad, D. P., and Simmons. M. J. (1997). *Principles of genetics* (2nd edn.). New York: Wiley.

Sokal, A. D. (1996a). Transgressing the boundaries. *Social Text*, 46–47, 217–252.

Sokal, A. D. (1996b). Transgressing the boundaries: An afterword. *Philosophy and Literature*, 20, 338–346.

Sonke, C. J., Poortinga, Y. H., and De Kuijer, J. H. J. (1999). Cross-cultural differences on cognitive task performance: The influence of stimulus familiarity. In W. J. Lonner, D. L. Dinnel, D. K. Forgays and S. A. Hayes (eds.), *Merging past, present, and future in cross-cultural psychology* (pp. 146–158). Lisse: Swets and Zeitlinger.

Sonke, C., Van Boxtel, G., Griesel, R., and Poortinga, Y. H. (2008). Brain wave concomitants of cross-cultural differences in scores on simple cognitive tasks. *Journal of Cross-Cultural Psychology*, 39, 37–54.

Sosis, R. (2003). Why aren't we all Hutterites? *Human Nature*, 14, 91–127.

Sosis, R., and Bressler, E. (2003). Cooperation and commune longevity: A test of the costly signaling theory of religion. *Cross Cultural Research*, 37, 211–239.

Sow, I. (1977). *Psychiatrie dynamique africaine* [African dynamic psychiatry]. Paris: Payot.

Sow, I. (1978). *Les structures anthropologiques de la folie en Afrique noire* [The anthropological structures of madness in black Africa]. Paris: Payot.

Spearman, C. (1927). *The abilities of man.* London: Macmillan.

Spector, P. E., Cooper, C. L., Sparks, K., *et al.* (2001). An international study of the psychometric properties of the Hofstede values survey module 1994: A comparison of individual and country/province level results. *Applied Psychology: An International Review*, 50, 269–281.

Spitzberg, B. H., and Chagnon, G. (2009). Conceptualizing intercultural competence. In D. K. Deardorff (ed.), *The SAGE handbook of intercultural competence* (pp. 2–52). Thousand Oaks, Calif.: Sage.

Sporer, S. L. (2001). Recognizing faces of other ethnic groups: Data in search of theory. *Psychology, Public Policy and Law*, 7, 36–97.

Sporer, S. L., Trinkl, B., and Guberova, E. (2007). Matching faces: Differences in processing sped of out-group faces by different ethnic groups. *Journal of Cross-Cultural Psychology*, 38, 398–412.

Stapel, D. A., and Semin, G. R. (2007). The magic spell of language: Linguistic categories and their perceptual consequences. *Journal of Personality and Social Psychology*, 93, 23–33.

Staudinger, U. M., and Dörner, J. (2007). Wisdom. In J. Birren (ed.), *Encyclopedia of gerontology* (2nd edn., pp. 674–683). Oxford: Elsevier.

Steers, R. M., Nardon, L., and Sanchez-Runde, C. (2009). Culture and organizational design: Strategy, structure, and decision-making. In R. S. Bhagat and R. M. Steers (eds.), *The Cambridge handbook of culture, organizations, and work* (pp. 71–117). Cambridge: Cambridge University Press.

Stefansson, H., Ophoff, R. A., Steinberg, S., *et al.* (2009). Common variants conferring risk of schizophrenia, *Nature*, 460, 744–747.

Steinberg, L. (2008). A social neuroscience perspective on adolescent risk-taking. *Developmental Review*, 28, 78–106.

Stephan, W., Renfro, C. L., Esses, V., Stephan, C., and Martin, T. (2005). The effects of feeling threatened on attitudes toward immigrants. *International Journal of Intercultural Relations*, 29, 1–19.

Stephenson, M. (2000). Development and validation of the Stephenson Multigroup Acculturation Scale (SMAS). *Psychological Assessment*, 12, 77–88.

Stern, J. M., Konner, M., Herman, T. N., and Reichlin, S. (1986). Nursing behaviour, prolactine and postpartum amenorrhea during prolonged lactation in American and !Kung mothers. *Clinical Endocrinology*, 25, 247–258.

Sternberg, R. J. (2002). Cultural explorations of human intelligence around the world. In W. J. Lonner, D. L. Dinnel, S. A. Hayes and D. N. Sattler (eds.), *Online Readings in Psychology and Culture* (Unit 5, Chapter 1). Retrieved August 9, 2010, from http://orpc.iaccp.org/

Sternberg, R. J. (2007). Intelligence and culture. In S. Kitayama and D. Cohen (eds.), *Handbook of cultural psychology* (pp. 547–568). New York: Guilford Press.

Sternberg, R. J. (2008). Successful intelligence as a framework for understanding cultural adaptation. In S. Ang and L. van Dyne (eds.), *Handbook of cultural intelligence: Theory, measurement, and applications* (pp. 306–317). Sharpe: New York.

Sternberg, R. J., and Grigorenko, E. (eds.) (1997a). *Intelligence, heredity and environment.* New York: Cambridge University Press.

Sternberg, R. J., and Grigorenko, E. (1997b). Are cognitive styles still in style? *American Psychologist*, 52, 700–712.

Sternberg, R. J., and Grigorenko, E. (eds.) (2004). *Culture and competence: Contexts of life success.* Washington, DC: APA Press.

Sternberg, R. J., Nokes, K., Geissler, P. W., Prince, R., Okatcha, F., Bundy, D. A., and Grigorenko, E. L. (2001). The relationship between academic and practical intelligence: A case study in Kenya. *Intelligence*, 29, 401–418.

Stevens, M., and Gielen, U. (eds.) (2007). *Toward a global psychology: Theory, research and pedagogy.* Mahwah, N.J.: Lawrence Erlbaum Associates.

Stevenson, B., and Wolfers, J. (2008). Economic growth and subjective well-being: Re-assessing the Easterlin paradox. *Brookings Papers on Economic Activities.* Retrieved January 17, 2010, from http://muse.jhu.edu/journals/brookings_papers_on_economic_activity/toc/eca.2008.1.html

Stewart, V. M. (1973). Tests of the "carpentered world" hypothesis by race and environment in America and Zambia. *International Journal of Psychology*, 8, 83–94.

Stompe, T., and Friedman, A. (2007). Culture and schizophrenia. In D. Bhugra and K. Bhui (eds.), *Textbook of cultural psychiatry* (pp. 314–322). Cambridge: Cambridge University Press.

Stompe, T., Friedmann, A., Ortwein, G., Stroble, R., Chaudry, H. R., Najam, N., and Chaudry, M. R. (1999). Comparison of delusions among schizophrenics in Austria and Pakistan. *Psychopathology*, 32, 225–234.

Stompe, T., Bauer, S., Ortwein-Swoboda, G., Schanda, H., Karakula, H., Rudalevicienne, P., Chaudhry, H. R., Idemudia, E. S., and Gschaider, S. (2006). Delusions of guilt: The attitudes of Christian and Islamic confessions towards good and evil and the responsibility of men. *Journal of Muslim Mental Health*, 1, 43–56.

Strauss, C., and Quinn, N. (1997). *A cognitive theory of cultural meaning.* Cambridge: Cambridge University Press.

Stroup, E. D. (1985). Navigating without instruments: The voyage of Hokule'a. *Oceanus*, 28, 68–75.

Stuart, J., Ward, C., Jose, P., and Narayanan, P. (in press). Working with and for communities: A collaborative study of harmony and conflict in well functioning acculturating families, *International Journal of Intercultural Relations.*

Sturtevant, W. (1964). Studies in ethnoscience. *American Anthropologist*, 66, 99–124.

Suárez-Orozco, C., and Suárez-Orozco, M. (1995). *Transformation: Immigration, family life and achievement motivation among Latino adolescents.* Palo Alto: Stanford University Press.

Suárez-Orozco, C., Pimentel, A., and Martin, M. (2009). The significance of relationships: Academic engagement and achievement among newcomer immigrant youth. *Teacher College Board*, 111, 712–749.

Suárez-Orozco, C., Suárez-Orozco, M., and Todorova, I. (2006). *Moving stories: Educational pathways of immigrant youth*. Cambridge, Mass.: Harvard University Press.

Suárez-Orozco, C., Suárez-Orozco, M., and Todorova, I. (2008). *Learning a new land: Immigrant students in American society*. Cambridge, Mass.: Harvard University Press.

Suinn, R. M., Ahuna, C., and Khoo, G. (1992). The Suinn-Lew Asian self-identity acculturation scale: Concurrent and factorial validation. *Educational and Psychological Measurement*, 52, 1041–1046.

Sulloway, F. (1996). *Born to rebel: Birth order, family dynamics, and creative lives*. New York: Pantheon Books.

Sumner, W. G. (1906). *Folkways*. New York: Ginn and Co.

Sung, B. L. (1985). Bicultural conflicts in Chinese immigrant children. *Journal of Comparative Family Studies*, 16, 255–269.

Super, C. M. (1976). Environmental effects on motor development: The case of "African infant precocity." *Developmental Medicine and Child Neurology*, 18, 561–567.

Super, C. M., and Harkness, S. (1986). The developmental niche: A conceptualization at the interface of child and culture. *International Journal of Behavioral Development*, 9, 545–569.

Super, C. M., and Harkness, S. (1997). The cultural structuring of child development. In J. W. Berry, P. R. Dasen and T. S. Saraswathi (eds.), *Handbook of cross-cultural psychology, Vol. II, Basic processes and human development* (pp. 1–39). Boston: Allyn & Bacon.

Super, C., and Harkness, S. (2008). Globalization and its discontents: Challenges to developmental theory and practice in Africa. *International Journal of Psychology*, 43, 107–113.

Super, C. M., and Harkness, S. (in press). Culture and infancy. In G. Bremner and T. D. Wachs (eds.), *Blackwell handbook of infant development*, Vol. I. Oxford: Blackwell.

Super, C. M., Harkness, S., Van Tijen, N., Vander Vlugt, E., Fintelman, M., and Dijkstra, J. (1996). The three R's of Dutch childrearing and the socialization of infant arousal. In S. Harkness and C. M. Super (eds.), *Parents' cultural belief systems: Their origins, expressions, and consequences* (pp. 447–465). New York: Guilford Press.

Surian, L., Caldi, S., and Sperber, D. (2007). Attribution of beliefs by 13-month-old infants. *Psychological Science*, 18, 580–586.

Sussman, N. M., and Rosenfeld, H. M. (1982). Influence of culture, language and sex on conversational distance. *Journal of Personality and Social Psychology*, 42, 66–74.

Swets, J. A. (ed.) (1964). *Signal detection and recognition by human observers*. New York: Wiley.

Tajfel, H. (1978). *The social psychology of minorities.* London: Minority Rights Group.

Tajfel, H. (1982). Social psychology of intergroup relations. *Annual Review of psychology,* 33, 1–39.

Tajfel, H. (ed.) (1978). *Differentiation between social groups.* London: Academic Press.

Tajfel, H., and Turner, J. (1986). The social identity theory of intergroup behavior. In S. Worchel and W. Austin (eds.), *Psychology of intergroup relations* (pp. 7–24). Chicago: Nelson-Hall.

Takano, Y., and Osaka, E. (1999). An unsupported common view: Comparing Japan and the U.S. on individualism/collectivism. *Asian Journal of Social Psychology,* 2, 311–341.

Tanaka-Matsumi, J. (1979). Cultural factors and social influence techniques in Naikan therapy: A Japanese self-observation method. *Psychotherapy: Theory, Research and Practice,* 16, 385–390.

Tanaka-Matsumi, J. (2004). Japanese forms of psychotherapy: Naikan therapy and Maritan therapy. In W. E. Gielen, J. M. Fish and J. G. Draguns (eds.), *Handbook of culture, therapy and healing* (pp. 277–292). Mahwah, N.J.: Erlbaum.

Tanaka-Matsumi, J. (2008). Functional approaches to evidence-based practice in multicultural counseling and therapy. In U. P. Gielen, J. D. Draguns and J. M. Fish (eds.), *Principles of multicultural counseling and therapy* (pp. 169–198). New York: Routledge.

Tanaka-Matsumi, J., and Draguns, J. (1997). Culture and psychopathology. In J. W. Berry, M. H. Segall and C. Kağitçibaşi (eds.), *Handbook of cross-cultural psychology, Vol. III, Social behavior and applications* (2nd edn., pp. 449–491). Boston: Allyn & Bacon.

Tanon, F. (1994). *A cultural view on planning: The case of weaving in Ivory Coast.* Tilburg: Tilburg University Press.

Tantam, D. (2007). Psychotherapy across cultures. In D. Bhugra and K. Bhui (eds.), *Textbook of cultural psychiatry* (pp. 414–423). Cambridge: Cambridge University Press.

Tarakeshwar, N., Stanton, J., and Pargament, K. I. (2003). Religion: An overlooked dimension in cross-cultural psychology. *Journal of Cross-Cultural Psychology,* 34, 377–394.

Tarique, I., and Takeuchi, R. (2008). Developing cultural intelligence: The role of international nonwork experiences. In S. Ang and L. van Dyne (eds.), *Handbook of cultural intelligence: Theory, measurement, and applications* (pp. 56–70). New York: Sharpe.

Tartakovsky, E. (2008). Psychological well-being and ethnic identities of Jewish adolescents planning emigration from Russia and Ukraine to Israel: Changes during the post-perestroika period. *International Journal of Intercultural Relations,* 32, 553–564.

Taylor, D. M. (1981). Stereotypes and intergroup relations. In R. C. Gardner and R. Kalin (eds.), *A Canadian social psychology of ethnic relations* (pp. 151–71). Toronto: Methuen.

Taylor, H. A., and Tversky, B. (1996). Perspective in spatial descriptions. *Journal of Memory and Language*, 35, 371–391.

Terracciano, A., and McCrae, R. R. (2006). How to measure national stereotypes? Response. *Science*, 311, 777–779.

Terracciano, A., and McCrae, R. R. (2007). Implications for understanding national character stereotypes. *Journal of Cross-Cultural Psychology*, 38, 695–710.

Terracciano, A., Abdel-Khalak, A. M., Ádám, N., *et al.* (2005). National character does not reflect mean personality trait levels in 49 cultures. *Science*, 310, 96–100.

Textor, R. (1967). *A cross-cultural summary.* New Haven, Conn.: Human Relations Area Files.

Thakker, J., and Ward, T. (1998). Culture and classification: The cross-cultural application of the DSM-IV. *Clinical Psychology Review*, 18, 501–529.

Thakker, J., Ward, T., and Strongman, K. T. (1999). Mental disorder and cross-cultural psychology: A constructivist perspective. *Clinical Psychology Review*, 19, 843–874.

Thara, R. (2004). Twenty-year course of schizophrenia. The Madras longitudinal study. *Canadian Journal of Psychiatry*, 49, 564–569.

Theron, C. (2007). Confessions, scapegoats and flying pigs: Psychometric testing and the law. *South African Journal of Industrial Psychology*, 33, 102–117.

Thomas, A., and Wagner, K. H. (1999). Von der Fremheidserfahrung zum interkulturellen Verstehen [From experiencing strangeness to intercultural understanding]. *Praxis*, 46, 227–236.

Thomas, F., Renaud, F., Benefice, E., De Meeus, T., and Guegan, J.-F. (2001). International variability of ages at menarche and menopause: Patterns and determinants. *Human Biology*, 73, 271–290.

Thornhill, N. (1991). An evolutionary analysis of rules regulating human inbreeding and marriage. *Behavioral and Brain Sciences*, 14, 247–293.

Thornicroft, G. (2008). Stigma and discrimination limit access to mental health care. *Epidemiologia e Psichiatria Sociale*, 17, 14–19.

Thouless, R. H. (1933). A racial difference in perception. *Journal of Social Psychology*, 4, 330–339.

Thurstone, L. L. (1938). Primary mental abilities. *Psychometric Monographs*, 1.

Thurnwald, R. (1932). The psychology of acculturation. *American Psychologist*, 34, 557–569.

Tinbergen, N. (1963). On aims and methods of ethology. *Zeitschrift fuer Tierpsychologie*, 20, 410–433.

Ting-Toomey, S. (1985). Toward a theory of conflict and culture. *International and Intercultural Communication Annual*, 9, 71–86.

Ting-Toomey, S. (2005a). *Understanding intercultural communication.* Los Angeles: Roxbury.

Ting-Toomey, S. (2005b). The matrix of face: An updated face-negotiation theory. In W. B. Gudykunst (ed.), *Theorizing about intercultural communication* (pp. 71–92). Thousand Oaks, Calif.: Sage.

Tinsley, C. H. (2001). How negotiators get to yes: Predicting the constellation of strategies used across cultures to negotiate conflict. *Journal of Applied Psychology*, 86, 583–593.

Titchener, E. B. (1916). On ethnological tests of sensation and perception. *Proceedings of the American Philisophical Society*, 55, 204–236.

Todd, Z., Nerlich, B., McKeown, S., and Clarke, D. D. (2004*). Mixing methods in psychology: The integration of qualitative and quantitative methods in theory and practice*. Hove: Psychology Press.

Tolman, W. (1971). The duplication theorem of social relationships as tested in the general population. *Psychological Review*, 78, 380–390.

Tomasello, M. (1999). *The cultural origins of human cognition*. Cambridge, Mass.: Harvard University Press.

Tomkins, S. S. (1962). *Affect, imaginary and consciousness, Vol. I, The positive emotions*. New York: Springer.

Tomkins, S. S. (1963). *Affect, imaginary and consciousness, Vol. II, The negative emotions*. New York: Springer.

Tooby, J., and Cosmides, L. (1990). The past explains the present: Emotional adaptations and the structure of ancestral environments. *Ethology and Sociobiology*, 11, 375–424.

Tooby, J., and Cosmides, L. (1992). The psychological foundations of culture. In J. Barkow, L. Cosmides and J. Tooby (eds.), *The adapted mind: Evolutionary psychology and the generation of culture* (pp. 19–136). New York: Oxford University Press.

Toovey, S., Jamieson, A., and Holloway, A. (2004). Travellers' knowledge, attitudes and practices on the prevention of infectious diseases: Results from a study at the Johannesburg airport. *Journal of Travel Medicine*, 11, 16–22.

Torbiörn, I. (1982). *Living abroad*. New York: Wiley.

Tov, W., and Diener, E. (2007). Culture and subjective well-being. In S. Kitayama and D. Cohen (eds.), *Handbook of cultural psychology* (pp. 691–713). New York: Guilford Press.

Townsend, J. W. (2003). Reproductive Behavior in the Context of Global Population. *American Psychologist*, 58, 197–204.

Tracy, J. L., and Robins, R. W. (2008). The nonverbal expression of pride: Evidence for cross-cultural recognition. *Journal of Personality and Social Psychology*, 94, 516–530.

Trafimow, D., Triandis, H., and Goto, S. (1991). Some tests of the distinction between the private self and the collective self. *Journal of Personality and Social Psychology*, 60, 649–655.

Triandis, H. C. (1975). Culture training, cognitive complexity and interpersonal attitudes. In R. W. Brislin, S. Bochner and W. Lonner (eds.), *Cross-cultural perspectives on learning* (pp. 39–77). Beverly Hills: Sage.

Triandis, H. C. (1989). The self and social behavior in differing cultural contexts. *Psychological Review*, 96, 506–520.

Triandis, H. C. (1994a). Cross-cultural industrial and organizational psychology. In H. C. Triandis, M. D. Dunnette and L. M. Hough (eds.), *Handbook of industrial and organizational psychology, Vol. IV* (2nd edn.). Palo Alto: Consulting Psychologists Press.

Triandis, H. C. (1994b). *Culture and social behavior.* New York: McGraw-Hill.

Triandis, H. C. (1995). *Individualism and collectivism.* Boulder, Colo.: Westview.

Triandis, H. C. (1996). The psychological measurement of cultural syndromes. *American Psychologist,* 51, 407–415.

Triandis, H. C. (2000a). Culture and conflict. *International Journal of Psychology,* 35, 145–152.

Triandis, H. C. (2000b). Dialectics between cultural and cross-cultural psychology. *Asian Journal of Social Psychology,* 3, 185–196.

Triandis, H. C. (2009). Ecological determinants of cultural variation. In R. Wyer, C. Chiu and Y. Hong (eds.), *Understanding culture: Theory, research and application* (pp. 189–210). Hove: Psychology Press.

Triandis, H. C., and Gelfand, M. (1998). Converging measurement of horizontal and vertical individualism and collectivism. *Journal of Personality and Social Psychology,* 74, 118–128.

Triandis, H. C., and Suh, E. M. (2002). Cultural influences on personality. *Annual Review of Psychology,* 53, 133–160.

Triandis, H. C., and Vassiliou, V. (1972). A comparative analysis of subjective culture. In H. C. Triandis (ed.), *The analysis of subjective culture* (pp. 299–335). New York: Wiley.

Triandis, H. C., Malpass, R., and Davidson, A. R. (1971a). Cross-cultural psychology. *Biennial Review of Anthropology,* 1, 1–84.

Triandis, H. C., Malpass, R., and Davidson, A. R. (1971b). Psychology and culture. *Annual Review of Psychology,* 24, 355–378.

Triandis, H. C., McCusker, C., and Hui, C. H. (1990). Multimethod probes of individualism and collectivism. *Journal of Personality and Social Psychology,* 59, 1006–1020.

Triandis, H. C., Kashima, E., Shimada, E., and Villareal, M. (1988). Acculturation indices as a means of confirming cultural differences. *International Journal of Psychology,* 21, 43–70.

Triandis, H. C., Leung, K., Villareal, M. V., and Clark, F. L. (1985). Allocentric versus idiocentric tendencies: Convergent and discriminant validation. *Journal of Research in Personality,* 19, 395–415.

Trivers, R. L. (1971). The evolution of reciprocal altruism. *Quartely Review of Biology,* 46, 35–57.

Trivers, R. L. (1972). Parental investment and sexual selection. In B. G. Campbell (ed.), *Sexual selection and the descent of man: 1871–1971* (pp. 136–179). Chicago: Aldine de Gruyter.

Trivers, R. L. (1974). Parent–offspring conflict. *American Zoologist,* 14, 249–264.

Trommsdorff, G., and Nauck, B. (eds.) (2005a). *The value of children in cross-cultural perspective: Case studies from eight societies.* Berlin: Pabst.

Trommsdorff, G., Kim, U., and Nauck, B. (eds.) (2005). Factors influencing value of children and intergenerational relations in times of social change: Analyses from psychological and socio-cultural perspectives. Introduction to the special issue. *Applied Psychology, An International Review*, 53, 313–316.

Tseng, W.-S. (2001). *Handbook of cultural psychiatry*. San Diego: Academic Press.

Tseng, W.-S. (2004). Culture and psychopathology. In W.-S. Tseng and J. Streltzer (eds.), *Cultural competence in clinical psychiatry* (pp. 181–189). Washington, DC: American Psychiatric Press.

Tseng, W.-S. (2007). Culture and psychopathology: General overview. In D. Bhugra and K. Bhui (eds.), *Textbook of cultural psychiatry* (pp. 95–112). Cambridge: Cambridge University Press.

Tsui, A. S., Nifadkar, S. S., and Ou, A. Y. (2007). Cross-national, cross-cultural organizational behavior research: Advances, gaps, and recommendations. *Journal of Management*, 33, 426–478.

Tucker, L. R. (1951). *A method for synthesis of factor analysis studies*. Personnel Research Section Report No. 984. Washington, DC: Department of the Army.

Tung, R. L. (1981). Selection and training of personnel for overseas assignments. *Columbia Journal of World Business*, Spring, 69–78.

Tung, R. L. (1998). American expatriates abroad: From neophytes to cosmopolitans. *Journal of World Business*, 33, 125–144.

Twaddle, A. (1994). Disease, illness and sickness revisited. In A. Twaddle and L. Nordenfelt (eds.), *Disease, illness and sickness: Three central concepts in the theory of health* (pp. 1–18). Linkøping: Studies on Health and Society.

Tylor, E. B. (1871). *Primitive culture* (2 vols.). London: Murray.

UNAIDS (2008). Global report on AIDS epidemic. Retrieved January 13, 2010, from www.unaids.org/en/KnowledgeCentre/HIVData/GlobalReport/2008/2008_Global_report.asp

UNDP (2009). Statistics of the human development report. Retrieved January 10, 2010, from http://hdr.undp.org/en/statistics/

United Nations (1948). *Universal Declaration of Human Rights*. New York: United Nations.

United Nations (2001). *United Nations millennium development goals*. New York: United Nations.

Uskul, A., Kitayama, S., and Nisbett, R. E. (2009). Ecocultural basis of cognition: Farmers and fishermen are more holistic than herders. *Proceedings of the (USA) National Academy of Science*, 105, 8552–8556.

Üstün, T. B., and Sartorius, N. (1995). *Mental illness in general health care: An international study*. Chichester: Wiley.

Vala, J. (ed.) (2009). Expressions of the "new" racism. Special issue, *International Journal of Psychology*, 44, 1–45.

Valentine, S. (2001). Self-esteem, cultural identity, and generation status as determinants of Hispanic acculturation. *Hispanic Journal of Behavioral Sciences*, 23, 459–468.

Valentine, T. (1991). A unified account of effects of distinctiveness, inversion and race on face recognition. *Quarterly Journal of Experimental Psychology*, 43A, 161–204.

Valentine, T., and Endo, M. (1992). Towards an exemplar model of face processing: The effects of race and distinctiveness. *Quarterly Journal of Experimental Psychology*, 44A, 671–703.

Valins, S. (1972). Cognitive effects of false heart-rate feedback. In R. S. Browne, H. E. Freeman, C. V. Hamilton, J. Kagan and A. Kimball Romney (eds.), *The social scene: A contemporary view of the social sciences* (pp. 87–98). Cambridge, Mass.: Winthrop Publishers.

Valsiner, J., and Rosa, A. (eds.) (2007). *The Cambridge handbook of sociocultural psychology*. Cambridge: Cambridge University Press.

Van Bezooijen, R., Otto, S. A., and Heenan, T. A. (1983). Recognition of vocal expressions of emotion: A three-nation study to identify universal characteristics. *Journal of Cross-Cultural Psychology*, 14, 387–406.

Van de Koppel, J. M. H., and Schoots, N. H. (1986). Why are all trains in Holland painted yellow? *Nederlands Tijdschrift voor de Psychologie*, 14, 189–196.

Van de Ven, N., Zeelenberg, M., and Pieters, R. (2009). Leveling up and down: The experiences of benign and malicious envy. *Emotion*, 9, 419–429.

Van de Vijver, F. J. R. (1997). Meta-analysis of cross-cultural comparisons of cognitive test performance. *Journal of Cross-Cultural Psychology*, 28, 678–709.

Van de Vijver, F. J. R. (2008). On the meaning of cross-cultural differences in simple cognitive measures. *Educational Research and Evaluation*, 14, 215–234.

Van de Vijver, F. J. R. (in press). Bias and real differences in cross-cultural differences: Neither friends nor foes. In F. J. R. Van de Vijver, A. Chasiotis and S. M. Breugelmans (eds.), *Fundamental questions in cross-cultural psychology*. Cambridge: Cambridge University Press.

Van de Vijver, F. J. R., and Breugelmans, S. M. (2008). Research foundations of cultural competency training. In R. H. Dana and J. Allen (eds.), *Cultural competency training in a global society* (pp. 117–133). New York: Springer.

Van de Vijver, F., and Chasiotis, A. (2010). Making methods meet: Mixed designs in cross-cultural research. In J. A. Harkness, M. Braun, B. Edwards, T. P. Johnson, L. Lyberg, P. P. Mohler, B. E. Pennell and T. W. Smith (eds.), *Survey methods in multinational, multiregional, and multicultural contexts* (pp. 455–473). Hoboken, N.J.: Wiley.

Van de Vijver, F. J. R., and Leung, K. (1997). *Methods and data analysis for cross-cultural research*. Newbury Park, Calif.: Sage.

Van de Vijver, F. J. R., and Leung, K. (2000). Methodological issues in research on culture. *Journal of Cross-Cultural Psychology*, 32, 33–51.

Van de Vijver, F. J. R., and Leung, K. (2009). Methodological issues in researching intercultural competence. In D. K. Deardorff (ed.), *The SAGE handbook of intercultural competence* (pp. 404–418). Thousand Oaks, Calif.: Sage.

Van de Vijver, F. J. R., and Leung, K. (in press). Equivalence and bias: A review of concepts, models, and data analytic procedures. In D. Matsumoto and F. J. R. van de Vijver (eds.), *Cross-cultural research methods in psychology*. Cambridge: Cambridge University Press.

Van de Vijver, F. J. R., and Phalet, K. (2004). Assessment in multicultural groups: The role of acculturation. *Applied Psychology: An International Review*, 53, 215–236.

Van de Vijver, F. J. R., and Poortinga, Y. H. (1982). Cross-cultural generalization and universality. *Journal of Cross-Cultural Psychology*, 13, 387–408.

Van de Vijver, F. J. R., and Poortinga, Y. H. (1997). Towards an integrated analysis of bias in cross-cultural assessment. *European Journal of Psychological Assessment*, 13, 21–29.

Van de Vijver, F. J. R., and Poortinga, Y. H. (2002). Structural equivalence in multilevel research. *Journal of Cross-Cultural Psychology*, 33, 141–156.

Van de Vijver, F. J. R., and Poortinga, Y. H. (2004). Conceptual and methodological issues in adapting tests. In R. K. Hambleton, P. F. Merenda and C. D. Spielberger (eds.), *Adapting educational and psychological tests for cross-cultural assessment* (pp. 39–63). Mahwah, N.J.: Erlbaum.

Van de Vijver, F. J. R., and Poortinga, Y. H. (2005). Conceptual and methodological issues in adapting tests. In R. K. Hambleton, P. F. Merenda and C. D. Spielberger (eds.), *Adapting educational and psychological tests for cross-cultural assessment* (pp. 39–63). Mahwah, N.J.: Erlbaum.

Van de Vijver, F. J. R., and Tanzer, N. (2004). Bias and equivalence in cross-cultural assessment: An overview. *Revue Européenne de Psychologie Appliquée*, 54, 119–135.

Van de Vijver, F. J. R., Breugelmans, S. M., and Schalk-Soekar, S. (2008). Multiculturalism: Construct validity and stability. *International Journal of Intercultural Relations*, 32, 93–104.

Van de Vijver, F. J. R., Chasiotis, A., and Breugelmans, S. M. (eds.) (in press). *Fundamental questions in cross-cultural psychology*. Cambridge: Cambridge University Press.

Van de Vijver, F. J. R., Van Hemert, D. A., and Poortinga, Y. H. (2008a). Conceptual issues in multilevel models. In F. J. R. Van de Vijver, D. A. Van Hemert and Y. H. Poortinga (eds.), *Individuals and cultures in multi-level analyisis* (pp. 3–26). Mahwah, N.J.: Erlbaum.

Van de Vijver, F. J. R., Van Hemert, D. A., and Poortinga, Y. H. (eds.) (2008b). *Individuals and cultures in multi-level analyisis* (pp. 3–26). Mahwah, N.J.: Erlbaum.

Van de Vliert, E. (2009). *Climate, affluence, and culture*. Cambridge: Cambridge University Press.

Van den Heuvel, K., and Poortinga, Y. H. (1999). Resource allocation by Greek and Dutch students: A test of three models. *International Journal of Psychology*, 34, 1–13.

Van der Zee, K. I., and Van Oudenhoven, J. P. (2000). The Multicultural Personality Questionnaire: A multidimensional instrument of multicultural effectiveness. *European Journal of Personality*, 14, 291–309.

Van der Zee, K. I., and Van Oudenhoven, J. P. (2001). The Multicultural Personality Questionnaire: Reliability and validity of self- and other ratings of multicultural effectiveness. *Journal of Research in Personality*, 35, 278–288.

Van Dyne, L., Ang, S., and Koh, C. (2008). Development and validation of the CQS: The cultural intelligence scale. In S. Ang and L. van Dyne (eds.), *Handbook of cultural intelligence: Theory, measurement, and applications* (pp. 16–38). New York: Sharpe.

Van Haaften, E. H., and Van de Vijver, F. J. R. (1996). Psychological consequences of environmental degradation. *Journal of Health Psychology*, 1, 411–429.

Van Haaften, E. H., and Van de Vijver, F. J. R. (1999). Dealing with extreme environmental degradation: Stress and marginalization of Sahel dwellers. *Social Psychiatry and Psychiatric Epidemiology*, 34, 376–382.

Van Hemert, D. A. (2003). *Patterns of cross-cultural differences in psychology: A meta-analytic approach*. Amsterdam: Dutch University Press.

Van Hemert, D. A. (in press). Cross-cultural meta-analysis. In D. Matsumoto and F. J. R. Van de Vijver (eds.), *Cross-cultural research methods in psychology*. Cambridge: Cambridge University Press.

Van Hemert, D., Poortinga, Y. H., and Van de Vijver, F. J. R. (2007). Emotion and culture: A meta-analysis. *Cognition & Emotion*, 21, 913–941.

Van Herk, H., Poortinga, Y. H., and Verhallen, T. M. M. (2004). Response styles in rating scales: Evidence of method bias in data from 6 EU countries. *Journal of Cross-Cultural Psychology*, 35, 346–360.

Van Ijzendoorn, M. H. (1995). Adult attachment representations, parental responsiveness, and infant attachment: A meta-analysis on the predictive validity of the adult attachment interview. *Psychological Bulletin*, 117, 387–403.

Van Leeuwen, M. S. (1978). A cross-cultural examination of psychological differentiation in males and females. *International Journal of Psychology*, 13, 87–122.

Van Muijen, J. J., Koopman, P. L., and De Witte, K. (1996). *Focus op organisatiecultuur* [Focus on organizational culture]. Schoonhoven: Academic Service.

Van Oudenhoven, J. P. (2006). Immigrants. In D. L. Sam and J. W. Berry (eds.), *The Cambridge handbook of acculturation psychology* (pp. 163–180). Cambridge: Cambridge University Press.

Van Oudenhoven, J. P., and Van der Zee, K. I. (2002). Predicting multicultural effectiveness of international students: The multicultural personality questionnaire. *Asian Journal of Social Psychology*, 6, 159–170.

Van Oudenhoven, J. P., Prins, K. S., and Buunk, B. P. (1998). Attitudes of minority and majority members towards adaptation of immigrants. *European Journal of Social Psychology*, 28, 995–1013.

Vandenberg, R. J., and Lance, C. E. (2000). A review and synthesis of the measurement invariance literature: Suggestions, practices, and recommendations for organizational research. *Organizational Research Methods*, 2, 4–70.

Vaughn, C. E., and Leff, J. P. (1976). The influence of family and social factors on the course of psychiatric illness: A comparison of schizophrenic and depressed neurotic patients. *British Journal of Psychiatry*, 129, 125–137.

Vedder, P. H., and Horenczyk, G. (2006). Acculturation and the school. In D. L. Sam and J. W. Berry (eds.), *The Cambridge handbook of acculturation psychology* (pp. 419–438). Cambridge: Cambridge University Press.

Vedder, P. H., Berry, J., Sabatier, C., and Sam, D. (2009). The intergenerational transmission of values in national and immigrant families: The role of Zeitgeist. *Journal of Youth Adolescence*, 38, 642–653.

Veenhoven, R. (1999). Quality-of-life in individualistic society: A comparison of 43 nations in the early 1990's. *Social Indicators Research*, 48, 157–186.

Veenhoven, R. (2000). Four qualities of life: Ordering concepts and measures of the good life. *Journal of Happiness Studies*, 1, 1–39.

Verkuyten, M. (2005a). Ethnic group identification and group evaluation among minority and majority groups: Testing the multiculturalism hypothesis. *Journal of Personality and Social Psychology*, 88, 121–138.

Verkuyten, M. (2005b). *The social psychology of ethnic identity*, London: Psychology Press.

Verkuyten, M. (in press). Understanding group identification of ethnic minority youth. In A. Masten, D. Hernandez and K. Liebkind (eds.), *Capitalizing on immigration: The potential of immigrant youth*. Cambridge: Cambridge University Press.

Vernon, P. E. (1969). *Intelligence and cultural environment*. London: Methuen.

Vernon, P. E. (1979). *Intelligence, heredity and environment*. San Francisco, Calif.: Freeman.

Verster, J. M. (1991). Speed of cognitive processing: Cross-cultural findings on structure and relation to intelligence, tempo, temperament, and brain function. In P. L. Dann, S. H. Irvine and J. M. Collis (eds.), *Advances in computer-based human assessment* (pp. 103–147). Dordrecht: Kluwer.

Vogel, F., and Motulsky, A. G. (1979). *Human genetics: Problems and approaches*. Berlin: Springer Verlag.

Voland, E. (1998). Evolutionary ecology of human reproduction. *Annual Review of Anthropology*, 27, 347–374.

Voland, E. (2009). The adaptationist perspective on religiosity, religiousness and religion. In E. Voland and W. Schiefenhövel (eds.), *The biological evolution of religious mind and behavior*. Heidelberg: Springer.

Voland, E., and Beise, J. (2002). Opposite effects of maternal and paternal grandmothers on infant survival in 558 historical Krummhörn. *Behavioral Ecology and Sociobiology*, 52, 435–443.

Voland, E., and Grammer, K. (eds.) (2003). *Evolutionary aesthetics*. Berlin: Springer.

Voland, E., Chasiotis, A., and Schiefenhövel, W. (2005). Grandmotherhood – An overview of three related fields of research on the evolutionary significance of postgenerative female life. In E. Voland, A. Chasiotis and W. Schiefenhövel (eds.), *Grandmotherhood: The evolutionary significance of the second half of female life* (pp. 1–17). New Brunswick, N.J.: Rutgers University Press.

Voland, E., Chasiotis, A., and Schiefenhövel, W. (eds.) (2005). *Grandmotherhood: The evolutionary significance of the second half of female life*. New Brunswick, N.J.: Rutgers University Press.

Voland, E., Dunbar, R. D., Engel, C., and Stephan, P. (1997). Population increase and sex biased parental investment in humans: Evidence from 18th and 19th century Germany. *Current Anthropology*, 38, 129–135.

Vorster, J., and Schuring, G. (1989). Language and thought: Developmental perspectives on counterfactual conditionals. *South African Journal of Psychology*, 19, 34–38.

Vul, E., Harris, C., Winkielman, P., and Pashler, H. (2009). Puzzlingly high correlations in fMRI studies of emotion, personality and social cognition. *Perspectives on Psychological Science*, 4, 274–290.

Vygotsky, L. S. (1978). *Mind in society: The development of higher psychological processes*. Cambridge, Mass.: Harvard University Press.

Vygotsky, L. (1997). *The collected works of L. S. Vygotsky, Vol. IV* (ed. R. Rieber). New York: Plenum.

Wagner, W., Duveen, G., Farr, R., Jovchelovitch, S., Lorenzi-Cioldi, F., Marková, I., and Rose, D. (1999). Theory and method of social representations. *Asian Journal of Social Psychology*, 2, 95–125.

Walker, E., and Tessner, K. (2008). Schizophrenia. *Perspectives on Psychological Science*, 3, 30–37.

Walsh Escarce, M. E. (1989). A cross-cultural study of Nepalese neonatal behaviour. In J. K. Nugent, B. M. Lester and T. B. Brazelton (eds.), *The cultural context of infancy* (pp. 65–86). Norwood: Ablex.

Wan, C., and Chiu, C. (2009). An intersubjective consensus approach to culture. In R. Wyer, C. Chiu and Y. Hong (eds.), *Understanding culture: Theory, research and application* (pp. 79–91). Hove: Psychology Press.

Wang, Q., Ceci, S., Williams, W., and Kopko, K. (2004). Culturally situated cognitive competence: A functional framework. In R. Sternberg and E. Grigorenko (eds.), *Culture and competence: Contexts of life success* (pp. 225–249). Washington, DC: APA Press.

Wang, Q., Leichtman, M. D., and Davies, K. I. (2000). Sharing memories and telling stories: American and Chinese mothers and their 3-year-olds. *Memory*, 8, 159–177.

Wanigartne, S., Salas, S., and Strang, J. (2007). Substance misuse. In D. Bhugra and K. Bhui (eds.), *Textbook of cultural psychiatry* (pp. 243–254). Cambridge: Cambridge University Press.

Ward, C. (1996). Acculturation. In D. Landis and R. Bhagat (eds.), *Handbook of intercultural training* (2nd edn., pp. 124–147). Thousand Oaks, Calif.: Sage.

Ward, C. (2001). The A, B, Cs of acculturation. In D. Matsumoto (ed.), *The handbook of culture and psychology* (pp. 411–445). Oxford: Oxford University Press.

Ward, C. (2004). Psychological theories of culture contact and their implications for intercultural training and interventions. In D. Landis, J. M. Bennett and M. J. Bennett (eds.), *Handbook of intercultural training* (pp. 185–216). Thousand Oaks, Calif.: Sage.

Ward, C. (2008). Thinking outside the Berry boxes: New perspectives on identity, acculturation and intercultural relations. *International Journal of Intercultural Relations*, 32, 105–114.

Ward, C., and Chang, W. C. (1997). "Cultural fit": A new perspective on personality and sojourner adjustment. *International Journal of Intercultural Relations*, 21, 525–533.

Ward, C., and Fischer, R. (2008). Personality, cultural intelligence and cross-cultural adaptation. In S. Ang and L. van Dyne (eds.), *Handbook of cultural intelligence: Theory, measurement, and applications* (pp. 159–173). New York: Sharpe.

Ward, C., and Kennedy, A. (1993). Where is the "culture" in cross-cultural transition? Comparative studies of sojourner adjustment. *Journal of Cross-Cultural Psychology*, 24, 221–249.

Ward, C., and Kennedy, A. (1994). Acculturation strategies, psychological adjustment, and sociocultural competence during cross-cultural transitions. *International Journal of Intercultural Relations*, 18, 329–343.

Ward, C., and Kennedy, A. (1999). The measurement of sociocultural adaptation. *International Journal of Intercultural Relations*, 56, 1–19.

Ward, C., and Leong, C.-H. (2006). Intercultural relations in plural societies. In D. Sam and J. W. Berry (eds.), *The Cambridge handbook of acculturation psychology* (pp. 484–503). Cambridge: Cambridge University Press.

Ward, C., and Masgoret, A.-M. (2009). Attitudes toward immigrants, immigration, and multiculturalism in New Zealand: A social psychological analysis. *International Migration Review*, 42, 222–243.

Ward, C., and Searle, W. (1991). The impact of value discrepancies and cultural identity on psychological and socio-cultural adjustment of sojourners. *International Journal of Intercultural Relations*, 15, 209–225.

Ward, C., Bochner, S., and Furnham, A. (2001). *The psychology of culture shock*. Hove: Routledge.

Ward, C., Chang, W., and Lopez-Nerney, S. (1999). Psychological and sociocultural adjustment of Filipina domestic workers in Singapore. In J. C. Lasry, J. Adair and K. Dion (eds.), *Latest contributions to cross-cultural psychology* (pp. 118–134). Lisse: Swets & Zeitlinger.

Ward, C., Leong, C.-H., and Low, M. (2004). Personality and sojourner adjustment: An exploration of the Big Five and the cultural fit proposition. *Journal of Cross-Cultural Psychology*, 35, 137–151.

Ward, C., Okura, Y., Kennedy, A., and Kojima, T. (1999). The U-curve on trial: A longitudinal study of psychological and sociocultural adjustment during cross-cultural transition. *International Journal of Intercultural Relations*, 22, 277–291.

Warneken, F., Chen F., and Tomasello, M. (2006). Cooperative activities in young children and chimpanzees. *Child Development*, 77, 640–663.

Warren, N., and Parkin, J. M. (1974). A neurological and behavioral comparison of African and European newborns in Uganda. *Child Development*, 45, 966–971.

Warwick, D. (1980). The politics and ethics of cross-cultural research. In H. C. Triandis and W. W. Lambert (eds.), *Handbook of cross-cultural psychology, Vol. I, Perspectives* (pp. 310–371). Boston: Allyn & Bacon.

Wassmann, J., and Dasen, P. R. (1994a). Yupno number system and counting. *Journal of Cross-Cultural Psychology*, 25, 78–94.

Wassmann, J., and Dasen, P. R. (1994b). "Hot" and "cold": Classification and sorting among the Yupno of Papua New Guinea. *International Journal of Psychology*, 29, 19–38.

Wassmann, J., and Dasen, P. R. (1998). Balinese spatial orientation: Some empirical evidence for moderate linguistic relativity. *The Journal of the Royal Anthropological Institute, incorporating Man (N.S.)*, 4, 689–711.

Wasti, S. A. (2008). Organizational commitment: Complication or clarification. In P. B. Smith, M. F. Peterson and D. C. Thomas (eds.), *The handbook of cross-cultural management research* (pp. 95–115). Los Angeles: Sage.

Watkins, D., Adair, J., Akande, A., Gerong, A., McInerney, D., Sunar, D., Watson, S., Wen, Q. F., and Wondimu, H. (1998). Individualism-collectivism, gender and the self-concept: A nine culture investigation. *Psychologia*, 41, 259–271.

Watkins, M., and Shulman, H. (2008). *Toward psychologies of liberation*. London: Palgrave Macmillan.

Watts, R., and Smolicz , J. (1997). *Cultural democracy and ethnic pluralism: Multicultural and multilingual policies in education*. Bern: Peter Lang.

Weber, E. U., and Hsee, C. K. (2000). Culture and individual decision making. *Applied Psychology: An International Review*, 49, 32–61.

Weber, M. (1905/1976). *The Protestant Ethic and the spirit of capitalism*. New York: Charles Scribner's Sons.

Wechsler, D. (1997). *Wechsler Adult Intelligence Scale – 3rd Edition (WAIS-3)*. San Antonio: Harcourt Assessment.

Weisner, T. S., and Gallimore, R. (1977). My brother's keeper: Child and sibling caretaking. *Current Anthropology*, 18, 169–190.

Wellings, K., Collumbien, M., Slaymaker, E., Singh, S., Hodges, Z., Patel, D., and Bajos, N. (2006). Sexual behaviour in context: A global perspective. *The Lancet*, 368, 1706–1728.

Wellman, H. M., Cross, D., and Watson, J. (2001). Meta Analysis of theory-of-mind development: The truth about false belief. *Child Development*, 72, 655–684.

Wells, G. L., Memon, A., and Penrod, S. D. (2006). Eye witness evidence: Improving its probative value. *Psychological Science in the Public Interest*, 7, 45–75.

Welzel, C., Inglehart, R., Klingemann, H.-D. (2003). The theory of human development: A cross-cultural analysis. *European Journal of Political Research*, 42, 341–379.

Westermarck, E. (1921). *The history of human marriage*. London: Macmillan.

Westin, C., Bastos, J., Dahinden, J., and Góis, P. (eds.) (2009). *Identity processes and dynamics in multi-ethnic Europe*. IMISCOE Series. Amsterdam: Amsterdam University Press.

Wexley, K. N., and Yukl, G. A. (1984). *Organizational behavior and personnel psychology* (revised edn.). Homewood, Ill.: Irwin.

Whitbourne, S. K., Zuschlag, M. K., Elliot, L. B., and Waterman, A. S. (1992). Psychosocial development in adulthood: A 22-year sequential study. *Journal of Personality and Social Psychology*, 63, 260–271.

Whiten, A., Horner, V., and Marshall-Pescini, S. (2003). Cultural panthropology. *Evolutionary Anthropology*, 12, 92–105.

Whiten, A., Goodall, J., McGrew, W. C., Nishida, T., Reynolds, V., Sugiyama, Y., Tutin, C. E. G., Wrangham, R. W., and Boesch, C. (1999). Cultures in chimpanzees. *Nature*, 399, 682–685.

Whiting, B. B. (1963). *Six cultures: Studies of child rearing.* New York: Wiley.

Whiting, B. B., and Whiting, J. W. M. (1975). *Children of six cultures: A psychocultural analysis.* Cambridge, Mass.: Harvard University Press.

Whiting, B. B., and Whiting, J. W. M. (1988). Foreword to Adolescents in a Changing World series. In V. C. Burbank (ed.), *Aboriginal adolescence: Maidenhood in an Australian community* (pp. vii–xiv). New Brunswick, N.J.: Rutgers University Press.

Whiting, J. W. M. (1954). The cross-cultural method. In G. Lindzey (ed.), *The handbook of social psychology, Vol. I* (pp. 523–531). Cambridge, Mass.: Addison-Wesley.

Whiting, J. W. M. (1968). Methods and problems in cross-cultural research. In G. Lindzey and E. Aronson (eds.), *Handbook of social psychology, Vol. II* (pp. 693–728). Reading: Addison-Wesley.

Whiting, J. W. M. (1974). A model for psychocultural research. *Annual report.* Washington, DC: American Anthropological Association.

Whiting, J. W. M. (1981). Environmental constraints on infant care practices. In R. L. Munroe, R. M. Munroe and B. B. Whiting (eds.), *Handbook of cross-cultural human development* (pp. 151–181). New York: Garland Press.

Whiting, J. W. M., and Child, I. (1953). *Child training and personality.* New Haven, Conn.: Yale University Press.

WHO (1948). Preamble to the Constitution of the World Health Organization as adopted by the International Health Conference, New York, June 19–22, 1946; signed on July 22, 1947 by the representatives of sixty-one States (Official Records of the World Health Organization, no. 2, p. 100); and entered into force on April 7, 1948.

WHO (1973). *Report of the international pilot study of schizophrenia vol. I.* Geneva: World Health Organization.

WHO (1978). *Primacy health care: Report of the international conference at Alma Ata.* Geneva: World Health Organization.

WHO (1979a). *Schizophrenia: An international follow-up study.* Chichester: Wiley.

WHO (1979b). *International Statistical Classification of Diseases and Related Health Problems 9th Revision Version.* Geneva: World Health Organization. Retrieved August 10, 2010, from www.lumrix.net/icd-9_info.php (The WHO no longer publishes and distributes the ICD-9.)

WHO (1982). *Medium term programme.* Geneva: World Health Organization.

WHO (1983). *Depressive disorders in different cultures.* Geneva: World Health Organization.

WHO (1986). Ottawa Charter for Health Promotion First International Conference on Health Promotion. Geneva: World Health Organization. Retrieved March 12, 2009, from www.who.int/hpr/NPH/docs/ottawa_charter_hp.pdf

WHO (2001). *The world health report 2001: Mental health: New understanding, new hope*. Geneva: World Health Organization. Retrieved February 20, 2010, from www.who.int/whr/2001/en/

WHO (2002). *The World Health Report 2002: Reducing risks, promoting healthy life*. Geneva: World Health Organization. Retrieved January 20, 2006, from www.who.int/whr/2002/en/index.html

WHO (2005). *Mental health: Facing the challenges, building solutions*. Report from the WHO European Ministerial Conference. Copenhagen: World Health Organization Regional Office for Europe.

WHO (2007a). *International Statistical Classification of Diseases and Related Health Problems 10th revision version for 2007*. Geneva: World Health Organization. Retrieved July 31, 2010, from www.who.int/classifications/icd/en/bluebook.pdf

WHO (2007b). *Mental health: Strengthening mental health promotion*. Geneva: World Health Organization. Retrieved July 12, 2010, from www.who.int/mediacentre/factsheets/fs220/en/print.html

WHO (2007c). *International Statistical Classification of Diseases and Related Health Problems 10th Revision Version for 2007*. Geneva: World Health Organization.

WHO (2008). *World malaria report*. Geneva: World Health Organization.

WHOQOL Group (1995). The World Health Organization Quality of Life Assessment. Position paper from the World Health Organization. *Social Science and Medicine*, 42, 1403–1409.

Whorf, B. L. (1956). *Language, thought and reality*. J. Carroll (ed.). Cambridge, Mass.: The MIT Press.

Widiger, T. A., and Clark, L. A. (2000). Towards DSM IV and the classification of psychopathology. *Psychological Bulletin*, 126, 946–963.

Wierzbicka, A. (1996). *Semantics: Primes and universals*. Oxford: Oxford University Press.

Wierzbicka, A. (1998). Angst. *Culture & Psychology*, 4, 161–188.

Wierzbicka, A. (1999). *Emotions across languages and cultures: Diversity and universals*. Cambridge: Cambridge University Press.

Wiggins, J. S. (1973). *Personality and prediction: Principles of personality assessment*. Menlo Park, Calif.: Addison-Wesley.

Willemsen, M. E., and Van de Vijver, F. J. R. (1997). Developmental expectations of Dutch, Turkish-Dutch, and Zambian mothers: Towards an explanation of cross-cultural differences. *International Journal of Behavioral Development*, 21, 837–854.

Williams, G. C. (1957). Pleiotropy, natural selection, and the evolution of senescence. *Evolution*, 11, 398–411.

Williams, G. C. (1966). *Adaptation and natural selection: A critique of some current evolutionary thought*. Princeton: Princeton University Press.

Williams, J. E., and Best, D. L. (1990). *Measuring sex stereotypes: A multination study*. Newbury Park, Calif.: Sage.

Willis, J. W., with Jost, M., and Nilakanta, R. (2007). *Foundations of qualitative research*. Thousand Oaks, Calif.: Sage.

Wilson, D. S. (2002). *Darwin's cathedral: Evolution, religion, and the nature of society*. Chicago: The University of Chicago Press.

Wilson, E. O. (1975). *Sociobiology: The new synthesis*. Cambridge, Mass.: Harvard University Press.

Wilson, J. (2009). The socio-cultural adaptation scale (SCAS) and its correlates: A meta analysis. Paper presented at the 6th Biennial conference of the International Academy of Intercultural Relations. Honolulu, Hawaii, August 15–19.

Wimmer, H., and Perner, J. (1983). Beliefs about beliefs: Representation and constraining function of wrong beliefs in young children's understanding of deception. *Cognition*, 13, 103–128.

Winkelman, M. (1992). *Shamans, priests and witches: A cross-cultural study of magico-religious practitioners. Anthropological Research Papers No. 44*. Tempe, Ariz.: Arizona State University Press.

Wissler, C. (1923). *Man and culture*. New York: Thomas Y. Crowell.

Witkin, H., and Berry, J. W. (1975). Psychological differentiation in cross-cultural perspective. *Journal of Cross-Cultural Psychology*, 6, 4–87.

Witkin, H. A., Goodenough, D. R., and Oltman, P. (1979). Psychological differentiation: Current status. *Journal of Personality and Social Psychology*, 37, 1127–1145.

Witkin, H. A., Dyk, R. B., Paterson, H. F., Goodenough, D. R., and Karp, S. (1962). *Psychological differentiation*. New York: Wiley.

Wober, M. (1966). Sensotypes. *Journal of Social Psychology*, 70, 181–189.

Wolf, A. P., and Huang, C. (1979). *Marriage and adoption in China, 1845–1945*. Stanford: Stanford University Press.

Wolff, P. H. (1972a). Ethnic differences in alcohol sensitivity. *Science*, 175, 449–450.

Wolff, P. H. (1972b). Vasomotor sensitivity to alcohol in diverse Mongoloid populations. *American Journal of Human Genetics*, 25, 193–199.

Wood, D., Bruner, J. S., and Ross, G. (1976). The role of tutoring in problem-solving. *Journal of Child Psychology and Psychiatry*, 17, 89–100.

World Mental Health (2010). The world health survey initiative. Retrieved February 10, 2010, from www.hcp.med.harvard.edu/wmh/

Wright, G. N. (1985). Organizational, group and individual decision making in cross-cultural perspective. In G. N. Wright (ed.), *Behavioral decision making* (pp. 149–165). New York: Plenum.

Wright, G. N., and Phillips, L. D. (1980). Cultural variation in probabilistic thinking: Alternative ways of dealing with uncertainty. *International Journal of Psychology*, 15, 239–257.

Wright, G. N., Phillips, L. D., and Wisudha, A. (1983). Cultural comparison on decision making under uncertainty. In J. B. Deregowski, S. Dziurawiec and R. C. Annis (eds.), *Expositions in cross-cultural psychology* (pp. 387–402). Lisse: Swets & Zeitlinger.

Wulff, D. M. (1997). *Psychology of religion: Classic and contemporary* (2nd edn.). New York, Wiley.

Wundt, W. (1893). *Grundzüge der physiologischen Psychologie, Vol. II* (4th edn.) [The basics of physiological psychology]. Leipzig: Engelmann.

Wundt, W. (1913). *Elemente der Völkerpsychologie* (2nd edn.) [Elements of Völkerpsychologie]. Leipzig: Alfred Kroner Verlag.

Wyer, R., Chiu, C., and Hong, Y. (eds.) (2009). *Understanding culture: Theory, research and application*. Hove: Psychology Press.

Wyndham, C. H. (1975). Ergonomic problems in the transition from peasant to industrial life in South Africa. In A. Chapanis (ed.), *Ethnic variables in human factors engineering* (pp. 115–134). Baltimore: Johns Hopkins University Press.

Yamagata, S., Suzuki, A., Ando, J., *et al.* (2006). Is the genetic structure of human personality universal? A cross-cultural twin study from North America, Europe, and Asia. *Journal of Personality and Social Psychology*, 90, 987–998.

Yamagishi, T., Hashimoto, H., and Schug, J. (2008). Preferences versus strategies as explanations for culture-specific behavior. *Psychological Science*, 19, 579–584.

Yamaguchi, S., and Ariizumi, Y. (2006). Close interpersonal relationships among Japanese: Amae as distinguished from attachment and dependence. In U. Kim, K.-S. Yang and K.-K. Hwang (eds.), *Indigenous and cultural psychology: Understanding people in context* (pp. 163–174). New York: Springer Science.

Yang, K.-S. (2000). Monocultural and cross-cultural indigenous approaches. *Asian Journal of Social Psychology*, 3, 241–263.

Yang, K.-S. (1999). Towards an indigenous Chinese psychology: A selective review of methodological, theoretical and empirical accomplishments. *Chinese Journal of Psychology*, 41, 181–211.

Yang, K.-S. (2003). Beyond Maslow's culture-bound linear theory: A preliminary statement of the double-Y model of basic human needs. In J. Berman and J. Berman (eds.), *Cross-cultural differences in perspectives on the self*, Vol. 49 of the Nebraska Symposium on Motivation (pp. 157–305). Lincoln, Nebr.: University of Nebraska Press.

Yang, K.-S. (2006). Indigenised conceptual and empirical analyses of selected Chinese psychological characteristics. *International Journal of Psychology*, 41, 298–303.

Yap, P. M. (1967). Classification of the culture-bound reactive syndromes. *Australian and New Zealand Journal of Psychiatry*, 1, 172–179.

Yates, J. F., Lee, J. W., Shinotsuka, H., Patalano, A. L., and Sieck, W. R. (1998). Cross-cultural variations in probability judgment accuracy: Beyond general knowledge overconfidence? *Organizational Behavior and Human Decision Processes*, 74, 89–117.

Yates, J. F., Lee, J.-W., Sieck, W. R., Choi, I., and Price, P. C. (2002). In T. Gilovich, D. Griffin and D. Kahneman (eds.), *Heuristics and biases: The psychology of intuitive judgment* (pp. 271–291). New York: Cambridge University Press.

Yates, J. F., Zhu, Y., Ronis, D. L., Wang, D.-F., Shinotsuka, H., and Toda, M. (1989). Probability judgment accuracy: China, Japan, and the United States. *Organizational Behavior and Human Decision Processes*, 43, 145–171.

Yijälä, A., and Jasinskaja-Lahti, I. (2010). Pre-migration acculturation attitudes among potential ethnic migrants from Russia to Finland. *International Journal of Intercultural Relations*, 34, 326–339.

Yovsi, R. D., and Keller, H. (2003). Breastfeeding: An adaptive process. *Ethos*, 31, 147–171.

Zahavi, A. (1975). Mate selection: A selection for a handicap. *Journal of Theoretical Biology*, 53, 205–214.

Zahavi, A., and Zahavi, A. (1997). *The handicap principle: A missing piece of Darwin's puzzle*. Oxford: Oxford University Press.

Zaman, A., and Zaman, R. (1994). Psychology and development: A conceptual itinerary. *Psychology and Developing Societies*, 6, 1–20.

Zebian, S., and Denny, P. (2001). Integrative cognitive style in Middle Eastern and western groups. *Journal of Cross-Cultural Psychology*, 32, 58–75.

Zebian, S., Alamuddin, R., Maalouf, M., and Chatila, Y. (2007). Developing an appropriate psychology through culturally sensitive research practice in the Arabic-speaking world. *Journal of Cross-Cultural Psychology*, 38, 91–122.

Zegers, F. E., and Ten Berge, J. M. F. (1985). A family of association coefficients for metric scales. *Psychometrika*, 50, 17–24.

Zhang, L.-F., and Sternberg, R. J. (2006). *The nature of intellectual styles*. Mahwah, N.J.: Erlbaum.

Zimba, R. F. (2002). Indigenous conceptions of childhood and social realities: Development in Southern Africa. In H. Keller, Y. H. Poortinga and A. Schölmerich (eds.), *Between biology and culture: Perspectives on ontogenetic development* (pp. 89–115). Cambridge: Cambridge University Press.

Zimmermann, L., Zimmermann, K. F., and Constant, A. (2007). Ethnic self identification of first-generation immigrants. *International Migration Review*, 41, 769–781.

Zinchenko, Y., and Pertenko, V. (eds.) (2008). *Psychology in Russia: State of the art*. Moscow: Moscow State University.

Zou, X., Tam, K.-P., Morris, M. W., Lee, S.-L., Lau, I. Y.-M., and Chiu, C.-Y. (2009). Culture as common sense: Perceived consensus versus personal beliefs as mechanisms of cultural influence. *Journal of Personality and Social Psychology*, 97, 579–597.

Author index

Subject index

Numbers in bold refer to page numbers where key terms are emphasized.
Additional topics to be found on the Internet are referred to by "I" followed by the chapter number.